British Bed & Breakfast

British Hotels & Inns

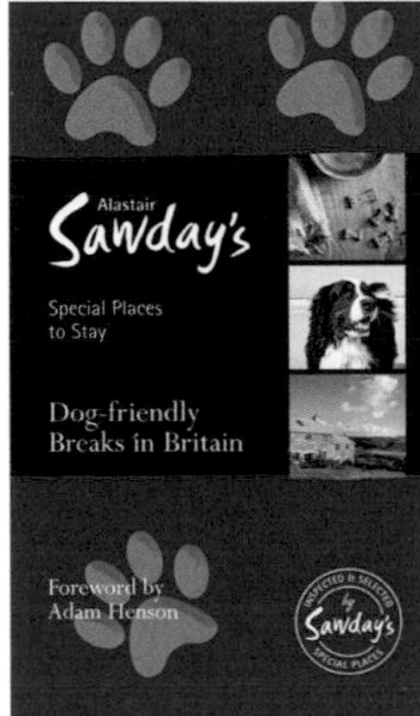

Dog-friendly Breaks in Britain

French Bed & Breakfast

Alastair Sawday's

Places to Stay

Fourteenth edition

Published in 2017
ISBN-13: 978-1-906136-82-6

Alastair Sawday Publishing Co. Ltd,
Merchant's House, Wapping Road,
Bristol BS1 4RW, UK
Tel: +44 (0)117 204 7810
Email: info@sawdays.co.uk
Web: www.sawdays.co.uk

A catalogue record for this book is available from the British Library. This publication is not included under licences issued by the Copyright Agency. No part of this publication may be used in any form of advertising, sales promotion or publicity.

We have made every effort to ensure the accuracy of the information in this book at the time of going to press. However, we cannot accept any responsibility for any loss, injury or inconvenience resulting from the use of information contained therein.

Series Editor Alastair Sawday
Editorial Gwen Vonthron
Production coordinator
Sarah Nuttall, Sarah Barratt
Senior Picture Editor Alec Studerus
Writing Jo Boissevain, Donald Greig, Helen Pickles, Sarah Barratt, Nicola Crosse, Carmen Cox, Sue Nottingham
Inspections Jan Adam, Colin Cheyne, Nicola Crosse, Beverley Jane Edge, Julie Franklin, Catherine Gledhill, Becca Harris, Paul Hennessy, Brian Jones, David Milne, Helen Pickles, Alastair Sawday, Annie Shillito, Kate Soar, Nicky Tennent, Gwen Vonthron, Rebecca Whewell, Matthew Woods
Thanks also to others who did an inspection or two.
Marketing & PR
Emily Enright, Tessa Glover
0117 204 7801
marketing@sawdays.co.uk

Alastair Sawday has asserted his right to be identified as the author of this work.

Production: Pagebypage Co. Ltd
Maps: Maidenhead Cartographic Services
Printing: Pureprint, Uckfield
UK distribution: The Travel Alliance, Bath
info@pelotongrey.com

Front cover photo credits
1. The Locksbrook Inn, entry 3 2. The Hoop, entry 201
3. The Royal Oak Inn, entry 481

Back cover photo credits
1. Hook Norton Brewery, entry 457 2. The Greyhound Inn, entry 429 3. The Mexico Inn, entry 98

Spine cover photo credit
The Stag at Offchurch, entry 587

Alastair Sawday's

Special Places

Pubs & Inns

of England & Wales

Contents

A word from Alastair Sawday

The river of change in the world of pubs tumbles down the valley, sweeping before it all that is weak, dated or un-rooted to the needs of the community. The river may occasionally subside but it will rise again. Change is now a permanent state.

Yet change can be invigorating and dynamic. Sawday's pubs have stood the test, flourishing because they are what is needed at the moment and nurtured by people who care for what they're doing, enjoy their customers, and aim to do more than simply sell beer and food and make a profit. They are, in a word, Special. And always open to change, to new ideas.

Photo: Tom Germain

True, there is concern for European staff who have added so much colour and character to pubs in recent years. Will recruitment become trickier after Brexit? We wait and see. But at least the lower pound has brought new tipplers into our pubs, especially in popular urban areas. Renewed efforts to delight guests with home-grown produce will perhaps counter the extra cost of imported chorizo, cheese and chardonnay.

There is much good news, too. Perhaps the best is the liberation of so many once-shackled pubs. Independent landlords are having a field-day, sourcing their food locally and experimenting with deliveries, selling more soft drinks for their newly-teetotal guests, and generally getting closer to their communities and their environment. Some even have their own land for growing purposes, and the results are often delicious.

You may have noticed that the micro-brewery revolution gathers pace, which is tremendous solace for those of us who fear the worst in this endlessly-changing world. There are several in this wonderful guide, along with community-owned pubs, gastro and firmly non-gastro pubs, and those that defy categorisation. We believe we have the most interesting and rewarding collection around – and invite you to stray from your familiar path to celebrate the diverse, the indulgent, the eclectic.

Alastair Sawday

How we choose our Special Places

Those who are familiar with our Special Places series know that we look for originality and authenticity, and disregard the anonymous and the banal. We also place great emphasis on the welcome – as important to us as the setting, the architecture, the atmosphere and the food.

The notion of 'special' is at the heart of what we do, and is highly subjective. We also recognise that one person's idea of special is not necessarily another's so there is a big variety of places in this book, from rural rustic to urban chic, from gastropub to cider house.

Inspections and subscriptions

We have visited every entry in this guide. We pick up those details that cannot be gleaned over the internet or by phone, and we write the descriptions ourselves, doing our best to avoid misinterpretation. If a pub is in, we think it's special, and the write-up should tell you if it's your sort of special.

Owners pay to appear in this guide. Their fee goes towards the high costs of inspecting, of maintaining our website and producing an all-colour book. We only include places that we find special for one reason or another, so it is not possible for anyone to buy their way onto these pages. Nor is it possible for the owner to write their own description. We say if the bedrooms are small, or if a main road is near. We do our best to avoid misleading people.

Photo: The Trout at Tadpole Bridge, entry 426

Feedback

Many of the pubs with rooms that appear in this guide are on our website, too. If you would like to tell us about your visit to any of these places, find them there and follow the link to the feedback form. For those that don't feature on our website, please email us with your feedback and tell us about your visit – the food, ales, staff and, crucially, the atmosphere. Write to info@sawdays.co.uk.

A lot of the new entries in each edition are recommended by our readers, so keep telling us about new places you've discovered, too.

Disclaimer

We make no claims to pure objectivity in choosing these places. They are here simply because we like them. Our opinions and tastes are ours alone and we hope you will share them. Do remember that the information in this book is a snapshot in time and may have changed since we published it; do call ahead to avoid being disappointed. Our website www.sawdays.co.uk has all the latest information, plenty more photos and details of special offers too.

You should know that we don't check such things as fire alarms, kitchen hygiene or any other regulation with which owners of properties receiving paying guests should comply. This is the responsibility of the owners.

Finding the right place for you

Drink, eat, sleep A growing number of pubs and inns combine atmosphere with good food and bedrooms to match – and at lower prices than many hotels. It's true that some pubs are virtually indistinguishable from some small hotels, but a lively bar serving real beer should put them into the classic inn category. Some pubs with rooms are more modest village affairs where the enthusiasm to get things right in the bar extends upstairs. (If you are worried about noise at weekends, you can ask for a room at the back or a room across the way.) So the next time you take a weekend or business break, dismiss those roadside lodges and impersonal hotels in favour of a friendly country inn.

Photo above: The Chequers Inn, entry 378
Photo right: The Duke of Wellington, entry 533

Pulled Pork on toast.
Burnt Ends.
Potato Skins with Pulled Pork.
Guacamole & Flat Breads
£6.50

Gastropubs and country dining pubs

Our best pubs are luring foodies away from pricier restaurants as a wave of casual dining enfolds the nation. Many backstreet boozers have been transformed, the fruit machines and beer-stained carpet being replaced by chalked-up menus and chunky tables. In the countryside, too, old-fashioned locals are being rejuvenated by landlords and chefs who believe that gastronomy is rooted in the soil and that food should be fresh, seasonal and sourced from the best local suppliers.

Our favourite food pubs in England and Wales are described within these pages; all strike a happy balance between restaurant and pub. (Note that booking is not always a given and you may have to take your chance with a table.)

Photo: The Roebuck, entry 73

Maps

The maps at the front of the book show the approximate position of each of our pubs and inns. The award winning pubs are marked with gold flags. The maps are for guidance only; use a detailed road map or you could lose yourself down a tangle of lanes.

Symbols

Below most entries you will see a line of symbols, which are explained at the very back of the book. They are based on the information given to us by the owners but things do change, so use the symbols as a guide rather than an absolute statement of fact. Please note that the symbols do not necessarily apply to the bedrooms. Double-check anything that is important to you. A fuller explanation of some symbols is given below.

Children – The symbol is given to pubs that accept children of any age. That doesn't mean that they can go everywhere in the pub, or that highchairs and special menus or small portions are provided. Nor does it mean that children should be anything less than well-behaved! Call to check details such as separate family rooms, whether children are allowed in the dining room and whether there is play equipment in the garden.

Dogs – The symbol is given to places where your dog can go into some part of the pub, generally the bar and garden. It is unlikely to include eating areas.

Wheelchairs – We use the symbol if we've been told those in wheelchairs can access the bar and a wc. The symbol does not apply to accommodation.

Pub awards

Every year we choose those pubs that we think deserve a special mention.
Our categories are:

- local, seasonal and organic produce
- authentic pub
- community pub
- favourite newcomer
- pub with rooms
- best all-rounder.

More details are given on pages 15-21, and all the award winners have been marked with a stamp.

Opening times

We list the hours pubs are closed during the afternoon and whether or not they are closed during particular lunchtimes and evenings. We do advise that you check before setting out, especially in winter.

Meals and meal prices

We give the approximate cost of main courses in the bar and/or restaurant. Note that some pubs charge extra for

Photo above: The Swan Hotel & Spal, entry 116
Photo below: The Oxney Gourmet Pie & Burger Bar, entry 313

side dishes, which significantly increases the main course price. Note that many pubs do fixed-price Sunday lunches, and that prices in general may change. Check when booking. We also state days or sessions when no food is served.

Bedrooms, bathrooms and breakfasts

If you're thinking of staying the night in a simple pub or inn, bear in mind that an early night may not be possible if folk are carousing below. A few bedrooms do not have en suite bathrooms – please ask on booking – and pub room check-ins are often late, eg. from 6.30pm. Breakfasts are generally included in the room price, and most places serve breakfast between 8am and 10am.

Bedroom prices

Prices are per room for two people sharing. If a price range is given, then the lowest price is for the least expensive room in low season and the highest for the most expensive room in high season. The single room rate (or the single occupancy of a double room) generally follows. Occasionally prices are for half board, ie. they include dinner, bed and breakfast. Do check.

Bookings and cancellations

Tables – At weekends, food pubs are often full and it is best to book a table well in advance; at other times, only tables in the dining rooms may be reserved. Tables in the bar may operate on a first-come, first-served basis. Some of the best gastropubs do not take reservations at all, wanting to hold on to their pubby origins. We applaud that, but it does mean you need to arrive early to bag a space. Always phone to double-check meal times.

Rooms – Most pubs and inns will ask for a credit card number and a contact phone number when you telephone to book a room. They may take a deposit at the time of booking, either by cheque or credit/debit card. If you cancel – depending on how much notice you give – you can lose all or part of this deposit unless your room is re-let. Ask the pub to explain their cancellation policy before booking so you understand where you stand; it may avoid a nasty surprise.

Tipping

It is not obligatory but it is appreciated, particularly in pubs with restaurants.

Photo left: The George, entry 614
Photo right: The Plough Inn, entry 221
Photo overleaf: The White Hart, entry 238

Sawday's Pub Awards

We have chosen six-of-the-best (which can't be beaten...) for our annual Sawday's Pub Awards. All the pubs featured in this book are special to us, but these have been chosen by our trusty team of inspectors as shining beacons in their particular category, and there's one best all-rounder.

Award categories:

Local, seasonal and organic produce

Authentic pub

Community pub

Favourite newcomer

Pub with rooms

Best all-rounder

www.sawdays.co.uk/pubawards

Local, seasonal and organic produce

Yummy food just whizzes out of this kitchen! Young, enthusiastic Ollie (MasterChef semi-finalist) and Lauren are firm believers in a farm-to-fork ethos so the menu is bursting with all things local: artisan charcuterie made by Ollie's dad on his nearby farm, craft lager, organic wines, homemade liqueurs. Treat yourselves to 'modern peasant food' in really comfortable surroundings, with maybe a pint of Ramsbury Gold.

The Wheatsheaf, Wiltshire
Entry 617

Sawday's Pub Awards 2017/18

Authentic pub

Like stepping back in time. Find flagstone floors at this long low pub which was once a row of five ancient cottages, the church tower peeking over them. Binka and David made it their mission to bring it back to life as the beating heart of the village and they've succeeded, brilliantly. The food is surprisingly modern and imaginative but this is a great village pub surrounded by glorious countryside.

The Ring of Bells, Devon
Entry 160

www.sawdays.co.uk/pubawards

Community pub

This little pub could have been a shameful statistic – another village local closed down. But luckily it was bought by the plucky village community and is now run by cheerful husband and wife team Ian and Lisa. A small blackboard menu (everything is cooked from scratch) concentrates on food from local producers and as much seasonal veg as possible comes from their own kitchen garden.

The Red Lion at Northmoor, Oxfordshire
Entry 445

Favourite newcomer

Lucky locals! The clever Cheshire Cat team have restored with extraordinary love, style – and a good dollop of Mediterranean rustic chic. Café tables, wine-red leather settles, mirrors and candles make a convivial backdrop for Toulouse sausage casserole, mackerel and orzo salad with orange and dill, a taste of some local craft beers. Bedrooms are filled with warmth and colour, one has a wood-burner.

The Roebuck, Cheshire
Entry 73

Pub with rooms

This is definitely not your average pub bedroom. Find a glamorous hideaway suite with soaring ceilings, big bed and deeply comfy sofas. Décor by local artisans, a modern kitchen, driftwood touches, beautiful throws and double doors that open onto your own terrace overlooking the brook. If you don't want to budge you can order up food, perhaps some champagne, and settle to soak up the view. Heaven.

The Millbrook Inn, Devon
Entry 135

Best all-rounder

A long, low coaching inn, beautifully restored by craftsmen using wood, slate and stone and painted in lovely colours. Inside you'll find bare wooden tables, comfy sofas, intimate alcoves, comfortable bedrooms and crackling fires. It's a delightful place to dine too – the chef does perfect justice to the slow-grown breeds of beef, pork and lamb produced on the 800-year-old Lowther Estate

George and Dragon, Cumbria
Entry 108

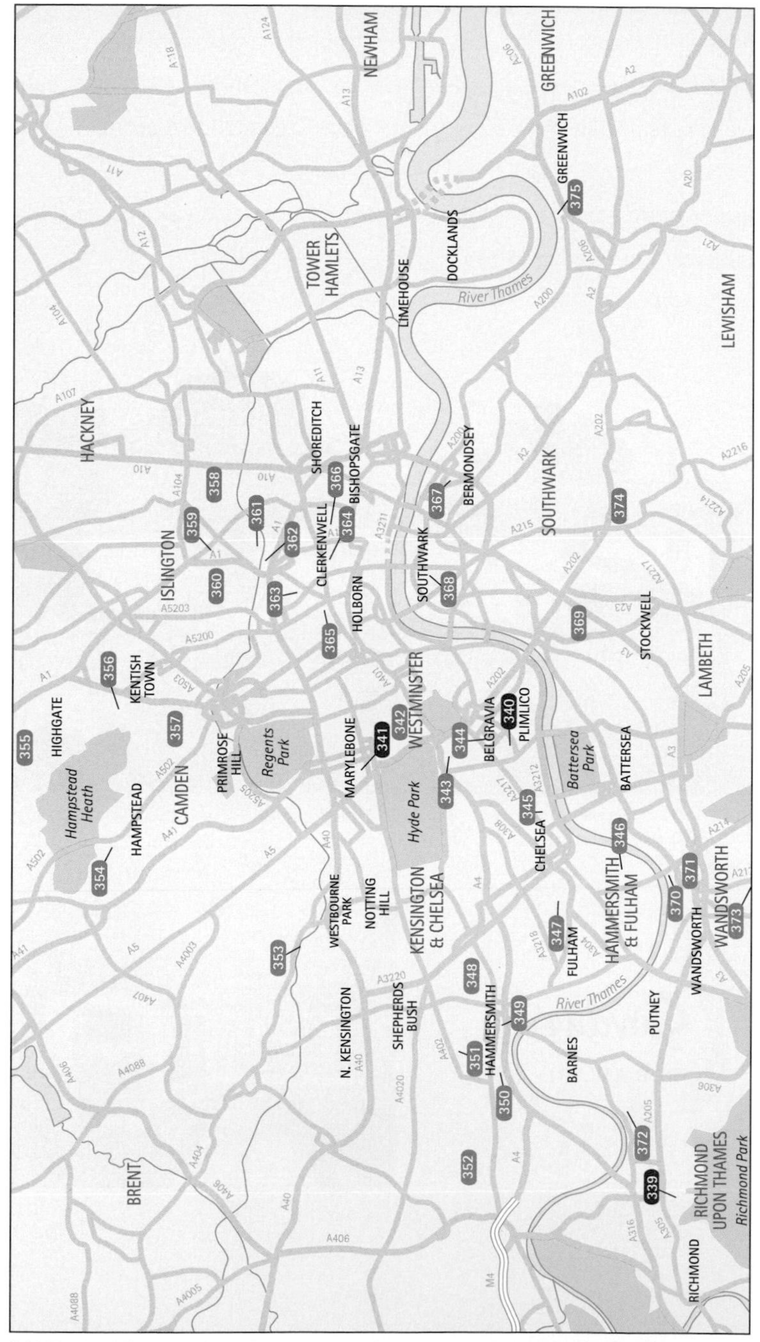
NEWHAM
GREENWICH
TOWER HAMLETS
LIMEHOUSE
DOCKLANDS
River Thames
GREENWICH
375
LEWISHAM
HACKNEY
SHOREDITCH
BISHOPSGATE
BERMONDSEY
SOUTHWARK
ISLINGTON
CLERKENWELL
HOLBORN
SOUTHWARK
STOCKWELL
LAMBETH
HIGHGATE
KENTISH TOWN
PRIMROSE HILL
Regents Park
MARYLEBONE
WESTMINSTER
BELGRAVIA
PLIMLICO
Battersea Park
BATTERSEA
Hampstead Heath
HAMPSTEAD
CAMDEN
Hyde Park
CHELSEA
HAMMERSMITH & FULHAM
WANDSWORTH
WESTBOURNE PARK
NOTTING HILL
KENSINGTON & CHELSEA
FULHAM
N. KENSINGTON
SHEPHERDS BUSH
HAMMERSMITH
BARNES
PUTNEY
WANDSWORTH
River Thames
BRENT
RICHMOND UPON THAMES
Richmond Park
RICHMOND
339
340
341
342
343
344
345
346
347
348
349
350
351
352
353
354
355
356
357
358
359
360
361
362
363
364
365
366
367
368
369
370
371
372
373
374

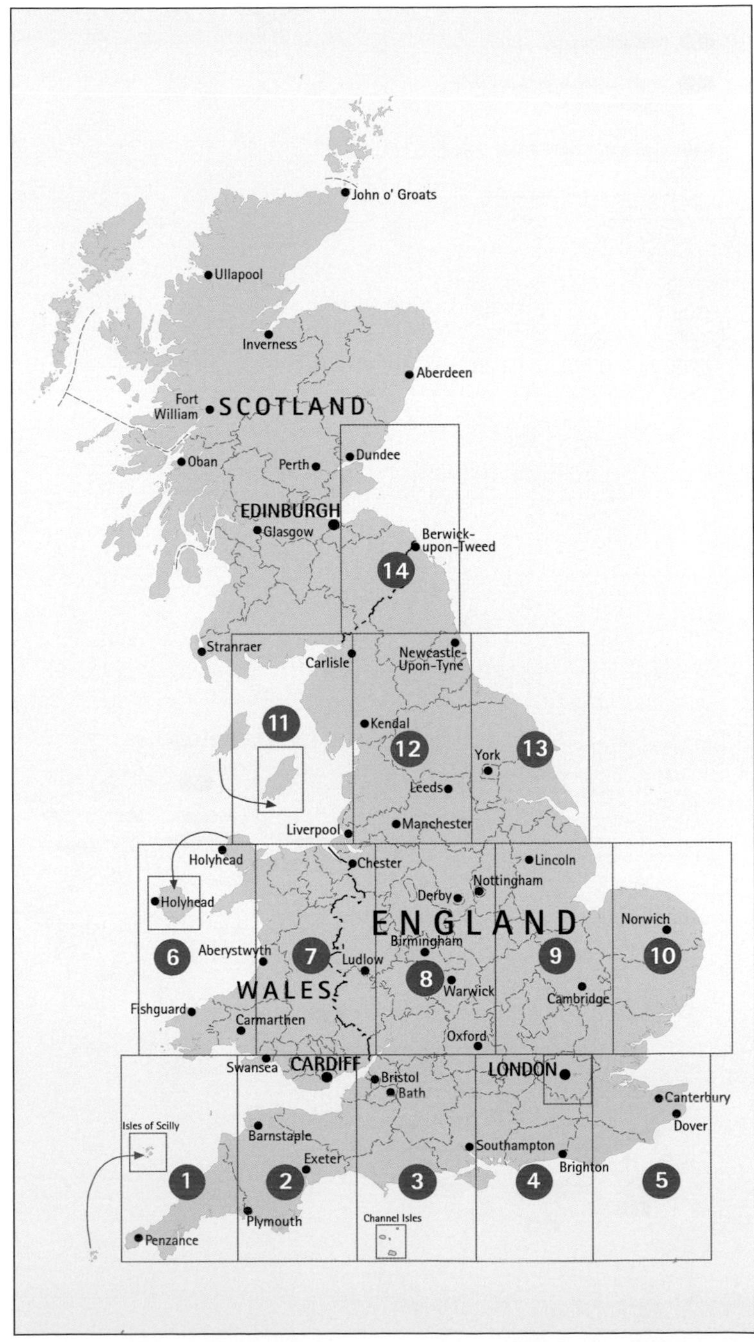
John o' Groats
Ullapool
Inverness
Aberdeen
Fort William
SCOTLAND
Oban
Perth
Dundee
EDINBURGH
Glasgow
Berwick-upon-Tweed
14
Stranraer
Carlisle
Newcastle-Upon-Tyne
11
Kendal
12
York
13
Leeds
Liverpool
Manchester
Holyhead
Chester
Lincoln
Holyhead
Nottingham
Derby
ENGLAND
Norwich
Birmingham
6
Aberystwyth
7
Ludlow
8
9
10
WALES
Warwick
Cambridge
Fishguard
Carmarthen
Oxford
Swansea
CARDIFF
Bristol
LONDON
Bath
Canterbury
Dover
Isles of Scilly
Barnstaple
Southampton
Exeter
Brighton
1
2
3
4
5
Plymouth
Channel Isles
Penzance

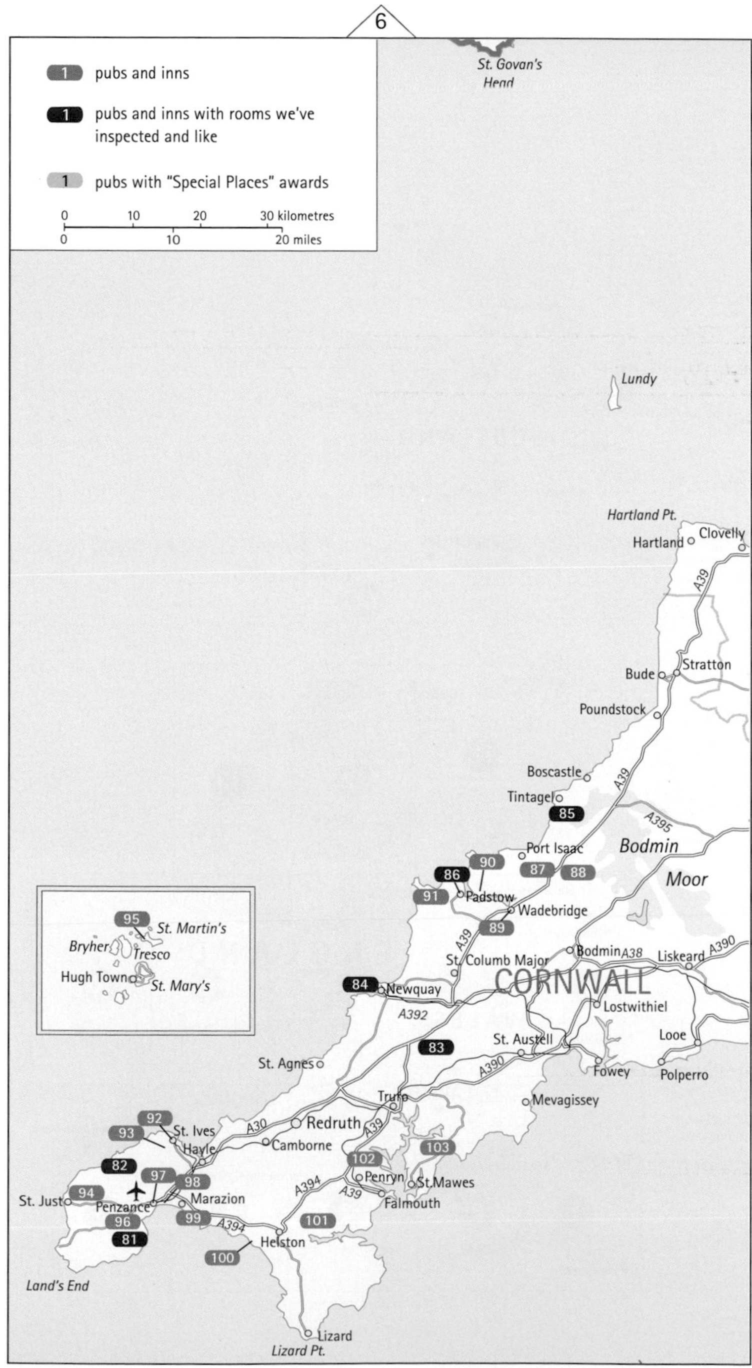
6
pubs and inns
pubs and inns with rooms we've inspected and like
pubs with "Special Places" awards
0 10 20 30 kilometres
0 10 20 miles
St. Govan's Head
Lundy
Hartland Pt.
Hartland
Clovelly
A39
Bude
Stratton
Poundstock
Boscastle
Tintagel
85
A395
Port Isaac
Bodmin
Moor
90
86
87
88
91
Padstow
Wadebridge
89
A39
St. Columb Major
Bodmin
A38
Liskeard
A390
84
Newquay
CORNWALL
Lostwithiel
A392
83
St. Austell
Looe
St. Agnes
A390
Fowey
Polperro
Truro
Mevagissey
92
93
St. Ives
A30
Redruth
A39
Hayle
Camborne
103
82
102
97
Penryn
St.Mawes
98
A394
St. Just
94
Penzance
Marazion
A39
Falmouth
96
99
A394
101
81
Helston
100
Land's End
Lizard
Lizard Pt.
95
St. Martin's
Bryher
Tresco
Hugh Town
St. Mary's

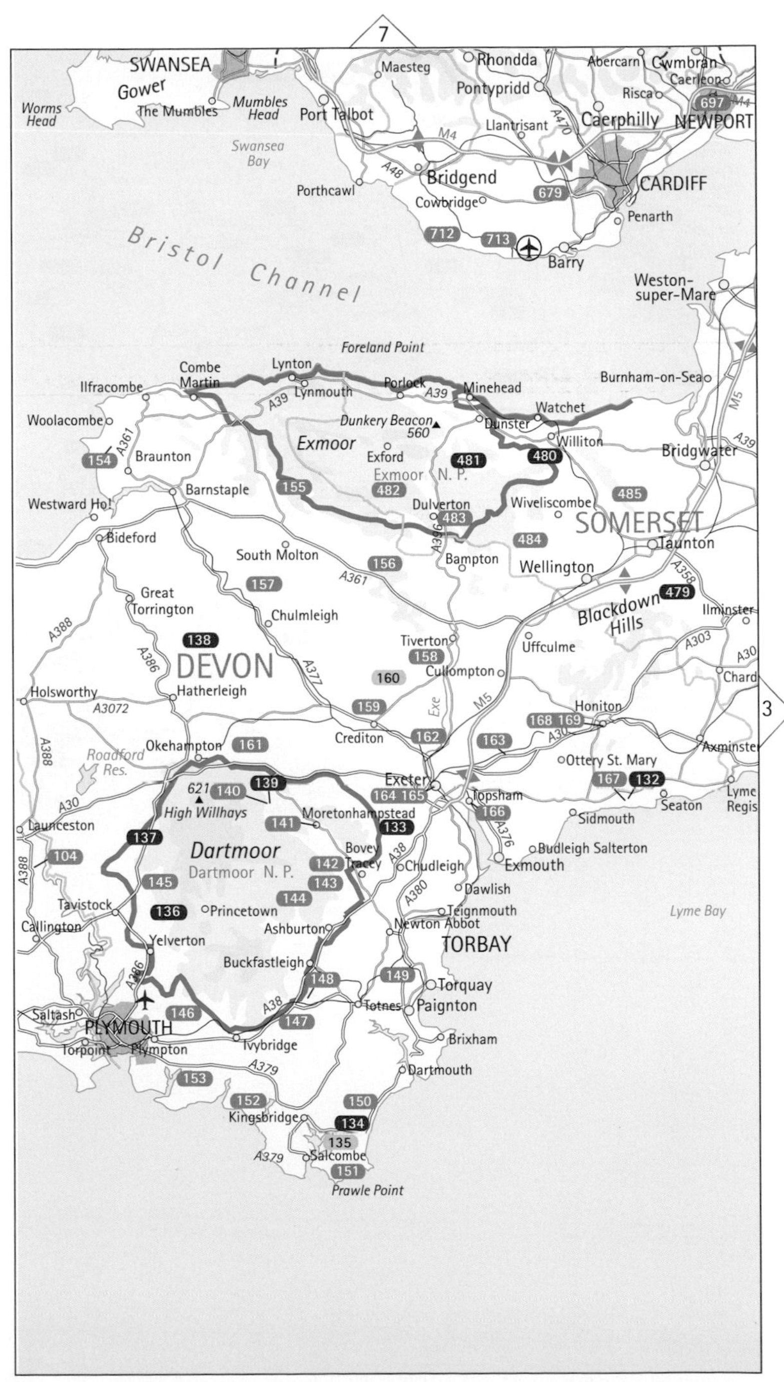
SWANSEA
Gower
Worms Head
The Mumbles
Mumbles Head
Swansea Bay
Port Talbot
Maesteg
Rhondda
Pontypridd
Abercarn
Cwmbran
Caerleon
Risca
NEWPORT
Caerphilly
Llantrisant
CARDIFF
Bridgend
Cowbridge
Porthcawl
Penarth
Barry
Bristol Channel
Weston-super-Mare
Foreland Point
Combe Martin
Lynton
Lynmouth
Porlock
Minehead
Watchet
Dunster
Williton
Burnham-on-Sea
Ilfracombe
Woolacombe
Braunton
Barnstaple
Westward Ho!
Bideford
Dunkery Beacon 560
Exmoor
Exford
Exmoor N. P.
Dulverton
Wiveliscombe
SOMERSET
Bridgwater
Taunton
Bampton
Wellington
South Molton
Great Torrington
Chulmleigh
Blackdown Hills
Ilminster
DEVON
Holsworthy
Hatherleigh
Tiverton
Uffculme
Cullompton
Chard
Honiton
Axminster
Crediton
Okehampton
Roadford Res.
Exeter
Topsham
Ottery St. Mary
Lyme Regis
Seaton
Sidmouth
High Willhays
621
Moretonhampstead
Launceston
Dartmoor
Dartmoor N. P.
Bovey Tracey
Chudleigh
Budleigh Salterton
Exmouth
Dawlish
Tavistock
Princetown
Teignmouth
Callington
Yelverton
Ashburton
Newton Abbot
TORBAY
Lyme Bay
Buckfastleigh
Torquay
Saltash
PLYMOUTH
Totnes
Paignton
Torpoint
Plympton
Ivybridge
Brixham
Dartmouth
Kingsbridge
Salcombe
Prawle Point

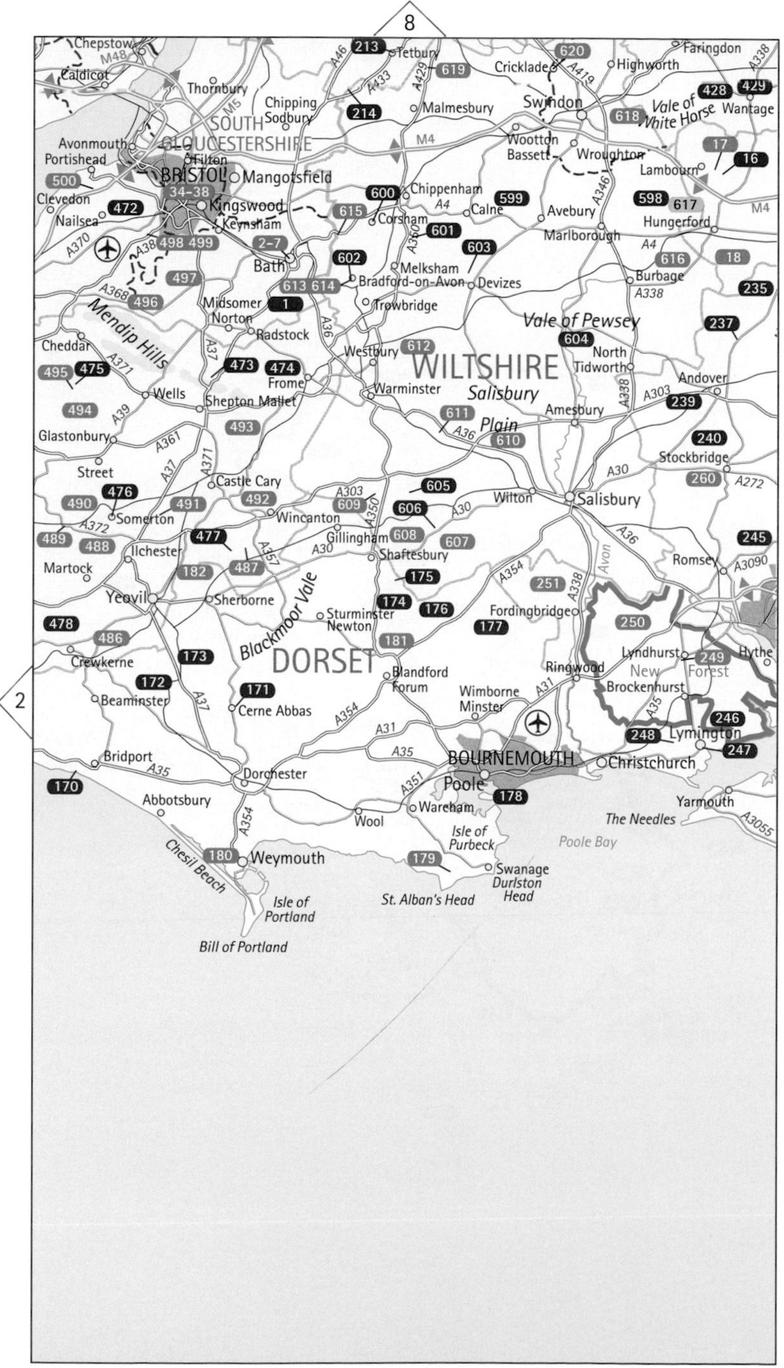
8
2
Chepstow
Caldicot
Thornbury
Chipping Sodbury
SOUTH GLOUCESTERSHIRE
Avonmouth
Portishead
Filton
BRISTOL
Mangotsfield
Clevedon
Nailsea
Kingswood
Keynsham
Bath
Tetbury
Malmesbury
Cricklade
Highworth
Faringdon
Swindon
Vale of White Horse
Wantage
Wootton Bassett
Wroughton
Lambourn
Chippenham
Corsham
Calne
Avebury
Marlborough
Hungerford
Melksham
Bradford-on-Avon
Devizes
Trowbridge
Burbage
Midsomer Norton
Radstock
Vale of Pewsey
Mendip Hills
Cheddar
Westbury
WILTSHIRE
North Tidworth
Frome
Wells
Warminster
Salisbury Plain
Andover
Shepton Mallet
Amesbury
Glastonbury
Stockbridge
Street
Castle Cary
Wilton
Salisbury
Somerton
Wincanton
Gillingham
Shaftesbury
Ilchester
Martock
Romsey
Yeovil
Sherborne
Blackmoor Vale
Sturminster Newton
Fordingbridge
Crewkerne
DORSET
Ringwood
Lyndhurst
New Forest
Hythe
Brockenhurst
Blandford Forum
Beaminster
Wimborne Minster
Cerne Abbas
Lymington
Bridport
BOURNEMOUTH
Christchurch
Poole
Dorchester
Abbotsbury
Wareham
Wool
Yarmouth
The Needles
Isle of Purbeck
Poole Bay
Chesil Beach
Weymouth
Swanage
Durlston Head
Isle of Portland
St. Alban's Head
Bill of Portland
Avon
M48
M5
M4
A4
A46
A433
A429
A419
A338
A370
A38
A368
A371
A37
A39
A361
A36
A350
A346
A303
A30
A372
A357
A354
A272
A3090
A31
A35
A351
A3055
213 619 620 428 429 214 618 17 16 500 472 600 615 599 598 617 498 499 2-7 601 603 616 18 34-38 602 497 613 614 235 496 1 237 604 612 495 475 473 474 494 239 493 611 610 240 476 605 260 490 491 492 609 606 489 488 477 608 607 245 487 182 175 251 174 176 478 250 486 181 177 249 173 172 171 246 248 247 170 178 180 179

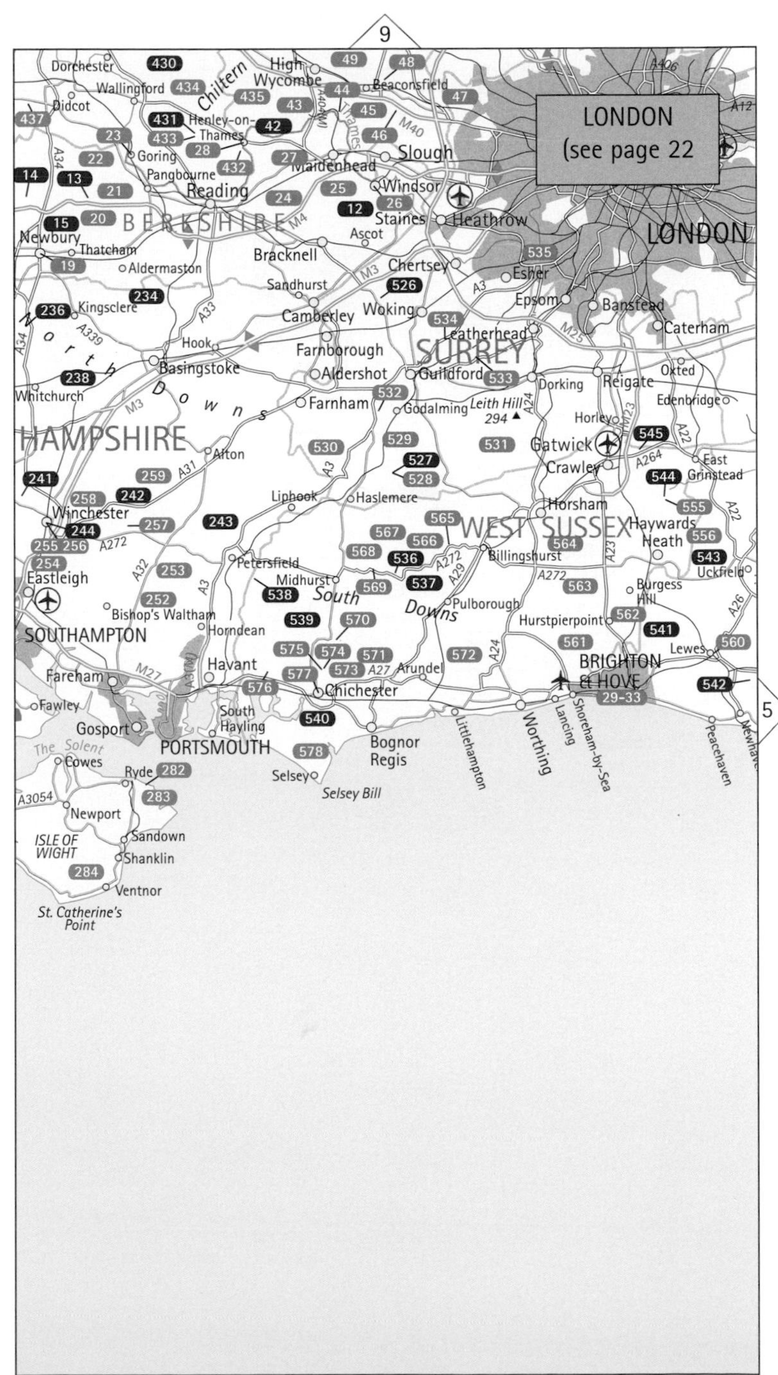

LONDON
(see page 22
LONDON
BERKSHIRE
SURREY
HAMPSHIRE
WEST SUSSEX
North Downs
South Downs
Chiltern
Reading
Slough
Windsor
Heathrow
Staines
Maidenhead
High Wycombe
Beaconsfield
Henley-on-Thames
Goring
Pangbourne
Wallingford
Didcot
Dorchester
Newbury
Thatcham
Aldermaston
Bracknell
Ascot
Chertsey
Esher
Epsom
Banstead
Caterham
Sandhurst
Camberley
Woking
Leatherhead
Kingsclere
Hook
Basingstoke
Farnborough
Aldershot
Guildford
Dorking
Reigate
Oxted
Edenbridge
Whitchurch
Farnham
Godalming
Leith Hill 294
Horley
Gatwick
Crawley
East Grinstead
Alton
Liphook
Haslemere
Horsham
Winchester
Haywards Heath
Billingshurst
Petersfield
Midhurst
Uckfield
Eastleigh
Burgess Hill
Pulborough
Bishop's Waltham
Hurstpierpoint
Horndean
SOUTHAMPTON
Lewes
Havant
Arundel
BRIGHTON & HOVE
Fareham
Chichester
Fawley
Gosport
South Hayling
PORTSMOUTH
Bognor Regis
Littlehampton
Worthing
Lancing
Shoreham-by-Sea
Peacehaven
The Solent
Cowes
Ryde
Selsey
Selsey Bill
Newport
Sandown
Shanklin
ISLE OF WIGHT
Ventnor
St. Catherine's Point
M4
M3
M40
M25
M23
M27
A3(M)
A404(M)
A3
A24
A22
A23
A26
A27
A29
A31
A32
A33
A34
A272
A264
A339
A3054
A406
A12
Thames
9
5
430 434 435 431 433 437 23 22 14 13 21 15 20 19 28 432 42 43 44 45 46 47 48 49 27 24 25 26 12
234 236 238 526 534 535 533 532 529 530 531 527 528 545 544 555 556 543
241 259 242 258 244 257 243 255 256 254 253 252 567 566 565 568 536 537 538 569 564 563 562 541 561 560
539 570 575 574 571 577 573 572 576 540 578 542 29-33 282 283 284

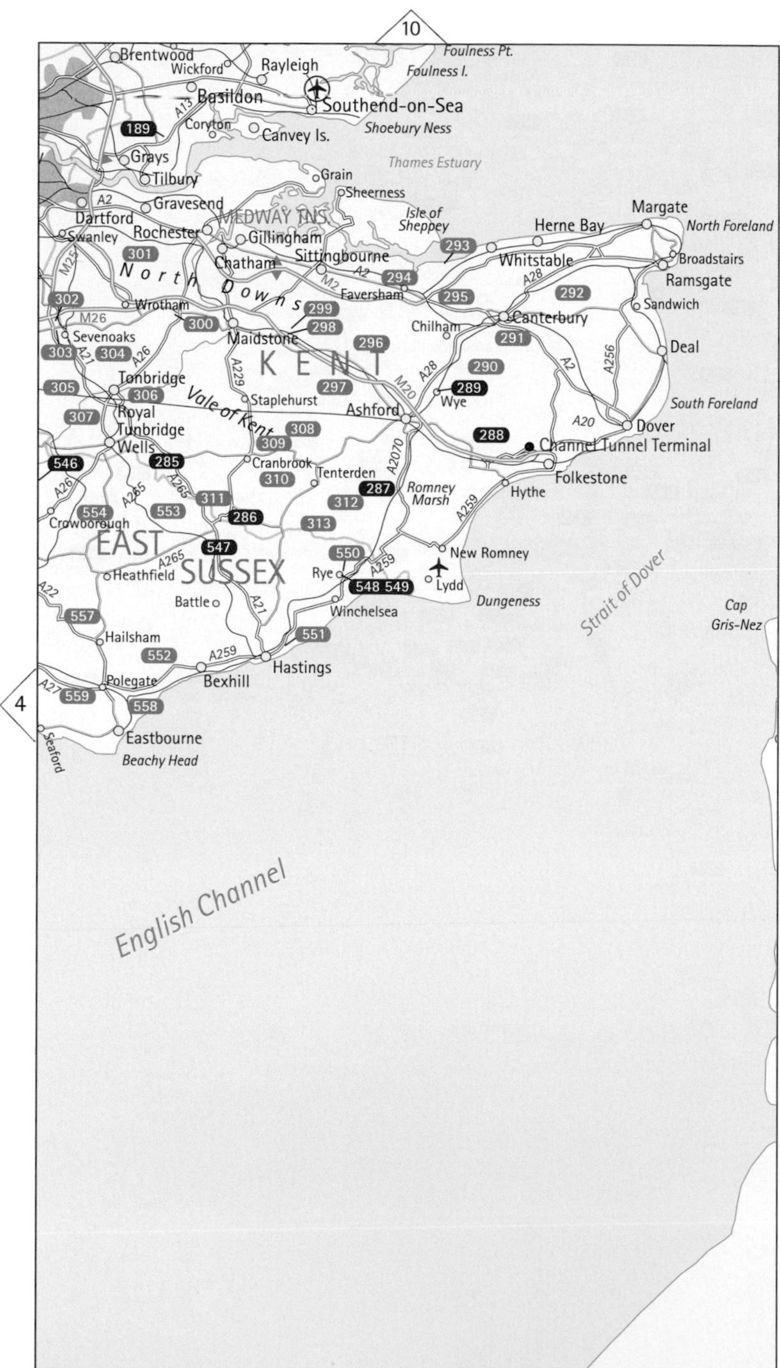
10
Foulness Pt.
Foulness I.
Brentwood
Wickford
Rayleigh
Basildon
Southend-on-Sea
Shoebury Ness
189
Coryton
Canvey Is.
Grays
Tilbury
Thames Estuary
Grain
Sheerness
A2
Gravesend
Dartford
MEDWAY TNS
Isle of Sheppey
Margate
Herne Bay
North Foreland
Swanley
Rochester
Gillingham
Chatham
Sittingbourne
293
Whitstable
Broadstairs
Ramsgate
301
North Downs
A2
M2
294
Faversham
A28
292
302
Wrotham
299
295
Sandwich
M26
300
298
Chilham
Canterbury
Sevenoaks
Maidstone
296
291
Deal
303
304
A26
KENT
A2
A256
A229
M20
A28
290
305
Tonbridge
297
289
306
Staplehurst
Wye
South Foreland
Royal Tunbridge Wells
Vale of Kent
Ashford
A20
Dover
307
308
288
Channel Tunnel Terminal
309
546
285
Cranbrook
A2070
Folkestone
Tenterden
310
287
Romney Marsh
Hythe
A26
A265
A265
311
312
554
553
A259
286
Crowborough
313
EAST SUSSEX
547
New Romney
550
A265
A259
Heathfield
Rye
Lydd
548 549
Dungeness
Strait of Dover
A22
Battle
A21
Winchelsea
Cap Gris-Nez
557
Hailsham
551
552
A259
Hastings
Polegate
Bexhill
A27
559
4
558
Eastbourne
Seaford
Beachy Head
English Channel

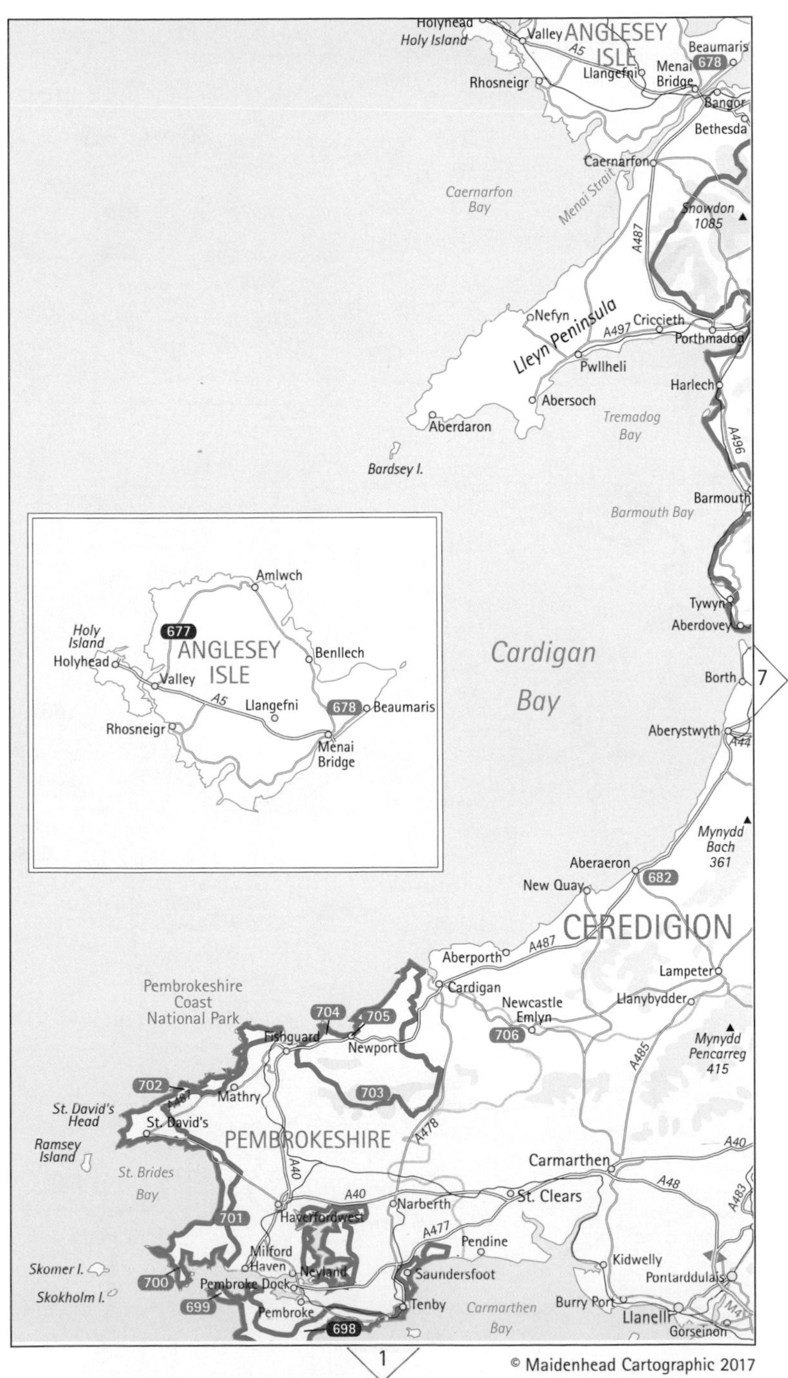
Holyhead
Holy Island
Valley
ANGLESEY ISLE
A5
Beaumaris
Menai Bridge
678
Llangefni
Rhosneigr
Bangor
Bethesda
Caernarfon
Caernarfon Bay
Menai Strait
Snowdon 1085
A487
Nefyn
Lleyn Peninsula
A497
Criccieth
Porthmadog
Pwllheli
Harlech
Abersoch
Aberdaron
Tremadog Bay
A496
Bardsey I.
Barmouth
Barmouth Bay
Amlwch
677
Holy Island
Holyhead
ANGLESEY ISLE
Benllech
Valley
A5
Llangefni
678
Beaumaris
Rhosneigr
Menai Bridge
Tywyn
Aberdovey
Cardigan Bay
Borth
7
Aberystwyth
A44
Mynydd Bach 361
Aberaeron
682
New Quay
CEREDIGION
Aberporth
A487
Lampeter
Cardigan
Pembrokeshire Coast National Park
704
705
Newcastle Emlyn
Llanybydder
706
Fishguard
Newport
Mynydd Pencarreg 415
A485
702
703
Mathry
A487
St. David's Head
St. David's
Ramsey Island
PEMBROKESHIRE
A478
A40
Carmarthen
St. Brides Bay
A40
A48
A483
A40
St. Clears
Narberth
701
Haverfordwest
A477
Pendine
Skomer I.
Milford Haven
Kidwelly
Neyland
Saundersfoot
Pontarddulais
700
Skokholm I.
Pembroke Dock
699
Tenby
Carmarthen Bay
Burry Port
M4
Llanelli
Pembroke
698
Gorseinon
1

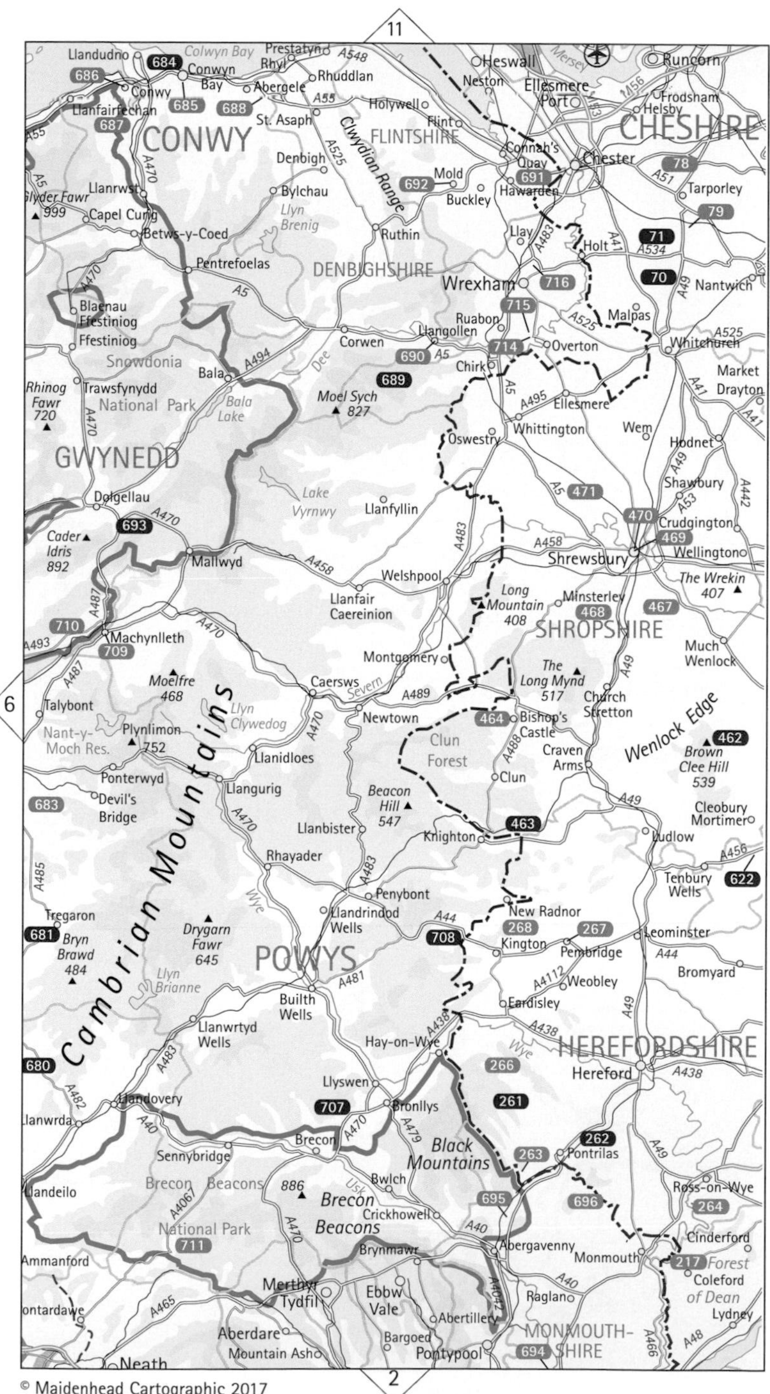

11
6
2
Llandudno
Colwyn Bay
Prestatyn
Rhyl
Conwy
Bay
Abergele
Rhuddlan
Holywell
Flint
Heswall
Neston
Ellesmere
Port
Runcorn
Frodsham
Helsby
Llanfairfechan
St. Asaph
CONWY
FLINTSHIRE
CHESHIRE
Clwydian Range
Connah's
Quay
Chester
Denbigh
Mold
Buckley
Hawarden
Tarporley
Llanrwst
Bylchau
Glyder Fawr
999
Capel Curig
Llyn
Brenig
Betws-y-Coed
Ruthin
Llay
Holt
Pentrefoelas
DENBIGHSHIRE
Wrexham
Nantwich
Blaenau
Ffestiniog
Ruabon
Malpas
Ffestiniog
Llangollen
Corwen
Overton
Whitchurch
Snowdonia
National Park
Chirk
Bala
Market
Drayton
Rhinog
Fawr
720
Trawsfynydd
Bala
Lake
Moel Sych
827
Ellesmere
Oswestry
Whittington
Wem
Hodnet
GWYNEDD
Shawbury
Lake
Vyrnwy
Dolgellau
Llanfyllin
Crudgington
Cader
Idris
892
Shrewsbury
Wellington
Mallwyd
Welshpool
The Wrekin
407
Llanfair
Caereinion
Long
Mountain
408
Minsterley
Machynlleth
SHROPSHIRE
Much
Wenlock
Montgomery
Moelfre
468
The
Long Mynd
517
Caersws
Severn
Church
Stretton
Talybont
Llyn
Clywedog
Newtown
Bishop's
Castle
Wenlock Edge
Nant-y-
Moch Res.
Plynlimon
752
Clun
Forest
Craven
Arms
Brown
Clee Hill
539
Llanidloes
Ponterwyd
Clun
Devil's
Bridge
Llangurig
Beacon
Hill
547
Cleobury
Mortimer
Llanbister
Knighton
Ludlow
Cambrian Mountains
Rhayader
Tenbury
Wells
Penybont
Tregaron
New Radnor
Llandrindod
Wells
Bryn
Brawd
484
Drygarn
Fawr
645
Kington
Pembridge
Leominster
POWYS
Bromyard
Llyn
Brianne
Weobley
Builth
Wells
Eardisley
Llanwrtyd
Wells
Hay-on-Wye
Wye
HEREFORDSHIRE
Hereford
Llyswen
Llandovery
Bronllys
Llanwrda
Black
Mountains
Brecon
Pontrilas
Sennybridge
Bwlch
Ross-on-Wye
Llandeilo
Brecon Beacons
National Park
886
Brecon
Beacons
Usk
Crickhowell
Abergavenny
Cinderford
Monmouth
Forest
of Dean
Ammanford
Brynmawr
Coleford
Merthyr
Tydfil
Ebbw
Vale
Raglan
Pontardawe
Abertillery
Lydney
Aberdare
Mountain Ash
Bargoed
MONMOUTH-
SHIRE
Neath
Pontypool
A548
A55
A5
A470
A525
A494
A483
A495
A41
A534
A49
A53
A442
A458
A487
A493
A489
A488
A485
A44
A481
A4112
A438
A482
A40
A479
A4067
A465
A4042
A466
A48
A456
A525
A51
M56
M53
684
686
685
688
687
692
691
78
79
71
70
716
715
714
690
689
693
471
470
469
468
467
710
709
464
462
683
463
622
681
268
267
708
680
266
261
707
262
263
695
696
264
711
217
694

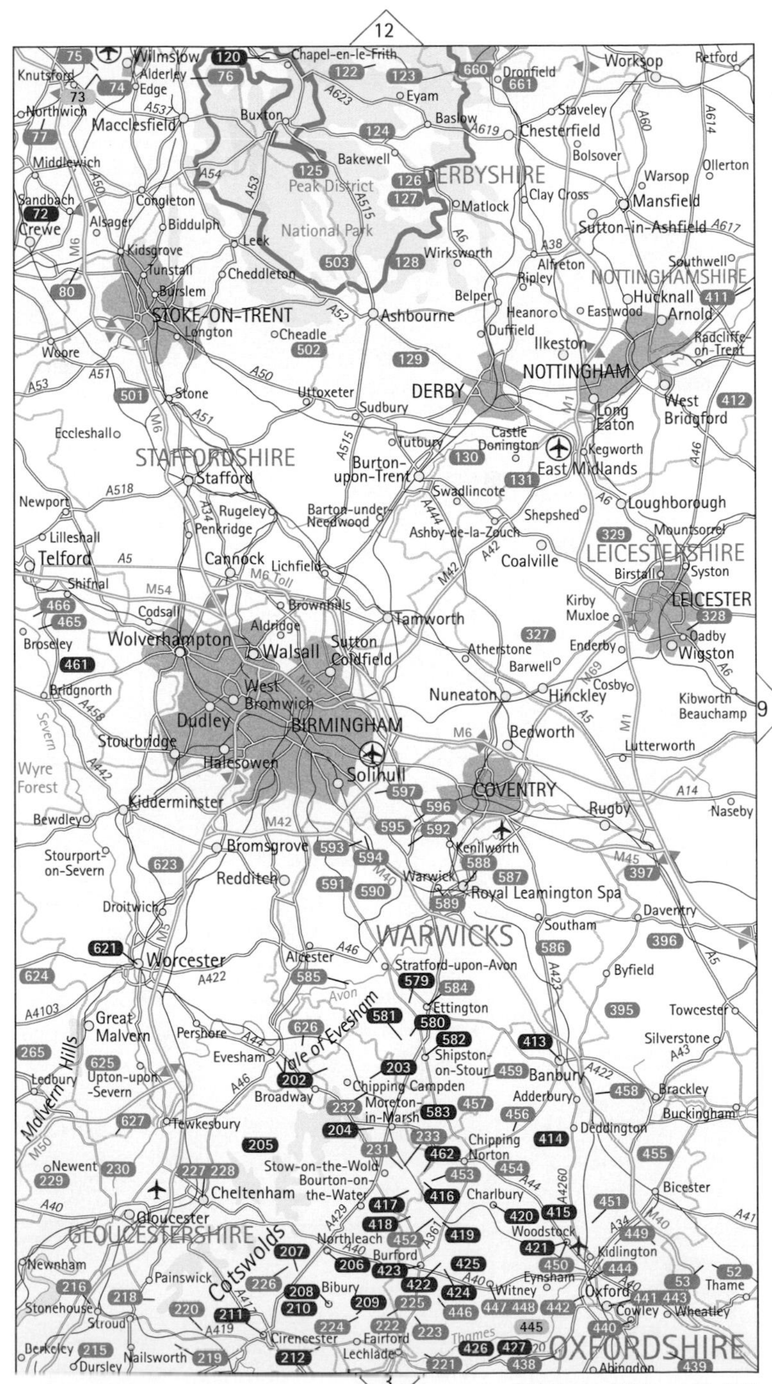
12
Peak District
National Park
DERBYSHIRE
NOTTINGHAMSHIRE
STAFFORDSHIRE
LEICESTERSHIRE
WARWICKS
GLOUCESTERSHIRE
OXFORDSHIRE
STOKE-ON-TRENT
DERBY
NOTTINGHAM
LEICESTER
BIRMINGHAM
COVENTRY
Cotswolds
Vale of Evesham
Malvern Hills
Wyre Forest
3
9

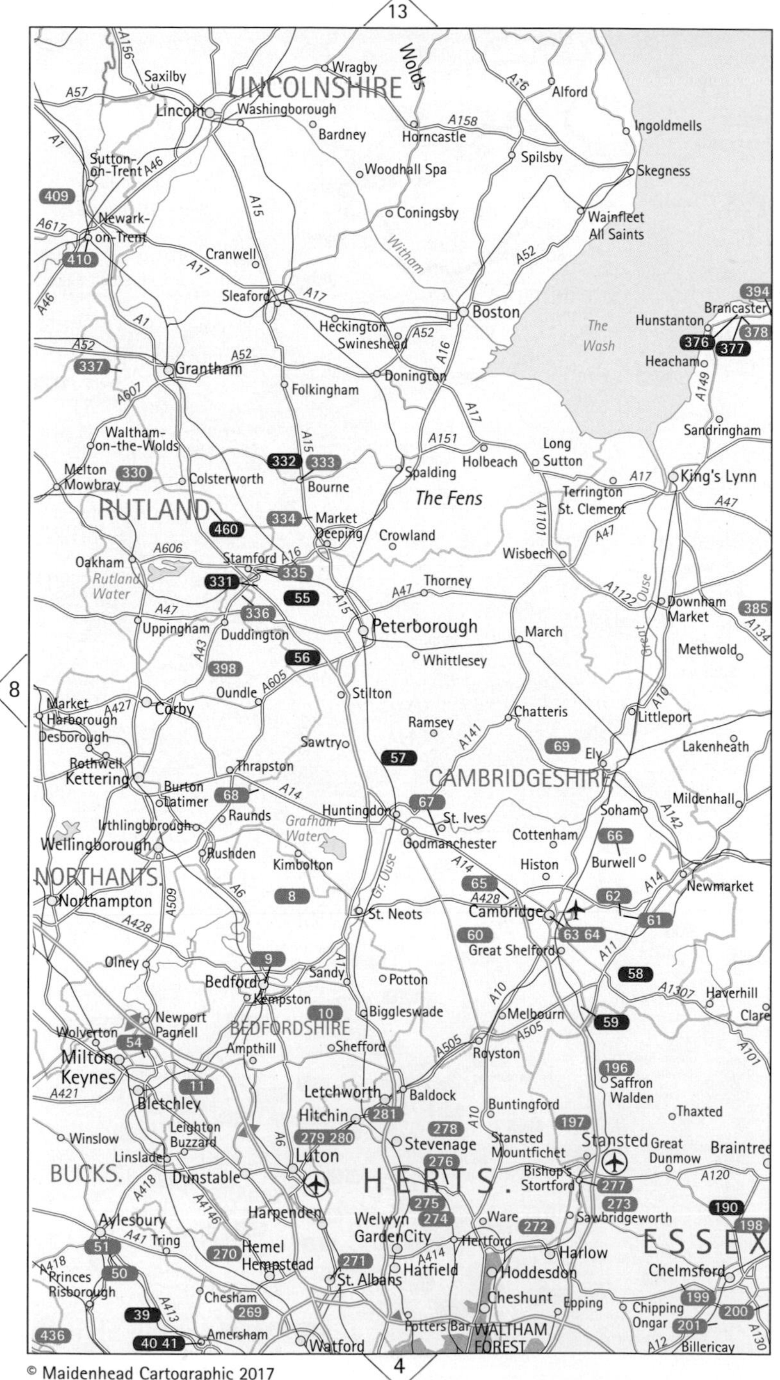
13
LINCOLNSHIRE
Saxilby
Wragby
Wolds
Alford
Lincoln
Washingborough
Bardney
Horncastle
Ingoldmells
Spilsby
Sutton-on-Trent
Woodhall Spa
Skegness
Coningsby
Newark-on-Trent
Wainfleet All Saints
Cranwell
Witham
Sleaford
Boston
Heckington
Swineshead
The Wash
Hunstanton
Brancaster
Heacham
Grantham
Donington
Folkingham
Sandringham
Waltham-on-the-Wolds
Long Sutton
Holbeach
Spalding
Melton Mowbray
Colsterworth
Bourne
King's Lynn
The Fens
Terrington St. Clement
RUTLAND
Market Deeping
Crowland
Wisbech
Oakham
Stamford
Rutland Water
Thorney
Downham Market
Uppingham
Duddington
Peterborough
March
Methwold
Whittlesey
Oundle
Stilton
8
Market Harborough
Corby
Chatteris
Littleport
Desborough
Ramsey
Sawtry
Lakenheath
Rothwell
Kettering
Thrapston
Ely
CAMBRIDGESHIRE
Burton Latimer
Huntingdon
St. Ives
Soham
Mildenhall
Raunds
Grafham Water
Irthlingborough
Godmanchester
Cottenham
Wellingborough
Rushden
Kimbolton
Histon
Burwell
NORTHANTS.
Newmarket
Northampton
St. Neots
Cambridge
Great Shelford
Olney
Bedford
Sandy
Potton
Haverhill
Kempston
Biggleswade
Melbourn
Clare
Newport Pagnell
BEDFORDSHIRE
Wolverton
Milton Keynes
Ampthill
Shefford
Royston
Saffron Walden
Letchworth
Baldock
Bletchley
Buntingford
Thaxted
Hitchin
Winslow
Leighton Buzzard
Stevenage
Stansted Mountfichet
Stansted
Great Dunmow
Braintree
Linslade
Luton
BUCKS.
Dunstable
HERTS.
Bishop's Stortford
Harpenden
Aylesbury
Ware
Sawbridgeworth
Tring
Welwyn Garden City
Hertford
ESSEX
Hemel Hempstead
Harlow
Princes Risborough
Hatfield
Hoddesdon
Chelmsford
St. Albans
Cheshunt
Chesham
Epping
Chipping Ongar
Potters Bar
WALTHAM FOREST
Amersham
Watford
Billericay
4
A156 A57 A1 A46 A617 A17 A15 A158 A16 A52 A607 A151 A606 A47 A43 A605 A427 A14 A141 A1101 A1122 Great Ouse A134 A10 A142 A509 A6 A428 Gr. Ouse A11 A1307 A101 A505 A421 A418 A4146 A41 A413 A414 A120 A12 A130
409 410 337 330 332 333 334 460 331 335 55 336 56 398 57 68 67 69 66 65 62 61 60 63 64 58 59 8 9 10 54 11 281 278 279 280 276 275 274 197 196 277 273 272 190 198 270 271 51 50 39 40 41 269 436 199 200 201 394 376 377 378 385

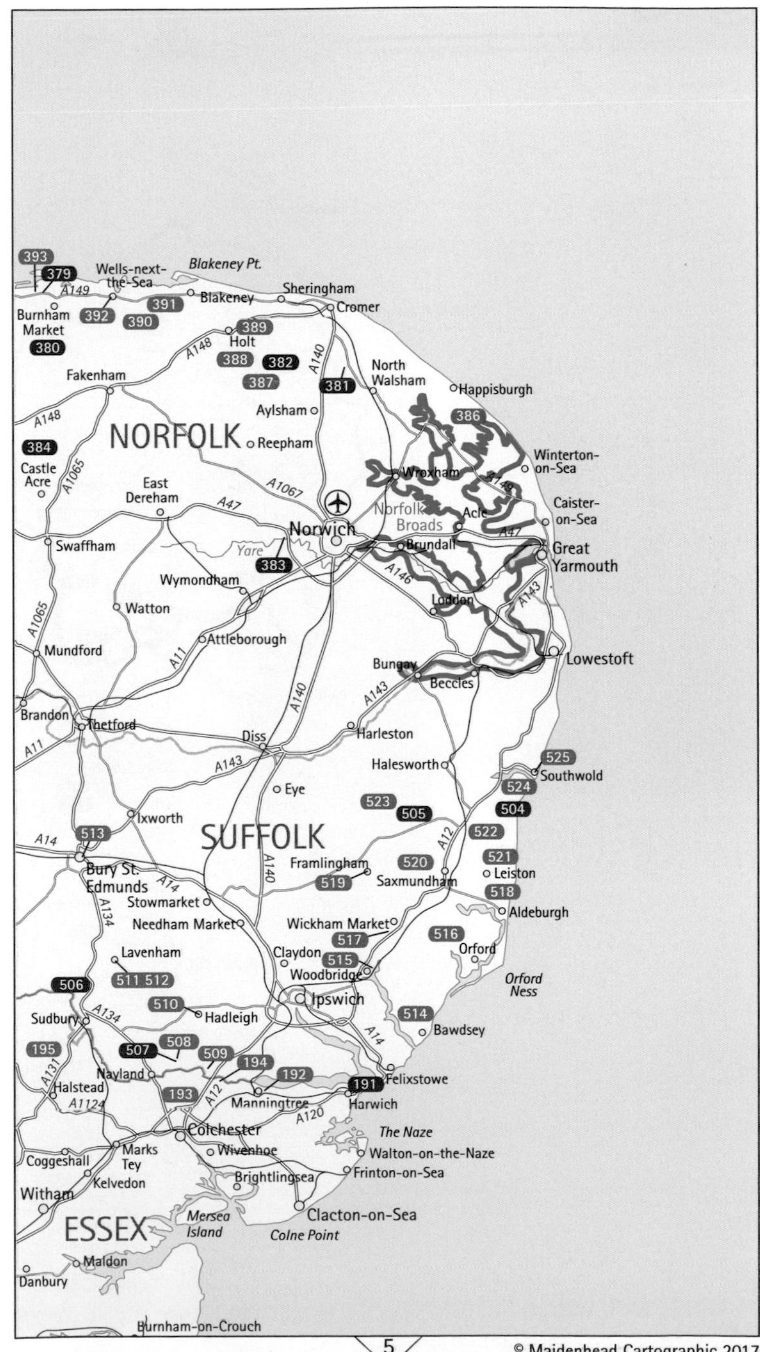

NORFOLK
SUFFOLK
ESSEX
Blakeney Pt.
Wells-next-the-Sea
Burnham Market
Blakeney
Sheringham
Cromer
Holt
Fakenham
North Walsham
Happisburgh
Aylsham
Reepham
Castle Acre
East Dereham
Winterton-on-Sea
Wroxham
Norfolk Broads
Acle
Caister-on-Sea
Norwich
Brundall
Great Yarmouth
Swaffham
Yare
Wymondham
Watton
Loddon
Attleborough
Mundford
Lowestoft
Bungay
Beccles
Brandon
Thetford
Diss
Harleston
Halesworth
Southwold
Eye
Ixworth
Framlingham
Saxmundham
Leiston
Bury St. Edmunds
Stowmarket
Aldeburgh
Needham Market
Wickham Market
Orford
Lavenham
Claydon
Woodbridge
Orford Ness
Ipswich
Sudbury
Hadleigh
Bawdsey
Nayland
Felixstowe
Halstead
Manningtree
Harwich
The Naze
Colchester
Walton-on-the-Naze
Coggeshall
Marks Tey
Wivenhoe
Frinton-on-Sea
Kelvedon
Brightlingsea
Witham
Clacton-on-Sea
Mersea Island
Colne Point
Maldon
Danbury
Burnham-on-Crouch
A149
A148
A140
A1067
A47
A1065
A146
A143
A11
A14
A12
A134
A131
A1124
A120
393
379
392
391
390
389
380
388
382
387
381
386
384
383
525
524
504
523
505
522
513
521
520
519
518
517
516
515
506
511 512
510
514
195
507
508
509
194
192
191
193
5

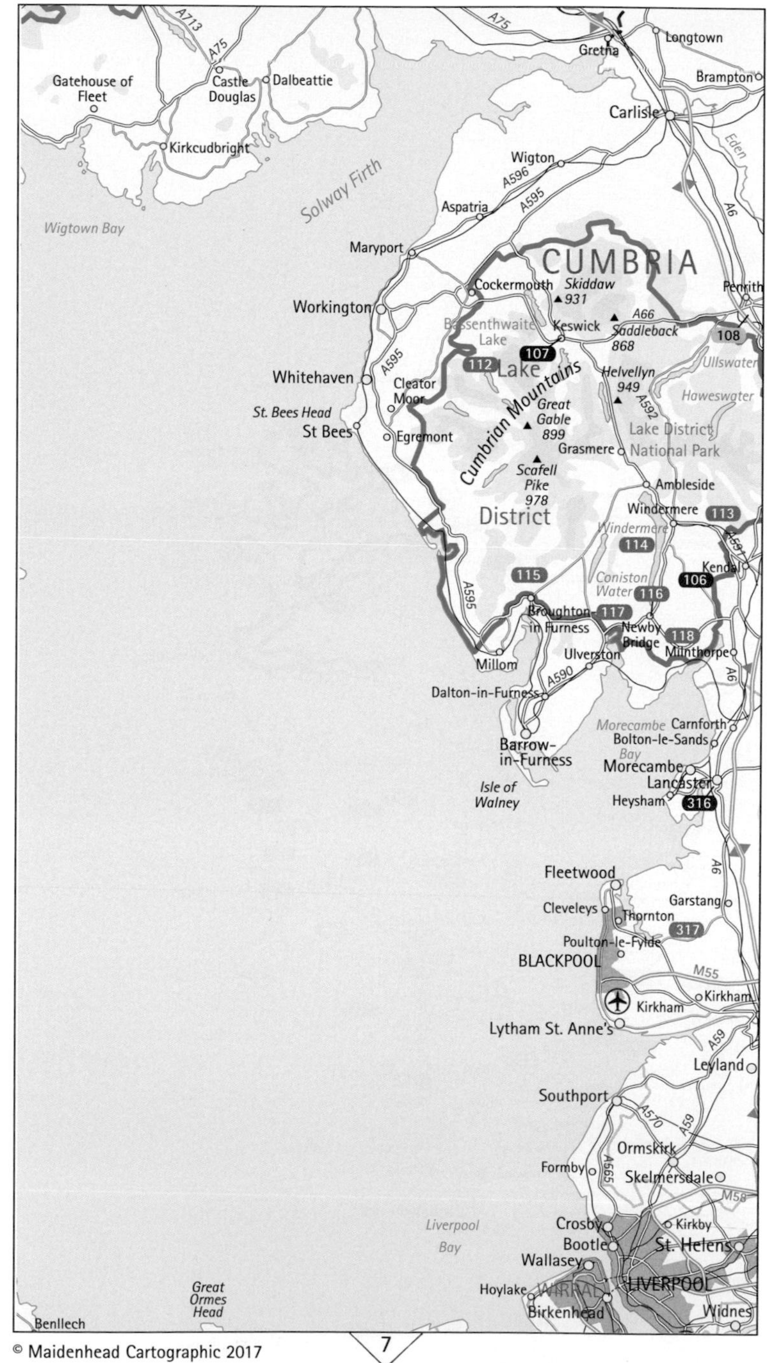
Gatehouse of Fleet
Castle Douglas
Dalbeattie
Kirkcudbright
Wigtown Bay
Solway Firth
Gretna
Longtown
Brampton
Carlisle
Eden
Wigton
A596
Aspatria
A595
A6
Maryport
CUMBRIA
Cockermouth
Skiddaw 931
Penrith
Workington
Bassenthwaite Lake
Keswick
A66
Saddleback 868
108
107
112
Lake
Ullswater
Whitehaven
A595
Cleator Moor
Cumbrian Mountains
Helvellyn 949
Haweswater
St. Bees Head
St Bees
Egremont
Great Gable 899
A592
Lake District National Park
Grasmere
Scafell Pike 978
Ambleside
Windermere
113
District
Windermere
114
A591
Kendal
115
Coniston Water
116
106
A595
Broughton-in Furness
117
Newby Bridge
118
Milnthorpe
Millom
Ulverston
A590
A6
Dalton-in-Furness
Morecambe Bay
Carnforth
Bolton-le-Sands
Barrow-in-Furness
Morecambe
Lancaster
Isle of Walney
Heysham
316
A6
Fleetwood
Garstang
Cleveleys
Thornton
317
Poulton-le-Fylde
BLACKPOOL
M55
Kirkham
Kirkham
Lytham St. Anne's
A59
Leyland
Southport
A570
A59
Ormskirk
Formby
A565
Skelmersdale
M58
Liverpool Bay
Crosby
Kirkby
Bootle
St. Helens
Wallasey
Great Ormes Head
Hoylake
WIRRAL
LIVERPOOL
Birkenhead
Widnes
Benllech
7

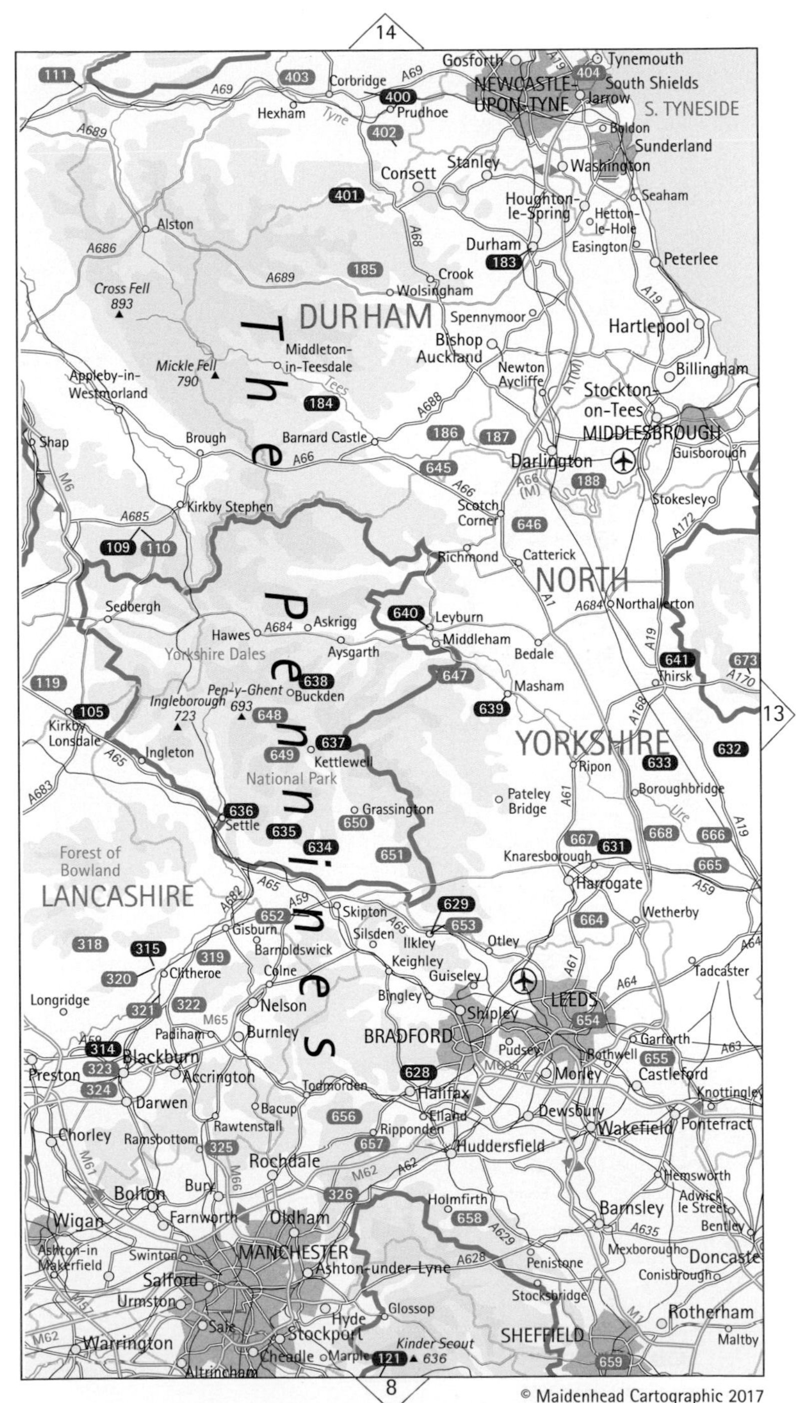
The Pennines
DURHAM
NORTH YORKSHIRE
LANCASHIRE
Yorkshire Dales National Park
Forest of Bowland
NEWCASTLE-UPON-TYNE
S. TYNESIDE
MIDDLESBROUGH
LEEDS
BRADFORD
MANCHESTER
SHEFFIELD
Kinder Scout 636
Cross Fell 893
Mickle Fell 790
Ingleborough 723
Pen-y-Ghent 693
© Maidenhead Cartographic 2017

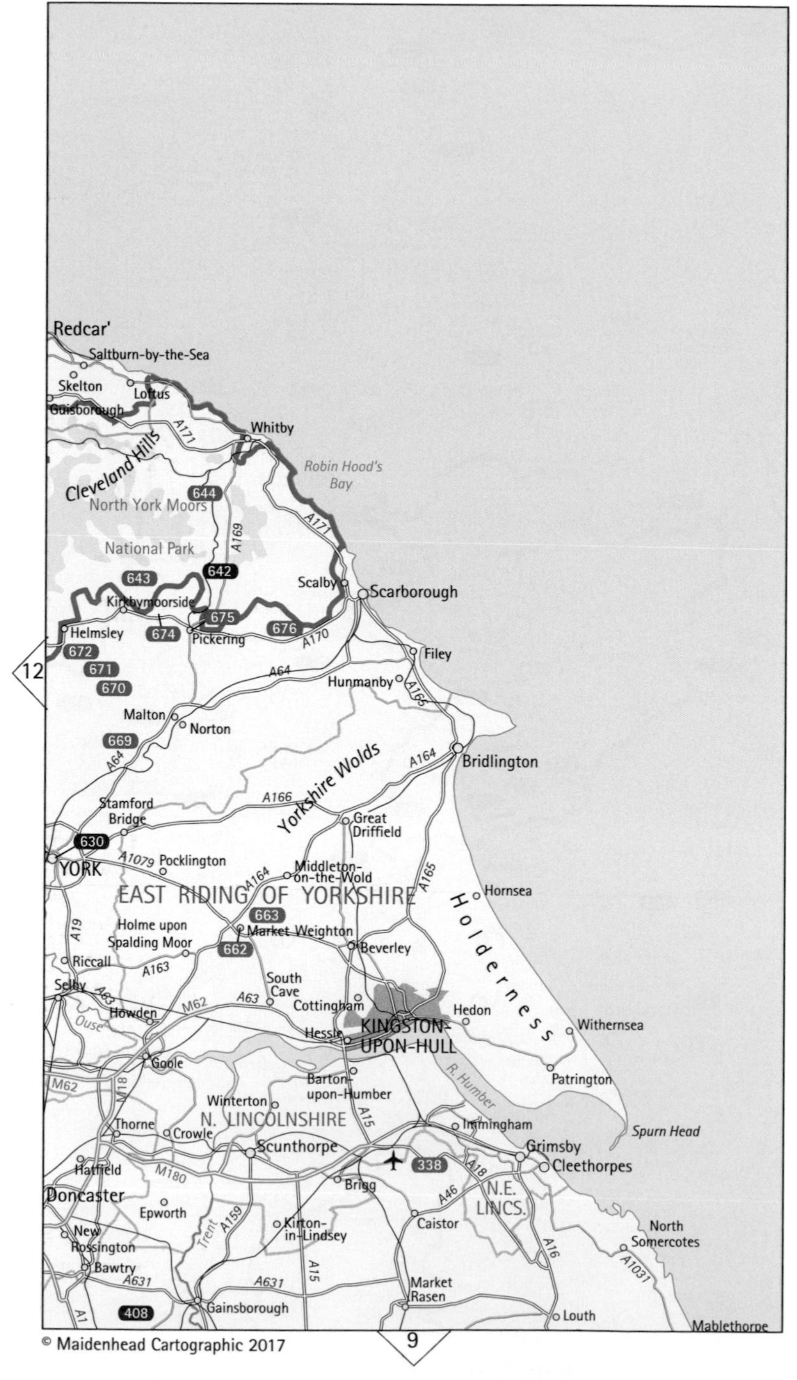
Redcar
Saltburn-by-the-Sea
Skelton
Loftus
Guisborough
Whitby
A171
Cleveland Hills
Robin Hood's Bay
644
North York Moors
National Park
A169
A171
642
643
Scalby
Scarborough
Kirkbymoorside
675
Helmsley
674
Pickering
676
A170
12
672
Filey
671
A64
Hunmanby
A165
670
Malton
Norton
669
Yorkshire Wolds
A164
Bridlington
A64
Stamford Bridge
A166
Great Driffield
630
YORK
A1079
Pocklington
Middleton-on-the-Wold
A164
A165
EAST RIDING OF YORKSHIRE
Hornsea
Holderness
663
A19
Holme upon Spalding Moor
Market Weighton
662
Beverley
Riccall
A163
Selby
A63
South Cave
Cottingham
Hedon
M62
A63
Howden
Ouse
Withernsea
Hessle
KINGSTON-UPON-HULL
Goole
R. Humber
Patrington
M62
M18
Barton-upon-Humber
Winterton
A15
N. LINCOLNSHIRE
Thorne
Crowle
Immingham
Spurn Head
Scunthorpe
Grimsby
338
Cleethorpes
Hatfield
M180
A18
Brigg
Doncaster
N.E. LINCS.
A46
Epworth
A159
Trent
Kirton-in-Lindsey
Caistor
North Somercotes
New Rossington
A16
A1031
Bawtry
A15
A631
A631
Market Rasen
408
A1
Gainsborough
Louth
Mablethorpe
9

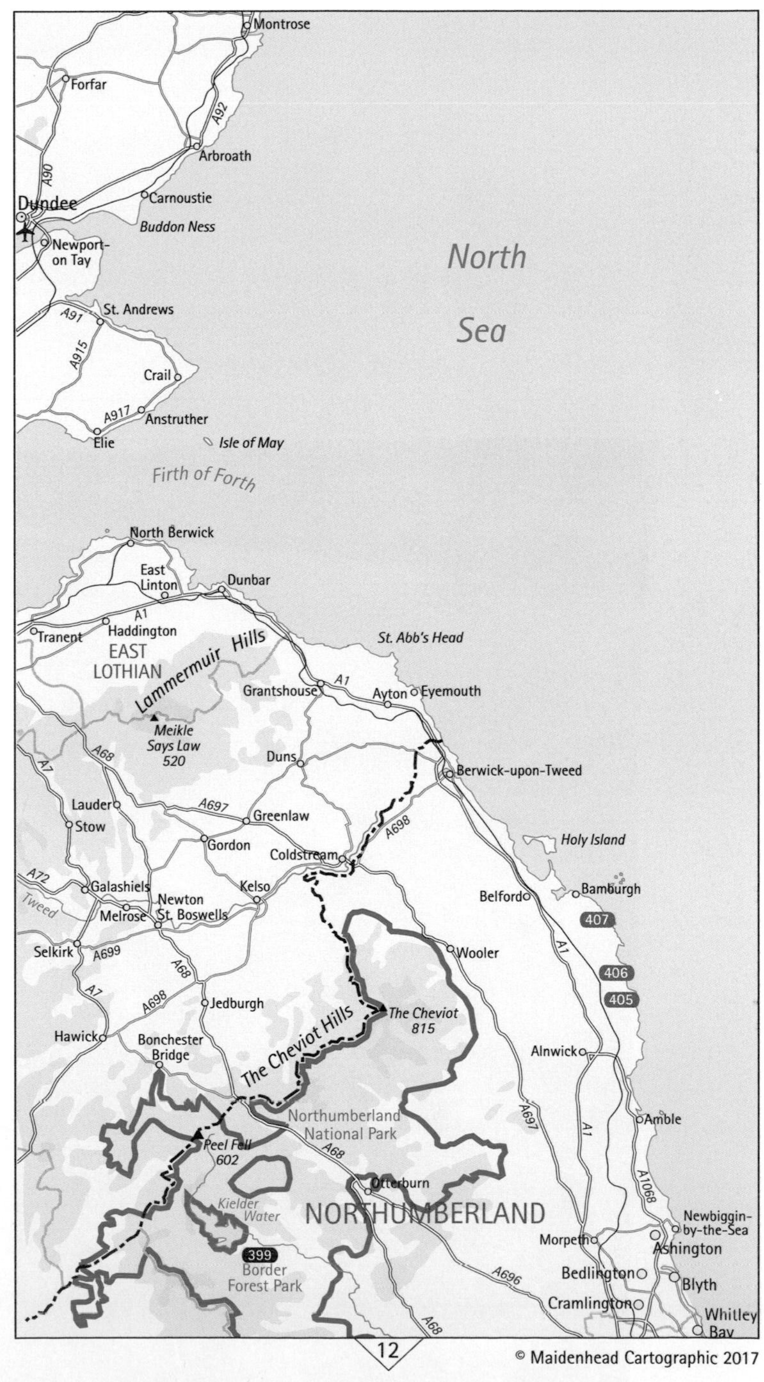
Montrose
Forfar
A92
Arbroath
A90
Dundee
Carnoustie
Buddon Ness
Newport-
on Tay
North
Sea
St. Andrews
A91
A915
Crail
A917
Anstruther
Elie
Isle of May
Firth of Forth
North Berwick
East
Linton
Dunbar
A1
Tranent
Haddington
EAST
LOTHIAN
Lammermuir Hills
St. Abb's Head
Grantshouse
A1
Ayton
Eyemouth
Meikle
Says Law
520
A68
A7
Duns
Berwick-upon-Tweed
Lauder
Stow
A697
Greenlaw
A698
Gordon
Holy Island
Coldstream
A72
Galashiels
Kelso
Tweed
Newton
St. Boswells
Melrose
Belford
Bamburgh
407
Selkirk
A699
Wooler
A68
A7
A1
406
405
A698
Jedburgh
The Cheviot
815
Hawick
Bonchester
Bridge
The Cheviot Hills
Alnwick
Amble
Northumberland
National Park
A697
A1
Peel Fell
602
A68
Otterburn
A1068
Kielder
Water
NORTHUMBERLAND
Newbiggin-
by-the-Sea
Morpeth
Ashington
399
Border
Forest Park
A696
Bedlington
Blyth
Cramlington
A68
Whitley
Bay
12

England

Photo: The Pheasant at Neenton, entry 462

The Wheatsheaf Combe Hay

Combe Hay

A hidden valley, a pretty village, a gorgeous inn, three fabulous rooms. Views from the lush terraced garden – replete with veg plot and hens – stretch across to a fine ridge of trees, the manor house and church jutting out of the woods below. In summer there are barbecues, lazy lunches, horses clopping by. This is a 15th-century farmhouse with later additions – it's all but impossible to spot the join – whose exterior comes clad in Farrow & Ball creams. Outside there are Indian benches with seagrass cushions; inside, big sofas in front of the fire. Gastropub interiors have neutral colours to soak up the light, sandblasted beams, halogen spotlights and Lloyd Loom wicker dining chairs. Steps outside lead down to three deeply comfy bedrooms in a stone building. All come in contemporary rustic style with light wood furniture, flat-screen TVs, Egyptian cotton and deluge showers; there are White Company oils and bathrobes too. Climb back up for seriously good food, perhaps pork belly with quince purée, skate wing with beetroot, parmesan and capers, and Valrhona chocolate fondant. Bath is a hike across the fields.

Rooms	3 doubles: £120-£150.
Meals	Lunch & dinner £16.50-£26.
Closed	3pm-6pm. Sun eves & Mon all day.

Ian & Adele Barton
The Wheatsheaf Combe Hay,
Combe Hay,
Bath, BA2 7EG
Tel +44 (0)1225 833504
Web www.wheatsheafcombehay.com

White Hart

Bath

A short walk from Bath Spa station, in mellow stone Widcombe, this big imposing pub has a pleasant courtyard garden for supping summer pints. With its reputation as one of the best places to eat in town, it still feels pubby, with a jolly bar, a pleasingly plain dining room and a mixed bag of tables. On rugby day it heaves, as pints of Butcombe Bitter and RCH Pitchfork are downed. Chef Rupert Pitt has worked in some of Bath's best restaurants and his menu is short and to the point, with five starters and mains. The food, well-priced and following the seasons, is delicious. Try the guinea fowl wrapped in bacon with roasted carrots and beetroot, or fillet of sea bream with runner beans, samphire and brown shrimps, or pan-fried goat's cheese and sundried tomato risotto cake. Heaven.

Meals: Lunch & dinner £10-£13.
Sunday lunch, 3 courses, £23.
No meals on Sunday eve.

Closed: Open all day.
Closed Sun eves in winter.

Rupert Pitt
White Hart,
Widcombe Hill,
Bath, BA2 6AA

Tel: +44 (0)1225 338053
Web: www.whitehartbath.co.uk

Entry 2 Map 3

Bath & N.E. Somerset

The Locksbrook Inn

Bath

Watch the canal boats putter up this leafy stretch of water, or settle into a comfy corner with the papers and a brunch fit for champions... The Bath Pub Company have played a blinder with this latest addition to their burgeoning group of classy gastropubs. Come in off the canal path via the stylish terrace, or through the front door to the bar where smiling staff will serve you local ales, ciders, smoothies or coffee while you tackle the task of choosing from the seasonal menu – splendid salads, posh burgers and hearty main courses buzzing with flavour – you'll be spoilt for choice. Add a fantastic Sunday roast and you're all set for a memorable visit. Oak floors, a long dining room glowing with light, snug corners, wood-burners and wonderful photographs that tell the history of Bath. A gem.

Meals: Starters from £5.
Lunch &nner from £9.
Dinner from £9.

Closed: Open all day.

Suzanne Pleshette
The Locksbrook Inn,
103 Locksbrook Road,
Bath, BA1 3EN

Tel: +44 (0)1225 427119
Web: www.thelocksbrookinn.com

Entry 3 Map 3

The Old Green Tree

Bath

In Bath centre, the oldest pub in Bath hums with life even before midday. Tim, Nick and their staff are fanatical about real ale – at least six guest beers are chalked up on the board. Squeeze through the narrow planked bar into a cabin-like room undecorated since panelling was installed in 1928 – this pub is part of our heritage and has no intention of changing! In three little low-ceilinged rooms, a mosaic of foreign coins are stuck up in frames behind the bar, along with local artists' work. The lunch menu includes hearty old English dishes and a daily chef's special; the chutneys are homemade, the pâtés too. They have a devoted following and the drink is not limited to beer – there are malts, wines and hot toddies too. *Cash only.*

Meals	Lunch £5.50-£10.
Closed	Open all day.

Tim Bethune
The Old Green Tree,
Bath, BA1 2JZ
Tel +44 (0)1225 448259

Entry 4 Map 3

Bath & N.E. Somerset

The Chequers

Bath

A lovely little Georgian pub tucked away close to the Circus, the Assembly Rooms and Royal Crescent. The ground floor bar and first floor dining room both have mirrored panels, parquet flooring, metro tiles and cushioned pew benches. A carefully curated wine list awaits at the bar, as do fine spirits, local ales and lagers. Do try a 'Chequers Classic' of salt and pepper squid then duck breast and confit leg, followed by chocolate fondant – this is five star fare served in a relaxed pub setting. Sunday lunch is not to be missed, but book ahead as locals know and love it here. The tasting menu is irresistible – seven courses of the chef team's finest seasonal dishes. Add happy, knowledgeable staff into the mix and you have a *bone fide* Bath gem.

Meals	Lunch & dinner £6.95-£23.50. Sunday lunch from £13.50.
Closed	Open all day (from 12pm).

Lianne Cooper
The Chequers,
50 Rivers Street,
Bath, BA1 2QA
Tel +44 (0)1225 360017
Web www.thechequersbath.com

Entry 5 Map 3

The Marlborough Tavern

Bath

A pint's throw from the Royal Crescent, The Tav is one of Bath's best food pubs, loved by locals and visitors alike. The 18th-century interiors tick all the gastropub boxes with sage green paintwork, feature wallpapers, polished boards and smartly snug corners. Wines include a fashionable palette of rosés, perfect for sipping in the lovely walled courtyard garden. As for the food, it is driven by the produce: seasonal and local are the buzzwords with producers and provenance listed. There's Chew Valley smoked salmon, 'Ruby Red' beef from Devon, Berkshire boar pork and fruit and veg from seventh generation Eades greengrocer's, just up the road. The freshest of fish arrives daily from Cornwall and Devon, Sunday lunches are the stuff of legend and booking is pretty much essential.

Meals Lunch & dinner, 2 courses, £12.
Closed Open all day.

Marco Leanza
The Marlborough Tavern,
35 Marlborough Buildings,
Bath, BA1 2LY
Tel +44 (0)1225 423731
Web www.marlborough-tavern.com

Entry 6 Map 3

Bath & N.E. Somerset

Hare & Hounds

Bath

Ten-mile views, excellent food and cool interiors at this beautifully renovated Victorian inn above Bath, looking across the city to Solsbury Hill. A conservatory, decked terrace, sprawling garden and a vast mullioned window in the bar all face the right way – you gaze on fields where vegetables for the restaurant are grown. You might find goat's cheese and honey terrine, beer-battered haddock and hand-cut chips, dark chocolate mousse and clementine purée. At the bar, traditionally brewed Butcombe and Hare & Hounds Ale stand side by side, backed up by excellent wines, many available by the glass. The pub is open all day, breakfast is served from 8.30am. There's a fire in the bar, a separate menu for children, and a private dining room for small parties. Perfectly located for those travelling to or from the M4 to the north of Bath. Gorgeous.

Meals Lunch & dinner £10.50-£22.
Sunday lunch £13.50-£15.50.
Closed Open all day.

Jennifer Blake
Hare & Hounds,
Lansdown Road,
Bath, BA1 5TJ
Tel +44 (0)1225 482682
Web www.hareandhoundsbath.com

Entry 7 Map 3

The Plough at Bolnhurst

Bolnhurst

A tavern has stood here since the 1400s. The last one burnt down, but tradition lives on in this unusually atmospheric reincarnation. Imagine nooks, crannies, stripped boards, blackened beams, leather armchairs, a bookcase stuffed with Sawday's tomes (yes!) and a welcome for all: foodies, families and old boys in for a pint. Chef-patron Martin Lee's grounding was with Raymond Blanc so the food, served in a barn open to the ceiling, is of note: Thai butternut squash soup with tempura prawns, grilled Ibérico pork cutlet, orange soufflé with caramel, cinnamon and ice cream, and a beautiful platter of cheeses. The wines are impressive, though the Gun Dog bitter also slips down a treat. All is loved and nurtured including the garden, with its little pond and decking, and picnic rugs for summer. A bright light in Bedfordshire.

Meals: Lunch & dinner from £13. Bar meals from £7.95. Sunday lunch £21-£25.

Closed: 3pm-6.30pm. Sun eves & Mon.

Martin & Jayne Lee & Michael Moscrop
The Plough at Bolnhurst,
Kimbolton Road, Bolnhurst,
Bedford, MK44 2EX

Tel: +44 (0)1234 376274
Web: www.bolnhurst.com

Entry 8 Map 9

Bedfordshire

The Park

Bedford

In a residential suburb near the park, the uninspiring 1900s exterior conceals an interior with a funky feel, following an inspired refurbishment by a small and passionate pub company. Traditional fireplaces, flagstones, beams and wood panelling blend effortlessly with quirky fabrics and furnishings in trendy-retro dining rooms that converge onto the bar area; lounge on a cool leather sofa or nurse a pint at the bar. The kitchen delivers great pub food: rabbit, cured ham and pistachio terrine, pressed pork belly with black pudding croquettes, and mint chocolate parfait, while the market-fresh fish and daily specials are listed on a brown paper roll on the wall. Tip-top ales from Bedford's Charles Wells brewery and a verdant heated patio garden area complete a very promising picture.

Meals: Breakfast from £4.50. Starters from £5.50. Mains from £11.50-£16. Sunday lunch from £13.25.

Closed: Open all day.

The Manager
The Park,
98 Kimbolton Road,
Bedford, MK40 2PF

Tel: +44 (0)1234 273929
Web: www.theparkbedford.co.uk

Entry 9 Map 9

Hare & Hounds

Old Warden

Set in a forested fold of countryside, with Emma and French chef Ben at the helm, the Hare & Hounds has a loyal following and a youthful spring in its step – from the cocktail list to the jaunty menu with "the freshest local ingredients we can get our mitts on". That might include venison and wild mushroom terrine with crushed walnuts, or slow braised hare with roasted garlic polenta and baby leeks. Hares loom large in the dècor – hares in hats, hares in ballgowns – and the overall feel is country-casual, while the rambling back garden melts away into the woods. It all feels just right for one of Bedfordshire's sweetest villages. Woburn and Whipsnade are in striking range, while the Shuttleworth Collection of vintage aircraft is just down the lane. You'd never believe you were only a 10-minute drive from the A1.

Meals	Starters from £5.25. Lunch, 2-3 courses, £12-£15. Dinner from £10.50.
Closed	Mondays.

Emma Amery, Ben Hars & Julie Witworth
Hare & Hounds,
The Village, Old Warden,
Biggleswade, SG18 9HQ
Tel +44 (0)1767 627225
Web www.hareandhoundsoldwarden.com

Entry 10 Map 9

Bedfordshire

The Black Horse

Woburn

The success of the Swan in sleepy Salford prompted Peach Pubs to take on the old Black Horse in posh Woburn. It looks every inch a small marketplace pub, yet the Georgian façade gives way to a big rambling interior. A lively front bar (wood floor and tables, high stools, Greene King ales) leads through to a big eating area, where red chairs, cushions and leather wall benches add colour to the beamed and informal dining room. Food combines classic pub dishes with modern brasserie meals and Peach's trademark deli boards: nibbles of cheese, charcuterie, fish and vegetarian treats, served with chutneys and artisan breads. Or choose potted duck livers; sea bass with lemon and fennel dressing; pear and blackberry crumble – best enjoyed in the secluded courtyard garden.

Meals	Lunch & dinner £10.75-£18.75.
Closed	Open all day.

Andrew Coath
The Black Horse,
1 Bedford Street,
Woburn, MK17 9QB
Tel +44 (0)1525 290210
Web www.blackhorsewoburn.co.uk

Entry 11 Map 9

The Winning Post

Winkfield

The old Cottage Inn has become Winkfield's hub, with a cute smokers' hut on the front terrace and a classy-rustic interior. This Upham Brewery pub is named (in part) after the stables that flank the drive, and there's a purpose-built extension with rooms at the back. Inside: dark planked floors and standing timbers, black lanterns fixed to low beams, a smattering of framed paintings, a roaring fire in the bar, copper pans by the wood-burner. It's nooked and crannied, cosy and inviting: a talented team has been at work. The staff are attentive and friendly; the food is flavourful modern European. Enjoy Newlyn crab with smoked salmon and crayfish, pork belly with black pudding mash, lemon posset with raspberry sorbet, and a liqueur coffee if you can find space. After a day at Henley Regatta it would be tempting to stay; bedrooms face the garden and one opens onto it; another is reached via outside steps. You get complementary tea, coffee, bottled water and fresh milk, the WiFi is fast, the beds are comfy, the rooms are peaceful, the kids are welcome, and breakfast is excellent.

Rooms	8 doubles, 2 twins: £85-£120.
Meals	Starters £7-£11. Mains £14-£24.
Closed	Open all day.

Brandon Kirby
The Winning Post,
Winkfield Street, Winkfield,
Windsor, SL4 4SW

Tel	+44 (0)1344 882242
Web	www.winningpostwinkfield.co.uk

The Royal Oak

Yattendon

Handsome centrepiece of a handsome village, the Royal Oak sits at its crossroads – the quintessential country inn. The bar is a back-in-time proposition of original checkerboard tiles, beams, brick and panelling, four hearths ablaze, offering superb pints of Good Old Boy and Mr Chubbs from the West Berkshire Brewery. But time has not stood still. The lobby's leather sofas and gleaming wooden floors, made homely by patterned rugs, project a smartness that carries through to the restaurant's terracotta reds and chunky beech furnishings where the likes of five-spiced duck salad with chicory, cucumber and sweet chilli and beetroot risotto, crispy sage and parmesan reflect an inventive use of local ingredients. Stay over and snuggle down in big comfy bedrooms, some classically kitted out with antiques and rich fabrics, others more contemporary. Choose between pretty views across the square or the walled garden; the quietest are at the back and three are in the old staff house. A garden ringed with herbs, shrubs and trellises includes smart wicker seating and is a boon for summer. Pub quizzes and family suppers underlie links to the community.

Rooms	8 doubles, 2 twin/doubles: £95-£135.
Meals	Lunch & dinner £11-£18.
Closed	Open all day.

Rob McGill
The Royal Oak,
The Square,
Yattendon, RG18 0UF
Tel +44 (0)1635 201325
Web www.royaloakyattendon.co.uk

Crab & Boar

Newbury

Shooting and fishing breaks can be arranged; Newbury Races are a short gallop away. Originally small and thatched, the Crab & Boar has been extended over the years, and stands alone in a rural spot alongside the fast road to Newbury (pick up a cab at the station!). Inside: a recent refurbishment has injected a relaxed feel and although the inn is large it still feels cosy. Contemporary but classy is their style: club chairs by the wood-burner, feature wallpapers, warm earthy colours, chocolate banquette seating. For wine by the glass or a pint of the best from local microbreweries there's a copper-topped, cream-panelled bar, then a big intimate restaurant for fine elegant food. Try seared haunch of venison or roast cod loin with chorizo pommes Anna, tomato and chickpeas. Behind: a marvellous garden furnished with oak tables that's abuzz on warm nights. If you stay, choose a room away from the road (ideally with a hot tub and a patio – a rare treat). Some have far-reaching views, some welcome dogs, all are comfortable, cosy and handsome.

Rooms	14 doubles: £110-£250.
Meals	Starters £7-£8. Mains £16-26.
Closed	Open all day.

The Manager
Crab & Boar,
Wantage Road,
Newbury, RG20 8UE

Tel	+44 (0)1635 247550
Web	www.crabandboar.com

The Bunk Inn

Curridge

Tucked peacefully away on the outskirts of Curridge is a two-storey brick building painted a pretty dove grey, with modern extensions behind. Outside is a large enclosed terrace, a heated hut for smokers and ample topiary; inside is an inviting bar. Find stripped pine tables fronting leather and felt banquettes, a leather sofa by the brick fireplace, wooden stools flanking the polished bar, and wide wood boards on the floor. Dogs are welcome, families are encouraged, and the menus are chalked up on the board. If you want to go posh then head for the dining room down the passage, Farrow & Ball'd in smart country style with pale carpeting and stable door partitioning. You can have 'lager and lime' mussels with spiced frites, aged beef burger with sticky white onions, and pork loin with smoked potato and cider cream. Stay the night in one of nine rooms, comfortable and contemporary and varying in size, the creakiest, and the more characterful, in the old part. Some have patios, all have tea and coffee making facilities, flat-screen TVs, mood lighting and top-notch mattresses.

Rooms	7 doubles, 2 twins: £85-£120.
Meals	Starters £6.50-£9. Mains £14-£19.
Closed	Open all day.

George Sallitt
The Bunk Inn,
Curridge,
Thatcham, RG18 9DS

Tel +44 (0)1635 200400
Web www.thebunkinn.co.uk

The Queens Arms

East Garston

A wiggly country road leads to the heart of racing country – just five minutes off the M4. But you don't have to be mad about horses to be seduced by the Queens Arms. The new hands-on owners run a top team, and you feel it the moment you enter. As tasty food is ferried to groups of jolly lunchers and Barbour-wearing owners of gun dogs, the occasional champion jockey may be spotted at the bar. Families descend for roasts on Sundays; Hennessy cocktails clink with champagne glasses during Gold Cup week. The food is hearty, the portions generous and on Fridays the fish lands straight from Looe. There's beef and Guinness pie, mussels with cream and chorizo, crab gratin with parmesan, game in season, scrumptious puds. The Queens is steeped in warmth and character, with a low-beamed bar, an intimate restaurant, an awned terrace facing west, and paddocks all around. A pity not to stay the night – and dogs get their own beds. If you like character go for the rooms in the pub. Ranging from cosy to large, they have coir floors, dark woods, deep mattresses, and lovely vibrant colours on the walls.

Rooms	7 doubles, 4 twin/doubles: £110-£130. 1 family room for 3: £110-£130.
Meals	Starters from £6. Lunch & dinner from £12.
Closed	Open all day.

Freddie & Sue Tulloch
The Queens Arms,
East Garston, RG17 7ET

Tel +44 (0)1488 648757
Web www.queensarmseastgarston.co.uk

The Eastbury Plough Inn

Eastbury

West Berkshire is surprisingly rural, its sloping green fields studded with sheep – and the village of Eastbury is exceedingly pretty, with thatch cottages, trees and a dreamy river running through. The pub is cream-coloured with grey windows; its benches out the front gaze on the river, and its back garden has a climbing frame for children. Step into a traditional bar, just big enough not to be pokey, where a fire glows in a real old brick fireplace, horseshoes and hops decorate beams and shelves, and drinkers order new wave lagers from Fuller's; there are also good local beers. To the right an arch opens into a swirly carpeted dining room, much-loved by families and locals. The menu is busy and the portions are generous; tuck into king scallops with foie gras and black pudding; pavé of Royal Berkshire venison; sumptuous roasts on Sundays.

Meals Lunch from £6. Dinner from £12.
Closed Monday. Tues-Sat 4pm-6pm.

Graham White & Louise Powell
The Eastbury Plough Inn,
Eastbury,
Lambourn, RG17 7JN
Tel +44 (0)1488 71312
Web www.eastburyplough.com

Entry 17 Map 3

Crown & Garter

Inkpen Common

Down winding country lanes is a red-brick beauty, with a long, trimmed beer garden overlooking the fields and an unexpectedly glamorous interior. There are gleaming floorboards, tartan curtains, a brick-lined hearth, bright pops of colour and atmospheric lighting. The bakery, from which croissants, cookies, cakes and breads flow, is a fabulous feature, and the café attracts the locals. As for the kitchen, it's led by Matthew Ambrose and the menu has something for all, from hearty club sandwiches for walkers, to elegant butternut squash risotto for vegetarians, to pan-fried sirloin of beef with fondant potatoes, served with ceremony from under silver cloches. Cockerels crow in the fields and in summer life spills onto a stone terrace. You can walk from the front door, try your luck at Newbury Races or watch the early morning gallops at Lambourn.

Meals Bar meals from £6.95.
Lunch & dinner from £9.95.
Sunday lunch £22.
No food on Sun eves.
Closed 3pm-5.30pm (5pm-7pm Sun).
Mon & Tues lunch.

Gill Hern & Christopher Box
Crown & Garter,
Great Common Road, Inkpen
Common, Hungerford, RG17 9QR
Tel +44 (0)1488 668325
Web www.crownandgarter.co.uk

Entry 18 Map 3

The Newbury

Newbury

Chef Clarke Oldfield, who helped set up the Albion in Bristol's Clifton village, has headed down the M4 to do the same for Newbury. With business partner Peter Lumber they have transformed the old Bricklayers Arms into a lively, laid-back and super-stylish venue. Expect vibrant colours, horse racing artwork, shelves groaning with cookery books (have a flick through), leather sofas for pints of Otter, and candles on sparkling wood tables. From an open kitchen Clarke delivers robust modern food – braised rabbit with pappardelle and parmesan; rib-eye with rocket and hollandaise sauce; rice pudding with fresh cherries. Pop in for coffee and pastries from 10am, super Sunday roasts, proper bar snacks (salt cod fritters, chorizo Scotch egg), and fresh bread and deli stuff to take home.

Meals	Lunch & dinner £11.50-£27. Sunday lunch £9.50-£26. No food on Sun eves.
Closed	Open all day.

Peter Lumber
The Newbury,
137 Bartholomew Street,
Newbury, RG14 5HB

Tel	+44 (0)1635 49000
Web	www.thenewburypub.co.uk

Entry 19 Map 4

Berkshire

The Pot Kiln

Frilsham

An isolated country pub with stunning views and a long history. Interiors are almost ramshackle but nonetheless well looked after, and the staff are all smiles. Food is characterful because it's based on what the owner (TV chef Mike Robinson) shoots, forages or buys locally; there are no predictable clichés on the menu. This is a food-led pub with great beer and a huge local following, a dedicated drinking area and a historic feel: in the tiny, basic bar are bare tables, a dartboard and foaming pints of Brick Kiln Bitter. If it's lovely in summer – the front garden looks onto fields – it's a treat in winter, when log fires and a menu strong on game come into their own; try venison pie with mash, follow with plum and almond tart. The wine list is both serious and affordable. Do book.

Meals	Lunch & dinner £12.50-£16. Bar meals £3.95-£10. Not food on Tuesdays.
Closed	3.30pm-6pm. Open all day Sat & Sun.

Mike & Katie Robinson
The Pot Kiln,
Frilsham,
Thatcham, RG18 0XX

Tel	+44 (0)1635 201366
Web	www.potkiln.org

Entry 20 Map 4

The Red Lion at Upper Basildon

Upper Basildon

Outside a small Berkshire village is a red brick pub with sash windows, 400 years old and charming. Original benching runs along the walls, hops froth across standing timbers, a new wood-burner keeps things cosy, and a big old fireplace divides restaurant from bar. All is historic but modern, and inviting. Lovers of Good Old Boy drop by, as do foodies and walkers. Kier is chef-patron, his passion drives the kitchen and his set lunches are superb value; the white and green asparagus with Parma ham and hollandaise was as gorgeous as the wild-garlic chicken Kiev with porcini mushrooms. There are burgers too, and onglet steaks, and battered fish and chips (skinny fries or triple-cooked, you choose), and rustic breads and tapas. Oh, and a melt-in-the-mouth red berry and almond tart. At the back is a large lovely garden with a veg patch.

Meals	Bar snacks from £3.50. Sandwiches from £7.50. Mains from £10.
Closed	Mon-Sat 3pm-5pm. Open all day Sun.

Kier Sheldon
The Red Lion at Upper Basildon,
Aldworth Road,
Upper Basildon, RG8 8NG

Tel +44 (0)1491 671234
Web www.theredlionupperbasildon.co.uk

Berkshire

The Bell Inn

Aldworth

The Bell has the style of village pubs long gone and has been in the family for 250 years. Plain benches, venerable dark-wood panelling, settles and an outside gents: it's an unspoilt place that visitors love. There's an old wood-burning stove in one room, a more impressive hearth in the main bar, and early evening drinkers cluster around a unique glass-hatched bar. Fifty years ago the regulars were agricultural workers; today piped music and mobile phones are fervently opposed. The food fits the image and they keep it simple: choose from warm rolls bursting with home-baked ham (or ox tongue or cheddar), treacle sponge and a winter soup of the day. Drink prices are another draw; the ales come from Arkell's and West Berkshire breweries. There's also a great big garden.

Meals	Bar meals £2.80-£6.50.
Closed	3pm-6pm (7pm Sun). Mon (except bank hols).

H E Macaulay
The Bell Inn,
Aldworth,
Reading, RG8 9SE

Tel +44 (0)1635 578272

Miller of Mansfield

Goring

A jog from the Thames is a 1700s brick inn with beautiful bay windows and a big walled courtyard to the rear. Inside: stripped floors, exposed walls, sherry barrels, real fires by leather sofas, elegance, warmth and the odd walker's dog. It's not a glamorous pub, although it's far from scruffy, and it's not a gastropub either. But there's Nick Galer in the kitchen, who's learned from the industry's best, and a perfect front of house in the shape of Mary. Nick (ex Fat Duck) is a great cook who uses wonderful produce, then adds his inimitable spin, so you could find line-caught hake with clams, crushed peas, pea purée and fennel, and lemon meringue tart with Earl Grey ganache. The restaurant is neater and plusher, great for a family roast lunch. In short, we loved it all, from the real ales to the 14 wines by the glass to the superb nibbles.

Meals	Lunch from £12.50. Dinner from £20.
Closed	Open all day.

Nick & Mary Galer
Miller of Mansfield,
High Street, Goring,
Reading, RG8 9AW

Tel	+44 (0)1491 872829
Web	www.millerofmansfield.com

Berkshire

The Bell

Waltham St Lawrence

Owned by Waltham St Lawrence village, deep in rural Berkshire, is a rare all-rounder. This 14th-century Wealden house, beamed inside and out, comes with low ceilings, creaking fireplaces, wattle and daub walls, a mishmash of furniture and candelabra lighting. It's a haven for ale fiends, five pumps rotating superbly kept local brews and a further six cask ciders held in cellar. A menu mounted above the hearth at midday and at 7pm offers one delicious constant – 'Bambi burger', minced on site from venison shot by a regular – alongside roast organic pumpkin with pearl barley, rocket and hazelnut salad and Spenwood ewe's milk cheese; wood pigeon and pork terrine; apple crumble – dictated daily by season and produce. Regulars are a crew of colourful eccentrics, making the Bell well-nigh perfect.

Meals	Lunch & dinner £10-£16.
Closed	3pm-5pm (Mon-Fri).

Iain Ganson
The Bell,
The Stree, Waltham St Lawrence,
Twyford, RG10 0JJ

Tel	+44 (0)118 934 1788
Web	thebellwalthamstlawrence.co.uk

The Royal Oak

White Waltham

Modest at first glance, there's star quality inside. Nick Parkinson (son of Michael) may have given this small inn a stylish lift, but he has managed to keep much of the traditional character... scrubbed wooden floors and stripped beams, timbers and panelling, the occasional music night. The bar is cosy and inviting, with solid wooden furniture, an open fire and a couple of armchairs, and the dining room's food, beautifully cooked by Dominic Chapman, is modern and classy, with a good choice of wines. Tuck into pickled South Devon mackerel with beetroot and watercress, peppered haunch of venison and creamy spinach, Yorkshire rhubarb trifle. And you can get a lovely pint of London Pride. The Royal Oak, friendly and well-run, opens its door to drinkers and diners with equal enthusiasm.

Meals — Lunch & dinner £12.50-£24.
Closed — 3pm-6pm. Sun eves.

Nick Parkinson
The Royal Oak,
Littlefield Green, White Waltham,
Maidenhead, SL6 3JN
Tel +44 (0)1628 620541
Web www.theroyaloakpaleystreet.com

Entry 25 Map 4

Berkshire

Two Brewers

Windsor

In Royal Windsor, next to the Cambridge Gate, is a charming centuries-old pub (one of Windsor's smallest) whose rooms meander around a panelled bar. There are magazines to dip into and walls crammed with press clippings, corks and wine boxes; on a blackboard above the fire, anecdotes commemorating each day are chalked up in preference to menu specials. Eyes peeled for one of the Castle's footmen... It's massively popular, but reserve a table and you won't go hungry. The compact menu follows a steady pub line, with daily specials, plates of cheese, a choice of five roasts on Sundays, and tapas on Friday and Saturday nights. Try oven baked loin of cod with caper and butter sauce, or warm spiced chicken Caesar salad with anchovies, or beetroot, pear and fig salad with ricotta. Dogs are welcome – but no under-18s; it's just too tiny.

Meals — Lunch & dinner £11-£19.50. Sunday lunch £12.50.
Closed — Open all day.

Robert Gillespie
Two Brewers,
34 Park Street,
Windsor, SL4 1LB
Tel +44 (0)1753 855426
Web www.twobrewerswindsor.co.uk

Entry 26 Map 4

The Crown

Burchett's Green

On the crossroads of a hamlet near Maidenhead is a very old pub with a back-to-basics fresh interior and a chef for whom food is a passion. The menu changes so often it has no time to make it to the website; instead, chalked up on the board, you find 'Artichokes like when in Provence', 'A Bowl of Arabic Grains with Harissa', 'Berkshire Pig with its own Chipolata'. Slaving away in the tiniest kitchen Simon Bonwick creates simple, gutsy, flawless classics inspired by market-fresh produce. The Ardennes pâté with gherkins, capers, shallots and home-baked bread was pink and robust; the salt marsh lamb rump was roasted with rosemary; the treacle sponge was as light as a cloud; and the Cashel Blue came with a beautiful Eccles cake. There are real ales, real ciders, and new front of house is son Dean – manning the bar, sorting the cellar. A foodie treat.

Meals Lunch from £10.
Dinner, 3 courses, £20.
Closed Open all day.

Simon Bonwick
The Crown,
Burchett's Green Road,
Burchett's Green, SL6 6QZ
Tel +44 (0)1628 826184
Web www.thecrownburchettsgreen.com

Entry 27 Map 4

The Little Angel

Henley-on-Thames

Winning a mention in 'The Haunted Pub Guide', the not-so-little Little Angel is one of the oldest pubs in Berkshire. Enter a huge bar to find sofas, vintage oars and pin-up portraits, and a log-burner lit on cool days. This handsome sash-windowed pub stands alongside a rowing club made famous by the likes of Pinsett and Redgrave (hence the oars) and the oldest part dates from the 1600s. If you bring your dog you can eat in the bar, or in the big-but-intimate 'barn'. There's a modern conservatory too, and a smart garden overlooking the cricket pitch that's perfect for a glass of prosecco in summer sunshine. Friendly staff ferry the likes of fillet of lamb with fondant potato and baby vegetables to a contented Henley crowd. Stroll to the river and catch a boat down the Thames, or simply linger and watch the world float by.

Meals Starters £5-£11.50.
Mains £10.95-£21.50.
Closed Open all day.

Lolly & Doug Green
The Little Angel,
Remenham Lane,
Henley-on-Thames, RG9 2LS
Tel +44 (0)1491 411008
Web www.thelittleangel.co.uk

Entry 28 Map 4

The Ginger Dog

Brighton

This gem of a pub is tucked away in Brighton's trendy Kemptown just a short stroll from the promenade. The Gingerman group have nailed it again with another trendy, chilled out, friendly sort of place. Expect hearty, traditional-with-a-modern-twist fare: beef jerky popcorn, mushroom soup with cep powder and parmesan, braised ox cheek with bone marrow polenta, and some very moreish liquid desserts! Outside it's an attractive townhouse – inside find classic stripped floorboards, a wood panelled bar and a wood-burner juxtaposed with interesting art (for sale) and bright red leather banquet seating. There's a mix of locals and out-of-towners who come to sample the menu or just for a drink, there's an exciting selection of local ales, wines and spirits. And the best of Brighton is right here: hit the arcades and the pier or shop till you drop.

Meals	Starters from £7. Mains from £13.50. Desserts from £7.50.
Closed	2.30pm-3pm.

Ben McKeller
The Ginger Dog,
12 College Place,
Brighton, BN2 1HN

Tel +44 (0)1273 620990
Web www.thegingerdog.com

Entry 29 Map 4

Brighton & Hove

The Ginger Pig

Hove

Everyone loves this pub minutes from the beach. The décor is fresh, contemporary and open-plan and the food is consistently brilliant. Whether it's poached skate wing terrine, a chargrilled rib-eye with horseradish and roast garlic butter and dripping chips, butter roast pork fillet with pig cheek croquette or a blackboard special (slow-braised lamb with spiced cabbage and garlic mash perhaps) this is a serious destination for those who love British food. In spite of gastropubby leanings, the friendly team has created a balanced mix of drinking bar frequented by locals and dining area decked with modern art. It's all down to experienced restaurateur Ben McKeller who, in transforming this building, has created the first in the funky, family-friendly Gingerman group. The paved, sheltered garden is a little oasis.

Meals	Lunch & dinner £9.50-£18.
Closed	Open all day.

Ben Mckellar
The Ginger Pig,
3 Hove Street,
Hove, BN3 2TR

Tel +44 (0)1273 736123
Web thegingerpigpub.com

Entry 30 Map 4

The Foragers

Hove

The laid-back Foragers in residential Hove combines the conviviality of a boozer with classy food from a talented team – you can glimpse the chefs at work from the front bar. Blackboard specials and printed menus are dependent on the seasons and raw materials are sourced from Sussex producers. There's a definite preference for organic, especially concerning meat (the Sunday roast always is). Everything bursts with flavour, from braised wild rabbit with buttered greens to Jerusalem artichoke and mushroom suet pudding; mash might be truffled or roast onion'd. There are sandwiches too, perhaps salt beef with dill pickle or steak with mayo, and Sussex Best Bitter to wash it all down. The interior revamp has created two distinct rooms with a relaxed, casual air – and the smart, decked all-weather garden is a popular draw.

Meals	Lunch £6-£14. Bar meals £4-£8. Dinner £19-£14. Sunday lunch, 3 courses, £21. No food Sunday eve.
Closed	Open all day.

Paul Hutchison & Sara Rottner Hutchison
The Foragers,
3 Stirling Place, Hove, BN3 3YU
Tel +44 (0)1273 733134
Web www.theforagerspub.co.uk

Entry 31 Map 4

The George Payne

Hove

Squirrelled away in residential Hove, the unpretentious George is a proper locals' pub. You're greeted by friendly, relaxed staff in the open plan bar/dining area. Find dark wood tables and chairs, squidgy leather sofas, wooden floors. With its 'chandelier' made from old tea cups and jars of sweets behind the bar, this is a place with a real sense of fun. Sip a pint of Harvey's Best Bitter as you peruse the brimming menus: there's a myriad of pub classics – the 'Sticky Stag' venison burger caught our eye – with daily specials chalked up on blackboards. Try the duck liver parfait with orange and onion marmalade, sea bass with samphire and caper butter, then top it off with apple and elderflower crumble. Dogs and small ones are welcome, and the patio garden is perfect for a summer pint. A short wobble from the station, leave the car and hop on the train.

Meals	Starters from £5.75. Mains from £12.
Closed	Open all day.

Zoe Rodgers
The George Payne,
18 Payne Avenue,
Hove, BN3 5HB
Tel +44 (0)1273 329563
Web www.thegeorgepayne.co.uk

Entry 32 Map 4

The Chimney House

Brighton

When exploring the maze of streets behind arty Severn Dials you don't expect a Victorian redbrick pub in among the painted stuccoed houses. Enter and be seduced. Planked floors, dark polished furniture, high ceilings, sash windows… there's a contemporary feel and the space is big, airy and light. With excellent beers, including Harveys, and 14 wines by the glass, it's a popular hangout for locals. But it's the food that's the star. A daily-changing menu zooms in on pub classics (cottage pie, sausages and mash) and Mediterranean-style dishes (fish soup with grey mullet, mussels and cockles) to attract diners in droves – and there's a sensible kid's menu. Pop in at lunchtime for soup and sandwiches, pick up some homemade bread or jars of jam and chutney to take home.

Meals: Lunch from £4.95. Dinner from £10.50. Sunday lunch £12.50.
Closed: 3pm-5pm (Tues-Thurs). All day Mon.

Helen & Andrew Coggings
The Chimney House,
28 Upper Hamilton Road,
Brighton, BN1 5DF
Tel: +44 (0)1273 556708
Web: www.chimneyhousebrighton.co.uk

Entry 33 Map 4

The Pump House

Bristol

Meander through Bristol's boatyards and find this grand ex-Victorian pumping station, with chef Toby Gritten at the helm. Inside: cool stone floors, high ceilings and big arched windows frame gorgeous harbour views. Local guest beers and ales abound behind the bar, but it's the gins that really pack a punch: there are over 400! Just ask the cool, young bar staff to guide your choosing. Upstairs it's both formal and fun; foodies travel far and wide to sample the tasting menu. Try seared Brixham scallops with sweetcorn and chicken wings, belly of suckling pig pork with apples, leeks and coco beans, then finish with a Tahitian vanilla brûlée. In summer, catch some rays out on the lavender-framed courtyard, tuck into a hearty ploughman's, watch the boats sail past, and see how many famous landmarks you can spot. The ss Great Britain and M Shed are close.

Meals: Starters from £5. Mains from £15.
Closed: Open all day.

Toby Gritten
The Pump House,
Merchants Road, Hotwells,
Bristol, BS8 4PZ
Tel: +44 (0)117 927 2229
Web: www.the-pumphouse.com

Entry 34 Map 3

The Lion

Bristol

On one of the steep narrow streets in the cosy Bristol community of Clifton Wood is a little pub that the locals love. Grandad on his barstool keeps a friendly watchful eye – this is a family affair. Bath Ales and Tribute are on tap and the food is all made to order – perhaps pie of the day, a delicious burger, a tasty risotto. The Welsh Black steaks are good and the Sunday lunch is legendary – come with the keenest appetite! Irish music rocks in the back bar on Fridays, there's a pub quiz on Wednesdays, open fires in winter and a happy weekend throng: families, couples, groups, dogs. Note the terrace to the side and the mini community park for children next door. One super-comforting local.

Meals	Lunch from £4.75. Dinner from £7.25. Sunday lunch £9.50.
Closed	Open all day.

Fiona & Charity Vincent & David Waddilove
The Lion, 19 Church Lane,
Clifton Wood, BS8 4TX

Tel	+44 (0)117 926 8492
Web	www.thelionclifton.com

Entry 35 Map 3

Bristol

The Greenbank

Bristol

Rescued from property developers by the local community and now headed up by Zazu's Kitchen – Bristol restaurateurs with a flair for good food – the Greenbank has it all. It's cool enough for a Friday night out (live music, cocktail list, friendly vibes), laid back enough for decent coffee and pastries on Saturday mornings; and serves up top-notch roasts on Sundays. It buzzes during the week too: come for scrummy stone-baked pizzas, real ales on tap, super local ciders, wines by the glass – head to the patio when the sun shines. Eat at a scrubbed table or comfy booth in the big open-plan space around the tiled central bar. Little ones are well looked after with toys, colouring in stuff, mini pizzas and small roast dinners. Staff are smiley and there's even a piano to tinkle.

Meals	Lunch from £8. Dinner from £10.
Closed	Open all day.

Toby Bywater
The Greenbank,
57 Belle Vue Road,
Bristol, BS5 6DP

Tel	+44 (0)117 939 3771
Web	www.thegreenbankbristol.co.uk

Entry 36 Map 3

The Grace

Bristol

This is the best independent shopping street in Bristol and The Grace sits happily amongst its trendy neighbours. Duck off the pavement and straight into the bar; take a pew around a scrubbed pine table and delve into the days menu. Choose from tapas, small plates or pizza; bring friends and share stuff. Perhaps salsify, goat curd, crispy kale and truffled honey or monkfish cheeks, cauliflower purée and almond butter. Finish off with a mouthwatering sorbet and a top-notch coffee. Or just pop in for a craft beer, real ale or tasty cocktail. Zazu's Kitchen (West Country restaurateurs) have done it again: cool bar, excellent (mostly local and organic) food, laid-back atmosphere. Everyone's welcome and best of all, there's a fab terrace out the back.

Meals — Lunch & dinner from £4.
Sunday lunch from £15.

Closed — Open all day.

Kristjan Bigland
The Grace,
197 Gloucester Road,
Bristol BS7 8BG

Tel — +44 (0)117 924 4334
Web — www.thegracebristol.uk

Entry 37 Map 3

Bristol

The Gloucester Old Spot

Bristol

Sitting beside a busy road in residential Horfield, the olive-hued Gloucester Old Spot is full of Bristolian pride and a real favourite with locals. Friendly landlady Amy sources everything from close by, from the charcuterie to the reclaimed furniture and funky salvaged mirrors lining the walls. Sink into a leather sofa or cosy up by the big brick fireplace – a pint of Exmoor ales Fox or Timothy Taylor's Landlord in hand – and let the day disappear. Peckish? There are hearty ciabatta sandwiches for lunch, pub classics for dinner (the sausages and mash are a firm favourite), and sharing boards to break bread over. Vegetarians are fed well here (no risotto!) and they do a cracking breakfast, too. With a handsome Wendy house in the garden, mini chocolate brownies and crayons to scribble with, the small ones will love it. A true community hub.

Meals — Small plates from £3.95.
Mains from £7.95.
Sunday lunch from £12.95.

Closed — Open all day.

Amy Devenish
The Gloucester Old Spot,
138-140 Kellaway Avenue,
Bristol, BS6 7YQ

Tel — +44 (0)117 924 7693
Web — theoldspotbristol.co.uk

Entry 38 Map 3

The Nags Head Inn

Little Kingshill

This was Roald Dahl's local – it features in *Fantastic Mr Fox*, half a mile out of Great Missenden. It's a beautiful old building built of red brick and flint under bright red pantiles, framed by the rolling hills of the Chilterns. At the back is a vast garden with plenty of trees under which to dream and picnic tables with umbrellas. Inside, a classic refurbishment from owner Alvin Michaels of the award-winning Bricklayers Arms, with food to match: the beloved 15th-century boozer has become a great dining pub. Now low dark beams and big inglenook blend with modern oak and lemon hues, there are salt and pepper mills on shining tables and boxed shelves guarding armagnacs. The food is faultless: try pan fried wood pigeon breast with black pudding and a dry sherry jus, or slow cooked pork hock on a bed of sweet & sour cabbage. Drinks cover every aspect of the grape and globe, including London Pride, and young staff are attentive. Bedrooms above are equally good, their creams and whites complementing ancient timbers. There are ironing boards, toiletries and full-length mirrors, and the bed linen is gorgeous.

Rooms	3 doubles, 2 twins: £90-£130.
Meals	Lunch & dinner from £10.95. Sunday lunch, 3 courses, £23.95.
Closed	Open all day.

Alvin Michaels
The Nags Head Inn,
London Road, Little Kingshill,
Great Missenden, HP16 0DG

Tel +44 (0)1494 862200
Web www.nagsheadbucks.com

The Crown Inn

Amersham

The Crown is where Hugh Grant got lucky with Andie MacDowell: *Four Weddings and a Funeral* was filmed here. But that was before Ilse Crawford's makeover. Now the Crown is an uber-chic dining pub in a plank-floored, New England style; the décor is charming, the cooking skilled and seasonal. Families are welcome, walkers' dogs doze, staff are friendly and obliging. The wines are global, the ale is local (Marlow's Rebellion), and the creaking, sloping floors are irresistible. There's a beamed bar decorated in muted colours, with cool wing chairs by a brick fireplace and sheepskins on new-old country seats, and two rustic-elegant dining rooms, one with long trestle tables. Twice Michelin-starred chef Atul Kochhar offers his take on British cuisine in both dining rooms and the bar, so start with Driftwood goat's cheese and baked beetroot carpaccio and follow with beautifully battered fish and chips. Bedrooms are understated and serene, those in the oldest part with the greatest character, those away from the kitchens the quietest. Breakfasts are fabulous.

Rooms	37 doubles: £110-£250. 1 family room for 3: £110-£120.
Meals	Sandwiches £6.50-£9.50. Starters £5-£9. Mains £7.50-£24.
Closed	Open all day.

David Ashfield
The Crown Inn,
16 High Street,
Amersham, HP7 0DH

Tel +44 (0)1494 721541
Web www.thecrownamersham.com

The Kings Arms

Amersham

Step in the footsteps of former guest Oliver Cromwell as you stroll along Amersham's classy High Street and turn in under the archway, as customers have done since the fifteenth century. Horses were once changed here in the cobbled courtyard, while guests alighted from their carriages for vittles. Much more recently the Kings Arms has featured in scenes for *Midsomer Murders* and *Four Weddings and a Funeral*. This lovely Tudor pub retains its historic roots, particularly in the snug bar with cosy seating areas, fire nooks and bare wood floors – black leather chairs and touches of purple velvet give it a modern twist. A new extension behind adds twenty smart bedrooms along a long corridor; for a more authentic inn stay, ask for a room in the stable block or main building, all dark wood furniture and beams, perhaps a four poster. Welcoming staff and friendly Irish owner David offer Brakspear and Rebellion beers on tap, and classic pub food. Fabulous for a weekend – check out David's hand painted map on the wall for local walks, discover the shops in this delightful market town or explore the Chilterns.

Rooms	28 doubles: £115-£145. 3 suites for 2: £175-£195. 2 suites for 4: £195-£225. 1 family room for 4: £155-£165.
Meals	Starters from £6. Lunch from £12. Dinner from £12.
Closed	Open all day.

David Ashfield
The Kings Arms,
30 High Street,
Amersham, HP7 0DJ

Tel	+44 (0)1753 534790
Web	www.kings-arms-hotel.com/contact

The Dog & Badger

Medmenham

Classic country pub on the outside, sleek and funky on the inside, the Dog & Badger proves that looks can be deceiving. Swish through glass doors and you're greeted by a shock of blue neon above the speedboat-inspired Riva Bar. Rub shoulders with the ultra trendy locals, slurp Carlingford Lough oysters and sip delectable cocktails, or choose from the vast, 400-strong wine list. In the restaurant, the fire roars against a backdrop of beams and plum-hued walls. Chef Shaun Rowlands sharpened his knives as head chef at Hix, and his carefully curated menu is mainly locally-sourced, seasonal perfection, even for the little ones (starting with polenta popcorn!). Gourmets might opt for Swaledale grouse with celeriac purée, or loin of Balmoral venison with foraged berries. At the bar, try wood roast shrimp with sriracha mayo. For pudding, poached plums with blackberry sorbet. Wash it all down with an espresso martini then retire next door to one of six indulgent bedrooms with spa-quality bathrooms for pampering between meals. Divine.

Rooms	4 doubles, 2 twin/doubles: £195-£350.
Meals	Nibbles £2.50-£4.50. Mains £7.50-£32.
Closed	Open all day.

Mo Hoffelner
The Dog & Badger,
Henley Road,
Medmenham, SL7 2HE

Tel +44 (0)1491 579944
Web www.thedogandbadger.com

The Royal Oak

Bovingdon Green

The old whitewashed cottage stands in a hamlet on the edge of the common – hard to believe that Marlow is just a mile away. It's a thriving dining pub (and sister pub to the Alford Arms, Herts). Beyond the terrace is a stylish open-plan bar, cheerful with cream-coloured walls, fresh flowers, rug-strewn boards, cushioned pews and crackling log fires. Order a pint of local Rebellion and check out the daily chalkboard or printed menu. You might start with breaded Cornish fishcake slider, mashed peas and tartar sauce before tucking into slow-cooked breaded lamb croquettes with sticky braised red cabbage, creamy mash and mint, saving room for lemon posset with hedgerow fruits and brandy snap cream. The sprawling gardens are perfect for a summer game of table tennis on the lawn.

Meals Lunch & dinner £11.75-£19.75.
Closed Open all day.

David & Becky Salisbury
The Royal Oak,
Frieth Road, Bovingdon Green,
Marlow, SL7 2JF
Tel +44 (0)1628 488611
Web www.royaloakmarlow.co.uk

Entry 43 Map 4

Buckinghamshire

The Garibaldi

Bourne End

The heart and soul of the community? That's incontrovertibly true of The Garibaldi, bought by the community in order to save their local. A solid Victorian coaching inn on a quiet road (views to the Chiltern Hills as you approach), the focus is on a relaxed welcome, a neighbourhood feel – four local beers plus artisan ciders – and interesting food. New chef Matt Lyons comes hot from The Jolly Cricketers and is cooking up a storm. You might find gin and coriander-cured salmon or beef shin with cardamom and ginger, while the shorter bar menu could include homemade burgers with smoked bacon or marinated halloumi with smoked aubergine, tomato and Jerez vinegar. This place is not about style but about warmth – lovely fire – comfort and genuine hospitality. Children, walkers and dogs welcome.

Meals Bar snacks from £3.50.
Starters from £6. Mains from £14.
Closed Open all day.

Amanda Baker & Chris Lillitou
The Garibaldi,
Hedsor Road,
Bourne End, SL8 5EE
Tel +44 (0)1628 522092
Web www.garibaldipub.co.uk

Entry 44 Map 4

Blackwood Arms

Burnham

This unassuming pub could be in the middle of the woods; indeed, it is near Burnham Beeches. There's a nose bag by the trees for horses, a dismounting block for riders and a dreamy garden bright with doves, pheasants and blackbirds that reaches down to a field of horses. Inside it is cottagey, quirky, full of character: plain boards, dark settles, hops on beams, old horsebrasses, stacked logs, and a basket of rugs for hardy drinkers. English Chancellors have patronised the Blackwood over the years (Profumo too) and *My Week with Marilyn* was filmed here. Children are welcomed and so are dogs; Sunday lunch is like Crufts. Ales, ciders, gins, wines by the glass, it's all waiting for you along with game from local shoots, tasty seafood grills, juicy burgers, nursery puds and a Moroccan chef; the bourek parcels are gorgeous.

Meals	Starters from £5.25. Mains from £7.50.
Closed	Mondays.

Sean Arnett
Blackwood Arms,
Common Lane, Littleworth Common,
Burnham, Slough, SL1 8PP

Tel +44 (0)1753 645672
Web www.theblackwoodarms.net

Entry 45 Map 4

Buckinghamshire

The White Horse

Hedgerley

In tiny Hedgerley village is a perfectly preserved slice of unspoiled pubbery. Whitewashed brick, horseshoes and cartwheels peer from shrubbery and window baskets, illuminated by ancient gas lamps on both street and façade. Inside, exposed wood is overlaid by carpet, while endless beams and supports for low ceilings are festooned with artefacts. As a serious ale house, seven ever-changing beers are drawn direct from cask and served via a hatch, the selection rotating on a seasonal basis. Food is from a pre deep-fryer age with ploughman's, quiches, cold meats and baps displayed at a chilled counter alongside the odd hot option of chunky lamb broth or maybe pheasant Wellington. A busy garden and marquee are a treat in summer – and house an aviary of finches.

Meals	Lunch £6-£10. No food in evenings.
Closed	Mon-Fri 2.30pm-5pm. Open all day Sat & Sun.

Doris Hobbs & Kevin Brooker
The White Horse,
Village Lane,
Hedgerley,
Slough, SL2 3UY

Tel +44 (0)1753 643225

Entry 46 Map 4

The Swan Inn

Denham

Swap the bland and everyday for the picture-book perfection of Denham village and the stylish Swan. Georgian, double-fronted, swathed in wisteria, the building is now in the capable hands of the Little Gems pub group. It's inviting and charming with rug-strewn boards, chunky tables, cushioned settles, a log fire and a fabulous terrace for outdoor meals. Food is modern British; choose from the 'small plates' list – a honey roast ham hock with baby gem and pea salad, soft boiled quail's egg with homemade salad cream. If you've nothing to rush for, enjoy pan-fried pork tenderloin with cider braised savoy cabbage and caramelised nectarine jus, accompanied by a pint of Rebellion IPA or one of 20 wines by the glass. The owners have thought of everything, and the gardens are big enough for the kids to go wild in.

Meals: Small plates from £5.25. Mains from £12.50-£19.75.
Closed: Open all day.

Mark Littlewood
The Swan Inn,
Village Road, Denham,
Uxbridge, UB9 5BH
Tel: +44 (0)1895 832085
Web: www.swaninndenham.co.uk

Entry 47 Map 4

Buckinghamshire

The Jolly Cricketers

Seer Green

When the Jolly Cricketers came on the market, Seer Green residents Chris and Amanda couldn't resist. Now pretty plants clamber up the brickwork outside, while behind the bar, optics have been replaced by sweet shop jars filled with roasted nuts, olives and lollipops – a picture of individuality matched by a freehouse ale selection that shows off the best of local breweries. Ornate fireplaces, oddment-cluttered shelves and pine tables create an unpretentious backdrop for cider-braised ham, crispy poached egg, pineapple chutney and triple-cooked chips; or succulent beef rump, tongue and cheek with potato purée. Coffee mornings, book clubs and pub quizzes contribute to a community spirit but do nothing to dilute this pub's new-found dining status.

Meals: Lunch from £6.50. Bar meals from £10.50. Dinner from £12.50.
Closed: Open all day.

Amanda Baker & Chris Lillitou
The Jolly Cricketers,
24 Chalfont Road, Seer Green,
Beaconsfield, HP9 2YG
Tel: +44 (0)1494 676308
Web: www.thejollycricketers.co.uk

Entry 48 Map 4

The Old Queens Head

Penn

Run by the small and intimate Little Gems group, this pub by the green oozes character and charm: dating from 1666, its old beams and timbers blend perfectly with a stylish and contemporary décor in both the rambling bar and the dining rooms. Find rug-strewn flags, polished boards, classic fabrics, lovely old oak, and innovative seasonal menus and chalkboard specials. Choices range from 'small plates' – confit duck leg, ham hock and apricot terrine with toasted rye bread and a ginger and plum salsa – to big dishes of slow-cooked shin of beef with saffron risotto, bone marrow crust and gremolata jus. For those who have room left, there's a tempting selection of puddings, classic raspberry Bakewell tart with clotted cream for one. To top it all, a parasol-strewn stone terrace, glorious garden, and walking in the ancient beech woodlands of Common and Penn Woods.

Meals	Small plates from £5.25.
Mains from £12.50-£21.50.

Closed	Open all day.

Tina Brown
The Old Queens Head,
Hammersley Lane, Penn,
High Wycombe, HP10 8EY

Tel	+44 (0)1494 813371

Web	www.oldqueensheadpenn.co.uk

Entry 49 Map 4

The Russell Arms

Butlers Cross

Sat neatly in the heart of Butlers Cross, this attractive 18th-century coach house was once the local for nearby Chequers' serving staff, and shares its name with the former owners of the prime minister's country retreat. Inside is smart and simple, with exposed beams, wooden furniture, politicians' portraits and the odd duck print cushion. You're spoilt for choice with drinks – the wine list is heaving, and the ales are local (Tring's Side Pocket is on tap) – while head chef Dan's menu champions local produce and keeps things seasonal. In the warmer months tuck into sea trout, chicory and Jersey royals on the sun terrace, and in winter nestle next to the fire and order the Kings Farm sausage and mash; hearty and warming. Finish with a warm chocolate pot or a large glass of red, then walk it off with a jaunt around the Chilterns. Divine.

Meals	Starters £4.95-£8.50.
Mains £12.95-£23.

Closed	Mondays all day.

James Penlington
The Russell Arms,
2 Chalkshire Road,
Butlers Cross, HP17 0TS

Tel	+44 (0)1296 624411

Web	www.therussellarms.co.uk

Entry 50 Map 9

The Bell

Stoke Mandeville

An attractive pub, built of brick around the turn of the last century, on the main road into Stoke Mandeville. Landlord James is engaging and affable, doing what he does best: creating a great name for The Bell. This is a pub where the food is the draw and the place was packed on a Tuesday lunch time in February. Beyond the big easy bar, with its dogs, WiFi and daily papers (reading glasses on tap!) is the dining room, large, lofty and light, a relaxed setting for modern, accomplished and seasonally-led food. Our guinea fowl with fondant potato, creamed cabbage and cep was top-notch. With a children's menu too, this is a brilliant venue for the family. Treat yourself to a pint of Bombardier by the log-burner, or a peach bellini in the lawned beer garden at the back.

Meals Lunch & dinner £11.75-£22.
Closed Open all day.

James Penlington
The Bell,
29 Lower Road, Stoke Mandeville,
Aylesbury, HP22 5XA
Tel +44 (0)1296 612434
Web www.bellstokemandeville.co.uk

Entry 51 Map 9

Buckinghamshire

The Hundred

Ashendon

With its walls of old brick and polished plaster and simple, soulful medley of furniture, it's not a swanky place and that is its charm. As if in sympathy with the inventive feel, local chef Matt (ex St John, London) knows how to make simple food taste special. Our dishes were spot on: a succulent starter of kohlrabi and pomegranate, another of squid, chilli and celery, then a robust beef and potato pie, and a melt-in-the-mouth braised lamb. There's an honesty and confidence about the food that demonstrates a skilful hand – and you have to love a pub with spotted dick and custard on the menu. The beers are Brill Gold and Tring, the wine list is short but very good. They say, 'bring your kids, your pets, your mates, your boots, your nan, your boss, your lover.' Brilliant!

Meals Lunch & dinner £5.50-£15.50.
Closed Mondays all day.
Tues-Fri 3pm-6pm.

Matt Gill & Pia Knight
The Hundred,
Lower End, Ashendon,
Aylesbury, HP18 0HE
Tel +44 (0)1296 651296
Web www.thehundred.co.uk

Entry 52 Map 8

The Pointer

Brill

The wine list is impressive, the ale and cider is local and the food is fresh, award-winning and modern. Brill is a pretty village, and the handsome Pointer, an inn since 1702, stands close to the church. Next door is their own butcher's shop and charcuterie, with local artisanal produce to take home. There are carefully restored sturdy oak beams and a reclaimed French oak bar, furs slung over chairs, modishly upholstered sofas and pictures on pale-hued walls. At the back of the pub, past the open plan kitchen is an attractive vaulted restaurant area at the back of the pub: try cannelloni of slow-cooked Longhorn beef with mushrooms, burnt onion and black radish, followed by blood orange sorbet and almond brittle. It's a sophisticated place but you can still bring the dog, and the garden is large and enclosed.

Meals Lunch £18-£45. Dinner £25-£45.
Closed Mondays all day.

Richard Smith
The Pointer,
27 Church Street, Brill,
Aylesbury, HP18 9RT
Tel +44 (0)1844 238339
Web www.thepointerbrill.co.uk

Entry 53 Map 8

Buckinghamshire

Swan Inn

Milton Keynes Village

A 13th-century beauty in the heart of a sprawling New Town; across roundabouts, through housing estates, to arrive at 'Milton Keynes Village'. Spruced up in a stylish gastropub style, keeping its beams, fireplaces and layout, the Swan has cool colours and scatter cushions, chic chairs in the snug and a glowing open fire in the bar. In the cosy dining room – wooden floors, chunky tables, open-to-view kitchen – a selection of sharing platters are on the menu alongside gammon, egg and chunky chips, or opt for a vegetarian treat of couscous-stuffed Romano pepper with goat's cheese. Some produce comes from local allotments (in return for a pint or two), while imaginative evening meals might include dishes such as gilt pork hock, Toulouse sausage and bean cassoulet. In summer you can eat on the sun terrace or in the pretty orchard garden.

Meals Starters from £5.50.
Mains from £9.50-£18.50.
Sunday lunch £14.95.
Closed Open all day.

Grant Owen
Swan Inn,
Broughton Road,
Milton Keynes Village, MK10 9AH
Tel +44 (0)1908 665240
Web www.theswan-mkvillage.co.uk

Entry 54 Map 9

The White Hart

Ufford

Wash up at the White Hart and mix with the locals drawn by the lovely lived-in farmhouse feel and the big, beamy bar. The ales are good too: Oakham Jeffrey Hudson, Woodforde Wherry, Tim Taylors, Grainstore's Red Kite. Farmers gather on Fridays, the cricket team drops by on Sundays; in summer life spills onto the terrace. Flags, floorboards and a crackling fire continue the rustic feel; railway signs, wooden pitch forks and hanging station lamps add colour. You can eat simply or more grandly, anything from a ploughman's to a three-course feast, with memorably good Sunday roasts full of flavour. Walk through rooms with lovely scrubbed tables to the orangery, a glass-gabled restaurant furnished with Lloyd Loom chairs. Bedrooms (four above the bar; six across the way) are simple and spotless, with crisp white linen and feather pillows, free WiFi and an honest price. One is airy and lovely, with period lounge chairs and views across the fields to the church; another has a four-poster bed. This forgotten slip of England – Stamford is five miles – is prettier than most imagine.

Rooms	8 doubles, 2 twins: £80-£120.
Meals	Lunch & dinner £10-£15. Bar meals £5.25-£8.75. Sunday lunch, 3 courses, £19.50. No food on Sun eve.
Closed	Sun eves from 9pm. Open all day.

Lisa Olver
The White Hart,
Main Street, Ufford,
Stamford, PE9 3BH

Tel +44 (0)1780 740250
Web www.whitehartufford.co.uk

The Crown Inn

Elton

A thatched inn built of mellow stone that stands on the green in this pretty village. Paths lead out into open country and you can follow the river up to Fotheringhay, where Mary Queen of Scots lost her head. Back at the pub, warm interiors mix style and tradition to great effect. The bar has stone walls, ancient beams, flagstone floors and a roaring fire; in summer you can decant onto the terrace and sip a pint of Black Sheep while watching village life pass by. Back inside, a beautiful new restaurant has recently appeared with golden stone walls, pale olive panelling and some very good food, anything from glazed ham and local eggs to oxtail lasagne, saddle of venison, sticky toffee tart with toffee sauce. You can also eat in the sitting-room bar on smart armchairs in front of another fire. Stylish bedrooms – some in the main house, others off the courtyard – are all different. You'll find smart colours, chic wallpapers, excellent bathrooms and good art. The bar hosts quiz nights, live music and the odd game of rugby on the telly, while on May Day there's a hog roast for the village fête.

Rooms	6 doubles, 2 twin/doubles: £120-£180. Singles from £55. Sofabed available, £30 per child per night.
Meals	Lunch & dinner £5-£25. No food Sun night; restaurant closed first week January.
Closed	Mon lunch.

Marcus Lamb
The Crown Inn,
8 Duck Street, Elton,
Peterborough, PE8 6RQ

Tel +44 (0)1832 280232
Web www.thecrowninn.org

The Abbot's Elm

Abbot's Ripton

Through force of personality and inspiration in the kitchen, John and Julia Abbey have managed to create a pub that caters for everyone without feeling like a compromise. Enter – passing a display case bearing tribute to John's carrying of the Olympic torch – to be faced with the deliciously tough decision of choosing between stylish pub grub in the bar and French-inspired cuisine in the restaurant. No fewer than 36 wines by the glass, including some made specially for the pub, will help you find something for any occasion: a quick lunch, a fancy evening out. The décor throughout the three-sectioned bar and the restaurant is smart and modern without being showy, while 17th-century character remains in the big beautiful hearth and towering beamed ceiling. The Abbot's Elm pulls a diverse crowd, from villagers to hikers to foodies. And if the brandy snap dessert means you end up wanting to stay, there are three ground-floor bedrooms available. Simple but smart, they have some antique items of furniture but comfort is favoured over grandiosity, especially when it comes to robes and towels!

Rooms	2 doubles, 1 twin/double: £75-£85.
Meals	Lunch & dinner from £9.50. .
Closed	Sunday eves.

John & Julia Abbey
The Abbot's Elm,
Abbot's Ripton,
Huntingdon, PE28 2PA
Tel +44 (0)1487 773773
Web www.theabbotselm.co.uk

The Black Bull Inn

Balsham

Buoyed by the success of the Red Lion at Hinxton, Alex has snapped up the 16th-century Black Bull in nearby Balsham. Unloved for years, it is now back on track as a pretty thatched pub. The beamed and timbered bar is spruced up, a new bar servery has been added, wooden floors gleam and there's a smart mix of old dining tables and leather sofas fronting the glowing log fire; so cosy up with a pint of Rusty Bucket on a winter evening. The ancient, high-raftered and adjoining barn has been restored and refurbished to perfection and is the place to sit and savour some cracking pub food; try the lamb shank with roasted garlic mash and rosemary jus, or the smoked haddock with tarragon foam. In the bar, tuck into roast beef and horseradish sandwiches or a plate of Suffolk ham, eggs and hand-cut chips. Comfortable rooms in the annexe, some overlooking the car park, sport oak floors and hand-made furniture, and huge duvets on king-size beds. Tiled bathrooms come with bath and shower. A peaceful bolthole with a sun-trap back garden, handy for the A11/M11, Cambridge, country walks and the Newmarket Races.

Rooms 5 twin/doubles: £125-£145.

Meals Lunch & dinner from £12.
Bar meals from £6.
Sunday lunch £13.

Closed Mon-Fri 3.30pm-5.30pm.

Alex Clarke
The Black Bull Inn,
27 High Street,
Balsham, Cambridge, CB21 4DJ

Tel +44 (0)1223 893844
Web www.blackbull-balsham.co.uk

Red Lion Inn

Hinxton

In pretty, peaceful Hinxton, close to Cambridge, the rambling Red Lion is a popular stopover in an area deprived of good inns. And its secluded garden, replete with dovecote, arbour and patio, overlooks the church: a lovely spot for peaceful summer sipping. Another draw is the buzzy atmosphere Alex has instilled in the beamed bar with its deep green chesterfields, worn wooden boards, cosy log fire and ticking clock. Own label ale Red & Black and others from the local micro brewery – Crafty Beers, Adnams, Woodfordes, Nethergate – add to the appeal, as do eclectic menus that list a range of classic pub dishes and more inventive specials, all at good prices. Pop in for a beef and horseradish sandwich or linger over venison with blackberry jus or wild mushroom fettuccine; tuck into delicious roast Norfolk chicken on Sunday. Puddings are to die for: sticky toffee pudding with caramel sauce, lemon tart with mango coulis. Named after local beers and ciders, new-build rooms are comfortable and smart with a fresh, contemporary feel – lightwood furniture, wooden floors, crisp cotton on top-quality beds, fully tiled bathrooms. Breakfasts are a serious treat.

Rooms	3 doubles, 5 twin/doubles: £129-£149.
Meals	Lunch & dinner £11-£25. Bar meals £4.50-£10.50. Sunday lunch £12.
Closed	Open all day.

Alex Clarke
Red Lion Inn,
32 High Street, Hinxton,
Saffron Walden, CB10 1QY
Tel +44 (0)1799 530601
Web www.redlionhinxton.co.uk

The Willow Tree

Bourn

Why use tea lights when you can stick candelabra on the table? Or light bulbs when you can hang four chandeliers above the bar? The Willow Tree mixes quirky design with heavenly food, a popular combination that has given the place a buzz. Expect a little metaphorical wrangling with the menu – you're going to want everything on it. From the bar order cocktails, mocktails, hot toddies, pints of Pegasus or a bottle of delicious French wine. As for the food, there's tapas (calamari, garlic prawns), sharing platters (venison and thyme meatballs), comfort food (fish pie, sausage and mash), pizzas, hot ciabattas, goat's cheese cake with beetroot crisps, venison stew with spiced red cabbage, mulled pear and fig tart with strawberry mascarpone. There are deckchairs under a willow tree in the garden and a take-out service for lucky locals. One of the best.

Meals Lunch from £6.50.
Dinner from £9.50.
Closed Open all day.

Craig & Shaina Galvin-Scott
The Willow Tree,
29 High Street,
Bourn, CB23 2SQ
Tel +44 (0)1954 719775
Web www.thewillowtreebourn.com

Entry 60 Map 9

Cambridgeshire

The Carpenters Arms

Great Wilbraham

A small, traditional, country pub where they brew their own beer and serve fabulous food, most of it French. Richard and Heather had an award-winning restaurant in France for six years, teaching the French a thing or two about food. Inside, the bar is authentic and characterful – low ceilings, bar billiards, padded pews, armchairs in front of the wood-burner. It's delightfully refreshing, a proper country local untouched by interior designers! Pick up a pint of Sauvignon Blond or Mild Manners, then fail to resist the menu. You might find coquilles St Jacques with a Provençal sauce, slow-roasted pork with apple and sage, chocolate amaretto truffle mousse. On Sundays, in season, the roast pheasant comes with parsnips and chestnuts, magical stuff; there are good French wines to wash it down. Walks start from the front door with Cambridge waiting across the fields. Brilliant.

Meals Starters from £3.
Mains from £13.95.
Closed Monday & Tuesday.

Richard Hurley
The Carpenters Arms,
10 High Street,
Great Wilbraham, CB21 5JD
Tel +44 (0)1223 882093
Web www.carpentersarmsgastropub.co.uk

Entry 61 Map 9

Hole in the Wall

Little Wilbraham

Hiding down a hundred lanes, this pretty village pub is in the inspired hands of Alex Rushmer, MasterChef winner 2010. It's clearly well-loved. Regulars drop by for a swift half in the big timbered bar – find horse brasses and country prints, junk-shop tables and log fires – or gather for lunch in the country room at the back. In contrast to all this old-fashioned rusticity the food is decidedly modern: ingredients as local and organic as can be and chalkboard specials changing regularly. Alex's cooking is inventive: seared scallops with Ibérico ham, cauliflower purée and apple jelly; Telmara Farm duck with potato and spring onion terrine and a spiced caramel sauce; hake with chorizo hash and Romesco sauce; Sunday roast rib with all the trimmings. On summery days, the front garden is glorious.

Meals Lunch & dinner £10.50-£17.50.
Closed 3pm-6.30pm. Sun eves & Mon.

Alex Rushmer & Ben Maude
Hole in the Wall,
Primrose Farm Road,
Little Wilbraham, Cambridge, CB21 5JY
Tel +44 (0)1223 812282
Web www.holeinthewallcambridge.com

Entry 62 Map 9

Cambridgeshire

Pint Shop

Cambridge

In the contemporary-rustic bar and dining rooms, and to the sheltered terrace, locals and tourists flock for 16 rotating beers, 100 gins, 100 whiskies and a seasonal menu that delivers delicious spit-roasted or chargrilled fish and meat. In the bar, wash down a scotch egg or hot garlic chicken and plum ketchup sandwich with a pint of Arise from Burning Sky Brewery, or look to the main menu for plaice with clams and cider, pork belly with beans and bacon, or an excellent steak; in the dining room, food is cooked over coals just the way it used to be. A trail-blazing concept that pays homage to an age-old tradition (the original beer houses or 'Tom and Jerry Shops' are believed by many to be the birthplace of today's pub) – this is the 19th-century beer house brilliantly reinvented.

Meals Lunch from £7.50.
Dinner from £12.
Closed Open all day.

Richard Holmes
Pint Shop,
10 Peas Hill,
Cambridge, CB2 3PN
Tel +44 (0)1223 352293
Web www.pintshop.co.uk

Entry 63 Map 9

The Punter

Cambridge

This is a pub that seems to wink conviviality. Maybe it's the suntrap courtyard at one side, with its flotsam of flowery crockery and pot plants, or the candles glowing in every window, enhancing the feeling that you are stepping back to an earlier age. Inside you'll find comely sofas, sturdy school chairs and and an artful jostle of kitschy paintings, with a matching mishmash of punters too – post-grads, dog lovers, creative types and determined townies who'll make the journey from across the river for their favourite dish at their favourite table. The regularly changing menu is a concise affair, blending quality pub staples with more eye-catching offerings: smoked eel with roast squash; venison sausages and mash; seabass with hazelnut crumble; cod loin with bulgur wheat. Best to book.

Meals	Mains £12.50-£16. Daily lunch special £5, weekdays only.
Closed	Open all day.

Sarah Lee
The Punter,
3 Pound Hill,
Cambridge, CB3 0AE

Tel +44 (0)1223 363322
Web www.thepuntercambridge.com

Entry 64 Map 9

Cambridgeshire

Three Horseshoes

Madingley

From the outside, the thatched pub is old; push the door and you embrace the new. It is simple, stylish, open, with pale wooden floors and chocolate and cream paintwork; there is lightness and space yet the familiar features remain. The bar has Adnams bitter and a guest ale on tap, a contemporary open fire and a menu that focuses on Italian country dishes and imaginative combinations: chargrilled lamb with cavolo nero and braised beans; roast pork belly with fagioli beans, lemon and spinach; white chocolate, mascarpone and pistachio cheesecake. Relaxed but excellent service matches the atmosphere of the busy bar while formality and white linen come together in the conservatory dining room, popular with business lunchers. In both rooms the choice of wines is superb – pity the designated driver!

Meals	Lunch & dinner £12-£25. Bar meals from £4. Sunday lunch, 3 courses, £26.
Closed	3pm-6pm. Open all day Sat & Sun in summer.

Richard Stokes
Three Horseshoes,
High Street, Madingley,
Cambridge, CB23 8AB

Tel +44 (0)1954 210221
Web www.threehorseshoesmadingley.co.uk

Entry 65 Map 9

Dyke's End

Reach

In a community hamlet in Fen country, this "splendid pub" (to quote the Prince of Wales) and former 17th-century farmhouse is a lovely old place with log fires, scrubbed pine tables and a relaxing vibe in the candlelit bar. George prides himself on serving beers from small regional breweries, and the pub even has a microbrewery at the back. After you've settled in for a pint, try one of the seasonal specialities from the oft-changing lunch and dinner menus. There's always fresh fish, as well as pub favourites such as local sausages and mash with onion gravy or beer-battered haddock and chips, and chef's daily specials. Finish with sticky toffee pudding with butterscotch sauce or crème caramel. There's al fresco dining on the lawn overlooking the village green, and memorable Sunday roasts – do book!

Meals	Lunch from £6.95. Dinner from £11.95. Sunday lunch, 3 courses, £21.95. No food Mon.
Closed	2pm-6pm & Mon lunch. Open all day Sat & Sun.

Catherine & George Gibson
Dyke's End,
8 Fair Green, Reach,
Cambridge, CB25 0JD
Tel +44 (0)1638 743816
Web www.dykesend.co.uk

Entry 66 Map 9

Cambridgeshire

The Cock

Hemingford Grey

A cracking country pub. First there's the pretty village that runs down to the river, then the tangle of footpaths and cycle tracks that wait beyond. As for this lovely 17th-century pub, it basks in its original simplicity – a bare-boarded bar, cosy low beams, a much-used log-burner, then four great ales from local breweries. Books and maps, the daily papers and happy staff all wait. For food, move into the airy restaurant where buttermilk walls and modern prints sit beautifully with wooden floors and tables. The menu is full of treats – crayfish cocktail, hake with chorizo, honey-glazed duck, roast plum crème brûlée. The chef makes his own sausages, there's local game in season, a fine cheese board and a much-praised Sunday lunch. Cambridge is close and you can walk across the fields to pretty St Ives.

Meals	Lunch from £5.50. Dinner from 11.50. Sunday lunch from £14.50.
Closed	3pm-6pm (4pm-6.30pm Sun).

Oliver Thain
The Cock, 47 High Street, Hemingford Grey, Huntingdon, PE28 9BJ
Tel +44 (0)1480 463609
Web www.cambscuisine.com/the-cock-hemingford

Entry 67 Map 9

The Pheasant

Keyston

This textbook country outpost does beams, open fires and comfy sofas better than anyone, yet never forgets it's a pub; two to three guest ales are on hand pump. John Hoskins bought the Pheasant in 2012 and chef/patron Simon Cadge is at the helm. The menu is English (give or take some gnocchi and tempura), the cooking is restorative, the meat is reared in the village, and if the mushroom man turns up with a colony of flavoursome fungi, then the menu will announce them. Add an enterprising list of wines and expertly kept ales and you have the Pheasant to a T. Try crab and prawn agnolotti, pork cheeks with puy lentils, parsnip purée and glazed brussels, and polenta cake with pineapple and coconut sorbet. If you don't want a full-blown meal, there's bar food instead. And beautiful unpasteurised British cheeses.

Meals	Lunch & dinner from £15. Sunday lunch, 3 courses, £25.
Closed	Monday all day & Sunday evenings.

Simon Cadge
The Pheasant,
Village Loop Road, Keyston,
Huntingdon, PE28 0RE
Tel +44 (0)1832 710241
Web www.thepheasant-keyston.co.uk

Cambridgeshire

The Anchor Inn

Sutton Gault

A real find, a 1650s ale house on Chatteris Fen, run by good people. Wedged between the bridge and the raised dyke, the little inn was built to bed and board the men conscripted to tame the vast watery tracts of swamp and scrub. These days cosy luxury infuses every corner. There are low beamed ceilings, timber-framed walls, raw dark panelling and terracotta-tiled floors. A wood-burner warms the bar, so stop for a pint of cask ale, then pick from a menu that is light, imaginative and surprising: hand-dressed crabs from Cromer in spring, asparagus and Bottisham hams in summer, wild duck from the marshes in winter. Footpaths flank the water; stroll down and you might see mallards or whooper swans, even a seal – the river is tidal to the Wash. Don't miss Ely (the bishop comes to eat).

Meals	Lunch, 2 courses, £13.95. Dinner, 3 courses, £25-£30. Sunday lunch from £12.95.
Closed	3pm-7pm (6.30pm Sat & Sun).

Majiec Bilewski
The Anchor Inn,
Bury Lane, Sutton Gault,
Ely, CB6 2BD
Tel +44 (0)1353 778537
Web www.anchor-inn-restaurant.co.uk

The Cholmondeley Arms

Cholmondeley

As prim and proper as a Victorian schoolmistress on the outside, as stylish as Beau Brummell within: the sandblasted brick walls of this old school house rise to raftered, vaulted ceilings and large windows pull natural light into every corner. Shelves of gin hover above fat radiators, cartoons and photos nestle amongst old sporting paraphernalia, and oriental rugs sprawl beneath an auction lot of tables, pews and chairs. The glorious carved oak bar dominates the main hall and apart from the malted charms of Cholmondeley Best Bitter and Merlin's Gold there are a staggering 200 varieties of ruinously good gin to discover, with the aid of a well-thumbed guide or one of the many charming staff. And when the dinner bell goes study the menus on antique blackboards and opt for devilled lamb's kidneys on toast, followed by baked cod with brown shrimps and lemon butter, or a spicy sausage and butternut squash hash cake. Rooms in the old headmaster's house behind are calm and civilised with all the comfort you need. Seldom has going back to school been this much fun.

Rooms	5 doubles, 1 twin: £60-£100.
Meals	Lunch & dinner £7.25-£17.95. Not Christmas Day.
Closed	Open all day.

Tim Moody
The Cholmondeley Arms,
Wrenbury Road, Cholmondeley,
Malpas, SY14 8HN

Tel +44 (0)1829 720300
Web www.cholmondeleyarms.co.uk

The Pheasant Inn

Higher Burwardsley

Pheasants scatter across the fields and the views, on a clear day, stretch to Liverpool. Gloriously positioned on a former farm in the Peckforton Hills, the Pheasant has been stylishly revamped. The old laid-back feel has survived the smartening up of dark beams in bustling bars where pots of jasmine scent the air and Weetwood Old Dog comes from the cask; for sheer cosiness, book a table by a fire (there are three). The food is more refined than your average pub grub, and is informally and delightfully served. Our lamb rump with broad beans, radish and apricots was full of flavour, our salmon with pancetta came with a creamy chive butter, and the sticky toffee pudding was pleasingly light. Deli boards and all-day hot beef sandwiches are also on the cards: just the job after hiking the Sandstone Trail. The staff are the best and if you stay the night – why wouldn't you! – the 12 bedrooms, some traditional (soft carpeting, sumptuous drapes, dark oak furniture), some contemporary (wide oak boards, exposed stone walls, atmospheric lighting) are split between the inn, the stone barn and the 'stables'; go for one with a view.

Rooms	8 twin/doubles: £95-£124. 3 suites for 2: £105-£140. 1 family room for 4: £135-£170. Singles from £65.
Meals	Lunch & dinner £6.75-£19.95. Bar meals £3.95-£8.50. Sunday lunch £12.50.
Closed	Open all day.

Andrew Nelson
The Pheasant Inn,
Higher Burwardsley, Tattenhall,
Chester, CH3 9PF
Tel +44 (0)1829 770434
Web www.thepheasantinn.co.uk

The Bear's Paw

Warmingham

Tucked into a pretty village is a dazzlingly refurbished 19th-century inn. There's an almost baronial feel to the Bear's Paw, thanks to the polished oak panelling, the huge fireplaces, the sweeping floors, the leather bucket chairs, bookshelves, old prints and vintage photos. No stuffiness here, just cheery staff making sure you are well-watered and well-fed. Six cask ales, several from Weetwood, all local, take centre stage on the bar; there are also premium brand spirits, 12 malts and an excellent wine list. At well-spaced wooden tables are menus that blend classics with modern twists. Try game and root vegetable pie served with hand-cut chips and pickled red cabbage; vegetarian lasagne with wild mushrooms, spinach and toasted pine nuts; posh poached egg with truffle sabayon. There are deli boards and fabulous sandwiches too. Staying the night? You have 17 superb bedrooms to choose from, each boutiquey, each flaunting funky fabrics, contemporary wallpapers, media hubs and designer fittings. Bathrooms are sleek with granite tops, rain showers, and the softest towels and robes.

Rooms	10 doubles, 7 twin/doubles: £80-£170.
Meals	Lunch & dinner £5.95-£19.95.
Closed	Open all day.

Andrew Nelson
The Bear's Paw,
School Lane, Warmingham,
Sandbach, CW11 3QN

Tel	+44 (0)1270 526317
Web	www.thebearspaw.co.uk

The Roebuck

Mobberley

From the cobbled pavement planted with little trees to the split-level terrace that catches the sun, you could believe you're in a French valley rather than an English village whose lucky residents now have a third offering from the Cheshire Cat team. The Roebuck dates back to 1708 and has been restored with extraordinary love and style. Rustic shutters, shipped from France along with the beds, sit prettily on the pink-brick masonry. Café tables, wine-red leather settles, mirrors, candles and a host of wine bottles make a colourful backdrop for tasty lunches and dinners with a Mediterranean flavour: Toulouse sausage cassoulet, classic croque monsieur, smoked mackerel and orzo salad with orange and dill. Sample local craft beers and ciders, or let the wine list tempt you. Six double bedrooms, two on the ground floor, four upstairs, are full of colour, warmth and texture: embroidered brocades, leather armchairs, even funky pony skins. All have sparkling bathrooms and the best (Bobal) has a woodburner between the bed and bath. A true gem.

Rooms	6 doubles: £130-£200.
Meals	Starters from £3.95. Lunch from £7.95. Dinner from £12.95.
Closed	Open all day.

Favourite newcomer

Jake Fuller
The Roebuck,
Mill Lane, Mobberley,
Knutsford, WA16 7HX
Tel +44 (0)1565 873939
Web roebuckinnmobberley.co.uk

The Bull's Head

Mobberley

You feel the warmth as soon as you walk through the door. Candles glow on the tables of this pretty village pub, fires crackle, and the staff couldn't be nicer. Under a low-beamed ceiling, seven hand pumps dispense the finest local ales from Storm, Wincle and Redwillow as well as the inimitable Mobberley Wobbly – ale is king! Add in a Highland extravaganza of over 80 whiskies and other tempting brews and you have the makings of a celebration. Chef Steve cooks 'pub classics from the heart' with full English flavours; the steak and ale pie is a fully encased masterpiece in itself, and the Irish whisky sticky toffee pudding too indulgent for words. With outside tables for sunny days, this is as good as it gets for a village pub.

Meals — Bar meals £2.85-£12.
Lunch £3.95-£19.95.
Sunday lunch £13.95.

Closed — Open all day.

Barry Lawlor
The Bull's Head,
Mill Lane,
Mobberley, WA16 7HX

Tel +44 (0)1565 873395

Web www.thebullsheadpub.co.uk

Entry 74 Map 8

Cheshire

The Church Inn

Mobberley

Tim Bird and Mary McLaughlin's mini-pub empire continues to thrive and grow with the addition of the 18th-century Church Inn. Sister pub to the Bull's Head, also in Mobberley, it has been fully restored and refurbished, retaining the small intimate dining rooms with their wood and tiled floors, exposed brick and beams, soft lamplight, and glowing candles. On a wild winter's day it's hard to leave, with four craft ales on tap and decent wines to quaff and some great food: sautéed lamb's kidneys followed by grilled hake with tarragon and white wine sauce, then a sticky date bread and butter pud. Or try lighter dishes like smoked haddock tart or a sirloin steak sandwich with roast tomatoes and chips. Summer terraces give views of the church or across rolling fields. A village gem.

Meals — Lunch & dinner £15-£24.95.

Closed — Open all day.

Simon Umpleby
The Church Inn,
Church Lane,
Mobberley, WA16 7RD

Tel +44 (0)1565 873178

Web www.churchinnmobberley.co.uk

Entry 75 Map 8

The Lord Clyde

Kerridge

Surrounded by fields, a short drive from the former silk town of Macclesfield, a young Cheshire gem. Vanilla walls, a gleaming bar and a spotless dining room with a log fire make a modest setting for food that is exciting, challenging and delicious. On the autumn menu we found celeriac and chicory with buttermilk and prune; rabbit with parsnip, wild mushrooms and pressed potato; 35-day aged rib-eye with fat chips and peppercorn sauce; bitter chocolate and quince with custard and crisp mousse. Owner-chef Ernst has a pedigree, and that includes Noma in Copenhagen. So push the boat out and sample the nine-course tasting menu – allow a glorious three hours. The bar is still a drinkers' domain (always Speckled Hen), wife Sarah runs a happy team, and if you fancy a sandwich, order one: the sourdough bread is out of this world.

Meals	Lunch £7.95-£20.95.
Closed	Mon lunch. Tues-Thurs 3pm-5pm. Open all day Fri-Sun.

Sarah Richmond & Ernst Van Zyl
The Lord Clyde,
36 Clarke Lane, Kerridge,
Bollington, SK10 5AH

Tel +44 (0)1625 562123
Web www.thelordclyde.co.uk

Entry 76 Map 8

Cheshire

The Three Greyhounds Inn

Allostock

The bright, many-bottled bar winks and glows as you enter, while host James has a welcome for all. Fat purple cushions soften wooden benches around a huge dual-facing fireplace; reach for the 'Brandy Bible' and settle in. The clever layout makes the space cosy and intimate, with snugs around every corner – four with firesides – and nooks and crannies aplenty. James is proud of the atmosphere, and rightly so. Families nibble and natter with relish, while walkers and couples take their time over delicious smoked haddock and leek tart or pan-fried lamb's kidneys. During annual Cheshire Game Week you can tuck into dishes such as pheasant breast with sautéed white pudding and red leg partridge croquette.... Deep in the Cheshire countryside, this well-restored pub is conveniently close to the M6.

Meals	Lunch & dinner from £10.50. Bar meals from £5.95.
Closed	Open all day.

James Griffiths
The Three Greyhounds Inn,
Holmes Chapel Road, Allostock,
Knutsford, WA16 9JY

Tel +44 (0)1565 723455
Web www.thethreegreyhoundsinn.co.uk

Entry 77 Map 8

The Fishpool Inn

Delamere

A vast renovation, a huge investment, the doors have opened and the results are impressive: this is a thriving gastropub that delivers consistently good food to 3,000 diners a week. The cosy, traditional feel of the original front rooms has been recreated using natural or reclaimed materials (oak beams, Victorian tiles, original sandstone), and the dining room extension has been gorgeously crafted and designed. The attention to detail throughout is extraordinary. It's still very much a pub; expect up to eight local ales on tap and a mix of pub classics and modern British dishes on the menu, which is eclectic, with homemade pizzas and pies, oxtail suet puddings, and platefuls of hot haddock and chips delivered from the open (and very organised) kitchen. Posh loos, afternoon teas, and a super terrace overlooking the fields complete the civilised picture.

Meals	Light lunch from £5.95. Mains £9.95-£22.95.
Closed	Open all day.

Andrew & Lucy Nelson
The Fishpool Inn,
Fishpool Road, Delamere,
Chester, CW8 2HP

Tel +44 (0)1606 883277
Web www.thefishpoolinn.co.uk

Entry 78 Map 7

Cheshire

The Dysart Arms

Bunbury

One of those rare places – all things to all people. And, with separate spaces clustered around a central bar, it feels open and cosy at the same time. The 18th-century building has a listed interior of scrubbed floorboards, solid tables and chairs, pictures, plants, and French windows opening to terrace and garden. There's an inglenook packed with logs, a dining area in a library, and superb beers and wines. They're proud too of their food, rightly so: pan-fried pheasant wrapped in bacon, crab cakes with shredded mooli and chilli jam, roasted aubergine, goat's cheese and red pepper lasagne, toasted bara brith with caramelised bananas and cinnamon ice cream. The cheeses are taken as seriously as the cask ales (try the local Weetwood or Purple Moose) and the wines are thoughtfully chosen. Warm, intimate, friendly, and running on well-oiled wheels.

Meals	Lunch from £4.50. Bar meals £4.50-£10.25. Dinner £7.95-£16.95.
Closed	Open all day.

Kate John
The Dysart Arms,
Bowes Gate Road, Bunbury,
Tarporley, CW6 9PH

Tel +44 (0)1829 260183
Web www.dysartarms-bunbury.co.uk

Entry 79 Map 7

The White Lion

Barthomley

An inn since 1614 and a siege site in the Civil War, the character-steeped White Lion – wonky black and white timbers, thick thatched roof – stands beside a cobbled track close to a sandstone church. Step in to find three gloriously unspoilt rooms, all woodsmoke and charm, wizened oak beams, ancient benches and twisted walls, tiny latticed windows and quarry-tiled floors. No music or electronic wizardry here, just the crackling of log fires and a happy hubbub. Lunchtime food is listed on chalkboards as walkers and locals settle on ancient settles at scrubbed tables for hot beef and onion baguettes with chips, hearty ploughman's and Sunday roasts, all washed down with well-kept pints of Marstons and Jennings real ale. Summer seating is at picnic benches on the cobbles, with pretty views onto the village.

Meals	Lunch & dinner £4.75-£7.95.
Closed	Open all day.

Laura Condliffe
The White Lion,
Barthomley,
Crewe, CW2 5PG

Tel +44 (0)1270 882242
Web www.whitelionbarthomley.com

Photo: Red Pump Inn, entry 315

The Old Coastguard

Mousehole

The Old Coastguard stands on the water in one of Cornwall's loveliest coastal villages. It's a super spot and rather peaceful – very little has happened here since the Spanish sacked the place in 1595. It's owned by Edmund and Charles Inkin, brothers who are past masters at running lovely small hotels; warm colours, attractive prices, great food and kind staff are their hallmarks. Downstairs, the airy bar and the dining room come together as one, the informality of open plan creating a great space to hang out. You get smart rustic tables, earthy colours, local ales and local art, then wooden floors and a crackling fire. Drop down a few steps to find a bank of sofas and a wall of glass framing sea views; in summer, doors open onto a decked terrace, a lush lawn, then the coastal path weaving down to the small harbour. Bedrooms hit the spot: warm colours, excellent beds, robes in fine bathrooms, books everywhere. Most have the view, eight have balconies. Don't miss dinner: salt and pepper monkfish, fish stew with mussels, chocolate mousse with tonka bean ice cream. Dogs are very welcome. *Ask about seasonal offers.*

Rooms	10 doubles, 3 twin/doubles: £135-£210. 1 suite for 2: £175-£225. 1 family room for 4: £190-£240. Dinner, B&B from £75 p.p.
Meals	Lunch from £6. Dinner, 3 courses, about £27. Sunday lunch from £12.50.
Closed	Open all day.

Charles & Edmund Inkin
The Old Coastguard,
The Parade, Mousehole,
Penzance, TR19 6PR

Tel +44 (0)1736 731222
Web www.oldcoastguardhotel.co.uk

The Gurnard's Head

Zennor

This quirky inn is one of the best, the sort of place you'd hope to find at the end of the road. Outside, the wild west coast weaves up to St Ives; secret beaches appear at low tide, cliffs tumble down to the water, wild flowers streak the land pink in summer. Inside, it's earthy, warm, stylish and friendly, with rustic interiors, colour-washed walls, stripped wooden floors and fires at both ends of the bar. Logs are piled high in an alcove, maps and art hang on the walls, books fill every shelf; if you pick one up and don't finish it, take it home and post it back. Cosy rooms have a warm colours and the odd antique, then Vi-Spring mattresses, crisp white linen, colourful throws and Roberts radios. Downstairs, you can scoff delicious food in the bar, the restaurant or out in the garden in good weather. Tasty snacks wait – pork pies, crab claws, half a pint of Atlantic prawns – as does more substantial fare, maybe grilled sardines, Cornish lamb with root vegetables, roasted apples and pears. Picnics can be arranged, there's bluegrass folk music in the bar most weeks. Dogs are very welcome. *Ask about seasonal offers.*

Rooms	3 doubles, 4 twin/doubles: £115-£180. Dinner, B&B from £75 p.p.
Meals	Lunch from £12. Dinner, 3 courses, from £26.50. Sunday lunch, 3 courses, £21.
Closed	Open all day.

Charles & Edmund Inkin
The Gurnard's Head,
Zennor,
St Ives, TR26 3DE
Tel +44 (0)1736 796928
Web www.gurnardshead.co.uk

The Plume of Feathers

Mitchell

One wonders what John Wesley would have thought about the place where he used to preach being turned into a stylish pub-restaurant! He certainly wouldn't have approved of the alcohol, but the food would be another matter. Properly-trained and friendly staff serve freshly cooked local produce at sensible prices – try Cornish fishcakes with sweet chilli sauce and dressed leaves, or grilled Dover sole with lemon butter. There are thick bacon sandwiches at lunch and delicious puddings after – the sticky toffee pudding is delicious. The central bar is lively with TV, piped music and Sharp's Doom Bar on tap. You'll also find low stripped beams, half-panelled walls hung with modern art, fresh flowers, candle-studded pine tables and thoughtful lighting. And if all this gets too much there are eight comfortable bedrooms, all on the ground floor. The biggest have squishy sofas, and all have sparkling bathrooms with nice things waiting for you. All the good food draws a big crowd so you certainly won't have the place to yourselves, especially in summer. Enjoy the buzz.

Rooms	5 doubles: £100-£140. 2 suites for 4: £140-£160. 1 family room for 4: £103-£150.
Meals	Lunch & bar meals from £10. Dinner from £15. Sunday lunch, 3 courses, £21.
Closed	Open all day.

Daniel Trotter
The Plume of Feathers,
Mitchell,
Newquay, TR8 5AX

Tel +44 (0)1637 870129
Web www.theplumemitchell.co.uk

Lewinnick Lodge

Newquay

Oh we do love to be beside the seaside! Poised above the cliff edge to a backdrop of rolling fields and hikers' trails (an inspiring setting for platefuls of St Austell mussels and Fowey oysters) this glass-fronted edifice overlooks the Atlantic; a mighty setting in all weathers. Polar opposite of the 'quaint local', Lewinnick Lodge is large and luminous with a friendly modern vibe. Find a wall of glass, a sweep of oak, a sparkling bar, an open fire, efficient staff who make everyone welcome and that includes your dog. You can eat in or out and they specialise in fish, cooked 'à point' just as it should be – haddock with ratatouille and pan-fried gnocchi burst with flavour – and the emphasis is on modern British favourites. Bedrooms are light, airy and have sea views, some with a bath overlooking the ocean, all with large comfortable beds and smartly tiled bathrooms. Wander down (latest time 11.30!) to a breakfast outside on the terrace if you want: full Cornish, or a Belgian waffle with caramelised banana, slices of Baker Tom's bread for toasting and excellent, freshly-roasted coffee. Walk it off on the coastal path.

Rooms 6 doubles,
2 twin/doubles: £145-£220.
2 suites for 2,
1 family room for 4: £190-£240.

Meals Breakfast from £3.50.
Lunch & bar meals from £5.50.
Dinner from £11.
Sunday lunch £10.50.

Closed Open all day.

Daniel Trotter
Lewinnick Lodge,
Pentire Headland,
Newquay, TR7 1QD
Tel +44 (0)1637 878117
Web www.lewinnicklodge.co.uk

The Mill House Inn

Trebarwith

Coast down the steep winding lane to a 1760s mill house in a woodland setting. Trebarwith's spectacular beach – all surf and sand – is a ten-minute walk away. It's quite a spot. Back at the inn, the bar combines the best of Cornish old and Cornish new: big flagged floor, wooden tables, chapel chairs, two leather sofas by a wood-burning stove. The swanky dining room overlooking the burbling mill stream is light, elegant and very modern. Settle down to some rather good food: firecracker prawns; fillet of sea trout with crushed potatoes, kale, roasted banana shallot, mussel & tarragon cream; coconut panna cotta, torched pineapple, rum sponge. Bar meals are more traditional, they do great barbecues in summer and (be warned) a band often plays at the weekend. In keeping with the seaside setting, bedrooms are simple and uncluttered, with good shower rooms in the smaller standard rooms. If you stay in the little cottage be ready for a steep staircase. Coastal trails lead to Tintagel, official home of the Arthurian legends, there's biking, surfing, crabbing… you couldn't possibly be bored.

Rooms	7 doubles, 1 twin/double: £75-£130. 1 family room for 4: £75-£130. 1 cottage for 2: £120-£160.
Meals	Lunch from £7.50. Dinner from £12. Sunday lunch, 3 courses, £17.85.
Closed	Open all day.

Mark & Kep Forbes
The Mill House Inn,
Trebarwith,
Tintagel, PL34 0HD

Tel +44 (0)1840 770200
Web www.themillhouseinn.co.uk

The Old Custom House

Padstow

You can't miss it: the big square Custom House opposite the car park, right on Padstow's quay. It is sturdy, delightful and no doubt has weathered many a storm. Inside: a large bar on two levels with planked floors and timbered ceiling, background music and a big screen for sport. There's a coffee shop on the ground floor and a hairdressers above. The place buzzes with trippers, locals, children, dogs, and if you fancy pushing the boat out book into the restaurant, modern and stylish with muted colours and views down over the harbour. The menu is fish-led – of course – and there's a daily changing specials board: they follow the seasons here. Try crispy fried camembert with chilli jam; cassoulet with roasted tomatoes; fish pie with creamy saffron sauce. Then catch the ferry to Rock, and tiny St Enodoc church where John Betjeman is buried. If you wish to linger, the bedrooms are very good, with their cream pattern carpets, heated towel rails, iPod docks and relaxed seaside décor. Splash out on one with a harbour or estuary view – corner rooms have both! The most peaceful are at the top.

Rooms	19 doubles, 4 twins: £115-£230.
Meals	Lunch & dinner £8.95-£13.95.
Closed	Open all day.

Linda Prior
The Old Custom House,
South Quay,
Padstow, PL28 8BL

Tel +44 (0)1841 532359
Web www.oldcustomhousepadstow.co.uk

St Kew Inn

St Kew

Lost down a maze of lanes in a secluded wooded valley, the St Kew is a grand old inn originally built in the 15th-century for the masons working on the church. It's an irresistibly friendly place with a huge range and a warming fire, a dark slate floor, winged settles and a terrific unspoilt atmosphere – no pub paraphernalia here but look out for the resident ghost who's been spotted in the past. Pewter tankards hang over the bar where local St Austell ales are dispensed, and soup and baguettes revive weary walkers. Elsewhere the food is bang up to date. Try cured salmon with beetroot and dill yogurt, chicken breast with smoked hog's pudding, sauté potatoes and Provençal sauce, marmalade pudding and custard. In summer, the big streamside garden is the place to be.

Meals: Lunch & bar meals from £5.50.
Dinner from £9.50.
Sunday lunch, 3 courses, £19.50.
Closed: 3pm-6pm.

Sarah Allen
St Kew Inn,
St Kew,
Bodmin, PL30 3HB
Tel: +44 (0)1208 841259
Web: www.stkewinn.co.uk

Cornwall

St Tudy Inn

St Tudy

Holiday walkers and cyclists from Padstow have long loved this little pub off the beaten track, with its new slate floors and its crackling fire, its Doom Bar and Tawny on tap. But it's the food that's been the biggest draw; it still is. Chef-patron Emily sailed in in 2015 with exciting plans, a friendly team and a rustic, seasonal menu. There are four cosy dining areas including the public bar and a terrace at the back, and the rooms are charming and countrified – a battered leather chair, a basket full of logs, a fine old settle. Emily heads the kitchen and creates disarmingly simple food from the best Cornish produce: lamb tagine with apricots; squash and fennel lasagne; lemon sole with new potatoes; treacle tart with clotted cream. Our sole goujons with citrus mayonnaise and a glass of white from Sicily totally hit the spot.

Meals: Lunch & bar meals from £8.95.
Dinner from £10.95.
Closed: Sun eve.

Emily Scott
St Tudy Inn,
St Tudy,
Bodmin, PL30 3NN
Tel: +44 (0)1208 850656
Web: www.sttudyinn.com

The Ship Inn

Wadebridge

Afloat after a superb refurbishment, one of the oldest pubs in town honours its maritime history in gilt-framed pictures on white stone walls. Padded banquettes blend with wooden stools, chairs, and tables to create an intimate bar area in which to sip a pint of Doom Bar or an ale from Padstow Brewing Company. There are books to read, board games to play, wood-burners and gentle music. Two dining areas, one a glorious open-raftered room with brass ship lights and a captain's table, are pleasant spaces in which to enjoy Darren Hardy's modern-traditional pub dishes; we loved the spiced mackerel with tomato and red onion salad, and the braised oxtail with horseradish mash. Little shipmates get menus, even your pooch can eat. There are bar snacks, Sunday roasts, great music nights – even Backgammon Club.

Meals Lunch & dinner £5-£18.95.
Closed 3pm-5pm Mon-Sat.

Rupert & Sarah Wilson
The Ship Inn,
Gonvena Hill,
Wadebridge, PL27 6DF
Tel +44 (0)1208 813845
Web www.shipinnwadebridge.co.uk

Entry 89 Map 1

Cornwall

The Mariners

Rock

Park in posh Rock's 'pay and display', or hop on the ferry from Padstow – what better than to arrive by boat! This big modern airy pub with sliding glass windows and bustling terrace is impossible to leave on a sunny day; the staff are trendy-friendly and the views are gorgeous. It's a major port of call for holiday makers, sailors, second-homers and all who love their food, and dogs and families are welcomed too. Inside are slate floors, stylish tables, an open-to-view kitchen and a small first-floor balcony for the privileged few (arrive early!). You can have bacon baps for breakfast, Porthilly oysters for lunch, and Sharp's beers (Doom Bar, Atlantic) all day. The menu is unashamedly fish-led and our cod fillet with salsa verde and lentils was super-fresh. We hear the steaks and roasts are rather good too.

Meals Bar snacks from £3.
Lunch from £8.50.
Dinner from £10.50.
Closed Open all day.

Nathan Outlaw & Paul Ripley
The Mariners,
Rock, PL27 6LD
Tel +44 (0)1208 863679
Web www.themarinersrock.com

Entry 90 Map 1

The Cornish Arms

St Merryn

It could be the blueprint for how a good country inn should be. It's unpretentious and authentic, there's a buzzy atmosphere with locals rubbing shoulders with walkers and holiday makers, and the food, as expected when Rick Stein is involved, doesn't miss a beat. We're not talking gastropub or fine dining but good honest dishes cooked well – scampi in the basket, rump steak and chips, treacle tart and custard. The atmospheric bar is where the locals down pints of Tribute – the pub is owned by the St Austell Brewery. There's a family room too, and a pool table and a wood-burner and a big garden for sunny days. The much missed canine star of Rick's TV shows would have loved a trip here, and no doubt have been thrilled by two of the beers on offer – Chalky's Bark and Chalky's Bite.

Meals — Lunch & dinner £9.95-£17.95. Sunday lunch £13.95 (winter only).

Closed — Open all day.

Rick & Jill Stein
The Cornish Arms, Churchtown,
St Merryn, Padstow, PL28 8ND
Tel +44 (0)1841 532700
Web www.rickstein.com/eat-with-us/the-cornish-arms

Cornwall

The Queen's Hotel

St Ives

A smart foodie pub set back from the harbour of St Ives, hung with flowers in season. Perch on a red bar stool at the impressive white marble-topped bar and choose from St Austell's fine ales – HSD will see you reeling – or some good old Cornish Rattler cider. Head to a well-scrubbed candlelit table, or a tartan bench seat by the fireplace; if you're lucky enough to land on a Friday evening there could be live music! Matt Perry's menus are constantly evolving and have big flavours based on rustic French and Italian recipes alongside sturdy old-fashioned English offerings: try lamb faggot with crispy belly pork, carrot purée, cabbage and bacon and onion gravy; finish with orange posset, marmalade ice cream and shortbread. Then stride south, along some of the finest coastline in Cornwall.

Meals — Lunch & bar meals from £5. Dinner from £8. Sunday lunch £9.50. No food on Mon eves (Nov-Feb).

Closed — Open all day.

Neythan Hayes
The Queen's Hotel,
High Street,
St Ives, TR26 1RR
Tel +44 (0)1736 796468
Web www.queenshotelstives.com

The Halsetown Inn

Halestown

Built by a Victorian philanthropist in 1831 this inn has impeccable eco credentials and has won awards for its efforts. Inside, comfort and character abound with a choice of cosy corners, two open fires, an old Cornish range, and deep red walls. Tuck into the likes of pan-fried scallops with caramelised cauliflower and apple, followed by slow roasted pork belly with black pudding and cheddar hash brown, spring greens, cider gravy and onion rings. Leave room for puddings, especially rosewater panna cotta with pistachio biscotti. Vegetarians are well-served, children have their own menu, and monthly Wine and Dine evenings draw a happy crowd. You can walk from St Ives if the spirit moves you, then sit at the bar with a pint of Doom Bar or Skinner's ale or even a Cornish gin or a pastis! A pub with huge soul and great character.

Meals: Starters from £3. Lunch & dinner from £11.
Closed: Rarely.

Morag Robertson
The Halsetown Inn,
Halestown,
St Ives, TR26 3NA
Tel: +44 (0)1736 795583
Web: www.halsetowninn.co.uk

Entry 93 Map 1

Cornwall

The Star Inn

St Just

Entrenched in the wild landscape close to Land's End is the 'last proper pub in Cornwall'. This 18th-century beauty, owned by the ex-mayor of St Just and its oldest and most authentic inn, proudly shirks the trappings of tourism and remains a drinkers' den. Bands of locals sink pints of Tinners Ale in the low-beamed, spick-and-span bar, old pub games thrive and the place is the hub of the local folk scene, with live music at least ten nights a month; singalongs and joke-telling are part of the Monday evening entertainment. The dim-lit bar is jam-packed with interest and walls are littered with seafaring and mining artefacts; coals glow in the grate on wild winter days. Come for St Austell ale and the 'craic'. There's a free juke box, mulled wine in winter and that pub rarity, a great family room.

Meals: No food served.
Closed: Open all day.

Johnny McFadden
The Star Inn,
1 Fore Street, St Just,
Penzance, TR19 7LL
Tel: +44 (0)1736 788767
Web: www.thestarinn-stjust.co.uk

Entry 94 Map 1

Seven Stones Inn

St Martin's

You cross the seven seas, wash up on a tiny island, follow a footpath up a forested hill, then discover this quirky pub and realise you're exactly where you want to be. Inside, wood panels, old settles and a wood-burner in the big stone fireplace give a lovely earthy feel. Well-kept Cornish ales wait at the bar, so order a pint, carry it onto the terrace, then lose your gaze in the magnificent view that shoots across the shimmering sea to St Mary's beyond. There's good pub grub, too: hearty ploughman's, crab sandwiches, tasty pies, freshly caught fish. Emily and Dominic orchestrate it all brilliantly – fire pits, live music, quiz nights and barbecues, even an October film festival. Locals love it, keeping it open a couple of nights a week off season. Paths lead out across the island, its northern point ringed by beaches. A very special place.

Meals Lunch from £5. Mains £9–£14.50.
Closed Low season: Closed on Mon, Tues and Thurs from Oct–April. Open all day in Summer.

Emily & Dominic Crees
Seven Stones Inn,
Lower Town,
St Martin's,
Scilly Isles, TR25 0QW
Tel +44 (0)1720 423777

Cornwall

The Tolcarne Inn

Newlyn

What might one expect on the menu at a pub in Newlyn, home to the Cornwall's biggest fish market? Ben Tunnicliffe, former chef at the Scarlet Hotel and the Abbey in Penzance (where he bagged a Michelin star) has set foodie hearts aflutter with his first solo venture. Fish, whatever's in season, is his thing – perfectly cooked and beautifully presented: roasted monkfish with linguine; wild mushrooms and truffle oil; fillet of brill with salsify; fish soup with rouille and crostini... it's great value too. This is a traditional fisherman's pub, simple, whitewashed and cosy and thankfully the locals are still coming. The pub is next to the sea wall and plans are afoot to raise the level of the terrace to take in the views over the bay. Bag a table outside and enjoy some of the best food in Cornwall.

Meals Lunch & dinner from £9.50.
Closed 3pm–5.30pm.

Ben Tunnicliffe
The Tolcarne Inn,
Newlyn,
Penzance, TR18 5PR
Tel +44 (0)1736 363074
Web www.tolcarneinn.co.uk

The Coldstreamer

Gulval

The Coldstreamer dates from 1895 and has one foot in the country and one foot in town – Penzance is a short drive or a good walk. There's a terrace at the front where you can catch the morning sun, a wood-burner in the bar for winter nights. Inside, all is cool and contemporary with grey-hued walls and retro fifties furniture. Choose from an extensive choice of ciders and ales at the bar, or head to the light, bright dining area with its exposed Cornish stone and fresh flowers on tables. Head chef Tom's menus are edgy, modern and worth travelling for: there's crab and crème fraîche sandwiches at lunch, or try blow-torched squid with risotto nero, pine oil and samphire, then gnocchi with purple sprouting broccoli, beetroot, porcini mushrooms and Bath Blue. Finish with cinnamon doughnuts, raspberry curd and Caramac. A real treat.

Meals	Lunch from £7.95. Dinner from £11.95.
Closed	Open all day.

Tom Franklin-Pryce
The Coldstreamer,
Gulval,
Penzance, TR18 3BB

Tel +44 (0)1736 362072
Web www.coldstreamer-penzance.co.uk

Entry 97 Map 1

Cornwall

The Mexico Inn

Longrock

Between Marazion and Penzance (an hour's walk between the two) is the Mexico Inn, an unlikely setting for a cracking food pub, and a feather in the cap for Longrock! This Cornish granite building, 200 years old and lovingly revived, faces the sea, with a small enclosed terrace at the rear. Tom Symons, ex Rick Stein, and partner chef Amy have infused the place with character and charm. Rustic plank floors run throughout, leather chairs gather round the wood-burner, and from the jolly bar doggie treats and pints of Tribute flow. Walls are pale granite, paintwork aqua-blue, up-cycled tables are rustic. Short seasonal menus promise whitebait and harissa mayo, celeriac and pancetta soup, haddock and chips, bangers and mash, superb Sunday roasts, vegetables cooked to perfection. The value is outstanding.

Meals	Starters from £5. Mains from £11.50. No food Sunday evenings.
Closed	Mondays.

Tom Symons
The Mexico Inn,
4 Riverside, Longrock,
Penzance, TR20 8JD

Tel +44 (0)1736 710625
Web www.themexicoinn.com

Entry 98 Map 1

The Victoria Inn

Perranuthnoe

With glorious Mount's Bay down the lane, this striking village inn draws the crowds. Arrive early and bag a seat in the stone-walled bar by the log-burner, or in the sunny sunken garden. Chef-landlord Nik Boyle is making waves locally, using the best Cornish ingredients for bang-up-to-date food. For ale-lovers there's Doom Bar or Sail Loft on tap, a perfect match for steamed Porthilly mussels. Cooking moves up a gear in the evenings, so try honey and truffle whipped goat's cheese mousse with chicory, pear and walnuts, followed by roasted artichoke and garden pea tagliatelle. Dogs will want to nab one of the biscuits behind the bar, jealously guarded by Monty the spaniel. Built originally to house the masons extending the church in the 12th century, this very old pub is one happy ship.

Meals Starters from £7. Mains from £13.
Closed Open all day.

Nik Boyle
The Victoria Inn,
Perranuthnoe,
Penzance, TR20 9NP
Tel +44 (0)1736 710309
Web www.victoriainn-penzance.co.uk

Entry 99 Map 1

The Ship

Porthleven

Imagine a weather-beaten pub hewn out of the rock on Cornwall's most southerly fishing harbour (thrilling on a stormy night). An ale-lovers' pub with a young and fun vibe, popular with salty sea dogs too, it's deluged with visitors in high summer, drawn to its position and its character. There's a cider festival in August and real ales all year round, from Surf Bum and Bal Maiden to Sharp's Coaster and Doom Bar. Inside, find granite walls, planked floors, church pews and an open fire. Drinks are drunk, songs are sung, and outside is a three-tier terrace – lower deck, bridge and crow's nest. You can have sandwiches, fish platters and spicy chicken wings, or fill up on crab cakes, lasagne, Thai curry, rump steak, battered hake with salad and fries. It's lovely grub, freshly homemade, and the fish comes straight from the sea.

Meals Starters from £4.95.
Mains from £8.95.
Closed Open all day.

Kate Preston
The Ship,
Mount Pleasant Road, Porthleven,
Helston, TR13 9JS
Tel +44 (0)1326 564204
Web www.theshipinncornwall.co.uk

Entry 100 Map 1

Trengilly Wartha Inn

Constantine

Well tucked down steep and twisting lanes, in the verdant heaven that is the Helford estuary, is this friendly Cornish inn. Choose a pint of Skinner's Trengilly Gold or St Austell HSD and enjoy a stroll in the six acres of old orchard with pond – and a gravelled pergola with ingenious underfloor heating. The main bar is a cracker with a wealth of mini-snugs formed by mid-height wooden settles, beer mats tacked to beams, cricketing memorabilia, local black and white photos and paintings, and a display of some of the 150 wines on offer; there are 40 malts too. Chef Nick Tyler has 20 years under his belt here and keeps it fresh, local and seasonal; a shame not to try the Falmouth river mussels with onion, white wine and cream, or the crab thermidor with homemade granary bread.

Meals	Lunch from £4.80. Bar meals & dinner from £7.20. Sunday lunch, 3 courses, £20.
Closed	3pm-6pm.

Lisa & William Lea
Trengilly Wartha Inn,
Constantine,
Falmouth, TR11 5RP

Tel	+44 (0)1326 340332
Web	www.trengilly.co.uk

Cornwall

The Pandora Inn

Mylor Bridge

Yachtsmen moor at the end of the pontoon that reaches into the creek. The building is special: thatched, 13th-century and rebuilt following a devastating fire. The pub is named in memory of the *Pandora*, a naval ship sent to Tahiti to capture the mutineers of Captain Bligh's *Bounty*. It keeps its traditional layout on several levels, along with panelled walls, polished flags, snug alcoves, log fires, maritime mementoes, and amazingly low wooden ceilings. The award-winning menu has something to please everyone, with fresh seafood dominating the specials board, and an indulgently long wine list. Arrive early in summer – by car or by boat; park nearby and walk (the car park isn't huge). On winter weekdays it's blissfully peaceful; the postprandial walking along wooded creekside paths is a delight.

Meals	Lunch & dinner £6-£19.
Closed	Open all day.

John Milan & Steve Bellman
The Pandora Inn,
Restronguet, Mylor Bridge,
Falmouth, TR11 5ST

Tel	+44 (0)1326 372678
Web	www.pandorainn.com

The Roseland Inn

Philleigh

Beside a peaceful parish church, two miles from the King Harry Ferry, a cob-built Cornish treasure with its own microbrewery (their Roseland Gullable is award winning). The front courtyard is bright with blossom in spring and climbing roses in summer. Indoors: old settles with scatter cushions, worn slate floors, low black beams and winter log fires. Local photographs, gig-racing memorabilia and a corner dedicated to rugby trophies scatter the walls. Spotlessly kept, it attracts locals and visitors in search of good food, such as local farm meats and fish landed at St Mawes. Dishes range from decent sandwiches to scallops with belly pork and white onion sauce, and roast duck with raspberry jus. Staff are full of smiles – even when the pub doubles as the Roseland Rugby Club clubhouse on winter Saturday nights.

Meals: Lunch & dinner £8.50-£13.95. Sunday lunch £9.95.

Closed: 3pm-6pm. Open all day Sat & Sun & in summer.

Phil Heslip
The Roseland Inn,
Philleigh,
Truro, TR2 5NB

Tel: +44 (0)1872 580254
Web: www.roselandinn.co.uk

Entry 103 Map 1

Cornwall

The Springer Spaniel

Treburley

Anton Piotrowski's food is modern and exciting with punchy rich flavours. This is a brilliant roadside stop for travellers from Exeter to Cornwall, and for local foodies too. In the bar, find a log-burner and bookcases full of books; in the dining room, simple colours and a medley of wooden furniture; the most romantic table is in the inglenook. The staff are wonderful, cheerful and knowledgeable, while muddy booted walkers and their dogs, in for a pint of Tribute, Proper Job or Cornish Rattler, are as welcome as the rest. Anton and head chef Ali are passionate about local and seasonal: note the pigeon Wellington with mushroom purée and sage and onion croquette, the Springer beef and venison burger with BBQ pulled ox cheek, triple cooked chips and onion rings, and the beautiful lemon sole with caper mash and fennel. Delightful.

Meals: Bar snacks from £3. Mains from £8.50. Sunday lunch, 2-3 courses, £18-£22.

Closed: Mon-Thurs 3pm-5pm. Open all day Fri-Sun.

Anton & Clare Piotrowski
The Springer Spaniel,
Treburley,
Launceston, PL15 9NS

Tel: +44 (0)1579 370424
Web: www.thespringerspaniel.co.uk

Entry 104 Map 2

The Sun Inn

Kirkby Lonsdale

This lovely old inn sits between the Dales and the Lakes in an ancient market town, one of the prettiest in the north. It backs onto St Mary's churchyard, where wild flowers flourish, and on the far side you'll find 'the fairest view in England', to quote John Ruskin. Herons fish the river Lune, lambs graze the fells beyond, a vast sky hangs above. Turner came to paint it in 1825 and benches wait for those who want to linger. As for the Sun, it does what good inns do – looks after you in style. There's lots of pretty old stuff – stone walls, rosewood panelling, wood-burners working overtime – and it's all kept spic and span, with warm colours, fresh flowers and the daily papers on hand. You find leather banquettes, local art and chairs in the dining room from Cunard's Mauretania, so eat in style, perhaps suckling pig, sea trout with mussel cream, chocolate and walnut tart. Bedrooms upstairs are stylishly uncluttered with warm colours, smart fabrics, stone walls and robes in good bathrooms. Car park permits come with your room and can be used far and wide. Market day is Thursday. *Minimum stay: 2 nights on weekends.*

Rooms	9 doubles, 2 twin/doubles: £135-£189. Singles from £76.
Meals	Lunch from £9.95. Dinner, 1-3 courses, £21-£34.
Closed	Mon lunch.

Iain & Jenny Black
The Sun Inn,
6 Market Street, Kirkby Lonsdale,
Carnforth, LA6 2AU

Tel +44 (0)1524 271965
Web www.sun inn.info

The Punch Bowl Inn

Crosthwaite

You're in the hills above Windermere in a pretty village encircled by lanes that defeat most tourists. It's a lovely spot, deeply rural, with ten-mile views down the valley and a church that stands next door; bell ringers practise on Friday mornings, the occasional bride glides out in summer. Yet while the Punch Bowl sits lost to the world, it is actually a deliciously funky inn. Rescued from neglect and renovated in great style, it now sparkles with a stylish mix of old and new. Outside, honeysuckle and roses ramble on stone walls. Inside, a clipped elegance runs throughout, with Farrow & Ball colours, rugs on wood floors and sofas in front of the wood-burner. Scott Fairweather's ambrosial food is a big draw, perhaps Lancashire cheese soufflé, loin of rabbit with crayfish mousse, pear soufflé and pecan ice-cream. Bedrooms are chic, all with beautiful linen, pretty fabrics and Roberts radios, while fabulous bathrooms have double-ended baths, separate showers and white robes. Four have the view, the suite is enormous, weekday prices are tempting. There's a terrace for lunch in the sun, too.

Rooms	5 doubles, 1 twin/double, 2 four-posters: £105-£235. 1 suite for 2: £180-£305. Singles from £75.
Meals	Lunch from £5. Dinner, 3 courses, £30-£35.
Closed	Open all day.

Richard Rose
The Punch Bowl Inn,
Crosthwaite,
Kendal, LA8 8HR

Tel	+44 (0)1539 568237
Web	www.the-punchbowl.co.uk

The Royal Oak at Keswick

Keswick

Step off a pedestrianised high street, into a cosily traditional haunt. This much-loved inn beside Keswick's old Moot Hall, with its old dark quarry tiles, long narrow bar, swish wallpapers and comfy seating attracts a diverse crowd: walkers, holiday makers, families, suits. Now it's pulling in diners too, with accessible menus and local supplies. The crispy duck spring rolls are delicious for kids, although they might be tempted by smaller portions of the hearty mains such as sausage and mash with cider apple chutney. Arrive early and pick a seat by a fire, then order homemade fish pie with parsley mash and mop up bread (winter doesn't get cosier than this). Leave room for pear and apple crumble. Most of Thwaites' cask ales are available, and well-kept. The wines are good, the landlord is interested, the staff are obliging, and there's always a water bowl for a walker's dog. There are delightful bedrooms too; all welcome dogs, and the largest are fabulous for families. They even have parking passes for further up the street – a boon in popular Keswick.

Rooms	19 doubles: £70-£140.
Meals	Starters from £4.95. Mains from £8.95.
Closed	Never.

Chris Lloyd
The Royal Oak at Keswick,
Main Street, Keswick, CA12 5HZ
Tel +44 (0)1768 773135
Web www.thwaites.co.uk/hotels-and-inns/inns/royal-oak-at-keswick

George and Dragon

Clifton

Charlie Lowther has found a chef who does perfect justice to the slow-grow breeds of beef, pork and lamb produced on the Lowther Estate – and you'll find lovely wines to match, 16 by the glass. Ales and cheeses are local, berries and mushrooms are foraged, vegetables are home-grown... and his signature starter, twice-baked cheese soufflé with a hint of spinach – is divine. As for the long low coaching inn, it's been beautifully restored by craftsmen using wood, slate and stone, and painted in colours in tune with the period. Bare wooden tables, comfy sofas, intimate alcoves and crackling fires make this a delightful place to dine and unwind; old prints and archive images tell stories of the 800-year-old estate's history. Outside is plenty of seating and a lawned play area beneath fruit trees. Upstairs are 11 bedrooms of varying sizes (some small, some large and some above the bar), perfectly decorated in classic country style. Carpeting is Cumbrian wool, beds are new, ornaments come with Lowther history, showers are walk-in, baths (there are two) are roll top, and breakfast is fresh and delicious.

Rooms	11 twin/doubles: £95-£155. Singles from £70.
Meals	Lunch & dinner from £12. Sunday lunch from £12.95.
Closed	Open all day.

Best all-rounder

Charlie Lowther
George and Dragon,
Clifton,
Penrith, CA10 2ER
Tel +44 (0)1768 865381
Web www.georgeanddragonclifton.co.uk

The King's Head

Ravenstonedale

Deep in the Upper Eden Valley, Ravenstonedale has the monumental Howgill Fells as its backdrop. This smartly refurbished 16th-century listed inn is the perfect place to start – or finish – a major walk; close to the river Eden, its exterior whitewash gleams. Inside, an earthy colour scheme adds to the warmth, with checked wool at period windows and on old settles, and furniture is mismatched in the best way, and dotted with newspapers and fresh flowers. Beams abound, and canine chums are welcome too. The menu changes regularly; there might be farmhouse cheese and onion soufflé or wood pigeon tart to start, followed by rump of Cumbrian lamb and braised red cabbage. Hobgoblin from the Wychwood Brewery and Jennings Cumberland are in top form on tap. Six stylish bedrooms await. Look forward to huge beds, perfect mattresses, deep baths… and soft colours in wool throws, tall padded headboards and pale carpets – and one or two nice vintage pieces: a table here, some china there. As for beams – they're everywhere!

Rooms 4 doubles, 2 twins: £80-£98.
Meals Lunch from £3.95.
Dinner, 3 courses, £22.
Closed Open all day.

Beverly Fothergill
The King's Head,
Ravenstonedale,
Kirkby Stephen, CA17 4NH
Tel +44 (0)1539 623050
Web www.kings-head.com

The Black Swan

Ravenstonedale

A lovely little inn in the middle of a pretty village, surrounded by wonderful walking country. It's all things to all men – a smart restaurant, a lively bar – and very dog-friendly. A stream runs through the big garden, where you can eat in good weather; free-range hens live in one corner. Inside, chic country interiors fit the mood perfectly. You get fresh flowers, tartan carpets, games and books galore. There's a bar for local ales, a sitting-room bar with an open fire, but the hub of the hotel is the bar in the middle, where village life gathers. You can eat wherever you want – there's an airy restaurant, too – so dig into delicious country fare, with meat from the hills around you, perhaps a tasty homemade soup, Galloway beef and root vegetable stew, sticky toffee pudding with vanilla ice cream. A very happy place.

Meals: Lunch from £4.95. Dinner, 3 courses, £20-£30.
Closed: Open all day.

Louise Dinnes
The Black Swan,
Ravenstonedale,
Kirkby Stephen, CA17 4NG
Tel +44 (0)1539 623204
Web www.blackswanhotel.com

Cumbria

The Samson Inn

Gilsland

On the Northumberland/Cumbria border, this Victorian pub is named after one of the first steam engines on the old Carlisle-Newcastle line. Red carpeting runs throughout, there are cushioned pews in corners, tub chairs around easy tables and a couple of log stoves. The more intimate dining room, with polished floors and dressed tables, is the backdrop to some refreshingly creative cooking. With the family farm certified organic, the emphasis is firmly on quality; our terrine of game with spiced fig compote was full of flavour. The wines are well considered, Brampton Bitter would be a nice accompaniment for sausages and mash; try roast hake in a bean and chickpea casserole, or a luscious chocolate torte. Finish with a whisky by the fire, surrounded by chat and good humour.

Meals: Lunch from £5. Dinner £10-£15. Packed lunch £6.
Closed: Sunday & Monday. Mid-November-February.

Liam McNulty & Lauren Harrison
The Samson Inn,
Gilsland,
Brampton, CA8 7DR
Tel +44 (0)1697 747962
Web www.thesamson.co.uk

Kirkstile Inn

Loweswater

Hard to imagine a more glorious setting than that of the Kirkstile Inn, tucked among the fells, next to an old church and a stream, a half mile from the lakes of Loweswater and Crummock. The whole place is authentic, traditional, well looked after: whitewashed walls, low beams, solid polished tables, cushioned settles, a well-stoked fire, plants, flowers and the odd horse harness to remind you of the past. Come for afternoon tea, or settle down with an unforgettable pint of Loweswater Gold or Melbreak Bitter or one of the Cumbrian Legendary Ales, brewed by Roger in Esthwaite Water near Hawkshead. Expect local produce and unfussy traditional dishes such as steak and ale pie, chicken breast stuffed with Cumberland sausage, sticky toffee pudding, a plate of local cheeses.

Meals	Lunch & dinner £8.95-£18.95. Bar meals from £4.50. Sunday lunch, 3 courses, £18.
Closed	Open all day.

Roger Humphreys
Kirkstile Inn,
Loweswater,
Cockermouth, CA13 0RU
Tel +44 (0)1900 85219
Web www.kirkstile.com

Entry 112 Map 11

Cumbria

The Beer Hall at Hawkshead Brewery

Staveley

Alex, an erstwhile BBC foreign correspondent, started his brewery in 2002 with little idea of the success he would find. But demand surged, and as Hawkshead Bitter established itself as one of the best pints in the Lakes, the need for greater space prompted a move across the lake to Mill Yard in Staveley (a micro-industrial park in the village). Then Alex developed The Beer Hall, adding food to the menu and now you can sup his ales and enjoy a hearty down-to-earth meal. You'll find the whole Hawkshead range at the bar and a menu that changes daily: stout and oxtail soup, wild local hare stew with dumplings, goat's cheese soufflé, omelette Arnold Bennett – and always, Brewers Lunch: a feast for carnivores. Tours of the brewery are available, and if you like what you drink, you can take some home.

Meals	Snacks from £2.50. Mains from £9.50.
Closed	Open from 12pm.

Chris Ramwell
The Beer Hall at Hawkshead Brewery,
Mill Yard, Staveley,
Kendal, LA8 9LR
Tel +44 (0)1539 825260
Web www.hawksheadbrewery.co.uk

Entry 113 Map 11

Tower Bank Arms

Near Sawrey

Just across from the ferry, next to Hilltop – Beatrix Potter's farm – is Jemima Puddleduck's inn. (She may not have caroused here, but she did waddle by.) Surrounded by glorious National Trust acres, whitewashed buildings make up the legendary village of Sawrey; a courteous staff handles the summer crowds. Enter a slate-flagged bar with a grand open range that throws out the heat on chilly days; further in it is carpeted and cosy. Flowers and shining bits and bobs make the place homely; the oak-floored dining room is set with white linen napkins and polished cutlery. Five local ales accompany dishes to please walkers: beef casseroled in ale, Woodall's Cumberland sausages and Cumbrian lamb. The puddings are scrumptious and the cheeses reflect Cumbria's producers. Special.

Meals: Lunch from £5.
Dinner from £11.50.
Sunday lunch, 3 courses, £18.95.

Closed: 3pm-5pm in winter.
Open all day Sat & Sun & in summer.

Anthony Hutton
Tower Bank Arms,
Near Sawrey,
Ambleside, LA22 0LF
Tel +44 (0)1539 436334
Web www.towerbankarms.co.uk

Entry 114 Map 11

Blacksmiths Arms

Broughton Mills

In the land of rugged hills and wooded valleys, you approach down a winding lane between high hedges; once round the final bend, the low-slung farmhouse-inn comes into view. Welcome to an utterly unspoilt little local. Inside: four small slate-floored rooms with beams and low ceilings, long settles and log fires, and a bar that is strictly for drinking – there's little room for anything else. Find three cask ales (two local, one guest) and traditional cider in summer. Across the passage: a room serving proper fresh food – snacks or full meals – and two dining rooms sparkling with glass and cutlery. The blackboard advertises dishes with a contemporary slant, and beef and Herdwick lamb reared in the valley. The food is so good it gets busy; in summer you can wander onto a flowery terrace.

Meals: Lunch & dinner £10.95-£14.95.
Lunch, 2 courses, £12.95.
Bar meals from £4.95.
No food on Mondays.

Closed: 2.30pm-5pm Tues-Fri
& Mon lunch (except bank hols).
Open all day Sat & Sun.

Michael & Sophie Lane
Blacksmiths Arms,
Broughton Mills,
Broughton-in-Furness, LA20 6AX
Tel +44 (0)1229 716824
Web www.theblacksmithsarms.com

Entry 115 Map 11

The Swan Hotel & Spa

Newby Bridge

This rather pretty hotel stands on the river Leven, a wide sweep of water that pours out of Windermere on its way south to Morecambe Bay. It's a fabulous spot and the Swan makes the most of it. The recent refurbishment breathed new life into the old bones of this 17th-century monastic farmhouse, with its stone terrace running along to an ancient packhorse bridge. Inside, airy interiors, sitting rooms, open fires, the daily papers, a lively bar and a good restaurant to keep you going. Dig into tasty food in the bar or brasserie, perhaps herb crusted salmon with spinach, roasted fennel and pink fir potatoes, or lamb hotpot with crinkled beetroot. Vegetarians are not forgotten: we enjoyed our chickpea and courgette fritters with chilli jam and grilled halloumi. You'll be spoilt for choice with delicious puddings too – or local cheeses.

Meals	Lunch from £5.95. Bar meals from £9.95. Dinner from £13.95. Sunday lunch £20-£27.
Closed	Open all day.

Lindsay Knaggs
The Swan Hotel & Spa,
Newby Bridge, LA12 8NB

Tel	+44 (0)1539 531681
Web	www.swanhotel.com

Entry 116 Map 11

White Hart Inn

Bouth

They stand four deep at the bar in summer, the promise of delicious food and local ales too good to miss. And it is too good to miss. The White Hart is a strand of English DNA, a traditional Lakeland pub in an untouched village. Outside, stone cottages abut fields that stretch across to the fells. Inside, traditional interiors have lots of charm with flagged floors, low ceilings, sofas in front of wood-burners, then an eccentric array of objects pinned to whitewashed walls: old hayforks, clay pipes, the odd stuffed fox. Beams drip with hops, brass shines brightly, hand pumps wait for pints of Hawkshead or Laughing Gravy. As for the food, it's delicious stuff, perhaps Morecambe Bay shrimps, haunch of venison, a plate of Cumberland cheeses. Fine walking starts from the front door. Peerless.

Meals	Lunch & dinner £10.75-£15.75.
Closed	Open all day.

Nigel & Kath Barton
White Hart Inn,
Bouth,
Ulverston, LA12 8JB

Tel	+44 (0)1229 861229
Web	www.whitehart-lakedistrict.co.uk

Entry 117 Map 11

The Derby Arms

Witherslack

Step into a stylish series of candlelit rooms, aglow with rug-strewn floors, cream and red walls, some rather grand paintings, polished period furniture, merry log fires, old stone fireplaces, dogs and booted walkers. The central bar heaves with hand pumps dispensing Cumbrian microbrewery ales (including Dent Aviator), hand-pressed juices from Witherslack, and heaps of wines by the glass. Bag a seat by the fire and settle in for supper; the changing menu announces a crowd-pleasing mix of traditional and modern pub dishes, much prepared from fresh local produce. Start with home cured dill salmon gravlax, follow with steak and ale pie or bubble and squeak cake, end with homemade apple custard. It's super civilised yet nicely laid-back, and you can take a spin to the splendid Sizergh Castle and Gardens.

Meals Lunch & dinner £8.95-£15.25.
Closed 3pm-5.30pm. Open all day Fri-Sun.

Nicola Harrison
The Derby Arms,
Witherslack,
Grange-over-Sands, LA11 6RN
Tel +44 (0)1539 552207
Web www.thederbyarms.co.uk

Entry 118 Map 11

Cumbria

The Plough

Lupton

This rambling 19th-century roadside inn goes from strength to strength with an enthusiastic team in charge. Outside is a pleasant paved patio with chunky furniture for lunch on a good day; inside is a vast open space full of comfortable corners, with open fires and stove. Expect nicely battered vintage furniture, polished oak floors and colourful rugs. For lunch, tuck into terrific sandwiches or grilled mackerel fillet with dill, caper and red onion salsa, washed down with a well-kept pint of local bitter. Or go for a Fisherman's or Ploughman's Board, both with generous portions and locally sourced. Main menu dishes are fantastic and puddings a treat; try vanilla panna cotta, Lyth Valley damson compote and "jammy dodger" shortbread. Wines from Kendal expert Frank Stainton, with plenty by the glass, boost a well-stocked bar.

Meals Lunch from £8.95.
Bar meals from £5.95.
Dinner from £10.50.
Closed Open all day.

Holly Duffy & Suzannah Harris
The Plough,
Cow Brow, Lupton,
Kirkby Lonsdale, LA6 1PJ
Tel +44 (0)1539 567700
Web www.theploughatlupton.co.uk

Entry 119 Map 12

The Old Hall Inn

Whitehough

Welcome to a glorious stone built 16th-century coaching inn and Elizabethan manor house, family run and country pub in character with reclaimed flagstones, chunky wooden furniture, padded pews, stools, real fires and local maps, blueprints and archive photos. Find a staggering ten cask ales on tap from local brewers Thornbridge, Bollington and Abbeydale amongst others, with their own to arrive as soon as Dan perfects the brew. Helpful staff will guide you through a multitude of bottled European and US craft beers, lagers and ciders, great wines, malts and cognacs. Food ranges from pub classics to more gourmet choices, provenance is impeccable; try locally shot game pie with braised red cabbage and handmade chips. The cheese board is special too. Eat in the main bar area or for a treat head next door to the old hall and dine beneath the beamed minstrels' gallery. You can stay here or at the charming sister pub, the Old Paper Mill, a stone's throw across the garden: all rooms have a modern country style with super patchwork quilts in some, oak furniture, wooden and brass beds and big colour photographs of gorgeous Derbyshire.

Rooms	8 doubles: £79-£115.
Meals	Lunch from £5.50. Bar meals & dinner from £8. Sunday lunch, 3 courses, £18.50.
Closed	Open all day.

Daniel Capper
The Old Hall Inn,
Whitehough,
Chinley, High Peak, SK23 6EJ
Tel +44 (0)1663 750529
Web www.old-hall-inn.co.uk

The Lamb Inn

Chinley

Just above Chinley, overlooking Cracken Edge, is the Lamb. The pub started life in 1769 as a row of quarrymen's cottages; later it became a coaching inn. Now it's cosy, characterful, much-loved, and owned by a husband and wife team. Low ceilings, leaded windows, log fires… they're all part of the charm, while staff are attentive and kind. Enjoy a bacon, brie and cranberry jelly baguette with a pint of Marston's Pedigree, or settle into a scrumptious cooked lunch: Whitby scampi with chips; steak and kidney pie; rabbit casserole; a vegetarian Moroccan tagine. Puds (sticky toffee pudding, Sicilian lemon pot) are to diet for. Sleep it off in one of three comfortable bedrooms: chunky wooden sleigh beds with cosy grey tartan blankets for snuggling; sturdy wardrobes and pretty flocked wallpaper in cool calm hues. Modern grey tiled shower rooms come with generous servings of lotions and potions and are worth lingering around for. For summer there's a long terrace out front, but parents please note, the road is just yards away.

Rooms	3 doubles: £95-£115.
Meals	Starters from £5.25. Mains from £10.50.
Closed	Mon-Fri 3pm-5.30pm. Open all day Sat & Sun.

David & Fiona Asquith
The Lamb Inn,
Hayfield Road,
Chinley, SK23 6AL
Tel +44 (0)1663 750519
Web www.goodfoodpeakdistrict.co.uk

The Samuel Fox Country Inn

Bradwell

Chef James Duckett has swapped a thriving Devon restaurant for a chance to reconnect with his north-country roots. His new project is a welcoming Hope Valley inn, its airy open-plan interior with splendid views and good art on the walls, warmed by wood-burners and – now that word has got around – filled with booted walkers, day-trippers and locals. The chalkboard menu suggests modern, imaginatively prepared pub dishes made with fresh local produce: there could be celeriac arancini with soused sardines, fennel and sumac; roast pheasant with parsnip bon bons and cavolo nero; Black Forest trifle for pudding. Extras like home-baked bread are beyond reproach. You'd be forgiven for thinking that this is more of a restaurant than a country pub, but drinkers are always welcome; there are two real ales from local microbreweries and 14 wines by the glass.

Meals	Lunch from £10. Mains from £13.50. Sunday lunch, 2-3 courses, £21-£26.
Closed	Mondays & Tuesdays.

James Duckett
The Samuel Fox Country Inn,
Stretfield Road, Bradwell,
Hope Valley, S33 9JT
Tel +44 (0)1433 621562
Web www.samuelfox.co.uk

Entry 122 Map 8

Derbyshire

The Plough

Hathersage

It's a great spot for walkers, this 16th-century former corn mill on the banks of the river, and the moment you enter you know you're in the right place. The sweeping tartan carpeting is cheering, the fires are crackling, the staff are chatty and engaging. Owner Bob, a lovely Dales man, continues to manage a brilliant team and that includes the chefs. Everything we tasted was well-presented and delicious, from the breast of duck with confit duck leg and celeriac wellington to the cheese platter and the apple crumble. The wine list is similarly good. A recent refurb sees warm red walls, scarlet-padded banquettes, and a baby grand at one end. You're on a main road but the large sloping gardens are safe for romping children, and are as gorgeous as the valley views.

Meals	Lunch & dinner £12.95-£19.95. Bar meals £9.95-£12.95.
Closed	Open all day.

Bob & Cynthia Emery
The Plough,
Leadmill, Hathersage,
Hope Valley, S32 1BA
Tel +44 (0)1433 650319
Web www.theploughinn-hathersage.co.uk

Entry 123 Map 8

The White Lion

Great Longstone

Greg and Libby Robinson have saved this handsome old village pub from a sorry end, lavishing love (and not a small amount of hard graft) into the very fabric of it. There are a handful of contemporary touches (splashy wallpaper, banquettes) but the beams, wood floors and open fire make it feel like a comfy nook to relax with a pint. The menu's pretty modern too; expect the likes of smoked chicken, chorizo and red pepper tian or gilt head bream with parsnip couscous alongside robust pub grub classics. Robinson's Dizzy Blonde is nicely kept; you can enjoy a pint in the cosy tap room with your canine chum, and a plate of bangers and mash. What's more, Sunday lunch is legendary! Just as well you're deep in the Derbyshire Dales, with super walks from the door.

Meals	Lunch & dinner from £11.95. Sunday lunch from £10.75
Closed	3pm-6pm Mon-Fri. Saturdays from 9pm. Sundays from 8pm.

Libby & Greg Robinson
The White Lion,
Main Street, Great Longstone,
Bakewell, DE45 1TA
Tel +44 (0)1629 640252
Web www.whiteliongreatlongstone.co.uk

Entry 124 Map 8

The Royal Oak

Hurdlow

This old boozer has been rescued and tenderly returned to award-winning life. In the old bar are beams, open fires, exposed stone walls and comfortable seating; there's an extra room, too, with scrubbed wooden tables and views over fields. Honest, straightforward pub grub flows from a spanking new kitchen, and everything's homemade and wholesome. Expect hand-raised pork and chicken pie; lamb chops with leek mash; goat's cheese and red onion tart. Local beers include Hartingtons, Wincles and the award-winning Thornbridge ales. There's a campsite and bunk barn on site and the stunning Tissington Trail is on the doorstep – just as well if you're going the whole hog and choose apple crumble and custard to finish.

Meals	Breakfast from £5.95. Lunch from £8.95. Dinner from £9.50. Sunday lunch, 2 courses, £15.25.
Closed	Open all day.

Paul White & Justin Heslop
The Royal Oak,
Hurdlow,
Buxton, SK17 9QJ
Tel +44 (0)1298 83288
Web www.peakpub.co.uk

Entry 125 Map 8

The Flying Childers Inn

Stanton-in-Peak

Standing proudly on a hill in pretty Stanton, in the Peak District National Park, this handsome, stone-built, 18th-century pub was once a row of farm labourers' cottages. Owned by the village aristocrats, it gets its name from a champion racehorse owned by the 4th Duke of Devonshire, reputedly unbeaten! Walk into the snug and a cosy fire greets you; slide into a corner and clock cricket team photos going back decades, slightly skew-whiff on wonky woodchip walls. Furniture is battered, nothing matches and pot tankards hang on blackened beams. The simple menu features homemade soup and game casseroles and ham-filled cobs with chunky chutney. Well-kept Wells Bombardier is permanently on tap, plus a couple of rotating guest ales.

Meals	Bar meals £2-£5.
Closed	2pm-7pm Wed-Fri. 3pm-7pm Sat-Sun. Mon-Tue lunch.

Stuart Redfern
The Flying Childers Inn,
Stanton-in-Peak,
Matlock, DE4 2LW

Tel +44 (0)1629 636333
Web www.flyingchilders.com

Entry 126 Map 8

Derbyshire

The Druid Inn

Birchover

A strangely enticing countryside of tors, crags, wooded knolls and stone circle-strewn moors erupts high above Matlock. In its midst stands the Druid, behind whose sober exterior lies a worn and well-loved bar, and a restaurant where the food does the talking. You're greeted by an array of ales in tip-top condition – then a small stone fireplace to the right, padded stools and eclectic art. The dining area with its lush purple wall is a light modern backdrop for innovative takes on traditional dishes; tuck into the likes of Druid smoky fish pie with cheddar mash and greens, or halibut rarebit. Rob and chef John are passionate about food and some items are named to keep guests guessing – what are Dixie's Three Little Piggies? Outside bench-tables deliver village views, ramblers rub shoulders with epicures, and there's a handsome beer garden.

Meals	Lunch & dinner £9-£21.
Closed	Open all day.

Rob Innes & Joyce Simpson
The Druid Inn,
Main Street,
Birchover, DE4 2BL

Tel +44 (0)1629 653836
Web www.druidinnbirchover.co.uk

Entry 127 Map 8

Ye Olde Gate Inn

Brassington

One of the most exquisite pubs in Derbyshire, built from timber salvaged from the Armada. Furnishings are plain: ancient settles, rush-seated chairs, gleaming copper, a clamorous clock, a collection of pewter. Mullioned windows look onto a sheltered back garden, perfect for warm summer evenings. In winter, a fire blazes in the blackened range that dominates the quarry-tiled bar; in the dim yet atmospheric snug are a glowing range and flickering candlelight. There's a daily specials board and traditional tucker: baguettes, steak and Guinness pie, liver and onions, beer-battered fish and chips, homemade bread and butter pudding. Come too for superbly kept Marston's Pedigree on hand pump and a number of malts.

Meals	Lunch from £7.95. Bar meals from £4.25. Dinner from £8.95. Sunday lunch, 2 courses, from £12.75. No food Sunday eve.
Closed	2.30pm-6pm (7pm Sun). Mon (except bank hols) & Tues lunch.

Peter Scragg
Ye Olde Gate Inn,
Well Street, Brassington,
Matlock, DE4 4HJ

Tel +44 (0)1629 540448
Web www.oldgateinnbrassington.co.uk

Entry 128 Map 8

Saracen's Head

Shirley

A pearl of a pub in unsung South Derbyshire. Renowned chef Robin Hunter and wife Terri have brought bags of gastropub style to the historic village, while cleverly holding on to an authentic pub feel. Slate floors give way to carpeting, light wood chairs are cushioned, an open roof space is stylishly decorated and fires crackle in cast-iron surrounds at either end. Greene King ales greet you at the bar and there's a good wine list. Linger over the menus as the smell of freshly baked breads wafts from the kitchen: modern English food and the best ingredients hold sway, and you can bring your own produce in to barter! There's rack of lamb with chorizo mash and olive and garlic jus, and lemon meringue roulade with vanilla bean ice cream – fit for Saladin himself.

Meals	Lunch & dinner from £9.25.
Closed	3pm-6pm (Mon-Sat). Open all day Sun.

Robin & Terri Hunter
Saracen's Head,
Church Lane, Shirley,
Ashbourne, DE6 3AS

Tel +44 (0)1335 360330
Web www.saracens-head-shirley.co.uk

Entry 129 Map 8

The Bulls Head

Repton

Once a derelict shell, the Bulls Head has been transformed by its owners, and the best of its old features brought to the fore. The downstairs is a jumble of connected rooms with wooden floors, stone flags, stripped timbers, chairs upholstered in cow hide, bulls heads made from bicycles, driftwood sculptures, steel pillars and, in the restaurant, 1930s gilt mirrors flanking a log-effect fire – amazing! Energetic staff flit hither and thither ferrying mouthwatering steaks and wood-fired pizzas and serious dinners: Indonesian fishcakes and seafood chowders; cannon of lamb with tomato and black olive salsa; apple, pear and blueberry crumble. There's a good kids' menu, too. It's hugely popular and the parking isn't easy, but it's one of the most exciting places in Derbyshire.

Meals	Lunch & dinner £8.95-£22.95. Sunday lunch £8.95.
Closed	Open all day.

Richard & Loren Pope
The Bulls Head,
84 High Street, Repton,
Derby, DE65 6GF

Tel +44 (0)1283 704422
Web www.thebullsheadrepton.co.uk

Entry 130 Map 8

Derbyshire

Three Horseshoes

Breedon on the Hill

Opposite the old 'village lock up', a listed village inn. Ian Davison and Jenny Ison have revitalised the old place and introduced a modern feel with a menu to match. Expect painted brickwork, seagrass matting, antique tables, Windsor chairs, eclectic pictures and masses of space. Smaller rooms include a simple quarry-tiled bar and an intimate red dining room with three tables; pride of place goes to a Victorian bar counter picked up years ago – now it displays chocolates and wine. Dishes are chalked up on boards in the bar and the award-winning formula includes such dishes as monkfish with capers and spinach, and pork and cider casserole. Marston's Pedigree on hand pump should satisfy those in for a swift half, while foodies can check out the farm shop – and the chocolate workshop across the yard.

Meals	Lunch & dinner £8.95-£26.50. Bar meals £4.95-£10.95.
Closed	Mon all day. Sun from 3pm.

Ian Davison & Jenny Ison
Three Horseshoes, 44-46 Main St,
Breedon on the Hill,
Derby, DE73 8AN

Tel +44 (0)1332 695129
Web www.thehorseshoes.com

Entry 131 Map 8

Masons Arms

Branscombe

Lose yourself in tiny lanes, follow them down towards the sea, pass the Norman church, roll up at the Masons Arms. It stands in a village half a mile back from the pebble beach surrounded by glorious country, with a stone terrace at the front from which to gaze upon lush hills. It dates back to 1350 – a cider house turned country pub – and the men who cut the stone for Exeter Cathedral drank here, hence the name. Inside, simple, authentic interiors are just the thing: timber frames, low beamed ceilings, pine cladding, whitewashed walls and a roaring fire over which the spit roast is cooked on Sundays. Some bedrooms are above the inn, others are behind on the hill. Those in the pub are small but cosy (warm yellows, check fabrics, leather bedheads, super bathrooms); those behind are bigger, quieter and more traditional; they overlook a garden and share a private terrace with valley views that tumble down to the sea. Footpaths lead out – over hills, along the coast – so follow your nose, then return for super food: seared scallops, lamb cutlets, saffron and honey crème brûlée. *Minimum stay: two nights at weekends in summer.*

Rooms	8 doubles, 6 twin/doubles, 6 four-posters: £80-£180. 1 family room for 4: £165-£195.
Meals	Lunch from £7.50. Bar meals from £9.95. Dinner, 3 courses, £20-£25. Sunday lunch from £9.95.
Closed	Open all day.

Alison Ede
Masons Arms,
Branscombe,
Seaton, EX12 3DJ
Tel +44 (0)1297 680300
Web www.masonsarms.co.uk

Nobody Inn

Doddiscombsleigh

Thankfully, little has changed since the current owners arrived in 2008; they run a happy ship. The wine and whisky lists remains over 200-strong, and the Devon cheese board continues to draw rural winers and diners from afar. Settles and tables are crammed into every corner, horse brasses brighten low beams, there's a cosy inglenook glowing with logs and part of the bar dates from Tudor times. Start with a bowl of Teign mussels, move on to rack of lamb with redcurrant and rosemary jus, finish with treacle tart: the food is beautiful, imaginative and locally sourced. Or try something traditional from the bar menu. To wash all this down: Nobody Bitter served in old pint glasses. A rare dram of Islay malt might be an excellent nightcap before retiring to one of five refurbished rooms upstairs, colour-themed according to name: Violet, Rose, Bluebell, Lily and Primrose. Quirky, fun, variously sized and extremely comfortable, they have soft carpets, super beds and decanters of sherry; bathrooms, smallish, are, bar one, en suite. The village is buried down a maze of lanes but is certainly worth the detour.

Rooms	3 doubles, 1 twin/double; 1 double with separate shower: £60-£95. Singles £45-£70.
Meals	Lunch & bar meals from £9.95. Dinner from £14.95. Sunday lunch from £9.95.
Closed	Open all day.

Sue Burdge
Nobody Inn,
Doddiscombsleigh,
Exeter, EX6 7PS
Tel +44 (0)1647 252394
Web www.nobodyinn.co.uk

Tradesmans Arms

Stokenham

A little cracker of a pub, 14th-century, part-thatched and two miles from the sea. Prop up the bar, bring the dogs, tuck into the fabulous food; head chef Kris Jury and his team are making a splash in remotest Devon, using fresh local produce, making seasonal changes to the menu. Formerly a brewhouse with three cottages, the pub stands in a sleepy village near Slapton Sands and takes its name from the tradesmen who trekked the coastal bridle path. Dark-beamed, slate-floored and charmingly rustic, the oldest part has a log-burner, antique tables and inviting bar stools, while the more hushed, more modern and slightly elevated dining room is red pattern-carpeted and dotted with gilt framed pictures. Outside: a beer garden with lush countryside views. Reasons to be here: superior malt whiskies, Otter and Tribute ales, top-notch breakfasts, an extensive wine list to suit all pockets, and a homemade pie with a beautiful glaze on its puff pastry lid. They also have a children's menu, and do a great vegetarian option. Cathy and her husband have now introduced four bedrooms with super bathrooms upstairs, the two at the front the biggest and the best.

Rooms	4 doubles: £100-£110.
Meals	Starters from £5.45. Mains from £10.50.
Closed	3pm-6pm.

Catherine Sanders
Tradesmans Arms,
Stokenham,
Kingsbridge, TQ7 2SZ
Tel +44 (0)1548 580996
Web www.thetradesmansarms.com

The Millbrook Inn

South Pool

Arrive before the boats do – they drop anchor a step away and the Millbrook is their first port of call. The atmosphere and food are quite something, and perfect ingredients are worshipped in best seasonal style. Tuck into pot-au-feu, a Devon take on traditional French stew with seasonal vegetables topped with pan-fried guinea fowl supreme and Montbéliard smoked sausage. Leave room for iced white chocolate meringue cake. In winter, a log fire warms the immediate bar area while padded settles and wheelback chairs cluster comfortably around tables in snugs. The stream-side terrace is tiny but assures entertainment in summer once the ducks are at play, so sit back and watch with a bowl of mussels and a pint of Tarka. At bedtime, as you wind your way up past beer barrels, you'll be delighted by your hideaway suite with its soaring ceilings, kingsize bed and deeply comfy sofas. Décor by local artisans, a modern kitchen, driftwood touches, beautiful throws and double doors that open onto your own terrace overlooking the brook. Order up a cheese platter, perhaps some champagne, and settle to soak up the view. Heaven.

Rooms	1 suite for 2: £150.
Meals	Starters from £7.50. Lunch from £7. Dinner from £14. Sunday lunch from £15.
Closed	Open all day.

Pub with rooms

Charlie Baker
The Millbrook Inn,
South Pool,
Kingsbridge, TQ7 2RW

Tel	+44 (0)1548 531581
Web	www.millbrookinnsouthpool.co.uk

The Elephant's Nest Inn

Mary Tavy

Travellers look happy as they enter the main bar, all dark beams, flagstone floors and crackling fires... you almost imagine a distant Baskerville hound baying. This is an atmospheric inn that serves delicious home-cooked food – local, seasonal and British with a twist. Tuck into antipasto of pastrami, rosette saucisson and Black Forest ham; South Devon sirloin with mushrooms, vine tomatoes and French fries; and Mrs Cook's fabulous lemon posset with blueberry compote. When suitably sated, slip off to the annexe and a nest of your own in one of three peaceful, very comfortable rooms, with gleaming oak floors heated underfoot; one room has its own private patio. Wake to a pretty garden with views to Brentor church and the moor, an exceptional breakfast and perhaps a cricket match to watch: the pub has its own ground and club. Settle back to the thwack of willow on leather with a pint of Palmer's IPA. There's Doom Bar too, Jail Ale from Princetown, and guest ales from Otter, Cotleigh, Teignworthy, Butcombe. What's more, the pub is a dog-friendly zone – check out their website for photos of the residents.

Rooms	3 twin/doubles: £88.
Meals	Lunch & dinner £8.95-£19.95.
Closed	3pm-6.30pm.

Hugh & Denise Cook
The Elephant's Nest Inn,
Horndon, Mary Tavy,
Tavistock, PL19 9NQ

Tel +44 (0)1822 810273
Web www.elephantsnest.co.uk

The Dartmoor Inn

Lydford

There aren't many inns where you can sink into Zoffany-clad winged armchairs in the dining room as you wait for the wild sea bass to crisp in the pan. Here you can: this Dartmoor inn is the template of deep-country chic, with a Cornish slate floor and a roaring log fire. Walkers and dogs stride in from the moors for Otter, Tribute and Devon Red cider on tap, real homemade crisps and hearty steak sandwiches. And fish and chips; fillet of hake with pork belly, black pudding and charcoal broccoli; vanilla panna cotta with passion fruit jelly and honeycomb. Real work has gone into forging links with local farmers and food artisans, and it pays off in fine dining style. The settles are smartly sandblasted, the gilded mirrors hang above fireplaces and the moors are on your doorstep (nearby is the thrilling Lydford Gorge). Upstairs, find three light, pretty bedrooms filled with candy-coloured brocade, toile de jouy cushions, French and British antique furniture. There's modern touches too, with Roberts radios and REN smellies in the bathrooms. Book a hearty breakfast before a walk in the wind, then eat, drink and unwind.

Rooms	3 doubles: £110-£120.
Meals	Lunch & dinner £10-£19.50. Sunday lunch £26.
Closed	2.30pm-6.30pm. Sun eves & Mon lunch.

Philip Burgess & Andrew Honey
The Dartmoor Inn,
Lydford,
Okehampton, EX20 4AY
Tel +44 (0)1822 820221
Web www.dartmoorinn.com

The Rams Head Inn Country Hotel

Dolton

A coaching inn in the 1600s – now a smart gastro inn and a hub for the village too. Simon and Darren have renovated throughout and have a real passion for the place. Simon is a bit of a magpie; he's been collecting market finds, prints, paintings, maps... for years, remembers the provenance of every piece and likes to shuffle things around. The bar and dining area has cushioned chairs, polished wood floors, pale sofas, wood-burners and tables laid with shiny glasses. You'll find rotating local brewery ales and Red Rock beers, a good range of gins and wine choice suggestions with the menu. Food is seasonal and mostly local: pigeon with lentils, Exmoor beef, lobster ravioli, followed by lemon tart or cinnamon apple crumble perhaps. Bedrooms are trad with a twist: floral and patterned wallpapers, dark furniture, and pristine white tubs and basins; one of the three ground floor ones has a big wood stove. The cheerful paved garden has red walls, pots of flowers and bunting. Dartmoor and Exmoor National Parks on the doorstep, sandy beaches 20 minutes; join the Tarka trail – dogs are welcome in all the rooms.

Rooms	4 doubles, 5 twin/doubles: £75-£155. 2 family rooms for 3: £95-£155. 1 single with separate bathroom: £59-£70.
Meals	Starters from £5.50. Lunch, 2-3 courses, £25-£28.50. Dinner from £12.50.
Closed	Monday lunchtime.

Simon Hunt
The Rams Head Inn Country Hotel,
South Street, Dolton,
Winkleigh, EX19 8QS

Tel +44 (0)1805 804255
Web www.theramsheadinn.co.uk

Three Crowns

Chagford

St Austell Brewery spent 19 months and oodles of cash restoring this eye-catching, 13th-century stone and thatch village beauty. Dominating Chagford, it now matches its more illustrious hotel neighbours for comfort, but realistic pricing and a relaxing informality make this swish flagship inn a choice Dartmoor bolthole. Mullioned windows, massive beams and a vast inglenook in the original bar blend with a spanking new atrium-conservatory dining room that opens to a sheltered courtyard. Wonky walls and floors upstairs lead to bedrooms in sympathy with the age and the charm. Find rich fabrics, contemporary wallpaper, cosy bathrooms in cleverly designed spaces and every modern comfort: iPod docks, flat-screens, fresh coffee, leaf tea. Book the suite for churchyard views – and a cute little sitting room perched above the old front porch. New rooms in smart new-build wings are equally good. Pop downstairs for pub classics, potted Brixham crab, Devon beef, plaice with parsley butter, and dark chocolate and orange tart. Moorland walks wait outside the door.

Rooms	20 twin/doubles: £95-£145. 1 suite for 2: £150-£190.
Meals	Lunch & dinner £8.95-£19.50.
Closed	Open all day.

John Milan & Steve Bellman
Three Crowns,
High Street,
Chagford, TQ13 8AJ

Tel +44 (0)1647 433444
Web www.threecrowns-chagford.co.uk

Chagford Inn

Chagford

In the pretty town of Chagford, enfolded by the lush hills of the National Park, is a small simple inn painted soft blue, with a black door and sparkling windows. Inside is warm and homely, friendly and quirky, and after a long walk up the Teign Valley the menu is a welcome sight. Art on the walls, logs in the burner… settle in and make yourself cosy. They bake their own bread, cure their own bresaola, buy local whenever it is possible, and bring fish in daily from the coast. The food is exciting and modern. Chef Russ, classically trained, is making big waves in Devon and his ethos is nose-to-tail, so there are pork croquettes with tarragon aïoli, roast ballotine of rabbit with a shallot ragù, and perfect rare roast beef ciabatta. The beers are local, the wine list is balanced, and everyone feels at home.

Meals	Starters from £5.50. Mains from £10.50.
Closed	Open all day.

John Freeman
Chagford Inn,
7 Mill Street,
Chagford, TQ13 8AW

Tel +44 (0)1647 433109
Web www.thechagfordinn.com

Entry 140 Map 2

Devon

The Horse

Moretonhampstead

The back room doubles as an art gallery, folk bands play once a month, a fabulous courtyard catches the sun. The Horse is all things to all men: friendly community centre, great little restaurant, the sort of local you'd move to the village for. And the menu offers home-smoked delights, from the Reuben sandwich with pastrami or the homecured salt beef bagel, and the freshest handmade breads. The front bar has charm – stripped boards, painted panelling, old settles, a wood-burner; follow the flagstones south past the open kitchen to the lofty dining room. You can spoil yourself variously with strong coffee, sparkling wine, local ale and a crispy pizza. Nigel and Malene escaped London for the country and have transformed the old biker's boozer into a foodie's joy. The welcome is second to none.

Meals	Lunch from £5.50. Dinner from £11.95.
Closed	Mondays & Sundays 12pm-5pm.

Nigel Hoyle & Malene Graulund
The Horse,
George Street, Moretonhampstead,
Newton Abbot, TQ13 8PG

Tel +44 (0)1647 440242
Web www.thehorsedartmoor.co.uk

Entry 141 Map 2

The Cleave Public House

Lustleigh

It's too pretty for words, this 15th-century longhouse on the edge of Dartmoor National Park. The main bar is classic to the core, with a granite fireplace, leather armchairs and Windsor chairs forming cosy huddles on red and gold carpeting, and a no-nonsense planked bar dispensing Otter Ales and local guests such as Yellowhammer. The head chef brings passion to the kitchen so menus are blessed with regional, seasonal produce. Bar meals don't get much better than the Dartmouth crab turnovers, or the double baked ham & gruyere soufflé, River Teign mussels and croque monsieur. There are homebaked baguettes for walkers, and good wines poured by cheerful staff. Plenty of dining tables at the back, but arrive early in summer: seats are like gold dust outside at the front.

Meals	Lunch & dinner £7.50-£15. Sunday lunch £9.95-£15.95.
Closed	Open all day.

Ben Whitton
The Cleave Public House,
Lustleigh, Newton Abbot,
Exeter, TQ13 9TJ

Tel	+44 (0)1647 277223
Web	www.thecleavelustleigh.uk.com

Devon

The Rock Inn

Haytor Vale

Originally an ale house for quarrymen and miners, the 300-year-old Rock Inn stands in a tiny village in a sheltered vale on Dartmoor's slopes. Run by the same family for 30 years, this civilised haven oozes Dickensian character; dark polished antique tables and settles on several levels, a grandfather clock and fresh flowers, cosy corners and at least two fires. Charming staff ensure it all ticks along very smoothly. Settle down in the compact carpeted bar and study a supper menu that highlights local, often organic, produce. All that fresh Dartmoor air will make you hungry, so tuck into Devon rump steak with garlic butter and chunky chips, and caramelised lemon tart with ginger ice cream. Lunchtime meals range from soup and sandwiches to local sausages in onion gravy. There's a pretty beer garden, too.

Meals	Lunch & dinner £7.50-£18.
Closed	Open all day.

Christopher & Susan Graves
The Rock Inn,
Haytor Vale,
Newton Abbot, TQ13 9XP

Tel	+44 (0)1364 661305
Web	www.rock-inn.co.uk

Rugglestone Inn

Widecombe in the Moor

Beside open moorland, within walking distance of the village, is a 200-year-old stone pub whose two tiny rooms lead off a stone-floored passageway; few of the daytrippers who descend on this idyllic village make it to the Rugglestone Inn. Low beams fill an old-fashioned parlour with simple furnishings and a deep-country feel. Both rooms are free of modern intrusions, the locals preferring cribbage, euchre and dominoes. The tiny bar serves local farm cider, while Teignworthy Moor Beer and Dartmoor Brewery Legend are tapped from the cask. From the kitchen comes proper home cooking – ploughman's lunches and soups, lamb shanks, fresh fish; across the babbling brook is a lawn with benches and peaceful moorland views. A modest slice of heaven.

Meals Bar snacks & starters from £4.95. Mains from £10.50.

Closed 3pm-6pm Mon-Thurs (3pm-5pm Fri). Open all day Sat & Sun

Richard & Vicki Palmer
Rugglestone Inn,
Widecombe in the Moor,
Newton Abbot, TQ13 7TF

Tel +44 (0)1364 621327

Web www.rugglestoneinn.co.uk

Entry 144 Map 2

The Peter Tavy Inn

Peter Tavy

Tough and sturdy, it's survived many a Dartmoor winter, this 15th-century inn at the end of a lane in little Peter Tavy. Inside is a pub of three rooms, with slate floors and log burners in wide granite fireplaces, and a hotch-potch of wooden chairs and tables. Find a cosy corner and contemplate your next hike over a pint – all is pleasingly rustic. They always have local ales alongside beer from Dartmoor Brewery; our halves of Jail Ale slipped down nicely. This is no gastropub but the food is homemade and hearty and comes in generous portions, from lamb cobbler to fishcakes to sizzling fajitas. There are lots of locals and everyone's friendly, families are welcome and so is your dog. For summer there's a charming beer garden out the back, with weathered picnic tables and white parasols.

Meals Lunch from £5.75. Dinner from £8.95.

Closed 2.30pm-6pm (3pm Sat & Sun).

Chris & Jo Wordingham
The Peter Tavy Inn,
Peter Tavy,
Tavistock, PL19 9NN

Tel +44 (0)1822 810348

Web www.petertavyinn.com

Entry 145 Map 2

The Treby Arms

Sparkwell

Behind the unremarkable exterior is a gastropub of surprises, a place of celebrity status. Anton Piotrowski, a joint MasterChef winner, heads a happy team. The cooking is tip top, of the moment and stunning to look at. There's pigeon en croûte with bubble and squeak; 'What Dad Got From the Garden' soup; gorgonzola with confit pear sorbet... these are just the starters. Step into a small dog-friendly bar for a pint of Tribute or one of many wines, then into the dining area where a young, happy and helpful staff ferry elegant plates to wooden tables. Or upstairs to the 45-cover restaurant; they're packed out every week. Pheasant, oxtail and black pudding terrine, roast sea trout with a crab bisque, Anton's famous carrot cake – our set lunch didn't miss a beat.

Meals	Midweek set lunch £20. Sunday set lunch £16.95. Taster menu, 6 courses, £55.
Closed	Mon all day.

Anton & Clare Piotrowski
The Treby Arms,
Sparkwell,
Plymouth, PL7 5DD

Tel +44 (0)1752 837363
Web www.thetrebyarms.co.uk

Entry 146 Map 2

Devon

Turtley Corn Mill

Avonwick

The mill has six acres sloping down to the lake and space for a multitude of picnic tables: order your hampers in advance. There are ducks too, and boules, croquet, Jenga and a ginormous chess set. Inside has been transformed to create a series of spacious interconnected areas: a bar with dark slate floors and doors to the garden; a wooden-floored 'library' lined with books; a mill room (turning wheel right outside) with a wood-burner, prints on white walls, oriental rugs and papers to read. The food is traditional and homemade, be it local game terrine, braised beef in red wine or sea bass with minted pea sauce. There's Princetown Jail Ale on tap and a raft of wines by the glass. The South Hams are close, as are the Dartmoor tors – and it's the perfect A38 stopover!

Meals	Breakfast from £4. Lunch & dinner £7.50-£17.95.
Closed	Open all day.

Samantha & Scott Colton
Turtley Corn Mill,
Avonwick,
South Brent, TQ10 9ES

Tel +44 (0)1364 646100
Web www.turtleycornmill.com

Entry 147 Map 2

The Church House Inn

South Bren

Once an ale house for 12th-century masons building the village church, the old place was 'modernised' in the 1600s; its big beams and fireplaces remain. Now it's one of the nicest pubs around, snapped up in 2015 by landlords John Edwards and son Will (a lovely pair). Horse-brasses line the bar, fires roar in winter, the produce comes from South Devon, the ales are Otter, Dartmoor and Shingle Bay, the cider's from Ashburton and the ginger beer is Luscombe. We loved the look of the monthly changing menu – short, fresh and seasonal – and all is imaginatively presented (our 'hog roast' sandwich, with apple sauce and crackling, was delicious). Bring the dog – it's a walkers' paradise, and the beer garden's tables overlook the South Hams hills.

Meals Lunch from £6.50.
Dinner from £11.50.
Closed Mondays.

William Edwards
The Church House Inn,
The Rattery,
South Bren, TQ10 9LD
Tel +44 (0)1364 642220
Web www.thechurchhouseinn.co.uk

Entry 148 Map 2

Devon

The Church House Inn

Marldon

The old village pub is a civilised place, popular with retired locals and ladies that lunch. Others come for a pint of well-kept Dartmoor Best and a chat by the fire – it's a proper all-rounder. The feel is one of a well-crafted, rustic elegance – stonework and beams, original strawberry gothic windows, crisp table settings and smiling service. The central bar has been partitioned into three areas, plus one four-tabled candlelit snug, perfect for a party, and there's a lovely sloping garden for summer. Food is modern British and locally sourced: baked hake with butterbean and chorizo ragoût, Dartmouth smoked fish platter, bramble Bakewell tart with blackberry compote. The pub originally housed the artisans who worked on Marldon Church; its ancient tower overlooks the hedged garden.

Meals Lunch & dinner £9-£19.95.
Sunday lunch £11.95.
Closed 2.30pm-5pm (3pm-5.30pm Sun).

Julian Cook
The Church House Inn,
Marldon,
Paignton, TQ3 1SL
Tel +44 (0)1803 558279
Web www.churchhousemarldon.com

Entry 149 Map 2

The Tower Inn

Slapton

Standing beside the ivy-clad ruins of a chantry tower, a flower-bedecked classic, a southern belle, loved by all who visit. Despite the hidden access and tricky parking, this 14th-century inn attracts not just locals but families from Slapton Sands. As for the low-beamed and stone-walled interior – all rustic dark-wood tables, old pews and fine stone fireplaces – it is hugely atmospheric by night, thanks to flickering candles and fires. Accompany golden, bitter-sweet Proper Job from the handpump with a plateful of Devon crab gnocchi, mussels in Addlestones cider cream broth, Start Bay scallops and locally-caught fish of the day. And for dessert, Salcombe Dairy ice cream from down the road; do book at weekends. A lovely, sleepy-village pub with a super landscaped garden at the back.

Meals	Lunch from £5. Dinner from £10. Sunday lunch, 3 courses, £22.
Closed	3pm-6pm. Sun eves in winter.

Thea Butler, Dan Cheshire & Kevin Tweddell
The Tower Inn,
Slapton, Kingsbridge, TQ7 2PN

Tel	+44 (0)1548 580216
Web	www.thetowerinn.com

Entry 150 Map 2

Pig's Nose Inn

East Prawle

Winding lanes with skyscraper hedges weave from the main road to the edge of the world. There are an awful lot of porcine references round these parts (South Hams, Gammon Head, Piglet Stores) and the Pig's Nose is Devon's most southerly pub. Filled with character, a wood-burner and quirky ephemera, it has an atmosphere all of its own. A pie, pint and a paper at lunchtime can give way at night to the entire pub joining in a singalong; Peter's connections entice legendary acts to play in the adjacent hall. Innovations include a flurry of fur 'smoking jackets' hanging in the porch and random pots of knitting inviting punters to 'do a line'. A one-off in a sea-view village that has barely changed since the thirties.

Meals	Lunch & dinner £6.50-£12.50.
Closed	2.30pm-6pm (7pm in winter). Sun eves & Mon all day in winter.

Peter & Lesley Webber
Pig's Nose Inn,
East Prawle,
Kingsbridge, TQ7 2BY

Tel	+44 (0)1548 511209
Web	www.pigsnoseinn.co.uk

Entry 151 Map 2

The Journey's End Inn

Ringmore

Down innumerable lanes where you can sniff the sea air is this: a 13th-century pub in a pretty thatched village. Four fires keep the original monks' mews snug and cosy, and each of the main areas has a different feel: a dark, rustic and flagged drinkers' bar – with a leather sofa-filled snug off it; a panelled room with a hatch bar; and a conservatory. Take your pick from many Devon ales, straight from the barrel, or Devonian cider; or choose from a great selection of whiskies and wines. Chef Conor has cooked in Thailand and at the Burgh Island Hotel, favours a refined simplicity, and menus change daily. When we were there on a cold February's day we were tempted by the slow-roast pork cheek with Bramley apple mash and buttered Savoy cabbage; and the charred beef rib-eye with a merlot reduction and a green peppercorn aïoli.

Meals: Lunch from £6.
Dinner £11.50-£19.95.
Sunday lunch £11.50-£13.75.
Bar meals £2-£6.50.

Closed: Mon all day.

Conor Heneghan & Tracy Brand
The Journey's End Inn,
Ringmore,
Kingsbridge, TQ7 4HL
Tel +44 (0)1548 810205
Web www.thejourneysendinn.co.uk

The Ship Inn

Noss Mayo

The Ship is gorgeous, so lovely it's almost unfair. It stands at the head of a tidal inlet, a 16th-century pub with majestic views over the water. Outside, a terrace flanked by olive trees and lavender draws a crowd in summer, but country-house interiors are just as good. You'll find wooden floors, country rugs, roaring fires and lovely art, with nautical curios scattered attractively throughout. Upstairs, the Library doubles as a private dining room, while the Bridge has weather-proofed views... not a bad spot for a good lunch, perhaps king prawns with sweet chilli sauce, seared scallops on saffron risotto, chocolate torte with vanilla ice cream. Local ales are downstairs, Jail Ale, Weather Station, or a pint of Tribute. The coast is on your doorstep, so bring your walking boots. One of the best.

Meals: Lunch & dinner £10.50-£18.95.
Bar meals £4.75-£11.95.
Sunday lunch, 3 courses, £20.

Closed: Open all day.

Charles & Lisa Bullock
The Ship Inn,
Noss Mayo,
Plymouth, PL8 1EW
Tel +44 (0)1752 872387
Web www.nossmayo.com

The King's Arms

Georgeham

A cracking little pub perched on a winding lane and perfect for everyone, from exhausted walkers and surfers to its very loyal locals (and their dogs). Passionate owner Steve Cave has worked really hard to make sure your welcome is hearty, your food is as local as possible (some homegrown), wines are interesting and reasonably priced (even if it's only the one glass) and you are entertained (plenty of board games for rainy afternoons and evenings, live music from a talented local pool, open mic nights and DJ evenings). The bar has sofas for flopping on, you can tuck in to burgers, bangers and mash, thickly sliced ham, eggs and chips, or go posh and try sticky lemongrass slow-cooked pork belly followed by passion fruit and coconut panna cotta. There's an outside seating area (rugs provided), extremely cheery staff and a smart dining room upstairs. Lovely.

Meals Starters £4.85-£7.
Mains £9.75.75-£22.

Closed Open all day.

Steve Cave
The King's Arms,
Chapel Street,
Georgeham, EX33 1JJ

Tel +44 (0)1271 890240
Web www.kingsarmsgeorgeham.co.uk

Entry 154 Map 2

Poltimore Arms

South Molton

Go off-grid and step back in time in gorgeous Exmoor countryside. This 13th-century pub has stood the test of time with more than a few stories to tell; just ask Steve, the knowledgeable landlord. Ivy-clad walls welcome you, and inside all is rustic and authentic: ancient wooden tables, a roaring fire, stacks of books, whitewashed walls, and a piano in the corner. There's jugs above the small bar and Steve might even let you pour your own pint! There's no mains electric, so evenings are cosy and candle-lit, and food is fresh and local, but you can bring your own if you want (Yarde Downe general store is next door). Try steak and mushroom pie or a ploughmans washed down with a pint of Otter or Butcombe. Outside, catch some rays in the beer garden where Steve hosts an annual music festival. Pitch a tent and join in! You can't get more authentic than this.

Meals Starters from £5.50.
Mains from £5.95.

Closed Open all day.

Steve Cotten
Poltimore Arms,
South Molton EX36 3HA

Tel +44 (0)1598 710381
Web www.poltimorearms.co.uk

Entry 155 Map 2

The Masons Arms

Knowstone

Thatched on the outside, with a beamed, flagged and inglenooked bar inside, is a classic Devon pub, the sort of place where farmers set the world to rights over pints of Cotleigh's Tawny Owl. Who would imagine, down a few worn steps, a smart light-filled extension and food from the former chef of the Waterside Inn? Mark Dodson's inspired cooking has made the Masons Arms a foodie haven. Michelin-starred menus revel in the region's fishermen, farmers and producers, so you could find roulade of pork belly with apple compote; fillet of brill with potato crust and salmon mousse; puff pastry of wild mushrooms with poached egg and pimento cream (rich, earthy and delicate all at the same time). Staff go to great lengths to make you feel at home, and if you are just here to drink, the garden is gorgeous.

Meals	Lunch, 2-3 courses, £21-£25. Dinner from £18.50; à la carte, 2 courses, from £45. Sunday lunch, 3 courses, £36.
Closed	3pm-6pm. Sun eves & Mon all day. Jan (2 weeks). Aug bank hol & following 10 days.

Mark & Sarah Dodson
The Masons Arms,
Knowstone,
South Molton, EX36 4RY

Tel +44 (0)1398 341231
Web www.masonsarmsdevon.co.uk

Entry 156 Map 2

Devon

The Grove Inn

Kings Nympton

The pub is in the heart of old Kings Nympton, a 'natural sacred grove' – raise a glass to your good fortune in being here. There are paintings of Devon countryside, a picture gallery of faces past and present, beams hung with bookmarks, stone walls, a slate floor, a wood-burner. Old and new combine with understated ease. Robert is the perfect host, Deborah uses the freshest produce to create her menus. Try roast May's Farm beef or Brewers Farm lamb for Sunday lunch, smoked trout with horseradish sauce, wild rabbit stew with mash, fish pie, and white chocolate cheesecake with Patrick's blackcurrants. Ales are from local breweries, ciders are Sam's Dry and Poundhouse, wine and champagnes come by the glass, and there are over 65 single malts.

Meals	Lunch & dinner £7-£17. Sunday lunch, 3 courses, £16.40.
Closed	3pm-6pm. Mon lunch (except bank hols). Sun eves.

Deborah & Robert Smallbone
The Grove Inn,
Kings Nympton, EX37 9ST

Tel +44 (0)1769 580406
Web www.thegroveinn.co.uk

Entry 157 Map 2

The Cadeleigh Arms

Cadeleigh

The villagers of Cadeleigh did not want to lose their local, so they stumped up the money and bought it! It's worth the drive down any number of lanes to get here. In the bar: ancient flagstones, high-backed benches, assorted scrubbed tables and a burner stocked with logs. In the dining room: orange carpeting, pale walls, rolling green views. There's a hillside beer garden, a skittle alley loved by kids, a room with a pool table, and ideal new landlords. They run a deli in Tiverton and keep a good house: find 16 good wines by the glass; Sam's Medium Devon Cider; and Tribute, Dartmoor Best and Legend on tap. There are juicy steaks too, and crab cakes (crispy outside, succulent within), and fabulous nut burgers for vegans. Our lamb koftas were a triumph... and the sticky toffee pudding comes with clotted cream.

Meals	Lunch & dinner from £8.95. No food Monday
Closed	Mon lunch. 2:30pm-6pm Tues-Sat. 3pm-7pm Sun.

Nick & Tina Hack
The Cadeleigh Arms,
Cadeleigh,
Tiverton, EX16 8HP

Tel +44 (0)1884 855238
Web www.thecadeleigharms.com

Entry 158 Map 2

Devon

The Lamb Inn

Sandford

This 16th-century inn is adored by locals and visitors alike. It's a proper inn in the old tradition with the odd touch of scruffiness to add authenticity to its earthy bones. It stands on a cobbled walkway in a village lost down tiny lanes, and those lucky enough to chance upon it leave reluctantly. Inside there are beams, but they are not sandblasted, red carpets with a little swirl, sofas in front of an open fire. Boarded menus trumpet irresistible food – carrot and orange soup, haunch of venison with a port jus, an excellent rhubarb crumble. You can eat wherever you want: in the bar, in the fancy restaurant, or out in the walled garden in good weather. There's a cobbled terrace, a skittle alley, maps for walkers and well-kept ales. Dartmoor waits, but you may well linger. Brilliant.

Meals	Lunch from £9. Dinner, 3 courses, £20-£30. Sunday lunch from £8.90.
Closed	Open all day.

Mark Hildyard & Katharine Lightfoot
The Lamb Inn,
Sandford, Crediton, EX17 4LW

Tel +44 (0)1363 773676
Web www.lambinnsandford.co.uk

Entry 159 Map 2

The Ring of Bells

Cheriton Fitzpaine

From its fetching thatch to its inventive menus, the Ring of Bells hits the right note every time. Binka and David made it their mission to restore the pub as the heart of the village, where it sits prettily as part of a long row of cottages, the church spire peeking over the top. A wood burner chases away chills in winter, and Binka will work her magic on the little garden come summer. You can tuck yourself into a corner with a pint of local cider and a ploughman's, or take a seat at one of the glowing tables where settings sparkle and menus tempt. Our pheasant skewers with miso marinade and baby gem were wonderfully light, followed by wild mallard with wild rice and kale, and the most delicious duck scotch eggs. Dog walkers and ramblers love it here, and so will you.

Meals	Starters from £4.95. Lunch from £10.50. Dinner from £16.
Closed	Sunday after 3pm. Monday all day.

Authentic pub

Dave Allen & Binka Caven
The Ring of Bells,
The Hayes, Cheriton Fitzpaine,
Crediton, EX17 4JG

Tel +44 (0)1363 860111
Web www.theringofbells.com

Entry 160 Map 2

Devon

Tom Cobley Tavern

Spreyton

They come by the hundreds to drink the ales at this shrine to the hop, and the front room – 1930s trapped in aspic – must qualify as one of the finest spots in the land to sample intoxicating potions. Roger treats his ales the way most of us treat our children, nurturing them with love before sending them out into the world. You'll find 14 waiting, most from the south west, with Tamar Black from Holsworthy, Legend, Jail Ale and Dragon's Breath from Dartmoor Brewery and Gun Dog from Teignworthy Brewery. Fishermen, hash runners and shooting parties drop by for a meal and dig into excellent, warming homemade pies and stews – the no-nonsense cooking goes down a treat. There's a big garden, and a thatched porch. As for Tom Cobley, he set off for Widecombe Fair from this very building.

Meals	Lunch & dinner £7.95-£15.95.
Closed	Mon all day. 12pm-3pm Tues-Sun

Roger & Carol Cudlip
Tom Cobley Tavern,
Spreyton,
Crediton, EX17 5AL

Tel +44 (0)1647 231314
Web www.tomcobleytavern.co.uk

Entry 161 Map 2

The Lazy Toad Inn

Brampford Speke

Stroll the banks of the river Exe and wind up at this listed inn. Slate tiles polished to a pewter hue gleam on floors around the bar where ales from Hanlon, Exeter Brewery and St Austell vie for attention, farming implements dot one wall, eclectic art another, and a mix of tables and chairs add pizzazz. Settle down by the fire and study head chef Steve Mabbutt's menus; featuring locally sourced and home produced food they change every day. How about pan fried hake, buttered spinach and mussel chowder, or loin of pork with a Jerusalem artichoke purée and salt baked celeriac? There's a great little menu for kids, too, a lovely walled cobbled courtyard outside, and more garden at the back.

Meals	Lunch from £5.35. Bar meals from £11.50. Dinner from £14. Sunday lunch, 3 courses, £25. No food Sunday eves.
Closed	Mondays all day.

Harriet & Mike Daly
The Lazy Toad Inn,
Brampford Speke,
Exeter, EX5 5DP
Tel +44 (0)1392 841591
Web www.thelazytoadinn.co.uk

Devon

The Jack in the Green

Rockbeare

Bustle and buzz in the light oak bar, with its flagstone floor, upholstered leather chairs and local brews on tap – Otter Ale, Butcombe Bitter. But this is more restaurant than pub: 'For those who live to eat' reads the sign. In a series of sumptuous plum-carpeted rooms, Matthew Mason's menu goes in for modern and mouthwatering variations of tried and trusted favourites: Scotch egg with mustard, fish and chips in real ale batter, homemade chicken liver parfait. More ambition is on display in the bright airy restaurant, where boned and rolled pork belly with black pudding and apple sauce or fillet of Cornish cod with saffron and River Exe mussels would make succulent choices. Note too the superb-value Totally Devon menu. Paul Parnell has been at the helm for nearly 25 years and this is one happy ship.

Meals	Lunch & dinner £11.50-£19.50. Bar meals from £4.95.
Closed	3pm-5.30pm (6pm Sat). Open all day Sun.

Paul Parnell
The Jack in the Green,
Rockbeare,
Exeter, EX5 2EE
Tel +44 (0)1404 822240
Web www.jackinthegreen.uk.com

The Fat Pig

Exeter

Tucked down a side street in an Exeter backwater, opposite warehouses and a 'pay and display', the pub holds a smokehouse, a brewery and the smallest commercial distillery in the UK, and the smell of hops and smoke (they brew in the cellar) pulls you inside. The vibe is friendly and fun: there's fine beer on tap (Mojo Hay, No 38 Summer), Rusty Pig Cider, and a dizzying array of whiskies. You can eat where you want on the best meat, fish and game that Devon can provide; take a look at the chalkboards! This is a wooden floorboards, no-printed-menus place, with a mishmash of tables and a sprinkling of Ikea, and a spillover room with purple and red walls. If beer's not your thing you'll love the food: halloumi and mozzarella salad, homemade smoked sausages, linguine with mussels, chocolate torte, Sunday roasts, Saturday brunch.

Meals	Starters £2-£7.50. Mains £12.50-£17.
Closed	Open all day.

Hamish Lothian
The Fat Pig,
2 John Street,
Exeter, EX1 1BL
Tel +44 (0)1392 214440
Web www.fatpig-exeter.co.uk

Entry 164 Map 2

Devon

Samuel Jones

Exeter

Who would guess this industrial Smoke and Ale House, inhabiting a stone warehouse on Exeter Quay, was an outpost of Cornish brewing giant St Austell? The Samuel Jones has not looked back since opening day in 2014, and everyone is welcome, including the dog. The setting is brilliant, the food is fresh, and if you like your beer there are guest draughts on offer (in pint and third-pint glasses) as well as a raft of craft beers. You enter a huge airy split-level space of polished copper, exposed pipes and reclaimed timbers, with bar stools at high tables, leather bench seating along exposed stone walls and occasional sofas; it's lively, but it feels intimate at the same time. Good food flows from the open-to-view kitchen starting with breakfast at 8.30am, the kids' menu boasts waffles with fresh fruit and the Devon-beef burgers are tip-top.

Meals	Starters from £5. Dinner from £9.
Closed	Open all day.

Rhys Heavens
Samuel Jones,
37 Commercial Road,
Exeter, EX2 4AE
Tel +44 (0)1392 345345
Web www.samueljonesexeter.co.uk

Entry 165 Map 2

The Bridge Inn

Topsham

Unchanged for most of the century – and in the family for as long – the 16th-century Bridge is for ale connoisseurs. And for all who love a pub furnished in the old-style: high-back settles, ancient floors, a simple hatch. Years ago it was a brewery and malthouse, Caroline's great-grandfather was the last publican to brew his own here and the Queen chose the Bridge for her first official 'visit to a pub'. This is beer-drinker heaven, with up to ten real ales served by gravity from the cask. There's cider and gooseberry wine, too. Cradle your pint to the background din of local chatter in the Inner Sanctum, or out in the garden by the steep river bank. Bread baked at the local farm, home-cooked hams, homemade chutneys, Devon cheeses: the Bridge's sandwiches, pork pies and ploughman's are first-class.

Meals	Lunch from £3.20. Bar meals £3.20-£7.
Closed	2pm-6pm (7pm Sun).

Caroline Cheffers-Heard
The Bridge Inn,
Bridge Hill, Topsham,
Exeter, EX3 0QQ
Tel +44 (0)1392 873862
Web www.cheffers.co.uk/bridge.html

Entry 166 Map 2

Devon

The Fountain Head

Branscombe

With an ale festival in June, they take their beer seriously here: local and top brew; the food is good too. There's not much to say about the history, except that the dining room was once a forge, but there is an authentic feel: big flagstones, wood-clad walls, dim-lit corners and a tap room that used to be the cellar. No TV screens, no fruit machines, just local babble and possibly a snoozing dog. (It's great walking country.) The restaurant is dominated by a central chimney and grate; tables are candlelit and horseshoes hang from beams, along with the landlord's boots. Locals and visitors tuck into honest pub food and plenty of it – half a pint of prawns, beef and Branoc Ale pie, curry of the day, barbecues on summer Sundays. Beers are brewed in the village, ciders are Green Valley and the staff are great.

Meals	Lunch & dinner £7.50-£12. Bar lunch £3.95-£5.95.
Closed	3pm-6pm.

Jon Woodley & Teresa Hoare
The Fountain Head,
Branscombe,
Seaton, EX12 3BG
Tel +44 (0)1297 680359
Web www.fountainheadinn.com

Entry 167 Map 2

The Holt

Honiton

So named (a holt = the lair of an otter) because the McCaigs own the Otter Brewery in the Blackdown Hills. Joe and chef Angus run the pub, and Otter brews come from the underground eco cellar: Bitter, Ale, Bright and Head. But the spruced-up boozer on Honiton's high street is much more than the brewery 'tap'. The vibrant bar and contemporary dining room upstairs play host to live music and film nights when food is off the menu. Angus delivers modern pub food from an open-plan kitchen, the emphasis being on local produce – farm meats, estate-shot game, and smoked meats and fish from the on-site smokehouse. On seasonal menus are beefburgers, confit duck leg and sandwiches for lunch; for dinner, bream with crab and coriander cream sauce, lamb shank with herb dumplings, chocolate brownies. A superb A30 pit-stop.

Meals	Lunch from £5.50. Dinner from £12.50.
Closed	3pm-5.30pm & all day Sun & Mon.

Joe & Angus McCaig
The Holt,
178 High Street,
Honiton, EX14 1LA

Tel +44 (0)1404 47707
Web www.theholt-honiton.com

Entry 168 Map 2

Devon

The Railway

Honiton

A gem of a pub, tucked just off the High Street in a vibrant market town. Built by GWR workers en route to Cornwall it has seen plenty of action; now a calmer vibe rules. The bar area is lounge style with long bench seats, Indian flagstones and café tables. The dining area beyond is upbeat and quirky with painted pulley wheels and lots of local art. Gorgeous food and an engaging atmosphere mix with a bistro-brasserie style and a wide-ranging menu: zucchini fritti, pressed ham hock terrine of local pedigree pork, fragrant chicken Vietnamese salad, traditional Louisiana jambalaya, pan-seared scallops, 'bucatini puttanesca' – dazzling. Drinkers have Branscombe Branoc and Bounders cider to discover.

Meals	Lunch from £6.95. Bar meals from £6.95. Dinner from £12.95.
Closed	Monday & Sunday all day.

Melanie Sancey
The Railway,
Queen Street,
Honiton, EX14 1HE

Tel +44 (0)1404 47976
Web www.therailwayhoniton.co.uk

Entry 169 Map 2

The Anchor Inn

Seatown

You're in a perfect spot here, smack-bang on the coastal path below Golden Cap; the Anchor is a thriving, lively inn that knows exactly how to make the most of its location. The big sun terrace and gardens overlook the pebbly beach; interiors evoke driftwood and nautical cosiness, with open fires around which you can enjoy a pint of Palmers and a crab sandwich, or a bowl of super fresh shellfish washed down with an excellent wine. If you've built up an appetite (there are walks from the doorstep) the menus will tempt you with inspiring, hearty and artisanal treats that make splendid use of locally sourced produce. Fish and lobsters direct from the beach make for the freshest of fresh dishes. Three bedrooms with deeply comfortable king-size beds are chic (a rusty tap as a coat hook, rope buoys, trunks turned into tables) with captivating sea views; you'll think you've stepped aboard an 18th-century schooner. Bathrooms have roll-top baths, walk-in showers, the fluffiest of white towels and glorious tiling, with top-notch oils and soaps. Terrific.

Rooms	3 doubles: £120-£170.
Meals	Starters from £5.95. Mains from £9.95
Closed	Open all day.

Paul Wiscombe
The Anchor Inn,
Seatown, Chideock,
Bridport, DT6 6JU

Tel	+44 (0)1297 489215
Web	www.theanchorinnseatown.co.uk

The New Inn Cerne Abbas

Cerne Abbas

The New Inn is most certainly new; it may date to the 16th century, but they have recently spent the best part of a year refurbishing the place and now it shines. Gone are the swirly green carpets; local slate has been laid in the bar. Lots of lovely old stuff remains – timber frames, mullioned windows, the odd settle – but the feel is fresh with warm colours, engineered oak floors and a smart new bar where you can order a pint of Dorset Gold or a glass of good wine. An open-plan feel runs throughout and you dig into local food wherever you want, perhaps fish from Brixham, local game, sticky toffee pudding. Bedrooms – some in the main house, others in the old stables – are good value for money. You'll find Hypnos mattresses, blond wood furniture and super little bathrooms. Those in the converted stables feel more contemporary: ground-floor rooms open onto the terrace, where you eat in good weather; those above are built into the eaves. The suites come with double-ended baths in the room. Don't miss the Giant. *Minimum stay: two nights at weekends.*

Rooms	7 doubles, 3 twin/doubles: £95-£140. 2 suites for 2: £160-£170. Singles from £75.
Meals	Lunch & dinner £5-£35.
Closed	Open all day.

Julian Dove & Annette Beardsmore
The New Inn Cerne Abbas,
Long Street,
Cerne Abbas, DT2 7JF

Tel +44 (0)1300 341274
Web www.thenewinncerneabbas.co.uk

The Acorn Inn

Evershot

Perfect Evershot and rolling countryside lie at the door of this 400-year-old gem in Thomas Hardy country. New owners Natalie and Richard took the reins to revive its fortunes, with head chef Guy Horley cooking hearty food. It's very much a traditional inn; locals sup pints of Otter Ale in the long flagstoned bar and guests sample good food sourced within 25 miles. In the dining room, the atmosphere changes to rural country house with smartly laid tables, terracotta tiles, soft lighting and elegant fireplaces. Good gastropub fare is taken seriously, be it an Acorn Inn homemade burger, or open lasagne of confit rabbit followed by twice cooked pork belly, and a warm sticky toffee pudding. Little ones have their own menu, and stacks of colouring books and crayons to keep them busy while they wait. Service is helpful and friendly. Bedrooms creak with age and style; there are antiques and fabric wall-coverings, super little bathrooms, perhaps a wonky floor or a lovely four-poster. It's worth splashing out on a larger room if you want space.

Rooms	4 doubles, 2 twin/doubles, 3 four-posters: £99-£160. 1 suite for 3: £160-£205. Singles £89-£205. Dinner, B&B £80-£133 per person. Extra bed/sofabed available £20 per person per night.
Meals	Lunch & dinner £5.25-£22.95. Bar meals from £4.95.
Closed	Open all day.

Natalie Read & Richard Legg
The Acorn Inn,
Evershot,
Dorchester, DT2 0JW
Tel +44 (0)1935 83228
Web www.acorn-inn.co.uk

The Chetnole Inn

Chetnole

This sweet little inn has the lot: a great position in a pretty village; lovely interiors that mix old and new; super food that draws a crowd, and three excellent, affordable bedrooms. Flagged floors, low ceilings and wood-burners keep things cosy inside, and you can eat in the dog-friendly bar or in the lively restaurant, even in the breakfast room if things get busy. The food is just what you want after a day in the hills, perhaps rabbit and pork rillettes with a pear and squash chutney, steak and ale pie with thick-cut chips, warm apple and 'Kingston black' crumble. Tea is served with homemade coconut ice, and the ales are locally sourced and constantly changing; try the Copper Hopper Gold Rush, brewed just three miles away. Spotless bedrooms upstairs fit the mood perfectly. All are big and come with comfy beds, pretty sofas, sparkling shower rooms with robes and lovely lotions. Sherborne is to the north, the coast to the south, and the Cerne Abbas giant between. Brilliant.

Rooms	2 doubles, 1 twin/double: £95. Singles £70.
Meals	Lunch & dinner £9.85-£21. Bar meals from £5. Sunday lunch from £10.50.
Closed	3pm-6.30pm. Sun eves & Mon (Oct-Apr).

Simon & Maria Hudson
The Chetnole Inn,
Village Street, Chetnole,
Sherborne, DT9 6NU
Tel +44 (0)1935 872337
Web www.thechetnoleinn.co.uk

The Fontmell

Fontmell Magna

After a year-long refurbishment, the former Crown opened up shop in 2011 – with a change of name and a stylish new feel. Colourful cushions and striped bar stools, striking red and blue walls, deep leather sofas and a table laden with magazines and games combine to create a super-cosy feel. Quaff Keystone Brewery's Sibeth Ale and mussels and chips at scrubbed tables – or follow glass-enclosed corridors across babbling Collyer's Brook to the dining room, furnished in relaxed country-house style. Jazzy rugs, old tables, a wall of shelves stacked with wine bottles and books create an easy mood, so settle down and enjoy chef Tom Shaw's imaginative cooking. Dishes include treats such as goat's curd cigar with roasted baby beetroot and truffle honey, Cornish fish stew, spaghetti alla Norma and banana tarte tatin. Delve into the wines – the list is eclectic – and stay the night. Fabulous rooms, named after 'butterfly' in various languages, ooze comfort and warmth. Rich colours and fabrics, fine linen and goose down, swish bathrooms and quirky details are there to seduce you; the best, Mallyshag has a fashionable roll top tub in the room.

Rooms	4 doubles, 1 twin/double: £75–£155. Singles £75–£130.
Meals	Lunch, bar meals & dinner from £9.25. Sunday lunch, 2–3 courses, £17–£23.
Closed	Open all day.

John Crompton
The Fontmell,
Fontmell Magna,
Shaftesbury, SP7 0PA
Tel +44 (0)1747 811441
Web www.thefontmell.com

King John Inn

Tollard Royal

You're on the Dorset/Wiltshire border, lost in blissful country, with paths that lead up into glorious hills. Tumble back down to this super inn, where every square inch has been refurbished, making the place shine. Expect airy interiors, a sober country feel, a sun-trapping terrace and a fire that crackles in winter. Originally a foundry, it opened as a brewery in 1859 and, when beer proved more popular than horseshoes, the inn was born. You'll find three local ales on tap and great wines too. As for the food, it's as local as can be: slow-braised red Devon beef pie with mash and vegetables; twice-baked Westcombe cheddar cheese soufflé; Earl Grey tea panna cotta with chocolate and hazelnut biscotti. Contemporary country bedrooms, three in the Coach House, are the final treat. Some are bigger than others but all come with modern fabrics, padded headboards, crisp linen and super bathrooms (one has a slipper bath). In summer, a terraced lawn gives views over a couple of rooftops onto the woods. A perfect spot.

Rooms	7 doubles: £90-£150. 1 suite for 2: £150-£190.
Meals	Lunch from £13.95. Bar meals from £8.95. Dinner, 3 courses, from about £35.
Closed	Christmas Day.

John Lacombe
King John Inn,
Tollard Royal,
Salisbury, SP5 5PS
Tel +44 (0)1725 516207
Web www.kingjohninn.co.uk

The Museum Inn

Farnham

In a village with roses round every door is one of the finest inns in England, built by the father of modern archaeology (whose museum, the Pitt Rivers, is in Oxford). Today, attentive staff keep the atmosphere warm and happy. Bedrooms – big in the main house, smaller in the stables, all super smart – have cool colours, crisp linen, fancy bathrooms (and hi-tech gadgetry in most). The big 17th-century bar has a period feel: flagstones, inglenook, fresh flowers and a fashionable mismatch of tables and chairs. There are cosy alcoves to hide in, a book-filled drawing room to browse and a smart white-raftered dining room. The head chef's dishes range from honey-glazed duck breast, seared duck liver and roasted Jersey Royals, to golden fried gnocchi with broad beans, pea purée, asparagus and rocket, sourced, of course, from the best ingredients; finish with poached rhubarb, Italian meringue, rosewater cream and strawberries. Popular with the barbour-and-dog set, the Museum Inn is quietest out of season but a treat all round.

Rooms	5 doubles, 2 twin/doubles, 1 four-poster: £90-£165.
Meals	Light lunch from £7.50. Mains from £12.95.
Closed	Open all day.

Lee Hart
The Museum Inn,
Farnham,
Blandford Forum, DT11 8DE
Tel +44 (0)1725 516261
Web www.museuminn.co.uk

The Inn at Cranborne

Cranborne

Aussie Jane's passion for the great English inn runs deep; she waved goodbye to her jet-setting career to take on the faded Fleur de Lys in the heart of pretty Cranborne. Now the Hall & Woodhouse inn glows. In the cosy bar – all panelled walls, rugs on woodblock or flagstone floors, warm heritage hues – say hello to Mikey and Poppy, Jane's characterful Jack Russells, then bag the smartly upholstered pew bench by the blazing wood-burner and enjoy Daniel Foy's seasonal menus. Tuck into a hearty smoked meat and fish platter, then spiced plum sausages with mustard and rapeseed mash, leaving room for sticky toffee pudding with salted caramel and honeycomb ice cream. Look to the bar menu for sandwiches and pub classics. Fancy staying the night? Upstairs, rooms have a classy contemporary feel, with cord carpets, fat radiators, painted furniture, and goose down duvets with Welsh blankets on big comfortable beds. Smart tiled bathrooms (the best have roll top baths) with posh Bramley toiletries have village views. Cranborne Chase and the New Forest (for walking and cycling), Salisbury and the Jurassic Coast are close.

Rooms	7 doubles, 2 twin/doubles: £85-£150.
Meals	Bar snacks from £2.50. Small plates from £4.95. Mains from £10.95.
Closed	Sun from 5pm. Mon all day.

Jane Gould
The Inn at Cranborne,
5 Wimborne Street, Cranborne,
Wimborne, BH21 5PP
Tel +44 (0)1725 551249
Web www.theinnatcranborne.co.uk

The Plantation

Poole

In a peaceful conservation area on the outskirts of Poole, within strolling distance of sweeping sands and sea, is a quick getaway from London. Come for the night, or stay the weekend. The Edwardian building with its gothicky turret has become a smart new dining venue with a colonial décor and a delightful young team. Beyond the suave banquettes, the pale wood tables and the bar stocked with Upham's ales and Orchard Pig cider is a large new conservatory with a decorative tiled floor and wrought iron chairs painted tasteful green. Nothing is too much trouble for the staff who ferry good-looking dishes to happy punters: roasted bass with Dorset cured ham; quinoa with creamed celeriac; beef burgers with bacon jam; clementine custard tart with coconut sorbet. Outside is a leafy garden with a hut for spoiled smokers; upstairs are ten snazzy, well-insulated rooms. Look forward to a deep soak or a waterfall shower, bathrobes, slippers and Ren toiletries, big comfy beds and perhaps the odd sofa. Breakfast is excellent: the full English, eggs any way you want them, homemade butter, yogurts and jams.

Rooms	3 doubles, 7 twin/doubles: £130-£170.
Meals	Starters £6.50-£9. Mains £12-£26.
Closed	Open all day.

Terry Cloutman
The Plantation,
53 Cliff Drive, Canford Cliffs,
Poole, BH13 7JF

Tel +44 (0)1202 701531
Web www.the-plantation.co.uk

The Square & Compass

Worth Matravers

The name honours those who cut stone from the nearby quarries. This splendid old pub has been in the family for generations and remains unchanged; a narrow, rare, drinking corridor leads to two hatches from where Palmer's Copper Ale and guest ales come from the cask. With a pint of home produced cider and a homemade pasty, you can chat in the flagged corridor or settle in the parlour; there are painted wooden panels, wall seats, local prints and cartoons, and a wood-burner to warm you on wild nights. The stone-walled main room has live music; there's cribbage and shove ha'penny and a fossil museum (the family's) next door. Gazing out across fields to the sea this pub and its sunny front terrace – occasionally dotted with roaming hens – is a popular stop for coastal path hikers. A national treasure!

Meals	Pasties £3.50.
Closed	3pm-6pm. Open all day Fri, Sat & Sun & every day July-Sept.

Charlie Newman & Kevin Hunt
The Square & Compass,
Worth Matravers,
Swanage, BH19 3LF

Tel +44 (0)1929 439229
Web www.squareandcompasspub.co.uk

Entry 179 Map 3

Dorset

The Red Lion

Weymouth

Just a buoy's throw away from Weymouth's off-shore lifeboat, this little pub has fed and watered lifeboat crews for nearly 150 years. Behind the central bar, locals and visiting seafarers quaff pints of Otter Bitter Lifeboat Ale whilst sharing plates of fresh seafood, surrounded by nautical ropes and Morse Code flags. In winter, cosy corners panelled with old rum barrels are a great place for warming dishes such as steak and ale pie served with minted 'not so mushy peas', and warm toffee apple cake with vanilla ice cream. Outside in summer, wooden tables with lanterns are perfect for al fresco eating in the square. Rain or shine, the bar with its collection of lifeboat memorabilia is still a focal point. Even if you can't decipher the flags you can toast the crews, with a tot of one of the pub's 80 rums.

Meals	Lunch & dinner £3.95-£14.95.
Closed	Open all day.

Brian McLaughlin
The Red Lion,
Hope Square,
Weymouth, DT4 8TR

Tel +44 (0)1305 786940
Web www.theredlionweymouth.co.uk

Entry 180 Map 3

The Anvil Inn

Pimperne

This pretty-as-a-peach thatched inn sits in the village of Pimperne and dates back to the 16th century. Friendly new owners (and Sawday's veterans) Karl and Zuzanna have breathed new life through the rafters: find traditional wooden tables, big fireplaces, a stone and brick bar and a mosaic floor of tiles and stone. Menus are unfussy and make the most of local produce: nestle into a corner with a book from the shelves and a pint of Tangle Foot while you tuck into Dorset cheddar sandwiches with real ale chutney. If it's heartier fare you're after, try the fresh Dorset crab on toasted sourdough, followed by steak and kidney pot pie. Dessert is a real treat and not to be missed: we loved the coffee crème brûlée with brown sugared doughnuts. In summer, bring the dog after a jaunt round Blandford Forum and sip proper cider by the garden pond.

Meals	Bar snacks from £2.50. Starters from £5.95. Sandwiches from £5.95. Mains from £11.95.
Closed	Open all day.

Karl Bashford & Zuzana Prekopova
The Anvil Inn,
Pimperne,
Blandford Forum, DT11 8UQ
Tel +44 (0)1258 451999
Web www.anvilpimperne.co.uk

Entry 181 Map 3

The Rose & Crown

Trent

In a sleepy estate village is a 15th-century pub, thatched and peaceful next to the church. Spruced up with style by tenant Heather, it remains refreshingly simple, with a rug-strewn stone floor, winter log fires, soothing colours, church candles, scrubbed tables, ticking grandfather clock, newspapers and books. Expect four gleaming handpumps (try the Bishops Tipple), squashy leather in the snug, impressive artwork in the conservatory dining room and sylvan views from the bar... and a welcoming wag from Archie. Young Marcus is cooking up a storm in the kitchen, offering pub classics with a twist at lunch and more adventurous evening dishes. Look forward to scallops with cauliflower purée, pressed potato and black pudding; duck breast and confit leg pie with carrot purée and salted pear; bakewell tart with jam sauce and almond ice cream.

Meals	Lunch from £7.95. Dinner from £9.95. Sunday lunch, 3 courses, from £19.95.
Closed	3pm-6pm Tues-Fri. Sun eves & Mon. Open all day Sat.

Nick Lamb & Michael Rust
The Rose & Crown,
Trent,
Sherborne, DT9 4SL
Tel +44 (0)1935 850776
Web www.roseandcrowntrent.co.uk

Entry 182 Map 3

The Victoria Inn

Durham

An old-school drinking bar in the middle of Durham: no music, no fruit machines, just original Victorian interiors trapped in aspic. There's a roaring fire, ancient wallpaper, pints of Big Lamp and lots of local banter. In the old days, shawled ladies would pop in to retrieve an errant husband. These days it's students, bar-room philosophers and beers lovers who drop by. It's not to everyone's taste – if you want boutique interiors and impeccable service, look elsewhere – but those who like to quaff a pint or two with the odd portrait of Queen Victoria hanging on the wall will love it. Bedrooms upstairs aren't huge, but have honest prices and are a good base for exploring the city. Most have been partially refurbished in the last two years and come with lots of colour and good bathrooms. Some have brass beds, others Fleur de Lys wallpaper; the family room up in the eaves is large and airy with a contemporary style. Big breakfasts wait downstairs, Durham starts at the front door: cobbled streets, riverside walks, university and cathedral. Good restaurants wait nearby, Hadrian's Wall is close.

Rooms	4 doubles, 1 twin: £75-£80. 1 family room for 4: £85. Singles £49-£68.
Meals	Toasted sandwiches £1.70.
Closed	Open all day.

Michael Webster
The Victoria Inn,
86 Hallgarth Street,
Durham, DH1 3AS

Tel	+44 (0)191 3865269
Web	www.victoriainn-durhamcity.co.uk

Rose & Crown

Romaldkirk

Romaldkirk is one of those lovely villages where little has changed in 200 years. It sits peacefully in the north Pennines, lost to the world and without great need of it. As for the Rose & Crown, it dates to 1733 and stands on the village green next to a Saxon Church. Roses ramble across stone walls at the front, so grab a pint of local ale, then sit in the sun and watch life pass by. Inside, you can roast away in front of a fire in the wonderfully old-school bar while reading the *Teesdale Mercury*. There's a peaceful sitting room for afternoon tea, then a panelled restaurant for excellent food, perhaps honey-glazed goats cheese with apple and hazelnut, shoulder of pork wrapped in Parma ham, banana Bakewell tart. Thomas and Cheryl bought the place in 2012 and have been spending money on it ever since: it has never looked better. Stylish rooms – some in the main house, others out back, a couple in a cottage next door – have warm colours, comfy beds, Bose sound systems and super bathrooms. Don't miss High Force waterfall, the magnificent Bowes Museum or the sausage sandwich at lunch. Dogs are very welcome.

Rooms	8 doubles, 3 twins: £115-£160. 3 suites for 2: £180-£200. Singles from £95. Dinner, B&B £110 p.p.
Meals	Lunch from £10.50. Dinner, 3 courses, from £27. Sunday lunch £19.50.
Closed	Open all day.

Thomas & Cheryl Robinson
Rose & Crown,
Romaldkirk,
Barnard Castle, DL12 9EB
Tel +44 (0)1833 650213
Web www.rose-and-crown.co.uk

Black Bull Inn

Frosterley

Ten paces from the atmospheric Weardale Railway: solid tables and cushioned settles, stone flags, ticking clocks, glowing ranges and a happy buzz. No lager in sight, just coffee and scones from 10.30am, cider from the cask and beers from a few villages away. The hop is treated with reverence – dark malty porter from Wylam Brewery, bitter from Allendale – and the good value food is a joy. Rather than devising a menu then searching for suppliers, Diane and Duncan source the produce first: local if possible, and in tune with the seasons. A rare rib of beef with lashings of homemade gravy, and crispy salmon on parsley with crushed new potatoes and chive cream is the sort of thing they do brilliantly here; and the sticky date pudding is unmissable. Regular classical, folk and jazz sessions, too… they even have their own peal of bells!

Meals	Lunch £7.95-£12.95. Dinner £11.95-£18.95. Sunday lunch from £9.95.
Closed	Mon-Wed all day. From 5pm Sun.

Duncan & Diane Davis
Black Bull Inn,
Bridge End, Frosterley,
Bishop Auckland, DL13 2SL
Tel +44 (0)1388 527784
Web www.blackbullfrosterley.com

Entry 185 Map 12

Durham

Bridgewater Arms

Winston

Out in beautiful Teesdale, a lovely pub with some very good food. Once the village school, it played host to a legendary performance of Jack and the Beanstalk in 1957, though these days the stars are more likely to pop in for a slap-up dinner or a pint of Keeper's Gold. Paul looks after things with an easy style, stopping to chat or talk you through the boarded menus. You'll find beautiful old windows, a vaulted ceiling, rich colours and the odd wall of books. As for the food, it's delicious stuff, the sort you crave after a morning on the fells, perhaps langoustine in garlic butter, rack of local lamb, saffron poached pears and ginger ice cream; there's a dining terrace for summer, too. Don't miss the exceptional Bowes Museum up the road in Barnard Castle – you'll find Goya, El Greco and Canaletto on the walls.

Meals	Lunch & dinner £10-£20.
Closed	2.30pm-6pm. Sun & Mon all day.

Paul Grundy
Bridgewater Arms,
Winston,
Darlington, DL2 3RN
Tel +44 (0)1325 730302
Web www.thebridgewaterarms.com

Entry 186 Map 12

The Fox Hole

Piercebridge

An 'old' stone-flagged bar at one end, a country-sleek restaurant at the other: the second you enter you unwind. This 'pub and kitchen' on the edge of Piercebridge was a hit the day it opened: the staff are delightful, the food is modern, and our roast fig and goat's cheese salad was fabulous. The drinks are of note too: ales on hand pump, organic wines, and a host of zippy new gins. Ellie Richmond is chef and naturally keen on provenance. The fish comes daily from Hartlepool, the bread is baked in Crook, the coffee is roasted 15 miles away and the lamb is from the other side of the road. You could have escabeche of beetroot with chorizo mayonnaise, rib-eye steak with béarnaise sauce, and lemon and thyme panna cotta. Sun streams into the restaurant, good dogs (on leads) relax by the fire, toddlers play on the fresh clipped grass.

Meals Starters from £5.25.
Mains from £7.50.
Sunday lunch £12.95.

Closed Open all day.

Jack Bowles & Ellie Richmond
The Fox Hole,
Piercebridge,
Darlington, DL2 3SJ
Tel +44 (0)1325 374286
Web www.the-foxhole.co.uk

Entry 187 Map 12

Durham

The Bay Horse

Hurworth

A pretty, bow-fronted building, painted cream under red pantiles, which sits happily at the end of a terrace with open countryside beyond. Inside is nicely pubby: comforting button-back wall seating, polished oak floor boards, local prints and soft wall lamps, quiet background jazz. At least two good cask ales are served (in dimpled tankards), and truly stunning food from chef Marcus Bennett is brought to you by friendly folk in crisp aprons; you eat in a dining room with antique tables and proper linen napkins. Try wild duck and pistachio terrine with fig chutney, smoked bacon, scrambled egg and toasted mushroom and onion brioche – the eggs come in a shell with a soldier! Puddings are irresistible – try caramelised rice pudding with spiced autumn berries, even the bread is home baked and there are private dining rooms upstairs.

Meals Lunch from £12.95.
Bar meals from £6.95.
Dinner from £13.95.
Sunday lunch, 3 courses, £21.95.

Closed Open all day.

Marcus Bennett & Jonathan Hall
The Bay Horse,
45 The Green, Hurworth,
Darlington, DL2 2AA
Tel +44 (0)1325 720663
Web www.thebayhorsehurworth.com

Entry 188 Map 12

The Bell Hotel

Horndon-on-the-Hill

A 600-year-old timber-framed coaching inn, as full of contented locals today as it was when pilgrims stopped on their way to Canterbury. Everything is a delight: hanging lanterns in the courtyard, stripped boards in the bar, superb staff in the restaurant, copious window boxes bursting with colour. It's a proper inn, warmly welcoming, with thick beams, country rugs, panelled walls and open fires. Stop for a pint of cask ale in the lively bar, then potter into the restaurant for top food, perhaps seared scallops with confit venison, grilled Dover sole, cherry parfait with chocolate brownie Alaska and popping candy. Christine grew up here, John joined her years ago; both are respected in the trade, as is Joanne, Master Sommelier and manager of many years. An infectious warmth runs through this ever-popular inn. As for the bedrooms, go for the suites above – or a new room in the grand Georgian property up the high street: cosily inviting, individual, quite funky. In the morning, breakfast with the papers at elegant Hill House, where further bedrooms, snazzily refurbished, lie. Then head north into Constable country.

Rooms	15 doubles, 3 twins: £50-£90. 9 suites for 2: £120-£145.
Meals	Lunch from £11.95. Bar meals from £8.95. Dinner à la carte, £30. Not bank holidays.
Closed	2.30pm-5.30pm (3pm Sat, 4pm-7pm Sun).

Christine & John Vereker
The Bell Hotel,
High Road, Horndon-on-the-Hill,
Stanford-le-Hope, SS17 8LD

Tel	+44 (0)1375 642463
Web	www.bell-inn.co.uk

The Compasses Inn

Littley Green

In a little hamlet tucked away from civilisation is The Compasses, a simple pub with a loyal following. The building is red brick and Victorian, the bar is plain (stone floors, wood tables, roaring fire: little has changed in 50 years) and it started life as the closest pub to the Ridley Brewery. Heritage is key; the family that run it have beer flowing through their veins and the Bishop Nick Ridley's Rite went down a treat. Off the bar is a dining room where freshly made food – chilli con carne, filled baked potatoes, ham, egg and chips – is chalked up on the board. The meat is local and the 'huffers' (traditional triangular baps) are huge, and stuffed with a choice of fillings. Ramblers, cyclists and the local shoots drop by, and if you come with children there's a garden with picnic tables at the back. Right next door is the biggest surprise, their new venture: five bedrooms, spacious, modern and on the ground floor. Make yourself at home among fresh new fabrics, pictures on white walls, excellent bathrooms and warm toasty floors. The big freshly cooked breakfast is served with a smile.

Rooms 2 doubles, 2 twin/doubles, 1 twin: £70-£90.
Meals Lunch from £3.50.
Closed Mondays-Wednesdays 3pm-5pm.

Jocelyn Ridley
The Compasses Inn,
Littley Green,
Chelmsford, CM3 1BU
Tel +44 (0)1245 362308
Web www.compasseslittleygreen.co.uk

The Alma Inn and Dining Rooms

Harwich

Yards from the sea at Harwich is a simple but great pub. Real ales, happy faces, sea shanties (Fridays), farmers, fishermen, families, dogs… and logs in the burner, a porthole in the bar, and crisply battered haddock sweet from the sea. Since 1850 the Alma has been a welcoming port of call. Now the planked floors and standing timbers are joined by upcycled curiosities and nautical oddities – quirky is the word. The blackboards are ever-changing so for lovers of fresh fish (skate wing, mussels, oysters, lobster, dressed crab, crab linguine, Dover sole) it's ace, and the tartare sauce is lovely too. They do good burgers – spiced for veggies, hand-pressed for carnivores – and a range of great puddings including a secret recipe chocolate brownie. Clean plates all round! So if you're too full up to go home then just pop upstairs to comfortable bedrooms (some larger than others) with fitted carpets, crisp white cotton, flat TVs on the wall, more wood and sparkling modern bathrooms with power showers. Beautifully presented breakfasts are worth getting up for – fill up again before you go off to explore the town

Rooms	4 doubles: £85-£95. 1 small double for 2: £75-£85.
Meals	Starters from £3.95. Lunch from £4.95. Dinner from £9.95
Closed	Open all day.

Nick May
The Alma Inn and Dining Rooms,
25 King's Head Street,
Harwich, CO12 3EE
Tel +44 (0)1255 318681
Web www.almaharwich.co.uk

The Mistley Thorn

Mistley

In Constable land: a perfect coastal village where Georgian cottages gather around a river estuary with wide, light views of water, bobbing boats and green hills beyond. David and Sherri (who have a cookery school next door) run the place beautifully: staff are young, and good, there are plenty of locals tossed into the mix and some impeccably behaved children. The mood is laid-back city wine bar rather than roadside country pub. Colours are soft and easy, the tables are of various shapes, candles flicker, modern art rubs along well with the odd antique and food is taken seriously but without reverence. There's lots of robust local fish and seafood – squid with chilli, crab cakes with mayonnaise, gurnard with black olive tapenade, brilliant chips – and a pudding list that includes cheesecake from Californian Sherri's mum.

Meals	Lunch from £6.25. Set lunch £11.95 & £15. Dinner, 3 courses, about £25.
Closed	3pm-6.30pm. Open all day Sat & Sun.

David McKay & Sherri Singleton
The Mistley Thorn,
High Street, Mistley,
Manningtree, CO11 1HE
Tel +44 (0)1206 392821
Web www.mistleythorn.co.uk

Entry 192 Map 10

Essex

The Shepherd

Langham

Esther and Richard have breathed style, metropolitan chic and gutsy food into this 1930s village pub without burying its roots. Walkers, cyclists, dogs, locals – and children – are welcome. Light and bright, with pine furnishings and tiled floors sassied up with modish paints and colourful cushions, the bar segues into the restaurant. Adnam's is on tap, as well as over 12 wines by the glass and a European menu that reflects Esther's esteemed cookery school training (Leith's, and then stints with London caterers). Break bread over an antipasti sharing platter filled with Mediterranean delights, then perhaps a grilled halloumi burger in brioche bun or a rump steak with chips and garlic mushrooms. There's always something going on here; quiz nights, curry nights, themed evenings. Try a Bloody Mary, we hear they're excellent!

Meals	Starters £6.25-£6.75. Mains £11-£19.50. Sharing platters £11.50-£17.
Closed	Open all day.

Richard & Esther Brunning
The Shepherd,
Moor Road,
Langham, CO4 5NR
Tel +44 (0)1206 272711
Web www.shepherdlangham.co.uk

Entry 193 Map 10

The Sun Inn

Dedham

Order a picnic at the inn, float down the Stour, then tie up on the bank for lunch al fresco. You're in Constable country, in an idyllic village made rich by mills in the 16th century, and you couldn't hope to wash up in a better place. Step in to find log fires in grand grates, board games on old tables, stripped floors, an easy elegance. A panelled lounge comes with sofas and armchairs, the bar is made from a slab of local elm and the dining room is beamed and airy. Delicious food is inspired by Italy: celeriac and black cabbage soup; pasta with red mullet, tomatoes, olives, chilli and thyme; baked hake with tomatoes, fennel and parsley; pork chop with cannellini beans and salsa verde. The cheeses are local and children can have small portions of whatever they fancy.

Meals	Lunch & dinner from £12. Bar meals from £6.85. Sunday lunch £24. No food 25 & 26 Dec.
Closed	Open all day.

Piers Baker
The Sun Inn,
High Street, Dedham,
Colchester, CO7 6DF

Tel	+44 (0)1206 323351
Web	www.thesuninndedham.com

Entry 194 Map 10

The Pheasant

Gestingthorpe

On the Essex/Suffolk border, with serene views over the Stour valley, the Pheasant thrives under James (former garden designer) and his wife Diana. Once a run-down boozer, it is now a well-loved food-led community pub. Two cosy countrified bars draw village folk in for quiz nights, wine tastings, monthly supper clubs, and the 'Thirsty Thursday Club', while well-informed foodies help swell the numbers, attracted by James's seasonal monthly menus. Tuck yourself next to a wood-burner with a pint of Pheasant Bitter then enjoy potted crab followed by lamb and smoked mushroom pie; finish with apple, pear and quince crumble. James also finds time to smoke fish, seafood and cheeses, and maintain his award-winning Chelsea show garden from which most of the fruit and vegetables flow, and where bees drone happily.

Meals	Bar meals from £5.95. Dinner from £10. Sunday lunch, 3 courses, £18.50.
Closed	2.30pm-6.30pm.

James & Diana Donoghue
The Pheasant,
Gestingthorpe,
Halstead, CO9 3AU

Tel	+44 (0)1787 461196
Web	www.thepheasant.net

Entry 195 Map 10

The Eight Bells

Saffron Walden

Leanne's first 'Cosy Pub' is a beautifully restored 16th-century wool merchant's house tucked away on a street lined with wonky timbered and painted houses, an easy stroll from the town centre. Find bowed beams, old wall timbers, crackling logs in a big brick fireplace, polished wooden floors, Farrow & Ball colours and chesterfield armchairs in cosy corners; the relaxing bars are perfect for quaffing pints of Taylor's Landlord and sharing a charcuterie grazing board. Arrive early to bag a table in the historic barn at the back, replete with vaulted ceiling and painted timbers. With two wood-burners keeping things toasty, tuck into baked camembert with rustic breads, lamb shank with redcurrant and rosemary jus, and blackberry Eton mess; or come on Sunday for a classic roast. Outside is a swish summer terrace.

Meals: Lunch & bar meals from £10.
Dinner from £20.
Sunday lunch, 2 courses, £13.50.

Closed: Open all day.

Leanne Langman
The Eight Bells,
18 Bridge Street,
Saffron Walden, CB10 1BU

Tel: +44 (0)1799 522790

Web: www.8bells-pub.co.uk

Entry 196 Map 9

The Cricketers Arms

Rickling Green

Having snapped up the Cricketers in 2011, Leanne Langman is working her magic and restoring the fortunes of this striking 200-year-old red-brick inn. The setting is tranquil and gorgeous, overlooking a vast village green and cricket pitch; arrive early on a summer Sunday to bag a bench and watch an innings or two with a pint of Wherry. Rickling Green became *the* venue for London society cricket matches in the 1880s and it's still taken seriously. There's a contemporary feel to the rambling bar and dining areas – old beams and timbers, wood and stone floors, chunky tables, colourful cushions on banquettes, sofas and easy chairs in front of a crackling log fire. Hungry? Tuck into grazing boards, risottos, fishcakes, lamb and mint pies, dry-aged steaks and sticky toffee puddings – out on the terrace on warm days.

Meals: Lunch & dinner £9.50-£16.95.

Closed: Open all day.

Leanne Langman
The Cricketers Arms,
Rickling Green,
Saffron Walden, CB11 3YG

Tel: +44 (0)1799 543210

Web: www.thecricketersarmsricklinggreen.co.uk

Entry 197 Map 9

The Square & Compasses

Fairstead

What's not to love? A country pub with wines by the glass and ales from the cask, modern British cooking that's delicious and well-priced, and a landlord who's knowledgeable and welcoming. This popular pub is owner-run and it shows. What's more, it's in a beautiful spot, overlooking the Essex Way. Walkers with dogs beat a path to its door, and so do lucky locals. Inside are black beams and log burners, crisp napkins on old wooden tables, a bookcase of antique tomes, and snugs with dark green walls. Our pigeon with black pudding served on a bed of red cabbage, washed down with a pint (you might try Crouch Vale or Mighty Oak) was full of flavour; the kitchen is known for its quality meats and locally sourced game, with some of the vegetables supplied by the villagers. All the pub classics are prepared from scratch too.

Meals	Bar meals from £4.95. Dinner from £11.95. Sunday lunch £14.95.
Closed	Open all day.

Victor Roome
The Square & Compasses,
Fuller Street,
Fairstead, CM3 2BB
Tel +44 (0)1245 361477
Web www.thesquareandcompasses.co.uk

Entry 198 Map 9

The Fox & Goose

Chelmsford

Next to a garden centre on the A414 (you can't miss it) is a warm, buzzing, much-loved pub. Enter a large open-plan space with a stone-slate floor, a wall of racked wines, a clutch of club chairs, a bar painted dove-grey. Delightful staff serve pints of Woodforde's Wherry, wines by the glass, and a sparkling selection of whiskies, rums, vodkas and gins. If you stop for a bite, you'll eat stylishly and well. Try Lambton & Jackson smoked salmon celeriac remoulade to start, then slow roasted belly of pork with mashed potato, Symonds cider jus and crispy crackling; the menu changes each day. A 'bakehouse' is attached (meet for lovely bagels, cakes, scones, tea or fizz), a wall of glass opens to a wicker-chaired terrace with sprawling views across the Essex countryside, and in winter the wood-burner glows.

Meals	Starters from £3.25. Lunch from £8.50. Dinner from £9.50.
Closed	Open all day.

Danielle Kirkham
The Fox & Goose,
Ongar Road,
Chelmsford, CM1 3SN
Tel +44 (0)1245 248245
Web www.foxandgoosepub.co.uk

Entry 199 Map 9

The Folly Bistro

East Hanningfield

The locals love their revamped pub – who wouldn't? It's smart but informal, customer focused and independently run. It started life as a butchery in 1642; now there's a log-burner in the inglenook, a modern striped carpet throughout and a fancy sign out front announcing its new bistro status. Food-driven they may be but they often match dishes to wines and they love their ales too – Puck's Folly from Brentwood Brewery is one of four residents. At solid polished tables in the bar and restaurant (checked curtains, standing timbers, dove-grey bar) diners tuck into satisfying platefuls of moules, sautéed wild mushrooms, pie of the day, chump of lamb, sweet chilli risotto, and warm chocolate brownies. In summer you can decant to the garden and terrace with your cider or bubbly. PS. The pork scratchings (with spiced apple sauce) are fabulous.

Meals: Lunch, 2-3 courses, £12.50-£15.50. Dinner from £11.50.
Closed: Open all day.

Danielle Kirkham
The Folly Bistro,
The Tye, East Hanningfield,
Chelmsford, CM3 8AA
Tel: +44 (0)1245 400315
Web: www.thefollybistro.co.uk

Entry 200 Map 9

The Hoop

Stock

History and heritage run deep at The Hoop; built in 1640 with timbers from the warships at Tilbury Docks, it's been a stalwart in the pretty village of Stock ever since. Inside, there's a huge fireplace, rustic wooden tables, wicker chairs. Enjoy wine from local New Hall Vineyard or a pint of Adnams before tucking into a pub classic in the bar area downstairs (we loved our 'toad in the Hoop' and mash). For a smarter experience, head up to The Oak Room, the light, bright, beautifully vaulted dining space. Phil's excellent, seasonal menus make the most of local produce: start with panko-crusted goat's cheese bonbons, follow with roast Goosnargh duck with pumpkin and burnt orange purée, then finish with chocolate fondant and salted caramel ice cream. If you're feeling particularly decadent, end the night with some of Phil's handmade chocolate truffles.

Meals: Starters from £6.95. Lunch from £10.95. Dinner from £15.95.
Closed: Open all day.

Phil Utz & Michelle Corrigan
The Hoop,
High Street,
Stock, CM4 9BD
Tel: +44 (0)1277 841137
Web: www.thehoop.co.uk

Entry 201 Map 9

The Seagrave Arms

Weston Subedge

Locked and unloved for nearly two years, this classic Cotswold coaching inn has been restored to its former Georgian glory. Worn flagstones draw you into the cosy, wood-floored bar, where leather armchairs by the inglenook provide the perfect spot to cradle a pint of Hooky, or to ponder the Seagrave chefs' mouthwatering modern menu. Served at old dining tables in two warm and inviting candlelit rooms is delicious food: monkfish with beetroot, turnip, parsnip and pear cider sauce; partridge with smoked bacon, chestnut and salsify; crème brûlée and rhubarb; a slate of cheeses with damson jelly. Meat and game are sourced from local farms and shoots; everything – breads, chutneys, lunchtime burgers – is freshly prepared. Immaculate, well-designed bedrooms are the icing on the cake, the ground-floor ones in the annexe, the quietest at the back. Look forward to top-notch linen and down, fresh coffee, and high-spec bathrooms with scented soaps and walk-in showers. You're 20 minutes from Stratford-upon-Avon, and strolling distance from Chipping Campden and the Cotswold Way.

Rooms	7 doubles: £70-£180. 1 suite for 3: £119-£165.
Meals	Lunch, 2 courses, £15. Dinner, 3 courses, about £35.
Closed	Open all day.

The Manager
The Seagrave Arms,
Friday Street, Weston Subedge,
Chipping Campden, GL55 6QH

Tel +44 (0)1386 840192
Web www.seagravearms.com

Ebrington Arms

Ebrington

The glorious gardens at Hidcote Manor and Kiftsgate Court are a ramble across fields from the Ebrington Arms, lovingly restored and revived by Claire and Jim. Little has changed in the 17th-century bar, hub of the community and beloved by locals and tourists alike, cosy with low beams and roaring fires. Bag a seat on the settle and share own-brewed Yubby, Goldie or Yawnie with the regulars, or seek out the fun dining room next door. Worn stone floors, fresh flowers and a delightful mishmash of tables set the scene for some terrific pub food cooked from mostly local produce. Dishes are simple yet full of flavour, so dive in to scallops with celeriac purée and black pudding; calves' liver with garlic mash and caramelised onions; and apple, strawberry and ginger crumble. No need to negotiate the route home when you can bed down here; bedrooms (up steepish stairs) are full of charm, with chunky wooden beds, colourful throws, plump pillows, smart bathrooms and deep window seats with village or country views. Stratford-upon-Avon is close, too. A properly unpretentious inn, run by the nicest people. One of the best. *Minimum stay: two nights at weekends.*

Rooms	5 doubles: £110-£170.
Meals	Lunch & dinner £9-£17.50. Limited menu Sunday eve.
Closed	Open all day.

Claire & Jim Alexander
Ebrington Arms,
Ebrington,
Chipping Campden, GL55 6NH

Tel +44 (0)1386 593223
Web www.theebringtonarms.co.uk

Horse and Groom

Bourton-on-the-Hill

A lovely pub, now in the capable hands of Cirrus Inns, serving up excellent food and home-brewed ale. It stands at the top of the hill with big views stretching over the Cotswolds. Outside, you can sit in the shade of damson trees and watch chefs gather carrots from the kitchen garden and berries from the fruit cage. Inside, open fires lure you to the generous bar with its glorious marble top and gleaming ranks of bottles. Locals love it: they come for the craic, a pint of home-brewed ale and some deliciously local food, perhaps whole roast mallard with celeriac purée, sautéed spinach and dauphinoise potatoes followed by apple and rhubarb flapjack crumble. Uncluttered bedrooms have a contemporary country-house style: crisp linen, good art, smart fabrics, sparkling bathrooms. None are small, three are big, the garden room opens onto the terrace, those at the front are soundproofed to minimise noise from the road. Breakfast is your final feast: Tamworth sausages, smoked haddock, freshly squeezed orange juice, breads and jams and Jersey butter. A real treat.

Rooms	5 doubles: £110-£190. Singles £80.
Meals	Starters from £5. Mains from £11.
Closed	Sunday evenings.

Karl Solomon
Horse and Groom,
Bourton-on-the-Hill,
Moreton-in-Marsh, GL56 9AQ
Tel +44 (0)1386 700413
Web www.horseandgroom.info

The Lion Inn

Winchcombe

The determination to restore this old inn's charms has been a joyous success. Push open the heavy oak door to reveal a beautiful main bar: rugs on pale-painted floors, candles at mullioned windows, rough stone walls, and a log fire crackling in a 15th-century inglenook. Jugs of fresh flowers, battered leather armchairs and grand gilt-framed paintings enhance the authentic feel. Review the papers over a pint of real ale, play scrabble, cards or one of the selection of games. Order from the seasonal menu: perhaps slow roast pork belly with creamed potatoes, savoy cabbage, red wine jus and prunes, followed by honey and almond panna cotta. Country-chic rooms upstairs – one with its own small balcony, one above the lively snug bar – are toasty-warm and TV-free, with inviting beds and soothing colours, upholstered armchairs and antique furniture. Bathrooms are just as good, with Bramley products and en-suite showers. Winchcombe is on the Cotswold Way; Chipping Campden, Broadway and Cheltenham are a short drive.

Rooms	7 doubles: £110-£185. 1 suite for 3: £150-£195.
Meals	Lunch from £12. Dinner, 3 courses, £28.
Closed	Open all day.

Sue Chalmers
The Lion Inn,
North Street, Winchcombe,
Cheltenham, GL54 5PS

Tel +44 (0)1242 603300
Web www.thelionwinchcombe.co.uk

The Wheatsheaf

Northleach

The Wheatsheaf stands at the vanguard of a cool new movement: the village local reborn in country-house style. It's a winning formula with locals and travellers flocking in for a heady mix of laid-back informality and chic English style. The inn stands between pretty hills in this ancient wool village on the Fosse Way. Inside, happy young staff flit about, throwing logs on the fire, ferrying food to diners, or simply stopping for a chat. Downstairs, you find armchairs in front of smouldering fires, noble portraits on panelled walls, cool tunes playing in the background. Outside, a smart courtyard garden draws a crowd in summer, so much so it has its own bar; English ales, jugs of Pimm's and lovely wines all wait. Back inside, beautiful bedrooms come as standard, some bigger than others, all fully loaded with comfort and style. Expect period colours, Hypnos beds, Bang & Olufsen TVs, and spectacular bathrooms with beautiful baths and/or power showers. As for the food, you feast on lovely local fare, perhaps devilled kidneys, coq au vin, pear and almond tart. Don't miss it.

Rooms	14 doubles: £120-£180. Singles from £100.
Meals	Lunch from £9. Dinner, 3 courses, about £30. Bar meals from £5.
Closed	Open all day.

James Parn
The Wheatsheaf,
West End, Northleach,
Cheltenham, GL54 3EZ

Tel +44 (0)1451 860244
Web www.cotswoldswheatsheaf.com

Inn at Fossebridge

Fossebridge

Here, on the old Roman road, rusticity and elegance achieve the perfect balance at this gorgeous 17th-century coaching inn run with aplomb by Dee Ludlow. Stone archways divide the bar, with its flagstone floors, open fires, beamed ceilings and a hubbub at lunchtime. Throw in real ales, roast lunches and a welcome for all and you have somewhere very special. This place prides itself on serving really good pub food: prawn cocktail, fish and chips, cottage pie, good puddings. The pub garden is one of the largest and most attractive in the Cotswolds with a two-acre lake, mature trees, and barbecues in summer. Country-smart bedrooms, decorated in Georgian style, range from smallish to spacious. There's no separate sitting room but plenty of places to sit and read a paper. The two splendid holiday cottages in the grounds are perfect for big families: Stable Cottage sleeps four plus two children; Lakeside House sleeps 10. Walk from the pub up the River Coln valley and revel in glorious countryside. *Ask about mid-week offers.*

Rooms	8 doubles: £110-£160. 1 family room for 3: £185.
Meals	Bar meals £5.75-£9.50. Lunch & dinner £11-£21.50. Sunday lunch £14.50.
Closed	Open all day.

Dee Ludlow
Inn at Fossebridge,
Fossebridge,
Cirencester, GL54 3JS
Tel +44 (0)1285 720721
Web www.fossebridgeinn.co.uk

The Catherine Wheel

Bibury

The 15th-century Catherine Wheel is the only pub in its perfect honeypot location, offering excellent food in a friendly atmosphere. Three small rooms circle the bar, so you can tuck into a private corner, while a larger dining area overlooks the orchard beer garden with trees for climbing (and apples that find their way into puddings when the harvest is good). The affordable menu is packed with those comforting classics we all love: steak and red wine pie, fish and chips, Gloucester Old Spot sausage and mash, as well as some seriously good vegetarian dishes (beetroot bourguignon with crispy confit parsnips took our fancy) and of course the local Bibury trout, here served with olive and caper mash, creamed greens and truffle oil. Chef-owner Jeremy has twenty years' experience and real passion for what he does; you'll eat well. The menu changes daily – all washed down with real ales or wines from an excellent list. Across the car park: four neatly unpretentious bedrooms with spotless shower rooms. The best treat is the setting; William Morris called Bibury 'the most beautiful village in England.' You'll have no trouble seeing why.

Rooms	8 twin/doubles: £65-£110.
Meals	Lunch & dinner £5-£14. Sunday lunch £16 & £19.50.
Closed	Open all day (from 9am).

Carole White
The Catherine Wheel,
Arlington, Bibury,
Cirencester, GL7 5ND

Tel +44 (0)1285 740250
Web www.catherinewheel-bibury.co.uk

The New Inn at Coln

Coln St Aldwyns

The New Inn is old – 1632 to be exact – but well-named nonetheless. The pub stands in a handsome Cotswold village with ivy roaming on original stone walls and a sun-trapping terrace where roses bloom in summer and fire pits warm in winter. Airy interiors have low ceilings, painted beams, flagged floors and fires that roar – perfect for supping pints of real ale with the famous New Inn burger, or lingering over sea bass with crushed haricot beans and salsa verde, chicken and leek pie followed by ginger parfait, plum and almonds, served in red-walled dining rooms by thoroughly delightful staff. Bedrooms are a treat, all warmly elegant with soft carpets, swish bed throws, perfect white linen in good little bathrooms (a couple with claw-foot baths). There are wonky floors and the odd beam in the main house, while those in the Dovecote come in bold colours and have views across water meadows to the river; walks start from the door. Bibury, Burford and Stow are all close, so spread your wings.

Rooms	14 doubles: £80-£170. 1 single: £65.
Meals	Starters from £5. Mains from £11. Sunday lunch from £16.
Closed	Open all day.

Steve Cook
The New Inn at Coln,
Main Street, Coln St Aldwyns,
Cirencester, GL7 5AN

Tel +44 (0)1285 750651
Web www.new inn.co.uk

The Village Pub

Barnsley

An old favourite of locals and faithfuls from far and wide, this civilised Cotswold bolthole has been given a gentle facelift by Calcot Health & Leisure – owners of Barnsley House, the country-house hotel across the road. Expect seasonal food based on the best local produce, good-quality Hook Norton ale and decent wines. There's even a service hatch to the heated patio at the back, so you can savour the sauvignon until the sun goes down. Cotswold stone and ancient flags sing the country theme; past bar and open fires, quiet alcoves provide a snug setting that entices you to stay. If you do, tuck into crab and leek tart, rib-eye steak with béarnaise sauce, or whole plaice with crab and parsley butter; sweet tooths will love the warm ginger cake with rum and raisin ice cream. Classy, spruced-up bedrooms are equally cosy and inviting, with soothing colours, stylish fabrics, plasma screens and iPod docks. Two stunning four-poster rooms have big bathrooms with claw-foot baths, walk-in showers, posh toiletries. Roman Cirencester and gorgeous Bibury are close by; this is classic Cotswold country.

Rooms	4 twin/doubles, 2 four-posters: £99-£174.
Meals	Starters from £6. Mains from £11.
Closed	Open all day.

Michele Mella
The Village Pub,
Barnsley,
Cirencester, GL7 5EF
Tel +44 (0)1285 740421
Web www.thevillagepub.co.uk

The Fleece at Cirencester

Cirencester

Charles II once stayed at this pretty coaching inn, posing as a manservant, so the story goes. Now it's had a refurb in classic English style, and bar, lounge and restaurant glow. Open all day, the Fleece has quite a buzz. Drop by for a wake-up coffee and eggs on toast; choose a deli board at lunchtime and a pint of Thwaites. There are daily specials and Sunday roasts; our steak and chips was delicious. As for the staff, they're charming, well-trained, smartly turned out. Set off into the Cotswolds for a hike with the dog, browse the antique shops and the chic little delis, then come back to the Fleece for the night – ask about parking before you arrive, and make sure you've booked for dinner; it can get busy! The more spacious 'Character' rooms, with their beamy, up-in-the-roof feeling – lots of stairs – are the best, but all are top-notch, with plush carpets and dark boards, beds antique and new, coordinated cushions, modish wallpapers, plump pillows... face the famous market square and watch the world go by, or settle more quietly into a room at the back. The Fleece is a crowd-pleaser from start to finish.

Rooms	18 doubles, 4 twin/doubles: £85-£125. 5 suites for 2: £115-£150. 1 family room for 4: £75-£150.
Meals	Lunch from £6.95. Bar meals from £4.95. Dinner from £8.95. Sunday lunch, 2 courses, £11.95.
Closed	Open all day.

Philip Mehrtens
The Fleece at Cirencester,
Market Place, Cirencester, GL7 2NZ

Tel	+44 (0)1285 650231
Web	www.thwaites.co.uk/hotels-and-inns/inns/fleece-at-cirencester

Masons Arms

Meysey Hampton

In a bustling Cotswolds village, the old pub owned by Arkells, the family brewery from Swindon, stands proudly by the village green. Paul Fallows first worked here aged 16; now he's head honcho and full of plans. Enter the bar, uncluttered in a stylish way, just low beams, scrubbed tables, a parquet floor, a couple of wood-burners... the sort of place where young mums meet for coffee (beans roasted in Cirencester) and business folk for breakfast. The restaurant seats 40, with shining glasses on small square tables and good pictures on white walls. As for the food, it's simple, modern, classy: slow roast celeriac with feta and hazelnut granola; sea bream with fennel, samphire and crab salad; dry aged steak with chips, roast tomato and garlic butter. There are burgers too, and a dark chocolate delice, and in summer you spill onto the green. Up above: simple comfortable bedrooms, a work in progress, great value, two for families. Paul's focus is on "a great bed, a great shower, and excellent WiFi" – who could argue with that?

Rooms	5 doubles: £90-£100. 1 family room for 3, 1 family room for 4: £140-£150.
Meals	Starters from £6. Dinner from £12.
Closed	Mon-Fri 3pm-5pm. Sat & Sun open all day. Open 12-2pm Christmas Day. Closed Boxing Day eve & New Year's Day eve.

Paul Fallows
Masons Arms,
28 High Street,
Meysey Hampton, GL7 5JT
Tel +44 (0)1285 850164
Web www.masonsarmsmeyseyhampton.com

The Royal Oak Tetbury

Tetbury

Resplendent after a full refurbishment this 17th-century coaching inn is abuzz with enthusiasm. Inside, reclaimed floorboards have been artfully fitted together, a salvaged carved oak bar has its own little 'Groucho snug' at one end. Exposed stone and a real fire co-exist with a pretty Art Deco piano whose ivories are often tinkled. Cheery staff will pull you a pint of Uley or Stroud ale – or perhaps an Orchard Pig cider – and on certain days you can even mix your own Bloody Mary. Treats in store on the menu from head chef Richard Simms feature pub classics with a twist: sharing or small plates, hearty salads, 'oak pots' with a veggie or meat option served with crusty bread or brown rice and plenty of choice for vegans. Up in the roof beneath massive beams is a more formal restaurant with a spacious, calm atmosphere. Across the cobbled yard are six bedrooms – three are dog-friendly – with a restful elegance, dreamy beds and bathrooms to linger in. And if a special occasion is the reason for your visit then the Oak Lodge room will not fail to get things off to a very good start. Enjoy the view from the garden, glass of wine in hand.

Rooms	6 doubles: £85-£170.
Meals	Lunch & dinner £5-£13.
Closed	Open all day.

Kate Lewis
The Royal Oak Tetbury,
1 Cirencester Road,
Tetbury, GL8 8EY
Tel +44 (0)1666 500021
Web www.theroyaloaktetbury.co.uk

The King's Arms

Didmarton

Next to the main road in Didmarton, close to Tetbury and the Badminton Estate, is this recently refurbished inn – a perfect place in the Cotswolds. Expect beams and stone-flagged floors, inviting dark green walls adorned with antlers, fat candles on dining tables, lovely painted settles, and photos showcasing local history. There's a big old fireplace for winter, darts and dominoes in the bar, a lovely walled garden and a wood-fired pizza oven that's doing brisk business. Blackboard menus on the walls are chalked up daily. Pop in for a deli pizza with cured and spiced meats, the King's burger with cheese and chorizo, or sautéed mixed nut and herb polenta with cherry tomatoes and basil – you won't go home disappointed. Wash down with a fine wine or a local tipple – Bath Gem, Uley Bitter, perhaps one of their guest beers. If you fancy staying over, rooms upstairs are cosy and stylish, with comfy beds, crisp linen, down duvets and spotless shower rooms. A couple of cottages suitable for larger groups await in the coaching stable.

Rooms	4 doubles, 1 twin/double: £95-£140. 1 single: £60-£65. 1 cottage for 6, 1 cottage for 4: £120-£250.
Meals	Light lunch from £6.50. Mains from £12.95. Wood-fired pizzas, £9.50 (summer only).
Closed	Open all day.

Mark Birchall
The King's Arms,
The Street, Didmarton,
Badminton, GL9 1DT
Tel +44 (0)1454 238 245
Web www.kingsarmsdidmarton.co.uk

The Old Spot

Dursley

Nudged by a car park and Dursley's bus station is the charming Old Spot. Built in 1776 as a farm cottage, the pub has since gained national recognition among those who make pilgrimages to sample the brews. Indeed, the Old Spot has become something of a showcase for the beers of Uley Brewery, including Pig's Ear and Old Ric, the latter named after a former landlord. Real ciders include Weston's and Ashton Press. No surprise, for a pub named after a rare-breed pig, that there are porcine figurines and pictures dotted around, alongside old prints and posters. New head chef Ben is moving the menu up a notch and lunch sandwiches are terrific; try roast topside of beef with caramelised onions and mozzarella. Friendly, no-nonsense, traditional and on the Cotswold Way. For ale-lovers – a joy.

Meals	Starters from £4.75. Lunch from £8.75. No food in evening.
Closed	Open all day.

Ellie Sainty
The Old Spot,
2 Hill Road, Dursley, GL11 4JQ
Tel +44 (0)1453 542870
Web www.oldspotinn.co.uk

Gloucestershire

Old Badger Inn

Springhill

From unloved boozer to village hub – that's some journey. The Old Badger's success is down to its owners who, friendly and laid back, have brought real beer to the village. Ellie has run pubs for over 20 years and knows her trade so everyone – farmers, office workers, walkers, old, young – goes home happy. Inside are stone and wood floors, a mishmash of tables, gleaming pumps at the bar and – of course – beer mats on the ceiling. There's a log burner for winter, a big garden and a heated patio, and a separate drinking/dining room that welcomes families. If you're here for the beer, and many are, they offer Butcombe and a wide-ranging choice of ever-changing ales, mostly local. (There's wine if you must! Twelve by the glass.) On the menu? Hearty pub grub, freshly cooked including the Pie of the Day, and lovely roasts on Sundays.

Meals	Starters from £5.85. Mains from £9.95.
Closed	Open all day.

Ellie Sainty
Old Badger Inn,
Alkerton Road, Springhill,
Eastington, GL10 3AT
Tel +44 (0)1453 822892
Web www.oldbadgerinn.co.uk

The Ostrich Inn

Newland

In the village of Newland the Ostrich is where the beer drinkers go, to sample eight changing ales. Across from All Saints Church, that 'Cathedral of the Forest', you mix with all sorts before a log fire. Walkers and trail bikers pile in for massive portions of delicious food, from Newland bread and cheese platter to rump of Welsh spring lamb with rich orange and cardamom sauce or spicy merguez sausages and crisp diced potato. The nicotine-brown ceiling that looks in danger of imminent collapse is supported by a massive oak pillar in front of the bar where the locals chatter and jazz CDs keep the place swinging. The weekly menu, served throughout the pub, takes a step up in class, and is excellent value. Energetic Kathryn and her team, including Alfie the pub dog, encourage the buzz. To the back is a walled garden – and the loos.

Meals — Lunch & dinner £12.50-£18.50. Bar meals £5.50-£10.50.
Closed — 3pm-6.30pm (6pm Sat).

Kathryn Horton
The Ostrich Inn,
Newland,
Coleford, GL16 8NP
Tel +44 (0)1594 833260
Web www.theostrichinn.com

Entry 217 Map 7

Gloucestershire

The Woolpack Inn

Slad

If you walk through the Slad Valley one midsummer morning be sure to stop off here and raise a glass of well-kept Stroud or Uley to Laurie Lee, whose image adorns the walls a century after his birth. Unashamedly authentic, this tiny, lively, community focused pub packs them in and serves up great entertainment and fresh, local food with a no-nonsense approach to constantly changing small menus. Munch on bacon sandwiches or char-grilled local rib-eye steak with roast field mushrooms and chips, or fat, juicy mussels in a cider, cream and parsley sauce – delicious! In summer the terrace is packed with those eager for the idyllic valley views and impromptu ukulele-themed jam nights are not unheard of either. Pizza on Mondays and live music Wednesdays.

Meals — Lunch & dinner £8.95-£16.50. Sunday lunch from £8.95.
Closed — Open all day.

Hannah Thompson
The Woolpack Inn,
Slad Road, Slad,
Stroud, GL6 7QA
Tel +44 (0)1452 813429
Web www.thewoolpackslad.com

Entry 218 Map 8

The Ragged Cot

Minchinhampton

The handsome old stone coaching inn stands alongside 600 acres of National Trust common land close to Gatcombe Park – ideal for walking off a fabulous lunch. The Cot's been on this spot since the 17th century so expect exposed stone walls, lovely low windows, thoughtful modern touches, and a light-filled dining room overlooking the big garden. Inside, you are blissfully snug, tucked into a corner by the log fire. You can pop in for a perfect cup of coffee (all too rare in many pubs, but not at the Cot), and it's hard to resist the lunch and dinner menus. Try roasted breast of chicken in thyme butter with crushed sweet potato, followed by apple and winter berry crumble with spiced topping and fresh custard. Wellies, dogs and children are all made welcome.

Meals Starters from £4.50.
Mains from £10.50.

Closed Open all day.

Stuart Hanson
The Ragged Cot,
Cirencester Road, Minchinhampton,
Stroud, GL6 8PE

Tel +44 (0)1453 884643

Web www.theraggedcot.co.uk

Entry 219 Map 8

The Butchers Arms

Oakridge Lynch

Alison and Philip are a great team for this lovely village pub with Philip front of house, a cheery soul and deeply efficient, and Alison (a trained chef) concentrating on good honest food, beautifully cooked and well presented: homemade fishcakes; deep-fried garlic mushrooms with chilli and lime aïoli; pan seared scallops, black pudding and pancetta served with curried cauliflower, greens and a saffron sauce; delightful puddings. Seasonal treats include a lamb burger topped with tomato, tzatziki, orange and mint chilli sauce. Settle in front of a roaring fire or a warming wood-burner with a choice of hand pumped ales or something from the well-priced wine menu. The Golden Valley is a mecca for walkers, and dogs and welly-wearing guests are welcome. Locals clearly love it here, and why not? It's a home from home.

Meals Lunch from £5.95.
Dinner from £9.95.

Closed Open all day.

Philip McLaughlin
The Butchers Arms,
Oakridge Lynch,
Stroud, GL6 7NZ

Tel +44 (0)1285 760371

Web www.butchersarmsoakridge.com

Entry 220 Map 8

The Plough Inn

Kelmscott

Once the summer haunt of William Morris, Kelmscott was to him 'a heaven on earth', and many today might well agree. Resolutely bucolic, it's the perfect spot for a few nights' break, to walk, tour the area, pop into town, or simply snooze away an afternoon on the banks of the Thames. It's also a place for foodies, who come for owner-chef Sebastian Snow's distinctive dishes: quail's eggs or monkfish, scampi and chips served in the bar, or 'mallard two ways' followed by dark rum and chocolate mousse in the restaurant. Real ales and wines by the glass or carafe feature on a worldly drinks menu. The old Cotswold stone building doesn't disappoint either, replete with flagstones, scrubbed pine tables, exposed beams and cosy corners. There are roaring fires in the winter and a garden for summer. Linger a while and make a day of it.

Meals	Lunch from £4.50. Dinner from £16. No food Monday evenings.
Closed	Open all day.

Sebastian & Lana Snow
The Plough Inn,
Kelmscott,
Lechlade, GL7 3HG

Tel +44 (0)1367 253543
Web www.theploughinnkelmscott.com

Entry 221 Map 8

Gloucestershire

The Swan at Southrop

Southrop

Welcome to a village inn on a village green with fires in the grate, dogs in the bar, and a potted pheasant so rich and gamey you'll find yourself asking for the recipe (our inspector did). Here on the Southrop Estate they keep their own chickens, grow their own salads and vegetables, bake their own bread, and employ a chef, Matt Wardman, who is brilliant at creating gutsy flavours from abundant local produce. Sip a pint of Doom Bar on the benches out front, enjoy the sun in the two new walled gardens with their outside bar, and then retire to the big, elegant, log-fired dining room for a slap-up meal; there's a kids' menu, too. The bar, full of quaffing locals on a Friday night, is similarly affable, and if you fancy a simple sandwich you know it will be first class.

Meals	Lunch & dinner £12.50-£17.
Closed	2.30pm-7pm (3pm-7pm Sat & Sun). Closed from 10pm every day.

Lydia Sheehan
The Swan at Southrop,
Southrop,
Lechlade, GL7 3NU

Tel +44 (0)1367 850205
Web www.theswanatsouthrop.co.uk

Entry 222 Map 8

The Five Alls

Filkins

The Snows have swapped the Swan at Southrop for a handsome 18th-century pub in postcard-pretty Filkins. The faded old coaching inn is back on track, once again full of warmth and personality. The bar throngs with locals and foaming pints of Brakspear, there are 15 wines by the glass and proper bar food: devilled kidneys on toast, hearty soups, fish and chips. Bright cotton cushions on cosy leather sofas front the inglenook, candles glow in lanterns and soft music plays; arrive early if you fancy a pre-dinner drink. Then it's into the dining room for Italian inspired British dishes – potted shrimps; roast lamb with beans, mash and salsa verde; drunken panna cotta with raspberries – served at old dining tables. Heaps of charm too, thanks to rugs on stone floors, modern art on stone walls and jugs of fresh flowers.

Meals: Lunch & dinner from £12. Set lunch £15 & £19. Sunday lunch £16.
Closed: Open all day.

Sebastian & Lana Snow
The Five Alls,
Filkins,
Lechlade, GL7 3JQ
Tel +44 (0)1367 860875
Web www.thefiveallsfilkins.co.uk

Entry 223 Map 8

Gloucestershire

The Keepers Arms

Quenington

It is sturdy, 18th century, refreshingly authentic and recently restored. Inside: a log-burner in a stone fireplace, earthy colours on the walls, pub furniture and one lovely large oak table. Landlord John has a sense of humour and loves his ale (Otter, Butcombe, Timothy Taylors...); Denzil the border terrier is an instant friend. You'll find yourself rubbing shoulders with locals sampling the pints, and enjoying straightforward, rib-stickin', filling good food. You might have a pint of prawns with Marie Rose dressing, or battered fish and chips with peas, or roast beef with all the trimmings, and find space for banoffee pie. Nine miles from Cirencester, the pub is in the centre of a charming village, with views over the Coln Valley to be enjoyed from the small stone terrace at the front.

Meals: Lunch & dinner £10.95-£16.50.
Closed: 3pm-6pm Wed-Sat. 4pm-7pm Sun. Mon-Tue open from 7pm.

Jon & Michelle Gardiner
The Keepers Arms,
Church Road, Quenington,
Cirencester, GL7 5BL
Tel +44 (0)1285 750349
Web www.thekeepersarms.co.uk

Entry 224 Map 8

The Victoria Inn

Eastleach Turville

The golden-stoned Victoria pulls in the locals – whatever their age, whatever the weather – propping up the bar, with or without dogs or tucking into home cooking by the log fire. A simple village hostelry on the outside, it's deceptively spacious inside, and the Richardsons, in spite of opening up the interior, have kept the character and cosiness intact. The low-ceilinged and flagstoned bar offers darts, conversation and pints of Arkells 3B, while the L-shaped dining room is the backdrop for tasty platefuls of fresh food: perhaps salmon fishcakes; pork and leek sausages; slow-roasted lamb shank with garlic potatoes and red wine sauce. There are picnic tables out at the front, from where you can look down onto the stone cottages of two pretty villages. A very charming spot for a country stroll.

Meals Lunch & dinner £7.95-£14.75.
Closed 3pm-7pm.

Stephen & Susan Richardson
The Victoria Inn,
Eastleach Turville,
Cirencester, GL7 3NQ
Tel +44 (0)1367 850277
Web www.victoriainneastleach.co.uk

Entry 225 Map 8

Gloucestershire

Seven Tuns

Chedworth

Hiding in a lush valley – you can see why the Romans chose this spot – are the protected mosaics of Chedworth, a huge draw. Nearby, down several winding lanes, is the Seven Tuns, a handsome Cotswolds pub, once lost and forlorn, now transformed – thanks to landlord Liz. Now there are dog biscuits behind the bar (along with Hooky and Otter), roaring fires in grates, and a warm and modern décor. Menus change regularly and the food is superb. Try wood pigeon with carrot relish and coriander, hake fillet with fennel and tomato compote, Longhorn burger with brioche and frites, "finest British cheeses," apple and berry crumble. Tuesday is steak night, Friday fish, and once a month you get a tasting menu paired with wines. It's a place for foodies that's for sure – but there's open mic night, skittles too, and even toys for kids. Fabulous.

Meals Starters from £6. Mains from £12.
Closed Mon-Thurs 3pm-6pm.
Open all day Fri-Sun.

Liz Henty
Seven Tuns,
Queen Street,
Chedworth, GL54 4AE
Tel +44 (0)1285 720630
Web www.seventuns.co.uk/home

Entry 226 Map 8

The Beehive

Cheltenham

Don't miss this: it's in Montpellier. Regency with Victorian additions, high ceilings, sash windows and a proper ale house feel. Dogs will head for the wood-burner downstairs while the Supper Room upstairs is a lofty gem, decked out with cast iron chandeliers, and long tables. "Custodian" Steve is another draw and his staff know their beers: no surprise the locals return. Pick a stool at the bar and order a Prescott brew or Cotswold Lion with your smoked salmon sandwiches, sausages with mash, or vegetable dahl with crusty bread; the food is executed with care and passion. Head upstairs for twice-cooked old spot belly pork with chorizo and bean cassoulet, followed by white chocolate cheesecake. In summer, spill out the back into the walled garden and let kids and dogs off leads. Perfect to unwind after a day at Cheltenham races.

Meals — Starters from £5. Lunch from £8. Dinner from £14. Sunday lunch, 1-3 courses, £12-£18.

Closed — Open all day.

Tommy Mark
The Beehive,
1-3 Montpellier Villas,
Cheltenham, GL50 2XE

Tel — +44 (0)1242 702270

Web — www.thebeehivemontpellier.com

Entry 227 Map 8

The Tavern

Cheltenham

From breakfasts of boiled eggs and soldiers to slow roast Sunday lunches and scrumptious Butts Farm burgers with slaw and fries, the menus say it all: this is a modern no-frills place with food to match. Bang in the middle of Cheltenham, it is a sister pub to the Cotswolds' Wheatsheaf Inn and attracts an urban crowd in search of cocktails and a plate or two to share; the food is modern American and British dishes with splashes of Asian and Mediterranean. The lower bar where you enter has high-legged metal chairs at reclaimed wooden tables and a warehousey brick wall; the more peaceful upstairs is a loft-like place with chunky trestle tables for sociable groups and an open kitchen so you can see the chefs perform. DJs on Saturdays, their own popcorn machine... this tavern is young and fun.

Meals — Starters £5-£6. Mains £6-£17.

Closed — Open all day.

The Manager
The Tavern,
5 Royal Well Place,
Cheltenham, GL50 3DN

Tel — +44 (0)1242 221212

Web — www.thetaverncheltenham.com

Entry 228 Map 8

The Kilcot Inn

Newent

Handsome and Grade II-listed, it's hard to believe that this pub once lay derelict and unloved. Now a real hive of activity, the Kilcot's had new life breathed into it by affable landlord Mark, bringing in families and foodies alike. Blond oak beams grace the ceiling, floors are flagged with stone and Wye Valley beer and Westons Organic cider feature behind the brick bar. Chef Richard knows every gamekeeper, farmer and fishmonger for miles, and his menus are full of the area's finest and freshest fare: start with wood pigeon pastrami, pickled beets, balsamic and orange jelly, feast on fillet of Blagdon Lake trout with sorrel hollandaise, linger over the gold-topped chocolate mousse cake. There's a pretty terrace with views for summer sipping, Ross-on-Wye and Ledbury are close and it's the perfect stop for walkers and cyclists.

Meals	Starters from £5.50. Lunch from £9.50. Dinner from £10.95.
Closed	Open all day.

Mark Lawrence
The Kilcot Inn,
Ross Road,
Newent, GL18 1NA
Tel +44 (0)1989 720707
Web www.kilcotinn.com

Gloucestershire

The Boat Inn

Ashleworth

This extraordinary, and tiny, pub has been in the family since Charles II granted them a licence – for liquor and exclusive ferrying rights. A peaceful rosy-brick cottage on the banks of the Severn, it's an ale-lover's paradise, an absolute gem. The choice of beer changes regularly and small local brewers are preferred. Settle back with a pint of Beowulf, Church End or Archer's in the gleaming front parlour, bright with garden flowers, a huge built-in settle and a deal table fronting an old kitchen range – or in the spotless bar. On sunny summer days you can laze by the river. Real ale straight from the cask, Westons farm cider, a bar of chocolate, a packet of crisps... There's no 'jus' here; lunchtime meals are fresh filled rolls with homemade chutney.

Meals	Filled rolls only.
Closed	2.30pm-7pm (3pm-7pm Sat & Sun). Wed lunch & all day Mon.

Mark Fox
The Boat Inn,
The Quay, Ashleworth,
Gloucester, GL19 4HZ
Tel +44 (0)1452 700272
Web www.boat-inn.co.uk

The Horse & Groom Village Inn

Upper Oddington

Cotswold stone, hanging baskets, hefty beams and flagstone floors, and logs around the double fireplace… is this a pub from central casting? It's 500 years old and Simon and Sally have rejuvenated without losing the charm. There's a good selection of guest ales, some from local microbreweries: choose from Wye Valley Best, Prescott Hill Climb, Chuffin Ale. Cider and lager, including Cotswold Premium, come from the Cotswold Brewing Co. nearby. The menu takes a tour of Europe, and there's traditional English too: shin of beef and root vegetable casserole; fillet of haddock topped with a chorizo, lime and parmesan crust; game from the Adlestrop Estate. Produce is organic whenever possible, breads and puddings are homemade, and there are 25 wines by the glass.

Meals	Bar meals from £4.50. Lunch & dinner from £12.50. Sunday lunch from £15.
Closed	3pm-5.30pm.

David Ashfield
The Horse & Groom Village Inn,
Upper Oddington, GL56 0XH
Tel +44 (0)1451 830584
Web www.horseandgroomoddington.com

Entry 231 Map 8

Gloucestershire

The Churchill Arms

Paxford

This lovely local sits in a tiny village with views across open country – you can follow footpaths across the fields to Chipping Campden. Outside, stone walls drip with wisteria. Inside you'll find a smart bar for local ales, low beamed ceilings, painted panelling and a roaring fire. It's exactly the sort of place lots of us love these days: stylish and informal with fantastic food. Nick, a Gordon Ramsay scholar who cooked at Soho House, hung up his London apron to come home and do his thing. Good food lies at the heart of it all – nothing overly complicated, just great produce cooked to perfection, perhaps smoked haddock soufflé, pork T-bone with apple and crackling, chocolate and salted caramel tart; the rare roast beef on Sundays is worth a detour. There's a small garden for summer days, and Stratford and Oxford are close.

Meals	Lunch from £5.95. Dinner, 3 courses, £25-£35. Sunday lunch from £14.50.
Closed	Sunday nights & Mondays.

Nick Deverell-Smith
The Churchill Arms,
Paxford,
Chipping Campden, GL55 6XH
Tel +44 (0)1386 593159
Web www.churchillarms.co

Entry 232 Map 8

The Fox Inn

Lower Oddington

Close to the grandeur of Cotswold country houses, the Fox evokes a sense of times past, all low ceilings, worn flagstones, log fire in winter and exciting, imaginative food. The bar has scrubbed pine tables topped with fresh flowers and candles, newspapers, magazines and ales on tap, and rag-washed ochre walls that date back years. Eat here or in the elegant, rose-red dining room, or on the terrace (heated on cool nights) of the cottage garden. We enjoyed a delicious, subtly spiced imam bayildi; cassoulet de luxe, a classic with a twist; a flavourful roasted red pepper tart; dark chocolate torte. Whatever you choose, there are 60 wines to match. Before you leave, explore the honeystone village and 11th-century church, known for its fascinating frescos. The Cotswolds wrap around you for walking, so you can indulge free from guilt.

Meals	Lunch & dinner £9.50-£19.50.
Closed	3.30pm-6pm (5pm-7pm Sun).

Graham Williams
The Fox Inn,
Lower Oddington,
Moreton-in-Marsh, GL56 0UR
Tel +44 (0)1451 870555
Web www.thefoxatoddington.com

Photo: The Mexico Inn, entry 98

The Wellington Arms

Baughurst

Lost down a web of lanes, the 'Welly' draws foodies from miles around. Cosy, relaxed and decorated in style – old dining tables, crystal decanters, terracotta floor – the newly extended bar-dining room fills quickly, so make sure you book to sample Jason's inventive modern cooking. Boards are chalked up daily and the produce mainly home-grown or organic. Kick off with home-grown courgette flowers stuffed with ricotta, parmesan and lemon zest, follow with rack of home-reared lamb with root vegetable mash and crab apple jelly, finish with elderflower jelly, strawberry and raspberry sorbet. Migrate to the huge garden for summer meals and views of the pub's small holding: seven little pigs, nine woolly sheep, a few bees and almost 100 assorted hens; buy the eggs at the bar. Stay over and get cosy in any one of the four rooms, housed in the former wine store and pig shed. Expect exposed brick and beams, vast Benchmark beds topped with goose down duvets, fresh flowers, coffee machines, mini-fridges, and slate tiled bathrooms with underfloor heating and walk-in rain showers. Breakfast too is a treat.

Rooms	4 doubles: £110-£200.
Meals	Set lunch £15.75 & £18.75. Dinner £11-£21.
Closed	Mondays-Saturdays 3pm-6pm. Sundays from 5pm.

Jason King & Simon Page
The Wellington Arms,
Baughurst Road,
Baughurst, RG26 5LP
Tel +44 (0)118 982 0110
Web www.thewellingtonarms.com

The Yew Tree

Highclere

The attractive brick Yew Tree stands beside the A343 south of the village and is perfect for visiting Highclere Castle (of Downton Abbey fame). A contemporary makeover stitches a rambling dining room into the old fabric of this 16th-century building, all inglenooks, timbers and uncluttered walls. Expect an elegant air, cracking log fires, rugs on red and black tiled floors, glowing candles on old dining tables, leather wall benches and wing chairs. From the beautiful copper-topped bar order great coffee or a pint of Upham ale and peruse the papers in a cosy corner. The best of British food is championed here: carpaccio of Trinley Estate White Park beef; cumin-spiced Faccombe partridge with turmeric and coriander rice, Brixham plaice with lemon brown butter; baked plum and mulled apple crumble. Cottagey rooms are compact and come with beams, statement William Morris wallpaper, tartan blankets, the finest linen and down, and fresh bathrooms with storm showers and bathrobes; ground floor rooms have dog beds and water bowls.

Rooms	8 doubles: £99-£129.
Meals	Light lunch from £6.95. Mains from £14.95. Sunday lunch from £10.95.
Closed	Open all day.

The Manager
The Yew Tree,
Hollington Cross, Andover Road,
Highclere, Newbury, RG20 9SE
Tel +44 (0)1635 253360
Web www.theyewtree.co.uk

Bel & the Dragon Kingsclere

Kingsclere

Today's version of this inviting red brick building is a happy mix of old and new, with friendly staff keen that both locals and visitors enjoy themselves. On a corner in the centre of Kingsclere, it has been a hostelry since the 15th-century when royalty galloped into town and, it's said, billeted their stable boys here. Now families and dog-lovers, country and business folk, gather in the different spaces of the bar: cosy with exposed brick and inglenook fire; casual with benches and wood block floor and rather smarter with blue velvet club chairs. And dine in the attractive beamed dining room with its booths and private spaces for parties, where pastel colours complement the red brick. Food is local where possible and menus follow the seasons, imaginatively. Wines are well-chosen; Sipsmith gin/vodka is the house brand. Those staying have a generous drawing room to retreat to with drinks and trendy grey cushion-backed sofas, a chess board, books and games. Bedrooms, not huge, are comfortably stylish and underfloor–heated, with white linen and throws in pretty blues, mauves and greens. Bathrooms are great, too.

Rooms	8 doubles: £95-£125.
Meals	Breakfast from £4. Lunch from £7. Dinner from £10.
Closed	Rarely.

The Manager
Bel & the Dragon Kingsclere,
Swan Street,
Kingsclere, RG20 5PP

Tel	+44 (0)1635 299342
Web	belandthedragon-kingsclere.co.uk

The George & Dragon

Hurstbourne Tarrant

Some places feel right the moment you step in; this is one of them. A handsome, 16th-century pub, it stands by the road in the village, its coaching inn spirit intact. Original fireplaces, windows, postal slots… all has been finely finessed. Inside are flagstone floors, old beams, curtains in tweed and check. There are two wood-burners, an open fire, a welcome for dogs, crayons for kids, and a tip-top pint of HBT Village Ale from Betteridge's. Chat at the bar, get cosy in a corner, book up a special meal… it's all so atmospheric you could imagine Jane Austen dropping by (she stayed up the road at Ibthorpe Manor). Staff are attentive and engaging, the menus are seasonal and the food is fabulous: charcuterie from Parsonage Farm, lemon and chickpea samosas, chargrilled rib-eye, fish from Cornwall, game from the shoots, dark chocolate torte. If you don't want to leave, then stay: eight rooms with charming sash windows, including one for families, wait above, stylish, serene and immaculate. Carpeting is soft, textiles are beautiful (lined curtains, wood blankets), small bathrooms are perfect.

Rooms	7 doubles: £75-£95. 1 family room for 4: £100-£125.
Meals	Starters £5.95-£9.50. Mains £7.95-£21.95.
Closed	Open all day.

Patrick Vaughan-Fowler
The George & Dragon,
The Square, Hurstbourne Tarrant,
Andover, SP11 0AA

Tel +44 (0)1264 736277
Web www.georgeanddragon.com

The White Hart

Overton

The White Hart, a listed building on the edge of a smart Hampshire town, is steeped in history: beams, wonky floors, Tudor carvings on a stone mantelpiece. It is also bang up to date. The terrace, family-friendly, and with a heated awning, is great for summer, while the lounge bar is cosy and atmospheric – delightful for a drink and a chat. There are comfy country armchairs in leather and stripes, antlers on the walls, board games to play, newspapers to browse… stay all day. If you like to eat, there are three restaurant areas (one a former magistrate's court room: elegant and photogenic); the food is classic British with a French twist, and the chef trained with Marco Pierre White. There's a kids' menu too. The pub's country-chic feel continues into the bedrooms, most of which, warm, wood-floored and dog-friendly, are in the stable block. Splash out if you can on a superior room in the pub itself, where ethic-inspired bedspreads blend with muted velvet upholstery and the bathrooms are fabulous. The Bombay Sapphire Distillery is a mile off, so book in for a cocktail master class, then head down here!

Rooms	2 doubles, 9 twin/doubles, 1 twin: £100-£170.
Meals	Lunch & dinner from £11.50.
Closed	Open all day from 7.30am Mon-Fri (from 8am Sat-Sun).

Helen Zivanovic
The White Hart,
London Road,
Overton, RG25 3NW
Tel +44 (0)1256 771431
Web www.whitehartoverton.co.uk

The Hawk Inn

Amport

Ales at the Hawk Inn haven't travelled far: the traditional pub was recently bought by Hampshire-based Upham Brewery and the public areas have had a complete makeover. Perch with a pint at the bar, settle into comfy fireside sofas or retreat to the Den, with its well-stocked bookshelves, for quiet meals away from the buzz of the restaurant. On sunny days head for the terrace out front, with views across the field to Pill Hill Brook. Food is modern and British, from light lunches to Sunday roasts: beetroot, watercress and shallot salad, venison and mushroom pie, sticky toffee pudding, plus interesting veggie dishes such as courgette pancakes with wild mushrooms, blue cheese, spinach and pistachios. Wine drinkers choose from an international selection by the glass. With the Hawk Conservancy, motorsports and Lutyens gardens nearby, it's worth staying over. Comfortable beds, quality linen, toiletries and fluffy towels are standard in the heather-hued rooms, all with fresh en suites. Expect a friendly welcome from Becky and her team, and a throng of people for cooked breakfast after a hearty morning walk.

Rooms	5 doubles, 1 twin/double, 1 twin: £90-£100. 2 suites for 4: £130.
Meals	Lunch from £6. Dinner from £11.50. Sunday lunch from £13.50.
Closed	Open all day.

Rebecca Anderson
The Hawk Inn,
Amport,
Andover, SP11 8AE
Tel +44 (0)1264 710371
Web www.hawkinnamport.co.uk

The Peat Spade

Longstock

Hampshire is as lovely as any county in England, deeply rural with lanes that snake through verdant countryside. As if to prove the point, the Peat Spade serves up a menu of boundless simplicity and elegance. First there's this dreamy thatched village in the Test valley, then there's the inn itself, always packed to the gunnels with lip-licking locals. Behind the lozenge-paned windows a Roberts radio on the bar brings news of English cricket, gilt mirrors sparkle above smouldering fires, candles illuminate chunky tables, and fishing rods hang from the ceiling – fishing packages can be arranged with local ghillies. There's a horseshoe bar, two private dining rooms, a roof terrace for summer breakfasts and the food is fabulous – mussels with cider and bacon; stone bass with chilli and crab risotto; sirloin steak with triple-cooked chips and peppercorn sauce. Lovely rooms above the bar and in the Peat House next door, come in fired earth colours with sisal matting, big wooden beds, top mattresses, crisp white linen – the works. Stroll the Test Valley Way, visit Stockbridge, Salisbury and Winchester, all are close.

Rooms	6 doubles, 2 twin/doubles: £100-£130.
Meals	Bar snacks £4.50. Starters £6-£9.50. Mains £12.50-£27.
Closed	Open all day.

Richard & Liza McBain
The Peat Spade,
Village Street, Longstock,
Stockbridge, SO20 6DR

Tel	+44 (0)1264 810612
Web	www.peatspadeinn.co.uk

The Running Horse

Littleton

The Upham pubs are known and admired for the age of their buildings and their retro-country makeovers. This one is no exception. Built in the 1850s and painted a stylish grey, the Running Horse, set back from the road into the village and with fields behind, is wonderfully close to Winchester. Enter to find a spacious interior of wooden floors and buttonback banquettes, mahogany bar stools with red leather tops, and smartly restored 1930s furniture. Chirpy staff serve well-kept Upham's ales, decently priced wines, malt whiskies, cocktails, real ciders, fancy sandwiches (focaccia, ciabatta or doorstep) and tasty pub food. You could choose prawn and chorizo pasta in a tomato sauce, or steak and ale pie with seasonal veg, and children have their own menu. Smokers are spoiled with a stylish, cushioned, heated hut. At the back lie nine peaceful, ground-floor bedrooms in a V-shaped annexe by the beer garden. Designer-decorated in simple rustic style, they come with brightly striped pillow cases and blinds, cafetières, free WiFi and spotless modern bathrooms.

Rooms	6 doubles, 2 twins: £105. 1 family room for 4: £135.
Meals	Starters £6-£9. Mains £12-£18.50.
Closed	Open all day.

Anita Peel
The Running Horse,
88 Main Road, Littleton,
Winchester, SO22 6QS

Tel	+44 (0)1962 880218
Web	www.runninghorseinn.co.uk

The Woolpack Inn

Totford

It's hard to fault this lovely little inn, deep in the Candover Valley. Its brick and flint exterior dates to 1880, views shoot across fields to a distant church, and there are terraces to the front and the side. Dogs doze by the fire, walkers and cyclists quench their thirst with pints of Woolpack, and shooting parties drop in by season. It's been refurbished in style, so expect striped banquettes and high-backed leather chairs in the dining room and a nice woody feel in the bar. The seasonal menu has a broad appeal, ranging from pub classics like burgers with smoked cheddar and Heineken-battered fish to more modish dishes like confit pork belly with potato gratin, and – of course! – game sourced within five miles. Sunday lunch is madly popular – don't forget to book. Hike, bike, visit Winchester Cathedral just over the hill, then return to cosy bedrooms named after game birds with brick and flint walls, big firm beds, gun cupboards and dark leather furnishings, storm showers and natural toiletries; those on the ground floor are ideal for dog owners.

Rooms	6 doubles: £100-£130. 1 suite for 4: £130.
Meals	Bar meals from £6. Mains from £12.50.
Closed	Open all day.

The Manager
The Woolpack Inn,
Totford, Northington,
Alresford, SO24 9TJ

Tel +44 (0)1962 734184
Web www.thewoolpackinn.co.uk

The Hawkley Inn

Hawkley

A chatty mix of farmers, walkers, dogs, and lovers of real ale beat a path to this little inn near Jane Austen's Chawton, in a sleepy village at the end of plunging lanes – blink and you miss it. The Hawkley's several front bars remain delightfully no-frills (a 'listed' carpet, scrubbed tables, a vast moose head above a roaring fire) while the rear extension adds a touch of modernity. Bag a pew, or a picnic table in summer, and check out the brews of Hampshire and West Sussex: Bowmans, Langhams, Flowerpots, Flack Manor (they know their beers). Or tuck into home-cooked pub grub of the tastiest kind: steak and kidney pie; pork belly with pea purée; partridge and duck in season; chickpea fritters with warm tomato salad; Sunday roasts. The wine list includes some excellent bottles and however busy it gets, the staff are the best. Problem is, once you've settled in, you can't leave, so tip-toe up the carpeted stairs to one of six bedrooms above. Pristine in creams and magnolias, two facing the beer garden, the rest the fields, they're comfy and cosy and offer decanters for wee drams of whiskey before bed!

Rooms	4 doubles, 1 twin: £85-£95. 1 family room for 4: £85-£95.
Meals	Starters & light bites from £4. Mains from £10. Sunday lunch from £13.
Closed	3pm-5.30pm. Open all day Sat & Sun.

Andy Ranson
The Hawkley Inn,
Pococks Lane,
Hawkley, Liss, GU33 6NE

Tel +44 (0)1730 827205
Web www.hawkleyinn.co.uk

The Old Vine

Winchester

You are in a small square overlooking the cathedral and mature trees. This red-bricked Georgian building has sash windows and hanging baskets – all tickety-boo and smart. Walk straight into the bustling bar with its beamed ceiling, upright timbers, open fires and a partly covered outdoor terrace for sunny days where a cheerful team serve Ringwood Best and three guest ales on rotation; the wine list has helpful comments to accompany the specials board. If you get peckish after all the quaffing, you can have anything from a hearty sandwich (Hampshire pork sausages and red onion relish) to Scottish salmon fillet with Hampshire watercress and crème fraîche sauce, then homemade butterscotch and treacle sponge pudding and custard or some excellent local cheese. Retire upstairs to rather posh bedrooms, with a mix of antique-looking and contemporary furniture. Colour schemes are muted with dashes of bold on throws and cushions, mahogany sleigh beds are deep and comfortable and you can splash about in bathrooms flaunting fluffy towels and gleaming taps.

Rooms	4 doubles, 1 twin/double: £120-£200. 1 annexe for 3: £160-£190.
Meals	Lunch & dinner £10.95-£19.50.
Closed	Open all day.

Ashton Gray
The Old Vine,
8 Great Minster Street,
Winchester, SO23 9HA
Tel +44 (0)1962 854616
Web www.oldvinewinchester.com

The King's Head

Hursley

The King's Head dates back to 1810 and stands opposite Hursley's ancient church. The pub was once a coaching inn linking London to the New Forest. These days the feel is half country pub, half country house. You find armchairs in front of roaring fires, shuttered windows in a Georgian dining room and, in the bar, excellent ales on tap. Elegant bedrooms are a treat. Two have slipper baths, all have warm colours, fancy bathrooms, soft carpeting and comfy beds. Some are smaller, as is reflected in the price; a couple have space for sofas. Back downstairs, delicious rustic fare awaits in bar and restaurant alike, try local Hursley venison loin with game faggot, beetroot and potato terrine and beetroot purée, or seaweed-wrapped hake with chorizo, baby potatoes, edamame and borlotti bean broth. Leave room for white chocolate and coconut truffle with pineapple carpaccio, rum and raisin ice cream and pineapple syrup. You get skittles every now and then, and wine tastings in a vaulted cellar. Richard Cromwell, Oliver's son, lived in the village.

Rooms	4 doubles, 2 twin/doubles: £110-£150. 1 suite for 2: £130-£155. 1 single: £85-£95.
Meals	Light lunch from £6.95. Mains from £13.50.
Closed	Open all day.

Mark & Penny Thornhill
The King's Head,
Main Road, Hursley,
Winchester, SO21 2JW
Tel +44 (0)1962 775208
Web www.kingsheadhursley.co.uk

The East End Arms

East End

A good little local hidden down New Forest lanes, winningly unpretentious and owned by John Illsley of Dire Straits. Walkers, wax jackets and locals congregate in the small, rustic Foresters Bar with its chatty community vibe, and walls come lined with the famous. The carpeted-cosy dining room, all cottagey furniture and roaring log fire, cocks a snook at gastropub remodelling, but the menus change twice daily – a rare treat – and make the best of seasonal produce. Try saddle of venison, whole baked seabass or locally caught Lymington crab. A paved terrace invites al fresco drinking, while bedrooms on the back add va-va-voom. Fresh, clean-lined and cosy, in fashionably neutral tones that bring the forest indoors, they sport roman blinds and Mulberry fabrics. Stylish bathrooms and paintings by John Illsley himself add warmth and class; fine breakfasts are the cherry on the cake. A great little find for anyone who loves the New Forest – neither new nor a forest, but fine open heathland nonetheless and excellent hiking terrain.

Rooms	5 twin/doubles: £110-£130.
Meals	Lunch from £5.50. Dinner from £10.50. Not Sunday eves.
Closed	3pm-6pm. Open all day Sun.

Danielle Ball
The East End Arms,
Lymington Road, East End,
Lymington, SO41 5SY
Tel +44 (0)1590 626223
Web www.eastendarms.co.uk

The Mayflower

Lymington

An imposing grey and blue building – a mix of brick and wattle and daub – opposite a row of pretty cottages, overlooking the Lymington slipway, in a residential area half a mile from the town centre. There's no forgetting you're in a renowned sailing resort, from the plush rooms (and smart bathrooms) named after ships to the associated paraphernalia: charts, pictures of boats, seashells, not forgetting the clientele – a mix of locals and well-heeled boat owners from the nearby marina. They come for the food and friendly welcome from the young staff. The menu is traditional (think scallops, pork belly, or aubergine and feta with couscous), the wine list wide-ranging with a good selection by the glass, and the décor new and shiny. Comfy armchairs, lead windows, parquet flooring, a wood burner and four separate eating areas help to keep it cosy and welcoming. Dynamic landlord Gary is working hard to make his mark, offering good value for the area and running events with the local community. There's a large garden to sit in, the whole of Hampshire and the New Forest to explore, and, of course, a spot of sailing, too.

Rooms	6 doubles: £95-£190.
Meals	Mains from £12.95. Dinner, 3 courses, £30-£35.
Closed	Open all day.

Gary Grant
The Mayflower,
King's Saltern Road,
Lymington, SO41 3QD
Tel +44 (0)1590 672160
Web www.themayflowerlymington.co.uk

The Mill at Gordleton

Sway

Another wormhole back to old England, a 400-year-old mill on Avon Water with mallards, lampreys and Indian runners to watch from the terrace in summer. The house stands in three acres of gardens that are filled with art and beautiful things. Inside, cosy interiors mix old and new delightfully: low ceilings, wonky walls, busts and mirrors, smouldering fires. Colour tumbles from pretty fabrics, there's a panelled bar for pre-dinner drinks, then bedrooms which are full of character. The suite above the wheelhouse has a fabulous bathroom, you'll find lots of colour, sheets and blankets, bowls of fruit. Three rooms have watery views (you can fall asleep to the sound of the river), most have fancy new bathrooms. The main suite has robes, all have White Company oils; and while a lane passes outside, you are more likely to be woken by birdsong. Downstairs, the beautifully refurbished restaurant continues to draw a happy crowd for its delicious local food, perhaps wild mushroom ravioli, Creedy Carver free-range duck, blackberry soufflé with apple crumble ice cream. The forest and coast are both on your doorstep.

Rooms	3 doubles, 3 twin/doubles: £150-£195. 2 suites for 2: £150-£275.
Meals	Lunch from £6.95. Sunday lunch from £21.50. Dinner £22.50-£27.50; à la carte about £40.
Closed	Open all day.

Stacey Crouch
The Mill at Gordleton,
Silver Street, Sway,
Lymington, SO41 6DJ
Tel +44 (0)1590 682219
Web www.themillatgordleton.co.uk

The Oak Inn

Bank

Aptly named (among the forest oaks), this 18th-century pub, with a double-bay frontage and a red phone box by the door, is a friendly and traditional little place. It's loved not just by locals but walkers and cyclists who pour in at weekends for 'classic British pub food with a modern twist' – and much of the produce has been reared or caught within the New Forest (note the symbols on the menu). Others drop in for a pint of Gales Seafarers in the low-beamed bar, or the little garden sheltered by a big yew. Blackboard specials might include whole baked John Dory or local venison sausages; doorstep sandwiches and homemade steak and ale pie catch the eye of the walkers. Come for dark red walls and winter fires, cottagey furniture and old-fashioned comfort.

Meals Lunch & dinner £8.95-£16.95.

Closed 3.30pm-6pm.
Open all day Sat & Sun.

Martin Sliva & Zuzana Slivova
The Oak Inn,
Pinkney Lane, Bank,
Lyndhurst, SO43 7FE
Tel +44 (0)23 8028 2350
Web www.oakinnlyndhurst.co.uk

Entry 249 Map 3

Hampshire

The Royal Oak

Fritham

Small, ancient, thatched and secluded is this ale-lover's retreat. No fruit machines, but lots of bonhomie. Locals chat around the bar; ramblers and dogs drop by. Huge fires crackle through the winter, demanding you linger. Neil and Pauline believe in local produce and deliver honest, unpretentious pub lunches: ploughman's with homemade pâté, French-dressed local crab, sausages from a local butcher, no chips. Though rustically simple, the three small rooms are perfect, with pale boards, solid tables and spindleback chairs, darts, dominoes and cribbage. Five local beers are drawn from the cask, including Hop Back Summer Lightning and Royal Oak by Bowman ales. There's more: a large garden for barbecues and a beer and food festival in September. Pub heaven?

Meals Lunch £6-£10.50.
No food in evening.

Closed 3pm-5.30pm;
open all day Jul-Sept.
Open all day Sat & Sun.

Neil & Pauline McCulloch
The Royal Oak,
Fritham,
Lyndhurst, SO43 7HJ
Tel +44 (0)23 8081 2606

Entry 250 Map 3

The Rose & Thistle

Rockbourne

Rockbourne is the kind of village where you might find Miss Marple trimming a rose bush. The pub is dreamy too, and started life as two thatched cottages; the two fireplaces should come as no surprise. It's a great mix of oak beams and timbers, carved benches and flagstones, country-style fabrics and tables strewn with magazines – an enchanting place to return to after visiting Rockbourne's Roman villa. Chris Chester-Sterne makes use of fresh local produce: estate game in season; pork with champ, black pudding and cider; veal with béarnaise sauce. In summer you can dine in the garden, perhaps smoked trout and scrambled eggs or steak and kidney pud. The changing chalkboard menu favours Cornish fish.

Meals Lunch & dinner £9.50-£19.50. Bar meals from £5.

Closed 3pm-6pm (Sun from 8pm Nov-Mar).

Chris Chester-Sterne
The Rose & Thistle,
Rockbourne,
Fordingbridge, SP6 3NL
Tel +44 (0)1725 518236
Web www.roseandthistle.co.uk

Entry 251 Map 3

The Bakers Arms

Droxford

Set in the attractive Meon Valley, this small village pub is a bit of a find for lovers of modern British cooking. For locals, there's the added plus of Droxford's Bowman Ales – and the post office and village stores parked on the side. Inside has a relaxed, traditional charm and a winter fire. The L-shaped, opened-up space is light and cheery, the customary miscellany of old wooden furniture and a few bar stools offset by a cosy dining room vibe. The kitchen's chalkboard menu pleases all with its use of prime local produce and seasonal dishes with punchy flavours and, in this rolling countryside, the local meats are a forte; organic Hyden Farm pork belly with smoked eel from the river Test, local sausages with mash and shallot gravy. An excellent meeting place for a civilised crowd.

Meals Lunch & dinner £10.95-£17.95.

Closed Sundays from 4pm.

Adam & Anna Cordery
The Bakers Arms,
High Street, Droxford,
Southampton, SO32 3PA
Tel +44 (0)1489 877533
Web www.thebakersarmsdroxford.com

Entry 252 Map 4

The Thomas Lord

West Meon

Named after the founder of Lord's Cricket Ground, the Thomas Lord is much loved and hard to fault. And, in spite of remodelling raising the gastro credentials, it keeps its endearing community vibe. Join locals (and dogs) over a trio of local Upham ales at the bar, or settle into leather armchairs around winter fires. Associated cricketing prints and paraphernalia still decorate the walls (old bats, balls, caps, shoes) while the darkly beamed bar's weathered wooden furniture gives way to a duo of preened, dedicated dining areas. Menus are rammed with local produce (including pickings from the pub's potager) and foodies relish it all, from the beef burgers and cottage pies to the more sophisticated dishes such as gurnard fillet with bacon and onion sauté potatoes, cauliflower purée and smoked mussels.

Meals	Starters £6-£10. Mains £12-£28.
Closed	Open all day.

Tabitha Money
The Thomas Lord,
West Meon,
Petersfield, GU32 1LN

Tel	+44 (0)1730 829244
Web	www.thethomaslord.co.uk

Entry 253 Map 4

Hampshire

The White Horse

Otterbourne

An inspired pit stop for the clued-up traveller – barely a mile from the M3 – and an on-cue village local. The large opened-up, L-shaped space has been imaginatively remodelled and comes in warm country style: varnished wood floors and black slate tiles, button-back banquettes and winged armchairs, smart sofas and winter fires… and a big-windowed dining area with exposed brick, objets d'art and an antler-style chandelier. Local ales and good wines accompany small plates such as squid fritto served with smoked paprika aïoli, and pub classics like sausage and mash. Pollock fillet served with a warm puy lentil salad, salt-baked beets and kale pesto offers more adventure. For summer: a terrace and a garden.

Meals	Lunch from £5. Dinner from £10.50.
Closed	Open all day.

Karen Light
The White Horse,
Main Road, Otterbourne,
Winchester, SO21 2EQ

Tel	+44 (0)1962 712830
Web	www.whitehorseotterbourne.co.uk

Entry 254 Map 4

The Wykeham Arms

Winchester

The old Wykeham is English to the core, full of its own traditions and hidden away between the cathedral and the city's famous school. Ceilings drip with memorabilia and bow-tied regulars, pints in hand, chat. It's grand, a throwback to the past and brimming with warm colours and atmosphere. There are small red-shaded lamps on graffiti-etched desks (ex-Winchester College), three roaring fires and two dining rooms. Food is not cheap, but certainly reliable, from posh sandwiches and cottage pie at lunch to daily-changing evening dishes, perhaps juniper infused venison saddle or aged Hampshire rib-eye steak with béarnaise sauce. The Fuller's Gales ales are good, the wine list is interesting (20 by the glass), and the staff are young and laid-back.

Meals	Lunch £7-£15. Bar meals £7-£10. Dinner £15-£24. Sunday lunch, 3 courses, £23.
Closed	Open all day.

Jon Howard
The Wykeham Arms,
75 Kingsgate Street,
Winchester, SO23 9PE
Tel +44 (0)1962 853834
Web www.wykehamarmswinchester.co.uk

Hampshire

The Green Man

Winchester

From outside, this Victorian pub – opposite the city's dinky cinema – looks much like any other. But the savvy Winchester set know it could win an Oscar for its gorgeous, interiors. An imaginative makeover delivers a successful marriage of original features with stylish frills, bold colours and comfy chairs, clever lighting and vintage bits and bobs. Upstairs the dining room has a romantic Victorian vibe with chandeliers, candlesticks and rich fabrics. Real ales line up alongside well-chosen wines, a handcrafted cocktail menu and a unique boutique spirits list. The food menu is wide – from light bites to hearty dishes, good old-fashioned pub food to eclectic modern trends – locally sourced as much as possible. The atmosphere here is great – and written on the wall – 'work hard and be nice to people.' Marvellous.

Meals	Lunch & dinner from £10.95. Set dinner menu from £24.95. Platters from £8.95.
Closed	Open all day.

Jayne Gillin
The Green Man,
53 Southgate Street,
Winchester, SO23 9EH
Tel +44 (0)1962 866809
Web www.greenmanwinchester.co.uk

The Flower Pots Inn

Cheriton

Ramblers and beer enthusiasts beat a path to Paul and Patricia's door, where award-winning pints of Flower Pots Bitter and Goodens Gold are brewed in the brewhouse across the car park. Open fires burn in two bars: one a wallpapered parlour, the other a quarry-tiled public bar with scrubbed pine and an illuminated, glass-topped well. Ales are tapped from casks behind a counter hung with hops, and drunk to the accompaniment of happy chat; no music or electronic wizardry here. In keeping with the simplicity of the place, the menu is short and straightforward: baps with home-cooked ham, sandwiches toasted or plain, home-cooked hotpots, spicy chilli with garlic bread, hearty winter soups – all served with a smile from a happy staff.

Meals	Lunch & dinner £5-£10. Not Sunday or bank holiday eves.
Closed	2.30pm-6pm (3pm-7pm Sun).

Paul Tickner & Patricia Bartlett
The Flower Pots Inn,
Cheriton,
Alresford, SO24 0QQ

Tel +44 (0)1962 771318
Web www.flowerpots-inn.co.uk

Hampshire

The Chestnut Horse

Easton

In the beautiful Itchen valley, this rather smart 16th-century dining pub is in the capable hands of Karen Wells. A decked terrace leads to a warren of snug rooms around a central bar, warmed by log fires, and at night it is cosy and candlelit. Eat in the low beamed 'red' room, with cushioned settles, a mix of dining tables and wood-burning stove, or in the panelled and memorabilia-filled 'green' room. Try the two-course menu (smoked mackerel pâté, sea bream with pesto dressing, apple and walnut pie) – great value. Or tuck into beer-battered fish and chips, vegetable potato cake with dressed leaves, or wild boar casserole with apple cobbler. There are great local ales, decent wines and champagne by the glass. A relaxed and civilised pub.

Meals	Lunch & dinner £10-£18. Sunday lunch £12.
Closed	Open all day (from 12pm).

Karen Wells
The Chestnut Horse,
Easton,
Winchester, SO21 1EG

Tel +44 (0)1962 779257
Web www.thechestnuthorse.com

The English Partridge

Bighton

The name gives a clue to the Partridge's countryside credentials, though not to its tucked-away village setting in Hampshire's huntin', shootin' and fishin' quarter. It's had a stylish revamp, but the modest property still retains the timeless air and charm of a proper local. Discover a cosy snug, a huge inglenook in the main bar, good solid furniture and sporting prints on the walls. A lighter and airier new extension has a dining vibe, but nevertheless fulfils the pukka country brief. Good British food is a strength here; try traditional classics like seared liver, bacon and mash or be more adventurous with fillet of cod, brown shrimp, samphire and new potatoes. Good ales abound and it is excellent value.

Meals Lunch & dinner £10-£18.
Closed Open all day.

David Young
The English Partridge,
Bighton,
Alresford, SO24 9RE
Tel +44 (0)1962 732859
Web www.englishpartridge.co.uk

Hampshire

The Greyhound on the Test

Stockbridge

Civilised, one-street Stockbridge is England's fly-fishing capital, and the colour-washed Greyhound reels in fishing folk and foodies. The 15th-century coaching inn is a dapper, food-and-wine-centred affair run with charm and panache by Lucy Townsend, while chef Alan produces modern dishes based on skill and impeccable produce. Try Dorset crab on toast; braised cod cheeks with linguine and curried saffron sauce; hake with lemon butter; rabbit cassoulet; chocolate fondant. In the bar are low dark beams and a big inglenook. In the open-plan dining area, wooden floors, more beams, and high stools at a walnut-topped bar: graze on oysters or potted shrimps. A garden at the back overlooks the Test; rest awhile with a glass of chablis – or cast a line.

Meals Lunch & dinner £12-£20.
No food on Sun.
Closed Open all day.

Lucy Townsend
The Greyhound on the Test,
31 High Street,
Stockbridge, SO20 6EY
Tel +44 (0)1264 810833
Web www.thegreyhoundonthetest.co.uk

The Bridge Inn

Michaelchurch Escley

Getting here is half the fun, in the wilds of Herefordshire (but it could be tricky in the dark). In a pretty spot down by the river, beneath the Black Hill of Bruce Chatwin fame, the 16th-century Bridge started life as a house, achingly lovely on its river side with willows weeping down the footbridge. Walkers descend, so do dogs, and families and shooting parties, and Glyn is the nicest host. Inside, hops hang from dark beams and the wood-burner belts out the heat, there are solid wooden pews, scrubbed pine tables and small bar stools on the other side. It's properly pubby yet there's an organic and fine wine menu. Eat in one of two dining areas with contemporary colours on the walls; our pints of Butty Bach slipped down nicely and our food – hake with seafood stew, and barbecue brisket – was very, very good. Stay the night? We would! Three super country bedrooms lie in the farmhouse a minute away, with antiques, thick carpets, deep window seats, and a dark panelled sitting room below. In summer you can camp in the field above the pub or – for romantics – in a super yurt with decking and a vintage interior up a wooded path.

Rooms	1 double, 2 twin/doubles: £95.
Meals	Lunch £8-£22. Dinner £12-£22.
Closed	Open all day.

Glyn Bufton & Gisela Vargas
The Bridge Inn,
Michaelchurch Escley,
Hereford, HR2 0JW
Tel +44 (0)1981 510646
Web www.thebridgeinnmichaelchurch.co.uk

The Kilpeck Inn

Kilpeck

Kilpeck – known for its Norman church – has a second string to its bow: a super little country inn with a facelift. It stands on the edge of the village overlooking beautiful fields, ten miles south of Hereford. Outside, smart white walls sparkle in the sun. Inside: old stone, slate floors and a warm contemporary feel. Find darts in the locals' bar, alongside the daily papers and a smouldering fire, and original beams, candle lanterns and painted panelling in the airy restaurant. Dig into the sort of food you'd hope to find in a country inn: River Exe mussels in a cider and sage cream sauce with hand cut chips; shepherd's pie, green beans, redcurrant and red wine jus. Rooms are above, crisp and comfortable. Named after local rivers, all have countryside views, plus pocket sprung mattresses, Egyptian cotton sheets and cloud-soft duvets. Bathrooms are spotless and sparkling. It's as local as possible and seriously green, what with low food miles, hi-spec insulation and a rainwater tank. Walkers rejoice: the Black Mountains and Offa's Dyke are close.

Rooms	3 doubles, 1 twin: £80-£110.
Meals	Lunch & bar meals from £5.95. Dinner £9.95-£17.95. Sunday lunch, 3 courses, £15.95. No food on Sun eves.
Closed	Mon-Sat 2.30pm-5.30pm.

Ross Williams
The Kilpeck Inn,
Kilpeck, HR2 9DN

Tel +44 (0)1981 570464
Web www.kilpeckinn.com

Carpenter's Arms

Walterstone

A little chapel-side pub in the middle of nowhere, hard to find but perfect in every way. Vera has been dispensing Wadworth 6X and Breconshire Golden Valley from the hatch for years and everyone gets a welcome: locals, walkers, families, babies. Through an ancient oak doorway is a tiny bar with a log-fired range and a dining area to the side. Floors are Welsh slate, settles polished oak, tables cast iron, walls open stone; it's as cared for as can be. On the menu: beef and Guinness pie, faggots and mash, bread and butter pudding – honest homemade food, some organic, at great prices. Beer is served from the drum, cider and perry from the flagon. Spill into the grassy garden and gaze up at the Skirrid, or pull on your hiking boots and climb it.

Meals	Lunch & dinner £10.95-£14.95. Bar meals from £5.
Closed	Open all day.

Vera Watkins
Carpenter's Arms,
Walterstone,
Hereford, HR2 0DX

Tel +44 (0)1873 890353
Web www.thecarpentersarmswalterstone.com

Entry 263 Map 7

Herefordshire

The Mill Race

Walford

As the 'ecclesiastical' door swings open, prepare yourself for a stylish place. A stainless steel kitchen glistens behind a granite-topped bar, there are counter-style bar tables and leather armchairs, a wood-burner divides the eating areas and a food provenance blackboard shows how seriously food is taken here. The kitchen team choose the meat and the game from their 1,000 acre farm and estate and help dig the vegetables; they'll even catch the trout for the table. Linger long over roast leg of red partridge with mash, bread sauce and watercress salad, or roast Gower pollock with crushed potatoes, wild mushrooms and parsley oil. A new carbon-neutral wood fired pizza oven, lit on certain days only, sits on the rear terrace. Look across the Wye to the ruins of Goodrich Castle, sip ales from the same valley. Fabulous.

Meals	Lunch & bar meals from £5. Dinner from £9.50. Sunday lunch £15-£18.
Closed	3pm-5pm. Open all day Sat & Sun.

Luke Freeman
The Mill Race,
Walford,
Ross-on-Wye, HR9 5QS

Tel +44 (0)1989 562891
Web www.millrace.info

Entry 264 Map 7

The Oak Inn

Staplow

Just west of the Malvern Hills – a freehouse dating from the 1600s, sympathetically refurbished. Farmhouse tables and chairs stand on polished flagstones, hops hang from beams and wood-burners crackle in exposed brick hearths – it's country pub to the core. There are ales from Bathams and Wye Valley and good ciders like Robinson's Flagon and Westons Stowford Press. Traditional home-cooked dishes with a modern twist are the order of the day; try local free-range pork belly with 'boozy' mustard mash or braised venison casserole with spiced red cabbage. Lighter options include deli boards with home-cured meats, sandwiches and golden beetroot soup with horseradish cream. The pretty garden is backed by orchards, while the fires and candles in the bar, two snugs and dining area are kept glowing by a bright and attentive team. A super little pub.

Meals: Starters & light meals from £5.50. Lunch & dinner from £12.50.
Closed: 3pm-5.30pm (Mon-Sat). 3pm-7pm (Sun).

Hylton Haylett & Julie Woollard
The Oak Inn,
Bromyard Road,
Staplow, Ledbury, HR8 1NP
Tel +44 (0)1531 640954
Web www.oakinnstaplow.co.uk

Entry 265 Map 8

Herefordshire

The Pandy Inn

Dorstone

Built in 1185... a half-timbered Herefordshire delight, a contender for 'oldest pub in the land'. Heavy beams, worn flagged floors, smoke-smudged stone and a vast oak lintel over the old log grate. This is the country of Golden Valley and Butty Bach ales and 'cloudy' scrumpy – no wonder there's a happy buzz. On the menus are organic Hereford beef steaks and delicious seasonal specials: try Welsh lamb shank with redcurrant and red wine sauce, hearty baguettes, walkers' soups, homemade fish pie and first-class bread. Families and dogs are welcome here and children can spin into a garden with picnic tables and a play area in summer. You are in the 'Golden Valley' so set off for Abbey Dore and Arthur's Stone, or bookish Hay-on-Wye, a short drive. Special place, special people.

Meals: Lunch from £4.95. Dinner from £10.95. Sunday lunch £10.95.
Closed: 3pm-6pm (6.30pm Sun). Mon in winter (except bank hols). Open all day Sat.

Bill & Magdalena Gannon
The Pandy Inn,
Dorstone,
Hereford, HR3 6AN
Tel +44 (0)1981 550273
Web www.pandyinn.co.uk

Entry 266 Map 7

The New Inn

Pembridge

Perfect for English heritage lovers with big appetites. The food is generously portioned, the building is as old as can be (1311), and Pembridge is a remarkable survivor; its market hall, where you can sup a pint in summer, could be in deepest France. It is a simple but great pleasure to amble into this ancient inn, order a drink and squeeze into the curved back settle in the flagstoned bar; in winter the logs are lit. This is the most timeless of old locals, with photos of village shenanigans up on the wall and a dart board put to good use. Upstairs has floral carpets, books and sofa – a reassuring spot in which to tuck into the comforting likes of smoked chicken and avocado salad, steak and ale pie, and seafood stew. Jane Melvin is happy doing what she does best.

Meals	Lunch £6.95-£12. Bar meals £5.95-£8.50. Dinner from £15. Sunday lunch, 3 courses, £16.
Closed	3pm-6pm.

Jane Melvin
The New Inn,
Market Square,
Pembridge,
Leominster, HR6 9DZ
Tel +44 (0)1544 388427

Herefordshire

The Stagg Inn

Titley

Deep in the wild Welsh borderlands lies the first British pub to have been awarded a Michelin star back in 2001. Gavroche-trained Steve Reynolds, defying all odds, ended up a Herefordshire food hero. As for provenance: the only thing you're not told is the name of the bird from which your pigeon breast (perfectly served on herb risotto) came. Most of the produce is very local, some is organic, with fresh fruit and vegetables from the kitchen garden. Seductive and restorative is the exceptional food: goat's cheese and fennel tart, saddle of venison with horseradish gnocchi and kummel, bread and butter pudding with clotted cream, a cheese trolley resplendent with 15 regional beauties. The intimate bar is perfect and dog-friendly, there's beer from Wye Valley Brewery, cider from Dunkerton's and some very classy wines.

Meals	Lunch & dinner from £25. Bar meals £9.80. Sunday lunch, 3 courses, £19.30.
Closed	Mon-Tues.

Steve & Nicola Reynolds
The Stagg Inn,
Titley,
Kington, HR5 3RL
Tel +44 (0)1544 230221
Web www.thestagg.co.uk

The Bricklayers Arms

Hogpits Bottom

Tucked away at a remote crossroads in the exotically named Hogpits Bottom ('hog' being local dialect for shale) is a pretty, ivy-strewn 18th-century building with low beams, blazing fires and timbered walls. Once a row of cottages and shops, and an ale house since 1832, this listed building is now rammed with diners daily and Alvin's staff are run off their feet. French chef Claude Pallait turns out local rare breed fillets of pork with apple compote and cider jus; Little Missenden lamb with a pea flan; home-smoked fish; good old steak and kidney pie. All are delicious, all are prepared from locally sourced or organic ingredients where possible. There's an excellent range of ales, and over 140 wines, ports and armagnacs. While away summer days in the garden, or watch the world go by from the benches out front.

Meals	Lunch & dinner £9.95-£24.95. Bar meals from £8.95.
Closed	Open all day.

Alvin Michaels
The Bricklayers Arms,
Hogpits Bottom, Flaunden,
Hemel Hempstead, HP3 0PH

Tel +44 (0)1442 833322
Web www.bricklayersarms.com

Entry 269 Map 9

Hertfordshire

The Alford Arms

Frithsden

It isn't easy to find, so come armed with precise directions before you set out! In a hamlet enfolded by acres of National Trust common land, David and Becky Salisbury's gastropub is worth any number of missed turns. Inside are two interlinked rooms, bright and airy, with soft colours, scrubbed pine tables, wooden and tile floors. Food is taken seriously and ingredients are as organic, free-range and delicious as can be. You might start with grilled Cornish mackerel, Bucksum Farm beetroot and horseradish salsa then move onto rabbit leg bourguignon with smoked pancetta and creamy mash, saving room for coconut panna cotta and crispy malt loaf. Wine drinkers have the choice of 22 by the glass; service is informed and friendly. Arrive early on a warm day to take your pick of the teak tables on the sun-trapping front terrace.

Meals	Lunch, bar meals & dinner £11.75-£19.75.
Closed	Open all day.

David & Becky Salisbury
The Alford Arms,
Frithsden,
Hemel Hempstead, HP1 3DD

Tel +44 (0)1442 864480
Web www.alfordarmsfrithsden.co.uk

Entry 270 Map 9

The Verulam Arms

St Albans

Sloe gin martini, elderflower champagne, woodruff and apple armagnac, horseradish schnapps: take your pick! The foragers who run The Verulam, a cosy corner pub in the heart of St Albans, make beautiful booze from the Hertfordshire hedgerows. They run foraging walks and wild tapas feasts, the meat and game come from a network of hunters and on Sundays they put their spin on the Great British Roast (foraged vegetables, wild herb seasonings). Enter a traditional interior of sage green and cream walls and plain tables, blackboards chalked up with seasonal menus, and, behind the bar, bio-dynamic wines, Tring and Adnams and their own 'wild' beers. From a tiny kitchen flow flower fritters and wild watercress gnocchi, venison burgers in brioche buns, rumps of local lamb with champ mash, and a wonderful sticky toffee pudding.

Meals — Starters from £7.
Mains from £15.5. Dessert from £7.
Sunday lunch from £13.50.

Closed — Open all day.

George Fredenham & Gerald Waldeck
The Verulam Arms, 41 Lower
Dagnall Street, St Albans, AL3 4QE

Tel — +44 (0)1727 836004

Web — www.the-foragers.com/the-verulam-arms

Entry 271 Map 9

Hertfordshire

The Fox & Hounds

Hunsdon

London chefs quitting fabulous establishments to transform country boozers may be two a penny, but few have managed it with the aplomb of James Rix. In the comfy laid-back bar: a log fire, the daily papers, local ales on tap and a menu that changes twice daily. Things step up a gear in the smart country-house-on-a-shoestring dining room with its cosy log-burner, that throws together polished old tables and crystal chandelier: a funky backdrop to black pudding from Normandy, wild mushrooms with a fried duck egg, or squid and chermoula, followed by whole grilled back bream, peperonata, monk beard and salsa verde. Puddings include salted caramel ice cream and biscotti. Even the focaccia is homemade. A recent refurb added a Josper charcoal oven, to the delight of diners. It is a treat to see an old pub in the right hands, and booking is recommended.

Meals — Lunch & dinner £9-£22.
Bar meals £4.95-£16.50.
Sunday lunch, 3 courses, £29.50.

Closed — 4pm-6pm.
Sun eves & Mon
(except bank hol lunches).

James Rix
The Fox & Hounds,
2 High Street, Hunsdon,
Ware, SG12 8NH

Tel — +44 (0)1279 843999

Web — www.foxandhounds-hunsdon.co.uk

Entry 272 Map 9

The Dukes Head

Hatfield Broad Oak

In the centre of Hatfield Broad Oak is a local loved not only for its great ales but also its food. Inside in the bar, cosy with cottage windows and wood-burning stoves, ales (Doom Bar, Timothy Taylor's Landlord) are on tap. At scrubbed wood tables you can tuck into Justin's hearty menus: crispy oriental duck salad with warm udon noodles; bubble and squeak with bacon, poached egg and hollandaise; Doom Bar beer battered Brixham haddock with thrice cooked chips and pea purée. One law that should be made here is to leave space for pudding. Justin's pastry-training produces elaborate treats. Try honeycomb parfait with chocolate 'soil', toffee pudding slice and popcorn, accompanied by an extensive pudding wine list. There's also a conservatory dining room for groups and a lovely garden in summer, where chickens cluck as contentedly as the guests.

Meals	Starters from £5. Mains from £11.75. Sunday lunch from £15.25.
Closed	Christmas & Boxing Day.

Liz & Justin Flodman
The Dukes Head,
High Street, Hatfield Broad Oak,
Bishops Stortford, CM22 7HH

Tel	+44 (0)1279 718598
Web	www.thedukeshead.co.uk

Entry 273 Map 9

Hertfordshire

The Grandison

Bramfield

A slick operation in rural surroundings, with a smart brick façade and fancy cars in the car park. The locals love the Grandison: families, business folk and ladies that lunch. The food is good-looking and the staff are great. What's more, children and dogs are welcome in the bar, and there's a big, buzzing, contemporary terrace. Find a small restaurant with high cottage windows, a modern brick bar fronted by orange leather armchairs and light wood tables, and a decked, black wicker furnished terrace; the old place had a complete overhaul in 2009. As for the food, it includes fried goat's cheese with truffle honey and hazelnuts; pork burgers in brioche buns; steamed stone bass with shitake mushrooms and crispy noodles; and a lovely, tangy lemon meringue pudding. Ales, wines and spirits are wide ranging; fruit teas are organic.

Meals	Starters £5.50-£7.95. Mains £10.50-£27.95.
Closed	Mondays (except Bank Holidays).

Aaron & Cheri Clayton
The Grandison,
Bury Lane, Bramfield,
Hertford, SG14 2QL

Tel	+44 (0)1992 554077
Web	www.thegrandisonbramfield.co.uk

Entry 274 Map 9

The Tilbury

Datchworth

Standing on the village crossroads, the Tilbury was once the Inn on the Green. Step into a bar of dark polished wood and real ales, and a dining room that is softer: pastel walls, chic wallpaper, cushions, leather chairs and gilt mirrors – a sanctuary for ladies that lunch. A fabulous place, too, for a special dinner: the food is a serious attraction. Chef Chas and his crew are dedicated to sourcing the best – locally reared meats and game, salt marsh lamb from Wales, Norfolk mussels from Blakeney Point. Tuck in to slow-cooked pig's cheek with pumpkin purée, honey-and-spice roast duck breast, and baked chocolate praline brownie. Unmissable is the delicious treacle-bread pot – and the barbecues in the big garden in summer. Worth going out of your way for.

Meals	Starters from £6.50. Mains from £12.
Closed	3pm-6pm. Sun eves.

James & Tom Bainbridge
The Tilbury,
Watton Road, Datchworth,
Knebworth, SG3 6TB
Tel +44 (0)1438 815550
Web www.thetilbury.co.uk

Entry 275 Map 9

Hertfordshire

The Bull

Watton-at-Stone

The timbered Bull is a wonderful time-warp gem of a village pub, oozing 15th-century charm. Its warren of rooms is filled with fresh flowers, glowing candles, and old dining tables on bare boards or slate-tiled floors. Menus champion seasonal British and rustic European dishes; classic pub favourites like fish and chips and pork belly with fennel and cider sauce vie for attention alongside tapas-style deli dishes (salt and pepper squid, crab beignets) and sun-dried tomato and garlic polenta. Leave room for Sicilian glazed lemon tart and wash a satisfying meal down with a pint of Wherry or Doom Bar. Open from 9.30am for perusing the papers over coffee and pastries, it is well worth the short trek from Stevenage, Welwyn or Ware. Don't miss a visit to nearby Knebworth House.

Meals	Light lunches from £7.50. Mains £9.95-£18.95.
Closed	Open all day.

Alastair & Anna Bramley
The Bull,
High Street, Watton-at-Stone,
Stevenage, SG14 3SB
Tel +44 (0)1920 831032
Web www.thebullwatton.co.uk

Entry 276 Map 9

Water Lane Bar & Restaurant

Bishops Stortford

Effortlessly urban and chic, this casual dining outpost occupies the old Hawkes Brewery site in sublime style. Downstairs, in an awesomely proportioned, stone-vaulted cellar bar, you can order cocktails, craft beers and spirits, and graze on tasty bar snacks. Then find a table in an industrial-look dining room with stripped back walls, exposed pipe work and copper lamps suspended from high ceilings. On the all-day menu: flavoursome flatbreads and burgers, mouth-watering steaks, sandwiches and soups, or strike out for salt baked pumpkin risotto, pulled lamb and chickpea masala, baked camembert to share... Leave room for Jaeger spiced roasted plums. Splendidly lazy and indulgent Sunday roasts, 'bottomless brunches', live Friday music... all is possible here.

Meals	Starters from £7. Lunch from £10. Dinner, 2-3 courses, £12.95-£15.95.
Closed	Open all day.

Cliff Nye & Family
Water Lane Bar & Restaurant,
31 Water Lane,
Bishops Stortford, CM23 2JZ

Tel +44 (0)1279 211888
Web www.waterlane.co

Entry 277 Map 9

Hertfordshire

The Jolly Waggoner

Ardeley

Not often is a pub run by a farm and this isn't the only unusual thing about the Jolly Waggoner. Church Farm also provides rare-breed meat and 'heritage' fruit and veg for the pub's menu. Nurse a pint of Buntingford's Highwayman in an armchair by the fire, or tuck into produce from 'over the road': hidden corners of the bar or smarter restaurant are perfect for enjoying seasonal soup with 'kitchen garden' vegetables, and slow-roasted rare-breed pork belly with mustard mash, crispy crackling and greens. On farm tours, you can walk off a final plate of apple crumble served with warm crème anglaise. Summertime brings beer lovers to the pretty garden and annual beer festival, and don't be surprised to find the vicar behind the bar. With 'guest landlord evenings' there's no knowing who might be pulling your pints!

Meals	Lunch & dinner £10.50-£19.95.
Closed	Open all day.

Tim Waygood
The Jolly Waggoner,
Church Farm, Ardeley,
Stevenage, SG2 7AH

Tel +44 (0)1438 861350
Web www.jollywaggoner.co.uk

Entry 278 Map 9

The Highlander

Hitchin

The Prutton family have been running this wonderful pub for over 30 years. Now the new generation – the Anglo-French partnership of Charlotte and Eric, back from several years in the Alps – add youthful energy and culinary skill to the family provenance. Their passion shines through. This is an unpretentious local that moves with the times and there's an informal Gallic bistro feel to the place. Stand over your pint at the bar, or settle back into one of the settles; read the papers, scan the menu. Behind the immaculate bar, all aubergine and white, wines are enticingly displayed, local art hangs on the walls. Eric's delicious food fuses the best traditions of France and England, from tasty ploughman's to duck leg confit with Sarladaise potatoes and red wine jus – and Sunday lunches worth missing breakfast for.

Meals: Lunch from £4.10. Dinner from £5.65.
Closed: 2.30pm–6pm (7pm Sun). Open all day Fri & Sat.

Charlotte Prutton & Eric Ransinangue
The Highlander,
45 Upper Tilehouse Street,
Hitchin, SG5 2EF
Tel +44 (0)1462 454612
Web www.highlanderpubhitchin.co.uk

Hertfordshire

Hermitage Rd

Hitchin

What a surprise: a former ballroom and nightclub in the heart of Hitchin; Anglian Country Inns opened its fourth dining venue in 2011. From the street and the coffee bar (all-day cakes, bagels, sandwiches) stairs lead up to a cavernous bar and dining room, funkily stripped back in New York loft style, with exposed brick walls, acres of oak floor, subtle lighting, arched floor-to-ceiling windows and open-to-view kitchen. Chill out with a cocktail or a pint of Brancaster Brewery ale, share a supper charcuterie board at high tables, or watch the food being cooked from the dining table – steaming Brancaster mussels; cauliflower cheese with almond and brioche crumb; pan fried sea bass with pumpkin, orange, spinach and red pepper risotto. Everyone is beating a path to Hermitage Rd – make sure you book!

Meals: Lunch, dinner & bar meals from £11. Sunday lunch, 2-3 courses, £22-£27.
Closed: Open all day.

Cliff Nye & Family
Hermitage Rd,
20-21 Hermitage Road,
Hitchin, SG5 1BT
Tel +44 (0)1462 433603
Web www.hermitagerd.co.uk

The Fox

Willian

Cliff and James's village pub has a fresh modern feel and a menu that showcases British ingredients, including seafood from the Norfolk coast and local farm meats. It could beat many neighbourhood restaurants into a cocked hat but part of its charm is that it's a place where beer drinkers are most definitely welcome – try a pint of Brancaster ale from the Nye family brewery. A cool, formal dining room sits astride a relaxed bar where Brancaster oysters in sesame tempura add glamour to a menu that includes beef and pork burgers with sweet onion and chilli relish. The restaurant is a mix of French bistro and British pub: braised beef cheeks with creamy garlic mash and red wine sauce, a couple of roasts on Sundays, chocolate orange fondant. This Fox is one you'd do well to hunt down.

Meals	Starters from £6.50. Mains from £12.
Closed	Open all day.

Cliff Nye & Family
The Fox,
Willian,
Letchworth, SG6 2AE

Tel +44 (0)1462 480233
Web www.foxatwillian.co.uk

Entry 281 Map 9

The Boathouse

Seaview

Walk up from Ryde, sit on a bench facing the sea with a pint of Ringwood Best and watch the fishing boats roll in with the day's catch; some of it may land on your plate. On the fringe of pretty Seaview village, this rambling Victorian seafront pub has long been part of the isle's defensive history, with a group of Dad's Army garden figurines a charming remnant of its previous incarnation. Inside, stretch back on one of the sofas and admire the little oddities: Art Nouveau touches in chair shapes and fireplace, an ornate gilt mirror, metal sail structures... and a varnished dinghy propped against a wall. It's a civilised backdrop for your lobster thermidor. Otherwise, the turf's as local as the surf, with Isle of Wight steaks and a trio of sausages and mash among the most popular dishes, together with the island's very own ploughman's.

Meals	Lunch from £5.50. Bar meals from £10.25. Dinner, 2 courses from £18.50.
Closed	Open all day.

Andrew McArthur
The Boathouse,
Springvale Road,
Seaview, PO34 5AW

Tel +44 (0)1983 810616
Web www.theboathouseiow.co.uk

Entry 282 Map 4

The Pilot Boat Inn

Bembridge

This amphibious-looking Bembridge Harbour landmark is ship-shape in more ways than one. Behind the nautical portholes and narrow Mackintosh windows of its Art Deco ship, award-winning landlord George has assembled friendly staff, good booze and generous plates of simple, fresh and often fishy pub cuisine. Snatch sea views from the side garden, savouring a speciality crab sandwich. Whether a dog walker, child-festooned parent or beachcomber with sand-tingled toes, warm welcomes await. Bar décor is eclectic, occasionally opulent. Floors and furnishings are dark wood, red walls frame vintage prints. Sofa seating is kitsch and comfy, board games beckon, bright fish somersault in tanks. Try an Island Brewery Yachtsman Ale, something from the wine list (decent mid-range options) or a draft Stowford Press, Grolsch or Guinness.

Meals Lunch & dinner £8-£20.
Closed Never.

George & Juliet Bristow
The Pilot Boat Inn,
Station Road,
Bembridge, PO35 5NN
Tel +44 (0)1983 872077
Web www.thepilotboatinn.com

Entry 283 Map 4

Isle of Wight

The Taverners

Godshill

A pub for all seasons: in summer take your pint (Taverners Own or a good guest beer) into a pretty rear garden with boules, picnic tables, vegetable beds and roaming chickens. In winter, hunker down by the front bar fire amid flagstone floors and wooden tables. There are a couple of sofas too for after lunch snoozers. Food is straightforward, fresh and local, skilfully cooked by Roger who used to head the kitchen at London's Haymarket Hotel; the family room has been converted into a shop selling home-baked goodies and island foodstuffs. Lovely to see hand-raised free-range pork pie, homemade pickles and 'my Nan's lemon meringue pie' on the simple menu; the wine list is short but well-chosen, there's freshly squeezed orange juice, and proper hot chocolate too.

Meals Lunch & dinner £8-£13.50.
Closed Sun eves from 5pm (except bank holidays & school holidays)

Roger Serjent
The Taverners,
High Street, Godshill,
Ventnor, PO38 3HZ
Tel +44 (0)1983 840707
Web www.thetavernersgodshill.co.uk

Entry 284 Map 4

The Vineyard

Lamberhurst Down

Real ales, real food and real English wines – from Lamberhurst Vineyard, naturally. Martial and Natasha Chaussy, who took over in 2012, have breathed new life into pub on the green, making the most of its 15th-century origins (low ceilings, beams, brick, flags, planked floor) and sprucing up the gorgeous interior with a smart, rustic-chic look – old rugs, leather sofas and wing chairs, colourful fabrics and fat church candles. Folk are drawn by the relaxed and friendly atmosphere, the winter fires, the local ales (from the barrel), the wines, the new dining room and the food. Menus combine pub classics with French brasserie-style dishes: baked camembert with shallot jam; a Kentish game board; sea bass with crayfish beurre blanc; pear and almond tart. Don't miss the Sunday roasts! New elegant bedrooms in four cottage-style suites added in 2013 have downstairs sitting areas and wet rooms (huge walk-in showers), with spiral staircases leading to bedrooms in the eaves. Expect low futon beds, quirky retro furnishings, leather sofas, iPod dock radios and private terraces. Close to Scotney Castle, Sissinghurst and Pashley Manor Gardens.

Rooms	4 doubles: £100-£110.
Meals	Lunch & dinner £9-£18. Bar meals from £7.
Closed	Open all day.

Martial & Natasha Chaussy
The Vineyard,
Lamberhurst Down, Lamberhurst,
Tunbridge Wells, TN3 8EU

Tel	+44 (0)1892 890222
Web	www.elitepubs.com/the_vineyard/

The Queen's Inn

Hawkshurst

Sharon and Sally Ann took on the run-down Queen's Inn in early 2014 having run a successful catering company for many years. Rather than deliver food to different venues across Kent, it was time to provide the venue to showcase Sally Ann's cooking and this rambling old village inn fitted the bill perfectly. Revived with panache, the wisteria-festooned Georgian façade hides a cosy, beamed 16th-century interior: a bar with wooden floor and huge fireplace, and upstairs, wonky corridors leading to quirky, hugely individual rooms. Expect a retro feel throughout with chunky dial phones, old-style radios, painted furniture and jazzy fabrics and lamps, plus goose down duvets, coffee and homemade brownies. Bathrooms are smart; room five boasts a free-standing tub in the room. Downstairs, rustic and modern combine in the dining room, with its ancient plank floor, brick fireplace and contemporary print wallpaper. In the bar, relax with a pint of Hophead or tuck into Moroccan spiced rack of lamb, sea bass with samphire, crab and chive sauce, Park Farm sausages and mash, baked vanilla cheesecake. National Trust treasures (Sissinghurst & Bodiam) and Pashley Manor Gardens are close.

Rooms	5 doubles: £95-£180. 1 family room for 4: £135.
Meals	Starters from £5. Mains from £12.50.
Closed	Open all day.

Sharon Retmanski
The Queen's Inn,
Rye Road,
Hawkshurst, TN18 4EY
Tel +44 (0)1580 754233
Web www.thequeensinnhawkhurst.co.uk

Woolpack Inn

Warehorne

Welcome to the latest in the Ramblinns' stable, in the heart of cycling country. An old inn in a beautiful setting, with views that reach for miles, it's cheery, chilled and loved by the locals. Modern colours and fabrics jostle with reinstated timbers and vintage country pieces and it seems the bar's not changed for 200 years. Logs are stacked for roaring fires, drinks include local ales, ciders, cocktails and 20 wines by the glass, and the kitchen is open to view. The team work with local producers; as they say on the prettily scrawled menu, "local families land the freshest fish daily so dishes change with wind, tide and season". Pizzas are baked over chestnut embers, steaks come from Sussex steer herds, and our skate wing with sautéed potatoes and capers was delicious. Note, no bookings are taken – hardly a problem if you stay the night. Five bedrooms upstairs burst with charm and arty-quirky style (one even has its own wood-burner). Find plants, planked floors, wool rugs, ornate mirrors, artisan toiletries and gleaming roll-top tubs, two in the bedrooms themselves.

Rooms	5 doubles: £60–£70.
Meals	Breakfast from £6. Lunch & dinner from £11.
Closed	Open all day.

Nina Katz
Woolpack Inn,
Church Lane, Warehorne,
Ashford, TN26 2LL
Tel +44 (0)1233 732900
Web www.woolpackinnwarehorne.com

Five Bells Inn

East Brabourne

Looking for somewhere that's quirky, full of character, champions local produce and has community spirit? Seek out this 15th-century village inn tucked beneath the North Downs. Alison and John revamped the building in 2011 and there's much to delight the eye: hopped beams, wood and tiled floors, exposed bricks walls, eclectic furnishings, blazing fires and individual touches – candles in upturned wine bottles, posh unisex loos. There's a local-produce shop at the bar, and the bar-cum-deli counter displays Kent ales, cider, olives, cheeses and Wye Bakery bread. Menus bristle with farm foods – Alkham beef and lamb, Potton Farm fruit and vegetables, estate game. Four swish bedrooms await, from the opulent 'Bacchus' with its own log fire to 'Fuggle' a breezy artist's attic conversion. Each has a big bed, three have freestanding baths; all are special. Downland walkers and lucky locals love the place, dropping by for breakfast from 9am, acoustic music, farmers' markets, craft fairs, and harvest supper.

Rooms	4 doubles: £60-£70.
Meals	Breakfast £5-£8. Lunch & dinner £10-£15.
Closed	Open all day.

The Manager
Five Bells Inn,
The Street, East Brabourne,
Ashford, TN25 5LP

Tel +44 (0)1303 813334
Web www.fivebellsinnbrabourne.com

The Kings Head

Wye

Welcome to a grand old pub in very pretty Wye run by "a couple of down to earth boys from the North" (their words). Mark and Scott have created an up-to-the-minute village pub where you're as welcome to drop by for coffee and croissants as order a glass of Sicilian wine. Or a good meal… the lemon-baked chicken with sweet potato and red pepper mash went down a treat and the pie of the day was tip-top. This pub is a cool place to be – suave pendant lighting, purple feature wall, open fire – but not so cool that they don't keep dog biscuits behind the bar (handmade by the chef). So settle into a leather wing back chair, rest your glasses on the vintage trunk and soak up the vibe. There's a welcome for all, and if you're going to hole up in the countryside, you'd do well to hole up here. Bedrooms upstairs are simple and uncluttered with a sunny feel; reclaimed and repainted furniture mixes with new; buttercup-coloured lamps and blankets add a touch of colour, there's robes to snuggle in, and bathrooms are stocked with nice toiletries and towels.

Rooms	3 doubles: £95-£105. 1 family room for 3: £100.
Meals	Lunch from £6. Dinner from £9. Sunday lunch from £12.
Closed	Open all day.

Mark Lightford & Scott Richardson
The Kings Head,
Church Street, Wye,
Kent, TN25 5BN
Tel +44 (0)1233 812418
Web www.kingsheadwye.com

The Compasses Inn

Crundale

"Half way between Petham and Waltham, take the right fork at the very small green with the pillar box," they say... Please follow their instructions, this is deepest Kent! Inside, the wood-burner glows and you can eat where you like. Beers are from the local brewery and superbly kept, and the wine list is good and global. Head chef Rob, and Donna who holds the fort front of house, are passionate about great, locally sourced food. Bread comes with home-churned butter, crispy lamb melts in the mouth, rabbit pie is outstanding, spuds are basted in dripping, and vegetables are given starring roles. We loved our venison ragù with mustard clotted cream and garlic crisp bread. Good dogs are welcome so spill into the big garden: brilliant for kids. Then walk off your indulgence on the Crundale Downs.

Meals Starters £6-£8.95.
Mains £11.95-£17.95.
Closed Open all day.

Rob & Donna Taylor
The Compasses Inn,
Sole Street, Crundale,
Canterbury, CT4 7ES
Tel +44 (0)1227 700300
Web www.thecompassescrundale.co.uk

The Granville

Lower Hardres

Straddling the divide between restaurant and pub, the Granville is an admirably up-to-date contemporary dining pub, a hop and a skip from Canterbury. The wood burner crackles, comfy leather sofas fill one corner and there's a separate drinkers' bar. It's a pleasure to sit back here, enjoying a pint of Whitstable Bay and admiring the interesting art that lines the walls. Seasonal menus tickle the taste buds with the likes of house-smoked duck breast with celeriac remoulade & hazelnut dressing, smoked haddock poached in cream and leeks with crushed new potatoes, and coffee and amaretto panna cotta. Pub classics have been updated with twists such as chargrilled lamb rump, roasted vegetables and pesto mash, and there are lots of lovely sharing platters. The beer garden is fab too! Great for walkers, foodies, families – and the Channel tunnel.

Meals Lunch & dinner £11.95-£19.95.
Closed 3pm-5.30pm. Open all day Sun.

Richard Borle
The Granville,
Faussett Hill, Street End,
Canterbury, CT4 7AL
Tel +44 (0)1227 700402
Web www.thegranvillecanterbury.co.uk

The Red Lion

Stodmarsh

Down rutted lanes that wind through bluebell woods is an enchanting village and a 15th-century pub. Step into tiny bare-boarded rooms with log fires, draped hops, prints, menus, wine bottles, milk churns, trugs, baskets, candles on every table and one bossy cat. New owner Mick Curtis has recently taken over and has promised to maintain the quirky country appeal that everyone loves. A basket of freshly laid eggs (chickens roam the garden), chutney and a sign for the sale of locally smoked ham add to the rural feel. Greene King IPA and Old Speckled Hen are tapped from barrels behind the bar and everyone is a regular, or looks like one. Menus change with the seasons and Kentish lamb with carrot and caraway purée and dauphinoise potatoes or roast vegetable tart will arrive on big painted plates. The quality is high. It doesn't get much better than this.

Meals	Lunch & dinner £10.95-£20.95.
Closed	Open all day.

Luke Edwards
The Red Lion,
Stodmarsh,
Canterbury, CT3 4BA
Tel +44 (0)1227 721339
Web www.theredlionstodmarsh.com

Entry 292 Map 5

Kent

The Sportsman

Seasalter

Brothers Steve and Phil Harris's pub is a Michelin starred haven amid marshland, beach huts and caravan sites, with the North Sea somewhere behind. The blackboard menu, short and sweet, promises everything seasonal and local; meat comes from farms within sight of the front door, Whitstable is just down the road. Order a native oyster or two to slurp while waiting for smoked mackerel with Bramley apple jelly or pork terrine. Roast chicken with bacon, sprouts and bread sauce is an old fashioned treat; apple sorbet and burnt cream makes a stunning finale. There's a tasting menu (book in advance), delicious bread, hams cured in the beer cellar, they churn their own butter and make their own salt. You eat at large chunky tables made from reclaimed wood in any of three airy rooms with marsh views. Exceptional.

Meals	Lunch & dinner £17.95-£22.95. Tasting menu £65. Not Sun eve or Mon.
Closed	3pm-6pm.

Phil & Stephen Harris
The Sportsman,
Faversham Road, Seasalter,
Whitstable, CT5 4BP
Tel +44 (0)1227 273370
Web www.thesportsmanseasalter.co.uk

Entry 293 Map 5

The Three Mariners

Oare

After a ramble across Oare marshes, welcome to a hideaway of good things. Food, mostly sourced from farms and day boats, is excellent value and it's the sort of place where you wish you could try everything that goes by. Potted crab, fish soup, and roast widgeon with red cabbage and parsnip potato cake represent contemporary pub classics, while a slow-roasted shoulder of lamb (for six to share at Sunday lunch) has a reassuringly timeless appeal. This 400-year-old pub comes with a laid-back medley of furniture and a double-sided log fire, cleverly dividing dining room from bar. It's simple and understated with an easy informality and lots of bare wood – a place to treasure; many do. There are Shepherd Neame ales and a modest and thoughtful selection of wines.

Meals	Lunch & dinner £12.50-£19. Set lunch, 2-3 courses, £11.95-£16.95. Set dinner, 3 courses, £16.95. Sunday lunch, 3 courses, £16.95.
Closed	Open all day.

John O'Riordan
The Three Mariners,
2 Church Road, Oare,
Faversham, ME13 0QA
Tel +44 (0)1795 533633
Web www.thethreemarinersoare.co.uk

Kent

The Red Lion

Hernhill

Sat on the village green in the pretty hamlet of Hernhill, this 14th-century former hall house is quintessentially Kentish. Through the impressive oak front door to beamed ceilings, flagstones and a red-brick fireplace that alludes to the Lion's historic past. A smattering of stylish cushions and hanging lamps add splashes of colour. Sip a pint of local Master Brew at the beam-framed bar while you peruse the specials chalked up on blackboards; try the whipped goats cheese and marinated beetroot, then poached salmon fillet with pernod and chive cream and follow with chocolate marquise with orange zest cream, a real treat. If you're ravenous, plump for the Butchers Block or Trawler sharing board. When the sun's out perch on benches and admire the nearby church, or lounge in the garden while the little ones play. Historic Canterbury is close.

Meals	Starters from £7. Mains from £10.50.
Closed	Open all day.

Joshua & Nicola White
The Red Lion,
Crockham Lane,
Hernhill, ME13 9JR
Tel +44 (0)1227 751207
Web theredlionhernhill.co.uk

The Plough

Stalisfield Green

Wonderful walks, Swale estuary views, a raft of lagers, ciders and Kentish ales, and land-rustic country cooking – just a few reasons for seeking out this 15th-century hall house hidden in a hamlet high on the North Downs. Beamed bars have wooden floors, old scrubbed pine tables, green and terracotta hues and glowing log fires. Doors in the light airy garden room can wander onto a peaceful patio for a pint of Hopdaemon ale or a heady Biddenden cider. Menus brim with local produce – saltmarsh lamb, rare-breed pork, delicious Angus beef from surrounding farms – while chef-patron Richard makes the bread, ice cream, pickles, sausages and home-smoked goodies. Typically, tuck into scallops with celeriac remoulade and apple caramel, lamb rump with baby beets and parsnip purée and banana tarte tatin. It's quite a find.

Meals	Lunch & dinner £10.95-£18.95.
Closed	Open all day.

Richard & Marianne Baker
The Plough,
Stalisfield Green,
Faversham, ME13 0HY

Tel +44 (0)1795 890256
Web www.theploughinnstalisfield.co.uk

Entry 296 Map 5

Kent

The Barrow House

Egerton

You get a little time travel at the Barrow House: a 14th century inn, 17th century timber frames, 21st century comfort and design. It's a great little place – friendly and stylish with super food and all sorts of libations waiting at the bar. It sits in a pretty village surrounded by open country with Leeds Castle up the road. Known as the George for centuries, it changed its name in deference to the Bronze Age barrow that rises in a field on the edge of the village. Back at the inn, there's a smart terrace for lunch in the sun, then a couple of open fires inside to keep things cosy. They serve their own ale, craft beers and well-priced wines but you can pop in for an espresso, too. As for the food, most is sourced within 20 miles. You'll find soups and sharing plates, burgers and fish and chips, or a three-course feast, perhaps smoked salmon, slow-cooked beef, marmalade Bakewell tart.

Meals	Starters from £6. Lunch from £8. Dinner from £10.
Closed	Open all day.

Dane & Sarah Allchorne
The Barrow House,
The Street,
Egerton, TN27 9DJ

Tel +44 (0)1233 756599
Web www.thebarrowhouse.co.uk

Entry 297 Map 5

The Windmill

Hollingbourne

In the village of Hollingbourne is a triple-gabled pub, behind whose façade is one of the best kitchens in Kent. It's headed by chef Richard Phillips, and serviced by impeccable staff. Enter a dog-friendly bar for a pint of Long Blond and a ploughman's platter, or the restaurant for a meal to remember. Hats hang from a silver antler above the huge inglenook, button banquettes line a wall, and tables are dark and polished. Start with a divine tart of braised chicory, confit shallots and melted blue cheese and black truffle honey dressing, move on to Madeira-infused roast chicken with tarragon gnocchi, end with coffee and chocs. The classics are covered – burgers, steaks, fish 'n' chips – the vegetables are Kent's finest, the puddings are to die for. Outside: a barbecue, a smokery and a child-friendly garden.

Meals	Bar snacks from £3.20. Starters from £5.95. Dinner from £12.95.
Closed	Open all day.

Richard Phillips
The Windmill,
32 Eyhorne Street,
Hollingbourne, ME17 1TR

Tel +44 (0)1622 889000
Web www.thewindmillbyrichardphillips.co.uk

Entry 298 Map 5

Kent

The Dirty Habit

Hollingbourne

Crackling fires in beamed bars, enjoyable food and pints of Harvey's lure walkers and foodies to this North Downs treasure by the Pilgrim's Way; monks once offered ale and lodgings to pilgrims en route to Canterbury. Elite Pubs have refurbished beautifully, restoring Georgian wall panelling in the bar and, in the Monks Corner room, preserving a 13th-century brick floor, rafters and bread oven. Daily menus make good use of local and seasonal and combine pub classics with Mediterranean dishes. You could start with devilled lamb's kidneys, move on to crab and crayfish linguine, or partridge with bacon and chestnut sauce, and finish with apple and orange tart. Sharing deli boards, afternoon teas and Sunday roasts complete the picture, there's a landscaped terrace too, and stunning downland walks that start from the door.

Meals	Lunch & dinner £9.50-£24.50.
Closed	Open all day.

Martial & Natasha Chaussy
The Dirty Habit, The Pilgrims Way,
Upper Street, Hollingbourne,
Maidstone, ME17 1UW

Tel +44 (0)1622 880880
Web www.elitepubs.com/the_dirtyhabit

Entry 299 Map 5

The Farm House

West Malling

The only village centre venue for Elite Pubs is a fine Elizabethan building on the High Street in West Malling, a busy little village west of Maidstone. The Farm House throngs with diners and drinkers, who spill out of the contemporary bar on warm days to share a charcuterie board and a bottle of Malbec at rustic tables on the terrace or in the pretty walled garden, which overlook a 15th-century barn. Escape the bar hub-bub and book a table in the smart, wood-floored dining room for scallops with pea and mint purée followed by crab linguini and apple and rhubarb crumble. All day sandwiches and pizzas, traditional afternoon teas, and Kentish ales on tap complete the thriving picture.

Meals	Lunch & dinner from £10.90. Sunday lunch from £11.90.
Closed	Open all day.

Martial & Natasha Chaussy
The Farm House,
97-99 High Street,
West Malling, ME19 6NA

Tel +44 (0)1732 843257
Web www.elitepubs.com/the_farmhouse/

Entry 300 Map 5

Kent

The Cricketers Inn

Meopham

Aptly named – Meopham is considered to be the birthplace of Kent cricket in 1776 this spick-and-span whitewashed pub overlooks the picture-book village green where the cricket club still play. Bag a bench on summer Sundays to watch the action with a pint of Harvey's Best and a round of tuna and horseradish mayonnaise sandwiches, or a steak and ale pie from the all day menu, or tuck into the full monty – sirloin of beef with roast duck fat potatoes and Yorkshire pud. In winter, hunker down beside the raised log fire in the bar with red-painted ceiling, wood floor and a wealth of cricketing memorabilia and dine heartily (salt and pepper squid; lamb shoulder; bread and butter pudding) in the impressive dining room extension. The posh heated terrace overlooks an early 19th-century smock mill.

Meals	Starters from £4.95. Mains from £9.50.
Closed	Open all day.

Brian Whiting
The Cricketers Inn,
Wrotham Road, Meopham,
Gravesend, DA13 0QA

Tel +44 (0)1474 812163
Web www.thecricketersinn.co.uk

Entry 301 Map 5

The George & Dragon

Chipstead

Ben James snapped up a failing boozer in leafy Chipstead, a 16th-century timbered gem, in 2009. Spruced up with style, minutes from Sevenoaks and the M25, it comes with log fires, timbers and beams, a classy daily menu bristling with produce from the larders of Kent and Sussex, and great wines. At lunch, accompany a pint of Westerham Grasshopper Ale with a succulent steak sandwich or share a deliboard of cured meats, cheeses and chutneys. At dinner, tuck into such delicacies as pigeon and pancetta salad; seared Chart Farm 'sika' venison; roast chicken breast with butterbeans and chorizo. Vegetarian dishes are very good: Blue Monday cheese, pear and walnut salad; wild mushroom risotto with truffle oil. Shun the motorway services – it's the best pit-stop for miles.

Meals	Lunch & dinner £9–£18.50.
Closed	Open all day.

Ben James
The George & Dragon,
39 High Street, Chipstead,
Sevenoaks, TN13 2RW

Tel	+44 (0)1732 779019
Web	www.georgeanddragonchipstead.com

Entry 302 Map 5

Kent

The Kings Head

Bessels Green

Brian Whiting pushed open the doors to the stylishly remodelled Kings Head in 2014, confident that the Whiting & Hammond trademark look and feel of the spruced-up interior and innovative pub menu would wow local diners. Rugs on bare boards, chunky church candles on old dining tables, walls of prints and posters lined with shelves of books, all set the scene for feasts of crab and lobster ravioli, smoked bacon and pea soup, toad-in-the-hole, Catalan fish and shellfish stew, and sticky toffee pudding. Local Westerham ales, great coffee, a sheltered rear terrace with posh tables and brollies, and three heated garden dining huts complete the promising picture. A cracking pit-stop close to the M25, the A21, Chartwell and Knole Park (NT), and Sevenoaks town centre.

Meals	Starters from £4.95. Mains from £9.50.
Closed	Open all day.

Brian Whiting
The Kings Head,
2 Westerham Road, Bessels Green,
Sevenoaks, TN13 2QA

Tel	+44 (0)1732 452081
Web	www.kingsheadbesselsgreen.co.uk

Entry 303 Map 5

The Chaser Inn

Shipbourne

Whiting & Hammond's flagship dining pub is a striking, colonial-style building beside the parish church with serene views over the village green. Its name is associated with the Fairlawne Estate where steeplechase horses, including the Queen Mother's, were trained. From the impressive porticoed frontage enter a warren of cosy, country-smart rooms – rugs on bare boards, fat candles on old tables, bookcases groaning with books. Browse the papers with a pint of Abbot by the fire or tuck into some hearty British food, best enjoyed in the timber-vaulted dining room. From the daily menu try potted rabbit or devilled lamb's kidneys then whole plaice with caper and citrus butter; top it all with lemon tart. Come for weekend breakfasts or Sunday roasts, then walk to Ightham Mote (NT) – the Greensand Way passes the front door.

Meals Lunch & dinner £9.95-£12.95.
Closed Open all day.

Paul Roser
The Chaser Inn,
Stumble Hill, Shipbourne,
Tonbridge, TN11 9PE
Tel +44 (0)1732 810360
Web www.thechaser.co.uk

Kent

The Little Brown Jug

Chiddingstone Causeway

Set beside a rural lane deep in the Kentish Weald, Whiting & Hammond's HQ and flagship pub makes a handy pit-stop after visiting nearby Penshurst Place, Chiddingstone Castle, or even Hever Castle; all are minutes away. Or, round off a cracking country walk with a pint of local ale in the beautiful garden. Tardis-like, the bar extends back into several inter-linked dining areas with intimate corners, book-filled shelves, old pictures and mirrors, rugs on wood floors, and old dining tables topped with candles. Seasonal daily menus combine hearty British pub classics with specials, perhaps braised shoulder of lamb, and traditional puds like sticky toffee pudding with vanilla ice cream. Heated garden huts with your own waiter/ess (seating eight) are perfect for family lunches at any time of year.

Meals Starters from £4.95.
Mains from £9.50.
Closed Open all day.

Brian Whiting
The Little Brown Jug,
Chiddingstone Causeway,
Tonbridge, TN11 8JJ
Tel +44 (0)1892 870318
Web www.thelittlebrownjug.co.uk

The Poacher and Partridge

Tudeley

In the peaceful flatlands of Kent, a two-minute drive from Tudeley's little church (famous for Chagall's exquisite stained-glass windows) is a new addition to Elite Pubs' classy stable. Through a new-timbered entrance enter a big airy space with new slates on the floor and a bright contemporary décor. Bentwood chairs at plain tables contrast with attractive upbeat fabrics and theatrical pops of colour; there's a specials board above the fire, a charming pair of partridges (stuffed) by a window, and a big rustic wood-fired oven from which pizzas and steaks flow. Service is attentive and the good-looking food ranges from rabbit and prune terrine to quinoa salad to broad bean risotto, chicken supreme, fish and chips and lot of lovely puds. Outside: a big terrace with views across fields, a summer bar and grill, and a super children's playground.

Meals	Small plates from £5.75. Mains from £11.95.
Closed	Open all day.

The Manager
The Poacher and Partridge, Hartlake Road, Tudeley, Tonbridge, TN11 0PH
Tel +44 (0)1732 358934
Web www.elitepubs.com/poacher_partridge/

Entry 306 Map 5

Kent

The Kentish Hare

Bidborough

In Bidborough is a reinvented local, a big busy gastropub enjoyed by the country set. From its pristine weatherboarding to its zinc-topped bar, it is delightful and dapper inside and out. The Tanner brothers opened their first restaurant in 1999 and this is their newest venture; find a sweep of hardwood floor, a long blue-grey bar, a log-burner by leather sofas, a large antler on a bare brick wall, a big paved garden. The range of drinks is broad (bottled beers, ciders, spirits, 30 wines by the glass) and the produce fresh, seasonal and Kentish; they champion the best. Old favourites appear on the menus (Bar, Set and Main) and are executed with a sure touch: devilled whitebait, scrumptious fish and chips, steak medallions with brandy cream, rice pudding with plum jam. Our burgers vanished in seconds.

Meals	Bar snacks from £3.95. Lunch from £7.50. Dinner from £13.95. Set menu, 2-3 courses, £15-£19.
Closed	Mondays. Sun from 6pm.

Chris & James Tanner
The Kentish Hare,
95 Bidborough Ridge, Bidborough, Royal Tunbridge Wells, TN3 0XB
Tel +44 (0)1892 525709
Web www.thekentishhare.com

Entry 307 Map 5

The Three Chimneys

Biddenden

Imagine tiny unspoilt rooms of stripped brick, faded paintwork, ancient timber and smouldering fires. During the Napoleonic wars French officers imprisoned nearby were allowed to wander as far as the point where the three paths meet (the 'trois chemins' – hence the name). There's farm cider and Adnams Best Bitter drawn straight from the cask, and the cooking is modern and tasty; parmesan and herb-crusted loin of lamb; chocolate and praline torte with pistachio ice cream. You can eat in the bars (though not the public one) as well as the charming restaurant with its stylish conservatory extension, or on the sheltered patio. They pretty much get the balance right between pub and restaurant here, so prop up the bar for as long as you like.

Meals: Lunch & dinner £11.95-£18.95.
Bar meals £3.95-£8.95.

Closed: 3pm-5.30pm (3.30pm-6pm Sun).

Craig Smith
The Three Chimneys,
Hareplain Road, Biddenden,
Ashford, TN27 8LW

Tel: +44 (0)1580 291472
Web: www.thethreechimneys.co.uk

Entry 308 Map 5

Kent

The Milk House

Sissinghurst

The gardens at Sissinghurst Castle were designed by Vita Sackville-West and they're some of the loveliest in the land. As for The Milk House, it's a great base from which to explore this deeply rural area – stylish, welcoming, nicely priced. It's also a place for a very good meal, seasonal and mostly sourced within 20 miles. In summer, you decant onto a smart terrace with an outside bar and wood-fired pizza oven, not a bad spot for a jug of Pimm's and a crispy margherita. There's a duck pond, lawns for a pint in the sun, then views over open country. Airy interiors have an easy style: woven willow lampshades hanging above the bar, a timber-framed dining room, where you dig into fabulous food, perhaps home-cured smoked salmon, free-range Park Farm beef, chocolate tart with kirsch-soaked cherries; there are matchless local cheeses, too. Marvellous.

Meals: Lunch from £5.
Dinner, 3 courses, from £35.
Sunday lunch from £15.

Closed: Open all day.

Dane & Sarah Allchorne
The Milk House,
The Street, Sissinghurst,
Cranbrook, TN17 2JG

Tel: +44 (0)1580 720200
Web: www.themilkhouse.co.uk

Entry 309 Map 5

The Bull

Benenden

Overlooking Benenden's large and lovely green, complete with cricket pitch and parish church, the 17th-century Bull draws an appreciative crowd, especially on match days. Behind the unusual paned windows, the appeal is obvious in this rustic-chic bar, all stripped wooden floors, fat church candles, scrubbed tables, cushioned settles, and a blazing fire in the inglenook. The dining room is equally informal and relaxed. Come for heady Biddenden cider or a cracking pint of Old Dairy Red Top, brewed along the road at Hole Park. The food is hearty and locally sourced – farm meats, Rye Bay seafood – and the menu holds such delights as scallops with sweet chilli butter, wild rabbit and bacon casserole, fish pie, treacle tart, and some rather good sandwiches. Once a month there's live music and the place heaves.

Meals: Lunch from £6.95.
Bar meals from £9.50.
Dinner from £10.50.
Sunday lunch £11.50.
No food Sunday eve.

Closed: Open all day.

Mark & Lucy Barron-Reid
The Bull,
Benenden,
Cranbrook, TN17 4DE

Tel: +44 (0)1580 240054

Web: www.thebullatbenenden.co.uk

Entry 310 Map 5

The Great House

Gills Green

In rolling Wealden countryside, the Elizabethan weatherboard cottages – now one smart cosy pub – invite you in with an alluring mix of old beams, wood floors and eclectic furnishings. There are log fires in the rambling bar, and a Mediterranean-style terrace (stone flower urns, Italian designer chairs) off the airy Orangery dining room. Menus combine a modern British and a French brasserie feel, so nibble on air-cured ham – sliced theatre-style from a huge leg on the butcher's block – then tuck into game stew from the Aga or halibut with tarragon mash and brown shrimp butter; make space for apple and plum crumble. Alternatively, pop in for a shared deli board (Kentish game), linger over afternoon tea or book in for Sunday roasts; it's all delicious. There are pints of Harvey's and 20 wines by the glass.

Meals: Lunch & dinner £9.50-£24.50.

Closed: Open all day.

Martial & Natasha Chaussy
The Great House,
Gills Green,
Cranbrook, TN18 5EJ

Tel: +44 (0)1580 753119

Web: www.elitepubs.com/the_greathouse

Entry 311 Map 5

The Ferry Inn

Stone in Oxney

Fairly remote and on the marshes is the misnamed Ferry Inn; the river changed its course and now everyone is landlocked. Beyond the picket fence that fronts the road, the inn is exceptionally pretty, with a Georgian brick façade and a beer garden behind, overlooking river and fields. Inside are scrubbed wood tables and hops above the bar, a big open fire, a more formal restaurant, and an enticing air of conviviality… and you can't fault the food, service or beer. There are Rye Bay scallops with crispy bacon and pea purée, marsh rack of lamb, spicy vegetable linguine, and a leek and potato soup that slipped down nicely with a well-kept pint of Harvey's. This is an amazing location for birders and wildlife walkers.

Meals	Starters from £5.95. Mains from £11.95.
Closed	Open all day.

Paul Withers-Green
The Ferry Inn,
Appledore Road,
Stone in Oxney, TN30 7JY

Tel	+44 (0)1233 758246
Web	www.oxneyferry.com

Kent

The Oxney Gourmet Pie & Burger Bar

Wittersham

Well, what a find: a sophisticated burger joint in the middle of the countryside. The Old Swan in Wittersham has had a rebrand, and everyone, it seems, loves it – from tourists in holiday season to locals to families to walkers with dogs. There are two plank-floored bars inside, one a light airy space with half-wall panelling and a solid new bar, the other with charming pine tables, a blackboard menu and a fat log-burner. It's a place for lovers of craft beers and Harvey's, and homemade burgers made from prime Scotch beef, flame-grilled to order and wrapped in a bun (brioche, granary, ciabatta). They offer chicken, lamb, mini and veggie burgers too. Expect Sunday roasts, the 'catch of the day', Thai fish cakes for kids, pecan treacle tart… best to book!

Meals	Starters from £5.45. Mains from £7.45.
Closed	Monday & Tuesday.

Paul Withers-Green
The Oxney Gourmet Pie & Burger Bar,
1 Swan St, Wittersham, TN30 7PH

Tel	+44 (0)1233 758246
Web	www.oxneygourmetpieand burgerbar.co.uk

Millstone at Mellor

Mellor

Modern meets traditional – in a handsome 18th-century coaching inn in a pretty village on the edge of the Ribble valley. There's a welcoming glow in the bar, with its oak beams and panelling, so get cosy by the roaring fire with a pint of local Thwaites Bitter and a crispy duck spring roll. Or eat in the stylish dining room with warm wood-panelled walls. Local ingredients are carefully sourced and the food is wholesome and unpretentious. Tuck into the likes of ham hock and Lancashire cheese croquette with chilli tomato chutney followed by Bowland steak, kidney and Wainwright pudding with mushy peas, fat chips and a jug of gravy. Or share a fishmonger's board of smoked Scottish salmon, crab bonbon, Thwaites ale battered haddock, crayfish … and freshly baked bread. Leave room for blackberry, rum and honey cheesecake with raspberry curd. Bedrooms ooze comfort: sumptuous fabrics and luxurious linen, digital radios and plasma TVs, high-spec bathrooms, umbrellas for wet days. No wonder it's popular.

Rooms	23 twin/doubles: £75-£125.
Meals	Lunch & dinner £8.95-£16.95.
Closed	Open all day.

Tim Parker
Millstone at Mellor,
Church Lane, Mellor, Blackburn, BB2 7JR

Tel	+44 (0)1254 813333
Web	www.thwaites.co.uk/hotels-and-inns/inns/millstone-at-mellor

Red Pump Inn

Bashall Eaves

Down meandering lanes in the lovely Ribble valley is a handsome roadside inn with a south-facing terrace tumbled with flowers. In the cosy snug bar: flag floors, crackling fires, oak settles and tables, and shuttered windows with green views. Changing cask ales might include Bowland Hen Harrier and Moorhouse's Pride of Pendle, while Jonathan hand-picks wines and malt whiskies. For lunch there are two rooms to choose from: one cosy with mustard walls, the other with bare oak tables and settles by the wood-burner. In the evening, sit in the large, beamed, candlelit restaurant and tuck in to something from the chargrill (steaks are to die for). The menu is warming, hearty and rich, and meat comes from Ginger Pig. Try lamb's kidneys with spinach and bacon, home cured salmon with caper and lemon dressing, slow roast pork belly and bean cassoulet. The eight bedrooms have Fran's design flair with French antique beds, wonderfully comfy mattresses and super wet room showers; hearty Irish breakfasts with white pudding await. Clitheroe Castle and the Forest of Bowland are nearby.

Rooms	8 twin/doubles: £95-£150.
Meals	Lunch & dinner £8.95-£24. Bar snacks from £2.50.
Closed	Christmas.

Jonathan & Fran Gledhill
Red Pump Inn,
Clitheroe Road, Bashall Eaves,
Clitheroe, BB7 3DA
Tel +44 (0)1254 826227
Web www.theredpumpinn.co.uk

Toll House Inn

Lancaster

This grand old city pub-hotel is bound to impress: high ceilings, stained-glass windows, huge Art Deco lights (yes, the originals) and ornate plasterwork abounds. And the elegant dining room with its vintage mismatch of furniture and gleaming parquet is a pleasing space from which to ponder a varied menu; locally potted shrimps, Lancashire hotpot, and steak and ale pudding all appeal. In the bar, sandwiches are packed with the likes of Lancashire cheese and chutney. Well-kept Thwaites cask beers await, and there's a selection of wines by the glass. Contemporary bedrooms of different shapes and sizes pick up on the period mood, and are comfortable and quiet, with drenching showers and triple-glazed windows, plasma TVs, snowy white linen; one has a beautiful listed wardrobe! Breakfast is full Lancashire – the works, and delicious. In short, a lovely friendly pub-hotel, and a fine place for a spot of retail therapy, slap in the throbbing heart of historic Lancaster.

Rooms	28 doubles: £70-£105. Singles from £64.
Meals	Breakfast £8.95. Lunch from £6.95. Bar meals from £5.95. Dinner from £8.95. Sunday lunch, 2 courses, £11.95.
Closed	Open all day.

Joe Ruddock
Toll House Inn,
Penny Street, Lancaster, LA1 1XT

Tel +44 (0)1524 599900
Web www.thwaites.co.uk/hotels-and-inns/inns/toll-house-at-lancaster

The Cartford Inn

Little Eccleston

Patrick and Julie know how to run a great little inn: whisk up some stunning food, throw in a pinch of quirky style then add impeccable service. The restaurant and inn overlook the river Wyre, with the Trough of Bowland a spectacular backdrop. The front bar, with its roaring fire and friendly locals is a great place to stop for a pint of local ale, though a courtyard garden will draw you out in good weather. In typically relaxed style you can eat whatever you want wherever you want: enjoy a traditional French tartiflette, then venison Wellington, followed by blackberry curd tart, perhaps. Afterwards, you can work it off by following the river; a two-mile circular walk will spin you round. Fantastic.

Meals	Lunch from £8.50. Dinner, 3 courses, £20-£30. No food Mon lunch.
Closed	Open all day.

Patrick & Julie Beaume
The Cartford Inn,
Cartford Lane, Little Eccleston,
Preston, PR3 0YP

Tel	+44 (0)1995 670166
Web	www.thecartfordinn.co.uk

Entry 317 Map 11

Lancashire

The Inn at Whitewell

Whitewell

The old deerkeeper's lodge sits just above the river Hodder with views across parkland to rising fells. Merchants used to stop by and fill up with wine, food and song before heading north through notorious bandit country. Now barbours and muddy dogs mix with frocks and suits. You can eat in the bar but the long restaurant and the outside terrace drink in the view – which will only increase your enjoyment of Bowland lamb with cassoulet of beans and root vegetables, homemade ice cream and fine wines (including their own well-priced Vintner's). In the bar, antiques, bric-a-brac, peat fires, old copies of *The Beano*, fish and chips, warm crab cakes and local bangers. At weekends it gets packed and if you want a table, the more formal restaurant takes bookings. You'll love it.

Meals	Bar meals from £8. Dinner £25-£35.
Closed	Open all day.

Charles Bowman
The Inn at Whitewell,
Dunsop Road, Whitewell,
Clitheroe, BB7 3AT

Tel	+44 (0)1200 448222
Web	www.innatwhitewell.com

Entry 318 Map 12

Assheton Arms

Downham

Delightful Downham is owned by the Clitheroes and they keep a close eye on 'modern' developments; seems they approve of the changes wrought by the Neve family to this historic pub. Gone is the fusty old warren of rooms; now you are welcomed by linked spaces full of light and warmth with stone floors, wood stoves, cheery duck-egg blue walls and oak furniture. Seafood is central to the menu; Chris Neve is from a long line of sea dogs and as a former trawlerman knows a thing or two about fish. Expect the likes of crab Waldorf salad, king prawn and shredded pork gyoza, or queenie scallops. Follow up with monkfish perhaps... meat eaters are nicely catered for too, with Goosnargh chicken pie and Gazegill lamb. With Black Sheep, Taylors and Thwaites on tap, it's the perfect place to drop into after a hike up Pendle Hill.

Meals	Lunch & dinner £8.50-£15.50.
Closed	3pm-7pm. Open all day Sat & Sun.

Joycelyn Neve
Assheton Arms,
Downham,
Clitheroe, BB7 4BJ
Tel +44 (0)1200 441227
Web www.asshetonarms.com

Entry 319 Map 12

Lancashire

The Lower Buck

Waddington

Look for the church as you enter the village and you'll discover an 18th-century treasure tucked behind – peaceful and unspoiled. Andrew Warburton took over the stone pub in 2005 and, while gently upgrading, has preserved the layout and atmosphere beautifully. Devoid of machines and music, each of the three rooms off the slate-tiled lobby has polished rug-strewn floors, cream walls, old prints, big mirrors, ticking clocks, crackling fires, and a mix of dark wood dining tables. Banter with the locals over a pint of Bowland Hen Harrier, or order from a menu that's chock full of pub classics made from local ingredients, including meat and veg from Longridge farms. Fancy Morecambe Bay potted shrimps, Lancashire hotpot, steak and kidney pie, plum and apple crumble? Perfect after a Ribble Valley ramble.

Meals	Lunch & dinner from £9.95.
Closed	Open all day.

Andrew Warburton
The Lower Buck,
Edisford Road, Waddington,
Clitheroe, BB7 3HU
Tel +44 (0)1200 423342
Web www.lowerbuckinn.co.uk

Entry 320 Map 12

The Three Fishes

Mitton

The suppliers and growers are listed on the back of every menu – Lancashire is a hotbed of food artisans – and the 17th-century village pub in the lovely Ribble Valley has taken gastropubbery to a mouthwatering level. This long whitewashed public house has been refurbed in rustic-smart fashion and is vast: up to 130 can be seated inside, a further 60 out. Walls are pale brick, floors stone, lighting subtle, winter logs glow, and the big new wing armchairs have been upholstered in tartan – fabulous! Wines are gorgeous, local ale and real cider is served and the beer-friendly food celebrates traditional British delicacies. We loved the game terrine with pear chutney, the Lancashire hotpot with braised red cabbage, and the chocolate tart with honeycomb. The places heaves so arrive early, especially on Sunday.

Meals	Lunch & dinner £9-£17.95. Sunday lunch £15-£19.50.
Closed	Open all day.

Nigel Haworth & Craig Bancroft
The Three Fishes,
Mitton Road,
Mitton, BB7 9PQ Clitheroe

Tel +44 (0)1254 826888
Web www.thethreefishes.com

Entry 321 Map 12

Lancashire

Freemasons at Wiswell

Wiswell

This old village pub has had a facelift; pots, plantings and a gravel drive swish it up. Inside, antique rugs on stone-flagged floors, gleaming oak furniture and beams, leather wing chairs, fires and fresh flowers. A series of rooms upstairs promise sophisticated dining at antique refectory tables set with white linen. Back down in the bar, Pride of Pendle and Blonde Witch are cask conditioned, whilst a cellar of 250 wines awaits. Local lad 'done good' (most recently at Stanley House Hotel), Steven Smith produces dishes bursting with seasonal ingredients: poached and roast wood pigeon with pressed leeks and hazelnuts; steamed game pudding; organic salmon fried in vanilla oil with Morecambe Bay mussels and fennel. Magners cider granita with hot cinnamon doughnuts rounds things off beautifully.

Meals	Lunch & dinner £10.95-£28.95. Seasonal set menu £13.95 & £15.95. Tasting menu £55.
Closed	Open all day.

Steven Smith
Freemasons at Wiswell,
8 Vicarage Fold, Wiswell,
Clitheroe, BB7 9DF

Tel +44 (0)1254 822218
Web www.freemasonsatwiswell.com

Entry 322 Map 12

The Clog and Billycock

Pleasington

Following the success of the Three Fishes and the Highwayman, another winner. Now the old boozer in this leafy village close to Blackburn has crackling fires, gleaming oak furniture and an eye-catching beamed atrium: a sensitively lit showcase for a collection of black and white photographs of the pub's esteemed growers and producers. The colour scheme is subtle and calming yet there's a great buzz to the place, as staff ferry beautiful food to cosy tables. Tuck into heather-fed lamb hotpot with pickled red cabbage, follow with jam roly poly and custard. With a great outside space, an inspiring children's menu, attentive staff and fine wines and ales, this pleasingly named pub is one to get excited about.

Meals Lunch & dinner £8.95-£19.75. Sunday lunch, 3 courses, £19.50.
Closed Open all day.

Nigel Haworth & Craig Bancroft
The Clog and Billycock,
Billinge End Road, Pleasington,
Blackburn, BB2 6QB
Tel +44 (0)1254 201163
Web www.theclogandbillycock.com

Entry 323 Map 12

Lancashire

The Oyster & Otter

Feniscowles

Joycelyn Neve, daughter of one of Fleetwood's most prominent fish merchants, has lavished money on this once boarded-up community boozer. The result is a swish contemporary dining pub, all blond wood floors, chunky tables, cushioned benches and modern art; business has boomed since day one. With the pick of the day's catch (and more) just a phone call away, to create a seafood-driven gastropub was the obvious direction; the appetite locally for quality fresh fish and seafood has been staggering. Fish lovers flock in for Malaysian seafood curry, tikka-spiced monkfish and classic haddock and chips (also available to take away), while carnivores tuck into Gazegill Organics slow-cooked lamb, or Pendle Hill 28-day dry aged steak with pepper sauce. Don't miss the seafood nights, with wine matched to each course – or the Sunday roast lunches.

Meals Lunch & dinner £9.50-£22.50.
Closed Open all day (from 12pm).

Joycelyn Neve
The Oyster & Otter,
631 Livesey Branch Road,
Feniscowles, Blackburn, BB2 5DQ
Tel +44 (0)1254 203200
Web www.oysterandotter.co.uk

Entry 324 Map 12

The Eagle & Child

Ramsbottom

Glen Duckett took a boarded-up pub with a bad reputation and transformed it into a thriving food-led pub in just over year. A passionate desire to do something different, and a clear vision from the start, to create a community pub with top-quality food, has been key to the pub's success. Menus focus on Lancashire's food heritage and classic local recipes and ingredients are given a modern twist. Hearty and affordable dishes include black pudding Scotch egg; braised beef shin and oxtail suet pudding; plum tart and clotted cream. Disadvantaged young local people are trained in the kitchen, and alongside community group Incredible Edible Ramsbottom, Glen has transformed former waste ground into a beer garden – a fabulous space for education, food production, drinking and dining.

Meals	Lunch from £5.95. Dinner from £12.95. Sunday lunch, 2 courses, £19.95.
Closed	January-March. Open all day April-December.

Glen Duckett
The Eagle & Child,
3 Whalley Road,
Ramsbottom, Bury, BL0 0DL

Tel +44 (0)1706 557181
Web www.eagle-and child.com

Entry 325 Map 12

Lancashire

The Rams Head Inn

Denshaw

You're on the border here and the views are glorious. High on the Saddleworth moors between Oldham and Ripponden, the Rams Head is two miles from the motorway but you'd never know. Unspoilt inside and out, there's an authentic, old-farmhouse feel. Small rooms, cosy with log fires in winter, are carpeted, half-panelled, beamed, and filled with memorabilia. With a range of cask ales served and wine by the glass drinkers are made very welcome. Menus announce a heart-warming selection of tasty food: game and venison in season, seafood, great steaks, puddings like treacle tart with ice cream as well as other classic British dishes. A wonderfully isolated Lancashire outpost, staffed by people who care, and with a farm shop, a deli and a tea room to boot.

Meals	Lunch & dinner £9.50-£17.95. Deli prices from £2.50.
Closed	Mondays all day.

G R Haigh
The Rams Head Inn,
Ripponden Road, Denshaw,
Oldham, OL3 5UN

Tel +44 (0)1457 874802
Web www.ramsheaddenshaw.co.uk

Entry 326 Map 12

The Hercules Revived

Sutton Cheney

Behind the charming painted façade of the 18th-century Hercules, opposite the church – you can't miss it – lies a totally refurbished pub. New oak beams and floors, and cream wall; this place has taken a dramatic change for the better. You can sit on a stylish tweed chair and enjoy a prosecco or espresso, or nurse a Guinness with the dog by the fire. It's neat and dandy, laid-back and friendly, and there's a rather posh restaurant upstairs. Pick an area to dine according to your mood… all have upholstered chairs and grey carpeting, and the area to the front left has a fine view across the field to the church. We hear good reports of the food: a beautiful shin of beef, a herb-crusted cod with crayfish linguini, a refreshing lemon and lime syllabub. A 'lovely bunch of producers' supply the goods, including Leicestershire cheeses.

Meals Lunch & dinner £10.95-£20.95.
Closed Open all day.

Oliver & Sian Warner
The Hercules Revived,
Main Street, Sutton Cheney,
Market Bosworth, CV13 0AG
Tel +44 (0)1455 699336
Web www.herculesrevived.co.uk

Entry 327 Map 8

Leicestershire

The Cow & Plough

Oadby

A one-storey pub housed in the former milking sheds of a working farm just outside Leicester. The Lounts founded it in 1989 and filled it with good beer and a hoard of brewery memorabilia: the back bars are stuffed with tin plate ads, mirrors and bottles, and there's a conservatory with piano and plants and beams decked with dried hops. It later became an outlet for their Steamin' Billy ales (named after Elizabeth's Jack Russell who 'steamed' after energetic country pursuits). In the farm's old visitor centre is the restaurant, its high beams draped with fairylights and lanterns, cosy backdrop to generous portions of pub classics and some more adventurous mains. The pub has won awards and become a place for shooting lunches; it's also popular with the Leicester rugby team supporters.

Meals Lunch from £10.95.
Bar meals from £6.95.
Dinner from £12.95.
Sunday lunch, 3 courses, £16.95.
Closed Open all day.

Leighton Turner
The Cow & Plough,
Stoughton Grange Farm, Gartree Road, Oadby, Leicester, LE2 2FB
Tel +44 (0)1162 720852
Web www.steamin-billy.co.uk

Entry 328 Map 8

The Curzon Arms

Woodhouse Eaves

In the village of Woodhouse Eaves is a pub that ticks almost every box. With four well-known real ales (Timothy Taylor's Landlord, Sharp's Doom Bar, York Guzzler and Bath Gem) and Westons Cider, this is the place to go for a pint! It attracts a crowd – suits and locals, friends and office parties, families at weekends, horses in summer, walkers en route. Refurbished in traditional style, with leather banquette seating and heritage colours, the interiors are warm and appealing. Painted beam ceilings and prints on the walls, a chesterfield sofa, a box of toys, log-burners belting out the heat. There are a 'pie of the day' and a 'catch of the day,' too, a cheese platter with tasting notes, wines to satisfy most, and chips crisp and hot. The terrace is attractive even on a winter's day and the garden is big enough to play in.

Meals	Lunch from £5.95. Dinner, 2-3 courses, £15.95-£18.95.
Closed	3pm-5:30pm Mon-Fri. Open all day Sat & Sun.

Ben Moore
The Curzon Arms,
44 Maplewell Road, Woodhouse
Eaves, Loughborough, LE12 8QZ
Tel +44 (0)1509 890377
Web www.thecurzonarms.com

Entry 329 Map 8

Leicestershire

The Berkeley Arms

Wymondham

In the middle of the village of Wymondham is an exemplary pub. Enter a low-beamed, pine-tabled, light-filled room, with an original terracotta tiled floor and a fire at the carpeted end. It's a wonderfully intimate place to drink and eat, and if you prefer to be more formal, there's a stylish dining room too. Owners Louise and Neil met at Hambleton Hall so the food is special and the suppliers are lovingly listed. Pigeons, tomatoes and rhubarb come from Ray and Pam Elsome; mint, marrows and flowers from Ken Hill. We tried the pâté of rabbit, pork and prune; the pasta with pickled walnuts, reblochon cheese and truffle oil; the pear and ginger crumble with pear sorbet – all were exquisite. In summer you can stroll in the garden and take in the pretty views. Staff are friendly, polite, perfect.

Meals	Lunch from £14.95. Bar meals from £10. Dinner from £25. Sunday lunch, 2 courses, £17.95.
Closed	Sun eves & all day Mon.

Neil & Louise Hitchen
The Berkeley Arms,
59 Main Street, Wymondham,
Melton Mowbray, LE14 2AG
Tel +44 (0)1572 787587
Web www.theberkeleyarms.co.uk

Entry 330 Map 9

The Bull & Swan at Burghley

Stamford

A magical renovation, an ancient inn that stands a short walk from the middle of glorious Stamford, part of the Burghley estate. The Order of Little Bedlam, a 17th-century aristocratic drinking club, would surely have popped in for the odd snifter. Not that they had it this good… step inside to discover varnished wood floors, golden stone walls, fires smouldering all over the place and newspapers hanging on poles. At the bar venison Scotch eggs are impossible to resist, as are a raft of local ales and splendid wines. Regal oils adorn the walls, leather-backed settles take the strain, and you eat wherever you want. As for beautiful bedrooms, they come in country-house style with huge beds, fabulous linen, warm colours and super-funky bathrooms. Most are big, all are delightful, two interconnect for families, and mattresses are divine. Back downstairs, delicious food waits, perhaps stilton on toast, Burghley game pie, apple and blueberry crumble. And don't miss Burghley, a five-minute stroll, one of Britain's finest houses.

Rooms	7 doubles, 2 twins: £100-£170. Half-board from £72.50 p.p.
Meals	Lunch from £6. Dinner, 3 courses, £25-£30.
Closed	Open all day.

Paul Brown
The Bull & Swan at Burghley,
St Martins,
Stamford, PE9 2LJ
Tel +44 (0)1780 766412
Web www.thebullandswan.co.uk

The Six Bells

Witham on the Hill

The latest venture from feted restaurateurs Jim and Sharon, and the trimmings in the front bar tell you everything about the place: mammoth barista machine at one end, champagne bucket beside the beer pumps, log-fired bread oven in the corner. This century-old village manor house has been made over with polished floors, wainscoting in Annie Sloan colours, and a trio of ceramic ducks flying ironically above the bar. The hipsterish staff ferry good-looking food to the table: signature steaks from butcher Owen Taylor; caramel crème brûlée with sweet and sour apples. Classy cooking for sure, but the Six Bells appeals to all: tuck in to homemade pizza for a tenner, ale from Star Brewing, and you can take home a loaf from that aromatic oven. Digest dinner by the woodburner with a complimentary tot of homemade mint vodka; it doesn't half soften the blow. Better still, retire upstairs to one of three newly primped bedrooms. Doubles are compact but tidily appointed, with carved beds and accent wallpapers, iPod docks and Nespresso makers. The star, though, is the Hayloft suite, with original windows and village views.

Rooms	2 doubles: £80-£95. 1 suite for 2: £120-£150.
Meals	Lunch from £7.50. Dinner, 2 courses, £20. Sunday lunch from £13.
Closed	Mondays.

Jim & Sharon Trevor
The Six Bells,
Main Street, Witham on the Hill,
Bourne, PE10 0JH

Tel +44 (0)1778 590360
Web www.sixbellswitham.co.uk

Smith's of Bourne

Bourne

For 140 years this was John Smith's Grocers, where four generations of men in crisp white overalls dispensed sugar, butter and bacon by the pound. You feel they would approve of its immaculate reinvention as a high street alehouse, from the beautiful green-and-gold picture windows to the panelled front bar, busy with intriguing bric-a-brac. A first visit to Smith's is an adventure, its warren of sepia-lit rooms bringing surprises at every door. There's an old-fashioned cook's pantry with titanic inglenook; a hop-hung minstrel's gallery; even a room done up like stables, with horses' troughs and tin buckets for lampshades. More importantly, the victuals here still bring the townsfolk flocking: six real ales from across the nation; hearty beef pie and pot-roast partridge sourced from local fields and served in vintage cookware.

Meals	Light lunch from £5. Mains £11-£19. Platter to share £16-£22. No food Sun eve.
Closed	Open all day.

Pat & Jane Taylor
Smith's of Bourne,
25 North Street, Bourne, PE10 9AE
Tel +44 (0)1778 426819
Web www.kneadpubs.co.uk/our-pubs/smiths-of-bourne

Lincolnshire

The White Horse

Baston

When a village campaign to save this 18th-century local foundered, farmer Mark Richardson rode to the rescue – and how. The stoutly rustic Spinning Wheel has become the rather slinky White Horse, enlivened by what Mark calls a 'meaty, manly menu' of Baston-reared produce and a smiling welcome from its young team. The bricks in the bay window are from the Richardson family farm, the stripped-back beams have been rifled from Grandad's barn, and (best of all) a handsome slice of felled sycamore serves as counter in the snug. Mark's real coup, though, was tempting Ben and Germaine Larter to come run the place: Ben bossing the kitchen with a chef's eye, Germaine keen as mustard that everyone has a great time. Don't miss their exemplary Sunday roasts, super value and famous with flavour.

Meals	Lunch £6.50-£9. Dinner £11.50-£16.50. Sunday lunch, 1-3 courses, £12-£18. No food Sun eve.
Closed	Mon & Tues lunch.

Ben & Germaine Larter
The White Horse,
4 Church Street, Baston,
Peterborough, PE6 9PE
Tel +44 (0)1778 560923
Web www.thewhitehorsebaston.co.uk

The Tobie Norris

Stamford

Built in 1280, remodelled in 1663 and 2006, the Tobie Norris draws you in to a warren of stunningly atmospheric rooms and takes you back to the old days – Cromwellian at least. Huge stone flags, oak settles and the smell of woodsmoke assail you as you leave the pavements behind. Between the main rooms is a staircase leading to three more, each with vast exposed timbers, little recesses and tiny doors, character and style. Find a church pew or a leather armchair and sit back with your Ufford Ales and Adnams – or a wine from a list of 21, each available by the glass. Dogs doze on bare boards, perfect staff ferry pizzas and plates of smoked salmon linguine, there are rotating ales on tap and you could stay here all day.

Meals	Lunch, bar meals & dinner from £9.95. No food Sunday eve.
Closed	Open all day.

Michael Thurlby & Will Fry
The Tobie Norris,
12 St Paul's St, Stamford, PE9 2BE

Tel	+44 (0)1780 753800
Web	www.kneadpubs.co.uk/our-pubs/the-tobie-norris

Entry 335 Map 9

Lincolnshire

The Exeter Arms

Easton on the Hill

A civilised pub that serves wonderful food. Discreetly modernised, it has a log-burner in the narrow bar and Ufford Ales on handpump. Soft pistachio colours, gentle lighting and polished wooden tables set the restaurant apart, but for a change of mood head for the Orangery with views onto the large, smart terrace; it has the same regularly changing menu and a sunny, contemporary feel. The cooking is classy yet simple, the kitchen moving deftly through a repertoire of modern dishes and pub classics: fish and chips or homemade sausages and creamy mash; pigeon breast with puy lentils and wild mushrooms; Grasmere Farm pork belly with potato cake and Mediterranean vegetables; rice pudding mousse with caramelised plums. Praise, too, for fair prices, 17 wines by the glass and a good, sensible children's menu.

Meals	Lunch & bar meals from £8.95. Dinner from £11.50. Sunday lunch, 3 courses, £18.95. .
Closed	Sunday after 6pm.

Michael Thurlby & Sue Olver
The Exeter Arms,
21 Stamford Rd, Easton on the Hill,
Stamford, PE9 3NS

Tel	+44 (0)1780 756321
Web	www.theexeterarms.net

Entry 336 Map 9

The Chequers Inn

Woolsthorpe

A perfect English inn with beautiful country all around and Belvoir castle looming over the fields as you drop down into the village. In summer, the cricket team play in the field behind, popping in to quench their thirst after a hard day's work. The Chequers started life as a bakery, but has been an inn for 200 years, and is now the hub of this estate village. With exposed timbers, a rug-strewn bar, Farrow & Ball colours and a flurry of open fires, it marries old-fashioned charm with rustic chic. The bar is beautifully busy with four hand-pumped ales, plenty of wines by the glass, 50 malt whiskies, and 30 gins. Food is eaten across four rooms, the robust dishes a satisfying mix of traditional and modern: quail and pigeon, rib of beef, fillet of bream with chive mash, mulled poached pear with cinnamon ice cream. The vale of Belvoir and its grand castle wait.

Meals: Lunch & dinner £9.50-£19.
Bar meals £4.95-£11.50.
Sunday lunch £13.95.

Closed: Open all day.

Justin & Joanne Chad
The Chequers Inn,
Main Street, Woolsthorpe,
Grantham, NG32 1LU
Tel +44 (0)1476 870701
Web www.chequersinn.net

Entry 337 Map 9

Lincolnshire

The New Inn

Great Limber

Beautifully refurbished village inn on the Brockelsby estate, built in the 16th century to welcome hungry travellers. Outside, you find a kitchen garden, a well-kept lawn and a smart terrace for lunch in the sun. Inside, a country-house feel runs through the restaurant – smart fabrics, pretty colours, art from the estate. The bar has attitude, too: grey panelling, red suede banquet, a roaring fire and pints of hand-drawn local ales. Back in the restaurant, delicious food waits. Ian Martin has worked alongside Gordon Ramsay, Raymond Blanc and Michael Caines, and much of what you eat is grown or reared on the estate, perhaps Jerusalem artichoke and truffle soup, saddle of venison with roasted root vegetables, caramelised pear with butterscotch sauce. Walk it off in the North Lincolnshire wolds; sublime, yet ignored, you'll probably have them all to yourself. Worth a detour.

Meals: Lunch, 2-3 courses £15-£18.
Bar menu from £3.50.
Dinner from £14.50.

Closed: Open all day.

Chloë Kirkby
The New Inn,
2 High Street,
Great Limber, DN37 8JL
Tel +44 (0)1469 569998
Web www.thenewinngreatlimber.co.uk

Entry 338 Map 13

The Victoria

London – Richmond

In the leafy suburb of Richmond, with a church and Sheen Common as neighbours, this long-established pub has been transformed by Greg Bellamy and Paul Merret. Find wooden floors, open brickwork, and sofas to flop on as you check out the menu for long, leisurely meals in the conservatory. Here, foodies and families tuck into crisp-battered Cornish squid with tomato, mint, chilli and lime; pan-roasted guinea fowl with spiced pastilla and smoked aubergine; pecan and walnut baklava with nectarine and honey ice cream. Beef comes from a small butcher in Devon, mussels from Norfolk and there's a forager for the elderflower and mushrooms! The wine list bursts with passion and helpful notes: a shame not to allow yourself to be led. The atmosphere is friendly, purposeful and fun, so stay a while: in the back wing are seven bedrooms in contemporary style, with iPod docks and WiFi; the quietest are at the top and the breakfasts are great. You are within striking distance of a cycle ride through Richmond Park, and ten minutes from Twickenham if rugby is your passion. And there's a play garden for children.

Rooms	5 doubles, 2 twin/doubles: £120-£150.
Meals	Lunch & bar meals from £6. Set menu, 2 courses, £12.50 (Mon-Thurs). Dinner from £13. Sunday lunch £24 & £28.
Closed	Open all day.

Bookings Team at The Victoria
The Victoria,
10 West Temple Sheen,
Richmond, London, SW14 7RT

Tel +44 (0)20 8876 4238
Web www.victoriasheen.co.uk

The Orange Public House & Hotel

London – Belgravia

Tall sash windows, lofty ceilings and distressed furniture and floorboards give The Orange its on-trend weathered good looks. The lovingly restored corner-sited Georgian building (a brewery in a past life) comes flooded by light and looks out over Orange Square, its bustling ground-floor bar delivering ales like Sussex Best, or well-chosen wines and seasonal cocktails to a well-heeled Sloaney crowd in its labyrinth of character rooms. Upstairs and downstairs this is one stylish, all-occasions affair, with a slightly more formal restaurant on the first floor and fashionable boutique bedrooms above. Smiley, clued-up young staff ferry dishes to and fro, the modern European menu changing with the seasons; take an opener pork, fennel and manchego scotch egg (with romesco sauce), and after that, maybe one of the wood-fired pizzas (Laverstoke Farm buffalo mozzarella, tomato and basil perhaps) or mains like Anglesey mussels in a bouillabaisse sauce with pomme frites. Of the four country-chic bedrooms – all pastel beige and sage green with lightwood floors, king-sized beds and marble bathrooms – one has a bathtub and pitched-roof ceiling crossed by beams. Breakfasts are a must.

Rooms	4 doubles: £205-£240.
Meals	Lunch from £6.50. Bar meals from £5. Dinner from £10.50. Sunday lunch, 3 courses, £30.
Closed	Open all day.

Nicolas Martin
The Orange Public House & Hotel,
37 Pimlico Road, Belgravia,
London, SW1W 8NE

Tel	+44 (0)20 7881 9844
Web	www.theorange.co.uk

The Grazing Goat

London – Marylebone

Where goats once grazed, smart boutiques flourish, but you barely know you're in the heart of town. Step inside, to a stylish serene space of light oak tables, sage green walls and beige textiles – more country cool than urban glitz. Graze on eggs Benedict at breakfast; at lunch, or dinner, move onto house cocktails and well-chosen wines. Dishes might include line-caught cod fillet with crushed baby potatoes, sautéed spinach and a pickled beetroot dressing, or 28-day dried Castle of Mey fillet steak from the grill. What's good about this intimate pub (little sister to the more characterful Thomas Cubitt and The Orange) is that it attracts a varied crowd, from chaps in suits to Portman village locals and tourists taking a break from Oxford Street. Ales include Doom Bar, juice is freshly squeezed, breakfasts are superb. There's a slightly more formal restaurant upstairs and eight bedrooms over a further three floors. Each comes in boutique country-house style; marble bathrooms have roll top tubs or powerful showers; cool neutral shades and sash-and-cord windows keep things super-fresh.

Rooms	8 doubles: £210-£250.
Meals	Lunch £9.50. Bar meals from £8. Dinner from £15.50. Sunday lunch, 3 courses, £30.
Closed	Open all day.

Guillermo Vidal
The Grazing Goat,
6 New Quebec Street, Marylebone,
London, W1H 7RQ
Tel +44 (0)20 7724 7243
Web www.thegrazinggoat.co.uk

The Punchbowl

London – Mayfair

Near the higgledy-piggledy streets of Shepherds Market is the Punchbowl, now spread over three floors and cunningly fusing Georgian tradition with up-to-the-minute glamour. Inside this former Court, the ground floor is a smart country-city pub, while upstairs is an art deco dining room. Up again to The Club for private parties in an opulent Victorian setting. At the bar or in the dining room, law-abiding Londoners sample pints of IPA Deuchars or the pub's own tipple '1750' with house ale-battered catch of the day, minted pea puree and hand cut chips, perhaps, or a hearty burger. You can feast on the likes of Norfolk chicken breast with forest mushrooms, celeriac, roasted garlic and truffled tarragon sauce, and there may be time to sneak in a rolo chocolate & blood orange fondant with honeycomb ice cream before the last cry of 'order'.

Meals: Mains from £13.50. Dinner, 3 courses, £30-35.
Closed: Open all day.

Ben Newton
The Punchbowl,
41 Farm Street,
Mayfair, London, W1J 5RP
Tel +44 (0)20 749 36841
Web www.punchbowllondon.com

Entry 342 Map 15

The Alfred Tennyson

London – Belgravia

This pretty Georgian 'public house and dining room' sits in a landmark location near Sloane Street, the perfect spot for people watching. Inside: mellow walls, oval sash windows, soft jazz and a big buzz – very SW1. Take your time; this isn't somewhere to pop into; punters are here for serious drinks and canapés in the private room upstairs, or for the food which is pricey but praiseworthy, upmarket pub grub. The breakfasts and weekend brunches (served until 4pm) caught our eye – how about sage and sweetcorn fritters, streaky bacon, avocado and heirloom tomatoes, or an open fillet steak sandwich with spinach, fried egg and béarnaise sauce. If you stay for lunch, you can indulge in Carlingford rock oysters, or settle in for one of their famous Sunday roasts which draw crowds of regulars. The bar is dog-friendly, and Knightsbridge beckons.

Meals: Starters from £8. Mains from £12. Sunday lunch from £16.50.
Closed: Open all day.

Jono Mark
The Alfred Tennyson,
10 Motcomb Street, Belgravia,
London, SW1X 8LA
Tel +44 (0)20 7730 6074
Web www.thealfredtennyson.co.uk

Entry 343 Map 15

The Thomas Cubitt

London – Belgravia

Simple, classic, and in the heart of Belgravia. Find high ceilings in the ground-floor bar, oak-block floors, fragrant lilies, tall windows that open to tables in the street and a bit of panelling thrown in for good measure. Buzzy crowds are drawn by the classic country-house feel, the real ales, the superb wines, and the kitchen, which puts more thought into what it produces than many a full-blown restaurant. In the bar is a reassuring selection of pub favourites, with specials on blackboards – organic beef burgers, grilled sausages with roasted red onion gravy and buttery mash – and the organic Sunday roasts are great. In the elegant dove-grey dining room upstairs the food is modern (take grilled tuna with red pepper and pearl barley and langoustine bisque). It's popular, and the friendliness of the staff, even under pressure, is a pleasure.

Meals	Lunch from £12. Dinner from £13.50. Sunday lunch from £17.
Closed	Open all day.

Tim Atkinson
The Thomas Cubitt,
44 Elizabeth Street, Belgravia,
London, SW1W 9PA
Tel +44 (0)20 77306060
Web www.thethomascubitt.co.uk

The Pig's Ear

London – Chelsea

Off the King's Road, a great little corner pub serving Uley Pig's Ear on tap and a zippy Bloody Mary – drinking is encouraged. In the chattering bar (this is Chelsea) are high ceilings, planked floors, big mirrors, a zinc-top bar and formica tables; upstairs, a cosy sash windowed dining room with twinkly lights and not a touch of Victoriana. Staff are knowledgeable, casually dressed and perky, in keeping with the spirit of the place. Cooking is rousingly rustic – part French, part English. The beef brisket and ox cheek casserole, topped with robust Jerusalem artichoke crisps, was deep flavoured and succulent; the orange panna cotta smooth, citrusy and decorated with a sesame tuile. There are cured herrings and rock oysters, and most nights it's rammed.

Meals	Lunch from £8.50. Bar meals from £5.50. Dinner from £14. Sunday lunch, 3 courses, £26.
Closed	Open all day.

Simon Cherry
The Pig's Ear,
35 Old Church Street,
Chelsea, London, SW3 5BS
Tel +44 (0)20 7352 2908
Web www.thepigsear.info

The Sands End

London – Fulham

Down a residential street off Wandsworth Bridge Road the faithful flock. One of the business partners was formerly an equerry to the Prince of Wales (sightings of the young Princes are not unfounded) but its popularity is most likely down to its menu, market-based, daily-changing and surprisingly affordable. The food zings with flavour – queen scallops with spinach and smoked gubbeen; braised beef, onion and mushroom pie; chocolate brownie – and complements the urban rusticity of scrubbed tables, planked floors and displays of bottled produce. While half the place is restaurant, the rest is old-fashioned bar, serving beers, wine and slices of hand-raised pork pie. For very special occasions, the private dining room with its lovely windows and chandelier is a treat. Staff are friendly and attitude-free

Meals	Lunch & dinner £12-£18. Bar meals from £3.
Closed	Open all day.

Eamonn Manson & Mark Dyer
The Sands End,
135-137 Stephendale Road,
Fulham, London, SW6 2PR
Tel +44 (0)20 7731 7823
Web www.thesandsend.co.uk

Entry 346 Map 15

London

The Harwood Arms

London – Fulham

A pint's throw from Fulham Broadway. There's an easy-on-the-eye modernity to this big-windowed gastropub on the corner, well-dressed with a Shaker-ish feel – and a Michelin star. Menus, driven by seasonality and provenance, revel in an intelligent simplicity, with game a speciality. The chef is Barry Fitzgerald (ex Arbutus and Wild Honey) – you're in mighty good hands. Expect to book days or weeks in advance – for game 'tea' served with a venison sausage roll; pheasant Kiev with champ and turnips glazed with mead; warm Bramley apple doughnuts with spiced sugar; sweet egg custard tart with drunk raisins. Hand-pump ales, well-chosen wines, tasty bar snacks and a laid-back but informed staff make this one civilised bolthole.

Meals	Lunch & dinner £16-18. Bar snacks £3-£8.
Closed	Mon lunch.

Brett Graham & Mike Robinson
The Harwood Arms,
Walham Grove, Fulham,
London, SW6 1QP
Tel +44 (0)20 7386 1847
Web www.harwoodarms.com

Entry 347 Map 15

Havelock Tavern

London – Brook Green

The staff are brilliant, the owners are new, and the dedication to wonderful food has not wavered. On the corner of a residential street behind Brook Green, this is not a restaurant in an old pub: it's a pub that serves good food. The kitchen hatch is ever open and the blackboard changes twice daily, the ales are numerous, so are the wines (many by the glass) and the room is abuzz with all ages. The floor is planked, there's a mishmash of tables, the sun adds a sparkle, a small fire crackles away. Chalked up on the board at lunch time we saw borlotti bean soup with parmesan, roast duck breast with a sorrel salad, crème brûlée with pistachio biscuits, platters of British cheeses... All of it thoughtfully sourced, all of it delicious. On Saturday afternoons the Kings Cross Jazz Club comes to play.

Meals	Starters from £5.50. Mains from £11.50. Dessert from £5.
Closed	Open all day.

Jonny Haughton & Pete Richnell
Havelock Tavern,
57 Masbro Road, Brook Green,
London, W14 0LS
Tel +44 (0)20 7603 5374
Web www.havelocktavern.com

Entry 348 Map 15

The Hampshire Hog

London – Hammersmith

Opposite the likes of Kings Kebabs & Pizzas, the little painted pig flies proudly out the front of this 'pantry-pub', fighting its quirky corner. This is a beacon on the Hammersmith/Ravenscourt border, a light bright refuge to which locals are drawn, from chatty office workers to breakfasting babies; at weekends, families descend. Wooden floors have been stripped and walls painted cream, wicker chairs have sheepskin throws, chandeliers twinkle and flowers top tables. To the left of the bar is the Pantry, its walls lined with lagers, wines, chutneys, breads, coffees and jams, its tables bright with fresh organic dishes. (Our rare chargrilled beef with shaved vegetables, green papaya and pomegranate salad was delicious.) The bar fronts an open-hatch kitchen; the dining area opens to a pretty garden. One for foodies.

Meals	Lunch & dinner £5.50-£22. Bar meals from £4.50. Sunday lunch £5.50-£19.
Closed	Sun eves.

Macarena Freire
The Hampshire Hog,
227 King Street, Hammersmith,
London, W6 9JT
Tel +44 (0)20 8748 3391
Web www.thehampshirehog.com

Entry 349 Map 15

The Carpenter's Arms

London – Hammersmith

An extraordinary distillation of gastropub and local in a charming backwater between King Street and the Great West Road (aka the A4). The glorious single bar has bare boards, plain tables, a fire that glows on chilly days and doors giving onto a sheltered little garden. And it's done well for itself, being a popular spot for a discerning mix while managing (just) to hold on to its pubby feel. An ever-changing seasonal menu sees inventive dishes popping up every day: seared scallops with butterbeans, pine nuts and saffron; rib-eye steak with fries and Café de Paris butter; apple tart 'fine' with nutmeg ice cream. Service is exuberant and warm, the atmosphere is laid back. It's a satisfying place to dine.

Meals Lunch & dinner £8-£16.95.
Closed Open all day.

Simon Cherry & Matt Jacomb
The Carpenter's Arms,
91 Black Lion Lane,
Hammersmith, London, W6 9BG
Tel +44 (0)20 8741 8386
Web www.carpentersarmsw6.co.uk

Entry 350 Map 15

London

The Anglesea Arms

London – Hammersmith

Everyone loves Hammersmith's long-running Anglesea – home to the well-heeled and the young at heart. Find an opened-up space and an endearingly shabby-chic interior, a log fire, a chesterfield, retro furniture and banquette seating. It's high octane but convivial, the bar delivering four ales and a score of wines by glass. As for the cooking, it's fabulous, ferried from an open theatre kitchen to a relaxed sky-lit dining area. Ticking all the local-and-seasonal boxes, dishes, chalked up on a daily-changing menu, are uncomplicated and flavour-driven: skate with butterbean casserole and salsa verde; panna cotta with winter berries; steamed orange pudding and custard. You can dine wherever you like, including the cordoned-off front terrace in summer. Lovely!

Meals Lunch from £10. Dinner from £14.
Sunday lunch from £15.50.
Closed Open all day.

Michael Mann
The Anglesea Arms,
35 Wingate Road,
Hammersmith, London, W6 0UR
Tel +44 (0)20 8749 1291
Web www.angleseaarmspub.co.uk

Entry 351 Map 15

The Swan

London – Chiswick

With window boxes, flower baskets and a green glazed frontage, the Swan is a cheery beacon in leafy Chiswick. Inside is just as good: high Victorian ceilings, big windows, planked floors, old chesterfields by the fire, original panelling around the bar. All ages drop by, for after-work drinks, board games over pints, a special meal out. Dogs are welcome, scruffy or sleek. There's a good range of draft beers, malt whiskies too, wines, port, Orchard Pig cider. The restaurant's the other side of the bar, with more of that warm polished panelling: a welcoming spot for risottos and roasts, French onion soup, cod with samphire, penne with spicy sausages, lemon tart. The staff are very friendly, and efficient, and at the back is a decked garden with lights in the trees: gorgeous on a summer's night.

Meals: Starters from £3. Mains from £13.50.

Closed: Open Mon-Fri 5pm-11pm; Sat 12.30pm-10.30pm; Sun 12.30pm-9pm.

Richard & George Manners
The Swan,
1 Evershed Walk, 119 Acton Lane,
Chiswick, London, W4 5HH

Tel: +44 (0)20 8994 8262
Web: www.theswanchiswick.co.uk

Entry 352 Map 15

London

Parlour

London – Kensal Greeen

Taking on this run-down Regent Street pub in July 2013, maverick chef Jesse Dunford Wood set about realising his vision for a modern-day city pub with passion and innovation; and started with the quirky and apt name 'Parlour'. Open from 10am for breakfast (unlimited toast and marmite), then 'funky British' brunch, lunch and dinner, his menus brims with humour and a huge dose of nostalgia – fish soup, chicken Kiev, marshmallow Wagon Wheel. The eclectic clientele like the unusual craft keg beers too, the fine wines, fancy cocktails, great coffee, the Sunday lunch sharing platters, and the Chef's Table for seven, where surprise dishes are delivered in theatrical style. Stylish, full of personality, refreshingly different, the Parlour is a game-changer to watch.

Meals: Lunch £4-£14.50. Dinner £9.50-£19.50.

Closed: Mondays all day.

Jesse Dunford Wood
Parlour,
5 Regent Street,
London, NW10 5LG

Tel: +44 (0)20 8969 2184
Web: www.parlourkensal.com

Entry 353 Map 15

Holly Bush

London – Hampstead

Down a Hampstead cul-de-sac, the stables once owned by painter George Romney have become a hugely loved pub. It's one of the most Dickensian places you could go for Sunday lunch in London: a labyrinth of corridors leading to treacle-coloured rooms, cosy corners, painted settles, tables set with board games, potted ferns on the bar. Ale rules at the Holly Bush, where the chef cooks not with wine but with beer and the aromas of beef and ale pie prove a temptation for drinkers to become diners. Guinness rarebit followed by sticky toffee pudding will educate the beer lover's palate, while Sunday roasts and scotch eggs are a hit with regulars. Upstairs in the dining room, all pistachio walls and wooden floors, the celebration of all things British continues. The staff are as happy as the punters. One of the best.

Meals Lunch & dinner £8-£15.
Bar meals £3.50-£6.
Closed Open all day.

Hannah Borkulak
Holly Bush,
22 Holly Mount, Hampstead,
London, NW3 6SG
Tel +44 (0)20 7435 2892
Web www.hollybushhampstead.co.uk

London

The Bull

London – Highgate

At Highgate's Bull, beer and food go hand in hand. In the cosy bar, homemade sausage rolls are stacked alongside pumps serving their own ales; we enjoyed our Beer Street and Highgate Winter. But that's just a hint at what goes on at the back. In the kitchen, master brewer Joanna keeps the beer flowing alongside chefs who work on the menus, many using the beers. By the open fire, locals tuck into ale-cured salmon, caper berries with Beer Street mustard dressing, and roast pork belly with artichoke purée, purple truffle potatoes and black pudding croquettes. It's worth taking a break before your pud of baked vanilla cheesecake with blood orange jelly to read the bar's vast blackboard explaining the brewing process. You can also visit the kitchen to see the mash tuns churning.

Meals Lunch & dinner £9.50-£23.
Closed Open all day.

Dan Fox
The Bull,
13 North Hill, Highgate,
London, N6 4AB
Tel +44 (0)20 8341 0510
Web www.thebullhighgate.co.uk

The Southampton Arms

London – Kentish Town

Where else in London has so many ciders (the real stuff) and ales, welcomes all comers (not just locals) and has a pub dog? You couldn't sit on your own here long without someone chatting to you. This little Victorian pub on Highgate Hill (a former Kentish Town dive) is long and thin with a table the length of the bar and a record player in the far corner that plays the blues; on sunny afternoons the sun hits the hand pumps and tankards, and there's no sign of Farrow & Ball. Along with the ever-changing ales from small breweries are sausage rolls, salami, pulled pork baps with warm crackling and vegetarian Scotch eggs, there are quiz nights on Mondays and the piano plays three times a week. They don't have a phone and don't reserve seats, tables 'or any of that caper'. It's perfect if you're skint. *Cash only.*

Meals Bar snacks from £2.
Closed Open all day.

Peter Holt
The Southampton Arms,
139 Highgate Road,
Kentish Town,
London, NW5 1LE
Web www.thesouthamptonarms.co.uk

Entry 356 Map 15

London

The Grafton

London – Kentish Town

The once dingy old boozer has been transformed to former Victorian glory by owners Susie and Joel. It is now a sanctuary for craft beer lovers. Behind the bar, knowledgeable staff pull firm favourites such as Hogs Back TEA, and also encourage you to try local brews such as Portobello Star. It's not just the array of beers that draws the crowds. Will Dee of the Fat Butcher, now the Grafton's resident chef, is passionate about doing 'interesting technical things" with meat. At scrubbed tables, cheddar and ale croquettes come with smoked ketchup, and 12-hour pork shoulder with crackling and apple sauce. Traditional apple pie and custard is another firm favourite. If you're sticking to pints, there may be some of Will's homemade salamis left to snack on; if not, spare a thought for them maturing in the cellar!

Meals Lunch & dinner £8.50–£15.50.
Closed Open all day.

Joel Czopor & Susie Clarke
The Grafton,
20 Prince of Wales Road,
Kentish Town, London, NW5 3LG
Tel +44 (0)20 74824466
Web www.thegraftonnw5.co.uk

Entry 357 Map 15

The Scolt Head

London – Islington

Imagine a fire in the grate, a hotch-potch of comfy seating, games, flowers, art and a scuffed wood floor, and delicious wafts emanating from the kitchen. This is an old-fashioned community pub, where the locals are friendly, kids and dogs are welcomed with open arms, and you mix with the odd celeb. In summer, you arrive to a triangular shaped garden out front, enclosed by high hedges, protected from showers by a big parasol, and great on a sunny day. Rosie and Richard turned the place around in 2006; now it's packed (get there early at weekends). Enjoy pale ale brewed in Dalston, Crouch Vale beer from Essex, well-chosen wines, and a menu that's short, seasonal, unfussy and high end: juicy burgers, wild mushroom pancakes, mussels with lemongrass, fish pie with kale, Neal's Yard cheeses, Eton Mess. Perfect.

Meals Starters from £5. Lunch from £8. Dinner from £11.
Closed Open all day.

Rich Haines & Rosie Wesemann
The Scolt Head,
107A Culford Road, De Beauvoir,
London, N1 4HT
Tel +44 (0)20 7254 3965
Web www.thescolthead.co.uk

Entry 358 Map 15

London

Smokehouse

London – Islington

Hard to imagine that behind this red brick pub lies a glorious selection of craft beers to challenge the palate, and salamis around the tiled bar for robust snacks. Scottish chef Neil Rankin knows his stuff and has great local craft beers and ales on tap. As for the food, in a dining room with simple plank tables, a 'beer blackboard' and a kitchen hatch, drinkers are lured into the gastronomic unknown. At first glance the menu follows tradition, but there are some surprising dishes too. Imagine crispy lobster frittata or foie gras with apple pie and duck egg to start, followed by roasted cod with masala cockles and clams, or peppered ox-cheek with gravy and cauliflower cheese. Then a pudding named 'Krun Chee Nut' – what can that be? The reviews are starry-eyed so visit and find out!

Meals Lunch & diner £12.50-£19.
Closed Open all day Sat & Sun. Open from 5pm Mon-Fri.

The Manager
Smokehouse,
63-69 Canonbury Road,
Islington, London, N1 2DG
Tel +44 (0)20 73541144
Web www.smokehouseislington.co.uk

Entry 359 Map 15

Drapers Arms

London – Islington

Reborn in 2009, the pared-back, opened-up Georgian building in a residential area of charming period houses has high ceilings, bare boards and an eclectic mix of wooden tables and chairs – expect a chilled fine dining vibe. The kitchen, under chef Gina Hopkins, fits the mood and ethic to a tee. Gutsy no-nonsense British dishes appear on twice-daily changing menus. Graze on pig's head croquettes with spicy nduja mayonnaise while you linger over the menu: maybe forerib of beef; duck breast, blood orange and chicory; suet crust lamb pie. Room should be left for the lemon posset and bergamot orange jelly and a generous plate of Neal's Yard cheeses and chutneys. There's a cracking fish menu to set your mouth watering, too. Hand-pump ales, enterprising wines, a cool candlelit dining room upstairs and a classy courtyard garden top a super-charged act.

Meals	Bar snacks from £3.50. Lunch from £13.50. Dinner from £13.50. Sunday lunch from £16.50.
Closed	Open all day.

Nick Gibson
Drapers Arms,
44 Barnsbury Street,
Islington, London, N1 1ER

Tel +44 (0)20 7619 0348
Web www.thedrapersarms.com

Entry 360 Map 15

London

Riverford at The Duke of Cambridge

London – Islington

Thanks to pioneering Geetie Singh, 'organic' and 'sustainable' are the watchwords at Britain's first organic pub, and British-rustic is the style. Wines, beers, spirits are certified organic and they buy as locally as they can to cut down on food miles. Most of the beers are brewed around London, meat comes from two farms, and fish is Marine Conservation Society-approved. Impeccable produce and menus change twice a day. It's a sprawling airy space with a comfortable, easy atmosphere; you could be alone happily here. Sit back and take your fill of broccoli, parsley & rosemary soup, pan-fried chorizo stuffed squid with puy lentils, Rhug estate "bangers" with colcannon mash, and blueberry and ricotta cheesecake with blueberry and elderflower sauce – in the lovely planked bar, or in the restaurant. Justifiably rammed.

Meals	Lunch & dinner £9-£22.
Closed	Open all day.

Geetie Singh
Riverford at The Duke of Cambridge,
30 St Peter's Street,
Islington, London, N1 8JT

Tel +44 (0)20 7359 3066
Web www.dukeorganic.co.uk

Entry 361 Map 15

Charles Lamb Public House

London – Islington

Everyone's welcome at Camille and Hobby's small pub, hidden down a tangle of streets behind Camden Passage. It's a dear little place that keeps its pubby feel, with two unshowy bar rooms and well-kept hand-pump beer. The blackboard menu – fresh, short, ever-changing – is a surprise. Eat informally at plainly set tables in either bar, on serrano ham with celeriac remoulade, or Lancashire hotpot; Camille is French so there may be duck confit too. On Sundays: all-day roast beef and Yorkshire pudding. It's good home-cooked food and you need to get here early: tables cannot be booked. Walk it all off with a stroll along the bosky banks of the Regent's Canal; seek out the house where essayist and poet Charles Lamb lived, two streets away.

Meals Bar snacks from £4. Starters £4.50. Mains £14.50. Dessert £5. Sunday lunch £16.

Closed Open all day Weds-Sun; from 4pm Mon & Tues.

Adam Devereux
Charles Lamb Public House,
16 Elia Street,
Islington, London, N1 8DE

Tel +44 (0)20 7837 5040
Web www.thecharleslambpub.com

Entry 362 Map 15

London

The Easton

London – Clerkenwell

Home from home for the Amnesty International crowd, whose headquarters are down the street, this may look like the classic London boozer but inside is airy and modern. Bare boards, plain windows, a long bar topped with fresh flowers, funky wallpaper at the far end... drinkers and diners mingle over pints of Timothy Taylor and global house-white and wonder what to pick from the ever-changing board. The kitchen goes in for rustic portions of chargrilled lemon and thyme pork chops; roast tomato and chorizo stew; Springbok sausages with spring onion champ and braised red cabbage. It's a godsend for the area, with pub tables spilling onto the pavement and a genuinely local feel. Staff are charming, even on Fridays when the drinkers descend and hearty dishes are replaced with tapas.

Meals Lunch & dinner £9-£16.

Closed Open all day.

Andrew Marshall
The Easton,
22 Easton Street, Clerkenwell,
London, WC1X 0DS

Tel +44 (0)20 7278 7608
Web www.theeastonpub.co.uk

Entry 363 Map 15

Jerusalem Tavern

London – Clerkenwell

There's so much atmosphere here you could bottle it up and take it home – along with one of the beers. Old Clerkenwell has reinvented itself and the tiny 1720 tavern epitomises all that is best about the place. The name is new, acquired when the St Peter's Brewery of Suffolk took it over and stocked it with their ales and fruit beers. Step in to a reincarnation of a nooked and crannied interior, candlelit at night with a winter fire; come before six if you want a table. Lunchtime food is simple and English (bangers and mash, a roast, a fine platter of cheese) with ingredients from Smithfield Market, and the pork scratchings are epic. Staff are friendly and know their beer, and the full range of St Peter's ales is all there, from the cask or the specially designed bottle.

Meals	Lunch £5-£10.
Closed	Sat & Sun. Open all day Mon-Fri.

Dave Hart
Jerusalem Tavern, 55 Britton Street, Clerkenwell, London, EC1M 5UQ

Tel	+44 (0)20 7490 4281
Web	www.stpetersbrewery.co.uk/london-pub/

Entry 364 Map 15

London

The Lady Ottoline

London – Bloomsbury

Tucked off the Gray's Inn Road is a pretty little pub with huge Georgian windows and a sun-dappled pavement for seats outside. Find a sedate interior of dark wood floors, dark leather banquettes and painted panelling. Candles are lit on dim days, spirits gleam behind a mahogany bar, and when the barman's not serving, he's polishing the pub's doors. It's an oasis for drinkers and dreamers and a wonderful place for a celebration. Up a narrow stair is a large lofty dining room painted petrol-blue, and, alongside, 'the cosiest dining room in Bloomsbury' (seats 12). They take their beers seriously, source wines from small growers, serve 25 gins and glorious roasts. All the produce is traceable and sustainable, from the Italian charcuterie to the Hereford Beef burgers to the zingy Dorset crab.

Meals	Starters from £6. Mains from £12.50.
Closed	Bank Holiday Mondays

Hannah Bonnell
The Lady Ottoline,
11A Northington Street,
London, WC1N 2JF

Tel	+44 (0)20 7831 0008
Web	www.theladyottoline.com

Entry 365 Map 15

The Jugged Hare

London – Barbican

An unexpected shrine in the City of London to the British countryside. The Jugged Hare, part of the old Whitbread Brewery, is not just about beer: stuffed creatures in glass cases around the bar tell of another passion. The very best of British meat is worshipped and with a kitchen supplied by rare-breed farmers and gamekeepers, there are some fabulous treats on the menu. The lively bar is ideal for sampling their own ales or Southwold Bitter, accompanied by black pudding croquettes with Guinness sauce, maybe. The pub's dining room, with its open hatch, is a fun place to fully indulge, so how about a fresh blue cheese, dandelion, walnut and fennel salad, then roast whole red-legged partridge with game chips, and apple junket with spiced shortbread to follow? Before leaving, pay homage to the birds and beasts of the land and check out the chefs' daily 'meat display'.

Meals Lunch & dinner £6.50-£27.
Closed Open all day.

The Manager
The Jugged Hare,
49 Chiswell Street,
London, EC1Y 4SA
Tel +44 (0)20 76140134
Web www.thejuggedhare.com

Entry 366 Map 15

London

The Garrison Public House

London – Bermondsey

The kitchen is open, staff are laid-back, decibels are high and tables are crammed. The Garrison bounces with bonhomie, more eaterie than pub. What's more, it has the confidence to be different: traditional benches and French boutique chairs, pistachio paintwork and quirky objets and the vegetables for the kitchen displayed in crates by the hatch. Earthy food reflects the décor (steak sandwich, chickpea and pumpkin tagine, Morecambe Bay potted shrimps) – classic British with a continental twist – most of it, from apricots to Orkney mussels, coming from the market down the road. Accompany a bottle of St Peter's with a rib-eye steak with watercress and roquefort butter. Arrive for breakfast, stay for dinner and a movie: there's a cinema downstairs and free screenings every Sunday.

Meals Lunch & dinner £9.50-£15.90.
Closed Open all day.

Clive Watson & Adam White
The Garrison Public House,
99 Bermondsey Street,
Bermondsey, London, SE1 3XB
Tel +44 (0)20 7089 9355
Web www.thegarrison.co.uk

Entry 367 Map 15

The Anchor & Hope

London – Southwark

Come for some of the plainest yet gutsiest cooking in London; chef Jonathan Jones attracts a crowd. The food is described as 'English bistro', and give or take the odd foreign exception (a chorizo broth, a melting pomme dauphinoise), it is just that. The menu is adventurous yet striking in its simplicity: warm snail and bacon salad, smoked herring with fennel and orange, slip soles with anchovy butter, rabbit with pearl barley and sherry, homemade liqueurs, blackberry meringue. The beer comes from Charles Wells, the wine list has 18 by the glass. Staff are youthful – and may be rushed. Décor is 1930s sober and the restaurant area glows by candlelight. No bookings bar Sunday lunch and a legend in the making – but arrive early (or late) and you may get a table.

Meals	Lunch & dinner £10-£20. Sunday lunch £30.
Closed	Mon lunch & Sun eves. Open all day Tues-Sat.

Robert Shaw
The Anchor & Hope,
36 The Cut,
Southwark, London, SE1 8LP

Tel	+44 (0)20 7928 9898
Web	www.anchorandhopepub.co.uk

Entry 368 Map 15

London

Canton Arms

London – Stockwell

In one of London's less salubrious zones is a high-ceilinged, screen-dominated bar, aimed at those in for a pint. Beyond: ox-red panelled walls, Edwardian mirrors, leaded windows, fat candles and diners of all ages. No bookings, it's first come first served, and you can linger as long as you like; note the teapots and the books. Trish Hilferty, 'unsung heroine of the gastropub scene', heads the kitchen. The foie gras toasties are legendary and the menu changes daily with lunch smaller than dinner: three starters, three mains, big rustic flavours and a special way with meat. Imagine slow-cooked Hereford beef shoulder with roasties, and panna cotta with grappa and quince. Drinks range from Bloody Mary to Black Sheep from Yorkshire to marvellous wines. A pub driven by passion, it's superb value. Give it a whirl.

Meals	Lunch from £8.80. Dinner from £14. Bar meals from £2.80. Sunday lunch £14. No food Sun eve.
Closed	Mon until 5pm.

Trish Hilferty
Canton Arms,
177 South Lambeth Road,
Stockwell, London, SW8 1XP

Tel	+44 (0)20 7582 8710
Web	www.cantonarms.com

Entry 369 Map 15

The Ship

London – Wandsworth

Drinking a pint of Young's Special next to a concrete works doesn't sound enticing, but the riverside terrace by Wandsworth Bridge is a dreamy spot. Chilly evenings still draw the crowds to this super old pub, so cosy inside with its warm-red and sage-green walls, and to its conservatory, with a central chopping-board table and a wood-burning stove. Chef Shaun Harrington sources fresh ingredients to create his seasonal menus. Try braised pork belly with caramelised white cabbage, fondant potato and bacon and herb dumplings; parsnip, tomato and goat's cheese gratin; Jerusalem artichoke and chestnut mushroom fricassée. The Ship opens its arms to all, there are live acoustic duos, Irish music on Tuesdays, and quiz nights. Families and friends gather merrily in summer.

Meals	Lunch & dinner £9.95-£19.95.
Closed	Open all day.

Oisin Rogers
The Ship,
41 Jews Row, Wandsworth,
London, SW18 1TB
Tel +44 (0)20 8870 9667
Web www.theship.co.uk

The Alma

London – Wandsworth

Exceedingly handsome in up-and-come Wandsworth, the much-loved Alma is named after a Crimean battle. Its green tiled façade is still intact, as are its parquet floors and mahogany bar. Above, a mirrored staircase looks down on the jolly hubbub below. The staff are relaxed but attentive and you can drink whatever you like – vodka, gin, malts, wines by the glass, Young's and guest ales. The restaurant is more formal – soft blue walls, blue check tweed chairs – but it's still mostly stuffed with locals enjoying the fresh, seasonal produce and the popular homemade pies. Tuck into good old-fashioned pub grub, or savour slowly the warm mushroom salad with pomegranates, the sea bream with prawn butter, the lemon tart with thyme sorbet.

Meals	Starters from £4.9.5. Mains from £11.95.
Closed	Open all day.

Sean Young
The Alma,
499 Old York Road, Wandsworth,
London, SW18 1TF
Tel +44 (0)20 8870 2537
Web www.almawandsworth.com

The Brown Dog

London – Barnes

Set the satnav to find a small, friendly gem, hiding down the streets of pretty Barnes 'village' – great after a Richmond Park romp. Post makeover it's opened-up and pared-back. Copper lights dangle from the red ceiling over the bar, there are floorboards, banquette seats and solid-wood furniture. Not a lot of passing trade here, just regulars with their families and their dogs (pig's ears are stocked behind the bar). It's as much gastro as pub, the kitchen driven by top seasonal ingredients and a light modish touch. Try the classics – shepherd's pie – or the posh: roasted monkfish tails with baked pumpkin, curly kale and sage pesto. Local-brewery cask ales and well-selected wines up the ante, while a rear terrace keeps al fresco lovers on board.

Meals	Lunch & dinner £8.25-£17.
Closed	Open all day.

Andrew Marshall
The Brown Dog,
28 Cross Street, Barnes,
London, SW13 0AP

Tel	+44 (0)20 8392 2200
Web	www.thebrowndog.co.uk

Entry 372 Map 15

The Jolly Gardeners

London – Wandsworth

The pub is home to the delightful Dhruv – born in Mexico, raised in India, winner of MasterChef 2010. Now, in an unprepossessing street in Earlsfield, he is pursuing his dream. Lucky locals: the food is a mix of modern Mediterranean, classic pub and exotic oriental. Now the old Victorian pub is packed every night. It's a building of two halves: handsome L-shaped front (bare boards, high ceilings, modish colours) and, at the back, a roofed conservatory with an open kitchen hatch. Sink into the soft leather sofa with an award-winning pint (Wandle, Northcote Blonde) or get stuck in to a gastronomic night. There's pork belly with carrot and cardamom purée; baked aubergine with Italian cheeses and hazelnut pesto; rhubarb and vanilla panna cotta. We chose spiced crab cakes with fennel and tamarind yoghurt and they were absolutely delicious.

Meals	Starters from £6.50. Mains from £11.50. Desserts from £7.
Closed	Sun from 6pm. Open all day Mon-Sat.

Stephen Robb
The Jolly Gardeners,
214 Garratt Lane, Wandsworth,
London, SW18 4EA

Tel	+44 (0)20 8870 8417
Web	www.thejollygardeners.co.uk

Entry 373 Map 15

The Crooked Well

London – Camberwell

Set up by a group of friends sharing a love of great food (and a training at Le Gavroche and Hotel du Vin) this new-wave neighbourhood pub stands between vibrant Camberwell and leafy Grove Lane. The commitment is to rustic British food, with the emphasis on shared dishes (such as rabbit and bacon pie) and family-roast platters on Sundays. On chef Matt's menu find scallop and squid ink risotto; Torbay sole with capers and anchovy; treacle tart with orange mascarpone. Basking in natural light, the elegant bar-dining room has a laid-back feel, with comfy armchairs in one corner. In the stylish dining section, Art Deco wallpaper and candles on eclectic tables. Cocktails, wine by the carafe, jazz nights, BYO wine dinners and fish-and-chip Fridays complete this pleasing picture.

Meals — Lunch & dinner £8.75-£17.90.
Closed — Open all day.

Hector Skinner & Jen Aries
The Crooked Well,
16 Grove Lane, Camberwell,
London, SE5 8SY
Tel +44 (0)20 7252 7798
Web www.thecrookedwell.com

Entry 374 Map 15

London

The Old Brewery

London – Greenwich

A one-off on the bank of the Thames, a brewery founded in 1717 when beer was drunk in favour of water. The interior is cavernous, listed, unique, and a shrine to the world's beers: taste before choosing your pint. Beyond are the restaurant and tea room, in a brewing area with vast gleaming tanks and funky beer bottle chandeliers. All is rich to reflect the warmth of the beers: dark woods, deep reds, terracottas; they also hold classes for aspiring brewers. Staff may be passionate about the golden brew but food is taken seriously too and the best of traditional British is served: fish from Billingsgate, meat from rare breeds, cheese from Neal's Yard. There's raspberry beer for jelly terrines and the spent brewing grain is used to make the bread.

Meals — Lunch & dinner from £10.
Bar meals from £5.50.
Closed — Open all day.

Alastair Hook
The Old Brewery, The Pepys Building,
The Old Royal Naval College,
Greenwich, London, SE10 9LW
Tel +44 (0)20 3327 1280
Web www.oldbrewerygreenwich.com

Entry 375 Map 15

The Lifeboat Inn

Thornham

You're in heaven here, under the big skies of Norfolk's north coast with its sweeping salt marshes, nature reserves and sandy beaches. The Lifeboat, newly captained by Agellus, sails a smooth and stylish path with glowing fires, scrumptious seafood and the comfiest of rooms. Tucked down a hidden lane in pretty Thornham, the inn's darkly-beamed bar conjures a smugglers retreat, while the conservatory and restaurant are light, bright and contemporary. Settle by a crackling fire with a pint of Woodforde's Wherry and plan a day's bird- or seal-spotting. In summer, the sun-trap courtyard beckons, or book one of two cedar wood pavilions for private dining. Wherever you settle, the menu will tempt you with seasonal specials, cream teas, hearty sandwiches and children's treats. Our Brancaster moules were the juiciest and tastiest we've eaten, and where else could you find roast beef in a Yorkshire pudding with horseradish sauce and a jug of gravy as a (bargain-priced) bar snack? Rooms (most are upstairs, one is on the ground floor) are wonderfully comfy with colour schemes that reflect the long landscape views. Bathrooms sparkle, and breakfasts are a treat.

Rooms	13 doubles: £120-£180. Pets by arrangement.
Meals	Starters from £6.25. Lunch from £6.50. Dinner from £9.95.
Closed	Open all day.

James Green
The Lifeboat Inn,
Ship Lane,
Thornham, PE36 6LT
Tel +44 (0)1485 512236
Web www.lifeboatinnthornham.com

The Orange Tree

Thornham

Nestled in one of Norfolk's loveliest coastal villages, The Orange Tree is a happy family-run gem with award-winning dishes that make delicious use of locally-sourced ingredients. From the wicker fencing fronting the garden to the sage-splashed front, the approach says it all; owners Mark and Jo have made subtle changes to this treasure off the village green. Step inside, to polished wood floors, cosy mulberry walls, log-stuffed fireplaces. Snuggle up at a cheeky table à deux in the bar, or be welcomed into one of two dining rooms. This is a fabulous area for food, the pub sources locally and well and there's something for everyone on Philip Milner's menu. Try lamb and apricot hotpot; salmon, chilli and crayfish cakes with ginger and soy dressing; garlic roasted halibut with passion fruit jus. Money and thought has been lavished on courtyard chalet bedrooms at the back, which, though small, are cosy, comfy and contemporary, with wooden floors, Farrow & Ball colours, coffee-makers and wet rooms. Breakfasts are sumptuous, with eggs Benedict, crêpes or the full English indulgence. If you're a birdwatcher, don't miss Titchwell Nature Reserve.

Rooms	5 twin/doubles: £69-£209. 1 family room for 4: £89-£190.
Meals	Lunch & dinner £10-£22.
Closed	Open all day.

Mark & Jo Goode
The Orange Tree,
High Street, Thornham,
Hunstanton, PE36 6LY
Tel +44 (0)1485 512213
Web www.theorangetreethornham.co.uk

The Chequers Inn

Thornham

Cheerful Chequers, beloved by locals and visitors alike, is thriving. General Manager Martin takes the helm and all is smooth sailing – with some of the best seafood you'll find in this lovely part of the world. Thornham is a pretty little village nestled along the coast, close to spectacular scenery and nature reserves, where Chequers gleams with its whitewashed walls and red pantiles. Inside, the fireplace glows and crackles, fresh flowers sit on scrubbed tables and the menu beckons. Our tempura of Brancaster mussels with tartar espuma and chilli vinegar (part of their Norfolk tapas range) was bursting with delicate flavours, but you might try slow-cooked crispy belly of pork with cider potato fondant, black cabbage, black pudding bonbon and grain mustard velouté. Pizzas are a treat too (crispy duck caught our eye) and there's private dining in the all-weather Pavilions outside. Rooms (most in the main building, two in a separate cottage) are stylish and spoiling – with sloe gin and homemade biscuits. Breakfasts are splendid, setting you up for a day of walking and exploring. Both Sandringham and Holkham Hall are close.

Rooms	11 doubles: £120-£195.
Meals	Breakfast from £15. Starters from £3.95. Tapas from £3.95. Lunch from £8.95. Mains from £13.95.
Closed	Never.

Martin Edwards
The Chequers Inn,
High Street, Thornham,
Hunstanton, PE36 6LY
Tel +44 (0)1485 512229
Web www.chequersinnthornham.com

The White Horse, Country Inn

Brancaster Staithe

A smart little inn on the North Norfolk coast with beautiful views that shoot across tidal marshes to Scolt Head Island. At high tide boats bob, birds swoop and the water laps at the garden edge; at low tide, the marshes appear and fishermen come to harvest the mussels and oysters. In summer you can eat on the terrace and drink it all in, then drop down to the coastal path at the bottom of the garden and follow your nose. But the view here is weather-proofed – a big conservatory restaurant looks out on it all. It's a popular haunt for locals and visitors alike, who come for consistently good food, perhaps oysters from the bay, sea bass with squid risotto, lemon tart with a chocolate macaroon. There's a sunken garden that catches the sun, then an open fire in the locals' bar, where you'll find well-kept ales, the daily papers, bar billiards and sofas for a game of scrabble. Chic, uncluttered bedrooms have seaside colours, robes for spotless bathrooms, good beds and fine linen. Some in the main house have the view, dog-friendly garden rooms have terraces. Sandringham is close. *Minimum stay: two nights at weekends.*

Rooms	11 doubles, 4 twins: £100-£230.
Meals	Lunch & bar meals from £8.95. Dinner from £13.95.
Closed	Open all day.

Cliff Nye & Family
The White Horse, Country Inn,
Brancaster Staithe, PE31 8BY
Tel +44 (0)1485 210262
Web www.whitehorsebrancaster.co.uk

The Duck Inn

Stanhoe

The Stanhoe Crown morphed into the Duck in 2010, and Ben and Sarah took on this much extended and spruced-up village local in 2013. Enter from the car park to find a slate-floored bar, with barrels of Elgood's ale on hand pump, and simple tables and benches for those who appreciate a well-kept pint of Cambridge Ale. Cosy dining rooms beyond are rustic-smart with their wood and slate floors, wood-burning stoves, candles on scrubbed tables, and really interesting local art adorning the walls. Expect memorable open sandwiches, seasonal dishes and fresh local fish on the menu, all beautifully prepared by Ben, perhaps scotch quail eggs with mustard and tarragon mayonnaise, baked Lowestoft cod with local brown shrimp, lemon and fennel risotto, or Norfolk beef sirloin with skinny fries. Leave room for brandy snaps with white chocolate and vanilla parfait, pistachio and celeriac. Bedrooms have a contemporary feel, with thick down duvets on big comfy beds, deep sofas, plasma screens, fresh coffee, and swish bathrooms with baths and walk-in showers. You are close to trendy Burnham Market, Brancaster Beach and the famous saltmarshes.

Rooms	2 twin/doubles: £110-£215. Singles £75-£105.
Meals	Lunch from £6.95. Dinner from £11.25. Sunday lunch £12.95.
Closed	Open all day.

Sarah & Ben Handley
The Duck Inn,
Burnham Road, Stanhoe,
King's Lynn, PE31 8QD

Tel +44 (0)1485 518330
Web www.duckinn.co.uk

The Gunton Arms

Thorpe Market

Click open the latch gate and enter Gunton Park. The beautifully restored Gunton Arms overlooks one thousand acres of lush and historic parkland and the setting is stunning. Art dealer Ivor Braka has lavished money on the once faded hotel and the results are impressive... who would not love the chic hunting-lodge style? Warm red hues, wooden floors, a blazing log fire in the traditional bar (dogs welcome too), elegant lounges with pretty views of deer from every window. Quaff pints of Wherry alongside gamekeepers and gentry; tuck into rib of beef cooked over the fire in the vaulted dining room. Stuart (ex-Mark Hix) champions locally sourced ingredients, so enjoy mixed grill of estate fallow deer served with crab apple jelly; Brancaster mussels and chilli tossed in linguine; Cromer crab in summer. Irresistible bedrooms ooze country-house charm: antiques, gorgeous fabrics, Persian rugs, old prints and paintings and indulgent marble-tiled bathrooms, some with deep tubs and walk-in showers... wake to parkland views. An unusual, hospitable, richly atmospheric find.

Rooms	12 doubles: £95-£240. 1 family room for 4: £230-£250.
Meals	Lunch & dinner from £10.50. Bar meals £1.50-£5.50.
Closed	Open all day.

Simone Baker & Stuart Tattersall
The Gunton Arms,
Cromer Road, Thorpe Market,
Norwich, NR11 8TZ

Tel +44 (0)1263 832010
Web www.theguntonarms.co.uk

Saracens Head

Wolterton

Lost in the lanes of deepest Norfolk, an English inn that's hard to match. Outside, Georgian red-brick walls stand to attention at the front, but nip round the back and find them at ease in a beautiful courtyard where you can knock back a pint of Wherry in the evening sun before slipping inside to eat. Tim and Janie upped sticks from the Alps, unable to resist the allure of this lovely old inn. A sympathetic refurbishment has worked its magic, but the spirit remains the same: this is a country-house pub with lovely staff who go the extra mile. Downstairs the bar hums with happy locals who come for Norfolk ales and good French wines, while the food in the restaurant is as good as ever: Norfolk pheasant and rabbit terrine, wild duck or Cromer crab, treacle tart and caramel ice-cream. Upstairs, there's a sitting room on the landing, then six pretty rooms. All have have smart carpets, wooden furniture, comfy beds and sparkling bathrooms. There's masses to do: ancient Norwich, the coast at Cromer, golf on the cliffs at Sheringham, Blickling Hall, a Jacobean pile. Don't miss Sunday lunch.

Rooms	5 twin/doubles: £100-£110. 1 family room for 4: £110-£140. Singles £70.
Meals	Lunch from £6.50. Dinner, 3 courses, £25-£35.
Closed	3pm-6pm. Mon (except bank hols) & Tues lunch (Oct-Jun).

Tim & Janie Elwes
Saracens Head,
Wolterton,
Norwich, NR11 7LZ

Tel +44 (0)1263 768909
Web www.saracenshead-norfolk.co.uk

King's Head

Bawburgh

Over the ancient humpback bridge is the village green and this large pub; built by a miller in 1602, it's been licensed since 1800. Inside is comfortable and full of character: pantiles and flag floors, nooks and crannies, wood-burners, low ceilings and sturdy ships' timbers. A vast inglenook fireplace divides restaurant from main bar (bar stools, rustic tables, black sofas). There's something for everyone here: in one room we met a shooting party with dogs, all standing up and drinking (not the dogs!), on a chilly Wednesday in December. The garden is perfect for families and the food is fresh and tasty, from sausage rolls and prawn and crayfish sandwiches to sea bass with rösti (delicious), generous Sunday roasts and good-looking desserts. Wines are numerous (15 by the glass) and ales include Adnams and Woodfordes. As for the bedrooms, they're spanking new, softly themed and double-glazed, with superb bathrooms and luxurious linens. One vaulted room has a private entrance and beams to die for. Breakfast – in the pub, by the fire – is ample and good.

Rooms	5 doubles: £100-£185. 1 single: £90.
Meals	Lunch from £6. Dinner from £11. Sunday lunch, 3 courses, £20. No food Sunday eve (Nov-Apr).
Closed	Open all day.

Anton & Tet Wimmer
King's Head,
Harts Lane, Bawburgh,
Norwich, NR9 3LS

Tel	+44 (0)1603 744977
Web	www.kingshead-bawburgh.co.uk

The Dabbling Duck

Great Massingham

After a campaign by villagers to buy their local in 2006, the neglected Rose & Crown became the Dabbling Duck and the pub was revived with panache and perches prettily by the green. Business has been brisk, food is the draw and beers from the barrel – well-kept Adnams and Woodforde's. As for the mood, it is warmly endearing. The bar has been cut from a single slice of ancient Norfolk oak, there are high-backed settles by a blazing log fire, sober hues, rug-strewn floors, chunky candles on scrubbed tables, and shelves lined with books and board games. Views are to the village. There's local Brancaster mussels, fish and chips, homemade pies. There's often game from the owner's farm on the menu too. The care and attention to detail extends upstairs to gorgeous bedrooms with big brass beds, colourful cushions and throws, plasma screens, Roberts radios and wood-floored bathrooms; cookies and fresh coffee on tap. All this, 20 minutes from the beach and the bird-rich saltmarshes.

Rooms	5 twin/doubles: £85. 1 single: £65.
Meals	Lunch from £5.75. Bar meals from £5. Dinner from £10.
Closed	Open all day (from 12pm).

Mark Dobby
The Dabbling Duck,
11 Abbey Road, Great Massingham,
King's Lynn, PE32 2HN

Tel +44 (0)1485 520827
Web www.thedabblingduck.co.uk

Bedingfeld Arms

Oxborough

Local farmers Stephen and Catkin rescued this striking 18th-century coaching inn, Oxborough's only pub, and have worked wonders, breathing new life into the bars and the big, open garden. Oxburgh Hall, the magnificent National Trust property, stands opposite. Expect a warm, relaxed feel throughout and a Pugin stone fireplace (naturally), flowers and fat lamps, fireside leather sofas and wing chairs in the wood-floored bar. Tuck into a Club sandwich or chicken and mushroom pie with an Adnams ale, or settle into the country-rustic dining rooms for the house terrine with pear and grape chutney, venison with red wine and blackcurrant jus, and baked orange cheesecake with cranberry jam. Everyone is welcome, even four-legged friends, and the friendly staff will recommend walks from the door. Sunday roasts are an indulgent treat.

Meals	Light lunch from £5.75. Mains £10-£18.
Closed	Open all day.

Stephen & Catkin Parker
Bedingfeld Arms,
Oxborough,
Downham Market, PE33 9PS

Tel +44 (0)1366 328300
Web www.bedingfeldarms.co.uk

Entry 385 Map 9

Norfolk

The Ingham Swan

Ingham

Down a wilderness of lanes, the Swan pleases foodies and lovers of Woodforde's Best – chef and owner Daniel Smith and Gregory Adjemian took over in 2010 and the locals have been flocking since. Inside, find a dining room of brick, flint, beams, wood-burners, suave leather chairs, a sofa'd snug in the bar and staff who are on the ball. The food is the real star of the show here, and much is grown and picked on their own farm. Daniel's menus will have you squealing with joy: our Cromer crab salad with avocado cream, crispy crab cake and King's Lynn brown shrimps was delicious, the Norfolk rhubarb and custard slice a grown-up version of a childhood treat. Sit outside on the terrace in summer with a glass of wine (their list is impressive). Perfect for a posh dinner after a stroll across the broads or the beaches.

Meals	Lunch from £11.95. Sunday lunch, 2 courses, £20.95. Dinner from £14.50. Tasting menu £47.50.
Closed	3pm-6pm.

Daniel Smith
The Ingham Swan,
Sea Palling Road, Ingham,
Norwich, NR12 9AB

Tel +44 (0)1692 581099
Web www.theinghamswan.co.uk

Entry 386 Map 10

The Walpole Arms

Itteringham

A local farming family bought this Norfolk food pub in 2012 and the unspoilt brick-and-timber cottage in sleepy Itteringham remains a favourite for first-class modern British food. Daily menus are utterly seasonal and delight in fresh local produce – pork, beef and pheasant reared on the Harrold farm, Cromer crab, Morston mussels and venison from the Gunton Estate. Typically, there's Norfolk Dapple soufflé; chicken, ham hock and leek pie with creamy mash; vanilla rice pudding with brandy poached apricots. You can eat in the bar, with rough brick walls, beamed ceilings, standing timbers and wood-burner, or in the stylish Garden Room. East Anglian ales too, from Adnams and Woodforde's, a first-class list of wines, a glorious vine-covered terrace for summer, and great walks from the door across the Blickling Estate.

Meals Lunch & dinner £9.95-£17.
Closed 3pm-6pm & Sun eves.

Oliver Harrold
The Walpole Arms,
The Common, Itteringham,
Norwich, NR11 7AR
Tel +44 (0)1263 587258
Web www.thewalpolearms.co.uk

Entry 387 Map 10

The Pigs

Edgefield

This gutsy gastropub stands for all we love. "Pig in charge" Tim Abbott, along with fellow foodie entrepreneurs, fights the corner for proudly British food locally sourced, and is ever on the look out for suppliers; barter your produce for a pint! This is the retro village pub of your dreams – decent ales, great wines and a menu that delivers tastes long forgotten. Try potted rabbit with redcurrant jelly, venison burgers on toasted muffins, slow-roast lamb shoulder with fresh thyme, caramelised rice pudding. It's brilliant for families: a new adventure play area, a playroom full of toys, and a menu for 'piglets' served with in-house lemonade. Bar 'iffits' (Norfolk tapas), homemade pork scratchings and mixed pickle pots are further enticements, as are quiz nights and pub games.

Meals Lunch & dinner £9.95-£14.50.
Closed 3pm-6pm (Mon-Sat).

Tim Abbott
The Pigs,
Norwich Road, Edgefield,
Melton Constable, NR24 2RL
Tel +44 (0)1263 587634
Web www.thepigs.org.uk

Entry 388 Map 10

The Dun Cow

Salthouse

Seasoned Norfolk landlord Dan Goff sold up in Blakeney (The White Horse) and has headed a few miles east to the Dun Cow. He has now revitalised this coastal gem beside the village green. Glorious views across Cley Marshes from the spruced-up bar and beer garden draw twitchers, tourists and coastal-path walkers in their droves. Cord matting and slate tiles have replaced swirly carpet and old pine, there are painted settles, fat radiators, nautical pictures on brick and flint walls, and a glowing wood-burner; it's a delicious atmosphere that few want to leave. Fresh, locally sourced food on seasonal menus (venison Scotch egg, Morston mussels, game stew, treacle tart), Adnams and Woodforde's ales on tap, and weekly quiz and music nights complete the pleasing picture. Mobbed in summer.

Meals: Bar snacks £4-£7.
Lunch & dinner £9-£17.

Closed: Open all day.

Dan Goff
The Dun Cow,
Salthouse,
Cromer, NR25 7XA

Tel: +44 (0)1263 740467
Web: www.salthouseduncow.com

Entry 389 Map 10

Norfolk

The Three Horseshoes

Warham

In a rural backwater, a rural treasure. This row of 18th-century cottages – now a pub – hides a mile from the coastal path and glorious salt marshes. Inside: three plain rooms that have barely changed since the Thirties – gas lights, deal tables, Victorian fireplaces and a pianola that performs once in a while. Vintage entertainment includes an intriguing American Mills one-armed bandit converted for modern coins and a rare Norfolk 'twister' set into the ceiling – for village roulette, apparently. The food is in keeping, just traditional English dishes based emphatically on Norfolk produce (locally shot game, hearty casseroles, shortcrust pies) enhanced by pints of Wherry straight from the cask. Alternatively, sample local cider or homemade lemonade.

Meals: Lunch from £4.20.
Bar meals & dinner from £7.80.
Sunday lunch £8.20.

Closed: 2.30pm-6pm.

Iain Salmon
The Three Horseshoes,
69 The Street, Warham,
Wells-next-the-Sea, NR23 1NL

Tel: +44 (0)1328 710547
Web: www.warhamhorseshoes.co.uk

Entry 390 Map 10

The Stiffkey Red Lion

Stiffkey

Tucked into the side of a hill, overlooking the meadows where beef cattle graze, is an inn that's a pleasure to step into, a warren of three small rooms with bare floorboards and 17th-century quarry tiles, sunflower yellow walls, open log fires and stripped settles, old pews and scrubbed tables. The pub attracts a loyal crowd for its fresh seafood – crab from Wells boats, mussels from Mark Randall in the village, beer-battered cod – and first-rate ales from brewers such as Woodforde's and Yetmans. Locals rub shoulders with booted walkers and birdwatchers recovering from the rigours of the Norfolk Coast Path and the Stiffkey marshes. After a day on the beach the large, airy conservatory is popular with families. Dogs, too, are made welcome.

Meals	Lunch, bar meals & dinner from £9.95. Sunday lunch, 3 courses, £20.
Closed	Open all day.

Stephen Franklin
The Stiffkey Red Lion,
44 Wells Road, Stiffkey,
Wells-next-the-Sea, NR23 1AJ
Tel +44 (0)1328 830552
Web www.stiffkey.com

Entry 391 Map 10

Norfolk

The Crown Hotel

Wells-next-the-Sea

The interior of this handsome 16th-century coaching inn has been neatly smarted up yet remains atmospheric with its open fires, bare boards and easy chairs. It's run by Chris Coubrough, an enterprising chef-landlord who knows how to cook. Order pub food at the bar and eat in the lounges or lovely modern conservatory: a hearty serving of Brancaster mussels, roast venison, or the Crown beefburger with pepper relish and a pint of Adnams Bitter. Bold colours, modern art and attractively laid tables give life to the restaurant where local ingredients are translated into global ideas: whole baked mackerel with lime and chilli butter; Ryburgh quail stuffed with chicken, sage and chestnut on beetroot risotto; raspberry and white chocolate cheesecake.

Meals	Lunch & dinner from £11.25. Set menu £12.95-£15.95. Sunday lunch £10.95.
Closed	Open all day.

Chris Coubrough
The Crown Hotel,
The Buttlands,
Wells-next-the-Sea, NR23 1EX
Tel +44 (0)1328 710209
Web www.crownhotelnorfolk.co.uk

Entry 392 Map 10

The Jolly Sailors

Brancaster Staithe

Cliff and James Nye have revived a 200-year-old coastal treasure. 'Eat, Drink and be Jolly' says it all: not only is this a community boozer geared to locals and families but it attracts all those who flock to Brancaster Bay, just across the road. In the classic bar, replete with beams, tiled floor, settles and a wood-burner pumping out the heat, adults can enjoy home-brewed Brancaster ales while kids can watch the pizzas being baked in the open-to-view oven. Hearty traditional pub dishes using fresh local produce include mussels cooked in wine, onion, garlic and cream; lamb and mint pie; gammon, egg and chips; and good ol' fish and chips (delicious). It's may be less classy than the Nyes' White Horse Inn down the road, but the Sailors is a great little pit stop for families, beach bums and walkers.

Meals	Lunch & bar meals from £8.50. Dinner from £9.50. Sunday lunch, 3 courses, £20.
Closed	Open all day.

Cliff Nye & Family
The Jolly Sailors,
Brancaster Staithe,
King's Lynn, PE31 8BJ
Tel +44 (0)1485 210314
Web www.jollysailorsbrancaster.co.uk

Entry 393 Map 10

The Ship Inn Hotel

Brancaster

The swanky Ship is smack on the coast road, a ten-minute walk from Brancaster beach. Once a grim boozer, this cosy coastal bolthole is now the first port of call for post-beach drinks and tucker; kids and dogs are welcome. Grab a pint of Adnams and a crab sandwich, or linger over game terrine with tomato compote… temptingly followed by venison casserole with creamy mash and kale, then sticky toffee pudding. The bar is stylish, the food locally sourced and the dining atmosphere relaxed and informal. Be wowed by a quirky-chic décor: jute blinds, driftwood lights, slate-topped tables, striped fabrics, antique mirrors, objets d'art, and map-of-Norfolk wallpaper in the Map Room – it's a fun place to end a glorious day on the beach.

Meals	Lunch from £6.95. Dinner from £12.45. Sunday lunch £15.95 & £19.95.
Closed	Open all day.

Chris Coubrough
The Ship Inn Hotel,
Brancaster,
King's Lynn, PE31 8AP
Tel +44 (0)1485 210333
Web www.shiphotelnorfolk.co.uk

Entry 394 Map 9

The Red Lion

Culworth

Culworth has it all: thatched cottages, sweet green, grand manor – and the Red Lion, a classic old local revived by chef Justin Lefevre. The 70s décor has gone; the stone and wood floors, the timbers and the fireplaces have been rediscovered; there's a rustic-chic feel. Now diners mingle with locals, booted walkers quaff pints of Tribute in the bar, dogs doze, and, if you bring in your surplus veg, you collect points towards a free meal! In keeping, the food is unpretentious and delicious. Try garlic and thyme-roasted Moreton Pinkney mushrooms on focaccia; Buckby beef burger topped with slow-cooked pulled rib of beef and house relish; sea bream on a potato and spring onion salad; blackberry crème brûlée with blackcurrant sorbet. The garden is huge with village views.

Meals Lunch & dinner £8.50-£16.

Closed 3pm-6pm. Monday.

Justin Lefevre
The Red Lion,
High Street, Culworth,
Banbury, OX17 2BD

Tel +44 (0)1295 760050

Web www.theredlionculworth.co.uk

Entry 395 Map 8

Northamptonshire

The Plough

Everdon

It's a family affair here; farmer owners Kim and Stephen keep sheep nearby and sell vintage furniture in the barn next door, leaving the bar in the capable hands of Uncle Barry. A seasoned, old-fashioned landlord and CAMRA-award winner, he welcomes both locals and strangers like old friends. Inside, character oozes: find a cosy log burner and open fire, exposed stone walls, quarry tiles and high wooden chairs at the bar. Ales change often but Doom Bar and Proper Job are regulars. The menus are short and locally-sourced: lunch on tart Provençal, dine on Everdon beef Bourguignon with dauphinoise potatoes, indulge in a treacle tart if you've room. The garden is a delight, with views for miles across the countryside, and there's even a play area for little ones. Bring the dog, too; all are warmly welcomed here.

Meals Starters from £5.50.
Lunch from £4.95.
Dinner from £11.95.

Closed Open all day.

Kim Hopewell
The Plough,
High Street,
Everdon, NN11 3BL

Tel +44 (0)1327 361606

Web theploughinneverdon.com

Entry 396 Map 8

The Olde Coach House

Ashby St Ledgers

With its tidy thatched cottages and handsome church, Ashby St Ledgers is a bit of a gem. It's ancient enough to get a mention in the Domesday Book, and its Manor House was owned by one of Guy Fawkes' plotters. This is an attractive pub with a modern country interior: wooden floors, feature wallpaper, logs by the wood-burner, a squishy leather sofa. Order a pint of Bombardier in the bar, take it to the huge and lovely garden, let the children and dogs frolic. Under white painted rafters, friendly approachable staff ferry platefuls of good-looking food to pine tables: French onion soup with cheese croutons, homemade fishcakes with tartare sauce, pizzas, steaks, burgers, and perhaps sticky toffee pudding. It's a really good place for business folk to meet – and, come the weekend, friends and families.

Meals Lunch & dinner £6.95-£17.95.
Closed Open all day.

Mark Butler
The Olde Coach House,
Main Street, Ashby St Ledgers,
Rugby, CV23 8UN
Tel +44 (0)1788 890349
Web www.oldecoachhouse.co.uk

Entry 397 Map 8

Northamptonshire

The Queen's Head

Bulwick

A mellow old stone pub opposite the church in a lovely village – you'll wish it was your local. The simple beamed, flagstoned bar rambles into country-styled dining rooms that deliver atmosphere and charm, their thick beams and timbers and wonky walls expressing a history that goes back 600 years. The landlords took over in 2011 and have kept things simple. They haven't lost the village pub feel – bell ringers still head across the road every Wednesday evening. There's a stone oven on the decked summer terrace, and you can expect traditional pub food with a modern twist – devilled lamb's kidneys; saddle of lamb with a sun-dried tomato and rosemary crust; apple and caramel tart. A cracking pit-stop should you find yourself thirsty on the A43.

Meals Lunch & dinner £9.95-£19.95.
Closed 3pm-6pm (5pm-7pm Sun). Mon all day.

Rob Windeler
The Queen's Head,
Bulwick,
Corby, NN17 3DY
Tel +44 (0)1780 450272
Web www.thequeensheadbulwick.co.uk

Entry 398 Map 9

The Pheasant Inn

Stannersburn

A super little inn lost in beautiful country, the kind you hope to chance upon. The Kershaws run it with great passion and an instinctive understanding of its traditions. The bars are wonderful. Brass beer taps glow, 100-year old photos of the local community hang on stone walls, the clock above the fire keeps perfect time. Fires burn, bowler hats and saddles pop up here and there, varnished ceilings shine. House ales are expertly kept, Timothy Taylor's and Wylam waiting for thirsty souls. Fruit and vegetables come from the garden, while Robin's lovely food hits the spot perfectly, perhaps twice-baked cheese soufflé, slow-roasted Northumberland lamb, brioche and marmalade bread and butter pudding; as for Sunday lunch, *The Observer* voted it 'Best in the North'. Bedrooms in the old hay barn are light and airy, cute and cosy, great value for money. You're in the Northumberland National Park – no traffic jams, not too much hurry. You can sail on the lake, cycle round it or take to the hills and walk. For £10 you can also gaze into the universe at the Kielder Observatory (best in winter). Brilliant. *Minimum stay: two nights at weekends.*

Rooms	4 doubles, 3 twins: £95-£100. 1 family room for 4: £95-£140. Singles £50-£65. Half-board from £70 p.p.
Meals	Bar meals from £9.95. Dinner, 3 courses, £18-£22.
Closed	3pm-6.30pm (7pm Sun). Mon & Tues Nov-Mar.

Walter, Irene & Robin Kershaw
The Pheasant Inn,
Stannersburn,
Hexham, NE48 1DD
Tel +44 (0)1434 240382
Web www.thepheasantinn.com

The Duke of Wellington

Newton

The village inn has been transformed. Now, at the back, is a generous L-shaped space for diners: exposed stone walls and sleek wooden floors keep things rural, white paintwork, crisp curtains and immaculate furniture add style, and French windows open to a big, sheltered, south-facing terrace with views across the valley. But it's still a pub at the front, with its smart stone-flagged bar, glowing log-burner and good old English darts. As for the food, expect traditional British comfort food made using local, seasonal produce including slow-cooked pork shoulder with sage and onion boulangère potatoes, and sausages with mustard mash. Food-lovers come for roast cod fillet with smoked haddock brandade; crispy parma ham and leek velouté; roast duck breast with butter roasted roots, fondant potato and wholegrain mustard; families can tuck into roast sirloin of Northumbrian beef – 'served pink' – on Sundays. Bedrooms excel; nothing has been overlooked. Expect top beds and bed linen, beams, baths and skylights with remote controls, and scatter rugs on polished wood floors. Only the best for innkeeper Rob Harris.

Rooms	6 doubles, 1 twin: £95-£120.
Meals	Lunch & dinner from £10.95. Sunday lunch from £11.95.
Closed	Open all day.

Rob Harris
The Duke of Wellington,
Newton,
Corbridge, NE43 7UL
Tel +44 (0)1661 844446
Web www.thedukeofwellingtoninn.co.uk

Lord Crewe Arms at Blanchland

Blanchland

Originally the abbot's lodge and kitchens (and its garden the cloisters), the Lord Crewe Arms has become a Grade II*-listed inn. The village, in a sheep-clad valley on the moors' edge, was built with stone from the abbey's ruins. Inside: ancient flags, inglenook fireplaces, fortress walls and a classy country décor. Public areas range from lofty to intimate and the atmospheric bar is in the vaulted crypt. With a head chef from Mark Hix's 'stable', the robust modern British menu includes steaks, chops and spit-roasted meats, fresh crab salad and ruby beets. Puddings hark back to ancient times: sea buckthorn posset, rhubarb fumble. Wines include great burgundies and clarets, ales range from Allendale's Golden Plover to Nel's Best from High House Farm, and there are water bowls for dogs in the garden. If you stay, you're in for a treat. Most rooms are divided between The Angel, a simple, beautiful, listed ex-inn across the way, and the former tied cottages. Some bedrooms have exposed stone walls and real fires, all have soft carpets, fine fabrics, divine beds and deep baths.

Rooms	19 doubles: £119-£192. 1 suite for 2: £144-£212. 1 family room for 4: £189-£252.
Meals	Lunch & dinner from £12.75. Sunday lunch, 2-3 courses, £18-£24.
Closed	Open all day.

Tommy Mark
Lord Crewe Arms at Blanchland,
The Square,
Blanchland, DH8 9SP
Tel +44 (0)1434 677100
Web www.lordcrewearmsblanchland.co.uk

The Feathers Inn

Hedley on the Hill

Helen and Rhian have worked hard to develop the Feathers' reputation as a destination for food, yet the pub has not lost its pubby feel. What a rare treat, west of Newcastle, to find such an authentic little place. In the two bars are old beams, exposed stone, open fires and a simple cottagey feel; you're as much at home browsing the papers as enjoying a fireside chat. Ale is excellent, with four cask beers from local or microbreweries, and wines are taken as seriously. As for the food – grilled mackerel with grain mustard butter and crispy shallots, black pudding stuffed local rabbit with cider cream sauce, wild cherry and kirsch Bakewell tart – it is cooked with passion and skill from locally sourced produce; Rhian will even let you in to the secrets of some of his recipes. A star in the making.

Meals	Lunch £9-£12. Dinner £11-£18. Sunday lunch, 3 courses, £20.
Closed	Mon lunch (except bank hols).

Helen Greer & Rhian Cradock
The Feathers Inn,
Hedley on the Hill,
Stocksfield, NE43 7SW

Tel	+44 (0)1661 843607
Web	www.thefeathers.net

Entry 402 Map 12

Northumberland

Rat Inn

Anick

Tucked into the south-facing hillside, overlooking the Tyne Valley, this hard-to-find old drovers' inn has an irresistible appeal. The bar is cosy, with gleaming dark oak, flagged floor, simple tables and chairs, a roaring fire: sup a pint of something local or a good glass of wine while you toy with the idea of nibbles or a sandwich (try honey roast ham and pease pudding) to appease your rumbling tum. Those who have yomped heartily to get here may be hungrier, so look to the blackboard and its excellent, mostly regional delights: roast Northumberland rib of beef with watercress and golden chips for two is delicious, and maybe rice pudding afterwards. The sun room has grand views of the spectacular valley, and on warm days you can spill out into the little garden with its benches and pretty shrubs.

Meals	Lunch & dinner £8.95-£18.95. Bar meals from £1.95. Sunday lunch £8.95.
Closed	Open all day.

Phil Mason & Karen Errington
Rat Inn,
Anick,
Hexham, NE46 4LN

Tel	+44 (0)1434 602814
Web	www.theratinn.com

Entry 403 Map 12

The Staith House

North Shields

Former MasterChef finalist John Calton and his family team bravely took on this failing fisherman's boozer in November 2013. Following a serious spruce up they haven't looked back, as the quirky interior (wood panelling with portholes, scrubbed brick, colourful chairs, maps on ceilings) and John's food soon found favour with the locals. The daily menu embraces the seasons and their relationship with Northumbrian farmers and skippers ensures only the best produce fills the fridges. Best to arrive early (it's a small place) to tuck into quay-landed fish and chips, hake with black pudding, chorizo and aïoli, and dark chocolate fondant. Or wash down a lamb and mint Scotch egg with an Old Speckled Hen at the bar. Monthly wine and food tasting menus and summer barbecues overlooking the harbour complete the pleasing picture. A cracking place.

Meals	Starters from £5. Mains from £10.50.
Closed	Open all day.

John Calton
The Staith House,
57 Low Lights,
North Shields Fish Quay, NE30 1JA
Tel +44 (0)191 2708441
Web www.thestaithhouse.co.uk

Entry 404 Map 12

Northumberland

The Jolly Fisherman Inn

Craster

A beautifully refurbished coastal pub that sits above the harbour at pretty Craster. The view from the dining room is hypnotic, a clean sweep out to sea and up the Northumbrian coast. It's a great spot for fresh seafood and a huge hit with the locals, who come for a bucket of Shetland mussels or the pub's famous crab sandwich. The attractive bar has wooden floors, leather banquettes, a fire that roars and old photographs on the walls. Outside, the garden looks the right way, perfect for lunch in summer. Pints of Timothy Taylor and Black Sheep wait at the bar alongside lots of good wines. Dinner is more extensive, perhaps crab soup, Northumbrian venison, meringues with black cherries and ice cream. Coastal walks start from the front door: south to Howick, north to Dunstanburgh Castle.

Meals	Lunch from £6.95. Dinner from £10.50. Sunday lunch from £10.95.
Closed	Open all day.

David Whitehead
The Jolly Fisherman Inn,
Haven Hill, Craster,
Alnwick, NE66 3TR
Tel +44 (0)1665 576461
Web www.thejollyfishermancraster.co.uk

Entry 405 Map 14

The Ship Inn

Low Newton-by-the-Sea

Film nights, folk nights, beer that's brewed ten paces from the front door, lovely staff, tasty food, and a beautiful position on the Northumbrian coast. The Ship is tiny, two wonderfully authentic rooms with stripped floors, stone walls, old settles and a wood-burner for winter. There are maps, the odd nautical touch, but mostly the happy chatter of hungry souls digging into a good lunch, perhaps a hand-picked crab sandwich or a bowl of homemade soup. Christine came north with no intention of running a pub, but as befalls most who visit, she fell under its spell; now it's a place of pilgrimage for many. The food is simple, scrumptious and as local as possible: crabs and kippers from Seahouses, free-range organic meat from the Borders. In summer, life spills onto the cobbles outside. Blissful.

Meals	Lunch £2-£8.95. Dinner £8.95-£23.
Closed	Open all day.

Christine Forsyth
The Ship Inn, The Square,
Low Newton-by-the-Sea,
Alnwick, NE66 3EL

Tel +44 (0)1665 576262
Web www.shipinnnewton.co.uk

Entry 406 Map 14

Northumberland

The Olde Ship

Seahouses

A nautical gem – of which the Glen dynasty has been at the helm for a century, their enthusiasm ever undimmed. The coastal inn sparkles with maritime memorabilia reminding you of Seahouses' heritage and the days when Grace Darling rowed through the waves to rescue stricken souls. Settle in by a glowing fire with a decent pint (no fewer than ten ales!). In the recently refurbished Cabin Bar you are treated to hearty pub food: ham hock terrine, chicken and mushroom casserole, fish chowder and bosun's fish stew, ginger trifle... then order coffee and mints in the lounge. The whole place creaks with history. Gaze across the harbour to the Farne Islands, catch the ferry, or set off for a bracing coastal walk to Bamburgh Castle.

Meals	Lunch from £8. Bar meals & dinner from £10. Sunday lunch, 3 courses, £11.50.
Closed	Open all day.

Judith Glen & David Swan
The Olde Ship,
7-9 Main Street,
Seahouses, NE68 7RD

Tel +44 (0)1665 720200
Web www.seahouses.co.uk

Entry 407 Map 14

The Blacksmiths

Clayworth

Following a stint in Switzerland, Will and Leah spent eight months refurbishing this 18th-century building, and it's quickly built a reputation for the quality of its local, seasonal food. Chef prefers 'to lead rather than follow', so expect dishes such as Jerusalem artichoke and Lincolnshire Poacher custard, monkfish loin with squid ink risotto, buttermilk panna cotta with Yorkshire rhubarb. For something simpler there's the blackboard menu with delicious pub classics: go for the fish and chips or wild mushroom wellington. Cosy up in front of the log burner in the spacious, stone-floored bar, dine at reclaimed wooden tables in the award-winning restaurant or sip a pint of real ale in the walled garden. There's a great selection of wines, too. Why not come for the weekend and book one of the stylish rooms in the gorgeous barn conversion; all have comfy beds, snow white linen and quirky, spotless bathrooms with Cowshed smellies. A breakfast hamper or cooked breakfast delivered to your door comes as standard. Fashionable, poised, self-assured, re-invigorated: The Blacksmiths is designed to please.

Rooms	1 double, 2 twin/doubles: £100-£150. 1 studio for 4: £180.
Meals	Starters from £5.50. Mains from £12.95. A la carte menu available.
Closed	Mondays.

Will & Leah Frankland
The Blacksmiths,
Town Street, Clayworth,
Retford, DN22 9AD
Tel +44 (0)1777 818171
Web www.blacksmithsclayworth.com

Caunton Beck

Caunton

Having hatched the successful Wig & Mitre in Lincoln, the Hopes looked for a rural equivalent and found one in this pretty village, then reconstructed the skeleton of the 16th-century Hole Arms. The elongated bar, with shining brass trimmings, frosted glass, scrubbed tables, serious tableware and rosebuds in tiny vases, is a hugely popular spot for breakfast with the papers from 8am, and later, sandwiches, daily blackboard lunches and set meals. It's deliciously rich comfort food (lamb and sage faggots, roast venison) with some oriental surprises, such as wok fried sesame and chilli chicken Singapore noodles. Puddings are fabulous. The dining room is less intimate, there's a cosy fire in winter, parasol picnic sets on the small front lawn in summer, and well-managed ales on hand pump all year around.

Meals	Lunch & dinner £9.50-£22.50.
Closed	Open all day.

Gill Woolsgrove
Caunton Beck, Main Street,
Caunton, Newark, NG23 6AB

Tel	+44 (0)1522 538902
Web	www.wigandmitre.com/the-caunton-beck/

Entry 409 Map 9

Nottinghamshire

The Prince Rupert

Newark

Now sympathetically restored, this 15th-century town-centre local creaks with history and has a deliciously pubby feel. It's just the kind of place you hope to chance upon – not grand, not scruffy, just right, where locals pile in for pints of local ale; as much thought goes into the beers here as the wines. The entrance opens to a series of small rooms where, among dark beams and polished wood, warmth and cosiness emanate from an open fire and a little seating spot snug enough for two. But upstairs is where the biggest treat lies: two rooms revealing the ancient building's glory – all beamed ceilings and timbered walls, and an ancient skylight exposed during the renovation. The regularly changing menu reveals further simple enticements: stone-baked pizzas; ham, eggs and sauté potatoes; beef lasagne.

Meals	Lunch & dinner from £6.95. Not Sunday.
Closed	Open all day.

Tony & Heidi Yale
The Prince Rupert,
46 Stodman Street,
Newark, NG24 1AW

Tel	+44 (0)1636 918121
Web	www.theprincerupert.co.uk

Entry 410 Map 9

The Full Moon

Morton

The Prices took on this creeper-clad Morton landmark in 2013, and have preserved the villagey friendliness: fish-and-chip takeaways, a toy cupboard for the kids, family fun-runs and an annual scarecrow trail. As for the food, chef James Stanton takes classic British ingredients and teeters them in elegant bonsai stacks on rustic hunks of slate. Eye-catching starters include pea, ham hock and truffle oil soup, and goat's cheese fondue with parsnip crisps, pine nuts and confit garlic; you can eat more substantially from the main-course lunch menu for under a tenner. There's a buzz in the bar, where locals hold court and the coal fire fizzes, but the trimmings are coolly contemporary: pale wood and pinstriped upholstery in tones of silver, blue and grey. A great little find – you can even get married here.

Meals	Lunch £5.50-£12. Dinner £11-£18.50. Sunday lunch, 2 courses, £16.
Closed	Open all day.

Richard & Alicia Price
The Full Moon,
Main Street,
Morton, NG25 0UT
Tel +44 (0)1636 830251
Web www.thefullmoonmorton.co.uk

Martin's Arms

Colston Bassett

An Elizabethan farmhouse that became an ale house around 1700, and an inn 100 years later. Today it is a deeply civilised pub. The front room exudes country-house charm – scatter cushions on sofas and settles, crackling logs in Jacobean fireplaces – and you can order a splendid ploughman's with Colston Bassett stilton from the dairy up the road (do visit). In the restaurant, menus change daily, while highlights include pan-fried scallops with Stafford black pudding; locally shot game with seasonal vegetables; delicious Sunday roast beef. Polish off with treacle sponge and butterscotch sauce with brandy butter ice cream. Behind the bar is an impressive range of well-kept real ales, cognacs and malts, with 20 wines (including sparkling and champagne) by the glass or carafe, and a further 22 by the bottle.

Meals	Lunch £5.95. Bar meals from £7.50. Dinner from £14.50. Sunday lunch £18.95 & £23.95. No food Christmas Day.
Closed	3pm-6pm Mon-Sat. 5pm-7pm Sun.

Lynne Strafford Bryan
& Salvatore Inguanta
Martin's Arms, School Lane, Colston Bassett, Nottingham, NG12 3FD
Tel +44 (0)1949 81361
Web www.themartinsarms.co.uk

The Three Pigeons Inn

Banbury

Close to the centre of busy Banbury town is this pretty thatched coaching inn, owned by Tina and Paul Laird. Recently refurbished with oak flooring, the original stone walls hark back to its beginnings while two attractive coal-effect gas burners (no logs allowed because of the thatch!), one snug in the old inglenook, lend warmth. At the rear of the pub is a large stone terrace with weathered oak seating for 60. The team is friendly and well-informed, serving a refreshing choice of old ales; they are also great on whiskies and wines by the glass. As for the menus, you'll find pigeon breasts with asparagus tips and wild mushrooms, Spring lamb rump with dauphinoise potatoes, and an array of super puddings including a truly indulgent white chocolate and raspberry cheesecake. Cheeses are served with homemade chutneys and port jelly. Upstairs and to the rear are three very smart bedrooms, with feature wallpapers and characterful beams, swish bathrooms and superb French-style beds. All overlook the courtyard, all are perfectly peaceful.

Rooms	3 doubles: £105-£125. Extra bed available in room 3: £30 extra per child; £40 extra per adult; max. 4 persons in room.
Meals	Lunch & dinner £12.95-£18.95.
Closed	3pm-6pm Mon-Sat. Sun eve.

Tina Laird
The Three Pigeons Inn,
3 Southam Road,
Banbury, OX16 2ED

Tel +44 (0)1295 275220
Web www.thethreepigeons.com

The White Horse Inn

Duns Tew

The White Horse has been on a roll since Michael and Josh arrived in 2014. The atmosphere is convivial, the food exceptional and the stables have been transformed. Old flagged floors, inglenooks and open fires, candles on wooden tables, a corner with a chesterfield, a snug for a private party, guest ales behind the bar. This handsome 17th-century building, tucked away in the pretty village of Duns Tew, is all you hope a Cotswolds pub to be. Beyond is the restaurant, less rustic but still atmospheric: dark chairs and tables, old standing timbers, a log-burner at one end. Expect braised squid with tomatoes and white wine aïoli; leek and Gruyère tart; cottage pie with greens. The menu changes daily, the fruit and veg are from North Aston Organics, the lamb is from the farm up the road (sweet, lean Zwartbles meat favoured by Rick Stein). No garden, but you can eat on the terrace in summer. As for the stables, they house fresh bedrooms, all stylish and delightful, with down-feather pillows and tartan wool throws. Breakfast is worth getting up for.

Rooms	11 doubles: £91-£131.
Meals	Starters from £5. Mains from £11.
Closed	Open all day.

Michael Regan
The White Horse Inn,
Daisy Hill,
Duns Tew OX25 6JS

Tel +44 (0)1869 340272
Web www.dunstewwhitehorse.co.uk

The Killingworth Castle

Wootton

The family behind the Ebrington Arms has renovated this 17th-century inn, around the corner from Blenheim Palace, to its former glory with beautifully restored bedrooms too. Wood floors sweep from side bar to main bar to dining room, burners in brick fireplaces belt out heat and the set menu is a steal. Smiling staff ferry own-brewed Yubby Bitter, Goldie and Yawnie to locals, dog walkers and drinkers; the rest are here for the food: roast venison and faggot croquette with beetroot dauphinoise, kale and juniper; blackberry and frangipane tart. And the best chips in Oxfordshire! Famous for their real ales, the focus is on small brewers; wines showcase independent makers; there's a nifty selection of malt whiskies, or try a pint of their home-brewed in the big beer garden. Oh, and the bedrooms! Some upstairs, some down, all with handpicked art, handmade sturdy beds and the softest linen. Muted tartan blankets keep you warm on winter nights, roll top baths sit on patterned tiled floors and there's a complementary decanter of sherry to start you off. Glorious.

Rooms 10 doubles: £99-£180.

Meals Starters £6-£8. Mains £13-£21. Midweek set menu, 2 courses, £11.95.

Closed Open all day.

Claire & Jim Alexander
The Killingworth Castle,
Glympton Road, Wootton,
Chipping Norton, OX20 1EJ

Tel +44 (0)1993 811401
Web www.thekillingworthcastle.com

The Kingham Plough

Kingham

You don't expect to find locals clamouring for a table in a country pub on a cold Tuesday in February, but different rules apply here. Emily, once junior sous-chef at the Fat Duck, is doing her own splendid thing and it's small wonder the locals approve. The tithe barn is an exquisite dining room, its ceilings open to ancient rafters, where attentive staff deliver sublime food. Try Adlington chicken breast and ballotine with local apricots, sweetcorn and runner beans followed by white chocolate burnt custard with cobnut caramel, raspberry ice cream and macaroon. Provenance is king here, so expect the best local ingredients cooked to perfection by a talented (and award-winning) team. The bar menu is temptingly long, there's a terrace for summer dining, and fruit trees, herbs and lavender in the garden. Charming bedrooms (which can be booked in adjoining pairs for families) have super-comfy beds with feather duvets and pillows, Egyptian cotton linen, armchairs, books and mini bars, and sparkling bathrooms with Neal's Yard potions. Arrive by train straight from London to be met by a bus that delivers you to the door. The Daylesford Organic farm shop/café is close. Exceptional.

Rooms	4 doubles, 2 twin/doubles: £145-£195. Singles from £75.
Meals	Lunch from £15. Bar meals from £5. Dinner, 3 courses, about £40. Sunday lunch from £17.
Closed	Open all day.

Emily Watkins & Miles Lampson
The Kingham Plough,
The Green, Kingham,
Chipping Norton, OX7 6YD
Tel +44 (0)1608 658327
Web www.thekinghamplough.co.uk

The Kings Head Inn

Bledington

The sort of inn that defines this country: a 16th-century cider house made of ancient stone that sits on the green in a Cotswold village with free-range hens strutting their stuff and a family of ducks bathing in the pond. Inside, locals gather to chew the cud, scoff great food and wash it down with a cleansing ale. The fire burns all year, you get low ceilings, painted stone walls, country rugs on flagstone floors. Bedrooms, all different, are scattered about; all are well priced. Those in the main house have more character, those in the courtyard are bigger (and quieter). You'll find painted wood, lots of colour, pretty fabrics, spotless bathrooms; most have great views, too. Breakfast and supper are taken in a pretty dining room (exposed stone walls, pale wood tables), while you can lunch by the fire in the bar on Cornish scallops, steak and ale pie, then a plate of British cheeses. There are lovely unpompous touches like jugs of cow parsley in the loo, and loads to do: antiques in Stow, golf at Burford, walking and riding through gorgeous terrain. The front terrace teems with life in summer.

Rooms	9 doubles, 3 twin/doubles: £100-£135. Singles from £70.
Meals	Lunch from £7.50. Dinner, 3 courses, about £30. Sunday lunch £15.
Closed	Open all day.

Archie & Nicola Orr-Ewing
The Kings Head Inn,
The Green, Bledington,
Chipping Norton, OX7 6XQ

Tel +44 (0)1608 658365
Web www.kingsheadinn.net

The Feathered Nest Country Inn

Nether Westcote

The village is tiny, the view is fantastic, the bar is lively, the rooms are a treat. This 300-year-old malthouse sits in 55 acres of green and pleasant land and is utterly gorgeous inside and out. The view from the garden is one of the best in the Cotswolds – a five-mile sweep across quilted fields to a distant ridge. Interiors are just as good. A warm rustic style mixes beautifully with original timbers and old stone walls. A fire smoulders in the lovely bar, doors in the restaurant open onto the terrace, the garden room has tartan walls and the white wine cellar on display. Bedrooms delight. One is enormous, two have the view, beds are dressed in crisp linen. Some have power showers, one has a claw-foot bath, all have robes. You get coffee machines and iPod docks, too. Delicious food waits downstairs, perhaps octopus with lemon and garlic, pollock with saffron and fennel, tarte tatin with vanilla ice cream. You eat on the terrace in summer looking out on the lake and distant farms. A couple of luxurious cabins are soon to be sprinkled across the grounds – Amanda and Tony do nothing by halves. Magical. *Minimum stay: two nights at weekends.*

Rooms	4 doubles: £235-£285.
Meals	Lunch & dinner £6.50-£30. No food Sunday eve.
Closed	Monday (except bank hols).

Tony & Amanda Timmer
The Feathered Nest Country Inn,
Nether Westcote,
Chipping Norton, OX7 6SD
Tel +44 (0)1993 833030
Web www.thefeatherednestinn.co.uk

The Shaven Crown

Shipton under Wychwood

The Great Hall, with its spectacular roof, dates back to 1368 – quite some sitting room. It was built by monks from Bruern Abbey, reborn as a royal hunting lodge after the Dissolution of the Monasteries, then gifted to the village as an inn. Phil and Evelyn rescued it from neglect, then spent a year restoring long-lost glories – no mean feat. Potter about and find parquet flooring in the airy bar, books and armchairs in the pretty snug, then mullioned windows in the restaurant, where you dig into some lovely local food; rabbit rillettes with pear purée, loin of venison with a port wine sauce, espresso mousse with rum ice cream or a William pear cheesecake. In summer you spill out into a gorgeous courtyard for afternoon tea in the sun. Bedrooms have an elegant simplicity: airy colours, stylish fabrics, beautiful beds, sparkling bathrooms. One has a beamed roof, a couple are smaller, but have courtyard views. You're right in the heart of the Cotswolds, with Stratford for Shakespeare, Cheltenham for the races and Oxford for the spires all within easy reach. There's even jazz in the hall once a month. Dogs are very welcome.

Rooms	4 doubles, 3 twin/doubles: £95-£135.
Meals	Starters £5.95-£8.25. Mains £13.75-£17.50.
Closed	Open all day.

Phil & Evelyn Roberts
The Shaven Crown,
High Street,
Shipton under Wychwood, OX7 6BA

Tel +44 (0)1993 830500
Web www.theshavencrown.co.uk

The Bull Inn

Charlbury

Hop on the train at Paddington for the Bull. The old pub sits on Sheep Street and ticks all the right boxes for lovers of Cotswolds' inns: great food, great service, gorgeous interiors. But it's the homely feel that pulls it into a class of its own. Warm up by log fires with a Bloody Mary (house speciality) or a pint of Fullers. The wine list is short and includes some great finds… Charlie (young, friendly, charming) recently ran a vineyard in France. Find kilim rugs on seagrass floors, white limed beams and rustic walls, a sparkling little bar with zinc tops, and wood panelling painted a Georgian slate blue. Everyone's welcome including kids and dogs, and the menu is short and delightful: baked gnocchi with mozzarella; battered whiting and chips; Pie of the Day with winter greens; chocolate sundae. The burgers (from local beef) are amazing. Upstairs are four bedrooms – with more to come in the barn – modern in feel, laid-back yet luxurious: white bathrooms, wonderful wallpapers, seagrass floors, vintage chests of drawers.

Rooms	4 doubles: £100-£180.
Meals	Starters from £5. Mains from £12.
Closed	Open all day.

Ellena Barnes
The Bull Inn,
Sheep Street,
Charlbury, OX7 3RR
Tel +44 (0)1608 810689
Web www.bullinn-charlbury.com

The Woodstock Arms

Woodstock

In Woodstock – picturesque estate town to magnificent Blenheim Palace – is an old pub with a new lease of life: Johnny and Damion, seasoned operators, have turned the former boozer around. Enter a large welcoming space, be-rugged and pattern floor-tiled, with a green-painted bar and a roaring fire beneath a copper hood, sturdy tables for eating and drinking, and wing-back chairs in elegant leather. Behind the bar: real ales, cocktails, well-priced wines, and an impressive selection of soft drinks. In the dark beamed restaurant is the best of old British with a firm eye on provenance: pints of crispy whitebait from Brixham, duck salads, hearty pies (including vegetarian), crumbles and brûlées. It's a pretty stone building on Market Street, blessed with a large courtyard behind, and if you're here for the palace and its gardens ('England's Versailles') stay the night. Three bedrooms wait above, carpeted, compact, light and bright, with stylish new bathrooms. Hypnos mattresses, Roberts radios, Tassimo coffee machines, smart TVs, laptop safes… all has been properly thought through.

Rooms	3 doubles: £120-£220.
Meals	Breakfast from £4.50. Starters from £7. Dinner from £9.
Closed	Open all day.

Damion Farah & Johnny Pugsley
The Woodstock Arms,
6-8 Market Street, Woodstock,
Oxford, OX20 1SX
Tel +44 (0)1993 811251
Web www.thewoodstockarms.com

The Swan

Swinbrook

Free-range bantams strut in the garden, a pint of Hooky waits at the bar. This lovely old pub sits on the river Windrush with the village cricket pitch waiting beyond. It started life as a water mill and stands on the Devonshire estate, hence the pictures of the Mitford sisters that hang on the walls. Outside, wisteria wanders across golden stone and creepers blush red in the autumn sun. Interiors hit the spot: low ceilings, open fires, beautiful windows, stone walls. Over the years thirsty feet on their way to the bar (including those belonging to prime ministers and presidents) have worn grooves into ancient flagstones. As for the food, seasonal menus brim with local produce, offering delicious delights, perhaps game terrine with pear chutney, roast partridge with a red wine jus, rhubarb and apple crumble. Bedrooms in the old forge have 15th-century walls and 21st-century interior design; those in the cottage across the lane are yards from the river. Expect crisp linen, comfy beds, warm colours and good art. Several have claw-foot baths, one has a pink chaise longue. Burford is close.

Rooms	4 doubles, 5 twin/doubles, 1 twin: £125-£150. 1 suite for 2: £180-£195. Singles from £70.
Meals	Lunch from £5. Dinner, 3 courses, about £30. Sunday lunch from £14.95.
Closed	Open all day.

Archie & Nicola Orr-Ewing
The Swan,
Swinbrook,
Burford, OX18 4DY

Tel +44 (0)1993 823339
Web www.theswanswinbrook.co.uk

The Angel at Burford

Burford

It's a Hook Norton house so they sell the excellent Hooky and stout, and a guest beer too. Take a pint to the sofa by the roaring log fire, or a good whisky or wine; this is what winter Sundays were made for. The Angel, listed and 16th-century, is tucked peacefully away from the broad beautiful high street. Take a look at the ever-changing blackboard menu with its focus on simplicity and quality, there's something for everyone: delicious pastrami sandwiches with French fries and dressed salad, moules marinière, rare-beef Sunday roasts, trios of cheeses and refreshing sorbets. Three big, comfortable and characterful rooms come with the requisite beams, sash windows and creaking wood floors, one overlooking the pretty courtyard and garden; cushioned window seats let you make the most of the view. In the summer, there are festivals, shire horses and music. Close to Oxford for a peek at the spires then back to your fireside armchair for a snooze. It must be the perfect Cotswolds' pub. *One-night weekend stays welcome.*

Rooms	2 doubles, 1 twin/double: £90-£120. Dinner B&B £130-£160.
Meals	Lunch & dinner £13.50-£21.50.
Closed	Open all day.

Gemma Finch & Terrance King
The Angel at Burford,
14 Witney Street,
Burford, OX18 4SN
Tel +44 (0)1993 822714
Web www.theangelatburford.co.uk

The Maytime Inn

Asthall

The setting is gorgeous, the village is historic, and the 17th-century coaching inn has its own smithy. Set off on a circular walk and end up in the bar. A cool young team run this rather posh pub, headed up by Dom who is involved in all areas of the business. Good food is sourced locally and freshly cooked in a modern, very British, way including pub classics and sandwiches. Drinks are taken seriously: an ever-growing choice of gins (over 80!), a beer menu with craft and world beers, ales and ciders from smaller independent breweries, and an excellent choice of wines and whiskeys. Dining areas are split level, a top-notch modern take on traditional, all new slate flag floors and tartan cushions, Windsor chairs and white-painted beams. Outside: a large terraced area, an outdoor bar, petanque, comfortable places to sit – and if you are chilly? A double-sided wood-burner and blankets take care of that. On the ground floor: handsome rooms with delicious beds, folding desks and all the technology. The quietest are away from the courtyard; go for a large room if you fancy a deep soak.

Rooms	6 doubles: £95-£150.
Meals	Starters from £6.50. Mains from £12.50.
Closed	Open all day.

Dominic Wood
The Maytime Inn,
Asthall,
Burford, OX18 4HW

Tel +44 (0)1993 822068
Web www.themaytime.com

Old Swan & Minster Mill

Old Minster Lovell

Understated magic abounds at this 16th-century riverside inn, a half-timbered beauty transformed into a charming gastropub. In the rambling bar are gnarled beams and timbers, bright kilims and stone-flagged floors, and crisp checked armchairs by big beautiful fireplaces – aromatic with logs in winter. In perfect sympathy with the mood, traditional British food is cooked with a modern approach; ingredients are of the best quality and the vegetables are home-grown. Menus change daily; try seared king scallops, Cotswold rack of lamb, rib-eye steak with horseradish mayonnaise… and for pudding, classic caramelised lemon tart. Steep twisting stairs lead to very fine bedrooms that combine solid darkwood antiques with every modern comfort – laundered linen and fine down, big beds, cafetières of coffee, decanters of sloe gin, bathrobes in lovely bathrooms. (There are many more rooms in the modern Minster Mill across the road, smaller but overlooking beautiful gardens.) Oxford and Burford are close

Rooms	57 doubles: £165-£275. 1 suite for 2: £350. 2 singles: £155.
Meals	Lunch from £9.50. Bar meals from £8.50. Dinner from £14.95. Sunday lunch, 3 courses, £30.
Closed	3pm-6.30pm.

Vicky Steedman
Old Swan & Minster Mill,
Old Minster Lovell,
Minster Lovell, Witney, OX29 0RN

Tel	+44 (0)1993 774441
Web	www.oldswanandminstermill.com

The Trout at Tadpole Bridge

Buckland Marsh

A 17th-century Cotswold inn on the banks of the Thames; pick up a pint, drift into the garden, watch the world float by. Inside you find all the trimmings of a lovely old pub: timber frames, exposed stone walls, a wood-burner to keep things toasty, local ales on tap at the bar. Logs are piled high in alcoves, good art hangs on the walls, old flagstones lead to the bar where delicious food ranges from classics to posh nosh, perhaps fish and chips, chargrilled rainbow trout, or liquorice glazed ox cheek. Finish with a hazelnut nougat parfait. Bedrooms at the back are away from the crowd; three open onto a small courtyard where wild roses ramble. You get smart fabrics, trim carpets, monsoon showers (two rooms have a claw-foot bath), DVD players and flat-screen TVs. Sleigh beds, brass beds, smartly upholstered armchairs... the suite has a roof terrace. You can watch boats pass as you indulge in a leisurely homemade breakfast with local teas and coffee. Oxford's cultural delights are a stone's throw away, there are maps for walkers, and you can even get married, riverside, in the garden. *Booking recommended.*

Rooms	2 doubles, 3 twin/doubles: £110-£170. 1 suite for 4: £140-£195.
Meals	Mains from £13.95. Dinner, 3 courses, about £30. Sunday lunch from £14.95.
Closed	Open all day.

Ricardo Canestra
The Trout at Tadpole Bridge,
Buckland Road, Buckland Marsh,
Faringdon, SN7 8RF
Tel +44 (0)1367 870382
Web www.troutinn.co.uk

The Lamb at Buckland

Buckland

Follow the signs through picture-perfect Buckland to the 18th-century Lamb, tucked into a green corner of this historic estate village. The combined talents and enthusiasms of Shelley and chef Richard have turned this little inn into one of the best; it's an absolute gem. Step into a simple, rustic bar to find crackling logs, low beams, fat candles, old dining tables, leather wing chairs, local ales and Cotswold gin. Beyond is the more refined dining room, where modern seasonal menus champion local suppliers (Kelmscott pork, home-grown vegetables, and local game). Beautiful food flows from the kitchen: duck balls with red cabbage; roasted fillet of pork with prunes and pancetta; butternut squash and sweet potato gallette with goat's cheese and mushroom cream sauce; warm chocolate and walnut brownies. The trio of bedrooms here is delightful: crisp cotton, down duvets, colourful throws, a mix of pine and painted furniture, iPod-radios, bathrooms fresh and simple. The Thames Path, William Morris's Kelmscott Manor and Oxford are close by.

Rooms	3 doubles: £80-£90.
Meals	Lunch from £9.50. Bar meals from £6. Dinner from £12.95. Sunday lunch from £12.
Closed	3pm-6pm. Sun eves & all day Mon (except bank hol lunch).

Richard & Shelley Terry
The Lamb at Buckland,
Lamb Lane, Buckland,
Faringdon, SN7 8QN
Tel +44 (0)1367 870484
Web www.lambatbuckland.co.uk

The Star Inn

Sparsholt

Set the sat nav to seek out this 300-year-old dining pub lost down lanes in a sleepy hamlet. Interior designer Caron Williams bought her faded and failing local and, with talented chef Matt Williams (ex Whatley Manor), has put it firmly on Oxfordshire's culinary map. It may be a foodie destination but the spruced up bar, with its wood floors, old pine tables and hop adorned beams, has a relaxed feel – dogs, walkers and cyclists are all welcome. Peruse the papers over a pint of Hooky and a bar snack (sandwiches, burger, scotch egg), or settle in for a memorable meal, Matt's food is top notch and the set menu is a steal: scorched mackerel fillet with pink grapefruit, sake and kohlrabi, followed by locally shot pheasant with artichoke, trompette mushrooms and hazelnut mashed potato, and yuzu tart with maple syrup ice cream and bourbon syrup. Refurbished rooms in the converted barn are contemporary and chic with rustic charm. Calm colours, rich fabrics, quality linen on big beds and smart tiled bathrooms with top toiletries. A star in the making.

Rooms	4 twin/doubles: £95-£105. 1 suite for 2: £125. 1 family room for 4: £135. 2 singles: £75.
Meals	Mains £16.50-£35.
Closed	Mondays all day. Tuesdays-Fridays 3pm-5pm.

Caron Williams
The Star Inn,
Watery Lane, Sparsholt,
Wantage, OX12 9PL
Tel +44 (0)1235 751873
Web www.thestarsparsholt.co.uk

The Greyhound Inn

Letcombe Regis

Close to the white chalk horse at Uffington – the walking is grand round here – is a beautiful red-brick pub on the quiet road that winds through Letcombe Regis. The new owners have kept the fine old windows and the irresistible fireplaces and have added a garden at the back, a bright, cheerful décor, and a diamond of a chef in Phil Currie. Whether you go for guinea fowl with truffle, choux gnocchi and consommé, or battered haddock and chips and salad, this is cooking of a high order. Our two-course 'Midweek Fix' was a steal: a cheddar and leek tart followed by new season lamb chunk steak, both delicious. If the pub is Georgian on the outside, it's country-trendy within; racing scenes adorn the walls, dog biscuits beautify the bar, and up the carpeted stairs are eight sympathetically, tastefully refurbished rooms. Our favourite is the family suite under the eaves (beams, sloping ceiling, simple country antiques, turquoise roll top tub). Beds are Hypnos, cushions are plush, bathrooms luxurious, breakfasts a treat. You can pop in for a latte, a well-kept pint, or a hedonistic meal: it's the sort of place we all love.

Rooms	4 doubles, 2 twin/doubles: £90-£135. 1 suite for 4, 1 suite for 5: £135-£195. Extra pull-out bed available.
Meals	Starters from £5.50. Lunch from £7. Dinner from £11.
Closed	Open all day.

Catriona Galbraith
The Greyhound Inn,
Main Street, Letcombe Regis,
Wantage, OX12 9JL
Tel +44 (0)1235 771969
Web www.thegreyhoundletcombe.co.uk

The Fat Fox Inn

Watlington

A stone's throw from the big smoke yet wonderfully rural. Historic Watlington is on the edge of the Chiltern Hills, red kites wheel above beech woods and the Ridgeway runs through. The 17th-century building has been part pub, butchers, bakery and shop in its day but is now an inn to the core. The bronze buddha on the bar gazes serenely over pumps with Brakspear Bitter and Oxford Gold, the carpeted bar is cosy and simple, there's an open fire, sofas and an elegant separate dining room with oriental rugs. Consider smoked chicken and foie gras terrine, fig chutney and sourdough toast; fillet of pollock, chick pea, chorizo and sherry stew with saffron aïoli; lemon financier and thyme ice cream – just some of the delights from chef Mark Gambles and quite simply divine. Staff and owner are delightful and the whole place hums along on this team's super-friendly and engaging manner. Set well behind the bustle in several old barns are a variety of bedrooms – some with signature beds and trappings, all with antiques, beams and small neat bathrooms.

Rooms	5 doubles, 4 twins: £75-£119.
Meals	Lunch from £12. Bar meals from £5. Dinner from £27. Sunday lunch, 2-3 courses, £20-£25.
Closed	Open all day.

John Riddell
The Fat Fox Inn,
13 Shirburn Street,
Watlington, OX49 5BU
Tel +44 (0)1491 613040
Web www.thefatfoxinn.co.uk

The Cherry Tree Inn

Stoke Row

A short drive from London (and Oxford) is a handsome old pub in Stoke Row, with food, service and bedrooms to match. It is one of three dining pubs in the Henley area run by the same operator. Throughout all is fresh, light and airy, with chunky wood tables and pale colours, and floors of stripped wood or stone; of the bars, the biggest is in the middle, warm and cosy with an open fire. You can eat where you like and the food is pub grub done well, with lots on the menu. Sunday lunches see two roasts as well as fish pie or sausages, and always a dish for vegetarians; there are tasty meals for little ones and puddings that sound suitably naughty. You could drop by for a pint of Brakspear and a platter of ham, salami, pork belly and chorizo, or tuck into tandoori chicken breast with all the trimmings, or beer-battered cod. In summer there are hog roasts in the beer garden. Crisp linen, cream walls, big beds, generous breakfasts… it's also a good weekend base for the area, with four ground-floor bedrooms in the wood-clad barn, a stagger away. Your dog can stay too.

Rooms	4 doubles: £85-£100.
Meals	Lunch from £6.95. Sunday lunch from £12.50. A la carte dinner £20-£30. No food Sunday eve.
Closed	Open all day.

Lolly & Doug Green
The Cherry Tree Inn,
Stoke Row,
Henley-on-Thames, RG9 5QA

Tel	+44 (0)1491 680430
Web	www.thecherrytreeinn.co.uk

The Plowden Arms

Shiplake

Inside has a 1920s feel; at any minute Agatha Christie might enter and order herself a gin fizz. Dark polished chairs sit on oak parquet, there's an open brick fireplace with hops above, and shining glasses on tables. And you'll find old forgotten favourites on the menu; Matthew worked at the Savoy Grill and calls himself 'unashamedly old-fashioned'. So tuck into herrings in oatmeal with sweet lemon salad, lamb cutlets cooked à la Reform Club in 1839, and barley cream with blackcurrant compote. The British cheeses with pear chutney are a delight (you can tell a lot from a cheeseboard) and if the slow-roast shoulder of pork is anything to go by, Matthew is a fabulous chef. Ales are in great condition, wines are mostly European, dogs are welcome, and the sloping garden next to fields is heaven on a summer's day.

Meals	Set menu, 2 courses, from £14.50. Sunday lunch, 2 courses, £22.50.
Closed	Mondays all day. 2.30pm-5pm Tuesday-Friday. 3pm-5pm Saturday. Open midday-4pm Sunday.

Matthew & Ruth Woodley
The Plowden Arms,
Reading Road,
Shiplake,
Henley-on-Thames, RG9 4BX
Web www.plowdenarmsshiplake.co.uk

Entry 432 Map 4

Oxfordshire

The Crooked Billet

Stoke Row

Dick Turpin apparently courted the landlord's daughter and Kate Winslet held her wedding breakfast here. Pints of Brakspear are drawn direct from the cask (there is no bar!) and the rusticity of the place charms all who manage to find it: beams and inglenooks, walls lined with bottles and baskets of spent corks, old pine. In the larger room, red walls display old photographs and mirrors; shelves are stacked with books... by candlelight it's irresistible. It's more restaurant than pub, so the menu is modern, eclectic and long: salt and pepper squid with chilli jam, Moroccan spiced lamb rump, Bakewell tart and custard. The food is founded on well-sourced raw materials (allotment holders are encouraged) and bolstered by a satisfying wine list. Weekly music, too, and a big garden bordering the beech woods where children may roam.

Meals	Lunch & dinner £12.50-£20.
Closed	2.30pm-7pm. Open all day Sat & Sun.

Paul Clerehugh
The Crooked Billet,
Newlands Lane, Stoke Row,
Henley-on-Thames, RG9 5PU
Tel +44 (0)1491 681048
Web www.thecrookedbillet.co.uk

Entry 433 Map 4

The Five Horseshoes

Maidensgrove

This cute pub-cottage sits on Maidensgrove Common, in a remote spot high in the Chilterns, on a lane that winds past Russell's Water near Stonor House. Arrive early for the best seat in the garden and the finest view in Oxfordshire: imagine gazing on rolling hills, pint of Brakspears to hand, red kites wheeling overhead, steaks sizzling on the chargrill. Windows in the conservatory dining room also get the view – or you can head for the rambling bars where roaring hearths warm the cockles. Find low crooked ceilings, beams, nooks, burgundy carpets, cushioned settles and tables that have been collected over years – a perfect place to tuck into fresh, plump mussels and chunks of homemade bread to mop up the juices. They make their own ginger beer and there are roasts on Sundays. Then head off into the hills.

Meals	Lunch & dinner £8.50-£16. Bar meals £5-£9.75. Sunday lunch £13.75.
Closed	Monday. Sunday eves.

Dan & Tracey Taverner
The Five Horseshoes,
Maidensgrove,
Henley-on-Thames, RG9 6EX
Tel +44 (0)1491 641282
Web www.thefivehorseshoes.co.uk

Entry 434 Map 4

Oxfordshire

The Frog

Skirmett

On the village main street, deep in the beautiful Hambledon valley, this 18th-century coaching inn is surrounded by open meadows and glorious walks. Head for the lovely secluded garden, pint of Marlow Rebellion in hand, gaze across the valley and watch the red kites wheel. Or choose a sofa by the cosy fire and mingle with locals and walkers. Wood floors, wall-mounted beer lists, bold mirrors and homogenous tables fill the dining areas where menus list hearty pub classics – steak, Guinness and mushroom pie, smoked haddock on champ with mustard sauce, lamb rump with port and redcurrant sauce – alongside the deli boards. Don't miss the sticky toffee pudding – or the once-a-month pub 'shop' selling Noelle's savoury pastries, cakes and chutneys.

Meals	Lunch & bar meals from £6.95. Dinner from £9.95.
Closed	3pm-6pm Mon-Sat.

Jim Crowe & Noelle Greene
The Frog,
Skirmett,
Henley-on-Thames, RG9 6TG
Tel +44 (0)1491 638996
Web www.thefrogatskirmett.co.uk

Entry 435 Map 4

Sir Charles Napier

Chinnor

In an enviable position high in the Chilterns, this attractive 18th-century brick and flint building oozes understated charisma. You'll feel beautifully cossetted here by Julie and her charming team as you loll on comfy sofas in front of huge log fires while easy-going jazz tinkles in the background and your eyes are drawn to Michael Cooper's sculptures (you can buy them too). The kitchen turns out delicious dishes of Michelin starred food: perhaps Orkney scallops with nasturtium or roast halibut with lobster followed by Amalfi lemon parfait and burnt meringue; the wine list is extensive and carefully chosen. Outside there are gorgeous gardens, a foliage-entwined terrace and surreal sculptures. This is a popular spot for well-heeled locals, and people travel especially from London and Oxford. Great walking and cycling abounds. Henley isn't far...

Meals	Starters from £9.50. Lunch, 2 courses, from £19.50. Dinner from £23.50.
Closed	Open all day.

Julie Griffiths
Sir Charles Napier,
Spriggs Alley,
Chinnor, OX39 4BX

Tel +44 (0)1494 483011
Web www.sircharlesnapier.co.uk

Entry 436 Map 9

Oxfordshire

The Eyston Arms

East Hendred

The Eystons have owned this pub since 1443! A renovation by the Daileys has brought a mix of the traditional and the new so step in to find flagstone floors and an original water pump, fresh flowers and chunky tables. It's a well-loved local, and the most regular regulars are immortalised in sketches on the dining room's papered walls. Come for happy chatter, first-class food, a good pint of London Pride. Chef Maria Jaremchuck earned her stripes here, left and has returned: the meat is properly hung for thick grilled steaks with triple-cooked chips, and rump of lamb with gratin dauphinoise, and desserts are just as good; we especially loved the lemon and saffron panna cotta. Daily specials are chalked up; Daisy Barton behind the bar knows her stuff. They look after you well here.

Meals	Lunch & dinner £11-£16.95. Sunday lunch £14.
Closed	3pm-6pm (from 7pm Sun).

George Dailey & Daisy Barton
The Eyston Arms,
High Street, East Hendred,
Wantage, OX12 8JY

Tel +44 (0)1235 833320
Web www.eystonarms.co.uk

Entry 437 Map 4

The White Hart

Fyfield

Stone mullioned windows, huge oak timbers and a magnificent arch-braced roof form a historic backdrop for oak settles, wrought-iron candle holders, white linen napkins and delicious food cooked by Mark. The menu is modern, British and changes from day to day depending upon what is fresh, in season and from the restaurant's kitchen garden that grows purple Shiraz mange tout, courgettes, fine beans, beetroot, Chantenay carrots, Swiss chard, cherries and more. There's scallops, black pudding beignet and piccalilli sauce; venison haunch and cottage pie with creamed cabbage and girolles; buttermilk panna cotta, caramelised orange and honeycomb crumble. Suppliers are mostly local and mentioned on the menu so you can see where everything's from. Enjoy four real ales and Cheddar valley cider, served by friendly staff who are capable and knowledgeable.

Meals: Lunch £13-£20. Bar meals £6-£20. Dinner £13-£20. Sunday lunch, 3 courses, £26. No food Sunday eve.

Closed: 3pm-5.30pm & Mon all day (except bank hols). Open all day Sat & Sun.

Mark & Kay Chandler
The White Hart,
Main Road, Fyfield,
Abingdon, OX13 5LW
Tel +44 (0)1865 390585
Web www.whitehart-fyfield.com

The Mole Inn

Toot Baldon

The Mole continues to wow Oxford foodies – it's packed most days. Expect an impeccable stone exterior, topiary in the garden and a ravishing bar. There are stripped beams and chunky walls, black leather sofas, logs in the grate and a dresser that groans with rustic breads and olive jars. Chic rusticity extends into three dining areas: fat candles on blond wood tables, thick terracotta floors, the sun angling in on a delicious plate of beef casserole. Daily specials point to a modern British menu peppered with eastern inspiration: devilled kidneys on a toasted muffin with tzatziki; crab risotto with chilli, ginger and lime. The cooking is excellent; we enjoyed a mixed grill of fish with fries and lime mayonnaise, and a terrific treacle tart. Warm, friendly staff complete the picture.

Meals: Lunch & dinner £12.95-£18. Bar meals £5.95-£9.95.

Closed: Open all day.

Gary Witchalls
The Mole Inn,
Toot Baldon,
Oxford, OX44 9NG
Tel +44 (0)1865 340001
Web www.moleinn.com/

The Magdalen Arms

Oxford

Suburban Oxford is not the most obvious setting for some of Britain's best pub food. But Anchor & Hope graduates Florence Fowler and Tony Abarno have created a hostelry worthy of foodie acclaim. Those fretting over another local hijacked for elaborate gastropubbery need not: half this pub's not inconsiderable space is cutlery free and, thanks to a billiards table, four well-kept real ales and cocktails that ooze class, drinkers will find much to like; plus a chop house-chic interior of advertising posters, scuffed wooden floor, mishmash wooden tables and bright streams of bunting – the antithesis of fine dining. Equally unpretentious is the food: gutsy, produce-led fare, as affordable as it is likeable. Knuckle down to Hereford beef with duck fat potato cake and béarnaise; braised shank of wild boar with polenta; boozy cherries and buttermilk pudding.

Meals	Lunch £15. Dinner from £25. Sunday lunch, 3 courses, £30.
Closed	Mon & Tues lunch.

Florence Fowler & Tony Abarno
The Magdalen Arms,
Iffley Road,
Oxford, OX4 1SJ

Tel	+44 (0)1865 243159
Web	www.magdalenarms.com

Entry 440 Map 8

The Rickety Press

Oxford

Jericho is a pretty quarter of Oxford and The Rickety Press, a big corner pub, is a quick cycle ride from the centre. It's the sort of place where you can eat bang up to date, faultless food in the restaurant or in the bar; we had pan-fried cod and chips with tartare sauce. The central bar is cool, contemporary, inviting, with antique stripped floors, background jazz and books on bold walls; the restaurant is at the back, similar but larger, with a log-burner. Staff love what they're doing and care about the details. You could have the foie gras and chicken liver pâté to start, then the deep-sea moules frites or the sharing rib from the grill. Made with love, no pretence. Note: if you bring the car, there's a Pay & Display a five-minute walk.

Meals	Lunch from £8. Dinner, 2 courses, from £12.50.
Closed	Open all day.

Leo Johnson & Christopher Manners
The Rickety Press, 67 Cranham Street,
Oxford, OX2 6DE

Tel	+44 (0)1865 424581
Web	www.therricketypress.com

Entry 441 Map 8

The Perch

Oxford

Off one of the main arteries into Oxford, you spin down a leafy lane for half a mile to arrive in a hamlet with two ways to go: 'the Perch and 'the Church'. At the former you find dogs in wax jackets, students with laptops and Londoners down for lunch. The building is listed, the fire is lit and the setting is idyllic, with a garden path arched by fairylights down to the river; Alice in Wonderland had its first reading here. You can eat at picnic tables by the willows or under the conservatory canopy, in the big beamy dining room or beneath the antler chandelier. The food is fantastic: potted rabbit and smoked bacon, globe artichoke and mint salad, crayfish cocktails, river trout fishcakes, English cheeses, seasonal sorbets, jam tarts for kids. What John doesn't know about hospitality could be written on the back of a stamp.

Meals	Starters £5.95-£9.95 Mains £12.95-£19.95. Sunday lunch £13.50-£16.95.
Closed	Open all day.

John Ellse
The Perch,
Binsey,
Oxford OX2 0NG

Tel +44 (0)1865 728891
Web www.the-perch.co.uk

Entry 442 Map 8

Oxfordshire

The Anchor Inn

Oxford

A pint of Wadworth, an Aspalls cider, a café latte or a glass of Domaine de la Renaudie – whatever you choose, it will charm you. In the Jericho district of North Oxford, this is one the city's best food pubs. Professors, professionals and canal-side walkers tuck into delights like grilled corn-fed chicken with winter leaves and aïoli, crunchy farro with squash, radicchio, taleggio and chestnuts, and steamed marmalade pudding with custard. Or try a simple Haggis scotch egg (ours was faultless). Two private dining rooms for parties, and there's a choice of four feasting menus for those in a sharing mood. Outside is a south-facing terrace, enclosed and child safe; dogs are most welcome too.

Meals	Lunch & dinner £9.50-£16. Bar meals £4-£7.85.
Closed	Open all day.

Julian Rosser
The Anchor Inn,
2 Hayfield Road, Walton Manor,
Oxford, OX2 6TT

Tel +44 (0)1865 510282
Web www.theanchoroxford.com

Entry 443 Map 8

Jacob's Inn

Wolvercote

From the Oxford sausages at breakfast to the home-cured meats and the home-baked focaccia, this is the place for nose-to-tail dining – and our rabbit ballotine with wild mushroom salad and truffle oil was fabulous. It's an old Cotswolds inn in a suburb of Oxford on the footpath to Port Meadow, and if you just fancy a pint and a pot of chipolatas, you're still in for a treat: the ales change daily and the chipolatas are from the garden (they keep pigs and hens). Inside all is airy, rustic, beautiful, with old tongue-and-groove walls and wide plank floors, books to read, chesterfields to recline on, and a fair few stuffed animals on the walls (very à la mode). Dogs doze by the fire, children tuck into baby burgers, and in summer you spill into the grounds, with picnic tables, deckchairs and great big terrace.

Meals Lunch from £3.50. Dinner from £7.
Closed Open all day.

Damion & Johnny
Jacob's Inn,
130 Godstow Road,
Wolvercote, OX2 8PG
Tel +44 (0)1865 514333
Web www.jacobs-inn.com

Entry 444 Map 8

Oxfordshire

The Red Lion at Northmoor

Northmoor

Drop in to the Red Lion, at the heart of the pretty village of Northmoor, for log fires in winter, generous garden in summer, and contemporary cooking all year round. This little pub was bought up by the village community, and is now run by cheerful husband and wife team Lisa and Ian. Check out the blackboard menu – it's not vast as Ian cooks everything from scratch using ingredients from nearby producers, seasonal vegetables from the kitchen garden, and eggs from their own hens. Starters might include a delicious game terrine or beetroot and homemade ricotta salad, followed up by a vegetarian risotto or braised Northmoor lamb with artichoke gratin. Lots of wines by the glass will slip down as you relax in the bar, with its beams and exposed Cotswold stone. To work up an appetite (or walk off your meal), the Thames trail is just down the road.

Meals Starters from £5.50.
Lunch from £5.50.
Dinner from £10.50
Closed Mondays all day.

Community pub

Ian & Lisa Neale
The Red Lion at Northmoor,
Standlake Road,
Northmoor, OX29 5SX
Tel +44 (0)1865 300301
Web theredlionnorthmoor.com

Entry 445 Map 8

The Shilton Rose & Crown

Shilton

Cosy, friendly, foodie, and run with great panache. The 16th-century Rose & Crown, set in an idyllic Cotswolds village, holds just two rooms: the bar itself, simple and unadorned, and a (slightly) larger extension built in 1701. There's an open fire in the inglenook, a medley of kitchen tables and chairs, well-kept beers, serious wines, and Martin, star of the show. With an impressive London pedigree behind him, he is warm, witty and passionate about food. Join a happy crowd for delicious, authentic renditions of parsnip and chestnut soup, roast partridge with haricot beans, bacon and garlic; steak ale and mushroom pie, bread and butter pudding and pear and almond tart. Cosiness and low beams for winter, a sheltered garden for summer, warmth and conviviality all year round. A gem.

Meals	Lunch £8.50-£19.50. Dinner £10-£19.50. Sunday lunch, 3 courses, £24.
Closed	3pm-6pm Mon-Fri.

Martin Coldicott
The Shilton Rose & Crown,
Shilton,
Burford, OX18 4AB
Tel +44 (0)1993 842280
Web www.roseandcrownshilton.com

Entry 446 Map 8

Oxfordshire

The Fleece

Witney

A half hour west of Oxford, on Witney's sweeping green, is the first outpost of what has become the hugely successful Peach Pubs. Step in to a sparkling gastropub interior – wooden floors, plum walls, squashy sofas, low tables – abuzz with continental opening hours that start with coffee and bacon sarnies at 8.30am. It's a humdinger of a place, with the bar at the front inviting casual drinkers in for pints of Greene King. Thumbs up too for the regularly changing wine list at sensible prices, and for the all-day sandwiches, salads and deli-board menu. Starters of charcuterie, olive tapenade, marinated chillies, guinea fowl salad, followed by such delights as braised shoulder of lamb with roasted winter roots, or sweet potato lasagne with jalapeño pesto, are ferried to packed tables by an enthusiastic and attentive staff.

Meals	Lunch from £7. Bar meals from £5. Dinner from £11. Sunday lunch £13.50.
Closed	Open all day.

Helen Sprason
The Fleece,
11 Church Green,
Witney, OX28 4AZ
Tel +44 (0)1993 892270
Web www.fleecewitney.co.uk

Entry 447 Map 8

The Hollybush

Witney

From the beer-battered gherkins to the Brixham plaice with samphire, the food at the Hollybush is amazing. Run by two local chaps, it's a gorgeous old pub on the Cotswolds' fringes in the market town of Witney, replete with homely touches: twinkling lights, modern log burner, candles in pewter holders. The staff are helpful and delightful, serving craft beers, sparkling wines, ciders, ales and home-cured gin, and a monthly changing menu using the best local ingredients. On Sundays, you have a choice of five roasts, or opt for a grazing platter with mini fish and chips, squid rings, garlic and chilli king prawns. Our smokey pigs' cheeks with pickled beets and black pudding was outstanding. Puddings are faultless; try vanilla panna cotta with poached rhubarb. Outside: a part-covered, heated courtyard, one more fabulous surprise.

Meals	Starters from £5.50. Mains from £12.50.
Closed	Open all day.

Alex Vaughan
The Hollybush,
35 Corn Street,
Witney, OX28 6BT

Tel +44 (0)1993 708073
Web www.hollybushwitney.com

Entry 448 Map 8

Nut Tree Inn

Kidlington

Find Michelin-starred food at this whitewashed thatched pub (idyllic!), breads and pork pies you can pre-book to take home and pigs out the back. Imogen and Mike are friendly and fun and operate their own version of *The Good Life*; they grow loads of lovely produce. The bar is soothing, relaxing, with an open fire, stools, leather chesterfields, cookery books to peruse. Off here: a big vaulted dining room. Choose from delicious bar food (smoked Loch Duart salmon, fillet steak, artisan cheeses) or take a look at the specials: tartare of Charolais beef; tea-smoked wild goose with mango purée; roast fillet of Cornish cod with green herb risotto; hot caramel soufflé with walnut ice cream. There's real ale, draught cider, a long wine list and a pretty terrace. The Nut Tree is a happy ship that caters effortlessly for all.

Meals	Lunch & dinner £12-£35. Bar meals £7-£12. Tasting menu, 8 courses, £60.
Closed	Sunday evening & all day Monday & Tuesday.

Michael & Imogen North
Nut Tree Inn,
Murcott,
Kidlington, OX5 2RE

Tel +44 (0)1865 331253
Web www.nuttreeinn.co.uk

Entry 449 Map 8

The Crown

Woodstock

In idyllic Woodstock, down the road from Blenheim Palace, is the listed, mellow old Crown. Inside? A large, light, bright, sleek, smiling place. Palest walls, orange lights, Nordic chairs, background music and a dog called Rory (belongs to the chef). There are two open fires, a sitting area with sofas and a stunning decorative sweep of Portuguese floor. Butcombe or Bellini, vodka, gin, champagne by the glass: the drinks are various and classy. So is the food; there's Provençal fish stew, roast rump of lamb with spinach, salmon with brown shrimp butter, and small plates that look sensational: Jerusalem artichokes with kale; wood-roast king prawns with chilli. The wood-fired pizzas are awesome as is the blood orange posset. Outside: a little furnished courtyard.

Meals — Small plates from £6. Mains from £9.
Closed — Open all day.

Julian Rosser
The Crown,
High Street,
Woodstock, OX20 1TE
Tel — +44 (0)1993 813339
Web — www.thecrownwoodstock.com

Entry 450 Map 8

The Oxford Arms

Kirtlington

A robust 19th-century dining pub tucked down a lane in a village eight miles from Oxford. Windows are sage-green, window boxes spill geraniums in summer and the coat of arms above the door shows an ox walking through a ford. The main bar faces south, the floors are flagged and boarded, wood smoke tinges the air; decide what to eat as you sip a half of Hooky Bitter or something excellent from the wine list. To one side is a candlelit dining area with large and small tables and comfy sofas, the other side is more pubby and informal with bar stools and farmhouse chairs. Wherever you decide to eat there's the convivial rumble of chat in the background and the food is good. Try potted shrimps with toast, Salcombe crabs with artisan bread, confit duck leg, roast pork belly with black pudding.

Meals — Lunch from £12. Bar meals from £6.50. Dinner from £12. Sunday lunch, 3 courses, £26.
Closed — 3pm-6pm. Sun eves.

Bryn Jones
The Oxford Arms,
Troy Lane,
Kirtlington, OX5 3HA
Tel — +44 (0)1869 350208
Web — www.oxford-arms.co.uk

Entry 451 Map 8

Milton Hare

Milton-under-Wychwood

At the heart of this pretty Cotswold village lies The Hare, its façade belying its stylish, contemporary interior. Beamed ceilings and exposed stone walls allude to its past, while the marble topped bar and splashes of colour – deep orange curtains, olive green corner seating – bring it forward to the 21st century. An eclectic mix of paintings, gold-framed mirrors and a pair of taxidermied hares are fun, quirky touches. Cosy up by the log burner with a pint of Hooky ale while you peruse menus chalked up on blackboards; head chef Matt serves up cracking modern food, with fresh fish the star of the show. Try griddled sardines on sourdough with wild garlic butter, sea bass in a white wine and tomato cream, then espresso crème brûlée and vanilla sugared doughnuts. With stacks of experience between them, you're in safe hands with landlords Rachel and Sue.

Meals Starters from £6. Mains from £14.
Closed Mon-Fri 3pm-5pm.

The Manager
Milton Hare,
3 High Street,
Milton-under-Wychwood, OX7 6LA
Tel +44 (0)1993 835763
Web www.themiltonhare.co.uk

Entry 452 Map 8

The Chequers

Churchill

Eye-catching with an immaculate frontage, the Chequers stands smartly on the village lane. Prepare for a dramatic, airy and open-plan interior of low beams, scrubbed tables on walker-friendly boards, stone walls, roaring wood-burner and a dart board put to good use. Soaring blue-green rafters and a vast dresser racked with wine bottles create an impression in the dining extension, where a blackboard up high announces the food: simple, British-traditional, and well priced. There are devilled kidneys on toast, steak and oyster pie, grilled lemon sole with brown butter, bavette steak with fries. The roasts are delicious, the service is terrific, but most exceptional are the beers: six real ales (Yankee from Roosters, Budding from Stroud) and six local keg beers. There are also ten wines by the glass.

Meals Lunch & dinner £4-£16.50.
Closed Open all day.

Sam Pearman
The Chequers,
Church Road, Churchill, OX7 6NJ
Chipping Norton
Tel +44 (0)1608 659393
Web www.thechequerschurchill.com

Entry 453 Map 8

The Crown Inn

Church Enstone

At the end of a row of houses this pretty pub in classic Cotswold stone is a real gem. Locals love the friendly feel – Tony and Caroline have been here since 2003 and know everybody. Menus change daily, wines come by the glass and you can expect fish or game specials in season. Tony's classic dishes are unpretentious but delicious; perhaps fishcakes with coriander and chilli mayo followed by slow braised beef in mushroom and red wine gravy. Meals are eaten in the red-walled restaurant or conservatory but the bar is the real draw here: flagged floors, exposed stone walls, rustic pine tables and chairs and a huge inglenook with roaring open fire. Settle yourself here with a pint of Hooky and a homemade Scotch egg after a long yomp in the Cotswolds. Blenheim Palace is only 15 minutes by car and Oxford's not much further.

Meals	Starters from £5.25. Lunch from £5.50. Dinner from £8.95. Puddings £5.50.
Closed	From 4pm Sundays.

Tony & Caroline Warburton
The Crown Inn,
Mill Lane, Church Enstone,
Chipping Norton, OX7 4NN
Tel +44 (0)1608 677262
Web www.crowninnenstone.co.uk

Entry 454 Map 8

The Muddy Duck

Hethe

In a remote but not too remote village is a handsome, honey-stoned pub. If you dropped by for a Hooky and homemade scratchings, it would be worth it just for the bar, a wonderful space with low beams and a roaring fire. The vaulted restaurant has been charmingly refurbished, with stripped wooden floors, 60 covers and an open kitchen. Friendly, knowledgeable staff ferry beautiful platefuls of (mostly local, often seasonal) food. Meat is raised to high welfare standards, fish (sustainable only) is cooked the day it's caught. You could have Cornish squid and avocado salsa to start, stuffed pork belly with roasted apples to follow, and fruits with iced chiboust crème to finish. Our Scotch egg with black pudding was brilliant. Outside: a rustically furnished stone terrace and a pizza oven.

Meals	Lunch & dinner £11.50-£48. No food Sun eve.
Closed	Open all day.

The Manager
The Muddy Duck,
Main Street, Hethe,
Bicester, OX27 8ES
Tel +44 (0)1869 278099
Web www.themuddyduckpub.co.uk

Entry 455 Map 8

Falkland Arms

Great Tew

Five hundred years on and the logs still glow in the stone-flagged bar under a low-slung timbered ceiling that drips with tankards and jugs. Tradition runs deep: the hop is treated with reverence, ales are changed weekly, old pump clips hang from the bar and they stock tins of snuff with names like Irish High Toast and Crumbs of Comfort. In summer Morris Men jingle in the lane outside and life spills out onto the terrace at the front and the lovely big garden behind. Dig into a homemade burger and ploughman's in front of the fire or hop next door to the tiny beamed dining room for such home-cooked delights as Guinness-baked ham hock with leek and sweetcorn champ. Perfect pub, perfect village, and blissfully short on modern trappings.

Meals: Lunch from £7.95.
Bar meals from £4.95.
Dinner from £8.95.
Sunday lunch, 3 courses, £17.95.

Closed: Open all day.

Kathryn Partridge & Richard Bennett
Falkland Arms,
19-21 The Green, Great Tew,
Chipping Norton, OX7 4DB

Tel: +44 (0)1608 683653
Web: www.falklandarms.co.uk

Oxfordshire

Hook Norton Brewery

Hook Norton

About 30 minutes north of Oxford, on the edge of pretty Hook Norton, is a Cotswolds' gem, a national treasure, in the family since 1849. Staff, distinguished by Hook Norton shirts, are engaging and knowledgeable, and the tours – six days a week – are fascinating. From the beer samplings in the old maltings to the shire horses in the yard, and the pizzas and pints in the cellar below, it's a brilliant day out. There's mashing at the top, boiling in the middle, and fermentation and racking at ground level; when steam pours out of the high chimneys it's like something out of Willy Wonka. The tour is a history lesson in Victorian engineering and brewing processes, from the original stream engine to the grist mill and open fermenting vessels. Yet Hook Norton is a vibrant and forward thinking company, and new recipes are being created all the time.

Meals: Bar snacks available.

Closed: Sundays.

Mark Graham
Hook Norton Brewery,
Brewery Lane,
Hook Norton, OX15 5NY

Tel: +44 (0)1608 730384
Web: www.hooky.co.uk

The White Horse

Kings Sutton

Explore the highways and byways of the Northamptonshire/Oxfordshire border and head for Kings Sutton, where The White Horse sits at the heart of the village with views to the parish church. Following refurbishment in 2013, Julie and Hendrik's pub is now the centre of local life, including live jazz and regular games evenings. Mellow Cotswold stone on the outside sets the tone for a warm and relaxed atmosphere inside, cocooned amid rug-covered floors, cushioned window seats, low beamed ceilings and warm pastel walls. Friendly Julie is out front, while Hendrik cooks, serving with flare everything from tasty bar snacks to serious restaurant food: think parfait of duck liver, whole baked Brixham plaice, and chocolate pavé and hazelnut ice cream. There are good vegetarian options, too. Brakspear and guest ales are on offer, plus traditional and New World wines.

Meals: Lunch from £4.50. Set lunch, 2-3 courses, £11-£13.95, Tues-Sat. Dinner from £11.50.
Closed: Mondays.

Julie Groves & Hendrik Dutson
The White Horse,
2 The Square, Kings Sutton,
Banbury, OX17 3RF
Tel: +44 (0)1295 812440
Web: www.whitehorseks.co.uk

Entry 458 Map 8

Oxfordshire

Wykham Arms

Sibford Gower

Another beautifully presented little pub in a Cotswolds village. You'd expect cushions and chintz, instead you get creams and deep reds, flag floors, two fires and a homely farmhouse feel. Life revolves around the central bar, and the menu, served through a warren of connected rooms, spills over with local seasonal produce, 'with one foot firmly in the past'. Tuck into Cornish scallops with celeriac remoulade; salmon with beetroot and artichoke salad; wild boar and apple sausages with beer mustard mash – flavours are strong, clean and uncomplicated. The fish is native to UK waters and there are lots of wines by the glass, excellent and affordable. Families and dogs are very welcome; for summer there's a big patio and a wooded garden.

Meals: Lunch from £10. Bar meals from £8.50. Dinner from £2 Sunday lunch, 3 courses, £20. No food Sunday eve.
Closed: 3pm-6pm. Monday.

Damian & Deborah Bradley
Wykham Arms,
Temple Mill Road, Sibford Gower,
Banbury, OX15 5RX
Tel: +44 (0)1295 788808
Web: www.wykhamarms.co.uk

Entry 459 Map 8

The Olive Branch

Clipsham

A lovely pub in a sleepy Rutland village, where bridle paths lead out across peaceful fields. It dates to the 17th century and is built of Clipsham stone, as is York Minster. Inside, a warm, informal, rustic chic hits the spot perfectly with open fires, old beams, stone walls and choir stalls in the bar. But there's more here than cool design. This is a place to come and eat great food, the lovely, local seasonal stuff that's cooked with passion by Sean and his brigade, perhaps potted pork and stilton with apple jelly, haunch of venison with a juniper fondant, then a boozy rhubarb trifle. Bedrooms in Beech House across the lane are gorgeous. Three have terraces, one has a free-standing bath, all come with crisp linen, pretty beds, Roberts radios and real coffee. Super breakfasts – smoothies, boiled eggs and soldiers, the full cooked works – are served in a stone-walled barn with flames leaping in the wood-burner. The front garden fills in summer, the sloe gin comes from local berries, and Newark is close for the biggest antiques market in Europe. Picnic hampers can be arranged. A total gem. *Ask about cookery demos.*

Rooms	5 doubles: £115-£195. 1 family room for 4: £115-£195. Singles from £97.50.
Meals	Bar meals £10.50. Dinner from £14.50. Sunday lunch £24.95.
Closed	3pm-6pm. Open all day Sat & Sun.

Ben Jones & Sean Hope
The Olive Branch,
Main Street, Clipsham,
Oakham, LE15 7SH
Tel +44 (0)1780 410355
Web www.theolivebranchpub.com

The Hundred House Hotel

Norton

The Phillips family has been at the helm for 25 years and Henry is an innkeeper with humour. As for the inn, having begun its life in the 14th century, it rambles charmingly inside as well as out. Enter a world of blazing log fires, soft brick walls, oak panelling and quarry-tiled floors. Dried flowers hang from beams, herbs sit in vases, and blackboard menus trumpet Hundred House fish pie, roast rack of Shropshire lamb and double chocolate mousse with orange anglaise. You are surrounded by Sylvia's wild and wonderful collage art hanging on the walls, and the fun continues in riotously patterned and floral bedrooms upstairs. Just go easy on the ale before you open the door: some have a swing hanging from the oak beams with a vibrant velvet seat. Lounge on antique beds – large, comfortable and wrapped in lavender-scented sheets. Wander out with a pint of Ironbridge Brewery and share a quiet moment with a few stone lions in the beautiful garden, a flight of fancy full of herbaceous plants and over a hundred herbs – a summer treat. You can tie the knot in the restored Tithe Barn.

Rooms	8 doubles, 1 twin/double: £79-£140. Singles from £55.
Meals	Lunch from £4.95. Dinner & bar meals from £8.95. Sunday lunch, 2 courses, £16.95.
Closed	Open all day.

Jo Phillips
The Hundred House Hotel,
Bridgnorth Road,
Norton, Shifnal, TF11 9EE
Tel +44 (0)1952 580240
Web www.hundredhouse.co.uk

The Pheasant at Neenton

Neenton

Opposite the pretty church, surrounded by picture-perfect Shropshire hills, is an 18th-century pub that's been remarkably reinstated; today, the Pheasant is owned by the locals. John is co-op chairman, Mark is chef, Sarah does front of house. The front bar is cosy (cushioned leather sofa and chairs, wood-burner in the chimney breast, rugs strewn on the tiled floor), the second bar is painted a deep chestnut, and the dining room is in an oak-framed extension at the back, its windows filling it with light. There's an orchard in the beer garden providing fruits for the kitchen, they tune their menus to the seasons and they seek out local suppliers (including lamb from the field next door). The beers include Hobson's and other Shropshire breweries, the wines are from Bibendum, and if you want to stay the night, you can. Three bedrooms, reached via an external stair, are spotless, sober, spanking new, and decorated in restful colours (whites, greys, olive greens). Bathrooms are immaculate with tip-top showers, one room wakes to splendid views, and we hear the breakfasts are fabulous.

Rooms	2 doubles, 1 twin/double: £75-£95.
Meals	Starters from £5.50. Dinner from £10.95. Sunday lunch £11.95-£16.95.
Closed	Mon-Fri 3pm-6pm.

Sarah Cowley & Mark Harris
The Pheasant at Neenton,
Neenton,
Bridgnorth, WV16 6RJ
Tel +44 (0)1746 787955
Web www.pheasantatneenton.co.uk

Baron at Bucknell

Bucknell

A stone's throw from Ludlow yet in the midst of the Shropshire Hills, the Baron sits at the base of Bucknell Mynd in a tranquil village by the Teme Valley. Peace reigns supreme and a flurry of super walks lead from the door: guides are behind the bar. Phil and Debbie have worked wonders on the bedrooms; all are well-groomed and tasteful with oak furniture, contemporary wallpaper, stylish lighting and fat mattresses to induce deep asleep; one has a Juliet balcony, all five have country views. Bathrooms are modern and white, one with a double-ended whirlpool bath. Ales from Hobson and Wye Valley await in the simple bar with its traditional carpet and wooden seating. Homemade pub food is the mantra here, uncomplicated and cooked to order. Start with glazed goat's cheese and beetroot salad with rocket, pine nuts and crusty bread, move on to slow-braised lamb shank with a fruity minty couscous. Eat in the restaurant beside a large millstone and grinding wheel and a huge wooden cider press dated 1770, or in the conservatory that overlooks the garden with boules pitches. You can camp, too!

Rooms	3 doubles, 2 twin/doubles: £90-£130.
Meals	Lunch & bar meals from £5.50. Dinner from £7.95. Sunday lunch, 2-3 courses, £14.90-£21.85.
Closed	Sun eves & Mon-Thurs lunch (except bank hols).

Phil & Debbie Wright
Baron at Bucknell,
Bucknell,
Ludlow, SY7 0AH

Tel +44 (0)1547 530549
Web www.baronatbucknell.co.uk

The Three Tuns

Bishops Castle

There's been a licensed brewery next door since 1642 (the oldest brewing license in the UK). Pub and brewery are now under separate ownership but the pub still sells up to four of their beers at any one time, and very good they are too. The place has an unassuming air, like the rest of this time-warp town. The separate snug, public bar and lounge are simply decorated with pale green paintwork, scrubbed tables, leather booths and old oak flooring. (In contrast are some impressive marble loos.) Or dine in the oak-framed, conservatory room, on grilled hake, chorizo, roasted pepper sauce with new potatoes and green beans, and, they say, the best rib-eye steaks in Shropshire. There's a great mix of regulars, from suits to bohemians, a real fire in the stone fireplace, and live music at weekends.

Meals	Lunch from £5.75. Dinner from £10.50. Sunday lunch £10.25. No food Sunday eve.
Closed	Open all day.

Tim & Catherine Curtis-Evans
The Three Tuns,
Salop Street,
Bishops Castle, SY9 5BW
Tel +44 (0)1588 638797
Web www.thethreetunsinn.co.uk

Entry 464 Map 7

Shropshire

The Woodbridge

Coalbridge

In the birthplace of the industrial revolution is this handsome pub, built in 1785 along with a wooden bridge to Coalport. It surveys the river Severn, and the cast-iron bridge that now spans it. A vast open-plan interior comes with plenty of cosy corners and the new garden room flows along the river bank. The abundance of cask ales would quench a furnace with Bishop's Castle, Hobson's, Tunfield and Phoenix Breweries well represented; there's Aspall Suffolk Cyder and a great wine list too. Daily changing menus feature modern British and pub classics, from a confit duck leg, bacon, butter bean and pearl barley cassoulet to steak and kidney suet pudding with English mustard mash, and a sweet potato, carrot and rocket quiche. A raised terrace and masses of seating strung out along the river is the icing on the cake.

Meals	Lunch & dinner £10.75-£25.95.
Closed	Open all day.

Jonathon Astle-Rowe
The Woodbridge,
Coalbridge, Telford, TF8 7JF
Tel +44 (0)1244 353070
Web www.brunningandprice.co.uk/woodbridge

Entry 465 Map 8

All Nations

Madeley

The old Victorian pub, spruce and white, could be an extension of the Victorian open air museum t'other side of the bridge. Step across the threshold and you're into timeworn-tavern territory – cast-iron tables, leatherette benches, coal fire at one end, log fire at the other. Old photographs of Ironbridge strew the walls, secondhand paperbacks ask to be taken home (donations to charity accepted), spotless loos await outside, and dogs doze. It's a chatty, friendly, ex-miners' ale house and some of the locals could have been here forever. Drink is own-brew, well-kept, low-cost Dabley from the hatch plus three others and a cider, while the menu encompasses several sorts of roll – black pudding perhaps, or cheese and onion, with tomato on request. Catch it before it's gone.

Meals Filled rolls £1.90-£3.
Closed Open all day.

Jim Birtwistle
All Nations,
20 Coalport Road,
Madeley,
Telford, TF7 5DP
Tel +44 (0)1952 585747

Entry 466 Map 8

Riverside Inn

Cound

There's a great buzz in this big comfortable huntin', shootin' and fishin' inn, standing on a magnificent bend of the Severn, looking out to the Wrekin and beyond. It's worth seeking out for its roaring wood-burner in winter and its dining conservatory – with views – all year round. In summer there's a pretty garden smartly furnished, from which you can fish from the bank for salmon and trout. The seasonal monthly menu might start with a winter vegetable and lentil broth, and move on to roast pork belly with an apricot and sage sauce, or a beef and Guinness shortcrust pie. There's port to accompany the cheese, and lovely Salopian beers and homemade puddings; we enjoyed the raspberry and thyme crème brûlée. It's all good value and comfortingly traditional.

Meals Lunch & dinner £7.75-£14.
Closed 3pm-6pm.
Open all day Sat & Sun May-Sept.

Peter Stanford-Davis
Riverside Inn,
Cound,
Shrewsbury, SY5 6AF
Tel +44 (0)1952 510900
Web www.theriversideinn.net

Entry 467 Map 7

White Horse Inn

Pulverbatch

The drive to get here is a treat, across the secret hills of Shropshire. This is a very old pub, with a restaurant built on at the back (scrubbed pine tables, oatmeal carpet, good art) but the old main bar is the most seductive, with wonky floors, a chesterfield here, a settle there, and a hint of woodsmoke from the big old grate. Walkers and cyclists, on their way to the Long Mynd, can recuperate with a trio of local-farm sausages on whole-grain mustard mash, or a casserole of Shropshire lamb. Steve's passion for food comes over strongly. Menus change monthly to reflect the best of each season, they rear their own pigs and lamb, and everything is made in-house from the bread to the ice cream. There's no garden, but smart new parasoled tables at the front, and you're surrounded by beautiful countryside.

Meals	Lunch & dinner £7.25–£14.95.
Closed	2pm–6.30pm & Mon lunch. Open all day Sat & Sun.

Steve & Vikki Nash
White Horse Inn,
Pulverbatch,
Shrewsbury, SY5 8DS

Tel +44 (0)1743 718247
Web www.thewhitehorseinnpulverbatch.co.uk

Shropshire

The Lion & Pheasant

Shrewsbury

Old meets new in this stunning transformation of a town centre inn with exposed beams, delicious log fire and a pale Scandinavian décor with rustic touches. Have a crack at Wood Shropshire Lad or Salopian Shropshire Gold while you peek at the menu, created by chef Matthew Strefford. Roast chestnut and thyme soup; crispy pork cheek terrine; roast hake, mussels, chickpeas and chorizo; British roast veal, soubise, sage and walnut pesto; this is food to linger over. The wine list is long and includes a dazzling array of dessert wines, port and different fizzes; the cocktails are works of art. When the sun shines, take to the terrace where canvas provides stylish shade, and artfully planted tubs add colour. Staff are young, friendly and efficient. Packed with character and atmosphere; decibels can be high.

Meals	Lunch & dinner £5–£21. Bar meals from £6.50.
Closed	Open all day.

Jim Littler
The Lion & Pheasant,
50 Wyle Cop,
Shrewsbury, SY1 1XJ

Tel +44 (0)1743 770345
Web www.lionandpheasant.co.uk

The Boathouse

Shrewsbury

Recently snapped up by the owners of the Lion & Pheasant in the centre of town and linked by a glorious riverside path, this huge historic pub stands on the banks of the Severn overlooking Quarry Park. Swamped in summer (and during very wet winters!), the decked terrace and big riverside garden now draw the crowds for cool drinks, pretty views, and top-notch bar food from the new Garden Bar and Kitchen. On cool days, arrive early to bag a fireside table or a river view in the spruced-up inside. Scandinavian colours, a rustic wooden floor, dark beams and cushioned benches set the scene for pints of Shropshire Gold and hearty plates of food – potted ham hock with red onion marmalade; charcoal-grilled steaks; towering burgers with chips and coleslaw served on wooden boards. With excellent service, it's great for events and private dinners, too.

Meals	Bar snacks from £4. Lunch from £6.50. Dinner from £11.
Closed	Open all day.

Jim Littler
The Boathouse,
New Street,
Shrewsbury, SY3 8JQ
Tel +44 (0)1743 231658
Web www.boathouseshrewsbury.co.uk

Entry 470 Map 7

New Inn

Baschurch

Outside, jolly hanging baskets and a whitewashed frontage. Inside, a sympathetic stripping back of old brick and beams and an open fire, comfortable sofas at one end, contemporary oak dining tables at the other and a big bar in between. In spite of the 48 covers, a well-placed wall and brick fireplace give the dining areas a certain intimacy. Five ales on the pump, and house wines served by Jenny Bean and her charming staff. In the kitchen, Marcus cooks up a storm: ham hock and parsley terrine with cheese scone and spiced apple chutney; roast duck breast with sweet plum and star anise jus; white chocolate and mascarpone cheesecake. It's delicious. In summer you spill out to sun shades and decking.

Meals	Lunch & dinner £9.50-£16.95. Bar meals £4.95-£8.50. Sunday lunch £14 & £17. No food Sunday eve.
Closed	3pm-6pm. Open all day Sat & Sun.

Marcus & Jenny Bean
New Inn,
Church Road, Baschurch,
Shrewsbury, SY4 2EF
Tel +44 (0)1939 260335
Web www.newinnbaschurch.com

Entry 471 Map 7

The Battleaxes

Wraxall

Originally a meeting place for workers on the Tyntesfield estate, this lovely inn now basks in a playful Victorian country-house style. Tasselled lampshades hang above the bar, the odd stately bust wears a flat cap, pot plants rise next to leather sofas. The painted bar, imaginatively stocked, features the inn's own Flatcappers Ale as well as other local brews, while The Club Room – once the village hall – is a lively dining room… though this is an informal place and you can eat wherever you want. And eat, you will. The food is excellent, lovely pub classics that are hard to resist, perhaps local gammon, free-range eggs and hand-cut chips or shepherd's pie with a white wine gravy and pickled red cabbage. Upstairs, a clutch of beautiful rooms wait. All come grandly adorned: lovely big beds, fat leather armchairs, fantastic walk-in showers. You get period wallpapers and lots of colour; one has a free-standing bath and a shower for two. Pick up the papers and sink into a sofa or spin across the road and walk on the Tyntesfield estate. The coast at Clevedon is close. Brilliant.

Rooms	6 doubles: £90-£140.
Meals	Lunch & dinner from £8.95. Sunday lunch, 3 courses, £19.95.
Closed	Open all day.

Tori Hill
The Battleaxes,
Wraxall,
Bristol, BS48 1LQ
Tel +44 (0)1275 857473
Web www.flatcappers.co.uk/the-battleaxes

The Redan Inn

Chilcompton

The sleepy village of Chilcompton has had a culinary reawakening, thanks to the arrival of this unsuspecting roadside inn. It's had a slick new makeover from the team behind The Pump House and The Bird in Hand, and all is fresh and new: find a sturdy blue bar with chunky wooden stools; board games, vintage signs and taxidermy; long benches, fresh flowers, grey cushions. There are over 30 gins behind the bar, and a good selection of local hand-pumped ales. Tuck into hearty fare from head chef Leon's seasonal menu – sausage rolls and ploughman's with homemade bread at lunch, slow braised brisket, caramelised onions and mash for dinner – or go all-out and choose something special from the à la carte menu: perhaps monkfish rolled in squid ink with clam velouté, fennel, and seaweed, followed by lemon meringue, tea sorbet, filo pastry. The roasts are cracking, too. Upstairs, seven stylish, spacious bedrooms gleam, and all have spotless en suite bathrooms with drenching showers and Bramley smellies. Tuck into a continental breakfast before a skip around the Mendips. You're just a short drive from Bristol and Bath.

Rooms	7 doubles: £70-£130.
Meals	Cooked breakfast available to non-residents, from £3. Bar snacks from £3. Lunch from £5. Dinner from £12.50.
Closed	Open all day.

Fred Maindron
The Redan Inn,
Fry's Well, Chilcompton,
Radstock, BA3 4HA

Tel	+44 (0)1761 258560
Web	www.theredaninn.co.uk

The Talbot Inn at Mells

Mells

The Talbot is an absolute stunner, one of the loveliest inns in the land. It sits in a timeless village lost in a tangle of country lanes, a 15th-century coaching inn reborn for the 21st-century. Sweep under the carriage arch and you enter a cobbled courtyard, where life gathers in good weather. There's a tithe-barn sitting room with big sofas and a Sunday cinema, then the Coach House Grill, where you eat at weekends under hanging beams. As for the main house, weave along ancient passageways and find stone walls, rugs on wood floors, crackling log fires and a low-ceilinged bar for a pint of Butcombe. The restaurant has colonised several cosy rooms and delicious food flies from the kitchen, perhaps white onion and cider soup, monkfish and mussel stew, chocolate and salted caramel sundae. Bedrooms are the best, some smaller, others huge with claw-foot baths, walk-in showers and modern four-posters. Add lovely staff to the mix and you have a slice of heaven. There's a colourful garden and great local walking, so bring your boots. The First World War poet, Siegfried Sassoon, is buried in the churchyard.

Rooms	8 doubles: £100-£160.
Meals	Lunch & dinner £10-£18. Sunday lunch, 2 courses, £15.
Closed	Open all day.

Matt Greenlees
The Talbot Inn at Mells,
Selwood Street,
Mells, Frome, BA11 3PN

Tel +44 (0)1373 812254
Web www.talbotinn.com

The Swan

Wedmore

The Swan is gorgeous, a contemporary take on a village local. It's part of a new wave of pubs that open all day and do so much more than serve a good pint. The locals love it. They come for breakfast, pop in to buy a loaf of bread, then return for afternoon tea and raid the cake stands. It's right on the bustling street, with a sprinkling of tables and chairs on the pavement in French-café style. Interiors mix old and new brilliantly. You get Farrow & Ball colours and cool lamps hanging above the bar, then lovely old rugs on boarded floors and a wood-burner to keep things toasty. Push inland to find an airy restaurant open to the rafters that overlooks the garden. Here you dig into Tom Blake's fabulous food (he's ex-River Cottage), anything from grilled Cornish herring to a three-course feast, maybe crispy Lyme Bay cuttlefish, slow cooked Quantock venison, chocolate and salted caramel tart. Bedrooms are lovely. Two have fancy baths in the room, you get vintage French furniture, iPod docks, colourful throws and walk-in power showers. Glastonbury is close, as are the Mendips.

Rooms	5 doubles, 2 twin/doubles: £75–£185. Extra bed £20. Cots available.
Meals	Lunch from £5. Dinner, 3 courses, about £25. Sunday lunch from £14. Bar meals only Sun night.
Closed	Open all day.

Natalie Zvonek-Little
The Swan,
Cheddar Road,
Wedmore, BS28 4EQ

Tel +44 (0)1934 710337
Web www.theswanwedmore.com

The White Hart

Somerton

Cool inns with lovely rooms in interesting parts of the land are a big hit with lots of us – we like the easy style, the local food, the good prices and the happy staff. The White Hart is a case in point, a beautifully refurbished inn. It sits on Somerton's ancient market square, 16th-century bricks and mortar, 21st-century lipstick and pearls. Inside, old and new mix beautifully: stone walls and parquet flooring, lovely sofas in front of the fire, funky lamps hanging above the bar. You'll find soft colours, padded window seats, country rugs, antler chandeliers. There's a cute booth in a stone turret, then lovely food waits, perhaps a chargrilled steak, Cornish crab cakes or wood roasted pork loin. In summer, you spill onto a smart courtyard or into the garden for views of open country. Upstairs, fabulous bedrooms await. You might find timber frames, a claw-foot bath, a wall of paper or stripped boards. All have super beds, flat-screen TVs, lovely bathrooms and a nice price. Beautiful Somerset is all around, don't miss it.

Rooms	8 doubles: £75-£165.
Meals	Breakfast £2.50-£7. Lunch & dinner £11-£19.
Closed	Rarely.

	Kirsty Schmidt The White Hart, Market Place, Somerton, TA11 7JX
Tel	+44 (0)1458 272273
Web	www.whitehartsomerton.com

The Queens Arms

Corton Denham

Stride across rolling fields, feast on Corton Denham lamb, retire to a perfect room. Buried down several Dorset/Somerset borders lanes, Gordon and Jeanette Reid's 18th-century stone pub has an elegant exterior – more country gentleman's house than pub. The bar, with its rug-strewn flagstones and bare boards, pew benches, deep sofas and crackling fire, is most charming. In the light, bright dining room that doubles up as a cinema on week nights, and on the terrace in summer, robust British dishes are distinguished by fresh ingredients from local suppliers. Try pheasant, pigeon and black pudding terrine, follow with monkfish with chive velouté, make room for a comforting crumble. Bedrooms are beautifully designed in soothing colours, and all have lovely views over the village and surrounding hills. New coach house rooms are super, too: underfloor heating, down duvets, brass and sleigh beds, iPod docks and immaculate wet rooms. Expect Gyle59 on tap, homemade pork pies on the bar, Gloucester Old Spot bacon at breakfast (from 8am daily), and stunning walks from the door.

Rooms	6 doubles, 2 twin/doubles: £110-£190. Singles from £80. Pets by arrangement only.
Meals	Lunch from £6.50. Dinner, 3 courses £25-£33.
Closed	Open all day.

Gordon & Jeanette Reid
The Queens Arms,
Corton Denham,
Sherborne, DT9 4LR
Tel +44 (0)1963 220317
Web www.thequeensarms.com

Lord Poulett Arms

Hinton St George

An idyllic inn that's hard to beat. It's like stepping onto the pages of a Jane Austen novel. A clipped country elegance runs throughout – old stone walls and period colours, then noble portraits on the walls and beautiful old settles to take the strain. There are drawbacks – sooner or later you will have to leave, probably with a touch of envy for the locals. Smart rusticity abounds. A fire burns on both sides in the dining room, where you eat under beams at antique tables. You'll find the daily papers, sofas in the locals' bar, a pile of logs at the back door, then an informal French garden with a piste for boules. Bedrooms upstairs have a lovely style with fancy flock wallpaper, pretty fabrics and fresh flowers, perhaps a small chandelier or a carved wooden bed. Two rooms have slipper baths in the room; two have claw-foot baths in bathrooms one step across the landing; the suite is enormous and has an open fire. The food is just as lovely, perhaps pea and ham soup, confit pork belly, praline fondant with coffee ice cream. Don't miss Sunday lunch or summer barbecues. An affordable treat.

Rooms	2 doubles; 2 doubles with separate bath: £85-£95. 1 suite for 3: £100-£150. Singles £60-£65.
Meals	Lunch & dinner £10-£25.
Closed	Open all day.

Steve & Michelle Hill
Lord Poulett Arms,
High Street,
Hinton St George, TA17 8SE
Tel +44 (0)1460 73149
Web www.lordpoulettarms.com

Farmers Arms

West Hatch

A lovely inn lost in peaceful hills on the Somerset Levels – a great base for a night or two of affordable luxury. Outside, free-range hens potter about, cows graze neighbouring fields and glorious views from the beer garden drift downhill for a couple of miles – a perfect spot for a pint in summer. Inside, you'll find friendly natives, sofas in front of an open fire and a timber-framed bar, where one airy room rolls into another giving a sense of space and light. There are beamed ceilings, boarded floors, tongue-and-groove panelling and logs piled high in alcoves. Bedrooms – some big, some huge – are just the ticket. They come with whitewashed walls, pretty beds, the odd chaise longue, then power showers or double-ended baths. One has a daybed, others have sofas, another has a private courtyard. Good food flies from the kitchen, perhaps ham hock terrine, crab and crayfish linguini, white chocolate and blackberry brûlée; in summer you can eat in the courtyard garden. There are local stables if you want to ride and great walking, so bring your boots. Taunton is close for cricket in summer.

Rooms	4 doubles, 1 twin/double: £105-£125. Singles from £75. Well-behaved dogs welcome.
Meals	Lunch & dinner £5-£35.
Closed	3pm-6pm (3pm-7pm Sat & Sun).

Alison Medley
Farmers Arms,
West Hatch,
Taunton, TA3 5RS

Tel	+44 (0)1823 480980
Web	www.farmersarmssomerset.co.uk

The Notley Arms Inn

Monksilver

In an Exmoor village with a 14th-century church is a recently refurbished inn – spruce on the outside, dapper within. They make their own bread, smoke their own fish, cure their own bacon, and, although the innovative menu changes every day, there's always beer-battered fish and chips to wolf down. They offer 25 wines by the glass with a global feel, an ale from St Austell brewed specially for the Notley, Exmoor Gold or Exmoor Stag, vodkas, lagers, and Black Rat cider; no wonder the country set descend. Simon is a host for whom nothing is too much trouble: when you want something, he's there. Find flagged floors, sturdy chesterfields, roaring wood-burners, and – ingenious touch – cloud-shaped cushions on the ceiling to absorb restaurant noise: no expense has been spared. Outside: a lawned garden bordered by a stream and a heated pavilion for summer dining. Six country-quiet bedrooms await in the two-storey coach house: a repro four-poster here, a gleaming leather bedhead there, top-notch wallpapers, hot water bottles, real coffee. Breakfasts are fresh and delicious.

Rooms	4 doubles, 2 twins: £65–£150.
Meals	Starters from £6. Mains from £8.
Closed	Open all day.

Simon & Caroline Murphy
The Notley Arms Inn,
Monksilver,
Taunton, TA4 4JB
Tel +44 (0)1984 656095
Web www.notleyarmsinn.co.uk

The Royal Oak Inn

Luxborough

After a walk in Chargot Woods with the pooches, what nicer than to drop in at the Royal Oak? Douglas (ex Hotel du Vin) is slowly restoring this pleasing red stone pub in a deep green valley in the Exmoor Country Park. Step in to find blackened beams, ancient flags, a hotch-potch of pine tables, a rustic oak settle: this bar is the place to be, especially when the wood-burner is roaring. There's a warren of rooms, a record player at the back, vinyl to play, and Latin lessons on Thursdays (Douglas knows how to keep the locals happy). As for the food, it comes with linen napkins and brings a smile to your face: mackerel quenelles with Melba toast; pheasant from the beat with allotment vegetables and crunchy roasties; apple crumble with homemade custard, and cheeses with homemade chutney. The beer is good, the wines are global, the service is fabulous. Bedrooms ramble around the first floor (one below with its own entrance; the suite with stunning views) and have cool neutral colours, sunken spotlights, smart tartan blinds, roll top tubs, drenching showers. Breakfast, the full cooked works, is delicious.

Rooms	5 doubles: £80-£100. 1 suite for 4: £120.
Meals	Bar snacks available. Starters from £4.75. Mains from £11. Sunday lunch, 2-3 courses, £14-£16.
Closed	3pm-6pm.

Douglas Yiend
The Royal Oak Inn,
Luxborough,
Watchet, TA23 0SH
Tel +44 (0)1984 641498
Web www.theroyaloakinnluxborough.co.uk

Tarr Farm Inn

Tarr Steps

No traffic lights, no mobile signals, peace for miles. Tucked into the Barle valley, a hop from the clapper bridge at Tarr Steps, this well-established 16th-century inn is surrounded by woodland above the hauntingly high spaces of Exmoor. The garden views are sublime – where better to test the best West Country cheeses followed by perfect coffee? Inside, the blue-carpeted, low-beamed main bar has comfy window seats and gleaming black leather sofas, and Exmoor Ale and Magner's cider flow as easily as the conversation. To fill the gap after a bracing walk the menu draws on local game (hunting and shooting are big here) so tuck into venison and rabbit casserole or pan-roasted partridge – partnered by a hundred French and New World wines.

Meals	Lunch £4.50-£14.95. Dinner from £5.50-£21. Sunday lunch £4.50-£14.95.
Closed	Open all day.

Hilary Lester
Tarr Farm Inn,
Tarr Steps,
Dulverton, TA22 9PY
Tel +44 (0)1643 851507
Web www.tarrfarm.co.uk

Somerset

Woods Bar & Dining Room

Dulverton

A warm and cosy place in a lively Exmoor village, replete with antlers and country paraphernalia, and the delight of wine-quaffing farmers and gentry. Foodies too have much to be grateful for. Find daily-changing modern menus and an emphasis on seasonal sourcing... perhaps roast tomato soup with serrano ham; roast Exmoor lamb with confit garlic and rosemary sauce; rich chocolate brownies. Or pop in for a stilton and onion marmalade baguette. A stable-like partition divides the space into two intimate seating areas, beyond which is a smart, soft-lit and deeply cosy bar: two wood-burners, lots of pine, a few barrel tables, exposed stone. Ales include Dartmoor Best and Devon Coast IPA but the wines are the thing, many by the glass. Friendly landlords Sally and Paddy welcome families and dogs.

Meals	Lunch & dinner £8.50-£16.50. Bar meals from £5.
Closed	3pm-6pm (7pm Sun).

Sally & Paddy Groves
Woods Bar & Dining Room,
4 Bank Square,
Dulverton, TA22 9BU
Tel +44 (0)1398 324007
Web www.woodsdulverton.co.uk

The Rock Inn

Waterrow

Tucked along the back road between Taunton and South Molton, built into the rockface by the river in a lush green valley, this 400-year-old gastro pub is thriving under Ruth and Daren's generous care. The food, beautifully sourced, cooked to perfection, draws the farmers from the hills and gourmets from further afield, and taps into a network of quality suppliers: free-range chicken and duck, Devon crab, Sunday roast of the day. On the menu: Somerset baked brie fondant; south coast hake grilled with a basil crust; feather blade of Angus beef marinated in black garlic. Local extends to the ales with Otter and Quantock on tap, as well as Cornish lagers. Special all round.

Meals: Lunch & dinner £7.95–£24.
Closed: Mondays all day. Tuesday lunchtimes. Sunday evenings.

Daren & Ruth Barclay
The Rock Inn,
Waterrow,
Taunton, TA4 2AX
Tel: +44 (0)1984 623293
Web: www.rockinnwaterrow.co.uk

Somerset

The Rising Sun Inn

Bagborough

In sleepy West Bagborough on the flanks of the Quantock Hills, the Rising Sun has been constructed around 16th-century cob walls and a magnificent door, with 80 tons of solid oak timbers and windows and a slate-floored bar. Add Art Nouveau features, spotlighting and swagged drapery and you find one very smart pub. There's Exmoor, guest local ales and Tribute to sample and, high in the rafters, a dining room with views that unfurl to Exmoor. It's an impressive setting for impressive food: Lyme Bay scallops with felt-baked heritage beetroot; steak-on-the-stone with gourmet salts and a peppercorn, blue cheese or red win jus; crème brûlée with lavender shortbread. All this and a new collection of vintage wines. Worth walking down the hill for.

Meals: Lunch from £9.50.
Bar meals from £5.95.
Dinner from £11.
Closed: Open all day.

Linda Palk
The Rising Sun Inn,
Bagborough,
Taunton, TA4 3EF
Tel: +44 (0)1823 432575
Web: www.risingsuninn.info

The White Horse

Haselbury Plucknett

In Haselbury Plucknett (the first part means Hazel Grove) in rural Somerset, owners Richard and Rebecca have brought culinary panache and first-class hospitality to this traditional pub. Flagstone floors, and, quite possibly, in front of the open fireplace, a slumbering dog. There are ales from Teignworthy and Butcombe, and feisty local scrumpy at the bar, and menus that feature pub classics as well as dishes with a Gallic twist. Snack on homemade focaccia; try saltmarsh lamb rump with pomme purée and spiced aubergine, tomato and tapenade sauce, or 38 day-hung Hereford steak; finish with chocolate terrine and pistachio ice cream. Or choose from a great selection of cheeses. A comprehensive wine list accompanies it all, there's a pretty garden with a re-opened well, and super friendly staff.

Meals: Lunch from £10. Bar meals from £5. Dinner £10-£25.
Closed: Sun eve, Mon & Tues.

Rebecca Robinson
The White Horse,
North Street, Haselbury Plucknett,
Yeovil, TA18 7RJ
Tel: +44 (0)1460 78873
Web: www.thewhitehorsehaselbury.co.uk

Entry 486 Map 3

Somerset

Kings Arms

Charlton Horethorne

A brilliantly run pub near Sherborne. With three dining pubs and a thriving food company behind them, Tony and Sarah are stars in the west country pub world, and the Kings Arms, with its bell ringers' lunches and local ciders and beers, has status as a proper local. The striking old façade opens to a contemporary-chic décor of wood and stone floors, good art, bold walls, vintage dining tables, cheery wood-burner, and squashy leather sofas. The restaurant has a coir-matted floor, arched mirrors – and outside is a terrace with views. On Sarah's daily-changing, local-produce menus, you find roasted pork belly with apple terrine; lamb rump with rosemary jus with butternut squash; ricotta ravioli with marjoram butter sauce; apple and calvados trifle. Delicious food for children too.

Meals: Lunch & dinner £8.95-£16.50. Sunday lunch £11.50.
Closed: Open all day.

Tony & Sarah Lethbridge
Kings Arms,
Charlton Horethorne,
Sherborne, DT9 4NL
Tel: +44 (0)1963 220281
Web: www.thekingsarms.co.uk

Entry 487 Map 3

The Devonshire Arms

Long Sutton

A lively English village with a well-kept green. The inn, 400 years old, was once a hunting lodge for the Dukes of Devonshire; a rather smart pillared porch survives at the front. These days open-plan interiors are warmly contemporary with high ceilings, blond floorboards and fresh flowers everywhere. Hop onto brown leather stools at the bar and order a pint of Moor Revival, or sink into sofas in front of the fire and crack open a bottle of wine. In summer, life spills onto the terrace at the front, the courtyard at the back and the lawned garden beyond. The hosts are engaging and the food's a joy; choose from ploughman's with homemade chutney or game burger and chips, linger over lamb rump with roast vegetables and puy lentils, dive into dark chocolate fondant. Then walk off your indulgence in style.

Meals	Lunch from £6.95. Dinner £11.50-£18.95.
Closed	3pm-6pm.

Philip & Sheila Mepham
The Devonshire Arms,
Long Sutton,
Langport, TA10 9LP
Tel +44 (0)1458 241271
Web www.thedevonshirearms.com

Entry 488 Map 3

Somerset

Rose & Crown Inn (Eli's)

Huish Episcopi

Quirky, unspoilt and in the family for over 140 years. The layout has evolved, gradually taking over the family home. There's no bar as such; you choose from the casks. Walk in and you step back to the 1930s; even the loos are historic. The cider and the beer (Glastonbury Mystery Tor) are tasty, the locals are lovely, the landlady is perfect; there are worn flagstones and aged panelling in four low parlours radiating off a central tap room, and an (almost modern) pool and juke box room. They do folk music nights and occasional quiz nights and Morris dancers drop by in summer. The food is brilliant value: creamy winter vegetable soup, a tasty pork, apple and cider cobbler, steak and ale pie, bread and butter pudding. Everyone's happy and children like the little play area outside.

Meals	Lunch & dinner £6.95-£7.95.
Closed	2.30pm-5.30pm Mon-Thurs. Open all day Fri-Sun.

Steve & Maureen Pittard & Patricia O'Malley
Rose & Crown Inn (Eli's),
Huish Episcopi,
Langport, TA10 9QT
Tel +44 (0)1458 250494

Entry 489 Map 3

Halfway House

Langport

First and foremost, the beer is second to none. As many as ten cask ales and ciders are lovingly nurtured by happy staff for grateful locals who love this pub. Inside, simple bricks and mortar require no embellishment: low ceilings, flagged floors, three smouldering fires and the constant flow of happy chatter. The food is as good as the beer. At lunch you dig into simple delights, perhaps deep-fried whitebait or a French onion tart, while at dinner you can try one of the pub's revered curries, washed down with a pint of Summer Lightning. Elsewhere, maps for walkers, the daily papers, a community notice board and a chesterfield by the fire. Children and dogs are very welcome. Simply wonderful.

Meals	Lunch & dinner £4.50-£10.95. No food Sun eve.
Closed	3pm-5.30pm. Open all day Sat & Sun.

Mark Phillips
Halfway House,
Pitney Hill,
Langport, TA10 9AB
Tel +44 (0)1458 252513
Web www.thehalfwayhouse.co.uk

Entry 490 Map 3

Somerset

The Red Lion Inn

Babcary

Dozing in sleepy Babcary, the Red Lion's transformation into a stylish inn is now complete. Clare and Charles's passion for this thatched local ensures it combines the best of pub tradition – a cosy rustic feel and local ales – with top-notch food. Hair-cord carpets, sofas and a blazing fire in the stove welcome you to the bar/lounge, while a dozen well-spaced country dining tables fill the beamed and flagstoned dining room. Daily menus offer pub classics like beef burger with home-made chutney, or confit chicken and black pudding terrine, roast partridge with parsnip purée, cabbage and bacon, and hot chocolate fondant. There's a terrific range of sandwiches too, not to mention the Red Lion's own take on a ploughman's which comes with wonderful warm bread. The best A303 stop-over for miles.

Meals	Lunch from £6.80. Bar meals from £5.95. Dinner from £8.50. Sunday lunch, 3 courses, £22.50.
Closed	Open all day.

Clare & Charles Garrard
The Red Lion Inn,
Babcary,
Somerton, TA11 7ED
Tel +44 (0)1458 223230
Web www.redlionbabcary.co.uk

Entry 491 Map 3

The Montague Inn

Shepton Montague

The O'Callaghans' 17th-century public house has been a stables, livery, grocery; now it is an inn in the true sense of the word. All remains beautiful, with Bath Ales and regional guests that may come from Butcombe and Blindman's Brewery, two wood-burners in the bar, candles on stripped pine tables and delicious produce from organic neighbouring farms. Chef Matt Dean's food is simple yet imaginative: chunky lunchtime ploughman's of local cheeses, and daily specials such as a hot pot on Tuesdays and fresh fish and chips on Fridays. Try the grilled local goat's cheese in a celery, apple and walnut salad, or seared fillet of local beef with garlic cream mash, bacon and lentil jus – all of it's brilliant. The restaurant and rear terrace have bosky views to Redlynch and Alfred's Tower.

Meals: Lunch from £4.95.
Bar meals from £4.95.
Dinner from £11.95.
Sunday lunch, 3 courses, £21.50.

Closed: 3pm-5pm Mon-Sat.
Sundays from 4pm.

Sean & Suzy O'Callaghan
The Montague Inn,
Shepton Montague,
Wincanton, BA9 8JW

Tel: +44 (0)1749 813213
Web: www.themontagueinn.co.uk

Entry 492 Map 3

Somerset

The Three Horseshoes Inn

Batcombe

A magnificent spot, England at its best. You get the full works here: a beautiful valley lost to the world, an English village impeccably preserved, a great little inn that sits in the shade of an ancient church tower. Inside, fires burn at both ends of the bar, there are low ceilings, window seats and a warm mix of traditional and contemporary. Rustic food hits the spot perfectly. Westcombe Cheddar sandwiches come with a real ale chutney, and if you want something more substantial, you can have it: pan-fried quail with ginger purée, tiger prawns in an Asian broth, Dorset mussels with lemongrass and chilli. In summer you slip outside and take your choice from a pretty courtyard where walls are clad in wisteria, and a lush lawn, where you can sip your pint as church bells chime. Great walks start from the front door.

Meals: Lunch from £6.
Dinner, 3 courses, £25-£30.
Sunday lunch from £11.50.

Closed: 3pm-6pm. Open all day Sat & Sun.

Kaveh Javvi
The Three Horseshoes Inn,
Batcombe,
Frome, BA4 6HE

Tel: +44 (0)1749 850359
Web: www.thethreehorseshoesinn.com

Entry 493 Map 3

The Sheppey Inn

Lower Godney

A funky country pub, one of the best in the west. Its exterior gives no hint of the wonders within – part cider house, part cool hotel. Low beamed ceilings in the bar, high white walls in the barn. There are cute booths, David Hockney prints, 50s retro furniture, the odd guitar waiting to be played. Music matters here: fantastic jazz, blues and funk bubbles away nicely, while a small stage hosts the odd travelling band. Local ales, scrumptious ciders, Belgian beers and lovely wines all wait, as does super food. Try French onion soup, a splendid fish stew or Somerset beef with Yorkshire pudding and red wine gravy. In summer, life decants onto a small terrace that hangs above a tiny river; otters pass, fields stretch out beyond. Glastonbury and the Somerset Levels wait. Out of this world.

Meals	Lunch from £5.95. Dinner from £8.95. Sunday lunch from £10.50.
Closed	3pm-5pm Tues-Fri.

Mark Hey & Liz Chamberlain
The Sheppey Inn,
Lower Godney,
Glastonbury, BA5 1RZ

Tel +44 (0)1458 831594
Web www.thesheppey.co.uk

Entry 494 Map 3

Somerset

The George

Wedmore

Wedmore's striking 15th-century coaching inn was lost in another century until Gordon Stevens took over. His vision for the vast stone building has breathed new life into a labyrinth of rooms that ooze character and charm. Wooden floors, half-panelled walls, stone fireplaces, old prints, warm greens and terracottas, wax-encrusted candlesticks on scrubbed dining tables... such is the setting for pints of Potholer and Orchard Pig cider. Food is hearty and locally sourced, and the menu ranges from crab sandwiches and afternoon teacakes with jam (yes!) to rack of Mendip lamb, beef and vegetable stew, and spicy pork curry. There's a cracking locals' bar, and a curry restaurant next door (in the bit that dates from 1760).

Meals	Lunch from £7. Bar meals £5. Dinner from £12. Sunday lunch, 2 courses, £18. No food Sun eves.
Closed	Open all day.

Gordon Stevens
The George,
Church Street, Wedmore,
Cheddar, BS28 4AB

Tel +44 (0)1934 712124
Web www.thegeorgewedmore.co.uk

Entry 495 Map 3

Ring O Bells

Compton Martin

Listed in the Domesday Book and rescued from decline by energetic quartet, Miles, Luca, Matt and Fiona, this lovely pub is now the local not only for Compton Martin but neighbouring Ubley, whose villagers have their own bar here, complete with one of Somerset's biggest inglenooks. A second bar serves locals who want a quiet quaff while the main dining area is abuzz with families, especially at weekends when the roast lunches do a roaring trade. Rightly so, since the food here is something special – Harlequin squash soup, Cornish sardines, smoky cheese burger with chilli jam – children are encouraged to order small portions from the main menu, great for little gourmets who can romp it off in the big gardens at the back. Miles, music guru, may persuade a famous artist or two to perform (Kylie did) while lovely Luca welcomes locals and visitors alike. A gem.

Meals	Bar snacks from £4. Lunch, 2 courses, £12. Dinner £10-£17.
Closed	Open all day.

The Manager
Ring O Bells,
The Street,
Compton Martin, BS40 6JE

Tel	+44 (0)1761 221284
Web	www.ringobellscomptonmartin.co.uk

Entry 496 Map 3

Somerset

The Pony & Trap

Chew Magna

Just outside pretty Chew Magna, a short drive from Bristol and Bath, is one of the best little gastropubs in the country. Josh Eggleton, who earned his spurs in France, Sicily and America, has won his first Michelin star. Provenance is all; from the blue cheese panna cotta to the fillet of pork with celeriac purée, almost every ingredient has travelled only a few miles to the plate. Deer is bought from a local marksman, eggs are from the chickens in the garden, berries from the hedges and perfect spears of asparagus straight from the patch. As for the views, they're stunning, and both the conservatory-style dining room and the large sloping garden – dine out on a summer's day – have them. For winter the bar is the place to be – super-cosy with wood panelling, old cider flagons and a cast-iron range.

Meals	Lunch from £9.50. Dinner £18-£23. Sunday lunch, 2-3 courses, £26-£30.
Closed	Open all day.

Josh Eggleton
The Pony & Trap,
Knowle Hill,
Chew Magna, BS40 8TQ

Tel	+44 (0)1275 332627
Web	www.theponyandtrap.co.uk

Entry 497 Map 3

The Bird in Hand

Long Ashton

The Bird in Hand is an unassuming little pub on Long Ashton's high street. Enter the bar, sparkling and new, for a pint of Gem or the guest ale of the week; turn right for plain tables and deep blue-grey walls. Owner Toby Gritten is as excited about foraged ingredients as he is about 'heritage vegetables, forgotten cuts and wild fish', and his sentiments are echoed by those of head chef Sylvester and manager Dominic. Elegant dishes are served on white plates by friendly staff – chargrilled tenderstem broccoli, soft boiled duck egg, Berkswell cheese; haunch of wild venison, juniper, carrots, fondant potato; figgy pudding, stout and toffee sauce, cinnamon ice cream. Come on Sunday for champagne rhubarb fizz and a choice of two roasts, or gnocchi with artichokes and salsify. The food is satisfying, unshowy and steeped in flavour.

Meals	Lunch & dinner from £9. Sunday lunch from £12.50.
Closed	Open all day (from 12pm).

Dominic Webster
The Bird in Hand,
17 Weston Road,
Long Ashton, BS41 9LA

Tel +44 (0)1275 395 222
Web www.bird-in-hand.co.uk

Entry 498 Map 3

Somerset

The Miner's Rest

Long Ashton

Trek up Providence Lane, then settle down here and lose yourself for the afternoon… Carol has run the Miners Rest for 23 years and little has changed. Find a refreshingly unpretentious pub with snug low ceilings, an open fire at each end, wooden tables on stone floors, brass lanterns, local mining pictures on the walls and an air of relaxed respite from all that ails. Carol keeps an eye out for everyone, staff are friendly; locals mix with passing ramblers, cyclists, cricketers; regulars help collect and chop wood for the fires. Beers include Butcombe and Doom Bar, and there's a good range of ciders. Food comes out of the kitchen at a rate, and is excellent value – generous Sunday roasts have heaps of spuds. There are a few tables outside, with views over fields and woodland. Perfect spot to escape the city, and let those deadlines whoosh past.

Meals	Lunch from £4.95. Mains from £7.95. Sunday lunch from £7.95.
Closed	Open all day.

Carol Rogers
The Miner's Rest,
42 Providence Lane,
Long Ashton, BS41 9DJ

Tel +44 (0)1275 393449

Entry 499 Map 3

The Black Horse

Clapton-in-Gordano

The Snug Bar once doubled as the village lock-up and, if it weren't for the electric lighting, you'd be hard pushed to remember you were in the 21st century. With flagstones and dark moody wood, the main room bears the scuffs of centuries of drinking. Settles and old tables sit around the walls; cottage windows with wobbly shutters let a little of the outside in. The fire roars in its vast hearth beneath a fine set of antique guns – pull off your muddy boots and settle in. Sepia prints of parish cricket teams and steam tractors clutter the walls and cask ales pour from the stone ledge behind the hatch bar. The food is unfancy bar fodder, with daily specials. Ale takes pride of place; beneath the chalkboard, six jacketed casks squat above drip pans. There are fine wines too, and plenty of garden.

Meals Lunch & dinner £3.50-£7.95.
Closed Open all day.

Nicholas Evans
The Black Horse, Clevedon Lane,
Clapton-in-Gordano,
Bristol, BS20 7RH
Tel +44 (0)1275 842105
Web www.thekicker.co.uk

Entry 500 Map 3

The Fitzherbert Arms

Swynnerton

In the old village of Swynnerton on Lord Stafford's estate is the once-forlorn Fitzherbert, all spruced up. If you've visited before you're in for a surprise: bar, lounge and snug entwine with an open-plan feel, warmed by three delicious fires. A friendly vivacious team makes the place tick as they ferry platefuls of flavoursome food to elegant tables: seafood platters, steak and stout pies, crumbles, brownies and port-poached pears. They do a great line in comfort food, have a good list of local suppliers, and Staffordshire ales star at the pumps. There are 30 ports (more than any other pub in the country!), 16 wines by the glass and a real cider, too: something to be proud of. The 1818 building once held a forge and the Anvil Room is enticing: leather wingback chairs, a forge-like fire, hops above a soft-lit wall.

Meals Bar snacks from £3.
Starters from £5.75.
Mains from £12.95.
Closed Open all day.

Leanne Wallis
The Fitzherbert Arms,
Swynnerton,
Stone, ST15 0RA
Tel +44 (0)1782 796782
Web fitzherbertarms.co.uk

Entry 501 Map 8

The Duncombe Arms

Ellastone

The bar is sleek and stylishly laid out, with rustic nooks to settle into, the music plays discreetly and the food is absolutely beautiful. Diners include many regulars and returning Londoners, even though this is Derbyshire. James is passionate about making the Duncombe excel, and excel it does: the staff are on the ball and there's a top team in the kitchen, headed by Gary Auld. Platefuls of flavoursome food, modern British with touches of rusticity, are delivered to inviting tables in dining areas cosy, lofty, private, airy or al fresco; take your pick. Our sea bass with crushed new potatoes and slow-cooked cherry tomatoes was faultless. There are wines from Bibendum, 13 top malts, Duncombe Ale on tap, and in summer you can spill into a huge garden with views across the Dove Valley.

Meals	Starters £5-£8. Mains £12-£20. Sunday lunch, 3 courses, £21.95.
Closed	Open all day.

James Oddy
The Duncombe Arms,
Ellastone,
Ashbourne, DE6 2GZ
Tel +44 (0)1335 324275
Web www.duncombearms.co.uk

Entry 502 Map 8

Staffordshire

The George

Alstonefield

A green sward ripples endlessly in this remote limestone village, perched on a plateau between the remarkable gorges of the rivers Dove and Manifold. Set amidst this verdant Eden, the handsome George is an ultra-reliable local, in the family for four decades and lovingly managed by Emily. As you walk into small, timeless rooms of old beams, gleaming quarry tiles and crackling log fire, you know you're in safe hands. It's an unhurried place, where everyone knows everyone else (or soon will), ramblers cram the benches out front and time passes slowly. The 18th-century coaching house is perfect for private parties. The welcome is warm, the beer's on song and the food is fab. Young chefs are creative with seasonal produce, so there's Devon crab, steak and real ale pie, and treacle tart.

Meals	Lunch £9-£30. Bar meals £5.50-£16. Dinner £11-£30.
Closed	3pm-6pm. Open all day Fri, Sat & Sun.

Emily Brighton
The George,
Alstonefield,
Ashbourne, DE6 2FX
Tel +44 (0)1335 310205
Web www.thegeorgeatalstonefield.com

Entry 503 Map 8

The Ship

Dunwich

Once a great port, Dunwich is now a tiny (but famous) village, gradually sinking into the sea. Its well-loved smugglers' inn, almost on the beach, overlooks the salt marsh and pulls in wind-blown walkers and birdwatchers from the Minsmere Reserve. In the old-fashioned bar – nautical bric-a-brac, flagged floors, simple furnishings and a stove that belts out the heat – you can tuck into legendary fish and chips washed down with Adnams. There's also a more modern dining room where hearty food combines with traditional dishes: try Lowestoft crispy cod cheeks with Romesco sauce, smoked paprika and rocket, or tuck into their terrific Scotch eggs: with black pudding and homemade piccalilli, or hot smoked salmon and horseradish. Up the fine Victorian staircase are spruced up bedrooms – simple, uncluttered – with period features, cord carpets, brass beds, old pine, little shower rooms. Rooms at the front have glorious salt marsh views, two new rooms overlook the garden, courtyard rooms are cosy with pine, and one of the family rooms is under the eaves is fabulous: single beds, a big futon-style bean bag, and a flat-screen for the kids. *Special midweek rates off season.*

Rooms	12 doubles, 1 twin: £120-£140. 3 family rooms for 4: £140.
Meals	Lunch from £4.95. Bar meals from £9.75. Dinner from £10.75. Sunday lunch £11.95.
Closed	Open all day.

Gareth Clarke
The Ship,
St James's Street, Dunwich,
Saxmundham, IP17 3DT

Tel +44 (0)1728 648219
Web www.shipatdunwich.co.uk

Sibton White Horse

Sibton

Step through the door of an unassuming pub and prepare for a surprise. The heart of this thriving village local is 16th-century and the bar is steeped in character: old pews, huge inglenook, horsebrasses on blackened beams, wonky walls, a fire in winter. (Take a peek through the window panel into the cellar to see a reclaimed Roman floor.) Ale drinkers will note the gleaming brass beer engines on the old oak servery and settle in for pints of Adnams and Woodforde's, or a weekly guest beer. Food is seasonal, with local game, meat from the next village and veg from the kitchen garden. There's chicken, tomato and herb terrine with tomato chutney; roast breast and confit leg of duck with wild mushroom jus; sticky toffee pudding. The bread is homemade, it's all delicious, and on sunny days you can spill onto the lawns. Thoroughly modern annexe bedrooms are furnished in old and new pine; beds are comfy; bathrooms fresh; views are to open countryside. You are 20 minutes from Aldeburgh and charming Southwold: enjoy beach cricket, a pint of prawns, a dip in the North Sea.

Rooms	5 twin/doubles: £80-£105.
Meals	Lunch from £7.50. Dinner from £13.25. Sunday lunch £14.25.
Closed	3pm-6pm. Monday lunch.

Neil & Gill Mason
Sibton White Horse,
Halesworth Road, Sibton,
Saxmundham, IP17 2JJ
Tel +44 (0)1728 660337
Web www.sibtonwhitehorseinn.co.uk

Long Melford Swan

Long Melford

Long Melford – home to TV's *Lovejoy* – is as achingly pretty as a Suffolk village can be, and the Swan is in the middle of it. Enter the airy bar, with blond oak beams and pale blue palette, an open fire, background music, original art, the odd dozing dog. In the restaurant: cool tartan carpeting and bold feature walls, shining glasses and upholstered chairs. As for the food, it's modern, Suffolk-local and executed with flair, from the eggs en cocotte at breakfast to the small plates for gourmets (the cockle popcorn with crab mayonnaise is fabulous) to a full-blown herb-crusted rack of lamb for two to share, with confit shallots and château potatoes. Parents can relax in the terraced, parasol'd garden; drinkers can choose whatever they fancy: a peachy bellini, an espresso Martini, a Sancerre rosé, a pint of Green King IPA. Stay the night? Yes please. Next door is Melford House with luxy bedrooms, each better than the last. Say wow to sumptuous headboards, gilt framed mirrors, subtle colours, atmospheric lighting and bathrooms with Noble Isle toiletries. You could hardly be more spoiled!

Rooms	7 doubles: £90-£175.
Meals	Bar snacks from £3.50. Starters from £6.75. Mains from £14.
Closed	Open all day.

Lorna Pissarro
Long Melford Swan,
Hall Street,
Long Melford, CO10 9JQ
Tel +44 (0)1787 464545
Web www.longmelfordswan.co.uk

The Crown

Stoke-by-Nayland

The Crown is all things to all men, a lovely country pub, a popular local restaurant, a small boutique hotel, a welcoming bolthole in Constable country. It sits in a pretty village with long views from its colourful terrace over the Box Valley, not a bad spot for a glass of Pimm's after a day exploring the area. It dates to 1560 and has old beams and timber frames, though interiors have youthful good looks: warm colours, tongue-and-groove panelling, terracotta-tiled floors, a fancy wine cellar behind a wall of glass. You'll find rugs and settles, the daily papers, leather armchairs in front of a wood-burner. Four ales wait at the bar, 30 wines come by the glass and there's seasonal food that will make you smile, perhaps confit duck leg ravioli, pan-roasted cod with chorizo and crayfish, popcorn panna cotta. Airy bedrooms are quietly hidden away at the bottom of the garden – excellent beds, lovely linen, a dash of colour and super bathrooms. All have armchairs or sofas, three have French windows that open onto private terraces with fine views. A great place to eat, sleep and potter.

Rooms	10 doubles: £145-£250. 1 suite for 2: £225-£295. Singles from £95.
Meals	Lunch & dinner £5-£25.
Closed	Open all day.

	Richard Sunderland The Crown, Park Street, Stoke-by-Nayland, Colchester, CO6 4SE
Tel	+44 (0)1206 262001
Web	www.crowninn.net

The Angel Inn

Stoke-by-Nayland

Soft lamplight glows in the windows of this 16th-century inn deep in 'Constable country'. Spruced up by Exclusive Inns, the bar divides into two. Find carved beams, open brickwork, log fires, polished wood tables, chesterfields and wing chairs, fresh flowers and candles, fine prints and paintings, and a few antique pieces to add to the appeal. The Angel fills early and menus include a good value lunchtime 'classics' choice – sausages with mash and onion gravy; battered haddock – and an imaginative carte. Tuck into Denham Estate venison scotch egg; pork belly with Madeira broth; treacle tart with white chocolate ice cream. Eat in the bar, the galleried restaurant (once a brewhouse) or at laid tables on the terrace at the back on warm summer evenings.

Meals	Lunch £13.95-£15.95. Dinner £14.50-£22.50. Sunday lunch, 2 courses, £16.95.
Closed	Open all day.

Bartholomew Bizbal
The Angel Inn,
Polstead Street, Stoke-by-Nayland,
Colchester, CO6 4SA

Tel +44 (0)1206 263245
Web www.angelinnsuffolk.co.uk

Entry 508 Map 10

Suffolk

The Swan

Stratford St Mary

Mark and Sophie Dorber's super Dedham Vale outpost (see The Anchor in Walberswick) is maturing apace. For beer buffs, tip-top hand-pulled ales and a global array of draught and bottled craft beers – a rare treat in Britain; wine lovers enjoy a stimulating esoteric list. Stephen Miles's food will not disappoint: try pig's head croquette; whole plaice with clams, bacon and celeriac chowder; bitter chocolate and salted caramel tart. The 16th century charm of this creaky old inn survives in its intimate rooms, sagging black beams, brick-parquet floors and requisite comforts of fat radiators and log fires; the gorgeous dining rooms come with obligatory wall timbers, antique tables and church candles. The exciting plans include a microbrewery plus regular tastings and feasting in the grounds.

Meals	Lunch from £5. Bar meals from £2. Dinner from £13.
Closed	Mon-Tues.

Mark Dorber
The Swan,
Lower Street, Stratford St Mary,
Ipswich, CO7 6JR

Tel +44 (0)1206 321244
Web www.stratfordswan.com

Entry 509 Map 10

The Hadleigh Ram

Hadleigh

In the market town of Hadleigh is a very good pub, country-classy and contemporary yet intimate and friendly: almost impossible to fault. The lighting is inviting, the bar is free-flowing, there's tongue and groove panelling and very helpful young staff. As for the food, it is serious, delicious and more beautiful with every course. They bake their own bread so the sandwiches are special, and they are passionate about seasonality and provenance. Set lunch is a steal: pheasant boudin with bacon crumb and endive perhaps, then pressed skate with mash and cockle cream, followed by ginger and lemon poached pear with coconut bavarois. Dogs are allowed in the enclosed courtyard and the bar; later they can romp on the banks of the Brett. It's a Greene King pub – but you may prefer a cocktail!

Meals	Set menu, 2-3 courses, £17.95-£21.95.
Closed	Open all day.

Lorna Pissarro & Oliver Macmillan
The Hadleigh Ram,
5 Market Place,
Hadleigh, IP7 5DL
Tel +44 (0)1473 822880
Web www.thehadleighram.co.uk

Entry 510 Map 10

Lavenham Greyhound

Lavenham

In the heart of pretty, half-timbered Lavenham, this beamed-and-cosy pub has been given a stylish makeover without losing character. Exposed brick walls, big fireplaces, tongue-and-groove panelling, and black-treacle wooden furnishings are jazzed up with bright stripes and indigo-coloured walls. There's a window-seat in the bar and exposed stone in the snug. Extensive menus include brunch, vegetarian, Sunday and children's with classic dishes given a local twist – Cromer crab quiche or house-smoked pulled-pork burgers. Wash down with Greene King ales or a good wines-by-the-glass choice. A friendly place that suits locals and visitors.

Meals	Bar snacks from £3.45. Lunch from £12.95. Sunday lunch, 2-3 courses, £19.95-£23.95.
Closed	Open all day.

Lorna Pissarro & Oliver Macmillan
Lavenham Greyhound,
97 High St, Lavenham,
Sudbury, CO10 9PZ
Tel +44 (0)1787 249553
Web www.lavenhamgreyhound.com

Entry 511 Map 10

The Angel Hotel

Lavenham

Little Lavenham, built on wool, is Suffolk's most celebrated town. It has 340 listed buildings, all limewashed timber and ochre, each one a gem, and enough tea shops to satisfy the nations's thirst. Welcome to the Angel, standing proud on the corner of Market Square since 1420. In 2014 Cosy Pubs gave it the sympathetic makeover it deserved: dark-grey woodwork, off-white render. Inside it shines. There's spruce wood in the bar, brown leather chesterfields around the inglenook, leather club armchairs in the cosy snug, and a window seat in the bay. The tourists flock and the locals are returning, for the warm service and the no-nonsense food: rare-breed pork sausages with silky mash; coq au vin with pearl onions; rump steak from the grill. The set lunches are good value and there's a sizeable garden at the rear.

Meals	Starters from £5.50. Mains from £12.
Closed	Open all day.

Alex Burgess
The Angel Hotel,
Market Place,
Lavenham, CO10 9QZ

Tel	+44 (0)1787 247388
Web	www.theangellavenham.co.uk

Entry 512 Map 10

Suffolk

The One Bull

Bury St Edmunds

Hats off to the One Bull! The staff are bright and knowledgeable, the food bursts with flavour, the wine list is well-informed. What's more, the One Bull is part of a family owned and run business including the craft brewery, Brewshed: try the 'American Blonde'. You enter this pretty sash-windowed pub to find a split-level interior of wood and tiled floors, tidy tables, brown sofas and leather high chairs at the bar, neat as a new pin, with sash windows and brick fireplace remaining. It's always busy and no surprise: the food looks tasty and the menu is adventurous. Perhaps beef scrumpets with root salad and horseradish vinegar then hake fillet with salsa verde. There are roasts on Sundays, cheeses from Suffolk and pudding grazing boards to share… who could resist tarte tatin with salted caramel? As for Bury, it's a great little market town steeped in history.

Meals	Starters from £6. Mains from £10.50. Puddings from £6. Children's menu available.
Closed	Sunday eves.

The Manager
The One Bull,
Angel Hill,
Bury St Edmunds, IP33 1UZ

Tel	+44 (0)1284 848220
Web	www.theonebull.co.uk

Entry 513 Map 10

The Ramsholt Arms

Ramsholt

In a setting that is all location, location, location (at the end of a lane, right beside a tidal beach overlooking the River Deben), this former farmhouse, ferryman's cottage and smugglers' inn is the place to be on a warm summer's evening. Watch the sun setting over the water and listen to the plaintive call of the curlew over the marshes, while you sup a pint of Adnams ale on the terrace, accompanied by a pulled pork bap from the barbecue. On wild winter days settle into the cosy atmosphere of the simply spruced up bar, with its big picture windows and watery views, and tuck into local estate game, braised shin of beef or sea bass with pea purée, followed by cherry and almond tart. Max and Polly are doing a grand job at this waterside gem. Rewarding riverside walks complete the picture.

Meals	Starters £4.50-£7. Mains £10-£16.
Closed	Until 5pm.

Max & Polly Durrant
The Ramsholt Arms,
Ramsholt,
Woodbridge, IP12 3AB

Tel	+44 (0)1394 411209
Web	www.theramsholtarms.com

Entry 514 Map 10

Suffolk

The Crown at Woodbridge

Woodbridge

Everyone loves Woodbridge's Crown, from its pastel façade to its cool laid-back interiors and humorous touches: beneath a sloping glass roof an immaculate wooden skiff is suspended. Welcome to a 400-year-old pub with great food, a long granite-topped bar and a cosmopolitan air. In intimate dining rooms, chef-patron Stephen David's menu trawls Europe for inspiration and draws as much as it can on Suffolk's natural larder. Look forward to hearty dishes full of flavour and some amazing taste combinations: grilled east coast skate wing with cockle and caper butter sauce; slow cooked rabbit and pappardelle in cider sauce with shaved parmesan and rocket. Wash it all down with Adnams or Meantime beers or delve into the wine list. As for the staff, nothing is too much trouble for them. A welcoming Suffolk bolthole – unmissable!

Meals	Lunch & dinner £6-£30. Sunday lunch from £12.50.
Closed	Open all day.

Laura Miles
The Crown at Woodbridge,
Thoroughfare,
Woodbridge, IP12 1AD

Tel	+44 (0)1394 384242
Web	www.thecrownatwoodbridge.co.uk

Entry 515 Map 10

The Froize

Chillesford

Impassioned by local produce before it became fashionable, David Grimwood lives in chef's whites or shooting tweeds – a Suffolk countryman too chivalrous to accept his reputation as East Anglia's best game cook. Off the beaten track, the path to these once charmingly remote 18th-century keepers' cottages is well worn by regulars. Blythburgh pork, Orford and Lowestoft fish, bags of local game (much of it retrieved by the landlord's black labs) combined with retro rustic cooking reflect the 'field, forest and foreshore' landscape. A perfect roast joint always stands alongside reworked classics such as devilled kidneys, stuffed skate wing or cider-braised rabbit and prunes, and the homemade puddings are legendary. Ales are the county's best, mostly Adnams. There's Aspall's cider, too.

Meals — Lunch & dinner from £13.50.
Closed — Monday (except bank hols).

David Grimwood
The Froize,
The Street, Chillesford,
Woodbridge, IP12 3PU
Tel +44 (0)1394 450282
Web www.froize.co.uk

Entry 516 Map 10

Suffolk

The Greyhound Inn

Pettistree

Stewart and Louise are reinventing one of the oldest boozers in Suffolk, and all who discover it, love it. It's a warm and friendly place to be, unspoilt and wood-floored, with a log-burner in the brick fireplace and a dining room with grey-panelled walls. Stewart – a Scot – knows his ales and his whiskies, and oversees a few Scottish gins too, while Louise cooks imaginative and seasonal food, including venison from her parents' estate. She cures her own salmon, then serves it with dill cream; whisks up homemade basil gnocchi and beautiful hake fishcakes on creamed leeks; offers curry nights on Thursdays and themed nights once a month. Families will be happy with small portions for kids and a safely fenced garden – and the elderflower panna cotta with poached gooseberries is to die for.

Meals — Starters from £5.95. Mains from £10.95.
Closed — Monday.

Louise & Stewart McKenzie
The Greyhound Inn,
The Street, Pettistree,
Woodbridge, IP13 0HP
Tel +44 (0)1728 746451
Web www.greyhoundinnpettistree.co.uk

Entry 517 Map 10

The Dolphin Inn

Thorpeness

Thorpeness is a one-off, the turn-of-the-century brainchild of G S Ogilvie, who set out to create a holiday resort free of piers and promenades and entirely safe for children. The Dolphin, in the middle of the village, is a great little inn. There are two lively bars, open fires and wooden floors in the dining room and, outside, a terrace and lawn for barbecues and al fresco dinners. No-nonsense food hits the spot, perhaps grilled sardines with basil pesto, chargrilled steak with chunky chips, a plate of local cheeses. Stay a while – you're spoiled for things to do: a great golf course, an unspoilt sand and pebble beach, and a 64-acre lake, the Meare, which is never more than three-feet deep and was inspired by the creator of *Peter Pan*; children can row, canoe up creeks and discover islands.

Meals Lunch & dinner £5-£30.
Closed 3pm-6pm Mon-Fri.

David James
The Dolphin Inn,
Peace Place,
Thorpeness, IP16 4FE
Tel +44 (0)1728 454994
Web www.thorpenessdolphin.com

Entry 518 Map 10

Suffolk

Station Hotel

Framlingham

The railway disappeared long ago. Now the former buildings are business units, but the Station Hotel continues to thrive. Cask ales (a classic Victorian bitter, a sweet, wintry porter) are perfect accompaniments for gutsy cooking. Chalked up on the board are a roast squash, chilli and ginger soup; confit duck leg; whole sea bass with chorizo, pepper and spinach casserole; lemongrass and ginger crème brûlée... all very good. Lunch is quiet but it bustles at night, helped along by chef Mike Jones and a friendly team. The building is shabby-boho, the interior is charming. Expect blackened stripped boards, cream papered walls, a stuffed head(!) and bone-handled knives partnering paper serviettes. Outside: a terrace sprinkled with tables under the tree.

Meals Lunch & dinner £4-£15.75.
Bar meals £3.25-£11.
Closed Open all day.

Mike Jones
Station Hotel,
Station Road, Framlingham,
Woodbridge, IP13 9EE
Tel +44 (0)1728 723455
Web www.thestationhotel.net

Entry 519 Map 10

The Sweffling White Horse

Sweffling

We love this old pub on the outskirts of Sweffling, rescued from oblivion by Mark and Marie. Inside is friendly, inviting and unspoilt. To the right, the Public Bar, to the left, the Lounge Bar, ahead, an upright piano for merry music nights. There's a quarry tiled floor and a mish-mash of chairs, books, games and cushions, a vibrant blue range in a big brick inglenook, and East Anglian beers served by gravity straight from the cask; tastings in small glasses are encouraged. On the food front they keep it simple. In summer, tasty toasties and ploughman's with Suffolk cheeses and chutneys, and when the range is roaring, crunchy pies and warm Huffer bread. The pub is well supported by locals and friends and there's a rustic beer garden hidden away at the back, lit by solar fairy lights. Fantastic.

Meals	Snacks from £1.50. Lunch & dinner from £5.
Closed	Tues-Thurs. Closed till 7pm Fri-Mon. Sun 3pm-7pm.

Marie Smith
The Sweffling White Horse,
Low Road, Sweffling,
Saxmundham, IP17 2BB
Tel +44 (0)1728 664178
Web swefflingwhitehorse.co.uk

Entry 520 Map 10

Suffolk

Eels Foot Inn

East Bridge

The sign depicts an eel wriggling out of an old boot. This plain-looking, oddly named backwater village pub lives up to its slightly eccentric reputation. It's a twitchers' pub where you find watchers and wardens from Minsmere RSPB Reserve swapping stories with visitors – walkers, cyclists, holidaymakers. All are drawn by the full-range of Adnams ales and the hearty food (beer battered cod, steak and ale pie, treacle tart), served in a cosy wood-floored bar with a log fire and simple furnishings; there's a homely upper dining area, too. Don't miss the craic on music nights – every Thursday is Squit Night (a folk, country and blues jamming session); the last Sunday of the month is folk night. The place is mobbed in summer... and there are new beer gardens to enjoy.

Meals	Lunch & dinner £5-£13.
Closed	3pm-6pm. Open all day Sat & Sun.

Julian Wallis
Eels Foot Inn,
East Bridge,
Leiston, IP16 4SN
Tel +44 (0)1728 830154
Web www.theeelsfootinn.co.uk

Entry 521 Map 10

The Westleton Crown

Westleton

One of England's oldest coaching inns, with 800 years of continuous service under its belt, in a village two miles from the sea. Aldeburgh and Southwold are close, Minsmere is a walk away. Inside, Farrow & Ball colours and leather sofas join panelled walls, stripped floors, ancient beams and spindle-back chairs. Weave around and find nooks and crannies in which to hide, flames flickering in open fires, a huge map on the wall for walkers. You can eat wherever you want – including the restaurant that opens onto charming terraced gardens and tasty barbecues. Enjoy slow-cooked rolled pork belly with Lyonnaise potatoes, wilted greens and apple purée with Aspall cyder, followed by pear frangipane tarte tatin, maple and pecan ice cream. The fish comes off the boats at Lowestoft, and the fish and chips are fabulous.

Meals	Lunch & bar meals from £5.50. Dinner from £11.95. Sunday lunch £26.
Closed	Open all day.

Gareth Clarke
The Westleton Crown,
The Street, Westleton,
Saxmundham, IP17 3AD

Tel	+44 (0)1728 648777
Web	www.westletoncrown.co.uk

Entry 522 Map 10

The King's Head

Laxfield

Known locally as the Low House because it lies in a dip below the churchyard, the 600-year-old pub is one of Suffolk's treasures. Little has changed in the last 100 years and its four rooms creak with character – expect narrow passageways, low ceilings, wood panelling and tiny fires for chilly eves. The simple parlour is dominated by a three-sided, high-backed settle and there's no bar – far too new-fangled a concept for this place. Instead, Adnams ales are served from barrels in the tap room. In keeping with the authenticity, the food is rustic, hearty and homemade, the short blackboard menu listing soup, sandwiches, hot dishes and puds. It's the sort of place where folk music starts up spontaneously and summer brings Morris men. The garden overlooking the brook at the back was once a bowling green – lovely.

Meals	Lunch & dinner £6.50-£9.50. Bar meals £4.25-£6.
Closed	3pm-6pm. Open all day in summer.

Robert Wilson
The King's Head,
Gorams Mill Lane, Laxfield,
Woodbridge, IP13 8DW

Tel	+44 (0)1986 798395
Web	www.laxfieldkingshead.co.uk

Entry 523 Map 10

The Anchor

Walberswick

Beer guru Mark and wife Sophie are doing wonders at this well-loved pub. To the sound of the sea crashing on the beach beyond, the vast lawn hosts summer soirées and barbecues. Inside, sand, stone and aqua tones are redolent of the ocean and open skies and add a contemporary touch, while Sophie's menus overflow with produce sourced from a rich vein of organic farms and top local butchers. Fresh food is definitely on the menu (ask about food safaris) and the allotment at the back has doubled in size. Their wine list is very impressive – exciting organic choices, delicious tasting options – and seasonal food to match: try game terrine with Flying Dog IPA, or roast cod, lentils and chorizo. Tempura rock oysters with a draught wheat beer are a summer treat, out on the sun terrace overlooking allotments, beach huts and distant sea.

Meals	Lunch from £6.50. Dinner from £13.25. Sunday lunch, 2 courses, £20.
Closed	Open all day.

Mark & Sophie Dorber
The Anchor,
Main Street, Walberswick,
Southwold, IP18 6UA
Tel +44 (0)1502 722112
Web www.anchoratwalberswick.com

Entry 524 Map 10

Suffolk

The Crown

Southwold

Well-heeled weekenders flock to Southwold most of the year; outside the season it's a gem. The Crown, stalwart of the dining pub world, oozes metro chic. Ceilings are elegantly beamed, walls are colourwashed and uncluttered, the bar is large and laid-back. Adnams is on home turf – you would struggle to find a smarter brewery tap. The wood-panelled rear snug is the province of traditionalists, the brasserie wine bar at the front is beloved of the urban crowd. As for the produce, it's fresh, local and seasonal, perhaps roast Gressingham duck breast with kumquats and a winter spice liqueur glaze, or slow-cooked pork belly and seared scallops with thyme marinated apples. And then a banoffee pain perdu: cinnamon roll, caramelised banana, candied almonds, toffee sauce. The wine list is an oenophiles' heaven.

Meals	Lunch from £8.95. Dinner from £12.95. Sunday lunch, 3 courses, £18.95.
Closed	3pm-6.30pm Mon-Fri in winter. Open all day Sat & Sun and in summer.

Lukas Juszczak
The Crown,
90 High Street,
Southwold, IP18 6DP
Tel +44 (0)1502 722275
Web adnams.co.uk/hotels/the-crown/

Entry 525 Map 10

The Inn West End

West End

Wine importer Gerry Price pulls the punters in from all over Surrey. Inside, the stylish bar area is light and modern with wooden floors and Shaker colours while the atmosphere's warm and friendly: monthly quiz nights; Sunday evening music sessions; summer barbecues in the garden. There are local beers – hand-pumped Fuller's and Young's – and the wine list is enticing, with a nod to Portuguese shores. Tuck in to lunch or dinner in the bar, or in the more traditional dining room. Seasonal menus announce fresh modern food, perhaps game casserole, or pan roasted cod in a mussel cream sauce. In autumn, there's pheasant, woodcock and teal. A pastry chef oversees the crumbles and tortes with South African vinegar pudding a house speciality, and the cheeses are farmhouse best. As for dogs, they're welcome in the bar – and in a couple of the rooms in the stable block behind (replete with clock tower). Enjoy modern oak beds with Hypnos mattresses, excellent wifi, swish wet rooms, even gun cupboards and safes. Breakfast is the final treat.

Rooms	12 doubles: £125-£150.
Meals	Lunch & dinner £5.25-£32.50. Sunday lunch £24.95.
Closed	3pm-5pm. Open all day Sat & Sun.

Gerry & Ann Price
The Inn West End,
42 Guildford Road, West End,
Woking, GU24 9PW
Tel +44 (0)1276 858652
Web www.the-inn.co.uk

The Swan Inn

Chiddingfold

After 20 years at Knightsbridge's revered Swag & Tails, Annemaria and Stuart escaped to the country to revive an old Surrey bolthole. What you find now are sparkling dining areas and a cool bar, wooden floors, blazing log fires, chunky tables and bags of style. It may be more classy eatery than traditional pub, but there's artisan ale from Surrey Hills Brewery, big smiles from attentive staff, and proper homemade burgers for those in for a bite. And more: beer-battered haddock with fries and pea purée; chargrilled rib-eye steak with caramelised shallots and béarnaise sauce; scallops with black pudding and smoked bacon risotto cake; braised beef cheeks with horseradish mash and curly kale – unpretentious dishes that juggle popular with modern. If you're staying, contemporary bedrooms are warm and cosy, with excellent linen and downy duvets, big beds and flat-screen TVs, sofas in spacious suites, and trendy bathrooms with power showers and toiletries. Outside: a super landscaped garden for summer socialising. In short, the Swan represents a relaxed revival of an old inn in a rather fetching village.

Rooms	8 doubles: £100-£135. 1 suite for 2: £150-£180. 1 family room for 4: £140-£165.
Meals	Lunch & dinner £7.50-19.95. Bar meals from £7.50. Sunday lunch, 3 courses, £26-£28.
Closed	Open all day.

Zach & Sinead Leach
The Swan Inn,
Petworth Road, Chiddingfold,
Godalming, GU8 4TY
Tel +44 (0)1428 684688
Web www.theswaninnchiddingfold.com

The Crown Inn

Chiddingfold

Beautifully restored in 2008, the Crown is a contender for the oldest hostelry in the country. Thirteenth-century bowed brick walls, warped weathered timbers, plaster ceilings and lattice windows… you could be back in the days of the highwaymen. The bar's stained-glass leaded lights – for which charming Chiddingfold was once famous – tell of 'the Lion and the Unicorn's fight for the Crown', while the pattern-carpeted main bar holds a fine stone fireplace from 1619 and a crackling winter fire. It's a fascinating place so, pint of Sharp's Doom in hand, take a wander and a gander at the small glass case of coins that date back to 1558. In keeping, the menu lists straightforward classic dishes – coq au vin, game pie, fish and chips, apple and rhubarb crumble – prepared from excellent ingredients.

Meals	Lunch & dinner £10-£20.
Closed	Open all day.

Marcus Tapping
The Crown Inn,
The Green, Chiddingfold,
Godalming, GU8 4TX

Tel	+44 (0)1428 682255
Web	www.thecrownchiddingfold.com

Entry 528 Map 4

Surrey

Dog & Pheasant

Brook

Safe in the hands of the two Davids, this popular roadside inn is full of bonhomie. The food may be the driving force, but the small bar heaves with locals in for a pint of Broadside or a glass of pinot noir. Smart and cosy it is, with black wood ceiling beams, striking wall timbers and warming winter fires. Service is friendly and upbeat. Chef Joseph Wright's lengthy repertoire should please all with classic and modern dishes, lots of fish (pan-fried fillet of rainbow trout with curly kale and roasted garlic sauce) and blackboard specials to complement the menu. Wednesday 'Grill Night' is not to be missed and sees Joseph cooking all the meats in the central inglenook fireplace. There's a terrace, a big garden and a private dining room upstairs.

Meals	Lunch & dinner £8-£17.
Closed	Open all day.

David Gough & David Hall
Dog & Pheasant,
Haslemere Road, Brook,
Godalming, GU8 5UJ

Tel	+44 (0)1428 682763
Web	www.dogandpheasant.com

Entry 529 Map 4

The Three Horseshoes

Thursley

Be sure to pack your boots as the walking is fantastic, especially when the leaves turn. Then slake your thirst with a pint from the Hog's Back or Surrey Hill's Breweries, or one of many wines by the glass. Gloriously old-fashioned and rambling – beams, brick fireplace, woodchip wallpaper hung with archive photos – it is run by a gregarious team who keep an often busy throng happy. Daily changing menus are unfussy and big on flavour. Favourites include pan-fried calves' liver with Wiltshire bacon, mashed potato and chantenay carrots; salmon and smoked haddock fishcakes with mixed salad and dill mayonnaise. There are hearty sandwiches, good desserts and British and French cheese boards with wines and ports to match. The large grassed garden has fine views, and there's a rather smart terrace.

Meals	Lunch & dinner £9.50-£21. Sunday lunch £14.50-£18.
Closed	3pm-5.30pm Mon-Fri. From 7pm Sun.

David Alders & Sandra Proni
The Three Horseshoes,
Dye House Road, Thursley,
Godalming, GU8 6QD
Tel +44 (0)1252 703268
Web www.threehorseshoesthursley.com

Entry 530 Map 4

The Parrot

Forest Green

Having left a mini-empire of London pubs for a livestock farm in the Surrey hills, Linda Gotto finds time too for her lovely, rambling, 17th-century pub overlooking the village green. She is passionate about food, its provenance and quality, and the Parrot showcases produce reared and grown on the farm – Shorthorn veal, Middlewhite pork, mutton from Dorset crosses, eggs from Copper Marans. Find them on the short imaginative menu – in the form of game pie; lamb rump with minted pea purée; roast belly pork with mash and braised cabbage – or in the farm shop next door. Elsewhere, beams, flagstones and lovely bits and bobs, old settles and blazing fires, London Pride on tap and 16 wines by the glass; they do weddings, too. The value is outstanding.

Meals	Lunch & dinner £9.50-£18. Bar meals from £5.50. Sunday lunch, 3 courses, £25. No food Sunday eve.
Closed	Open all day.

Linda Gotto
The Parrot,
Forest Green,
Dorking, RH5 5RZ
Tel +44 (0)1306 621339
Web www.theparrot.co.uk

Entry 531 Map 4

The Stag on the River

Eashing

Through Eashing, to a small bridge with a warning that heavy loads might lead to its demise; this pretty stone structure built by 13th-century monks forms an essential link to the Stag on the River. With a lease dating back to 1771, the pub is an atmospheric place to discover home cooking, real ales and a happy buzz. Produce is fresh and local and succulent meats include the new standard of local beef, 'Surrey Beef'. Try lamb rump with bean cassoulet and red wine jus or winter vegetable tagine; finish with warm chocolate and walnut brownies. In spring and summer the teak-furnished terrace by the water makes a languorous spot for supping a pint of Surrey Hills Shere Drop; in winter you can seek out a cosy corner in one of several rambling rooms, where wood and brick floors and open fires blend with modern tables and stylishly upholstered wingback chairs.

Meals Lunch & dinner £10.75-£22.95.
Closed Open all day.

Mark Robson
The Stag on the River,
Lower Eashing Lane, Eashing,
Godalming, GU7 2QG
Tel +44 (0)1483 421568
Web www.stagontherivereashing.co.uk

Surrey

The Duke of Wellington

East Horsley

Set back from the road, surrounded by leafy loveliness, is a big sturdy pub with a Regency façade and neo Byzantine wings. Inside is equally unique: an open-plan space with a fire at its heart, a planked floor, a hotch-potch of furniture, a brick wall hung with old mirrors. It's cool décor with a theatrical twist. There's a formal dining room, exciting modern lighting, and a cosy corner with leather club chairs, trendy bookshelf wallpaper and a fire in the grate. Sundays are rammed and the lunches are sought after, with excellent roasts and Yorkshires to die for. House-smoked brisket is a speciality, there are pulled pork buns, warm crab salads, treats for vegetarians. Drinks range from guest beers to craft beers to prosecco. They love kids and dogs, and cyclists get free coffee on the terrace at weekends.

Meals Bar snacks from £5.
Starters from £3.50.
Mains from £12.95.
Closed Open all day.

Glyn Roberts
The Duke of Wellington,
Guildford Road,
East Horsley, KT24 6AA
Tel +44 (0)1483 282312
Web www.dukeofw.com

The Anchor

Ripley

The clued-up Ripley set will know the Anchor is related to renowned restaurant 'Drake's' just across the High Street. Though its Michelin-starred patron Steve Drake moved his head chef (Mike Wall-Palmer) over to run the pub kitchen, the Anchor isn't all flashy dining pretension, rather a relaxed, inviting place turning out simple, creative food alongside good ales and interesting wines. This listed pub (once almshouses) has been spruced up; find comfy armchairs round a log-burner, fashionable dark wood furniture, slate floors and original features in interlinked areas. Enjoy innovative snacks such as puffed pork skin with apple sauce, or opt for something heartier like slow cooked duck leg, savoy cabbage, mash potato and liquorice sauce.

Meals — Lunch, 2-3 courses, £15-£19 (Tues-Sat). Dinner £18. Sunday lunch £15.
Closed — Monday.

Abilio Oliveria
The Anchor,
High Street, Ripley,
Woking GU23 6AE
Tel +44 (0)1483 211866
Web www.ripleyanchor.co.uk

Entry 534 Map 4

Surrey

The Canbury Arms

Kingston upon Thames

Much has changed since Michael and Charlotte bought the dilapidated Canbury Arms a decade ago – then they could only feed guests grilled chorizo ciabattas from a barbecue. Now, visitors can enjoy real ales, good wines and delicious treats in this handsome corner pub. Built in the late 1800s to feed and water Victorian white collar workers, it's remained popular with locals who pop in for pints of Twickenham's Naked Ladies and a Canbury Scotch egg. You can eat in the main bar or garden room; there's a pretty terrace in summer for hog roasts and pints as the sun goes down. Try slow-smoked Scottish salmon with quail egg and dill mayonnaise to start, followed by corn-fed chicken breast with chanterelles, leek and pancetta, perhaps. The railway workers may have gone, but the breakfasts are popular – from full English to warm croissants with preserves made in the Canbury kitchen.

Meals — Bar meals £5. Mains from £11. Sunday lunch from £14.
Closed — Open all day.

The Manager
The Canbury Arms,
49 Canbury Park Road,
Kingston upon Thames, KT2 6LQ
Tel +44 (0)20 8255 9129
Web www.thecanburyarms.com

Entry 535 Map 4

The Horse Guards Inn

Tillington

After a visit to Petworth House, head for the pub on the park's western edge. Up from the tiny lane, views sweep towards the South Downs from the pub's hammock'd garden. Inside: a series of rambling and intimate rooms furnished with quirky pieces, fresh flowers, wonky beams, brick floors, painted panelling, old pine tables and four log fires – one in an old back range. Sam and Misha love this pub and their passion is reflected in the homemade treats on sale by the door and the chalkboards championing the producers (the latest a goat farmer with a dairy). Beautiful dishes include summer soup of local berries with mint and crème fraîche, gazpacho of heritage tomatoes, potted rabbit, a rich fish pie. Our hot beef sandwich, served with homemade horseradish sauce, was delicious. Each of the three bedrooms is simple, characterful and contemporary, from the smallish brass-bedded double with a sloping floor and a view of the church to the wonderfully romantic cottage. Hand-made chocolates are on the house; bathrooms stock local treats. A very happy place in a sleepy Sussex village.

Rooms	2 twin/doubles: £85-£120. 1 double: £105-£140.
Meals	Starters from £6. Mains from £15.50.
Closed	Open all day.

Sam & Misha Beard
The Horse Guards Inn,
Tillington,
Petworth, GU28 9AF
Tel +44 (0)1798 342332
Web www.thehorseguardsinn.co.uk

The Welldiggers Arms

Petworth

A true country classic where the views stretch for miles and the staff are warm, friendly and attentive. The kitchen turns out delicious modern British dishes; start with duck hash, hen's egg and crispy bacon crumb followed by pan-fried hake with spiced lentils and pot-roasted cauliflower and fennel. Finish up with a moreish pudding and coffee. Or just pop in for a drink and a bar snack: the large convivial space is full of happy diners making the most of the knock out views over the South Downs. The bar and dining area of this 300-year-old stone, slate-roofed inn has a fresh yet traditional feel: roaring fire, bespoke oak furniture, local art. Drink in the picture-perfect vistas or spill onto the terrace. And they've got 14 en suite bedrooms, some in the pub and some in a separate courtyard. The calm contemporary rooms have top quality Hypnos beds with attractive upholstered headboards; and all of them make the most of the scenery, while some windows frame spectacular views. Excellent walking all around; Chichester, sailing and National Trust properties are close.

Rooms	14 doubles: £90-£155. Extra beds available.
Meals	Bar snacks from £3.95. Starters from £7. Mains from £11.95.
Closed	Open all day.

The Manager
The Welldiggers Arms,
Low Heath,
Petworth, GU28 0HG

Tel +44 (0)1798 344288
Web www.thewelldiggersarms.co.uk

The White Hart

South Harting

Inside this rural pub all feels cosy and welcoming, with antlers above the fireplace, logs stacked by the burner and a happy mix of tables, lamps and chairs: the pub manager is a self-confessed rummager! As they lie somewhat in the middle of nowhere they stock food essentials as well as all the good things behind the bar: local ales, unusual spirits, nice wines, great coffee. Walkers drop by for sandwiches, locals for pints, builders for pies (crisp, delicious ones) and everyone loves the garden in summer. In the kitchen the focus is on high quality pub food, from house pâté with chutney to pork chops on sweet potato mash to fruit crumbles with ice cream or custard; children get small portions and much is vegetarian. Dogs are welcome and the garden's great, with 30 bird boxes and feeders, and tea lights hanging from the spreading magnolia. The family room, perfect for a stopover, has a king-sized bed and bunk beds for the little ones. Great views, and great coffee in the morning. Marvellous.

Rooms	5 doubles, 1 twin: £90-£110.
Meals	Starters £5.50-£8.50. Mains £12.50-£23.
Closed	Open all day.

Dana Tase
The White Hart,
The Street,
South Harting, GU31 5QB
Tel +44 (0)1730 825124
Web www.the-whitehart.co.uk

The White Horse

Chilgrove

Beautiful Sussex downland provides a backcloth to this very English inn close to Chichester. Long, low and whitewashed, it dates from 1768 and was once a staging post; now it's the perfect place for foodies and wine buffs to be fed and watered in style. The relaxing timbered bar and dining room combines contemporary-smart with traditional charm: blazing wood-burners, heritage hues, fat candles on scrubbed tables, rugs on upholstered benches. There are serious wines (flick through the 'Red Book') and a delicious monthly menu – fishfinger sandwiches, oxtail linguini, venison and mustard ragù, whole lemon sole, rhubarb and almond crumble. A secluded courtyard and spacious garden rooms blend rustic-chic with modern design, featuring steamer trunks, architectural four-poster beds, striking wall coverings, posh linen, sheepskin rugs and iconic retro furnishings. Bathrooms are swish; two have hot tubs on private patios. Glorious Goodwood draws the racing set, while stunning downland rambles radiate from the front door.

Rooms	15 doubles: £90-£175. Pets by arrangement.
Meals	Starters from £5.50. Small plates, 3-5 dishes, from £16-£25.50. Mains from £13.95.
Closed	Open all day.

Niki Burr
The White Horse,
High Street,
Chilgrove, PO18 9HX
Tel +44 (0)1243 519 444
Web www.thewhitehorse.co.uk

The Blacksmiths

Chichester

A beautiful little pub, freshly painted and as spruce as can be, run by the nicest people. There are crackling fires, pale floors, seating upholstered in charcoal leather and benches topped with sheepskins and throws: very modern and Nordic. It's the sort of place where you come for a business lunch – or tip up with the kids and the dogs on the way to the Witterings; in summer the garden is fabulous. There are long Sussex views, a raised fire pit for tasty morsels, and two patios, one with a sail-like awning. Overlooking the garden is the restaurant, slightly more formal but equally stylish. Based around fresh local ingredients, the menu ranges from huge open sandwiches to venison sausages to warm chocolate brownies, and there are mini homemade burgers (with Birds Eye peas!) for the children. Up a teensy stair are the lovely bedrooms, Skylark, Lapwing and Barn Owl, each with exquisite bird-traced wallpapers and pale wood furniture. You'll love them all: the crisp white linen, the light-filled bathrooms, the Cowshed lotions, the grey-painted boards, and the soothing views of endless green fields.

Rooms	3 doubles: £120-£150.
Meals	Starters from £5.50. Mains from £10.95. Sunday lunch from £12.50.
Closed	Christmas, New Year.

The Manager
The Blacksmiths,
Selsey Road,
Chichester, PO20 7PR
Tel +44 (0)1243 785578
Web www.the-blacksmiths.co.uk

The Bull

Ditchling

This 16th-century inn on the South Downs has lots to offer – a cracking bar, four fancy bedrooms, tasty local food and an excellent array of ales and craft beers from across the globe. Step inside and it's like travelling back to Dickensian England. Light is rationed on aesthetic grounds, beams sag, fires roar and happy locals gather for a pint of Bedlam, the pub's own brew. You can eat wherever you want – meat from Sussex farms, game from local estates, fish from short-range boats – perhaps cider steamed mussels with pancetta, venison pie with chestnut mash, steamed ginger and treacle sponge. Upstairs, four stylish bedrooms have recently been refurbished (two larger, two above the bar), with four more coming soon. Expect Farrow & Ball colours, chic fabrics, old-style radiators and comfy beds. Bigger rooms have sofas, you might find timber frames, a cow-hide rug or a low beamed ceiling. All have digital radios, flat-screen TVs and smart little bathrooms. Bring walking boots and mountain bikes and scale the Ditchling Beacon for big views. Brighton and Gatwick are close. Don't miss Sunday lunch.

Rooms	3 doubles, 1 twin/double: £100-£160.
Meals	Lunch & dinner from £10.
Closed	Open all day.

Dominic Worrall
The Bull,
2 High Street, Ditchling,
Hassocks, BN6 8TA

Tel +44 (0)1273 843147
Web www.thebullditchling.com

The Ram Inn

Firle

The road runs out once it reaches Firle village nestling beneath the South Downs... hard to believe now, but this quiet backwater was once a staging post. Built of brick and flint, the inn reveals a fascinating history – the Georgian part was once a courthouse and the kitchen goes back 500 years. Rescued from closure in 2006, the Ram Inn is once again thriving. Its three rooms have been decorated in rustic-chic style – bare boards and parquet, coal fires in old brick fireplaces, chunky candles on darkwood tables. Walkers stomp in from the Downs for pints of Harveys Sussex and hot steak sandwiches; foodies flock after dark for great fresh food, perhaps ham and pea broth, rump of Hankham Farm organic lamb with red wine jus, and sticky toffee pudding. Retire upstairs to quirky, individual rooms with bold colours, exposed beams, super comfortable beds, fluffy bathrobes in tiled bathrooms, and dreamy village or South Downs views. And there's a splendid flint-walled garden for peaceful summer supping. Handy for Charleston Farmhouse, country home to the Bloomsbury set.

Rooms	2 doubles, 2 twin/doubles: £90-£145.
Meals	Lunch & dinner £9.95-£16.95. Sunday lunch £11.95.
Closed	Open all day.

Hayley Bayes
The Ram Inn,
The Street, Firle,
Lewes, BN8 6NS

Tel +44 (0)1273 858222
Web www.raminn.co.uk

The Griffin Inn

Fletching

It's not often you end up discussing the death of Athenian democracy with a barman, but that sort of thing is quite common here. The Griffin is English to its core, a posh inn with a streak of scruffiness, a community local that draws a devoted crowd. They come for the lively bar, the attractive restaurant and the club room for racing on Saturdays. In summer, life spills onto a smart terrace for local food cooked in a wood-fired oven. There's a bar in the garden, weekend barbecues, deckchairs scattered across the lawns for ten-mile views over Pooh Bear's Ashdown forest to Sheffield Park. Quirky bedrooms are nicely-priced. Some have wonky floors, others a four-poster, you'll find timber frames, lovely old furniture, then robes and free-standing baths; those in the coach house are quieter. Seasonal menus offer tasty rustic food, perhaps rabbit gnocchi, local pheasant, dark chocolate tort with honey ice cream; excellent wines help you wash it all down. The pub has three cricket teams that travel the world in pursuit of glory – you may find them in the bar on a summer evening after a hot day in the field.

Rooms	6 doubles, 7 four-posters: £85-£150. Singles £60-£80 (Sun-Thur).
Meals	Bar meals from £11. Dinner, 3 courses, £30-£40. Not 1st Jan eve.
Closed	Open all day.

Nigel & James Pullan
The Griffin Inn,
Fletching,
Uckfield, TN22 3SS

Tel +44 (0)1825 722890
Web www.thegriffininn.co.uk

The Cat

West Hoathly

Owner Andrew swapped grand Gravetye Manor for the buzzy, pubby atmosphere of The Cat in 2009; he hasn't looked back. The 16th-century building, a fine medieval hall house with a Victorian extension, has been comfortably modernised without losing its character. Inside are beamed ceilings and panelling, planked floors, splendid inglenooks, and an airy room that leads to a garden at the back, furnished with teak and posh parasols. Harvey's Ale and some top-notch pub food, passionately put together from fresh local ingredients by chef Max Leonard, attract a solid, old-fashioned crowd: retired locals, foodies and walkers. Tuck into rare roast beef and horseradish sandwiches, Rye Bay sea bass with brown shrimp and caper butter, South Downs lamb chops with dauphinoise (and leave room for treacle tart!). The setting is idyllic, in a pretty village opposite a 12th-century church – best viewed from two of four bright and comfortable bedrooms. Crisp linen on big beds, rich fabrics, fawn carpets, fresh bathrooms and antique touches illustrate the style. A sweet retreat in a charming village backwater.

Rooms	4 doubles: £125-£165.
Meals	Lunch & dinner from £12. Bar meals from £6. Sunday lunch, 3 courses, £26.
Closed	Sun eves from 5pm.

Andrew Russell
The Cat,
Queen's Square, West Hoathly,
East Grinstead, RH19 4PP
Tel +44 (0)1342 810369
Web www.catinn.co.uk

The Old House Inn

Copthorne

The wonky tiled roof and the black-and-white timbered façade draw the eye to this former farmworker's cottage – and entice one in. It stands beside a B-road that services Crawley and Gatwick, so step inside and leave the modern day behind. The 16th-century Old House is heaped with charm, in latticed windows, bowed oak beams, wonky walls, sloping floors, and cosy nooks and alcoves. This is now a stunning modern inn with a new bar and dining area, transformed from a former faded French restaurant. We love the warm textured fabrics and comfy banquettes, the chunky leather armchairs by log burners, the fat candles on old dining tables, and the retro pub artefacts. Equally up-to-date is the menu, a modern British choice with pub classics (rib-eye burger with triple cooked fat chips and house slaw) alongside such dishes as chargrilled chicken, grilled halloumi, chilli, chorizo and Israeli tomato couscous, or lamb rump, pesto gnocchi, bean medley and mint jus. Rooms in the converted barn are named after local woods and sport earthy hues, big wooden beds, the best linen and down. Bathrooms are spoiling, two with claw-foot baths.

Rooms	5 doubles, 1 twin/double: £99-£159.
Meals	Seasonal lunchtime offers available. Mains from £11.95. Dinner, 3 courses, from £30.
Closed	Open all day.

Stephen Godsave
The Old House Inn,
Effingham Road,
Copthorne, Crawley, RH10 3JB

Tel +44 (0)1342 718529
Web www.theoldhouseinn.co.uk

The Dorset Arms

Withyham

Set back from the road, the striking façade of the Dorset Arms oozes history and charm. Inside: thick beams, wall studs, an ancient Sussex oak floor, and an enormous log fire in the bar. An ale house since 1735, its fortunes have been revived by the current Lord De La Warr, with Lady De La Warr lending her astute eye for detail to the rooms. Locals love the candles on old tables, colourful cushions on benches, and family paintings and photos. Ale from local Larkins, Tonbridge and Black Cat micro-breweries and a changing menu from the Buckhurst Estate. Try pan-seared scallops with smoked bacon, peas and saffron cream sauce, then venison steak with stilton mash, and vanilla panna cotta to finish. Or go for the locally famous Buckhurst Park sausages, made to the Lord's own recipe reminiscent of his childhood. Six lovely bedrooms are housed in the attractive red brick cottage detached from the pub; beautifully comfy beds with upholstered headboards, spotless bathrooms, and a shared sitting room on the ground floor. Marvellous.

Rooms 6 doubles: £105-£120.

Meals Starters from £5. Mains from £10. Sunday lunch from £14.

Closed Open all day.

Charlie Blundell
The Dorset Arms,
Buckhurst Park,
Withyham, TN7 4BD
Tel +44 (0)1892 770278
Web www.dorset-arms.co.uk

The George Inn

Robertsbridge

This handsome old inn in pretty Robertsbridge has a warm welcome for all. The bare-boarded, earthy-hued bar/dining area is the perfect setting for richly textured fabrics, wool and leather chairs and sofas, painted tables and beautiful period pieces. Family portraits gaze serenely down as you enjoy a pint of Rother Valley Level Best and get cosy by the brick inglenook – famously favoured by Hilaire Belloc. If you're peckish, look to the chalkboards for the day's local and seasonal dishes: locally landed lemon sole, Rye Bay scallops, slow-roasted pork belly with Bramley apple spiced compote, chargrilled lamb rump with minted rösti. Or opt for a chargrilled rib eye steak, cut to size and order. Leave room for lovely puddings, especially the chocolatey ones. Upstairs, money has been lavished on four gorgeous luxury-steeped rooms with superb Hypnos beds, signature wallpapers, rich fabrics, antique furniture and beautiful en suite shower rooms. Perfect for visiting nearby Battle, Bodiam Castle, Pashley Manor Gardens and more besides.

Rooms	4 twin/doubles: £95-£130. Singles £80-£100.
Meals	Lunch from £5. Bar meals from £9.75. Dinner from £10. Sunday lunch £10.75. No food Sun eve.
Closed	Mondays.

John & Jane Turner
The George Inn,
High Street,
Robertsbridge, Battle, TN32 5AW

Tel	+44 (0)1580 880315
Web	www.thegeorgerobertsbridge.co.uk

The Ship Inn

Rye

The 16th-century smuggler's warehouse stands by the quay at the bottom of cobbled Mermaid Street. Climb the church tower for stunning coast and marsh views, then retreat to the laid-back warmth of the Ship's rustic bars. Cosy nooks, ancient timbers, blazing fires and a quirky delicious décor characterise this place; there are battered leather sofas, simple café-style chairs, old pine tables and good paintings and prints. Quaff a pint of Harvey's Sussex or local farm cider, leaf through the daily papers, play one of the board games – there are heaps. Lunch and dinner menus are short and imaginative and make good use of local ingredients, so tuck into confit duck with grilled aubergine and saffron yoghurt, roast sea bream with buttered samphire, warm salad of squid, fennel and chorizo, and fresh Rye Bay fish. The relaxed funky feel extends to bright and beachy bedrooms upstairs: find painted wooden floors, jazzy wall coverings, comfortable beds, splashes of colour. Quirky extras include Roberts radios, sticks of rock, and rubber ducks in simple bathrooms. And they love dogs.

Rooms	10 doubles: £80-£125.
Meals	Lunch & dinner £11.75-£18.50.
Closed	Open all day.

Karen Northcote
The Ship Inn,
The Strand,
Rye, TN31 7DB

Tel +44 (0)1797 222233
Web www.theshipinnrye.co.uk

The George in Rye

Rye

Rye is beautiful, old England trapped in aspic. It was a Cinque Port, Henry James lived here and the oldest church clock in England chimes at the top of the hill. The George stands on its cobbled High Street right in the thick of things. Built in 1575 from reclaimed ships' timbers, its exposed beams and panelled walls remain on display. Inside, old and new mix beautifully – expect Jane Austen in the 21st century. There's a roaring fire in the bar, screen prints of the Beatles on the walls in reception, a sun-trapping courtyard for lunch in summer. Beautiful bedrooms come in all shapes and sizes (a couple are small), but chic fabrics, Frette linen and Vi-Spring mattresses are standard, as are good books, fine bathrooms, white robes and cashmere covers on hot water bottles. Some are huge with zinc baths in the room, one has a round bed. You eat in the George Grill, an open kitchen on display, perhaps Provençal fish soup, grilled rib-eye with hand-cut chips, gooseberry soufflé with bay leaf ice cream. Walk it off by following the river down to the sea. *Mapp and Lucia* was filmed in the town.

Rooms	8 doubles, 21 twin/doubles: £135-£195. 5 suites for 2: £295-£325.
Meals	Starters £6-£10. Mains £10-£22.
Closed	Open all day.

Alex & Katie Clarke
The George in Rye,
98 High Street,
Rye, TN31 7JT
Tel +44 (0)1797 222114
Web www.thegeorgeinrye.com

The Globe Inn Marsh

Rye

Expect the unexpected at this quirky clapboard-covered boozer on the edge of Rye. Bought to life by the Rogers family (who also run the Five Bells at East Brabourne) there's much to catch the eye inside from corrugated iron walls, hanging buoys and glowing oil lamps to wine bottle candelabras and lobster pot lampshades. You won't find a 'proper' bar, instead a line of pumps dispensing top-notch Sussex and Kent ales. Menus are hand-scribbled, but don't let that deceive you – food is taken seriously here. Come for brunch or lunch with friends, order a pizza from the wood-fired oven, or choose one of the 'Daily Doings', handsome local offerings that change as regularly as the sun rises – Rye Bay scallops, Dungeness sea bass, Romney salt marsh lamb. Three blazing winter log fires and a super side terrace for summer drinking add to the year-round appeal.

Meals	Lunch from £6.50. Dinner from £11.
Closed	3pm-6pm Mon-Thurs. Open all day Fri-Sun.

Alison Roger
The Globe Inn Marsh,
10 Military Road,
Rye, TN31 7NX

Tel +44 (0)1797 225220
Web www.globeinnmarshrye.com

Entry 550 Map 5

Sussex

The Crown

Hastings

Just a short stroll up from the beach, this old corner boozer oozes artful charm and hipster-cool. Décor is shabby-chic, the mood is laid-back, and the craft beer list is curated by an expert palate. With Tess and Andrew at the helm, the Crown celebrates fantastic local produce and menus bristle with local artisan producers: cured delights from Moon's Green in Northiam, meat from Winchelsea and homemade bread by Emmanuel Hadjiandreou. Enjoy a pint of Three Legs Pale with local herring fillet, beetroot and sour cream and horseradish croquette, or go the whole hog and tuck into Romney Salt Marsh lamb suet pie with roast carrots, greens and mash. Community spirit rings throughout and everyone is welcome, including the dog. Anything goes, from live music, monthly quizzes and board games to regular events such as storytelling and craft groups.

Meals	Starters £4-£9. Mains £10-£16. Puddings £3-£7.
Closed	Open all day.

Tess Eaton & Andrew Swan
The Crown,
64-66 All Saints Street,
Hastings, TN34 3BN

Tel +44 (0)1424 465100
Web www.thecrownhastings.co.uk

Entry 551 Map 5

The Lamb Inn

Wartling

James, Joanna and son Charlie bought the deeply rural Lamb in 2012, and spruced it up with panache. Now appreciative crowds beat a path to its door, for good food, good beer and good cheer, and Charlie's eclectic vinyl collection – select and play your favourite album. There's a wood-floored bar with a wood-burner, milk churns for bar stools and a deep sofa to sink into with a pint of Harvey's Best, a rich-panelled eating area with candles on old tables, and more dining in the converted stables. Monthly menus and chalkboard specials brim with local produce. Try Rye Bay scallops, rump of salt marsh lamb with minted mash and jus, wild boar and apple sausages, and fish from the Sussex coast. Good cheeses can follow, as can honeycomb and vanilla cheesecake, and lemon tart with raspberry coulis.

Meals	Lunch & dinner £8.95-£17.95. Bar meals £5.75-£12.95. Sunday lunch, 3 courses, £15.50.
Closed	Open all day.

Charlie & Ned Braxton
The Lamb Inn,
Wartling,
Hailsham, BN27 1RY

Tel +44 (0)1323 832116
Web www.lambinnwartling.co.uk

Entry 552 Map 5

Sussex

The Bell

Ticehurst

Rescued, restored and reinvented, the old Bell is back: a community hub, a dining pub and a fun, fabulous place to stay. Enter to find oodles of 16th-century charm – rugs on bare boards, gilt-framed paintings on red walls, bowed beams, crackling logs in a brick inglenook. In the gorgeous bar-dining room and the cosy snug are innumerable and original design details: top-hat lampshades, spilling piles of floor-to-ceiling books, French Horn urinals in the gents, witty anecdotes in antique scripts, a stuffed squirrel on a rocking chair. Enjoy Harveys ales and delicious pub dishes on modern seasonal menus – Rye Bay scallops, lamb chops with bubble and squeak, Cambridge burnt cream. The 'stable with the table' hosts table talks (debates), wine tastings and supplier dinners... an amazing community inn!

Meals	Lunch & dinner £6.50-£21.50.
Closed	Open all day.

Howard Canning
The Bell,
High Street,
Ticehurst, TN5 7AS

Tel +44 (0)1580 200234
Web www.thebellinticehurst.com

Entry 553 Map 5

The Mark Cross Inn

Mark Cross

Set back from the A267 south of Tunbridge Wells, this whitewashed old inn makes the most of its lofty location in Mark Cross. On warm summer days arrive early to bag a table in the garden and savour the glorious rolling views across the Sussex Weald, best enjoyed with a pint of Harvey's Sussex in hand. Retreat inside in winter to find rambling rooms with old tables on rug-strewn wood floors and every inch of wall space filled with old paintings and prints and shelves groaning with books. The atmosphere is relaxed, the staff happy, and diners, children and dogs will all feel pampered. Daily menus run the gamut of pub classics and modern gastropub dishes – ham, egg and chips, moules and chips, confit pork belly with bubble and squeak, thyme and smoked garlic sauce, and sea bass with crab and crayfish risotto.

Meals — Starters from £4.95. Mains from £10.95.
Closed — Open all day.

Brian Whiting
The Mark Cross Inn,
Mark Cross,
Crowborough, TN6 3NP
Tel +44 (0)1892 852423
Web www.themarkcross.co.uk

Entry 554 Map 5

Sussex

The Fox Eating and Drinking House

West Hoathly

It's hard to miss this pub, a row of former cottages at the junction of two country lanes. Its interior is equally unmissable. A fun collection of ephemera, that stays just the right side of crazy – a pillar of books, a collection of road signs, a letter-box, wine-bottle chandeliers – is set against a backdrop of exposed brick, colourful walls and scrubbed wooden tables. The small central bar has three changing real ales and a wine list (ten by the glass) chosen with food in mind. Tim's daily changing menu (partner Claire is front-of house) is well-executed, modern comfort food – pan-fried hake, duck confit – with interesting vegetarian and lighter options. Not your average rustic pub, there's a popular Sunday lunch with pianist, plus monthly music and quiz nights. Warm and inviting – three fireplaces – this place is as serious about food as drink.

Meals — Lunch from £8. Dinner from £14.
Closed — Mondays.

Claire Kacy
The Fox Eating and Drinking House,
Highbrook Lane,
West Hoathly, RH19 4PJ
Tel +44 (0)1342 810644
Web www.thefoxwesthoathly.co.uk

Entry 555 Map 4

The Coach & Horses

Haywards Heath

With ale on tap from Harveys in Lewes, fresh fish, honey from their own bees, and lamb from the field opposite, this is one special pub. The central bar is its throbbing hub, wooden panelling and open fires the backdrop for jugs of mulled wine in winter-cosy rooms. During the rest of the year the big raised garden comes into its own; sit out on the stone terrace and watch horses frolic in the pretty adjoining fields. Whatever the weather, the food attracts folk from far and wide. In the stable block restaurant a changing seasonal menu from chef Dan Hockaday places the emphasis on quality rather than quantity; smoked chicken terrine with harissa, roast confit duck, braised Danehill spiced lamb with roasted sweet potato and greens. Delicious! A lovely rural pub, a true local.

Meals: Lunch & dinner £10.50-£19.95. Bar meals £6.75-£10.50 (lunchtime only).

Closed: 3pm-5.30pm Mon-Fri. Open all day Sat & Sun.

Ian & Catherine Philpots
The Coach & Horses,
Coach & Horses Lane, Danehill,
Haywards Heath, RH17 7JF

Tel: +44 (0)1825 740369
Web: www.coachandhorses.co

Entry 556 Map 4

The Gun

Gun Hill

Winding lanes lead to a 16th-century farmhouse with glorious views across rolling countryside. Its name originates from the cannon foundries that were located at Gun Hill. Expect a neat open-plan interior with comfortably furnished alcoves, several log fires and an Aga in the cosy main bar. Plank floors, thick candles on scrubbed tables, fresh flowers and bold artwork create a civilised feel, menus champion local produce and every dish is freshly prepared. Kick off with a game terrine with red onion compote, follow with pan-fried halibut with tarragon sauce, finish with a warm chocolate fondant. Worth hunting down in all seasons, it has a terrace and lawn for summer days. Pick up the 'Gun Walk' leaflet and explore the surrounding footpaths.

Meals: Lunch from £8.95. Dinner from £11.50. Bar meals from £5.60.

Closed: 3pm-6pm in winter. Open all day Sat, Sun & in summer.

Alex Tudor
The Gun,
Gun Hill,
Heathfield, TN21 0JU

Tel: +44 (0)1825 872361
Web: www.thegunhouse.co.uk

Entry 557 Map 5

Farm @ Friday Street

Langney

The imposing 17th-century building and its name are the sole reminders that it was a fully functioning farm until the early 1980s. Houses have replaced the fields and Langney has morphed into a suburb of Eastbourne, yet the old farmhouse continues to thrive as a pub serving good food to hungry residents. Beams and timbers abound, log fires blaze in brick fireplaces and fat candles flicker in the rambling and atmospheric old rooms. The dining extension, with soaring rafters and tables on two levels, has a private dining room and an open kitchen, delivering sausages and mash with onion gravy, battered cod with chunky chips, confit pork belly with garlic mash and mustard sauce, and sticky toffee pud. All day sandwiches (steak and red onion marmalade), best washed down with a pint of Landlord, complete the picture.

Meals: Starters from £5.95. Mains from £9.95.
Closed: Open all day.

Brian Whiting
Farm @ Friday Street,
15 Friday Street, Langney,
Eastbourne, BN23 8AP
Tel: +44 (0)1323 766049
Web: www.farmfridaystreet.com

Entry 558 Map 5

Sussex

The Sussex Ox

Polegate

Just below the South Downs, the Sussex Ox is a popular retreat with ramblers and A27 escapees – time it right and you'll catch a sunset from the garden. Jonny has invested well in refurbishing the rambling old place, and now there's a clean and civilised feel: cream walls, wonky timbers, wood or worn-brick floors, painted panelling, vases overflowing with lilies. Find a cushioned pew at a scrubbed pine table in the Garden Room for the best of the sweeping views. Daily printed menus list hearty, locally sourced choices – lunchtime sandwiches and soups, grilled whole plaice with sautéed potatoes, spinach and parmesan gnocchi, chocolate brownie with homemade banana and rum ice, artisan cheeses. Ales come from the Longman and Harveys breweries, best enjoyed in summer on the decked terrace. Views stretch over Firle Beacon and Cuckmere Valley.

Meals: Starters from £6.50. Mains from £12.95.
Closed: Open all day.

Jonny Bunt
The Sussex Ox,
Milton Street,
Polegate, BN26 5RL
Tel: +44 (0)1323 870840
Web: www.thesussexox.co.uk

Entry 559 Map 5

The Snowdrop Inn

Lewes

The former Victorian bargeman's pub is tucked away down a dead-end lane on the edge of town, semi-derelict with a rough reputation when Tony and Dominic took over in 2009. Now it's the heart of the community, a colourful local that appeals to all, welcoming families and dogs, ale aficionados and music lovers. The quirky barge theme to the décor creates a warm and cosy atmosphere, there's a passion for craft beers and Sussex ales, and the cooking is a big surprise. Daily menus offer good value fresh food prepared from local and organic ingredients – sweet potato and ginger soup, home-reared pork, Hophead ale sausages, Irish stew, apple crumble and custard. It's the base for the South Street Bonfire Society and they organise a brilliant beer festival as part of Lewes's Octoberfeast.

Meals Lunch & dinner from £10.50.
Sunday lunch from £10.50.

Closed Open all day.

Tony Leonard & Dominic McCartan
The Snowdrop Inn,
119 South Street,
Lewes, BN7 2BU

Tel +44 (0)1273 471018

Web www.thesnowdropinn.com

Entry 560 Map 4

Sussex

The Shepherd & Dog

Fulking

On a hill beside a stream in the heart of the Sussex Downs is a freehouse that started life as three cottages, now dedicated to food, cider and beer; it heaves at weekends and the setting is idyllic. Sit in the garden on a summer's day with a pint of Saxon brewed in Horsham or a sparkling cider from Orchard Pig, and let the children frolic. They're welcomed with swings and a fab menu, as indeed are you: drunken mussels; pan-roasted Sussex lamb rump with baby green veg; a hearty ploughman's. For winter there's an open fire at one end and a wood-burner at the other, for summer, a sloping lawned garden with a fabulous view; and a cracking barn extension for special occasions. Thanks to gin and jazz festivals, Sunday roasts "with dripping potatoes and honey parsnips," David, Emily and their lovely staff, this is one special pub.

Meals Bar snacks from £2.
Dinner from £12.50.

Closed Open all day.

David & Emily Pearse
The Shepherd & Dog,
The Street, Fulking,
Henfield, BN5 9LU

Tel +44 (0)1273 857382

Web www.shepherdanddogpub.co.uk

Entry 561 Map 4

The Ginger Fox

Albourne

This country pub looks splendidly traditional, its thatch crowned by a fox stalking a pheasant. The second of Ben McKeller's Sussex Gingerman pubs, it has a contemporary zing. Both its aim (to create modern British dishes from the finest produce) and its look (armchairs, stone floors, open fires) are close to the Hove original – a cool uncluttered style blends with the old. Chalked-up menus are short and to the point: wood pigeon with bacon and foie gras croquette; brill fillet, cuttlefish, creamed leeks and salsify; and Redlands Farm beef fillet with cauliflower cheese purée. For veggies there's a splendid tasting platter: Guinness and cheddar soup; goat's cheese croquettes with walnut pesto; poached egg with spinach and hollandaise, beetroot, celeriac and apple salad. A favourite with well-heeled locals, so make sure you book; it gets busy!

Meals	Lunch & dinner £10.50-£16.50.
Closed	Open all day.

Ben Mckellar
The Ginger Fox,
Muddleswood Road, Albourne,
Hassocks, BN6 9EA
Tel +44 (0)1273 857888
Web thegingerfox.com

Entry 562 Map 4

Sussex

Royal Oak

Wineham

The part-tiled, part-timbered cottage – almost lost down a country road – is six centuries old and has been refreshing locals for two. In the charming bar and tiny rear room are brick and boarded floors, a huge log-fired inglenook, sturdy rustic furniture, and antique corkscrews, pottery jugs and aged artefacts hanging from low-slung beams. Michael and Sharon Bailey have changed little since taking over in 2007, drawing Harveys Best straight from the cask (no pumps) and, in keeping with ale house tradition, delivering a menu of freshly made pub food using locally sourced produce. Expect an updated full menu as well as a light lunch: sandwiches, ploughman's, hearty soups. No music or electronic hubbub, just traditional pub games, makes this heart-warmer a rural survivor.

Meals	Lunch & dinner £8.95-£15.95.
Closed	2.30pm-5.30pm (3.30pm-6pm Sat, 4pm-7pm Sun).

Michael & Sharon Bailey
Royal Oak,
Wineham Lane,
Wineham, BN5 9AY
Tel +44 (0)1444 881252

Entry 563 Map 4

The Crabtree

Lower Beeding

Welcome to a former haunt of Hilaire Belloc, who'd sit in the garden munching bread and Sussex cheese. You can do the same, on benches topped with fleeces, with bread from the on-site bakery. This country pub has it all: a vast inglenook stacked with logs, lots of cosy flagstone'd corners, a daily menu that supports local producers, and a rather stylish wine list. Pop in for a pint and a pie, a scrumptious snack (Scotch egg and curried mayo, red pepper hummus with spiced flatbread) or three beautifully presented courses. There are great Sunday lunches too, and a kids' menu that will delight. Get chatty in the open bar filled with light from the big sash window; find a wicker chair in the sunshiney Garden Room, where a dresser overflows with biscotti and crabapple jellies. There are local events on Fridays, sweet Sussex views and the staff are totally on the ball.

Meals	Lunch from £10. Dinner from £12. Sunday lunch, 2 courses, £16.
Closed	Open all day.

Simon Hope
The Crabtree,
Brighton Road, Lower Beeding,
Horsham, RH13 6PT

Tel +44 (0)1403 892666
Web www.crabtreesussex.co.uk

Entry 564 Map 4

The Three Crowns

Wisborough Green

Landlord Tim Skinner's bonhomie helps to keep the customers coming at this convenient and convivial roadside pub. Exposed brick walls, parquet flooring and wooden beams give an old-time feel but it's bright and welcoming in the summer, cosy by the fire on cooler days. Relax in a comfy chair for afternoon tea, dine from wooden tables, or settle down beneath a heater on the large terrace to the rear. Local ingredients are used in innovative ways for the international and seasonal menu: chicken satay and Thai spiced crab; Sussex smoked haddock, seafood platter or Portobello mushroom burger. Sunday roasts come with their own mini versions for children. For grown-up tipples, try the Crown Inn Glory or guest ales. The gin menu – with nutmeg, with hibiscus, with grains of paradise – rather hits the spot.

Meals	Starters from £7. Dinner from £10.
Closed	Open all day.

Tim Skinner
The Three Crowns,
Billingshurst Road,
Wisborough Green, RH14 0DX

Tel +44 (0)1403 700239
Web www.thethreecrownsinn.com

Entry 565 Map 4

The Stag

Balls Cross

The quintessential Sussex pub – some might say (and often do), the best pub in the world. Beneath 16th-century beams by a crackling fire – or out in the garden in summer – riders, walkers and locals enjoy a natter over well-kept Badger and Sussex Bitter. Wholesome home-cooked food is another draw, the traditional suet puddings and jam roly polys being the biggest temptation; note too a fine mutton and pearl barley broth. A sweet shop in a former life, this little inn still pulls the children in; today there's a room in which they may play undisturbed. Lots for adults too: a darts team, jazz nights in summer, the Mummers at Christmas. Find a 17th-century stone-floored bar, a large old clock that ticks above the inglenook, a dining room carpeted and cosy, and a tethering post should you drop by with your horse.

Meals	Lunch & dinner £7.50-£18. Bar meals £6-£18. Not Sun or Mon eves.
Closed	3pm-6pm Mon-Fri. Open all day Sat & Sun.

Erika Godsland
The Stag,
Balls Cross,
Petworth, GU28 9JP
Tel +44 (0)1403 820241
Web staginnpetworth.co.uk

Entry 566 Map 4

Noah's Ark

Lurgashall

In an idyllic setting – beside village pond and churchyard, overlooking a cricket green – the Ark restores faith in the future of the English country pub. In Henry and Amy's hands, this old village boozer has become a place of charm; no more darts, but a surprise at every turn. From bar to cosy dining areas – and one barn-like room – are beams, parquet flooring, open fires, traditional country furniture and a sprinkling of modern leather. The kitchen's insistence on good-quality (local, seasonal) produce results in a roll-call of British dishes; come evening, the simple bar menu is bolstered by such dishes as pan-fried wood pigeon breast with sautéed savoy cabbage and crispy pancetta. A cottagey garden to the side and picnic tables out front complete the very pleasing package.

Meals	Bar meals £6-£7.50. Mains £12.50-£22.50. Sunday lunch, 3 courses, £30.
Closed	Open all day.

Henry Coghlan & Amy Whitmore
Noah's Ark,
Lurgashall,
Petworth, GU28 9ET
Tel +44 (0)1428 707346
Web www.noahsarkinn.co.uk

Entry 567 Map 4

The Duke of Cumberland Arms

Henley

In the spring the Duke looks divine, its cottage walls engulfed by flowering wisteria. Beyond is the tiered garden, with babbling pools and huge Weald views. Latch doors lead to two tiny bars that creak with character – well-worn tongue-and-groove walls, low ceilings, scrubbed tables, log fires in the grate. Choose a pint of Hip Hop or Goodwood Organic Blonde from the cask. Rescued from closure by a local a few years back, the Duke has Simon Goodman as chef-landlord (2010 Pub Chef of the Year), and the new dining room, a light, modern, country confection with a big fire, is a show-stopper. And there's a terrace with a marvellous view. Daily menus rely on fresh local produce, including Goodwood organic rib-eye steak, estate venison and South Downs lamb; Sunday roasts are brought as a joint to the table and the fresh Irish oyster platter is a treasure.

Meals: Lunch £7.95-£28.95.
Dinner £16.95-£28.95.
Dessert £7-£9.50.

Closed: 3pm-5pm in winter.
Open all day in summer.

Simon Goodman
The Duke of Cumberland Arms,
Henley,
Haslemere, GU27 3HQ

Tel: +44 (0)1428 652280
Web: www.dukeofcumberland.com

Entry 568 Map 4

Sussex

Halfway Bridge Inn

Halfway Bridge

Fancy visiting Petworth House or a walk on Wittering Beach? Sam Bakose has set to work his magic on this mellow old coaching inn deep in polo country, just back from the A272. A series of spruced-up rooms comes with cosy corners and split levels, the bar with a modern look, the rest more traditional: scrubbed tables, crackling fires, fat candles. Thirsts are quenched by local Langham and Long Man beers and 25 wines by the glass, and the food is a satisfying mix of traditional and modern British, the menus evolving with the seasons. Tuck into moules and chips at the bar or pork belly and black pudding terrine, or baked bream with clam and caper butter – and leave room for prune and armagnac tart! For summer there's a sheltered patio with posh tables and parasols.

Meals: Lunch & dinner £14.50-£28.
Bar meals £6.50-£12.50.

Closed: Open all day.

Sam Bakose
Halfway Bridge Inn,
Halfway Bridge, Lodsworth,
Petworth, GU28 9BP

Tel: +44 (0)1798 861281
Web: www.halfwaybridge.co.uk

Entry 569 Map 4

The Fox Goes Free

Charlton

King William III may have stopped off here to refresh his hunting parties. Now this 400-year-old flint pub, secreted away in the South Downs, is home to fine ales from local breweries. Settle down by a blazing fire under beamed ceilings for a pint of Ballards Best and the pub's own Fox Goes Free; in summer you have a garden with farmland views. The traditional bar food suits the surroundings, with scrubbed tables and choir chairs. Everything from the chips to the ice cream is homemade; tuck into Cumberland sausages with bubble and squeak and onion marmalade, or whole baked camembert, confit garlic and toast fingers. Main courses are tempting too, with locally reared Tamworth pork or roasted monkfish. Goodwood racecourse is up the hill, downland walks start from the door.

Meals	Lunch & dinner £10.95-£17.50. Bar meals £10.95-£12.50. Sunday lunch £10.50-£15.95.
Closed	Open all day. Not 26 Dec eve or 1 Jan eve.

David Coxon
The Fox Goes Free,
Charlton,
Chichester, PO18 0HU
Tel +44 (0)1243 811461
Web www.thefoxgoesfree.com

Entry 570 Map 4

The George

Eartham

Tucked away in the South Downs is a very English cosy pub. It's not just the Cath Kidston country kitchen bar and the Saint George references that wave the British flag; behind the bar are artisan beers, stouts, meads, cordials, and British and Commonwealth wines. Well-kept beers such as Goodwood Organic Sussex Ale make a fine accompaniment to the locally sourced dishes: Sussex rarebit on artisan bread; pork chops with butternut squash mash, leeks and apple and ale gravy; seasonal fruit crumbles. In summer there's a pretty garden for barbecues and James's annual beer festival. What's more, you're so near the glorious South Downs (they know all the routes) that there's every excuse for a spot of Sussex cheese board indulgence before striding uphill.

Meals	Lunch & dinner £9.50-£17.95.
Closed	Open all day.

James Anthony Thompson
The George,
Eartham,
Chichester, PO18 0LT
Tel +44 (0)1243 814340
Web www.thegeorgeeartham.com

Entry 571 Map 4

The George at Burpham

Burpham

Tucked away in a sleepy South Downs village, this wonderful little pub that dates from the 1700s was facing extinction – until the locals bought it. Now it's back, run by locals, supplied by locals, and refurbished by locals too. By the welcoming fire, with a pint of the pub's own beer and homemade pork scratchings, it's easy to see why this was once a haunt for smugglers. Now folk enjoy simple and delicious dishes in the cosy bar or the cottagey dining areas; try game terrine with cranberry compote, and house beef burger with Welsh rarebit topping. The pub's motto may be 'by the locals, for the locals, of the locals' but visitors are extremely welcome. Which is just as well – if not, the treacle sponge with salted caramel ice cream would have to be smuggled out!

Meals	Lunch & dinner £9.75-£23.95.
Closed	3pm-6pm Mon-Fri.

Martin Bear
The George at Burpham,
Main Street, Burpham,
Arundel, BN18 9RR
Tel +44 (0)1903 883131
Web www.georgeatburpham.co.uk

Entry 572 Map 4

Anglesey Arms at Halnaker

Halnaker

Laid back, relaxed, free of airs and graces, a Georgian brick pub in charming West Sussex. This cracking local is lovingly run by George and Jools Jackson, both committed to keeping it charming and old-fashioned. Expect varnished and stripped pine, flagstones, beams and panelling, crackling log fires, locals at the bar, and a cosier, smarter dining room. Guest ales are local, food is fresh and home-cooked using great local produce – crab and lobster from Selsey, traceable meats in hearty pies: organic South Downs lamb and pork; well-hung beef from the Goodwood estate; venison and game from local shoots. Even the ciders, wines and spirits are organic. A great little local, with inter-pub cricket, golf and quizzes and regular 'moules and boules' events in the two-acre garden. Perfect for lazy summer afternoons.

Meals	Starters from £4.15. Mains from £7. Sunday lunch £13.
Closed	3pm-5.30pm. Open all day Sun.

George & Jools Jackson
Anglesey Arms at Halnaker,
Halnaker,
Chichester, PO18 0NQ
Tel +44 (0)1243 773474
Web www.angleseyarms.co.uk

Entry 573 Map 4

The Royal Oak Inn

East Lavant

There's a cheery wine-bar feel to the Royal Oak; locals and young professionals come with their children and it's as countrified as can be. Inside, a modern-rustic look with traditional touches prevails: stripped floors, exposed brickwork, dark leather sofas, open fires and racing pictures on the walls: this was once part of the Goodwood estate. The dining area is big, light and airy, with a conservatory from which you can amble out onto a terrace that's warmed by outdoor lamps on summer nights. At scrubbed-top tables you can tuck into delicious trio of Barbary duck, seared scallops on pumpkin purée, fig tart with pistachio ice cream. Staff are attentive, a secret garden looks over cornfields, and you're well-placed for Chichester Theatre and the boats at pretty Bosham.

Meals — Lunch from £7.95.
Dinner, 3 courses, about £35.
Sunday lunch £25-£29.

Closed — Open all day.

Charles Ullmann
The Royal Oak Inn,
Pook Lane, East Lavant,
Chichester, PO18 0AX
Tel +44 (0)1243 527434
Web www.royaloakeastlavant.co.uk

Entry 574 Map 4

The Earl of March

Lavant

Having been taken over by ex-Ritz chef Giles Thompson, this is one snappy performer. It's a clean-lined, fashionable space with a cosmopolitan vibe: modern leather seating in the bar area, high-backed suede chairs in the dining room, and sepia prints of racing cars and aircraft on the walls. Bolstered by specials, the up-tempo dining roster delivers game in season and wonderful fresh seafood. On the summer Champagne & Seafood menu are dressed Selsey crab salad, king prawns with mayonnaise, whole smoked mackerel with saffron rouille. There's a bar and terrace menu, too (Sussex ham and eggs, beer-battered haddock) and great South Downs views from terrace and the dining area. Faultless service, gorgeous food, and it's child friendly.

Meals — Lunch from £12.50.
Bar meals from £10.50.
Dinner from £18.50.
Sunday lunch, 3 courses, £21.50.

Closed — Open all day.

Giles Thompson
The Earl of March,
Lavant,
Chichester, PO18 0BQ
Tel +44 (0)1243 533 993
Web www.theearlofmarch.com

Entry 575 Map 4

Richmond Arms

West Ashling

This little beauty may hide away in an idyllic red-roofed village, but it's barely ten minutes from Chichester. The Jacks' conversion is warm, modern and hugely appealing, thanks to mellow pastel colours, a real fire in winter and chunky oak tables. There are local ales at the pint-sized central bar, and a feature wine rack to one side that announces the dining credentials; most come here to eat. The bar blackboard bubbles with fashionable grazing plates, from chorizo and lemon-crumbed sprats to Thai-spiced fish tempura, and all is produced with imagination and skill. Enjoy Sussex saltmarsh rib-eye (cooked over charcoal) with beef-dripping chips and béarnaise sauce, and peanut butter and chocolate fondant. Marvellous.

Meals	Lunch from £6.95. Bar meals from £4.95. Dinner from £15.95. Sunday lunch, 2-3 courses, £22.90-£29.65.
Closed	Sun eves. Mon & Tues. Christmas & New Year until mid-Jan.

William & Emma Jack
Richmond Arms,
Mill Road, West Ashling,
Chichester, PO18 8EA
Tel +44 (0)1243 572046
Web www.therichmondarms.co.uk

Entry 576 Map 4

The Crate & Apple

Chichester

Opened in 2016, it's a hit with everyone already: foodies, families, shoppers, sailors. Enter the pretty corner building to find a stylish open-plan space with pale walls and high ceilings, striking lamps above a zinc bar, an assortment of scrubbed wooden tables and a couple of smart brown chesterfields. Charlotte is front of house, Martin runs the kitchen, and seasonality is the key. This is inventive cooking of the most enjoyable kind and our Selsey crab Scotch egg was delicious. On the menu: fillets of bass, bavette steaks and Funtington pork, lunchtime sandwiches, handmade burgers, and a gorgeous baked aubergine with chickpea fritters. Summer puds include roast peaches, breakfast runs from 10 till 12, and drinks range from Hophead Beer to Belvoir Elderflower to a number of gins. And there's a big walled garden for barbecues.

Meals	Starters from £5.50. Lunch from £6. Dinner from £12.
Closed	Open all day.

Martin Bull
The Crate & Apple,
12-14 Westgate,
Chichester, PO19 3EU
Tel +44 (0)1243 539336
Web www.crateandapple.co.uk

Entry 577 Map 4

The Crab & Lobster

Sidlesham

Backing directly onto Pagham Harbour and the bird-rich marshes, the gentle Crab flaunts an inglenook fireplace and ancient flagstones that blend effortlessly with dark leather banquettes, ornate mirrors and vintage photos. This sparkling pub is managed by Sam but is often driven by the locals; Burns Night and wine evenings are big events. Windows offer endless sea views and there's a fishy focus to the menu, as you might expect – crab and lobster ravioli, organic sea trout with niçoise salad, Cornish sardines with black olive butter. Carnivores can tuck into lamb cutlets with roasted garlic and thyme jus, and all is served on stylish white plates. Enjoy a pint of local Sussex and choose a seat on the back terrace for views of sheep-grazed meadows and marshes.

Meals	Lunch from £10.50. Bar meals from £6.50. Dinner from £16.95. Sunday lunch, 2-3 courses, £24-£35.
Closed	Open all day.

Sam Bakose
The Crab & Lobster,
Mill Lane, Sidlesham,
Chichester, PO20 7NB
Tel +44 (0)1243 641233
Web www.crab-lobster.co.uk

Entry 578 Map 4

Photo: The Royal Oak Inn, entry 481

The Bell Alderminster

Alderminster

A lively inn on the Alscot estate with gardens that run down to a small river. There's a beautiful terrace, too, a popular spot for lunch in the sun, washed down by a pint of home-brewed ale. Inside, chic interiors mix of old and new to great effect – low beamed ceilings and exposed brick walls, then lots of colour and leather banquettes. You'll find candles everywhere, armchairs in front of the fire, black-and-white screen prints of estate life. Recent additions include an airy new restaurant with a wall of glass that opens onto the terrace, then a balcony above, where you can scoff afternoon tea while gazing out on open country. There's good food, too, with lamb and beef straight from the estate. You'll find sharing plates, soups and salads, perhaps seared tuna with chilli fritters, rump steak with a pepper sauce, banana sponge with toffee ice cream. Stylish bedrooms have smart fabrics, crisp linen, sofas or armchairs if there's room. Two are small, the suites are enormous and have gorgeous bathrooms. A road passes to the front, quietly at night. Stratford waits up the road for all things Shakespeare.

Rooms	5 doubles, 2 twins: £100-£145. 2 suites for 2: £150-£170. Singles from £75.
Meals	Bar meals from £7. Lunch, 2 courses, from £14.50. Dinner, 3 courses, from £18. Sunday lunch, 3 courses, £25.
Closed	Open all day.

The Manager
The Bell Alderminster,
Shipston Road, Alderminster,
Stratford-upon-Avon, CV37 8NY
Tel +44 (0)1789 450414
Web www.thebellald.co.uk

The Fuzzy Duck

Armscote

Nestled in the rolling folds of the Cotswold countryside, close to Stratford-upon-Avon, is this 18th-century coaching inn, polished to perfection by Tania, Adrian and their team. Beautiful fireplaces and gleaming tables, fine china and big sprays of wild flowers tell a tale of comfort and luxury, while the smiling staff are rightly proud of this gem of a pub. You dine like kings and queens in the sparkling bar, or in the clever conversion at the back, overlooking grounds that are part-orchard, part-walled-garden. Try Cotswold chicken breast with slow-cooked chorizo and white bean stew, or a splendid ploughman's with warm Scotch quail's egg. For pudding, try the zingy lemon posset, or treacle tart with orange scented milk ice. If you over-indulge, borrow wellies in your size for a bracing walk then back to your beautiful bed above the bar; rooms are sound-proofed and two have double loft beds (up very vertical ladders) for families. Best of all, the generous team has provided indulgent treats: lovely slippers; a nightcap tipple – come prepared to be spoiled. Bliss.

Rooms	2 doubles: £110-£140. 2 family rooms for 4: £180-£200.
Meals	Starters from £4.50. Mains from £9.95.
Closed	Monday until 6.30pm.

The Manager
The Fuzzy Duck,
Ilmington Road, Armscote,
Stratford-upon-Avon, CV37 8DD

Tel +44 (0)1608 682 635
Web www.fuzzyduckarmscote.com

The Howard Arms

Ilmington

The Howard stands on Ilmington Green, eight miles south of Stratford-upon-Avon. It was built at roughly the same time as Shakespeare wrote *King Lear* and little has changed since. It's a lovely country inn and comes with original fixtures and fittings: polished flagstones, heavy beams, mellow stone walls, a crackling fire. Outside, roses ramble on golden stone walls, while a pretty garden waits at the back. Good food comes as standard, perhaps ham hock terrine with homemade piccalilli, marinated duck breast with bok choy, apple tart tatin with mascarpone cream; there's fish and chips and a good burger, too. Elsewhere, you find oils on walls, books on shelves, settles in alcoves, beautiful bay windows. A colourful dining room floods with light courtesy of fine arched windows that overlook the green. Bedrooms in the main house have a charming old-world feel, garden rooms are more contemporary with excellent bathrooms. You can walk across fields to Chipping Campden; Simon de Montfort once owned this land. The village church dates to the 11th century and has Thompson mice within.

Rooms	5 doubles, 3 twin/doubles: £110-£130. Singles £75.
Meals	Lunch from £4.50. Dinner from £10.50.
Closed	Open all day.

Robert Jeal
The Howard Arms,
Lower Green,
Ilmington, CV36 4LT

Tel	+44 (0)1608 682226
Web	www.howardarms.com

The George Townhouse

Shipston-on-Stour

Celebrate the refurbishment of this gloriously handsome inn with a pint of Brakspear Best Bitter at the long bar that gleams with speciality gins and wonderful wines. Slap-bang in the centre of pretty Shipston, the new-look George is a treat of a place to eat, drink and be merry. Full of snug corners to settle and private spaces for family gatherings, you'll struggle to find a more cheering spot so close to Stratford and the lure of the Cotswolds. With deep blue velvet banquettes and mustard yellow velvet chairs, colourful rugs and a choice of log burners to sit beside as you tuck into menus that make the most of local suppliers (pork and beef from the award-winning Todenham Manor Farm; artisan bread). Our Welsh rarebit with roasted tomato was excellent, topped up with a hearty mug of potato and leek soup, but you might fancy wild mushroom and tarragon risotto with spring onions and truffled crispy egg, or the locals' favourite fishcakes. Bedrooms are above – some cosy, others spacious – all with kingsize beds, Feather & Black mattresses and blackout blinds to ensure a good night's sleep. The Cotswolds Distillery is nearby, as is the Wychwood Brewery. Smashing.

Rooms	14 doubles: £100-£180. 1 suite for 2: £200-£240.
Meals	Starters from £5. Lunch & dinner from £9.
Closed	Open all day.

Emma Sweet
The George Townhouse,
8 High Street,
Shipston-on-Stour, CV36 4AJ

Tel +44 (0)1608 661453
Web www.thegeorgeshipston.co.uk

The Red Lion

Long Compton

Dogs are welcome in this ancient warren of a pub where canine sketches adorn the walls; 'the Landlady' – the pub's own chocolate lab – is often around. Enter to a mouthwatering aroma of imaginative dishes from chef/co-patron Sarah Keightley. Crispy-battered cod and chips with caper berries and mushy peas are served on *The Red Lion Times*, and pork tenderloin comes wrapped in pancetta with apple purée and black pudding. A meltingly warm pear and ginger pudding with toffee sauce rounds it all off nicely. Easy to find, this characterful pub has benefited from a wonderful refurb and there's space for everyone, from the pool room to the restaurant to the beautiful flagged bar with fire and wood-burning stove. There are five bedrooms too, the quietest at the back, which reflect the unfussy approach: natural colours and crisp ginghams; comfort and attention to quality make up for their size, though the King Room has an ante chamber should anyone snore! It is cheerful, hospitable, and breakfasts are worth waking up for.

Rooms	2 doubles, 1 twin: £95-£130. 1 family room for 4: £115-£150. 1 single: £60.
Meals	Lunch & dinner £11.95-£18.95.
Closed	2.30pm-6pm Mon-Thurs. Open all day Fri-Sun & bank hols.

Lisa Phipps & Sarah Keightley
The Red Lion,
Main Street, Long Compton,
Shipston-on-Stour, CV36 5JS
Tel +44 (0)1608 684221
Web www.redlion-longcompton.co.uk

The Chequers Inn

Ettington

New life has been breathed into this north Cotswold pub by Kirstin and James – and how! A bold style of classic British meets country French thanks to rich tapestries, gilt mirrors, padded chairs, round tables and aged wooden flooring throughout. There is a proper glowing wood bar with St Austell Tribute and London Pride on tap; plus Stowford Press cider, an impressive wine selection and several varieties of fizz for special occasions. The calm, elegant Provençal dining area at the back overlooks a well-planted and sheltered garden which hides the chef's veg patch. Start with honey-glazed crispy duck salad with hoisin dressing and cashew nuts, move on to brill with buttered mash and gremolata. The puds will also tempt, and then there's freshly ground coffee. Different, slightly decadent, and definitely worth a visit.

Meals	Lunch & bar meals from £4.50. Dinner £9.50-£16.95. Set lunch, 3 courses, £23.45.
Closed	3pm-5pm. Sun eves & Mon.

James & Kirstin Viggers
The Chequers Inn,
91 Banbury Road, Ettington,
Stratford-upon-Avon, CV37 7SR
Tel +44 (0)1789 740387
Web www.the-chequers-ettington.co.uk

Entry 584 Map 8

Bell Inn

Welford-on-Avon

If things Shakespearian inspire you, then the timbered high street's 17th-century Bell will not disappoint. There is a richness about the natural oak beams and settles, the stone floors strewn with Persian rugs, the dog-grates cradling glowing embers. This is a historic village inn that serves top-quality, locally sourced food, be it simple pub favourites such as pork loin with sausage and bean cassoulet or a more Gallic beef bourguignon served with mash. Don't miss the Indian-inspired Fridays, or the excellent wine list. If you're into food provenance, every supplier is listed on the back of the menu and they are almost all small independents. Staff are happy, attentive and long-serving. Cask ales, kids' portions – a wonderful traditional English pub.

Meals	Lunch & dinner £9.95-£18.50. Bar meals from £5. Sunday lunch £12.95-£13.75.
Closed	3pm-6pm. Open all day Sat & Sun.

Colin & Teresa Ombler
Bell Inn,
Binton Road, Welford-on-Avon,
Stratford-upon-Avon, CV37 8EB
Tel +44 (0)1789 750353
Web www.thebellwelford.co.uk

Entry 585 Map 8

The Bell Inn

Ladbroke

A pub with a pleasing front and a respectable air, and one that's easy to find. It stands opposite a lovely Tudor thatch house and its young owners attract a diverse crowd: tweedy checkshirts, comfortable couples, young mums with their laptops. The aim is to cook the best seasonal produce and to keep it simple, and the service is quick, attentive and cheerful – perfect. Huw knows his food and is attuned to the talents of his chef, Steve. Our fillet of plaice with dill sauce couldn't have been fresher, and the berry-and-apple crumble came with a delicious jug of just-made custard. There's a bistro pub feel, nothing too heavy or too shiny, with open fires in the bar in winter and a dining area that leads seamlessly to the back. The garden potters to a small stream – enjoy a pint of Boon Doggle, but keep an eye on little ones!

Meals	Lunch & dinner £13.50-£16.50.
Closed	Mondays all day.

Ruth & Huw Griffiths
The Bell Inn,
Banbury Road,
Ladbroke, CV47 2BY

Tel	+44 (0)1926 811224
Web	www.thebellinnladbroke.co.uk

Entry 586 Map 8

Warwickshire

The Stag at Offchurch

Offchurch

This lovely old thatched building tempts you to step inside. You'll probably stay for lunch or supper, the food is a real draw, perhaps roasted beetroot and locally cured Oxprings ham salad, followed by roasted turbot with crushed new potatoes, fine green beans and a clam and Pernod emulsion, finished off with white chocolate and vodka parfait. The copper bar gleams, walls and beams are painted cream to maximise the light and a couple of wallpapered feature walls add interest. Happy attentive staff make everything run smoothly, so pull up a colourful tub chair and sit at dark wooden tables on stripped floors in the bar, cosy up by the wood-burner or open fire; or spill onto the terrace, you're on the outskirts of the pretty village of Offspring with neat Warwickshire countryside all around. Well-heeled locals make the place feel nicely busy.

Meals	Lunch from £6.50. Dinner from £12.50.
Closed	Open all day.

Lizzie Harris
The Stag at Offchurch,
Welsh Road, Offchurch,
Leamington Spa, CV33 9AQ

Tel	+44 (0)1926 425801
Web	www.thestagatoffchurch.com

Entry 587 Map 8

The Drawing Board

Leamington Spa

It's a great place to live is Leamington Spa: shops, cafés, bars, open spaces, Regency houses and now The Drawing Board to enjoy. Theatregoers and foodies love it, and the décor is just like the youthful staff: vibrant and fun. The exterior is white stucco with sash windows, the interiors large and open plan. Spread over two floors, squishy leather sofas and glossy chesterfields mix with steel-legged stools and quirky zinc touches. There are log-burners, vintage annuals, plants (stylish ones), a pretty antler, a bike (of course) and old comic books framed on the walls. Pop in for a malt, a macchiato, a local ale, and stay: the food is seasonal, trendy and exciting. Breast of Barbury duck with potato terrine, braised endive and orange, or a rare roast beef dripping-dipped brioche. Dogs are more than welcome, too.

Meals — Small plates from £4.50.
Dinner from £10.95.

Closed — Open all day.

Sam Cornwall-Jones
The Drawing Board,
18 Newbold Street,
Leamington Spa, CV32 4HN
Tel +44 (0)1926 330636
Web www.thedrawingboard.pub

Entry 588 Map 8

Warwickshire

The Rose & Crown

Warwick

Peach Pubs' flagship Rose and Crown opens for bacon sarnies at breakfast and stays open all day. Enter the cheery front bar with its red and white walls, big leather sofas, and a crackling winter fire. To the back is the bustling eating area and a private room for parties. The food is scrummy and children enjoy downsized versions from the main menu. The tapas-style portions of cheeses, hams, mixed olives and rustic breads slip down easily with a pint of Purity Gold or a glass of pinot, while hot dishes are modern British with a Mediterranean slant. Try roast cod with pea purée, smoked haddock and prawn pie with winter greens, or Cornish lamb casserole with creamy mash. Young, fun and conveniently central for Warwick, which has history in spades.

Meals — Lunch from £7. Bar meals £5.
Dinner from £11.
Sunday lunch £13.50.

Closed — Open all day.

Suzie Ayling
The Rose & Crown,
30 Market Place,
Warwick, CV34 4SH
Tel +44 (0)1926 411117
Web www.roseandcrownwarwick.co.uk

Entry 589 Map 8

The Crabmill

Preston Bagot

The lovely, rambling building, with tiny leaded windows and wonky beams, once contained a cider press. Later a pub, now it's a gastro haven with a dining room for every mood – one stone and scented with lilies, another brown, its walls hung with risqué drawings; the third is a candlelit mushroom-cream. There's a steely bar with sandblasted glass panels, great flagstones and a winter fire. At the back, a split-level lounge with wooden floors, elegant tub chairs and a garden that heads off into open countryside; there's also a stylish paved area outside. The food is popular and the dishes imaginative and colourful, from simple soup to ploughman's with pork pie and pickles to roast pork belly with black pudding.

Meals: Lunch & dinner £5.95-£18.95. Sunday lunch £12.75.
Closed: Open all day. Closed Sun from 6pm.

Sally Coll
The Crabmill,
Preston Bagot,
Henley-in-Arden, B95 5EE
Tel +44 (0)1926 843342
Web www.thecrabmill.co.uk

Entry 590 Map 8

The Bluebell

Henley-in-Arden

Leigh and Duncan Taylor went to town updating this 500-year-old coaching inn – one of the most distinctive bistro pubs in the country. A clever combination of country casual and urban chic means atmosphere and style are delivered in spades: bold colours and striking furniture meet ancient beams, flagstones and a big fireplace. Real ales, wines and an irresistible menu draw keen diners from far and near, ingredients are sourced with care, vegetables are grown on the owners' allotment. The menu combines colourful modern dishes – dill-cured Loch Duart salmon, Salcombe crab fritter, and Jimmy Butler's free-range pork for two (loin, belly, cheeks, crackling). Beer-battered haddock with hand-cooked chips is a favourite. Lunch on the decked area is sublime.

Meals: Lunch & dinner £13-£19. Set menu £15 & £18. Sunday lunch £13.95. Afternoon tea £15. No food on Sun eves.
Closed: Mon (except bank hols).

Duncan & Leigh Taylor
The Bluebell,
93 High Street,
Henley-in-Arden, B95 5AT
Tel +44 (0)1564 793049
Web www.bluebellhenley.co.uk

Entry 591 Map 8

The Case is Altered

Five Ways

No food, no mobiles and a Sopwith Pup propeller suspended from the ceiling – a Warwickshire treasure. There's even a vintage bar billiards machine, operated by sixpences from behind the bar. In the main room are terracotta tiles, leather-covered settles and walls covered in yellowing posters offering beverages at a penny a pint. Jackie does not open her arms to children or dogs: this is a place for liquid refreshment only – and devotees travel some distance for the homemade pork scratchings and the expertly kept beer. The sign used to show lawyers arguing but the name has nothing to do with the law; once it was, simply, 'The Case', and so small that it was not eligible for a spirit licence. Later it was made larger, the name was changed, and everyone was happy. They've been that way ever since.

Meals	No food served.
Closed	2.30pm-6pm (2.15pm-7pm Sun).

Jackie & Charlie Willacy
The Case is Altered,
Case Lane, Five Ways,
Hatton,
Warwick, CV35 7JD

Tel +44 (0)1926 484206

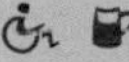

Entry 592 Map 8

Warwickshire

The Boot Inn

Lapworth

The Boot was here long before the canal that runs past the back garden. With its exposed timbers, quarry floors, open fires and daily papers it combines old-fashioned charm with rustic chic. Under the guidance of Paul Salisbury and James Elliot, the once down-at-heel boozer became one of the first gastropubs of the Midlands. Menus have a distinct touch of Mediterranean and Pacific rim: fresh tian of spiced crab; Asian five-spice duck breast; dukkah-spiced rack of lamb; great Greek sharing plates topped with olives. Ingredients are as fresh as can be and seafood dishes are a speciality. Eat in the lounge or in the stylishly revamped dining room upstairs. In summer, go al fresco: there's a lovely terrace to the side.

Meals	Lunch from £6. Dinner from £9. Sunday lunch £12.95.
Closed	Open all day.

Paul Salisbury & James Elliot
The Boot Inn,
Old Warwick Road, Lapworth,
Solihull, B94 6JU

Tel +44 (0)1564 782464
Web www.lovelypubs.co.uk

Entry 593 Map 8

The Punchbowl

Lapworth

The Punchbowl comes with a big pubby fire and a friendly bar dispensing Timothy Taylor's Landlord. But the building is new; the original burnt down a few years ago. James Feeney has a flair for design and from simple materials has created contemporary opulence: candelabra on long tables, ornate mirrors on brick walls, and windows swept by crushed velvet. And the food is really delicious – we chose a sharing platter of seared scallops with dressed crab, grilled prawns and fishcakes. Beef Wellington comes with wilted spinach and smoked potato purée, Gressingham duck breast with potato rösti, maple and black pepper. Thatcher's Gold cider washes it all down beautifully, there's a vegetarian dish of the day and the glassed-in patio has a conservatory feel.

Meals Lunch from £5.95.
Dinner from £9.95.
Closed Open all day.

James Feeney
The Punchbowl,
Mill Lane, Lapworth,
Solihull, B94 6HR
Tel +44 (0)1564 784564
Web www.thepunchbowllapworth.com

Entry 594 Map 8

Warwickshire

The Orange Tree

Chadwick End

The flagship pub of Classic Country Pubs has a striking interior. You'll love the earthy colours, the low limewashed beams, the log fires, big lamps, deep sofas around low tables and the airy dining rooms. This tastefully rustic décor, Mediterranean with oriental touches, is matched by an ambitious, Italian-inspired menu – note the gorgeous Italian-style deli counter showing off breads, cheeses and vintage oils. Food-lovers descend in droves for authentic fired pizzas and full-flavoured meat dishes cooked on the on-view rotisserie spit. There's homemade pasta, delicious warm salads, fish specials. All this plus great wines by the bottle or glass, real ales, a heated patio dotted with teak tables and all-day opening hours.

Meals Lunch & bar meals from £5.95.
Dinner £7.95-£25.95.
Sunday lunch from £12.95.
No food on Sun eves.
Closed Open all day.

Paul Hales
The Orange Tree,
Warwick Road, Chadwick End,
Solihull, B93 0BN
Tel +44 (0)1564 785364
Web www.theorangetreepub.co.uk

Entry 595 Map 8

The Almanack

Kenilworth

Clever Peach Pubs continues to reinvent the gastropub. This, their tenth venture, is a swish new-build beneath apartments in Kenilworth town centre. It opened in 2009 and business has boomed since. Although more trendy bar-restaurant than pub, there's a vast island bar, lots of spacious informal seating and local Purity ales on tap. Expect a cool retro feel, with vintage 60s and 70s armchairs and sofas and a colourfully eclectic décor throughout. Pop in for breakfast or coffee and cake and settle down to free WiFi – or graze from a modern pub menu. In the all-day, open-to-view kitchen, corned beef hash and BLT sandwiches are created, along with substantial lunches and suppers: a daily roast, coq au vin with creamy mash, a fish deli-board, duck with redcurrant jus. Young and fun.

Meals	Lunch from £6.75. Bar meals from £5. Dinner from £11. Sunday lunch £13.95.
Closed	Open all day.

Jonathan Carter
The Almanack,
Abbey End North,
Kenilworth, CV8 1QJ
Tel +44 (0)1926 353637
Web www.thealmanack-kenilworth.co.uk

Entry 596 Map 8

The Malt Shovel at Barston

Barston

A smart, bright, food-driven place that knows its market and caters to it well. Whether you're ensconced in the powder-blue and cream bar (with a fire in the grate at the far end), on the trellis-shaded terrace in summer, or in the country restaurant, the food is to savour, and the Tribute and Old Speckled Hen are matched by decent wines. The menu covers international as well as pubby treats (Aberdeenshire rump steak; crayfish and cress breaded scampi with lemon and lavender dressing; sticky toffee pudding with clotted cream ice cream) and executes both with aplomb. The culinary innovation extends to the vegetarian options, perhaps a filo tart of crushed carrot topped with a poached egg, courgette strips and rocket pesto. A slick operation out in the country, warm, friendly and relaxed.

Meals	Lunch & dinner £11.95–£21.50. Not Sun eve.
Closed	Open all day.

Helen Somerfield
The Malt Shovel at Barston,
Barston Lane, Barston,
Solihull, B92 0JP
Tel +44 (0)1675 443223
Web www.themaltshovelatbarston.com

Entry 597 Map 8

The Bell at Ramsbury

Ramsbury

New owners have snapped up The Bell, creating a classy new-wave inn and one that showcases Ramsbury Estate produce. Come for Ramsbury beers, kitchen garden fruit and veg, and seasonal game. Completing this pleasing picture are nine stunning bedrooms named after game birds and fish. Cosy lodgings for fishermen, and for those exploring the glorious Marlborough Downs, they come with soothing Farrow & Ball colours, rich fabrics, down duvets, big beds, vintage books, and super bathrooms with rain showers, White Company lotions and heated slate floors. Back downstairs, accompany your fish and chips with a pint of Gold in the smart, hop-adorned bar, or bag the sofa in the library-style lounge and entertain yourself with a copy of *The Field*. Or pop into the stylish restaurant for assiette of spring lamb, followed by lemon ice mousse perhaps. There's also a wonderful little café (Café Bella) at the back serving teas, coffee and cakes during the day. As for the village, it's really pretty, and the pub, sprucely off the main square, is 100 yards from the river bank.

Rooms	7 doubles, 2 twins: £110-£150.
Meals	Lunch £20-£25. Bar meals £7-£17. Dinner £30-£45. Sunday lunch, 2 courses, £19.50.
Closed	Open all day.

Ramsbury Estates
The Bell at Ramsbury,
The Square, Ramsbury,
Marlborough, SN8 2PE

Tel +44 (0)1672 520230
Web www.thebellramsbury.com

The White Horse Inn

Compton Bassett

Whitewashed walls echo the chalk horse that gave its name to this very handsome village inn. Inside all is as neat as a new pin. Lovingly polished parquet glows beneath scrubbed wooden tables, while padded bar stools and assorted chairs – some antique and carved – are well spaced around the reclaimed oak bar, a beautiful piece of recycling. Having been a grocer's shop, a bakery and an inn during its long life the pub now focuses on what it does best: providing great food and drink to villagers and visitors. Eat by the sturdy wood-burner in the bar or in the elegant terracotta dining area with its beams and mullioned windows. Lunches are relaxed affairs of sandwiches and pub classics. Dinner lists pork and game from the pub's own farm in season – and children are well looked after. In the old stable lie eight simple but comfortable rooms, with pine furniture and pretty fabrics. Many have views to paddocks, sheep and geese, all are blissfully peaceful at night. A super pub from start to finish – very friendly, too.

Rooms	3 doubles: £85-£95. 3 family rooms for 4: £110-£120. 2 singles: £75-£85.
Meals	Lunch from £9.95. Bar meals from £5.95. Dinner from £11.95. Sunday lunch from £10.95.
Closed	Sunday eves & Monday.

Eva Novakova
The White Horse Inn,
Compton Bassett,
Calne, SN11 8RG

Tel +44 (0)1249 813118
Web www.whitehorse-comptonbassett.co.uk

Methuen Arms Hotel

Corsham

The Methuen has always changed with the times. It started life as a 14th-century nunnery, turned into a coaching inn and brewery in 1608, had a Georgian facelift in the late 1700s, then became a boutique hotel in 2010. It's a lovely little place – cosy and stylish with some gorgeous food. It sits on the edge of the village, with an avenue of trees around the corner leading up to Corsham Court, an Elizabethan pile. As for the hotel, there's a beautiful courtyard at the back where you can eat in summer, a restaurant that opens onto the garden, a locals' bar where the main currency is gossip, then a sitting-room bar where you can sink into an armchair in front of the wood-burner and enjoy a pint of Otter. Chic bedrooms are scattered about. You'll find warm colours, padded bedheads, good art, Roberts radios. There are robes in fine bathrooms, four of which have claw-foot baths, one of which is in the bedroom. Don't miss the excellent food, perhaps cream of shallot soup, monkfish wrapped in Parma ham, chocolate mousse with caramelized oranges. Sunday lunch draws a crowd. Bath is close.

Rooms	11 doubles, 2 twin/doubles: £140-£175. 1 family room for 4: £150-£220. Singles from £90.
Meals	Lunch from £5.95. Dinner, 3 courses, about £30. Sunday lunch £17.95-£21.95.
Closed	Open all day.

Drew Reilly-Sanderson
Methuen Arms Hotel,
2 High Street,
Corsham, SN13 0HB
Tel +44 (0)1249 717060
Web www.themethuenarms.com

Sign of the Angel

Lacock

You might find the cast of Downton Abbey staying at this 15th-century coaching inn – and for method actors, it must be a dream. Occupying centre-stage in one the prettiest of all Cotswold villages, the Sign of the Angel is a genuine period piece: all chalky whitewash and wonky beams, artful oak furniture and flagstoned passageways. The inn was taken over by energetic young brothers Tom and Jack last year, and has been impeccably renovated to trumpet its age. The owners are from farming stock, and it shows in Chef Patron Jon's menu: everything from the bread to the sorbets are locally sourced and homemade: warm mackerel rarebit, brioche and heritage tomato salad; baked tenderloin in local bacon stuffed with pear and Bath cheese; Bramley crumble with toffee apple ice cream. Upstairs, the bedrooms let the antique architecture do the talking: pretty box windows and wainscotting; beams that extend into the bathrooms as well as the bedrooms. The duck-feather bed linen is a narcoleptic's nightmare, and the chef's home-made cookies are waiting on your tea tray.

Rooms	5 doubles: £120-£140.
Meals	Lunch from £5.50. Dinner from £16. Sunday lunch, 2-3 courses £19-£22. Cream teas from £7.50.
Closed	Sunday evening & Monday all day.

Tom Nicholas
Sign of the Angel,
6 Church Street,
Lacock, SN15 2LB
Tel +44 (0)1249 730230
Web www.signoftheangel.co.uk

The Castle Inn

Bradford-on-Avon

On top of the hill that dips down to the mellow heart of Bradford-on-Avon, this heart-warming renovation of a neglected Bath stone inn is the work of Flatcappers, who, in their first foray into the world of real pubs, struck gold. Enter a warren of planked rooms – one large, three small – in muted greys, reds and greens, lovingly and imaginatively restored. Expect solid stone walls and little log fires, recycled chairs and long farmhouse tables, a leather sofa to sink into, books on the shelves, prints on the walls and a youthful vibe. Six ales from local breweries dominate the bar as locals pop in for a pint and the papers, and muted jazz plays. An Anglo-Saxon take on tapas stands alongside British pub classics, the specials are special (rabbit ragoût with handmade pappardelle) and our Sunday sirloin with Yorkshire pud was heaven. Above, four equally characterful bedrooms have modish wallpapers and stylish hues, wonky door frames and period fireplaces, stunning walk-in bathrooms and wide-reaching views of the church, or the White Horse on the Wiltshire hills. And breakfast lasts until 12!

Rooms	3 doubles: £100-£140. 1 family room for 4: £100-£140.
Meals	Lunch & dinner £7.95-£18.95.
Closed	Open all day.

Tori Hill
The Castle Inn,
Mount Pleasant,
Bradford-on-Avon, BA15 1SJ

Tel	+44 (0)1225 865 657
Web	www.flatcappers.co.uk/the-castle-inn/

The George & Dragon

Rowde

Behind the whitewashed exterior hides a low-ceilinged bar, its stone fireplace ablaze in winter, its half-panelled walls lined with old paintings, its antique clock ticking away the hours. Furnishings are authentically period, there are wooden boards in the dining room, painted walls and plenty of dark timber. The kitchen's chutneys and preserves are for sale, international bottled beers and organic ciders line the shelves and hand-pumped Butcombe Bitter announces itself on the bar. Experienced owners are maintaining the pub's reputation for fish delivered fresh from Cornwall – with the odd concession to meat eaters. There are puddings to diet for, and specials such as delectable chargrilled scallops with black pudding brochettes or whole grilled mackerel with anchovy butter. Rooms are charming and individual – Country, Classic or Funky – with wall timbers and wonky floors, contemporary wall coverings, White Company duvets and linen on wooden or brass beds; bathrooms are the business; the complimentary breakfast is continental. Great value, and a treat to come back to after a long walk along the Kennet & Avon Canal.

Rooms	2 twin/doubles: £75-£125. 1 family room for 2: £95-£125.
Meals	Lunch & dinner £9.95-£18.50. Sunday lunch £19.50.
Closed	Sunday eves.

Christopher Day
The George & Dragon,
High Street, Rowde,
Devizes, SN10 2PN
Tel +44 (0)1380 723053
Web www.thegeorgeanddragonrowde.co.uk

Red Lion Freehouse & Troutbeck Guest House

East Chisenbury

Unless you found yourself lost on Salisbury Plain, chances are you wouldn't stumble upon the Red Lion. You'd be missing much: this smart thatched village inn is a local serving ale from Wiltshire microbreweries, a restaurant drawing food lovers from far and wide, and, since December 2012, a glorious place to stay, with the addition of ultra cosy rooms in a spruced up property (Troutbeck) just down the lane. Having worked under Thomas Keller at the breathtaking Per Se restaurant in New York, owner-chefs Guy and Brittany Manning apply cutting-edge cookery techniques to simple rustic dishes and the results are very special. The Michelin-starred menu offers the likes of chicken liver pâté with madeira jelly, braised ox cheek with mash, bacon, and red wine, and caramel poached apples with candied walnuts and sage ice cream. Indulge yourself and then retire to one of the five very individual rooms; all have luxury Somnus beds, the finest cotton and down, Bang & Olufsen flatscreens, fluffy bathrobes and organic smellies in natural stone bathrooms, and a private deck with serene rural views across the Avon chalk stream. Bliss.

Rooms	5 doubles: £180-£265.
Meals	Lunch & dinner £15-£20. Bar meals from £7. Sunday lunch, 2 courses, £20.
Closed	Open all day.

Guy & Brittany Manning
Red Lion Freehouse & Troutbeck Guest House, East Chisenbury,
Pewsey, SN9 6AQ

Tel +44 (0)1980 671124
Web www.redlionfreehouse.com

The Beckford Arms

Fonthill Gifford

A country-house inn on the Fonthill estate. You sweep in under the Triumphal Arch, which seems appropriate – this is one of the loveliest inns in the land. Outside, in the garden, you find hammocks in the trees and parasols on the terrace, then a church spire soaring beyond. Georgian interiors are no less lovely, a mix of original features and 21st-century style. There's a drawing room with facing sofas in front of a roaring fire; a restaurant with a wall of glass that opens onto the terrace; a bar with parquet flooring for an excellent local pint. Potter about and chance upon the odd chandelier, roaming wisteria and a rather grand mahogany table in the private dining room. Bedrooms are small but perfectly formed with prices to match: white walls, the best linen, sisal matting, good bathrooms. If you want something bigger try the pavilions on the estate; former guests include Byron and Nelson, though we doubt they had it so good. As for the food, it's lovely stuff, perhaps Brixham clam chowder, whole lemon sole, chocolate and Cointreau delice with blood orange sorbet. One of the best.

Rooms	7 doubles, 1 twin/double: £95-£120. 2 pavilions for 2: £175-£195.
Meals	Main courses £9.95-£13.75.
Closed	Open all day.

Charlie Luxton
The Beckford Arms,
Fonthill Gifford,
Tisbury, Salisbury, SP3 6PX
Tel +44 (0)1747 870385
Web www.beckfordarms.com

The Royal Oak Inn

Swallowcliffe

Philanthropic gestures don't come much better than a group of locals financing the renovation of this once-disused village pub. That's what happened to the Royal Oak, now happily restored to the heart of the community. On a quiet village lane stands this whitewashed building with thatched roof and porch. Inside, neutral walls and a pastel palette are complemented by light oak furniture from a local carpenter and a cornucopia of beams in the dining room. All is airy and bright with floor to ceiling windows on two walls – a great spot for breakfasts of fresh fruit, muesli, or a full English with local sourdough bread. Bedrooms calm and soothe, each designed individually, with heavenly beds, Egyptian cotton linen, carefully toned fabrics and throws, and sparkling bathrooms. Open all day, this is somewhere to whittle away the hours reading the papers, playing board games, supping the local ales, brandy and cider, and tucking into great food with a local provenance. Head out to walk the surrounding countryside, visit stately homes, or explore Stonehenge, Shaftesbury and Hardy's Wessex.

Rooms	4 doubles, 2 twin/doubles: £100-£150.
Meals	Lunch from £5.25. Dinner from £10.95. Sunday lunch from £15.95.
Closed	Open all day.

Mark Treasure
The Royal Oak Inn,
Swallowcliffe,
Salisbury, SP3 5PA

Tel +44 (0)1747 870211
Web www.royaloakswallowcliffe.com

The Horseshoe Inn

Ebbesbourne Wake

The Ebble Valley and Ebbesbourne Wake appear to have escaped the modern age. A bucolic charm pervades this village inn, dozing down tiny lanes close to the Dorset border and run as a 'proper country pub' by the Bath family for 30 years. Climbing roses cling to the 17th-century brick façade, while the traditional layout – two bars around a central servery – survives. Old farming implements and country bygones fill every available cranny and a mix of furniture is arranged around the crackling winter fire. Beer is tapped straight from the cask and food is hearty and wholesome, prepared by Pat Bath using local meat and veg, and game from the shoots. Tuck into steak and kidney pie, fresh fish bake, nursery puddings and three roasts on Sundays (do book). Benches and flowers fill the garden.

Meals	Lunch & dinner £9.95-£17. Bar meals £4.95-£12.95. Sunday lunch from £9.50. Tues eve 'Simple Supper' £10.
Closed	3pm-6.30pm. Sun from 4pm & Mon until 7pm.

Anthony & Patricia Bath
The Horseshoe Inn,
The Cross, Ebbesbourne Wake,
Salisbury, SP5 5JF
Tel +44 (0)1722 780474
Web www.thehorseshoe-inn.co.uk

Entry 607 Map 3

Wiltshire

The Forester Inn

Donhead St Andrew

Tiny lanes frothing with cowparsley twist down to this wonderful little pub. The revitalised 600-year-old inn has rustic walls and low dark beams, logs in the inglenook and planked floors; colours are muted, there's not an ounce of flounce and locals still prop up the bar of a late weekday lunchtime. People travel some way for Andrew Kilburn's cooking: a trio of lamb chops with bubble and squeak, a goat's cheese omelette, a pudding cooked to order; the food is seriously good. Andrew uses local Rushmore venison, Old Spot pork and specialises in fresh Cornish seafood – brill with shellfish bisque and mussels, skate wing with brown butter and capers. Lucky dogs get delicious gravy bones, the garden terrace has views, there are three ales on tap, Westons Organic cider and ten gorgeous wines by the glass.

Meals	Lunch from £7.50. Bar meals from £7. Dinner from £12.50. Sunday lunch, 3 courses, £25.50.
Closed	3pm-6.30pm. Sun from 4pm.

Chris & Lizzie Matthews
The Forester Inn,
Lower Street, Donhead St Andrew,
Shaftesbury, SP7 9EE
Tel +44 (0)1747 828038
Web www.theforesterdonheadstandrew.co.uk

Entry 608 Map 3

Fox & Hounds

East Knoyle

Beech trees and high ridges: make time for a walk with views over the vale, then land at the 17th-century thatched pub on the green. Inside are two areas: one bright and conservatory-like, with a great view, the other older and cosier, its fireplace flanked by small red leather sofas. There are warming ales from Palmers and Butcombe, and Hop Back's inimitable Summer Lightning, and a well-presented wine card that tells you exactly what you'll get. No-nonsense New Zealander Murray cooks in an eclectic, untypical gastro style. Tuck into a chorizo, bean and red pepper casserole in red wine with belly pork, or a sweet onion, ricotta and parmesan tart, and follow with melting chocolate fondant and mascarpone cream; no need to feel sinful. Then stay till the pub closes.

Meals Lunch & dinner £9-£17.
Closed 3pm-5.30pm.

Murray Seator
Fox & Hounds,
The Green, East Knoyle,
Salisbury, SP3 6BN
Tel +44 (0)1747 830573
Web www.foxandhounds-eastknoyle.co.uk

Entry 609 Map 3

Wiltshire

The Boot

Berwick St James

In the pretty village of Berwick St James in the Till valley, sits this 'real British inn' where Giles and Cathy are working a quiet magic with food, ales and happy locals. The striking building – 17th-century Grade II listed, with flint and limestone bands – was once owned by Lord Malmesbury and later home to a boot and shoemaker who gave it its name. Inside, it's richly atmospheric, and very welcoming. You can sit snugly at the fireside with a ploughman's and a pint, or bring the family for Sunday lunch. Lush gardens, great Wadworth beers and proper pub food cooked with passion draws visitors and walkers. Tuck into lavender and cider roast ham with eggs and home-cut wedges, or Barnsley chop with bubble and squeak; for the more adventurous, try crab, whisky and sweetcorn risotto. Dogs and children welcome.

Meals Light lunches from £6.
Mains from £13.
Closed Mondays all day
(except Bank Holidays).

Giles & Cathy Dickinson
The Boot,
High Street, Berwick St James,
Salisbury, SP3 4TN
Tel +44 (0)1722 790243
Web www.theboot.pub

Entry 610 Map 3

The Prince Leopold Inn

Warminster

Named after Queen Victoria's youngest son 'The Leo' has, over the 150 years of its existence, been many things but has now perhaps reached its apogee. Step in to find a craftsman-built bar with super stylish stools on which to down a pint of London Pride or Otter ale. A Victorian snug and some cosy parlour rooms lead off here; at the back is a contemporary dining room with views across the river Wyle to water meadows. Here – and in the bar – you can sample mezze style plates available as starters, mains or to share: perhaps grilled figs and halloumi cheese on a bed of leaves with a balsamic glaze, or oven-baked sardines with chilli, lemon and garlic. From pub classics to fine dining, from sandwiches and puddings, it's good news all the way.

Meals Lunch & dinner £10.50-£19.

Closed Open all day.

Liza Kearney
The Prince Leopold Inn,
Upton Lovell,
Warminster, BA12 0JP
Tel +44 (0)1985 850460
Web www.princeleopold.co.uk

Wiltshire

The Three Daggers

Edington

Superb pub, sparkling brewery, and first-class farm shop across the yard. Restored, renamed and rejuvenated, the Three Daggers thrives as a village local, and a stop-off for conscientious foodies. Find stripped beams, slate tiles, church candles on old dining tables, chapel chairs, cushioned benches, a blazing log fire and a new conservatory for dining. Flick through the papers with a pint of Stonehenge or tuck straight into Hayley's food. A sharing board laden with game goodies, a lamb shank shepherd's pie, a plate of pork belly with a cider and thyme sauce – it's all delicious, and so is the sticky toffee pudding. Sample their wares on brewery nights, every Thursday. Check out the farm shop before you go, magnificent inside and out; and don't miss Edington's church.

Meals Lunch from £9.50.
Bar meals from £6.50.
Dinner from £12.

Closed 3pm-5pm Oct-Mar.
Open all day Sat & Sun.

Robin Brown
The Three Daggers,
Westbury Road, Edington,
Westbury, BA13 4PG
Tel +44 (0)1380 830940
Web www.threedaggers.co.uk

Timbrell's Yard

Bradford-on-Avon

The latest inn from Draco Pub Co is in the loveliest of spots; recently refurbished, this 18th-century listed building has beautiful views across the river to the churchyard, its outdoor terrace the perfect place to sip something delicious, nibble on a tasty bar snack and bask in the sun. Inside you'll find a winning combination of lovely food and well-kept ales, stripped floors, hanging lamps, exposed stone walls and sofas in front of an open fire. Helpful staff weave about, delivering food that makes you smile; Cornish crab cakes with chilli slaw, pork belly with sea salt crackling, rhubarb & custard tart with crème fraîche sorbet. Peruse the bar menu if you're after something simpler – try the cider battered fish and chips. All is simple, fresh and local, and you can even get a cup of coffee and a slice of homemade cake.

Meals	Starters £5.50-£8. Mains £12.50-£23.50.
Closed	Open all day.

Henry Gray
Timbrell's Yard,
49 St Margaret's Street,
Bradford-on-Avon, BA15 1DE

Tel +44 (0)1225 869492
Web www.timbrellsyard.com

Entry 613 Map 3

Wiltshire

The George

Bradford-on-Avon

The beef wellington says it all: prime fillet of beef topped with mushroom duxelle and liver parfait and cooked in pastry, laid on a bed of allotment greens and dauphinoise potatoes, and finished with a red wine sauce. The old boozer in the hamlet of Woolly Green has been gutted and transformed by Alex Venables, chef with a pedigree, and Alison, dynamic front of house. Enter to find comfy leather chesterfields and a long panelled bar, open fires, scrubbed pine tables, smart tartan touches, and an antlered head on a tasteful grey wall. The ales are local, the wines are global and eclectic, and you can watch the chefs create marvels from the open-to-view kitchen: fish hotpot; osso buco; belly of pork; ravioli filled with mushrooms and cream cheese, served on wilted spinach and finished with truffle oil. The beer garden is a suntrap in summer.

Meals	Starters from £5.50. Mains from £13.50.
Closed	Mon-Thurs 3pm-5.30pm. Sun eves. Open all day Fri & Sat.

Alison Ward-Baptiste
The George,
67 Woolley Street,
Bradford on Avon, BA15 1AQ

Tel +44 (0)1225 865650
Web thegeorgebradfordonavon.co.uk

Entry 614 Map 3

Quarrymans Arms

Box

A fine old pub lost in pretty hills with views that stretch across lush country. As the name suggests, it once served the miners from the local quarry; fascinating maps and pictures adorn the walls, as does some scary-looking stonecutting equipment. From the tiny terrace at the front you can watch farmers and walkers weave through the hamlet, but it's the big garden at the back where the faithful gather in summer – where better to consume a plate of rare roast beef and a pint of Butcombe on a sunny Sunday? Traditional interiors fit the bill (old beams, exposed stone, open fire), while tasty rustic food includes homemade pies, Wiltshire ham, perhaps lemon sole or roast spatchcock. A great fuel stop for cyclists, walkers and potholers; some of the mines are accessible to all and tours can be arranged.

Meals	Lunch from £4.50. Bar meals from £2.95. Dinner from £7.95. Sunday lunch, 3 courses, £16.
Closed	Open all day.

John & Ginny Arundel
Quarrymans Arms,
Box Hill, Box,
Corsham, SN13 8HN

Tel +44 (0)1225 743569
Web www.quarrymans-arms.co.uk

Entry 615 Map 3

Wiltshire

The Three Tuns Freehouse

Great Bedwyn

Drive through woodland from Marlborough to arrive at a pretty village and this late 18th-century pub in the capable hands of a young husband and wife team. James has gained experience in London, Seattle and Italy and places a very homemade emphasis on his modern and classic pub dishes. Begin with golden beetroot soup, horseradish crème fraîche and homemade bread, before bavette steak with chop house butter and bordelaise sauce, then perhaps poached rhubarb and passion fruit mess. The cheeses are good too. The bar has a well-loved traditional feel with a glorious brick fireplace, old floorboards and panelling, beams and rustic signage. A lovely place to raise a pint of Butcombe or Ramsbury ale, poured by smiley Ashley. Plus a small garden with boules pitch and Savernake Forest nearby.

Meals	Lunch & dinner £12-£22; starters £6-£9.
Closed	Monday.

Ashley & James Wilsey
The Three Tuns Freehouse,
1 High Street, Great Bedwyn,
Marlborough, SN8 3NU

Tel +44 (0)1672 870280
Web www.tunsfreehouse.com

Entry 616 Map 3

The Wheatsheaf

Chilton Foliat

Ollie (MasterChef semi-finalist) and Lauren are brimming with energy and ideas for their flavourful pub. From the art adorning the walls (much is Ollie's) to the live music (Lauren's also a musician) to the yummy food whizzing out of the kitchen they do it all with flair. Deep in Wiltshire's horse-racing country The Wheatsheaf – thatched, 1750s – sits in a peaceful village; the cosy carpeted bar has a traditional feel with wood-burners, a small piano and locals supping Ramsbury Gold. Don't miss Ollie's 'modern peasant food', perhaps red pepper and tomato stew with duck egg, kale and sourdough followed by cobnut and white chocolate cheesecake. They believe in a farm-to-fork ethos so the menu is bursting with all things local: charcuterie made by Ollie's dad on his nearby farm, craft lager, organic wines, homemade liqueurs. And they have great live music nights.

Meals: Starters from £3.50. Lunch & dinner from £13.

Closed: Open all day.

Local, seasonal and organic produce

Kate Hamilton
The Wheatsheaf,
Chilton Foliat, RG17 0TE
Tel +44 (0)1488 680936
Web www.thewheatsheafchiltonfoliat.co.uk

Entry 617 Map 3

Wiltshire

Helen Browning's Royal Oak

Bishopstone

Passionately organic, delightfully unpreachy. In 2005 the simple pub in the idyllic village was taken on by farmer Helen Browning and has been flying the flag ever since. There's food bartering with locals, a wild garden, an outdoor pizza oven and a barbecue, open days with hay bales for kids to romp on, and pig races and live music in summer. The planked, beamed open-plan bar has mismatched furniture and a roaring fire and the staff are friendly. But best of all is the menu that changes twice a day: crayfish from the Thames served with Bishopstone watercress, home-cured bacon from home-reared pigs, asparagus from Lotmead down the road, fish from the boats out of Newlyn, gooseberries from the garden. Perfect ingredients, perfect food, beer from Arkells and six wines by the glass.

Meals: Lunch & dinner £8-£20. Bar meals £6-£8. Sunday lunch from £15-£25.

Closed: 3pm-6pm. Open all day Sat & Sun.

Helen Browning & Tim Finney
Helen Browning's Royal Oak,
Easterbrook Farm, Bishopstone,
Swindon, SN6 8PP
Tel +44 (0)1793 790481
Web www.helenbrowningsorganic.co.uk/pub.html

Entry 618 Map 3

The Potting Shed Pub

Crudwell

From the outside this may look like a quiet village inn, but step through the pretty white doors to reveal a treasure trove of quirk and vintage. Open fireplaces and kilim sofas fat with cushions make you feel at home, while door handles fashioned from trowels, hand pumps from fork handles and old butchers' block tables will have you smiling. Eat in the big airy dining room with mix 'n' match antiques, or in one of the cosy corners around the bar. The food is exuberantly British, from dressed Cornish crab on sourdough to ribeye steaks with rich béarnaise. Two acres and an apple orchard at the back have been turned into an organic vegetable patch, while local ales, and dog treats on the bar reflect the focus on real-pub values and friendliness. There's an excellent children's menu and puds to warm your heart; try the egg custard tart with clove honey.

Meals	Lunch from £5.50. Dinner from £11.95.
Closed	Open all day.

Kate Hamilton
The Potting Shed Pub,
Crudwell,
Malmesbury, SN16 9EW

Tel	+44 (0)1666 577833
Web	www.thepottingshedpub.com

Entry 619 Map 3

Wiltshire

The Red Lion Inn

Cricklade

Specialising in seasonal, local and often organic food, this rambling old inn off the Thames path combines contemporary features with a charming 16th-century fabric and extends its welcome to all (including your dog). In the red-carpeted bar, all low beams, stone walls, wood settles and log fires, treat yourself to a pint of ale (the choice is mind-boggling, from Arbor Motueka to Butcombe Bitter), or try something from their own microbrewery. Lunches involve the best of English classics: real burgers with triple-cooked chips; chicken and locally foraged wild mushroom pie; great homemade bread... and a beer to match each and every dish. Served at reclaimed tables in the elegant restaurant, you might enjoy tea-smoked salmon; roast local pork with crispy potatoes and black pudding; rhubarb and ginger crumble.

Meals	Lunch & bar meals from £6. Dinner from £9. Sunday lunch, 3 courses, £19.95.
Closed	Sun eves.

Tom Gee
The Red Lion Inn,
74 High Street,
Cricklade, SN6 6DD

Tel	+44 (0)1793 750776
Web	www.theredlioncricklade.co.uk

Entry 620 Map 3

The Cardinal's Hat

Worcester

Wines to suit Spanish charcuterie, luscious local ciders, and a small terrace out back; welcome to the oldest pub in Worcester. Most of it is 18th-century – fine brickwork, sash windows – but it originates from the 14th and stands on a street of Tudor houses close to the cathedral. Step in to find an oak-planked bar and a carpeted 'snug' from whose easy chairs and leaded windows you can watch the world go by. The most atmospheric room is at the back, where dark wood panelling glows in the candlelight and the burner roars in the fireplace. As for the food, they keep it simple and authentic: hot pork pies, smoked kippers on toast, platters of fine local cheeses. Accompaniments include spicy chutneys, quince jellies, and ever-changing ales... how about Hobson's Old Prickly? Then it's up to one of the best bedrooms in Worcestershire. Immerse yourself in a world of soft carpets, polished antiques, glam wallpapers, and bathrooms that are state of the art (one with a tub in the room itself). Continental breakfast is delivered to your door, but there's full English at Mac & Jac's across the street.

Rooms	4 doubles: £80-£125.
Meals	Bar snacks from £4.20. Platters from £8.95.
Closed	Monday until 4pm.

Nigel Smith
The Cardinal's Hat,
31 Friar Street,
Worcester, WR1 2NA
Tel +44 (0)1905 724006
Web www.the-cardinals-hat.co.uk

Talbot Inn

Newnham Bridge

This fine 19th-century red brick coaching inn once welcomed hop and apple pickers to the Teme Valley for a season's work. Now, after a meticulous renovation, it caters for weary travellers' needs in the best possible manner. Grab an armchair by the fire with a pint of Wye Valley or Hobson's Ale, and admire photos of local rural heritage. Menus operate from a specials board and have a rustic-contemporary appeal: start with chicken liver parfait, pear & ginger preserve, before monkfish tail, spiced pearl barley, sultana and kale. The sirloin steaks are a favourite, as is the sticky toffee pudding. There's a peaceful lounge, a panelled dining room and charming staff and owners will see that your stay is just right. Bedrooms are calm, uncluttered and stylish with soft carpets, bespoke headboards and one-off pieces of furniture: bathrooms are equally sleek, with limestone tiling and White Company toiletries. All are a good size, have super-thick curtains to absorb a small amount of road noise, and beds for the sweetest of dreams.

Rooms	7 doubles: £90-£140.
Meals	Lunch & dinner £9.95-£14.95. Sunday lunch £16.50 & £19.95.
Closed	Open all day.

Barney Williams
Talbot Inn,
Newnham Bridge,
Tenbury Wells, WR15 8JF
Tel +44 (0)1584 781941
Web www.talbotinnnewnhambridge.co.uk

The Chequers

Cutnall Green

The Chequers was rebuilt in the 1930s on the site of an ancient coaching inn. You'd never know: its open fires, comfy sofas and snug little booths have evolved as smoothly as its menu. While the thirsty gather round the church-panel bar with pints of Timothy Taylor's, the hungry head for the dining room, cosy and candlelit with cranberry walls, blond beams and a huge display of wines. Make the most of a vibrant 'mod Brit' menu from award-winning chef Roger Narbett: the food bursts with flavour. There's chicken liver parfait with plum compote, pot-roasted belly pork with crackling and duck-fat potatoes, and apple tarte tatin. And if the liqueur coffees catch your fancy, slip off and savour one in the Players' Lounge, a small room that has photos of Roger's Football Chef days.

Meals	Lunch & dinner from £9.50. Bar meals from £5.50.
Closed	Open all day.

Roger & Jo Narbett
The Chequers,
Kidderminster Road, Cutnall Green,
Droitwich, WR9 0PJ

Tel	+44 (0)1562 730319
Web	www.chequerscutnallgreen.co.uk

Entry 623 Map 8

Worcestershire

The Live & Let Live

Bringsty Common

Well off the beaten track and reached down a stone road this 300-year-old thatched pub sits splendidly isolated and with views over the Bringsty common all the way to the Malvern Hills in the distance. Beautifully restored by Sue Dovey it now hums with life: the single-room bar is a refuge for locals and walkers and is quaint with pale gnarled beams, flagstones, dusky pink walls, stoneware bottles and a huge roaring fire for chilly days. Upstairs is a dear little restaurant open all week, bookings allowing. On sunny days, outside is best – there's a pretty little garden with views. Wherever you perch you can tuck into delicious beer, cider and perry from nearby, and good grub – an ever-changing seasonal menu bursting with local ingredients, and some old favourites like fish and chips, steak and ale pie, decent burgers.

Meals	Lunch & dinner £9.95-£18.95.
Closed	2.30pm-5pm & Mon (except bank hols). Open all day Fri-Sun.

Sue Dovey
The Live & Let Live,
Bringsty Common,
Bringsty, WR6 5UW

Tel	+44 (0)1886 821462
Web	www.liveandletlive-bringsty.co.uk

Entry 624 Map 8

The Inn at Welland

Welland

David and Gillian have created a 'contemporary traditional' style that flows together effortlessly. Those who just want to sup their Butty Bach or Otter bitter can retire to eclectic dining furniture. The main sweep has gorgeous limestone tile flooring and a mix of tables and chairs: a bleached wooden sideboard dispenses Provençal olives and artisan breads and beside it a stack of wine cases filled with bin end bottles – for later perhaps? The kitchen team (now with a dedicated pastry chef) serve up a proper gastro medley with homemade desserts, ice creams, sorbets and petit fours. Enjoy pan-fried Cornish scallops, pea mint purée, crisp lardons and tomato oil followed by crisp belly pork, garlic mash, pak choi, orange and ginger jus. There are log fires and, in the garden, one of the terraces has a glass veranda with a wood-burner. Welcome back!

Meals Lunch & dinner from £11.
Bar meals from £6.50.
Sunday lunch £21.50 & £26.

Closed Mon & Sun eves.

David & Gillian Pinchbeck
The Inn at Welland,
Drake Street, Welland,
Malvern, WR13 6LN
Tel +44 (0)1684 592317
Web www.theinnatwelland.co.uk

Entry 625 Map 8

Worcestershire

The Fleece Inn

Bretforton

'No potato crisps to be sold in the bar'. So ordered Lola Taplin when The Fleece was bequeathed to the National Trust after 500 years in her family. It's the sort of tradition that thrives in this quintessential English pub where you pitch up for fresh local food, ales from Uley and the Fleece Inn's home-brewed cider. Local sausages with red onion marmalade with red wine gravy, Tewkesbury mustard mash vegetables and orchard apple crumble may tempt you but there is more. The Asparagus Festival commences in the courtyard, with an auction on the last Sunday in May and summer festivals twirl with Morris dancers. The medieval barn, the perfect setting for weddings, is stuffed with historical artefacts, stone flagged floors, big log fires, ancient beams and a wonderful collection of pewter.

Meals Lunch & dinner from £8.75.
Bar meals from £5.25.
Dinner from £8.75.

Closed Open all day.

Nigel Smith
The Fleece Inn,
The Cross, Bretforton,
Evesham, WR11 7JE
Tel +44 (0)1386 831173
Web thefleeceinn.co.uk

Entry 626 Map 8

Butchers Arms
Eldersfield

A 16th-century pub for Slow Foodies – with a lovely big garden where you can relax and enjoy the surroundings. The Butchers is a place for regulars popping in for pints of Wye Valley Bitter from the cask and Herefordshire cider; now there's a Michelin star. Elizabeth does friendly front of house, James has a hands-on philosophy and cooks single-handedly for just 18 covers. His gutsy British dishes use local produce from named suppliers, so you can swoon over aged fillet of Hereford beef with oxtail in pastry, girolle mushrooms and fondant potato, or that old English delicacy Bath chap, served with potato scone and grain mustard. The finale? Seville orange marmalade pudding with Drambuie custard, should you fancy. A marvellous little place for some 'nose to tail' dining.

Meals	Lunch & dinner £16-£24. Bookings only at lunch.
Closed	2.30pm-7pm. Sun eves & Mon all day. Closed 10 days in Aug & Jan.

James & Elizabeth Winter
Butchers Arms,
Lime Street, Eldersfield,
Gloucester, GL19 4NX

Tel	+44 (0)1452 840381
Web	www.thebutchersarms.net

Photo: The Duke of Wellington, entry 533

The Shibden Mill Inn

Shibden

The rambling and beautifully renovated old corn mill is hidden in a tranquil wooded valley overlooking Red Beck, just minutes from the hustle and bustle of Halifax; at night, the peaceful stream-side terrace is floodlit and heated, for idyllic summer drinking. An unstuffy integrity lies at the heart of Simon Heaton's welcoming inn, from the front-of-house warmth to the pubby bar where locals gather for a natter over a pint of Shibden Bitter. From the modern British kitchen innovative dishes flow: potted pork with pickled quail eggs, sorrel and mushroom ketchup; lamb rump and kidney gratin with butternut squash; mallard and curried pigeon Wellington; banana soufflé with toffee ice cream. There are beams and timbers, roaring log fires and stone-flagged floors, deep sofas and soothing colours in the cosy, candlelit bar and dining rooms, and the wine list is impressive. Refurbished bedrooms are comfortable, individual and decorated with warmth and style, with big beds, bold colours, Roberts radios and smart tiled bathrooms.

Rooms	10 doubles: £95-£149. 1 suite for 2: £165-£195. Singles £85-£140.
Meals	Lunch & dinner £11.50-£19. Sunday lunch £12.95.
Closed	2.30pm-5.30pm. Open all day Sat & Sun.

Simon Heaton
The Shibden Mill Inn,
Shibden Mill Fold,
Shibden, Halifax, HX3 7UL

Tel +44 (0)1422 365840
Web www.shibdenmillinn.com

The Crescent Inn

Ilkley

The handsome Victorian building wrapped round a corner on the high street in Ilkley has been restored to its former glory – and it feels as though it's always been this way. Smooth walls are a vibrant blue, reflected in upholstered settles and checked wool curtains at tall windows; floors are in old oak and a glorious fire at the end of the comfortable bar belts out the heat. Choose from an impressive list of speciality beers and ciders, seven cask ales and wines by the glass. The value-for-money menu includes a gourmet British beef burger with skinny fries and a ploughman's platter that positively groans under the weight of local pork pie, ham off the bone and scrumptious Yorkshire cheeses. Pub classics are chalked up on boards, so tuck in to steak, ale and mushroom pie or fish and chips. At the top of an elegant curved staircase peaceful, high-ceilinged, boutiquey bedrooms await, some in the French country style, all with sumptuous linen, fat mattresses and sleek state of the art bathrooms. In short, the perfect spot in which to relax after a bracing yomp on the moors (or round Ilkley's fabulous shops!).

Rooms	11 doubles: £75-£145.
Meals	Lunch from £9.95. Bar meals from £5.95. Dinner from £13.90. Sunday lunch £11.95-£13.95.
Closed	Open all day.

Richard Paterson
The Crescent Inn,
Brook Street,
Ilkley, LS29 8DG
Tel +44 (0)1943 811250
Web www.thecrescentinn.co.uk

Judge's Lodging

York

In the centre of York is a handsome Georgian townhouse with a strikingly luxurious interior. In the cellar: vaulted rooms, cool tunes, stone floors, Farrow & Ball colours, quirky mismatched furniture. Upstairs: a pair of dining rooms, grand, elegant and eye-catching. Vintage grey-blue panelling, tall sash windows, semi-circular sofas, illuminated sculptures. All is cosy but classy, and the service is informal but attentive. The food is impressive too, and packed with flavour so tuck into the likes of slow cooked beef and Thwaites ale pie with clapshot potatoes and buttered kale, or a warming helping of moules frites. The wines are wide-ranging and the beers are Thwaites. Join the punters on the galleried decked terrace and unwind, then treat yourself to a stay in a room with feature wallpapers and fabulous beds. The garden rooms in the courtyard are small and can be noisy, so pay more for the smartest and quietest at the top of the house, one with an original marble fireplace and a York Minster view. Breakfasts are generous.

Rooms	21 doubles: £110-£125.
Meals	Starters from £4.95. Mains from £8.95.
Closed	Open all day.

Rachel Guy
Judge's Lodging,
9 Lendal, York, YO1 8AQ
Tel +44 (0)1904 638733
Web www.thwaites.co.uk/hotels-and-inns/inns/judges-lodging-at-york

The General Tarleton

Ferrensby

John and Claire run this old coaching inn with an easy charm. It's a community hub, a default destination for locals in search of good food and drink. The stylish low-beamed brasserie-bar mixes rough stone walls with leather chairs, period colours and a roaring fire. You'll find a pint of hand-pumped Black Sheep, then a dozen well-chosen wines by the glass. Good food with Yorkshire roots ranges from pub classics to posh nosh, anything from cheese soufflé to warm rabbit terrine, fish pie to haunch of venison, dark chocolate fondant with Horlicks ice cream to mascarpone panna cotta. There's a beautiful sitting room with comfy sofas and a log burner or a stone terrace in summer for lunch in the sun. Expect a good buzz and delightful staff. If you're tempted to stay, comfortable, well-equipped bedrooms in a purpose-built extension have recently been refurbished in elegant style: smart colours, crisp linen and homemade biscuits, with Molton Brown oils in good bathrooms. But the food is the thing – it's fabulous – as are the breakfasts. York, Harrogate, the Dales and the Moors wait.

Rooms	11 doubles, 2 twins: £129.
Meals	Lunch & dinner from £12 (brasserie). Dinner, 3 courses, £28. Sunday lunch £18.50-£22.50.
Closed	3pm-5.30pm.

John Topham
The General Tarleton,
Boroughbridge Road, Ferrensby,
Knaresborough, HG5 0PZ
Tel +44 (0)1423 340284
Web www.generaltarleton.co.uk

The Durham Ox

Crayke

At the picturesque top of the Grand Old Duke of York's hill is an L-shaped bar of flagstones and rose walls, worn leather armchairs, carved panelling and big fires. On the other side of the bar you'll find a new wood floored extension with exposed brickwork and a dapper wine-themed restaurant that draws all and sundry. Chalkboards and menus reflect the freshest and best local ingredients of each season. They also bake all their own bread and petit fours here. Puddings are tempting too – try sunken 'gooey' chocolate cake. Set lunches, early birds and Sunday roasts are inevitably popular, and there are three private dining rooms – great for family celebrations and weddings. No need to drive home either: the delightfully quirky rooms in the old farmworkers' cottages have been renovated in contemporary, country-house style. Expect original quarry-tile floors, warmly painted walls, beams and revamped bathrooms, and a new room in the pub, The Studio, reached via its own outside staircase. The long views across the valley are stunning; in summer, flowers burst from stone troughs. Dog-friendly peacefulness 20 minutes outside York.

Rooms	1 cottage for 4, 4 cottages for 2: £120-£180. 1 studio for 2: £150
Meals	Lunch & dinner £8.95-£26.95. Bar meals from £6.95. Sunday lunch from £14.95.
Closed	Open all day.

Michael Ibbotson
The Durham Ox,
Westway,
Crayke, York, YO61 4TE

Tel +44 (0)1347 821506
Web www.thedurhamox.com

The Oak Tree Inn

Helperby

Helperby is a historic spot and this new village pub is the jewel in its crown. The mellow brick exterior has scrubbed up nicely and a big paved area at the back is a great place to eat out on a sunny day. Inside, the old snug remains, complete with its open fire, oak floors and beams. Two bright and airy dining spaces, one by the rather sophisticated bar, strike a more clubby note: tartan check wool on wing chairs, ruby-red walls, dark elegant tables. An impressive line of brews beckon, including Timothy Taylor and Theakstons, so enjoy a pint by the fire while you choose your food. Souped-up pub classics are chalked on boards: home-cured salmon with capers, shallots and lemon dressing perhaps, followed by local venison with sautéed wild mushrooms and red wine sauce. Upstairs, soak any aches and pains away in a deep bath bubbling with L'Occitane treats. The six sumptuous bedrooms have funky wine-glass chandeliers, huge beds and fine linen, generously padded headboards and monster mirrors. After a spot of retail therapy in nearby Thirsk, Knaresborough or York, the Oak Tree is a pleasure to come home to.

Rooms	5 doubles, 1 twin/double: £85-£150.
Meals	Lunch from £6.95. Dinner from £12.95.
Closed	Open all day (from 8am).

Michael Ibbotson
The Oak Tree Inn,
Raskelf Road,
Helperby, York, YO61 2PH
Tel +44 (0)1423 789189
Web www.theoaktreehelperby.com

The Angel Inn

Hetton

This cute little drover's inn has an old-school feel and sits in a tiny hamlet that's surrounded by glorious country – views stretch across fields of sheep to Rylstone Fell. Outside, there's a terrace for lunch in the sun, inside you find locals gossiping over a pint of Hetton pale ale in the half-panelled bar. It's all very cosy – beamed ceilings, mullioned windows, exposed stone walls, even a working Yorkshire range. There's colourful art on the walls, nooks and crannies to hide away in. The feel is bright and breezy, especially in the dining room, where you dig into delicious food, perhaps seafood parcels with a lobster sauce, chargrilled local beef, a legendary sticky toffee pudding; there's Yapas, too – tapas Yorkshire style! Rooms are scattered about. The suites across the lane have a more traditional feel (half testers, window seats, papered walls, the odd claw-foot bath); those next door in Sycamore House are more contemporary (stylish fabrics, big beds, a sofa if there's room). All have robes in good bathrooms. Jazz bands play at summer barbecues, glorious walks wait.

Rooms	9 doubles: £150-£175. 5 suites for 2: £175-£200. Singles from £125.
Meals	Lunch from £12.95. Bar meals from £15.95. Dinner £15.95-£38.50. Sunday lunch £24.50.
Closed	3pm-6pm. Open all day Fri-Sat (reduced choice menu).

Juliet Watkins
The Angel Inn,
Hetton,
Skipton, BD23 6LT
Tel +44 (0)1756 730263
Web www.angelhetton.co.uk

The Lister Arms at Malham

Malham

You'll be hard pushed to find a finer looking pub in a more gorgeous village. The National Trust's Malham is a favourite with potholers (this part of Yorkshire is rich with caverns) but there are many surface pleasures to be had. Sitting on the edge of the village green, the 17th-century coaching inn was once home to the first Lord of Ribblesdale and very grand it looks too. Don't stand on ceremony: inside are flagged floors, wood-burning stoves and well-kept local ales. Darren also puts an interesting menu together using mostly local produce. You could start with game galantine, and move onto blackened prawn and salmon stroganoff; if you have room, finish with rum soaked apple and sultana crumble. Staying the night? Choose a contemporary new room in the cottage, or head upstairs to one of the comfy bedrooms with calm colours, lovely linen and pristine bathrooms; many have views over the village green to the hills beyond. The newly opened barn has beautiful bedrooms, a shared lounge with a wood burner, and a warm welcome for dogs.

Rooms	12 doubles, 6 twins: £80-£182. 5 family rooms for 4: £110-£182. Singles £59-£79.
Meals	Lunch & dinner from £10.50. Bar meals from £6.95. Sunday lunch, 3 courses, £15.50.
Closed	Open all day.

Darren Dunn
The Lister Arms at Malham,
Malham, Skipton, BD23 4DB

Tel	+44 (0)1729 830444
Web	www.thwaites.co.uk/hotels-and-inns/inns/lister-arms-malham

The Lion at Settle

Settle

Generations of travellers have enjoyed the welcome at this grand 17th-century coaching inn; following a recent renovation its doors are open to all. Original features have been saved, including smooth oak floors, a fabulous inglenook fireplace in the grand entrance hall and the graceful sweeping staircase; comfortable sofas and chairs are upholstered in checked tartan wool. Locally sourced ingredients dominate a menu which places its emphasis on comfort: try Settle Pudding (tender braised beef with a suet lid) and homemade fish pie with parsley mash, and, if you can find room, the sticky toffee pudding is a must. The elegant but cosy dining room with its pleasingly mismatched furniture, panelled walls and old photos buzzes with friendly chat. If you're a Three Peaks bagger, a devotee of the stunning Settle to Carlisle railway or simply want to get away from it all you can stay in characterful bedrooms with five-star mattresses, white cotton bed linen, immaculate bathrooms, smart TV's and fresh milk for your morning cuppa. The historic town is worth exploring: lose yourself in its cobbled alleyways.

Rooms: 14 twin/doubles: £75-£130. Family room from £100.

Meals: Lunch from £6.95. Bar meals from £5.95. Dinner from £8.95.

Closed: Open all day.

Peter Barton
The Lion at Settle,
Duke Street, Settle, BD24 9DU
Tel +44 (0)1729 822203
Web www.thwaites.co.uk/hotels-and-inns/inns/lion-at-settle

The Kings Head

Kettlewell

It's worth dropping by for the fireplace alone – irresistible, monumental and smouldering on 18th-century flags. You could have a pint of Hetton Pale Ale, a Montrachet by the glass, a proper espresso... and pigeon breast salad with black pudding bon bons, the black pudding as light as a feather. Owner Michael Pighills has 20 years' cheffing under his belt and his short inspired menu, chalked up on a board, changes every two days. Local fishermen bring trout to the door and the meat is from Jacksons of Cracoe. There are rare beef sandwiches, heritage potatoes and delicious Goosnargh chicken with Wensleydale cheese. If you can't bear to leave then you must stay, in one of five white-and-grey bedrooms above, two overlooking the stream. Colours are muted, beds are wide, bathrooms are snazzy, there are flat screens, books, homemade biscuits, and wonky walls abound. The pub, in one of the cutest villages in the Dales, sits on a lane opposite the church. The parking may be difficult but the setting is idyllic, and the Tour de France passed right by in 2014.

Rooms	4 doubles, 1 twin: £90.
Meals	Starters £4.95-£6.50. Mains £10.95-£18.95.
Closed	Mondays.

Michael & Jenny Pighills
The Kings Head,
The Green, Kettlewell,
Skipton, BD23 5RD
Tel +44 (0)1756 761600
Web www.thekingsheadkettlewell.co.uk

The White Lion

Cray

Green fields all around, the river Wharfe across the road: a very fine spot for an old drovers' inn. Inside: open fires, flagged floors, sturdy tables, the minimum of ephemera. Leave muddy boots in the porch and catch the barman's eye, for a pint of Black Sheep and a hot beef sandwich. You can eat where you like, in the bar or in the snug, aptly named with books, games, wood-burner and sofa. Locals Dennis and Amelia, natural born hosts, fell in love with the White Lion and haven't looked back. Their chef's style is rustic and much of her produce is locally sourced; enjoy homemade chicken liver pâté served with onion marmalade, or sizzling Jacksons of Cracoe sausages. Portions are Yorkshire generous, vegetarians are not ignored, and if you love the countryside, consider an overnight stay. The fleshpots of Skipton are 20 miles away and this is rural, so check out the bedrooms, and book in. You get plaid wool carpets, high padded headboards, comfy beds, great little showers, and butlers trays of tea, coffee and the pub's spring water. Views are worth waking up for, cooked breakfasts are a treat. Cyclists, ramblers, walkers with dogs: welcome to one of the best!

Rooms	8 doubles, 1 twin: £100-£130.
Meals	Starters from £6. Lunch from £6. Dinner from £14.
Closed	Open all day.

Amelia Johnson & Dennis Peacock
The White Lion,
Cray,
Skipton, BD23 5JB
Tel +44 (0)1756 760262
Web www.bestpubinthedales.co.uk

The White Bear Five Star Country Inn

Masham

At five o'clock on a Friday evening there's only one place to be in Masham: the tap room at the White Bear, home of Theakston's beer. The great and the good gather to mark the end of the week, the odd pint is sunk, the air is thick with gossip. Interior design is 1920s trapped in aspic – red leather, polished brass, a crackling fire. But there's more here – a country-house dining room for lovely food; a handsome bar with stripped boards; a flower-filled terrace for lunch in the sun. Bedrooms are lovely, a touch of 21st-century luxury. They occupy the old Lightfoot brewery and come in contemporary style with good fabrics, warm colours, excellent beds and fancy bathrooms. Some have views across town, the vast penthouse suite is open to the rafters and worth splashing out on. There's a courtyard for guests, a sitting room, too; staff will bring drinks if you want privacy and peace. Delicious food waits in the restaurant, perhaps shellfish soup, steak and ale pie, treacle sponge pudding. Tours of the brewery are easily arranged, with a pint of your choice at the end. The Dales are all around.

Rooms	13 twin/doubles: £120. 1 suite for 2: £200-£220.
Meals	Lunch from £4.95. Dinner, 3 courses, about £30.
Closed	Open all day.

Sue Thomas
The White Bear Five Star Country Inn,
Wellgarth, Masham,
Ripon, HG4 4EN

Tel	+44 (0)1765 689319
Web	www.thewhitebearhotel.co.uk

Sandpiper Inn

Leyburn

Leyburn is lovely, a fine old market town on the edge of the Yorkshire Dales. As for the Sandpiper, this 17th-century stone inn sits peacefully on the square. Inside, cosy interiors have low ceilings, the odd beam and the best food in town. Jonathan, a Roux scholar, has cooked for presidents and prime ministers, robust food that elates. In the bar, locals put the world to rights over pints of Black Sheep while contemplating irresistible menus: salted squid or roasted chorizo if you fancy Yorkshire tapas; battered haddock or omelette Arnold Bennett if you want to explore the bar menu; or the full works in an attractive dining room, perhaps cheese soufflé, Swinton venison, dark chocolate marquise with white chocolate ice cream. Whisky lovers will appreciate the large collection of malts behind the bar. Upstairs, two simple bedrooms have a warm country feel with robes and good showers in the bathrooms. The Dales is one of the most beautiful places in England. Don't miss the roast rib of beef for Sunday lunch or the market in the square on Fridays.

Rooms	2 doubles: £95-£110.
Meals	Lunch from £6. Dinner £7.50-£22.
Closed	3pm-6pm (7pm Sun). Mon (& Tues in winter).

Jonathan & Janine Harrison
Sandpiper Inn,
Railway Street,
Leyburn, DL8 5AT
Tel +44 (0)1969 622206
Web www.sandpiperinn.co.uk

The Carpenters Arms

Felixkirk

Peace has returned to sleepy Felixkirk following a dramatic transformation by Provenance Inns. Michael and Sasha Ibbotson have worked hard to create one rather stylish country inn, keeping period detail in the traditional bar whilst adding a decked terrace and eight garden suites. Built into the hillside below the church, set around a landscaped garden, these stunningly swish rooms have private patios and picture windows for a view that stretches across the Vale of Mowbray to the Dales. Inside are sweeping floors, gas fires and honesty bars, big beds topped with duckdown and bathrooms with toasty floors. Back in the pub, stone floors, wonky beams, open fires, scarlet walls and comfy old furniture – an inviting backdrop for tasty food. Try scallops with garlic and parsley butter; pork fillet wrapped in Serrano ham with apple mash and mustard sauce; rib-eye steak with dauphinoise potatoes and Madeira jus. There's a cracking wine list, an intimate private dining room, and the staff are local and lovely. Fabulous moorland walking, too; bring the boots.

Rooms	8 doubles, 2 twin/doubles: £99-£185.
Meals	Lunch & dinner £10.95-£19.95. Bar meals £3.95-£8.95. Sunday lunch from £13.95.
Closed	Open all day (from 8am).

Michael Ibbotson
The Carpenters Arms,
Felixkirk,
Thirsk, YO7 2DP
Tel +44 (0)1845 537369
Web www.thecarpentersarmsfelixkirk.com

The Horseshoe Inn

Levisham

This handsome old stone built, pantile roofed pub takes pride of place at the head of stunning, broad-laned Levisham, a magnet for train enthusiasts – the North Yorks Moors railway runs through the bottom of the valley a mile down the road. You're guaranteed the warmest of welcomes in the Horseshoe with its oak-floored, beamed bar, and a pleasing pub grub menu promises the likes of Whitby haddock with chunky chips, and steak and ale pie. Well-kept Black Sheep Best Bitter and Yorkshire Moors from the local Cropton Brewery keeps the real ale lovers happy – park yourself in front of a roaring open fire with a pint and the paper after a stroll through nearby Dalby Forest. There's so much to do and see locally you might want to make a night or two of it; opt for one of the luxurious, contemporary rooms with big beds, fat mattresses and spanking new bathrooms. If you fancy a fabulous view down the village, take a cosy, spotless room above the pub. Either way, this is the ideal base for some serious yomping (terrific walks start from the door), or a trip down memory lane on the steam train.

Rooms	6 doubles, 5 twin/doubles: £85-£125. Singles from £75.
Meals	Lunch from £4.95. Bar meals from £5.95. Dinner from £10.50. Sunday lunch, 3 courses, £20.
Closed	Open all day.

Charles & Toby Wood
The Horseshoe Inn,
Main Street, Levisham,
Pickering, YO18 7NL
Tel +44 (0)1751 460240
Web www.horseshoelevisham.co.uk

The Blacksmith's Arms

Lastingham

Low black beams, glowing fires, antique saddles, a ghost called Ella and a pint of Copper Dragon. You almost slide down to the lovely little village, so deeply is it sunk into the valley. This low, rambling, dimly-lit pub has provided shelter and comfort to monks and shepherds since 1693; now it is visited by gamekeepers, walkers and church enthusiasts: ancient St Mary's sits next door and a secret tunnel runs between the two. Once an impoverished priest with 13 children ran both the pub and church; the current landlord is approved by all. The little dining rooms are not quite as atmospheric as the bar with its lit range, but this is a great place for a gossip and a pint – and a proper Yorkshire portion of game casserole or lamb and mint pie. Delicious.

Meals Lunch & dinner £8.95-£14.95.
Closed Tues lunch.

Peter & Hilary Trafford
The Blacksmith's Arms,
Front Street,
Lastingham, York, YO62 6TL
Tel +44 (0)1751 417247
Web www.blacksmithslastingham.co.uk

Entry 643 Map 13

Yorkshire

The Birch Hall

Beck Hole

Two small bars with a shop in between, unaltered for 70 years. Wooded hillsides and a stone bridge straddling the rushing river and, inside, a glimpse of life before World War II. The Big Bar has been beautifully repapered and has a little open fire, dominoes, darts and service from a hatch; benches come from the station waiting room at Beck Hole. The shop (postcards, traditional sweets) has its original fittings, as does the Little Bar with its handpumps for three cask ales. The original 19th-century enamel sign hangs above the door. Food is simple and authentic: local pies, baked stotties, homemade scones, delicious beer cake. Steep steps take you to the terraced garden that looks over the inn and across the valley. Parking is scarce so show patience and courtesy in this old-fashioned place.

Meals Sandwiches & pies from £1.90.
Closed 3pm-7.30pm.
Mon eves & Tues in winter.
Open all day in summer.

Glenys & Neil Crampton
The Birch Hall,
Beck Hole,
Whitby, YO22 5LE
Tel +44 (0)1947 896245
Web www.beckhole.info

Entry 644 Map 13

The Oak Tree Inn

Hutton Magna

A tiny Dales' cottage at the end of a row, masquerading as a pub, the Oak Tree was discovered by the Rosses. Alastair trained at The Savoy, and together they have created a relaxed and welcoming gem. The front bar has its original panelling and whitewashed stone, a medley of tables, squishy leather sofas, newspapers, fresh flowers, an open fire. The dark green dining area at the back is cosily lit, its tables separated by pews. Locally shot game appears on the menu in season and the produce is as fresh as can be. Try prosecco-poached shellfish with crab and cucumber mayonnaise; herb-crusted saddle of lamb with garlic and rosemary potatoes, sweet peppers, aubergine and fennel; hot chocolate fondant with delice and pistachio ice cream. The food is always a joy.

Meals	Dinner, 3 courses, from £33.
Closed	Tues-Sun lunch & Mon.

Alastair & Claire Ross
The Oak Tree Inn,
Hutton Magna,
Richmond, DL11 7HH
Tel +44 (0)1833 627371

Yorkshire

The Black Bull

Moulton

The Black Bull – a famous old name in Yorkshire dining – is the latest addition to Provenance Inns and its collection of fine hostelries. It's received the trademark makeover to bring it into the 21st century, the most notable addition being a smart restaurant, where walls of glass open onto a terrace for lunch in good weather. Inside, there's a panelled bar with armchairs in front of a wood-burner where you can sink a pint of Black Sheep (brewed down the road). Then there's the excellent food. Menus are extensive, a smörgåsbord of fresh, local produce, with fish and chips and a good burger sitting alongside East Coast lobster and charcoaled steaks. You'll find chateaubriand too, and an excellent wine list to help wash them down. There are monthly music nights, tapas nights on Fridays, even the odd Murder Mystery evening.

Meals	Starters & light bites from £6.95. Market Menu lunch, 1-3 courses, £13-£20. Mains from £13.95. Sunday lunch from £14.95.
Closed	Open all day.

Michael Ibbotson
The Black Bull,
Moulton,
Richmond, DL10 6QJ
Tel +44 (0)1347 821506
Web www.theblackbullmoulton.com

The Blue Lion

East Witton

The front bar at the Blue Lion is one of the best in the land – little has changed since it was built at the end of the 18th century. It's a delightful mix of flagged floors, open fires, beautiful old settles, newspapers on poles, polished beer taps for Yorkshire ale, bunches of dried flowers hanging from beams. It's a bustling place that serves delicious food and no one seems in a hurry to leave. The two restaurants have boarded floors and shuttered Georgian windows, log fires and candles everywhere. Food is hearty and deliciously English, perhaps potted partridge with red onion marmalade, whole roast grouse with bread sauce, apple crumble with toffee custard. There's an excellent wine list, too, and a garden at the back for Pimm's in summer. Jervaulx Abbey is a mile away, and you can follow the river up to Middleham with stepping stones to help you cross.

Meals Lunch & dinner £10.50-£27.50.
Closed Open all day.

Paul & Helen Klein
The Blue Lion,
East Witton,
Leyburn, DL8 4SN
Tel +44 (0)1969 624273
Web www.thebluelion.co.uk

Entry 647 Map 12

Yorkshire

Queens Arms

Litton

It's a happy day for everyone when a country pub re-opens. This one sits in Litton, one of the most remote villages in this corner of the Dales and as pretty as it gets, with a smattering of handsome, thick-walled 17th-century houses, wildflower meadows and the river Skirfare burbling through. The Queens Arms, long, low and freshly whitewashed, is a fabulous find after a lovely walk. A lick of paint has smartened the inside without routing tradition; flagged floors, open fire, beams and stone walls remain. There's a new regime in the tiny kitchen, and a short but appealing menu. Seared Littondale mallard breast with homemade carrot and ginger chutney makes a substantial starter, while pot roast wild rabbit with prunes will set you up nicely for a stroll – particularly if you finish with treacle sponge.

Meals Lunch & dinner £4.95-£12.95.
Closed Mon (open Bank Hols).
3pm-6pm Tues-Fri.
Open all day Sat & Sun.

John Younger
Queens Arms,
Litton,
Skipton, BD23 5QJ
Tel +44 (0)1756 770096
Web www.queensarmslitton.co.uk

Entry 648 Map 12

The Falcon Inn

Arncliffe

The Falcon is tucked onto the village green of Arncliffe in Littondale, one of the most remote of Yorkshire's dales. Several generations of Millers have been licensees here, preserving a way of life almost lost. The fine bay-windowed building looks more private house than village local; inside find few frills and old-fashioned hospitality. The entrance passageway leads to a small hallway at the foot of the stairs, there's a tiny bar counter facing you, and a small simple lounge, a log fire and haphazard pictures. The sunny back room looks across the garden to open fells and the loos are out the back. Timothy Taylor Boltmaker is served straight from the cask in a large jug, then dispensed into pint glasses at the bar, and at lunchtime you can order pie and peas, sandwiches and ploughman's. Deeply traditional. A Yorkshire gem.

Meals	Bar meals £2.50-£6, lunchtime only.
Closed	3pm-7pm. Reduced winter opening times, phone to check.

Joanne & Steven Hodgson
The Falcon Inn,
Arncliffe,
Skipton, BD23 5QE

Tel +44 (0)1756 770205
Web www.thefalconinn.com

Entry 649 Map 12

Yorkshire

Fountaine Inn

Linton

Linton, a heartbeat from the fleshpots of Grassington, has the whole caboodle, including Vanbrugh's stunning Fountaine Hospital and almshouses. Here is a village green complete with ducks and tiny humpback bridge; on its edge sits the historic Fountaine Inn. Inside, a warren of attractive rooms includes a chic snug with comfortable high-backed banquettes, beams and a cracking open fire. Theakstons, Thwaites and John Smiths are on tap while the crowd-pleasing menu features smoked haddock rarebit, Kilney smoked trout niçoise and pot roast poussin with leeks. In the winter, beef braised in Fountaine Pale Ale is a rib-sticking winner. This is perhaps the 'pubbiest' of the Clarksons' Skipton-based group – the kind of place you want on your doorstep.

Meals	Lunch & dinner £7.50-£14. Set menus £9.95.
Closed	Open all day.

Chris Gregson
Fountaine Inn,
Linton,
Skipton, BD23 5HJ

Tel +44 (0)1756 752210
Web www.fountaineinnatlinton.co.uk

Entry 650 Map 12

Craven Arms

Appletreewick

Authentically restored, this ancient rustic, creeper-clad pub (built in 1548) stands among gorgeous hills overlooking Wharfedale. It's a favourite with walkers so you could end up wagging a chin with them by the glowing cast-iron range in the stone-flagged bar. Just plain settles, panelled walls, thick beams, nothing more; beyond, a snug with simple benches and valley views, and a homely dining room. The final treat are the Wharfedale ales – Folly Gold, Executioner. Head out back to the loo to take a peek at the amazing function room housed in a replica medieval barn. Back in the bar, free of music and flashing games, find hot sandwiches and a legendary slow-roasted and minted lamb shoulder. Just the job after a blustery hike or cycle ride across the moors.

Meals	Lunch & dinner £8.95–£15.25. Bar meals £7.50–£10.50.
Closed	Open all day.

Mark Cooper
Craven Arms,
Appletreewick,
Skipton, BD23 6DA
Tel +44 (0)1756 720270
Web www.craven-cruckbarn.co.uk

Entry 651 Map 12

The Bull

Broughton

Off the main road to Skipton is this handsome, sprawling, mellow stone pub, with a big attractive patio at the back. The Bull is a great 'celebration' pub, and tops for Sunday lunch too. Being part of the Ribble Valley Inns group, it shares the same plush-but-relaxed décor that draws a crowd (smart flagged floors, chunky wood tables, open fires) and the same passion for local artisan producers, whose commissioned photographs hang on the walls. Attentive young staff deliver good-looking dishes that are packed with flavour, including duck and black pudding hash cakes, and chargrilled rump burgers with homemade piccalilli. There are ten wines by the glass and cask ales too – local, of course.

Meals	Starters from £4. Lunch from £6.50. Dinner from £9.
Closed	Open all day.

Nigel Haworth & Craig Bancroft
The Bull,
Broughton,
Skipton, BD23 3AE
Tel +44 (0)1756 792065
Web www.thebullatbroughton.com

Entry 652 Map 12

Ilkley Moor Vaults

Ilkley

A stone's throw from the centre of genteel, elegant, bustling Ilkley town is an establishment known for years as 'the Taps'. Though Jo and the loyal team have spruced it up you can still whet your whistle with a good pint of local ale, but there's so much more to enjoy. Joining the stone flagged floors, the scrubbed pine tables and the crackling fires are kitschy standard lamps with tasselled shades and a menu that promises robust dishes with a twist – and delivers. Out back is a smoker and kitchen garden, so air miles don't exist. You could happily take root here all day. When hunger hits, tuck into the likes of beef and ale pie, wild mushroom and spinach omelette, Vaults rarebit and tomato chutney, or a whole pheasant pie to share. The vibe is young but completely inclusive. Don't hesitate, just go.

Meals	Lunch & dinner £5.95-£9.95. Bar meals from £4.95. Sunday lunch from £10.95.
Closed	3pm-5pm. Mon. Open all day Sat & Sun.

Jo Zezulka
Ilkley Moor Vaults,
Stockeld Road,
Ilkley, LS29 9HD

Tel +44 (0)1943 607012
Web www.ilkleymoorvaults.co.uk

Entry 653 Map 12

Friends of Ham Leeds

Leeds

Beers, cheeses, charcuterie: that's all they do, but boy they do it well! Off the narrow dusty approach to the main train station is a big airy bar of scrubbed 'school' tables, designer chairs, funky swine prints and a fabulous buzz. Downstairs: a long, low, atmospheric room with benched tables, sofa-ed corners, bookshelf wallpapers and warm lighting; it's hipster-friendly and extremely inviting. We had hot-smoked Bath chaps (pigs' cheeks), Ibérico de Bellota (the king of Spanish ham), Jésus du Pays Basque (French salami with rum), and Vacherin, Comté and Stichelton cheeses. All were delightful. Beers are draft and bottled and global, from chocolate stouts to floral ales; wines are from interesting vineyards. Freshen up with a spring green salad, or round off your indulgence with chocolate panettone – served with crème patissière and rhubarb purée.

Meals	Small plates from £5.50. Sharing boards from £12.50.
Closed	Open all day.

Claire & Anthony Kitching
Friends of Ham Leeds,
4 New Station Street,
Leeds, LS1 5DL

Tel +44 (0)113 242 0275
Web www.friendsofham.com

Entry 654 Map 12

The Chequers Inn

Ledsham

Fires glow, horse brasses gleam… this honey-stone village inn could be in the Dales. In fact, you're a couple of miles from the A1. Panelled, carpeted rooms radiating off the central bar are cosy with log fires and plush red upholstery; faded photographs are a reminder of an earlier age. Rare hand-pumped ales from the Brown Cow Brewery at Selby do justice to good English food of Yorkshire proportions: steaming platefuls of loin of venison and red cabbage, wild boar with onion confit and sweet potato mash… just when you think you're replete, along comes chocolate torte with cream. The pub has been welcoming travellers since the 18th century and still closes on Sundays: in 1832 the lady of Ledsham Hall, confronting a drunken farmer on her way to church, insisted they close on the Sabbath!

Meals Lunch & dinner £5.50-£19.95.

Closed Sun.

Chris Wraith
The Chequers Inn,
Claypit Lane,
Ledsham, Leeds, LS25 5LP

Tel +44 (0)1977 683135

Web www.thechequersinn.com

Entry 655 Map 12

The Hinchliffe Arms

Cragg Vale

Wind down a leafy, quiet lane and find the handsome Hinchliffe nestled on the valley floor. On a sunny day you'll find all sorts of folk enjoying a drink outside; walkers, horse riders and cyclists. Locals, and newcomers to the trade, Miles and Linda Laprell have created a jolly, welcoming atmosphere, with a designated drinking area at the long oak bar where regulars (and their dogs!) convene nightly, enjoying the likes of Ilkley Stout Mary, Purity UBU and Oakham Citra. In the cosy dining room (warmed by a wood stove during cold months) dig into a menu that offers homely pub grub; it also features strikingly good-looking options should you want to push the boat out. White onion and coffee risotto, pan-fried halibut with potatoes anyone?

Meals Tea-time special £5.
Lunch & dinner £7-£25.

Closed Mon (except bank hols).
Tues until 5pm.
Wed-Thurs 3pm-5pm.
Fri until 4.30pm.

Miles & Linda Laprell
The Hinchliffe Arms,
Cragg Vale,
Halifax, HX7 5TA

Tel +44 (0)1422 883256

Web www.hinchliffearmscraggvale.co.uk

Entry 656 Map 12

The Old Bridge Inn

Ripponden

An ancient packhorse bridge and a little low inn… such is the setting. Friendly Tim and Lindsay's involvement over decades has resulted in a thoroughly civilised, unspoilt little local. Three carpeted, panelled, split-level rooms – dimly lit – are furnished with old oak settles and rush-seated chairs. The small green-walled snug at the top is atmospheric; the bar has a lofty ceiling with exposed timbers and a huge fireplace with a log-burning stove; the lower room is good for dining. Lindsay's buffet lunches are as popular as ever, and the evening menu reveals sound English cooking (pan seared hake; pie of the day with chips; Scotch eggs and curried eggs; Yorkshire cheeses) with a modern slant. The bar is well used by locals who come for Timothy Taylor's Best Bitter, Landlord and Golden Best. The wines are good, too.

Meals	Lunch £4.50-£14.50. Dinner from £9. No food Sun eves.
Closed	3pm-5.30pm. Open all day Fri-Sun.

Tim & Lindsay Eaton Walker
The Old Bridge Inn,
Priest Lane,
Ripponden, HX6 4DF
Tel +44 (0)1422 822595
Web www.theoldbridgeinn.co.uk

Entry 657 Map 12

Butchers Arms

Holmfirth

Up a steep hill in the middle of the village, a 250-year old pub with flagstone floors, blazing fires and cushioned settles around scrubbed tables. Well-travelled owner/chef Mark and his partner Caroline offer a mixed menu of French provincial and Thai dishes: meat is sourced from a nearby farm while Asian ingredients come from Manchester's Chinatown. Tuck into Salade Périgourdine or risotto with locally foraged mushrooms followed by frangipane with homemade ice cream. Come for Sunday roasts, brunch once a month and BBQs on special occasions. A huge effort goes in to keeping things interesting at this remote spot: lots of entertainment and events are organised, from brass band evenings to school quizzes and French communal evenings. Parking is limited so catch the bus or come on foot and make the most of the handpumped ales. It's ideal for walkers.

Meals	Lunch & dinner £13.95-£17.95.
Closed	Monday until 3pm.

Mark Hogan & Caroline Kimber
Butchers Arms,
38 Towngate, Hepworth,
Holmfirth, HD9 1TF
Tel +44 (0)1484 687147
Web www.thebutchersarms-hepworth.co.uk

Entry 658 Map 12

Broadfield Ale House

Sheffield

Not too long ago, this gnarly old city pub was a sticky-carpeted, nicotine-drenched dive, but the forward-thinking team from the Sheffield-based Forum group have completely turned it around. Lots of period features remain; stunning stained and etched glass, oak floors and open fires in all three rooms and they've added great beer and a simple but very inviting menu. Featuring prominently are homemade sausages and pies – ham, leek and cider, or beef, ale and mushroom – served with fat chips and of course mushy peas. Elsewhere, the likes of maple-glazed ham hock and slow beer-braised brisket will delight – all this and nicely kept pints of Abbeydale Moonshine and Bradfield Farmer's Pale Ale among half a dozen others. It's good to see the Broadfield has got its mojo back.

Meals	Lunch & dinner £7.50-£10.
Closed	Open all day.

Mark Simcox
Broadfield Ale House,
452 Abbeydale Road,
Sheffield, S7 1FR

Tel	+44 (0)114 255 0200
Web	www.thebroadfield.co.uk

Entry 659 Map 12

Yorkshire

The Cricket Inn

Totley

'Children, dogs, muddy boots welcome!' says this old stone pub, next to the cricket pitch in a leafy Sheffield suburb; the feel is rural. After a walk in the woods, put up your feet by the fire with the papers and pick up a pint of specially brewed Jaipur. Or take a ringside seat by the pitch in summer. Local restaurateurs Richard and Victoria Smith have joined forces with Thornbridge Brewery to create a laid-back, welcoming dining pub with stone floors, tongue-and-groove walls and open fires. They have a Portuguese chef now and their own smoker, so you can enjoy smoked beef brisket, smoked haddock risotto, smoked chicken... or mini Scotch eggs, beef jerky with black garlic aïoli, Portuguese fish stew. The food is pricey but praiseworthy, the service is warm and there's a great vibe.

Meals	Sandwiches from £5. Lunch & dinner £12-£20. Set menu £25. Sunday lunch from £13.50.
Closed	Open all day.

Richard Smith
The Cricket Inn,
Penny Lane, Totley,
Sheffield, S17 3AZ

Tel	+44 (0)114 236 5256
Web	www.relaxeatanddrink.com

Entry 660 Map 8

The Inn at Troway

Troway

High on a hill with rolling country views sits a 1930s mock Tudor pub with an arms-open-to-all approach. Inside, polished wood and terracotta sweep you towards a bar primed with Thornbridge Wild Swan and Jaipur alongside Black Sheep and Cocker Hoop ales. On either side are open-plan areas with red leather sofas, padded bench seats, period fireplaces and modern cartoon prints on walls. Enthusiastic staff settle you in and blackboards list the great meal offers for families, from grills, fish and chips and sandwiches to modern pub classics – perhaps Yorkshire pheasant with parsnip purée and buttered vegetables. Great homemade desserts as well, and pork crackling with apple sauce (the real deal!). There's a separate games room, lots of fresh flowers and treats for children on arrival.

Meals	Lunch & dinner from £8. Bar meals from £2. Sunday lunch from £10.
Closed	Open all day.

Richard Smith
The Inn at Troway,
Snowdon Lane, Troway,
Sheffield, S21 5RU

Tel +44 (0)1246 290751
Web www.relaxeatanddrink.com

Entry 661 Map 8

Yorkshire

The Star at Sancton

Sancton

Once upon a time, every farming village in the Yorkshire Wolds had a pub that was the beating heart of the community. Thanks to Ben and Lindsey Cox, this 800-year-old building is just that: the welcome is warm, the fires are lit and the comfortable, laid-back vibe is just wonderful. It's still very much a place for locals to pop in for a pint – beer is from the Copper Dragon and Wold Top breweries – but you must stay to eat. Ben is making a name for himself and the menu is tempting. Try Yorkshire pudding with confit oxtail and onion gravy (after all, Ben was the Yorkshire Pudding champion for two year's running) or Anna's Happy Trotter belly pork, braised kale and bacon with black pudding and Harrogate Blue bonbon and cyder reduction. Much of the produce comes from their allotment and orchard – a real treat.

Meals	Lunch & dinner £13.95-£21.95. Bar meals £4.95-£11.95. Set lunch £16.95 & £18.95.
Closed	Monday.

Ben & Lindsey Cox
The Star at Sancton,
Sancton,
Market Weighton, YO43 4QP

Tel +44 (0)1430 827269
Web www.thestaratsancton.co.uk

Entry 662 Map 13

The Goodmanham Arms

Goodmanham

In the middle of a village of whitewashed cottages, in yet-to-be-discovered 'Hockneyshire', is a simple red brick pub. Built in the 1800s it's handsome enough, with a pantile roof and a beer garden at the back. Inside is another story! Enter a wood-clad wonder of settles and wheel-back chairs, ticking clocks and roaring fires, brasses, baskets, books and candles, and All Hallows ales behind the bar: Abbie and Vito have a craft brewery out the back (Dark Mild, Gold and Porter). They're CAMRA award-winners too, so there's Ragged Robin and Old Peculier and guest beers that rotate weekly. In one of three linking rooms (one housing Vito's motorbikes), is a magnificent range on which they do the cooking. Arrive early if you want a table; the Gypsy Pot, tender beef cooked in ale, is sublime. Old-fashioned, timeless, and with a welcome second to none.

Meals Lunch & dinner from £8.95.
Closed Open all day.

Vito Logozzi
The Goodmanham Arms,
Main Street, Goodmanham,
Market Weighton, YO43 3JA
Tel +44 (0)1430 873849
Web www.goodmanhamarms.co.uk

Entry 663 Map 13

The Shoulder of Mutton

Kirkby Overblow

A handsome old inn between Harrogate and Harewood House with views rolling south over green hills to Wharfe Valley. Warm, stylish interiors mix old and new to great effect – original stone walls and low ceilings, then contemporary fabrics and a wall or two of paper. There's an open fire at one end, a wood burner at the other, stone flags and oak floors in between. As for the chattering band of happy locals, they flock in for fine Yorkshire ales, a glass of good wine and a tasty plate of comfort cooking, perhaps butterfly king prawns with chilli dipping sauce followed with shoulder of Masham lamb, then sticky toffee pudding with caramel sauce. In summer, you decant into a child-friendly garden and eat in the shade of ancient trees. Sunday lunch is a feast, with local walks to help you atone.

Meals Lunch & dinner £10.95-£19.50.
Early bird menu, 2-3 courses, £13.95-£16.95.
Sunday lunch, 3 courses, £18.95.
Gluten-free menu available.
Closed Monday.

Kate Deacon
The Shoulder of Mutton,
Main Street, Kirkby Overblow,
Harrogate, HG3 1HD
Tel +44 (0)1423 871205
Web www.shoulderofmuttonharrogate.co.uk

Entry 664 Map 12

The Alice Hawthorn

Nun Monkton

Pretty Nun Monkton: church, duck pond, village green, and the tallest maypole in England. The pub, named after a racehorse, was built in the late 1800s, but step in and the past falls away. In the bar, lavish banquettes, a stone flagged floor, a real fire. In the dining room, reindeer skins on a cushioned settle, a fireplace with a gleaming hood, fresh heather in zinc buckets. In the snug, tweedy chairs and rustic tables, each one different. Drinks are impressive, cooking is skilful and we didn't want our meal to end… homemade bread, butter on a stone slab, fish casserole with chorizo, beef-fried chips served in a little copper pan, crumble from apples from the neighbour five doors down. Spill onto the lawns in summer, for barbecues and pizzas from the oven. It's pubby and fun and opens its heart to everyone.

Meals	Lunch, 1-3 courses, £13.95-£21.95. Mains from £9.95.
Closed	Mondays.

Katherine Doughty
The Alice Hawthorn,
Nun Monkton,
York, YO26 8EW

Tel +44 (0)1423 330303
Web www.thealicehawthorn.com

Entry 665 Map 12

Yorkshire

Dawnay Arms

Newton on Ouse

The script on the lintel reads 1778. This stately building in a very pretty village has been rescued by Kerry and Martel, who have taken a step sideways from their Leeds brasserie. Now the old boozer is a shrine to modernity. Stone flagged floors and massive fireplaces have been kept, and church pews and chunky tables (constructed from timber pilfered from a Durham post office) sit stylishly against a pale backdrop enlivened by bright funky cushions and modern art in rococo frames. Faultless food scrupulously sourced flows from a kitchen run by maestro Martel – steak and kidney pudding with root vegetables and ale sauce; treacle tart with butterscotch ice cream. There's a glorious riverside garden for lazy summer days.

Meals	Lunch from £7.95-£14.95. Dinner from £9.95-£16.95. Sunday lunch, 3 courses, £17.95.
Closed	3pm-6pm. Mon. Open all day Sat & Sun.

Kerry Smith
Dawnay Arms,
Newton on Ouse,
York, YO30 2BR

Tel +44 (0)1347 848345
Web www.thedawnayatnewton.co.uk

Entry 666 Map 12

The Malt Shovel

Brearton

A warm convivial atmosphere permeates this restored building, where stone floors, open fires and beams abound. Set in the Mountgarret Estate, it's the perfect rest-stop for walkers and ramblers alike; there's a leather sofa in the hallway to take your muddy boots off (weary punters often roam the pub in their socks). Choose from three eating spaces – the bar with its salvaged church panelling and candles, the dining room stuffed with vintage finds, or the conservatory. Local ingredients are put to ambitious use in a menu that includes home-cured pancetta, while the sharing platter features home-smoked fish. There are several gruyère dishes on the bistro menu, and the oxtail and kidney pudding is a winner on a damp Yorkshire day. Ales are well-kept, the wines are a cut above the norm. Ask the friendly staff for their favourite walks while you lace up your boots on the way out.

Meals	Lunch & dinner from £10.95. Bar meals from £6.95. Dinner from £10.95. Sunday lunch, 3 courses, £20. No food Sun eve.
Closed	3pm-5.30pm. All day Mon.

Matt Marriott
The Malt Shovel,
Main Street, Brearton,
Harrogate, HG3 3BX
Tel +44 (0)1765 279188
Web www.themaltshovelbrearton.co.uk

Entry 667 Map 12

Yorkshire

The Punch Bowl Inn

Marton

The good people of Marton have got back their lovely local, thanks to the care and skill of Sasha and Michael Ibbotson. A gleaming coat of whitewash invites you in and the light lofty bar with its stunning cruck-barn ceiling tells of 16th-century origins. There's a very pleasing mix of oak settles and smart velvet chairs, open fires, polished wood floors and ruby-red walls. Tuck into twice-baked blue cheese soufflé with cauliflower purée or more substantially, confit shoulder of lamb. Veggies are well-served: try autumn field mushroom risotto or roast cherry vine tomato and sweet basil penne. Puds are a treat – bitter lemon posset with chantilly cream; apple and berry crumble with proper custard. In summer, a stylish courtyard at the back is a suntrap – a fab spot for a glass of something chilled.

Meals	Lunch from £7.95. Dinner from £12.75. Sunday lunch from £14.95.
Closed	Open all day.

Michael Ibbotson
The Punch Bowl Inn,
Marton, Marton-cum-Grafton,
York, YO51 9QY
Tel +44 (0)1423 322519
Web www.thepunchbowlmartoncumgrafton.com

Entry 668 Map 12

The Crown & Cushion

Welburn

Provenance Inns go from strength to strength. The latest addition to the stable bears all their trademarks (good beer, many wines by the glass, a pleasing value for money menu and a big welcome) but this nicely spruced-up old village pub, just a mile from the roaring A64, feels subtly different. Maybe it's the moss green palette, the coal fires, or the tap room? Whatever; it's a very pleasant spot for a pint of Black Sheep Bitter and a plate of local beef carpaccio, or the cracking Crown & Cushion pie. Gird your loins with treacle sponge and custard if you've planned to take advantage of one of the wonderful walks from the door. Outside, a flagged, be-shrubbed garden, a lovely place to sit out on a good day, with long views across the rolling Howardian Hills.

Meals	Starters from £5.95. Mains from £11.95. Sunday lunch from £14.95.
Closed	Open all day.

Michael Ibbotson
The Crown & Cushion,
Welburn,
York, YO60 7DZ

Tel +44 (0)1653 618777
Web www.thecrownandcushionwelburn.com

Entry 669 Map 13

Yorkshire

The Grapes Inn

Slingsby

Sometimes you walk into a pub and know it's a classic in the making. Locals Leigh and Catharine Spooner, a couple with no previous experience in the trade but a ton of enthusiasm took a chance and bought this handsome but run-down Georgian village boozer and have transformed it. All the good bits remain – stone floors, period windows, open fires – and they've filled it full of fabulous antique furniture of the period, plus a smattering of kitsch vintage finds. With jugs of fresh flowers, light jazz in the background and a short homely menu chalked on a board (the steak pie with herb suet crust is a winner) it's a fabulous spot to sit with a pint of Timothy Taylor Landlord before a tour round nearby Castle Howard.

Meals	Starters £4.95. Dinner from £9.95. Sandwiches £5.50, only at lunchtime. No food Sun eve.
Closed	Mon all day. Wed-Fri 2.30-5.30pm.

Leigh & Catharine Spooner
The Grapes Inn,
Railway Street,
Slingsby, YO62 4AL

Tel +44 (0)1653 628076
Web www.thegrapesinn-slingsby.co.uk

Entry 670 Map 13

The Royal Oak

Nunnington

In a distractingly pretty village is a handsome stone pub, once neglected, now revived, and loved by all who visit. Jill and Abbi (Italophiles both) are introducing Italy to North Yorks. No surprise that families are given a big welcome, and fish and chips join arms with the 'menu al giorno' (there's Yorkshire rarebit, gammon and pineapple, sticky toffee pudding and Sunday roasts, too). Plates of Tuscan deliciousness are ferried from the kitchen to the dining bar, which is shambolic in the nicest way. Tartan wool carpets, standing timbers, scrubbed tables, old mirrors, fresh flowers, tons of books, a wall of old keys, an eclectic mix of music on the stereo – seems like they've been here for years! There's a games room with bar billiards, a patio at the back and cosy fires for dogs. Cask ales, wines, local craft beers, espresso... marvellous.

Meals Starters from £4.50.
Mains from £9.50.
Closed Monday & Tuesday.

Jill & Abbi Greetham
The Royal Oak,
Church Street,
Nunnington, York, YO62 5US
Tel +44 (0)1439 748271
Web www.nunningtonroyaloak.co.uk

Entry 671 Map 13

Yorkshire

The Star Inn

Harome

You know you've hit the jackpot as soon as you step into the 14th-century Star – low ceilings, flagged floors, gleaming oak, flickering fire. Andrew's food is rooted in Yorkshire tradition, refined with French flair and written in plain English on ever-changing menus that brim with local produce. Swoon over the likes of white onion and smoked salmon soup with chestnut chantilly; risotto of partridge with black trumpet mushrooms; mutton and caper suet pudding; dark chocolate and satsuma tart; cheeses of the week. There's a bar with a Sunday papers-and-pint feel, a coffee loft in the eaves, their deli across the road, and now a new dining room with acres of white linen and lovely French windows to the garden. Even the schnapps is homemade.

Meals Lunch & dinner £16-£24.
Closed Mon lunch.

Andrew Pern
The Star Inn,
High Street, Harome,
Helmsley, YO62 5JE
Tel +44 (0)1439 770397
Web www.thestaratharome.co.uk

Entry 672 Map 13

The Hare

Scawton

You're on the brink of spectacular Sutton Bank here and it's pretty lofty, though the pretty pub with its freshly whitewashed front and cheery pantile roof nestles into the hillside. It's thought to date back to the 13th century and monks, knights, pilgrims and marauding Scots are said to have enjoyed its hospitality; enjoy a welcome today from owners Paul and Liz Jackson. Wood stoves, rich red walls and beams signal a traditional, rural pub but there's a surprise in store. Paul's skills in the kitchen produce fine tasting menus along the lines of scallop with smoked eel, apple and celeriac. You don't have to dress to the nines though; call by after a walk round nearby Rievaulx Abbey and settle down to a leisurely lunch; start with the Sutton Bank Dexter with watercress, macadamia, smoked oil and bone marrow. A classic in the making.

Meals	Lunch & dinner taster menu £45-£60.
Closed	3pm-6pm. Sun eves & Mon.

Paul & Liz Jackson
The Hare,
Scawton,
Thirsk, YO7 2HG

Tel	+44 (0)1845 597769
Web	www.thehare-inn.com

Yorkshire

The Fox & Hounds

Sinnington

The 18th-century coaching inn sits on the main street in sleepy Sinnington, on the edge of the North Yorkshire moors; the mounting block by the front door hints at its past. You feel embraced by the place the moment you walk in: Andrew, Catherine and their young team have got hospitality down to a fine art. The feel is utterly traditional, all oak settles, open fires and hops hanging from beams; relax with a pint of Copper Dragon or a seasonal brew from Black Sheep brewery while choosing your lunch. The attractive menu includes the likes of Lincolnshire poacher soufflé with golden beets and pine nut salad, and shoulder of lamb with pesto dumplings. If you can find room – portions are generous – the assiette of puddings is perfect for sharing. Wonderful in every way.

Meals	Light lunch & early supper £8.95. Dinner £11.50-£23.75. Sunday lunch, 3 courses, £22.
Closed	2pm-5pm.

Andrew & Catherine Stephens
The Fox & Hounds,
Main Street,
Sinnington, York, YO62 6SQ

Tel	+44 (0)1751 431577
Web	www.thefoxandhoundsinn.co.uk

The White Swan Inn

Pickering

Victor swapped the City for the North Yorkshire Moors and this old coaching inn; the place oozes comfort and style. Duck in through the front door to a tiny, cosy, panelled tap room serving real Yorkshire ales, with smart country furniture, fine wines and eager young staff. In the dining room, find heaven on a plate as you dig into supper. Try seared hand-dived king scallops with air-dried ham, Levisham mutton with Irish cabbage, poached rhubarb on toasted brioche and homemade ice cream. Menus change monthly and 80% of the ingredients are locally sourced, with meat coming from the legendary Ginger Pig. Don't miss the beamed club room for a roaring fire, board games and an honesty bar. Castle Howard is nearby, the moors are wild, the steam railway is fun.

Meals	Lunch from £5.25. Dinner £13-£24. Sunday lunch £22.50.
Closed	Open all day.

Claire Beaumont
The White Swan Inn,
Market Place,
Pickering, YO18 7AA

Tel +44 (0)1751 472288
Web www.white-swan.co.uk

The Anvil Inn

Sawdon

The fact that this village is not on a bus route suggests you may be in the back of beyond – but we urge you to beat a path to its very cosy door. The Anvil was a working forge until the mid 1980s, the building is over 200 years old and the lofty, all-stone workshop has become a bar – an unusual centrepiece to a great little pub. Partner-chefs Mark and Alexandra have pulled the place up by its bootstraps and have created an environment to linger long in. Settle into an old oak pew, lounge by the wood-burner in a leather tub chair, order a pint – Daleside, Wold Top – and scan the menu. Invention without pretension is the philosophy here, and thoughtfully executed, locally sourced food flows from the kitchen. A classic in the making.

Meals	Lunch & dinner from £9.50-£15.45. Sunday lunch £11.50.
Closed	Mon & Tues all day. 2.30pm-6.30pm.

Mark & Alex Wilson
The Anvil Inn,
Main Street, Sawdon,
Scarborough, YO13 9DY

Tel +44 (0)1723 859896
Web www.theanvilinnsawdon.co.uk

Photo: Alec Studerus

Wales

Photo: The Dolaucothi Arms, entry 680

The Black Lion Inn

Holyhead

The lion roars again thanks to the hard work of owners Mari and Leigh who have transformed this once derelict late 18th-century country inn into an award-winning local champion. Contemporary slate tiles wrap round a modern bar, lime rendered walls host modern pictures – one a fabulous collage of local wildlife. French windows open to a paved patio with views across the car park to fields, one of which grow vegetables and herbs for the kitchen. Ales from local Welsh breweries and interesting wines set you up for modern British dishes made with locally grown, foraged and reared produce. Try fresh-as-can-be seared scallops with black pudding, pancetta and pea purée, or braised shoulder of local lamb with a root vegetable rösti. Upstairs are two hugely comfortable rooms with open rafters, thick carpets and handmade oak furniture: the mattresses are top of the range, the bathrooms gleam with white tiles, mosaic inlay and sleek chrome. You are beside a road but thick walls and small windows ensure blissful calm, while eco-energy keeps you snug. Glorious Anglesey awaits.

Rooms	1 double: £115. 1 family room for 4: 140
Meals	Lunch & dinner £6-£19.
Closed	3-6pm Mon-Fri. Open all day Sat-Sun. From Nov to Easter, closed Mon-Tues.

Leigh & Mari Faulkner
The Black Lion Inn,
Llanfaethlu,
Holyhead, LL65 4NL
Tel +44 (0)1407 730718
Web www.blacklionanglesey.com

Anglesey

Ye Olde Bulls Head Inn

Beaumaris

The former haunt of Johnson and Dickens now attracts drinkers and foodies like bees to clover. In the rambling, snug-alcoved bar there's draught Bass on offer; in the modern brasserie in the stables are ten wines by the glass – and tasty food to go with it, perhaps Moroccan fish stew or confit duck leg. Upstairs sees a sophisticated remodelling, in the intimate Loft Restaurant – along with pieces of ancient weaponry and an antique ducking stool. Here, Welsh dishes are designed around seafood from the Menai Strait, and as much beef, lamb and game as the chefs can source on the island. The results: lamb loin rolled in thyme and garlic with coriander jus; wild turbot with braised pigs cheeks, fondant potato and glazed vegetables... seasoned as required with Anglesey sea salt. Service comes with warmth and charm.

Meals: Lunch & dinner in brasserie £5-£30. Dinner in restaurant, 3 courses, £45 (Tues-Sat only).
Closed: Open all day.

David Robertson
Ye Olde Bulls Head Inn,
Castle Street,
Beaumaris, LL58 8AP
Tel: +44 (0)1248 810329
Web: www.bullsheadinn.co.uk

Entry 678 Map 6

Cardiff

The Longhouse

Cardiff

Welcome to the 'God's pantry' that is Wales, where the menu shouts seasonal and the produce is as local as can be. This 17th-century longhouse is heaped with character in exposed stone walls and flagstone floors, there's a game park opposite and gorgeous countryside all around. Sunshine pours onto new chesterfields and old pews, a friendly bookcase partitions the rooms, and wood-burners roar. Nicky keeps the wine list exciting and Andy cooks meals which are earthy and enticing: tuck into roasted quail with ceps, egg, bacon and sorrel followed by Halen Môn sea-salted chocolate-hazelnut torte. Don't fret if you prefer old-fashioned pub classics: there are Welsh beef burgers in brioche buns, ocean-fresh fish 'n' chips, and keg ales from the Vale of Glamorgan. For summer: a large roadside terrace at the front.

Meals: Starters from £6. Mains from £13.
Closed: Monday.

Andy Aston
The Longhouse,
The Tumble, St Nicholas,
Cardiff, CF5 6SA
Tel: +44 (0)29 2115 7754
Web: www.longhousewales.com

Entry 679 Map 2

The Dolaucothi Arms

Pumpsaint

Tucked away in the heart of the Carmarthenshire countryside, this gem of a pub shines bright. Lovely Esther and Dave have brought the Dolaucothi back to life – notice little touches like handsome floral reupholstering on the mix-and-match dining chairs, and clutches of blooms in jugs and antique bottles on tables and sills. Dave's gorgeous gardens flank the walk up the little path; as you come in, there's a happy buzz in the air and the tempting scent of fresh home cooking; nearly everything is lovingly cooked from scratch! The dining room and bar are all in warm neutrals, with terracotta tiles and wood-burners. Sink into the velvety green chesterfield in the snug with a bottle of local brew or a glass of wine – Esther and Dave can advise. Food wise, try lamb reared by Dolaucothi farmer Gary, or the homemade pies; both are local and delicious. Hop up the little staircase, and you'll find three quiet bedrooms with garden views in soft tones of olive or wild rose. Snuggle up with wool duvets and pillows topped with colourful Welsh blankets, and enjoy the peace. There's even a little tipple on the chest of drawers for a nightcap.

Rooms	3 doubles: £75-£80.
Meals	Lunch from £5. Dinner £7-£15.
Closed	Monday. Tuesday until 6.30pm.

David Joy & Esther Hubert
The Dolaucothi Arms,
Pumpsaint, Llanwrda, SA19 8UW
Tel +44 (0)1558 650237
Web www.thedolaucothiarms.co.uk

Y Talbot

Tregaron

In the centre of tiny Tregaron, the crisply Georgian frontage of Y Talbot makes a big impression, part modern-rustic drover's inn and part old-fashioned hotel. Inside the inn: an enormous inglenook with bread oven, slate floors, thick walls gleaming with hanging brass and copper. You dine in what was once the stable, with oak furniture and soapstone sculptures, where everything is light and bright. The hotel is all white corridors and glass doors, its curved wooden staircase leading to rooms which are cool and white and comfortable, with big smart bathrooms. The rooms on the top floor are cosiest, with low windows to views over the square. New airy rooms at the rear of the pub are big enough for families. Friendly Mick and Nia will point you towards the best walks or rambles while head chef Dafydd Watkin (who worked under Marco Pierre White) does a mean Cambrian lamb shoulder, and works wonders with the day's fresh fish catch. All this and local tipples such as Purple Moose, Gwynt y Ddraig cider and Mantle from the latest micro brewery on the block.

Rooms	8 twin/doubles: £85-£120. 3 family rooms for 4: £110-£160. 2 singles: £50-£70.
Meals	Starters from £4.75. Mains £9-£18.
Closed	Open all day.

Mick Taylor
Y Talbot,
Tregaron, SY25 6JL
Tel +44 (0)1974 298208
Web www.ytalbot.com

Harbourmaster

Aberaeron

Lobster boats at lunch, twinkling harbour lights at dinner, real ale, well-chosen wines, dazzling service. The old harbourmaster's residence has become decidedly chic with an inspirational restaurant and bar. Step in to find a space that's cosy but cool: soft shades, zinc-topped tables. In the celebrated bistro, daily menus are studded with the best local produce and the dishes delight: roast Blaencamel Farm beetroot with honeycomb and feta; Carlingford oysters; fillet of cod, samphire, chard, cockles and tomato; thyme roast peach with Glyn Aeron honey ice cream. In the bar (open for breakfast from 8am) tuck into local crab, chilli and garlic linguine, Welsh rib-eye steak or a stone-baked pizza. The Heulyns' dedication to all that is best about Wales shines forth. Cycle tracks spin off into the hills, coastal paths lead north and south.

Meals: Lunch & bar meals from £9.50. Dinner from £16. Sunday lunch, 3 courses, £21.

Closed: Open all day.

Dai Morgan
Harbourmaster,
Pen Cei,
Aberaeron, SA46 0BT

Tel: +44 (0)1545 570755
Web: www.harbour-master.com

Entry 682 Map 6

Ceredigion

Y Ffarmers

Llanfihangel y Creuddyn

The drive to this pretty village, once a silver and lead mining community, is well worth it. Previously a farm and tax collector's office, Y Ffarmers has found its true calling under the delightful stewardship of chef Rhodri and wife Esther. You can walk into the quarry-tiled bar with mud on your boots and not an eyelid will be batted; enjoy a pint of Evan Evans or Felinfoel. The dining rooms next door have polished oak flooring, an assortment of tables, books on Wales, and terrific local art on walls, with regular choral or harp evenings adding a real Welsh flavour. Everything is made from scratch, from bread and rolls to relishes and puddings. Menus range from Penlan gammon, egg and chips to lamb tagine with medjool dates, and a pomegranate and mint couscous too.

Meals: Lunch & dinner £5-£18.50. Sunday lunch £16-£19.50.

Closed: Mondays all day, except school summer holidays.

Esther Prytherch
Y Ffarmers,
Llanfihangel y Creuddyn,
Aberystwyth, SY23 4LA

Tel: +44 (0)1974 261275
Web: www.yffarmers.co.uk

Entry 683 Map 7

The Queen's Head

Glanwydden

The old wheelwright's cottage has gone up in the world. Now there are low beams, polished tables, smart tartan carpeting, walls strewn with maps and a roaring fire in the bar. The food is good, the portions generous and you can see the cooks at work through the open hatch. This is home-cooked pub food with a modern twist; in summer there'll be fresh Conwy crab and Great Orme lobster. Friendly, smartly turned-out staff serve starters of crispy duck leg or Conwy fish soup, then salmon and coriander fishcakes, then Welsh rump steaks with garlic butter... desserts might include raspberry and amaretto trifle. Robert and Sally Cureton have been here for over 30 years, nurturing a country local that puts those of Llandudno to shame. Complete the treat by booking a night in the old parish storehouse across the road, a sweet retreat for two and recently revamped. A gallery bedroom under white-painted eaves, a bathroom lavishly tiled, a small private garden for breakfast coffee and fresh croissants... a perfect set up for a romantic break. *Self-catering available.*

Rooms	1 cottage for 2: £90-£150.
Meals	Lunch & dinner £9.95-£21.95. Sunday lunch £10.95.
Closed	Open all day.

Robert & Sally Cureton
The Queen's Head,
Glanwydden,
Llandudno Junction, LL31 9JP
Tel +44 (0)1492 546570
Web www.queensheadglanwydden.co.uk

Pen-y-Bryn

Colwyn Bay

Oak floors and bookcases, open fires and Turkey rugs – welcome to the make-believe world of Brunning & Price. Staff are well-informed and never too busy to share their knowledge, of the food and its provenance. Menus are enticing and generously priced: braised shoulder of lamb with dauphinoise potatoes and rosemary gravy; warming leek and potato soup with crusty bread. Pork and lamb is local, cheeses fly the Principality's flag and plump mussels come from down the coast. You're high up on Colwyn Heights here but a few glasses of Purple Moose's Snowdonia or Salopian Black Heart Stout will soon warm your toes. Sturdy wooden furniture in the garden fits in well with the neighbourhood's residential air... and there are wonderful views over the sea.

Meals	Lunch & dinner £6.25-£16.95. Bar meals £4.50-£9.25. Sunday lunch £10.25.
Closed	Open all day.

Andrew Grant
Pen-y-Bryn,
Wentworth Avenue,
Colwyn Bay, LL29 6DD

Tel +44 (0)1492 533360
Web www.penybryn-colwynbay.co.uk

Entry 685 Map 7

The Albion

Conwy

For lovers of real ale and lively chat no visit to Conwy would be complete without raising a glass here. Tucked just beside the ancient town walls by one of the narrow stone gateways is an unassuming pub. Inside is spacious with roaring fires and comfy interiors: Tiffany style lamps and chandeliers, an antique banquette, dark polished wood floorboards and Art Deco touches. Run as a joint venture by the Conwy, Great Orme, Nant and Purple Moose Breweries the real ale on offer is outstanding and there's no food to interfere with the flow, just handmade pork pies and pickled eggs. There's a neat central courtyard for warmer days and it's super dog-friendly too. The Albion buzzes with humanity and good cheer, and staff know their beer-led business.

Meals	Bar snacks only.
Closed	Open all day.

Stuart Chapman-Edwards
The Albion,
Upper Gate Street,
Conwy LL32 8RF

Tel +44 (0)1492 582484
Web www.conwybrewery.co.uk

Entry 686 Map 7

The Groes Inn

Ty'n-y-Groes

The first licensed house in Wales (1573) is splendidly old-fashioned, with rambling bars, nooks and crannies, and low beams and doorways that demand heads be bowed. Painted stonework is hung with local prints and pictures, there are displays of teacups and Victorian postcards, a red carpet, a polished dresser, a wood-burner to keep things toasty. Our pint of Orme's Best – brewed by Justin's cousin – went down a treat, as did the prime-beef burger in its great toasted bap, with a crisp mixed salad and delicious hand-cut chips. In the more elegant restaurant, 32 wines accompany award-winning dishes: baked field mushrooms, Conway crab and Anglesey oysters, sweet Welsh lamb with rich rosemary jus, chocolate-scented pancakes with sumptuous ice cream. For summer there's a pretty garden with mountain views.

Meals	Lunch & dinner from £13.25. Bar meals from £9.65.
Closed	3pm-6pm.

Dawn & Justin Humphreys
The Groes Inn,
Ty'n-y-Groes, LL32 8TN

Tel +44 (0)1492 650545
Web www.groesinn.com

Entry 687 Map 7

Conwy

The Kinmel Arms

St George

In a tiny hamlet – yet easily reachable from the A55 – the Kinmel Arms shines like a culinary beacon. Lynn and Tim arrived a decade ago and the place continues to delight. Walk in to an open-plan space of cool neutral colours, hardwood floors and a central bar with stained-glass above; then through to a conservatory restaurant, painted a cheery yellow and decorated with Tim's photographs. Seasonal brasserie-style menus champion local producers – Welsh beef fillet with Penderyn whisky sauce; Asian-spiced sea bass with crispy squid in a coconut and lentil cream. All is beautifully presented, and the slate-topped bar dispenses top quality local ales and great value bin-end wines. This is a hop from the stunning North Wales coast and Snowdonia; great walks start from the door.

Meals	Lunch £6.95-£17.50. Dinner £14.95-£24.95.
Closed	3pm-6pm. Sun & Mon all day.

Tim Watson & Lynn Cunnah-Watson
The Kinmel Arms,
The Village, St George,
Abergele, LL22 9BP

Tel +44 (0)1745 832207
Web www.thekinmelarms.co.uk

Entry 688 Map 7

The Hand at Llanarmon

Llanarmon Dyffryn Ceiriog

The Hand sits in glorious country – vast skies, rolling hills, country lanes that deliver you into the middle of nowhere. It's a popular spot with walkers, mountain bikers and wildlife spotters, who spend their days having fun in the hills before rolling down to this 16th-century drovers' inn for the pleasures of a country local. A coal fire burns on the range in reception, a wood fire crackles in the front bar, a wood-burner keeps things cosy in the restaurant. Expect stone walls, low beamed ceilings, old pine settles and candles on the mantelpiece. There's a locals' bar for darts and pool, then a quiet sitting room for maps and books, which doubles as a treatment room. Delicious food draws a crowd, so grab a table and dig into excellent country fare, perhaps Welsh Cheddar brûlée, roast rump of local lamb, sticky toffee pudding with caramel sauce. Airy rooms, all recently refurbished, have a contemporary feel with Welsh woollen throws on good beds and views of village and hill. Those in the main house are a little bigger, a couple have claw-foot-baths, three are dog friendly. Special indeed.

Rooms	11 doubles: £95-£135. 1 suite for 4: £150. Singles from £52.50.
Meals	Lunch from £4.75. Bar meals from £9.50. Sunday lunch from £15. Dinner, 3 courses, £25-£30.
Closed	Open all day.

Jackie & Jonathan Greatorex
The Hand at Llanarmon,
Llanarmon Dyffryn Ceiriog,
Llangollen, LL20 7LD
Tel +44 (0)1691 600666
Web www.thehandhotel.co.uk

The Corn Mill

Llangollen

The 18th century has been left far behind in this renovated corn mill beside the swift flowing Dee. Not only is the interior airy and well-designed but the menu is laced with contemporary ideas. There are gorgeous views onto the river whether you're quaffing your pint of Phoenix in the fabulous bar, or sitting down to eat in one of the upper dining areas. The decked veranda-cum-walkway is stunning, built out over cascading rapids with a gangway overhanging one end beyond a revolving water wheel. Watch dippers and wagtails as you tuck into smoked haddock and mozzarella rarebit, Welsh pork sausages with spring onion mash, king prawn salad with chilli dressing – the Brunning & Price formula is known for its 'something-for-everyone' appeal.

Meals Lunch & dinner £8.95-£16.50.
Closed Open all day.

Andrew Barker
The Corn Mill,
Castle Street,
Llangollen, LL20 8PN
Tel +44 (0)1978 869555
Web www.cornmill-llangollen.co.uk

Entry 690 Map 7

The Glynne Arms

Hawarden

This handsome Georgian coaching inn was built in 1812 and takes its name from the Glynne family whose ancestral seat was Hawarden Castle. From the outset it was a place for the village, more 'house of refreshment' than drinking den. Today that is as true as ever, with outstanding produce from the estate's farm shop finding its way to the kitchen. There's grilled sea bream on crushed new potatoes with curly kale and a crayfish and thermidor sauce; grills, antipasti and ploughman's platters and more. The pub itself has undergone a stunning renovation and has a retro-quirky character with bold rugs, framed period posters, bills and letters, crossed axes, antlers and a bust encircled with a footy scarf – get the picture? Charming staff make you feel welcome, and being here is a treat.

Meals Lunch & dinner £6.95-£23.50.
Closed Open all day.

Martin Hurd
The Glynne Arms,
3 Glynne Way,
Hawarden, CH5 3NS
Tel +44 (0)1244 569988
Web www.theglynnearms.co.uk

Entry 691 Map 7

Glasfryn

Sychdyn

Drawing a diverse crowd, this solid red brick pub – a former judges' residence with an Arts & Crafts pedigree – sits on a south-facing slope with views over the town to the Clwydian range. A stunning makeover has led to acres of oak flooring, Indian rugs, book-lined walls and locally themed pictures and prints. Real ale aficionados will thrill to eight cask ales. Purple Moose's Snowdonia ale delivers a crisp, citrus beer; Flowers Original is brewing heritage in a glass. Foodies are not forgotten... find mint-braised shoulder of lamb with mustard mash and broccoli; quiche with roasted squash, goat's cheese and red onion; white chocolate cheesecake. You get 80 malts, every spirit imaginable and coffee made by an Italian – need we say more? It's abuzz, and the staff are attentive and helpful.

Meals	Lunch & dinner £8.50-£15.95.
Closed	Open all day.

Andrew Grant
Glasfryn,
Raikes Lane, Sychdyn,
Mold, CH7 6LR

Tel	+44 (0)1352 750500
Web	www.glasfryn-mold.co.uk

Entry 692 Map 7

Photo: The Butchers Arms, entry 220

Cross Foxes

Brithdir

Nicol and Dewi have worked wonders breathing new life into this stone built former farmhouse. A steel and glass entrance leads through to a modern bar where flagstones, exposed stonework and beams mingle with contemporary sofas, designer bar stools and sleek lighting. In summer, sup Purple Moose's Snowdonia Ale on the terrace and gaze up at lofty Cadair Idris – a giant's seat indeed. Food from the open kitchen comes with impeccable local credentials and the char-grill compliments the meats perfectly. What could be more local than Conwy mussels, leeks and cream followed by confit leg of Welsh lamb, rosemary and honey gravy, potatoes and seasonal vegetables? There are great Sunday roasts too, light bites, and afternoon teas. Upstairs the comfort factor scales new heights as natural stone, beams and antiques blend with a crisp modernity; there are beds for dreaming in and mountain views through windows. Gorgeous bathrooms, with Thierry Mugler lotions and thick robes, soothe those who have stretched their muscles in the surrounding hills. A 15-minute drive brings you to delightful Barmouth and the coast.

Rooms	2 doubles, 2 twin/doubles, 2 suites for 2: £90-£135.
Meals	Lunch from £4.95. Dinner & bar meals from £9.95. Sunday lunch, 2 courses, £12.95.
Closed	Open all day.

Nicol Gwynne
Cross Foxes,
Brithdir,
Dolgellau, LL40 2SG
Tel +44 (0)1341 421001
Web www.crossfoxes.co.uk

Newbridge On Usk

Tredunnock

As darkness falls, the old stone bridge is floodlit, its arches reflected in the waters of the Usk. The setting is seductive, the garden runs down to the river bank, and the views from the window are stunning. Inside is what a gastropub should be; warm, inviting and beautifully turned out. In several rooms on several levels, pots of flowers or collections of squashes reflect the seasons, big leather sofas invite you to linger, and the design reveals the polished beauty of floorboards and beams. You don't have to eat here but if you do the set lunch is a steal. Ingredients are sourced from around the UK and with care; try woodland mushroom and white truffle risotto, Brecon venison wrapped in smoked bacon, a wicked sticky toffee pudding. Private groups can sit down to an indulgent feasting menu in the atmospheric wine store.

Meals: Set lunch, 2 courses, from £15.95. Dinner, 3 courses, from £30.
Closed: Open all day.

James Lewis
Newbridge On Usk,
Tredunnock, Usk, NP15 1LY
Tel: +44 (0)1633 410262
Web: www.celtic-manor.com/newbridge-on-usk-restaurant

Entry 694 Map 2

Monmouthshire

The Crown at Pantygelli

Pantygelli

On a quiet lane above the Usk Valley between the Sugarloaf and Skirrid mountains, a whitewashed building with tables and umbrellas outside and hanging baskets framing a slate-roofed porch. Step in to a traditional pub with oak beams, dogs lazing on the floor and a series of red-carpeted rooms with white stone walls and wood burners. Landlords Steve and Cherrie run a real community pub thanks to a convivial atmosphere, regular events and a menu of hearty old favourites made from local produce wherever possible: prawn marie rose to start, perhaps, followed by beef and bubble or goat's cheese tart, rounded off with fudge muffin with chocolate sauce, and all accompanied by handpumped ales or a choice of wines by the glass. There's a cracking specials menu, too. Play a board game, listen to one of the locals on the piano, or just settle in with the papers.

Meals: Starters from £5. Mains from £10. Desserts from £5.50. Baguettes from £4.50.
Closed: Mondays.

Steve & Cherrie Chadwick
The Crown at Pantygelli,
Old Hereford Road, Pantygelli,
Abergavenny, NP7 7HR
Tel: +44 (0)1873 853314
Web: www.thecrownatpantygelli.com

Entry 695 Map 7

The Bell at Skenfrith

Skenfrith

The Bell stands by an ancient stone bridge in a little-known valley with beautiful hills rising behind and a Norman castle paddling in the river a hundred yards from the front door. A sublime spot – and the inn is as good. In the locals' bar you find slate floors, open fires, plump-cushioned armchairs and polished oak. In summer, life decants onto the terrace at the back; priceless views of wood and hill interrupted only by the odd chef pottering past on his way to a rather impressive kitchen garden. Stripped boards in the restaurant give an airy feel, so stop for delicious food served by young, attentive staff, perhaps chicken liver parfait, duck with chorizo and mixed bean cassoulet, and chocolate fondant with caramelised banana and white chocolate ice cream. Finish with a fine cognac – the list is long.

Meals Lunch from £18.
Sunday lunch from £22.
Dinner, 3 courses, around £35.

Closed Open all day.
Closed Tues Nov-Mar.

Richard Ireton & Sarah Hudson
The Bell at Skenfrith,
Skenfrith,
Abergavenny, NP7 8UH

Tel +44 (0)1600 750235
Web www.skenfrith.co.uk

Entry 696 Map 7

The Ridgeway Bar & Kitchen

Newport

Minutes from the M4 this former 1960s watering hole has been transformed into a stylish concern in a residential suburb. The bar area is for drink and chat only and has a smart lounge feel, all padded banquettes, polished slate tiles and a mix of wood and painted furniture. Cheery staff dispense Sharps, St Austell and Wye Valley ales and cocktails are coming soon. The dining areas are spacious and comfortable with New England tones on painted panelling and here you can enjoy chef Rickie's modern British food. There are good old-fashioned methods in the preparation and no corner-cutting. Start with Somerset cider-steamed mussels mopped up with toasted artisan bread, and move on to braised beef shin with chantenay carrots, wilted spinach, fondant potato and roasting jus. Quality is king.

Meals Lunch & dinner £8.50-£15.

Closed Open all day.

David Pell
The Ridgeway Bar & Kitchen,
No. 2 Ridgeway Avenue,
Newport, NP20 5AJ

Tel +44 (0)1633 266053
Web www.storyinns.com

Entry 697 Map 2

Stackpole Inn

Stackpole

This lovely inn sits in a pretty village that's marooned in beautiful country. It's a few miles back from the sea, with Barafundle Bay – one of the finest beaches in Britain – a short walk away. You can pick up the coastal path, too, and follow it round past Stackpole Quay and St Govan's Chapel to the cliffs at Linney Head, then the surfers at Freshwater West. It's pure heaven, one of those sleepy areas you drop into for a couple of days and hardly use your car. As for the Stackpole, it's a great little base – stylish and welcoming with tasty rustic food, perhaps deep-fried whitebait, rib of local beef, almond and hazelnut tart. Outside, the pub is drenched in honeysuckle and there's a small garden to the front for a drop of Welsh ale in summer. Inside, you find low wooden ceilings, exposed stone walls, a hard-working wood-burner and four hand pumps at the slate bar. Super bedrooms have comfy beds, stripped floors, seaside colours and excellent bathrooms. All have sofabeds, two have velux windows for star gazing. Dogs and children are very welcome.

Rooms	2 twin/doubles: £90. 2 family rooms for 4: £90-£120. Singles from £60.
Meals	Lunch from £5. Dinner, 3 courses, £25-£30. Sunday lunch, 3 courses, £18.95.
Closed	3pm-6pm & Sun eves in winter. Open all day Sat & Sun in summer.

Gary & Becky Evans
Stackpole Inn,
Stackpole,
Pembroke, SA71 5DF

Tel +44 (0)1646 672324
Web www.stackpoleinn.co.uk

The Old Point House Inn

Angle

Lonely, windswept, so close to the sea they're cut off at spring tide. Weary fishermen have beaten a path to the inn's door for centuries; part-built with shipwreck timbers, it started life as a bakehouse for ships' biscuits. The tiny, low-beamed bar, its bare walls papered with old navigation charts, is utterly authentic, the restaurant is cosy by night, and in fine weather you can sit out and devour prawn sandwiches. Everyone is welcome here, from weathered regulars meeting over pints of Felinfoel to families in for Sunday lunch. Naturally, menus favours fish, with local Milford cod, sea bass and a delicious peppery fish chowder, all chalked up on the board. Further crowd-pleasers rib-eye steak with red wine sauce and piles of chips.

Meals	Lunch & bar meals £5.50-£10.50. Dinner £5.50-£19.95. Sunday lunch, 3 courses, £12.50. No food on Weds (Nov-Feb).
Closed	3pm-6pm. Mon & Tues in winter. Open all day in summer.

John Noble
The Old Point House Inn,
Angle Village,
Angle,
Pembroke, SA71 5AS
Tel +44 (0)1646 641205

Entry 699 Map 6

Pembrokeshire

Griffin Inn

Dale

Dale's last, very old pub – there were once 15 – sits defiantly close to the water and has seen out some stormy seas. The stone sea wall in front is known as 'the longest bar in Pembrokeshire' and what better place to be on a warm day with a pint of Tenby Harbwr's North Star or Tomos Watkin's Cwrw Haf, both from local breweries, as you watch the day's catch being unloaded from responsible day boats. Fresh fish, lobster and shellfish are hugely popular here and make the short distance from beach to Simon and Sian's home-cooked menus. Inside are red quarry tiles, painted stone, wood panelling and an open fire in the cosy, traditional bar. An additional restaurant and roof terrace have been added to make the most of the great views across the bay and up the Haven, kids love to play on the pontoon, and the coastal walks are superb.

Meals	Starters from £5.95. Mains from £9.25.
Closed	Open all day.

Simon & Sian Vickers
Griffin Inn,
Dale,
Haverfordwest, SA62 3RB
Tel +44 (0)1646 636227
Web www.griffininndale.co.uk

Entry 700 Map 6

The Swan Inn

Little Haven

Little Haven is jumbled into the seaward end of a narrow valley with glorious views across St Bride's Bay. Trek up the cobbled path to reach the Swan, whose fabric and fortunes have been restored by Paul Morris. Original features abound in the uncluttered sideroom snug and the blue-painted dining room, alongside bare boards and stone, simple wood furniture and glowing stoves for wild days. Equally warming is the delicious food: at lunch, homemade sodabread topped with smoked salmon maybe, or a traditional Welsh cawl with Caerfai cheese. In the evening: pan-fried scallops with chorizo, roasted sea bass with caper butter and samphire. For summer there's a broad wall to lounge on and a tiny terrace, so settle in for the day with a foaming pint of Bass and take in the views – they're stupendous.

Meals	Lunch from £5.50. Dinner from £12.
Closed	Open all day.

Paul & Tracey Morris
The Swan Inn,
Point Road, Little Haven,
Haverfordwest, SA62 3UL
Tel +44 (0)1437 781880
Web www.theswanlittlehaven.co.uk

Entry 701 Map 6

Pembrokeshire

The Sloop

Porthgain

Perfectly in keeping with its seawashed setting, the Sloop has been welcoming fisherfolk since 1743. The village remains a fishing harbour – the landlord catches his own lobster, mackerel and crab, and dives for scallops – but, until the Thirties, Porthgain was more famous for bricks and granite. Weatherbeaten on the outside, with a little seating area at the front, the old Sloop is surprisingly cosy within. Expect bare beams, some bare boards, a happy melée of furniture, a canoe suspended from the ceiling and a board announcing daily specials. Tuck into homemade mackerel pâté, lobster thermidor or Welsh Black steak; breakfast too (open to all) sounds a treat. Holiday makers descend in summer but the rest of the year this is a community pub, with a proper games room and real fires.

Meals	Lunch & dinner £5.35-£18.
Closed	Open all day.

Matthew Blakiston
The Sloop,
Porthgain,
Haverfordwest, SA62 5BN
Tel +44 (0)1348 831449
Web www.sloop.co.uk

Entry 702 Map 6

Tafarn Sinc

Rosebush

The highest pub in Pembrokeshire is the quirkiest pub in the world – a corrugated crimson shed. It was speedily erected in 1876 as a hotel on the GWR railway; now this huge zinc building with a panorama of the Preseli Hills oversees a railway platform complete with mannequin-travellers. It is beautifully tended, with a profusion of planters and picnic sets outside and an arresting Alpine-panelled bar within. Hams and lamps hang from the ceiling, there's sawdust on the floors and two wood-burners that belch out heat. It's warm and welcoming and full of merry walkers. Hafwen the perfect landlady, and husband Brian, oversee the cosy constant buzz and serve a solidly traditional menu (Preseli lamb burgers; faggots with onion gravy), and their own excellent beer. No further introduction is needed – just go.

Meals: Lunch & dinner £9.80-£16.50. Sunday lunch, 3 courses, £12.95.

Closed: Open all day. Closed Mon in winter.

Brian & Hafwen Davies
Tafarn Sinc,
Rosebush,
Clynderwen, SA66 7QU

Tel: +44 (0)1437 532214
Web: www.tafarnsinc.com

Entry 703 Map 6

The Old Sailor's

Newport

A quick zig and a zag off the coast road and you are rewarded with a sublime waterside setting, a stunning walk around Dinas Head and superb seafood at this 500-year old pub. Formerly called the Sailors' Safety, it once kept a light burning as a guide for ships. Dylan Thomas visited at least once and so must you! It's no beauty from the outside but inside is comfortingly traditional with a dark wood carved bar, quarry tiles, sturdy tables and chairs, rough-rendered white walls and nautical bits: a fitting place for a Felinfoel ale pulled by long-term landlord Langley, who will tell you about the best fish of the day on the specials boards; the shellfish, crabs and lobster are good too. The dining area is more formal and has great views across the garden to Fishguard.

Meals: Starters from £4.95. Mains from £9.

Closed: Mondays all day.

Langley Forrest
The Old Sailor's,
Pwllgwaelod,
Dinas Cross,
Newport, SA42 0SE

Tel: +44 (0)1348 811491

Entry 704 Map 6

Llys Meddyg

Newport

This fabulous restaurant has a bit of everything: cool rooms that pack a designer punch, super food in a sparkling restaurant, a cellar bar for drinks before dinner, a fabulous garden for summer treats. It's a very friendly place with charming staff on hand to help, and it draws in a local crowd who come for the seriously good food, perhaps mussel and saffron soup, rib of Welsh beef with hand-cut chips, cherry soufflé with pistachio ice-cream. You eat in style with a fire burning at one end of the restaurant and good art hanging on the walls. Best of all is the back garden with a mountain-fed stream pouring past. In summer, a café/bistro opens up out here – coffee and cake or steak and chips – with doors that open onto the garden. Don't miss Pembrokeshire's fabulous coastal path for its windswept cliffs, sandy beaches and secluded coves.

Meals	Lunch from £7. Dinner from £14.
Closed	Mondays all day.

Louise & Edward Sykes
Llys Meddyg,
East Street,
Newport, SA42 0SY

Tel +44 (0)1239 820008
Web www.llysmeddyg.com

Entry 705 Map 6

Pembrokeshire

Nag's Head Inn

Abercych

Behind the vibrant orange exterior is a feast of bare wood and stone. The lighting is soft and warm, there's a rustic chicken-wire sideboard crammed with old beer bottles, a glass cabinet displaying the famous 'rat' of Abercych (a stuffed coypu) and a photo of old Emrys, the treasured regular after whom the home-brew is named. The Nag's Head has a simple, tasteful charm, is full of old tales, curios and quirkery and serves the best kind of hearty food, from whitebait and fresh soups to steak and kidney pudding, treacle tart, and Sunday roasts. Come with the family and explore the pushchair-friendly Clynfyw sculpture trail – it starts from here. There's a play area too, in the lovely riverside garden. By a bridge on the river bank, at the bottom of a steep hill, the setting alone is worth the trip.

Meals	Lunch & dinner £8-£15. Sunday lunch, 3 courses, £13.95.
Closed	3pm-6pm. Open all day Sun.

Sam Jamieson
Nag's Head Inn,
Abercych,
Boncath, SA37 0HJ

Tel +44 (0)1239 841200
Web www.nagsheadabercych.co.uk

Entry 706 Map 6

The Felin Fach Griffin

Felin Fach

It's quirky, homespun, and thrives on a mix of relaxed informality and colourful style. The low-ceilinged bar resembles the sitting room of a small hip country house, with timber frames, cool tunes and comfy sofas in front of a smouldering fire. Painted stone walls come in blocks of colour, there's live music on Sunday nights, and you dine informally in the white-walled restaurant, with stock pots simmering on an Aga. The food is excellent, perhaps dressed Portland crab, rump of Welsh beef, treacle tart with bergamot sorbet; much of what you eat comes from a half-acre kitchen garden, with meat and game from the hills around you. Bedrooms above have style and substance: comfy beds wrapped in crisp linen, good bathrooms with fluffy towels, Roberts radios, a smattering of books, but no TV unless you ask. Breakfast is served in the dining room; wallow with the papers, make your own toast, scoff the full Welsh. A main road passes outside, but quietly at night, while lanes lead into the hills, so walk, ride, bike, canoe. Hay is close for books galore. Don't miss excellent off-season deals.

Rooms	2 doubles, 2 twin/doubles, 2 four-posters: £130-£170. 1 family room for 3: £170.
Meals	Lunch from £7. Dinner, 3 courses, about £30. Sunday lunch from £20.
Closed	Open all day.

Charles & Edmund Inkin
The Felin Fach Griffin,
Felin Fach,
Brecon, LD3 0UB

Tel +44 (0)1874 620111
Web www.felinfachgriffin.co.uk

The Harp
Old Radnor

For the last seven years Chris and Angela have been running this ancient Welsh longhouse tucked up a lane near the parish church, and there are no plans to change. The wonderful interior is spick-and-span timeless: 14th-century slate flooring in the bar, tongue-and-groove in a room that fits a dozen diners, crannies crammed with memorabilia, an ancient curved settle, an antique reader's chair, two fires and a happy crowd. Accompany a pint of Wye Valley or Three Tuns bitter with a Welsh Black rump steak with chips, or sea bass with salsa verde. Or take a ploughman's to a seat in the garden and gaze on the spectacular Radnor Valley. Five comfy rooms have countryside views, colourful Welsh blankets on the beds, bright bathrooms (some are shower rooms) and a farmhouse feel. Bracingly full breakfasts set you up for a day of exploring the wonderful Radnor Valley, or dipping into the shops of Hay-on-Wye. Life in this tiny village, like its glorious pub, remains delightfully unchanged.

Rooms	4 doubles; 1 double with separate bath: £95-£105.
Meals	Lunch from £5. Dinner from £10. Sunday lunch, 3 courses, from £22.
Closed	Weds-Thurs lunch. 3pm-6pm Sat & Sun. Mon & Tues all day.

Chris & Angela Ireland
The Harp,
Old Radnor,
Presteigne, LD8 2RH
Tel +44 (0)1544 350655
Web www.harpinnradnor.co.uk

Wynnstay Hotel

Machynlleth

In the quaint first capital of Wales, you'll be charmed to discover this old coaching inn. It may be more hotel than pub, but there's a great big bar with old oak floors and beams, scrubbed tables and candles, and it buzzes. Bag a seat by the woodburner in winter and study Gareth Johns's menus over a pint of Welsh ale. He applies his skills to the finest local produce: Conwy mussels, Borth lobster, salmon from the river Dyfi, beef and lamb from the valley. Try scallops with dijon velouté and truffle dressing, then Marches venison with root vegetables, colcannon, red wine and chocolate; and you can finish with a slate of Welsh cheeses. Some wonderful wines from small producers too, and, surprisingly, a real pizzeria at the back. Stroll off any excess with a walk and the dog.

Meals	Lunch £7.95-£15.95. Dinner from £11.95. Sunday lunch, 3 courses, £16.50.
Closed	Open all day.

Gareth & Paul Johns
Wynnstay Hotel,
Heol Maengwyn,
Machynlleth, SY20 8AE

Tel +44 (0)1654 702941
Web www.wynnstay-hotel.com

Entry 709 Map 7

Powys

Riverside Hotel

Pennal

Between the bohemian market town of Machynlleth and charming Aberdyfi by the sea is a handsome village inn, the focal point of little Pennal. New pumps shine behind the well-polished counter, the carpeted lounge is smart with mini sofas. Even the restaurant is spruce with new slate floors and matching tables, and there's a roaring wood-burner between the two. Look forward to great ales and malts, good wines by the glass and delicious food that never lets you down. Whether you go for a Welsh Black sirloin steak or a spicy vegetable stew, you know it's from local suppliers. The fish cakes were spot on and served with skinny fries; the chicken liver pâté, a smooth parfait with a lovely lingering taste, was served with berry chutney. Folks flock for the Sunday lunches, families love the riverside garden.

Meals	Starters from £5. Mains from £9.50.
Closed	Open all day.

Glyn & Corina Davies
Riverside Hotel,
Pennal,
Machynlleth, SY20 9DW

Tel +44 (0)1654 791285
Web www.riversidehotel-pennal.co.uk

Entry 710 Map 7

Pen y Cae Inn

Pen-y-Cae

Everything about the Pen y Cae is pristine, from the multi-levelled garden at the back to the claret sofas and wood-burner in the bar. They've even created a new upper floor, reached by a wooden staircase, supported by chunky beams. It's an exceptionally lovely interior, the best of old and new, and you feast under rafters. French windows open to the Brecon Beacons in summer, informed staff are delightful and there's food to match, from classic pub grub at lunch to liver with crispy pancetta on creamed potatoes at dinner. Find too Welsh Black rib-eye steak with dauphinoise potatoes, and rump of Breconshire lamb with chive mash and roasted vegetables. Wash it all down with a bottled beer from Tomos Watkin, Wales's fastest growing brewery, and trundle off home – charmed, well-fed and happy.

Meals	Lunch, bar meals & dinner £4.95. Sunday lunch from £9.95.
Closed	3pm-6pm. Sun eves & Mon. Open all day Sat.

Anthony Christopher
Pen y Cae Inn,
Brecon Road, Pen-y-Cae, SA9 1FA

Tel	+44 (0)1639 730100
Web	www.penycaeinn.com

Entry 711 Map 7

Plough & Harrow

Monknash

Originally part of a monastic grange, well off the beaten track, the Plough & Harrow is hugely convivial. Ancient low white walls lead to the front door, then you dip into two dim-lit, low-ceilinged, character-oozing rooms, their rustic fireplaces filled with church candles or crackling logs. There are cheerful yellow walls, original floors, church pews, smiling staff and a small bar area with a big array of handpumps – up to 11 ales are served. Traditionalists will smile to see gammon and chips on the lunch menu while the more adventurous may plump for summer crab salad, moules marinière or roast belly pork with mustard mash and sweet cider sauce. A brilliant atmosphere, a great find, the kind of pub you wish was your local – and as friendly to single drinkers as to groups.

Meals	Lunch & dinner £6.95-£13.95.
Closed	Open all day.

Paula Jones
Plough & Harrow,
Monknash,
Cowbridge, CF71 7QQ

Tel	+44 (0)1656 890209

Entry 712 Map 2

The Blue Anchor

East Aberthaw

Inglenooks and open log fires, stories of smugglers and derring-do – it's rich in atmosphere. Inside is a warm warren of little rooms and doorways less than five feet high. The Colemans have nurtured this 700-year-old place for 66 years and restored the pub following a fire in 2004. Dine in winter on pheasant from the shoot, in summer on sewin from Swansea Bay and salads from the vegetable garden. Pop in for a bowl of mussels and a moreish pint of Wye Valley – or dip into the chef's selection of regional cheeses. Under the eaves of a classic thatched roof, the restaurant delivers hake with chorizo and roasted red pepper risotto, duck with savoy cabbage, pancetta and redcurrant jus, lemon and sultana cheesecake, and roasts on Sundays (do book). It's pubby, good looking and wonderful at doing what it knows best.

Meals	Lunch £8.95-£10.95. Dinner £12.50-£17.85.
Closed	Open all day.

Jeremy Coleman
The Blue Anchor,
East Aberthaw, Barry, CF62 3DD

Tel	+44 (0)1446 750329
Web	www.blueanchoraberthaw.com

The Boat

Erbistock

Be sure to study your map and arrive on the right bank of the Dee as the old winch ferry no longer operates to pull you across to this riverside beauty. It's part 17th-century with worn stone floors, heavy oak beams, open fires and nooks to snuggle up in, part conservatory extension where you eat on marble-topped tables under open rafters. Daily changing menus reflect the chef's passion for fish and game and the choice is extensive. Share a platter of fruits of the river and sea or confit duck with orange and cointreau gravy; there are good desserts and plenty for children to enjoy. Arrive early if the sun is shining and grab a picnic bench by the fast flowing river to enjoy a pint of Weetwood Ale. You can even camp nearby and may see the otter family at play. A waterside delight.

Meals	Main courses £10.95-£19.95. Bar meals £4.95-£9.95.
Closed	Open all day.

Katerina Novotna
The Boat,
Erbistock, LL13 0DL

Tel	+44 (0)1978 780666
Web	www.boatondee.com

The Cross Foxes

Erbistock

It's on a travellers' crossroads, as the highway crosses the waters of the Dee and man and fish move in either direction, depending on the season. Rest on the terrace with a pint of Marston's Burton Bitter or Ringwood's Huffkin and soak up the views from this timeless spot. Inside, a log fire throws light on a well-carved bar front, polished wood tables and quarry tiles, while on the shelves glows the finest whisky and armagnac collection for many a mile: cockle-warming stuff. The big blackboard at the end of the bar is scrawled with good things to eat, from Cumberland sausage with black pudding mash to venison and pheasant meat loaf with juniper sauce. Settle into the wood-panelled area, the fireside snug or the conservatory. Enjoy a genuine classic.

Meals Lunch & dinner £9.50-£16.95. Bar meals from £4.75.
Closed Open all day.

Ian Pritchard-Jones
The Cross Foxes,
Erbistock, LL13 0DR
Tel +44 (0)1978 780380
Web www.crossfoxes-erbistock.co.uk

Pant-yr-Ochain

Gresford

A long drive snakes through landscaped parkland to a magnificent multi-gabled country house sheltered by trees, to one side of which a huge conservatory opens up views across terraces to the estate lake. Inside, a jigsaw of richly panelled rooms and drinking areas lures drinkers and diners alike: note the nine real ales. There are intimate corners, comfy alcoves and private snugs, open fires, quarry tiles and bare boards below an eccentric ceiling-line. Everywhere, a cornucopia of bric-a-brac: penny slots and cases of clay pipes, caricatures and prints. It sounds OTT but it fits comfortably here, and the ever-reliable Brunning & Price menus feature enjoyable dishes: venison, orange and thyme burger; smoked haddock and salmon fishcakes. Outside? A flower-filled, lakeside garden.

Meals Lunch & dinner £5.75-£16.95.
Closed Open all day.

James Meakin
Pant-yr-Ochain, Old Wrexham Rd,
Gresford, Wrexham, LL12 8TY
Tel +44 (0)1978 853525
Web www.brunningandprice.co.uk/pantyrochain/

Photo: Y Ffarmers, entry 683

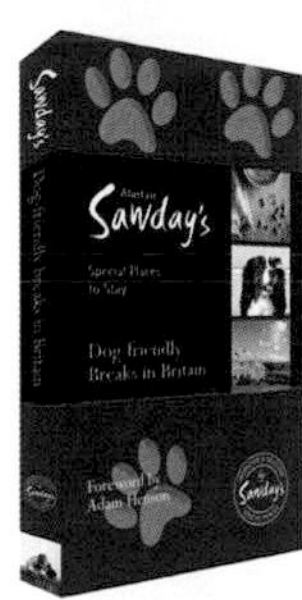

Alastair Sawday has been publishing books for over 20 years, finding Special Places to Stay in Britain and abroad. All our properties are inspected by us and are chosen for their charm and individuality. And there are many more to explore on our perennially popular website: www.sawdays.co.uk. You can buy any of our books at a reader discount of 25%* on the RRP.

List of titles:	RRP	Discount price
British Bed & Breakfast	£15.99	£11.99
British Hotels and Inns	£15.99	£11.99
Pubs & Inns of England & Wales	£15.99	£11.99
Dog-friendly Breaks in Britain	£14.99	£11.24
French Bed & Breakfast	£15.99	£11.99
French Châteaux & Hotels	£15.99	£11.99
Italy	£15.99	£11.99

*postage and packaging is added to each order

How to order:

You can order online at: www.sawdays.co.uk/bookshop/
or call: +44 (0)117 204 7810

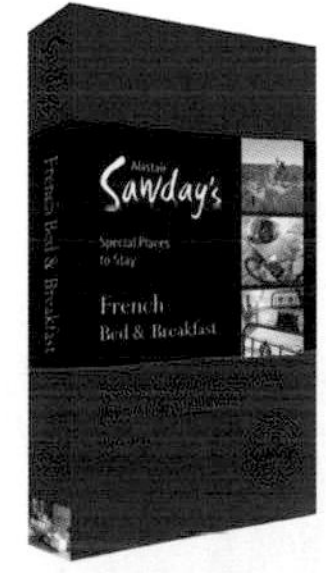

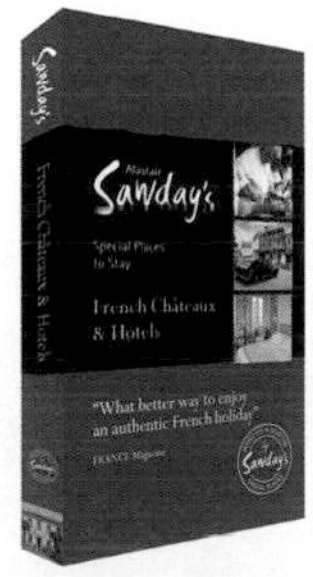

BREAD
PETERS
& SONS.
83 QUEENS PARK
BRIGHTON.

BOTTLED VINTAGE
2008

Photo: The Royal Oak Inn, entry 574

Photo: The Seven Tuns, entry 226

BEER
If you can't happy at least you can drunk

Photo: The George Townhouse, entry 582